Peter & Olson
Consumer Behavior and Marketing Strategy
Seventh Edition

Purvis & Burton
Which Ad Pulled Best?
Ninth Edition

Quelch, Rangan, & Lal
Marketing Management Text and Cases
First Edition

Rayport & Jaworski
Introduction to e-Commerce
Second Edition

Rayport & Jaworski
e-Commerce
First Edition

Rayport & Jaworski
Cases in e-Commerce
First Edition

Richardson
Internet Marketing
First Edition

Roberts
Internet Marketing: Integrating Online and Offline Strategies
First Edition

Spiro, Stanton, & Rich
Management of a Sales Force
Eleventh Edition

Stock & Lambert
Strategic Logistics Management
Fourth Edition

Ulrich & Eppinger
Product Design and Development
Third Edition

Walker, Boyd, Mullins, & Larreche
Marketing Strategy: A Decision-Focused Approach
Fourth Edition

Weitz, Castleberry, & Tanner
Selling: Building Partnerships
Fifth Edition

Zeithaml & Bitner
Services Marketing
Third Edition

Consumer Behavior and
Marketing Strategy

McGraw-Hill/Irwin Series in Marketing

Consumer Behavior and Marketing Strategy

Seventh Edition

J. Paul Peter

University of Wisconsin, Madison

Jerry C. Olson

Pennsylvania State University
Olson Zaltman Associates

Boston   Burr Ridge, IL   Dubuque, IA   Madison, WI   New York   San Francisco   St. Louis
Bangkok   Bogotá   Caracas   Kuala Lumpur   Lisbon   London   Madrid   Mexico City
Milan   Montreal   New Delhi   Santiago   Seoul   Singapore   Sydney   Taipei   Toronto

**McGraw-Hill
Irwin**

CONSUMER BEHAVIOR AND MARKETING STRATEGY

Published by McGraw-Hill/Irwin, a business unit of The McGraw-Hill Companies, Inc., 1221
Avenue of the Americas, New York, NY, 10020. Copyright © 2005, 2002, 1999, 1996, 1993,
1990, 1987 by The McGraw-Hill Companies, Inc. All rights reserved. No part of this publication
may be reproduced or distributed in any form or by any means, or stored in a database or retrieval
system, without the prior written consent of The McGraw-Hill Companies, Inc., including, but
not limited to, in any network or other electronic storage or transmission, or broadcast for
distance learning.

Some ancillaries, including electronic and print components, may not be available to customers
outside the United States.

This book is printed on acid-free paper.

1 2 3 4 5 6 7 8 9 0 DOW/DOW 0 9 8 7 6 5 4

ISBN   0-07-286487-7

Editorial director: *John E. Biernat*
Executive editor: *Linda Schreiber*
Sponsoring editor: *Barrett Koger*
Developmental editor: *Sarah Crago*
Executive marketing manager: *Ellen Cleary*
Media producer: *Craig Atkins*
Project manager: *Jim Labeots*
Senior production supervisor: *Michael R. McCormick*
Freelance design coordinator: *Kami Carter*
Photo research coordinator: *Judy Kausal*
Photo researcher: *Photosearch, Inc., NY*
Senior supplement producer: *Rose M. Range*
Senior digital content specialist: *Brian Nacik*
Cover design: *JoAnne Schopler*
Cover illustration: *© Paul Turnbaugh*
Typeface: *10/12 New Caledonia*
Compositor: *GTS—York, PA Campus*
Printer: *R. R. Donnelley*

Library of Congress Cataloging-in-Publication Data

Peter, J. Paul.
    Consumer behavior and marketing strategy / by J. Paul Peter, Jerry C. Olson.—7th ed.
        p. cm.—(McGraw-Hill/Irwin series in marketing)
    Various multi-media instructional materials are available to supplement the text.
    ISBN 0-07-286487-7 (alk. paper)
    1. Consumer behavior. 2. Marketing. I. Olson, Jerry C. (Jerry Corrie), 1944– II. Title.
    III. Series.
    HF5415.3.P468 2005
    658.8'342—dc22

www.mhhe.com   2003071083

Rose and Angie
Becky, Matt, and Seth

About the Authors

J. Paul Peter

J. Paul Peter is James R. McManus-Bascom Professor and Chair of the Marketing Department at the University of Wisconsin–Madison. He was a member of the faculty at Indiana State, Ohio State, and Washington University before joining the Wisconsin faculty in 1981. While at Ohio State, he was named Outstanding Marketing Professor by the students and has won the John R. Larson Teaching Award at Wisconsin. He has taught a variety of courses, including Consumer Behavior, Marketing Management, Marketing Strategy, Marketing Research, and Marketing Theory, among others, and has taught in a variety of executive programs.

Professor Peter's research has appeared in the *Journal of Marketing, Journal of Marketing Research, Journal of Consumer Research, Journal of Retailing,* and *Academy of Management Journal,* among others. His article on construct validity won the prestigious William O'Dell Award from the *Journal of Marketing Research,* and he was a finalist for this award on two other occasions. He is an author of more than thirty books, including *A Preface to Marketing Management,* ninth edition; *Marketing Management: Knowledge and Skills,* seventh edition; *Consumer Behavior and Marketing Strategy,* seventh edition; *Strategic Management: Concepts and Applications,* third edition; and *Marketing: Creating Value for Customers,* second edition. Citation research indicates that he is one of the most cited authors in the marketing literature.

Professor Peter has served on the review boards of the *Journal of Marketing, Journal of Marketing Research, Journal of Consumer Research,* and *Journal of Business Research* and was Measurement Editor for JMR and Professional Publications Editor for the American Marketing Association. He has consulted for several corporations as well as the Federal Trade Commission.

Jerry C. Olson

Jerry C. Olson is the Earl P. Strong Executive Education Professor of Marketing at Pennsylvania State University and a founding partner of Olson Zaltman Associates. He joined Penn State in 1971 after receiving his Ph.D. in consumer psychology from Purdue University. At Penn State, he has taught Consumer Behavior, Marketing Management, Advertising and Promotion Management, Research Methods, and Marketing Theory.

Professor Olson's research has been published in the *Journal of Consumer Research, Journal of Marketing Research, Journal of Marketing, Journal of Applied Psychology,* and *International Journal of Research in Marketing.* He is author or editor of a number of books, including *Consumer Behavior and Marketing Strategy, Understanding Consumer Behavior, Perceived Quality,* and *Advertising and Consumer Behavior,* as well as several conference proceedings.

Professor Olson has served as President of the Association for Consumer Research, the major professional organization for consumer researchers. He has served on the editorial review boards of most of the major journals in the marketing and consumer behavior field. As partner in Olson Zaltman Associates, Professor Olson is an active consultant to a number of consumer products companies, helping them develop a deep understanding of their customers. He also has consulted for the Federal Trade Commission.

In his spare time, Professor Olson enjoys traveling with his wife, Becky, and skiing, biking, reading, and making music with his collection of antique banjos.

Preface

We continue to be pleased that so many undergraduate and graduate instructors and students have found our book useful for teaching and learning the fascinating field of consumer behavior. We appreciate their sentiments that our book does the best job of integrating consumer behavior into the marketing curriculum. Since the objective of the book is to give students the knowledge and skills necessary to perform useful consumer analyses in developing effective marketing strategies, we are encouraged that the book is accomplishing its objective.

The seventh edition of *Consumer Behavior and Marketing Strategy* continues to reflect our firm belief that the Wheel of Consumer Analysis is a powerful tool not only for organizing consumer behavior knowledge but also for understanding consumers and for guiding the development of successful marketing strategies. In fact, it has been used by marketing consultants and practitioners to do so. The four major parts of the Wheel of Consumer Analysis are consumer affect and cognition, consumer behavior, consumer environment, and marketing strategy. Each of these components is the topic of one of the four major sections of this book.

After Section One, which provides an overview of the model, Section Two discusses affect and cognition, which refers to how consumers think and feel about various things, such as products and brands. Section Three discusses consumer behavior, which refers to the physical actions of consumers, such as purchasing products and brands. Section Four discusses the consumer environment, which is everything external to consumers that influences how they think, feel, and act, such as advertisements or price information. Section Five discusses marketing strategies by which marketing stimuli, such as products, packages, advertisements, sales promotions, stores, websites, and price information, are placed in consumer environments to influence consumers' affect, cognition and behavior.

Text Pedagogy
This book contains a variety of pedagogical aids to enhance student learning and facilitate the application of consumer behavior concepts to marketing practice:

- **Introductory scenarios.** Each chapter begins with an interesting example that discusses a real-world situation involving some aspect of consumer behavior.

Then each chapter ends with a "Back To . . ." section that summarizes how the chapter material relates to the opening example. This clearly shows students how the chapter concepts are relevant to marketing strategy decisions. This feature has been very successful in generating student interest and increasing understanding of the chapter material.

- **Examples.** Reviewers have applauded the inclusion of many examples of marketing strategies used by actual companies. These examples demonstrate how marketers use consumer behavior concepts. Also, they increase student interest in the material.
- **Highlights.** Each chapter contains longer examples called Highlights that show the relevance of consumer behavior concepts and give students real-life examples of marketing strategies. All Highlights are referenced in the text but are self-contained for individual study.
- **Key terms and concepts.** We include a list of key terms and concepts and the page on which they are discussed at the end of each chapter to facilitate study of the material. These terms and concepts are also boldfaced within the chapter text.
- **Marketing Strategy in Action.** Each chapter concludes with a case that focuses on consumer analysis issues facing real companies. These short cases help to integrate consumer behavior information into the marketing strategy development process. The discussion questions accompanying the cases can be used for written assignments or to stimulate in-class discussion.
- **Review and discussion questions.** Each chapter contains a series of review and discussion questions that emphasize the understanding and application of chapter material to strategic marketing issues. These can be used for written assignments, in-class discussions, essay exam questions, or student self-study.
- **Notes.** Notes for the most current and useful references and additional sources of information are provided at the end of the book. These sources illustrate and expand on topics in each chapter of the text.
- **Glossary.** The text contains a glossary of key consumer behavior terms. Many of these definitions were previously prepared by the authors for the American Marketing Association's *Dictionary of Marketing Terms*.

Many of the introductory scenarios, Marketing Strategy in Action cases, and Highlight examples are new to this edition; the remaining are updated as appropriate. While the previous ones were praised by instructors and students for the insights they provided, the new features are intended to better capture consumer behavior and marketing strategy issues in today's global economy.

Instructional Aids

The text package contains five instructional aids.

- **Instructor's Manual.** This manual is widely recognized as one of the best ever developed for any marketing or consumer behavior text. It contains a variety of useful information and suggestions for teaching each chapter in the text as well as examples not included in the text. It includes mini-lectures, projects, in-class exercises, notes for the Marketing Strategy in Action cases, and notes for the discussion questions. It also includes notes for each of the available video segments. It is an excellent resource for increasing student interest in and learning of consumer behavior.
- **Videos.** The instructional package contains 10 video segments on various companies that can be used in class to involve students in important consumer

behavior and marketing strategy issues. Segments average 15 minutes in length, and discussion notes are included for each.

- **Manual of Tests.** The revised Manual of Tests consists of 2,000 multiple-choice and short-answer questions. Rationales for the answers to the more difficult questions are included. The Manual of Tests has been thoroughly reviewed to ensure a reliable, high-quality test item set.
- **PowerPoint Presentation.** PowerPoint presentation slides of exhibits from the text and from other sources enhance lectures and discussions.
- **Instructor's Resource CD-ROM** The CD-ROM includes CompuTest, which offers instructors the option to construct a computer-generated test from the questions in the Manual of Tests.

Acknowledgments

We are indebted to the many people who contributed to the development of the current and previous editions of this book. First, we thank our professors, colleagues, and students for their contribution to our education. Second, we thank the many consumer behavior researchers whose work is reflected in the pages of this text and the companies whose strategies are used as examples of consumer analysis and marketing strategy development. Third, we thank Linda Schreiber, Executive Editor, and Sarah Crago, Developmental Editor, for their encouragement, constructive criticism, and patience throughout the preparation of this edition. Fourth, we thank James Forr from Olson Zaltman Associates for his assistance. Finally, we thank the following reviewers of this text for the time, effort, and insights they offered.

Reviewers for Previous Editions

Dr. Ronald J. Adams
University of North Florida

Dr. Paul J. Albanese
Kent State University

M. Wayne Alexander
Moorhead State University

Dr. Mark G. Anderson
University of Kentucky

Dr. Subir Bandyopadhyay
McGill University

Delores Barsellotti
California State Polytechnic University–Pomona

Mickey Belch
San Diego State University

Russell Belk
University of Utah

Dr. Lauren Block
New York University

Tom Boyd
Miami University

Ray Burke
University of Pennsylvania

James Cagley
The University of Tulsa

Louis M. Capella
Mississippi State University

Auleen Carson
University of New Brunswick (Canada)

Ellen Day
University of Georgia

Aimee Drolet
Anderson School at UCLA

Professor Sunil Erevelles
University of California

Mike Etzel
University of Notre Dame

Andrew M. Forman
Hofstra University

Bill Gaidis
Marquette University

Meryl Gardner
New York University

Peter L. Gillett
University of Central Florida

Dr. Ronald Goldsmith
Florida State University

Audrey Guskey
Duquesne University

Kenneth A. Heischmidt
Southeast Missouri State University

Robert M. Isotalo
Lakehead University

Dr. Ann T. Kuzma
Mankato State University

Steven Lysonski
Marquette University

Deborah Mitchell
Temple University

Dr. Lois A. Mohr
Georgia State University

Dr. James Munch
University of Texas–Arlington

Walter Nord
*University of
South Florida*

Professor Kathy O'Malley
University of Idaho

Betty J. Parker
University of Missouri

William S. Piper
*The University of Southern
Mississippi–Gulf Park*

Dr. Akshay R. Rao
University of Minnesota

Maria Sannella
Boston College

David W. Schumann
University of Tennessee

Richard A. Spreng
Michigan State University

Shirley M. Stretch
*California State University,
Los Angeles*

Cathie H. Tinney
*University of Texas of the
Permian Basin*

Gail Tom
California State University

J. Dennis White
Florida State University

Dr. David B. Whitlark
Brigham Young University

Tommy E. Whittler
University of Kentucky

Arch Woodside
Tulane University

In addition to the reviewers named above, we also found feedback from individual users of the first six editions—both instructors and students—to be useful for improving the seventh edition. We continue to value your comments and suggestions for the continuous improvement of this work.

J. Paul Peter
jppeter@bus.wisc.edu

Jerry C. Olson
jco@psu.edu

Brief Table of Contents

Contents

Section 3
Behavior and Marketing Strategy

Section 4

The Environment and Marketing Strategy

one

A Perspective on Consumer Behavior

1

Introduction to Consumer Behavior and Marketing Strategy

Cyberconsumers: A Growing Group in the New Millennium

Marketing to consumers via the Internet has many advantages for marketers. It allows products and services to be offered 24 hours a day, 7 days a week, 365 days a year; it allows products and services to be offered globally in an efficient manner; it is cost efficient in that it saves the need for stores, paper catalogs, and salespeople; it provides a means for developing one-on-one relationships with consumers and establishing consumer databases for conducting online research. Online Business-to-Consumer (B2C) marketing requires marketers to understand consumers and deliver the products and services consumers want and need, just as traditional marketing does. In 2003, many marketers proved their ability to serve consumers online, and total Internet sales to consumers reached $95 billion. While this figure is dwarfed by the $2.4 trillion in Internet business-to-business (B2B) sales, it is close to the forecasts for B2C sales years

earlier. Although the e-commerce shakeout in the early 2000s led many analysts to declare that the Internet was overhyped as a marketing tool, it is now firmly established as a critical element of overall marketing strategy.

One major criticism of B2C marketing was that it reached only a small segment of the population. In 1996, the profile of the typical Internet shopper was young, relatively wealthy, and 62 percent male. However, more recent research shows that current online shoppers are 49 percent male and 51 percent female, reflecting the same ratio listed in the 2000 U.S. census. Likewise, in 1996, the average household income for the online population was $62,700 and five years later reached $49,800, close to the average household income of the general population in the 2000 U.S. census. Thus, Internet marketers are now reaching a much broader market than they did only a few years ago.

A second major criticism of B2C marketing was that consumers would shop on the Web to collect information about

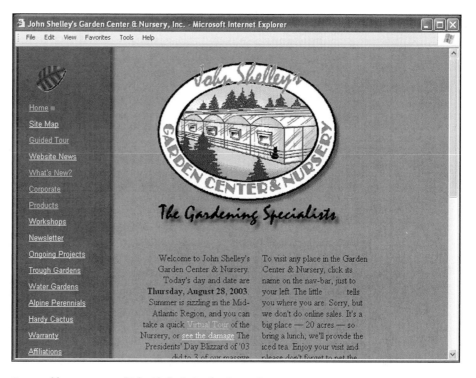

Reprinted by permission of John Shelley's Garden Center & Nursery, Inc.

products and services but would not buy. Reasons consumers gave for not buying included that they preferred to shop in person at stores and they did not want to risk giving hackers access to credit card or personal information sent online. However, recent research by ACNielsen found that almost one-half of shoppers with Internet access actually made a purchase on the Web. Apparently, improved security on the Web has assuaged the fears of many online shoppers.

So what do cyberconsumers buy online? According to an ACNielsen study, books top the list (42 percent of buyers), followed by CD/DVD/video purchases (38 percent). Computer software (29 percent), travel-related services (28 percent), clothing and apparel (27 percent), and specialty gift items like flowers (24 percent) account for a signifi-

cant portion of web-based purchases. Still ranking in the double digits are computer hardware (18 percent), entertainment-related services (17 percent), and houseware items (16 percent).

Others use the Web for the vast selection of products and services available. If you are looking for unusual plants and landscaping, including miniature Alpine plants from Oregon or 40 varieties of cacti grown from seedlings collected from the Grand Canyon, contact John Shelley's Garden Center & Nursery in Winterstown, Pennsylvania, at **http://www.gdnctr.com**. Looking for high-end mountain bike components and accessories, the kind you can't find in local shops? If so, contact Aardvark Cycles in Provo, Utah, at **http://www.aardvarkcycles.com**. If you want to bid on collectibles, such as an early 60s Barbie or a Lionel train set from the 1950s, contact eBay at **http://www.ebay.com**. Looking for a new horse? If so, contact Equisearch, which lists 700 horses that sell for an average of $10,000 each at **http://www.equisearch.com**.

Sources: Timothy J. Mullaney, Heather Green, Michael Arndt, Robert D. Hof, and Linda Hilelstein, "The E-Biz Surprise," *BusinessWeek,* May 12, 2003, pp. 60–68; Ken Cimino, "Reports Paint Profile of an Internet Shopper," EcommerceTimes.com, July 13, 2001; acnielsen.com.

How can consumer behavior research help Internet marketers increase their chances of success? Marketers have long argued that the **marketing concept** is the appropriate philosophy for conducting business. Simply stated, the marketing concept suggests an organization should satisfy consumer needs and wants to make profits. To implement the marketing concept, organizations must understand their customers and stay close to them to provide products and services that consumers will purchase and use appropriately.

For many years, the marketing concept was not fully understood or implemented properly by U.S. firms. Often, even firms that accepted the marketing concept in principle did not recognize that the marketing concept required the organization to change its existing practices dramatically. In general, these firms viewed implementing the marketing concept as a marketing task rather than something in which the entire organization had to be involved. Although these companies conducted marketing and consumer research, this research was seldom used as the basis for designing not just the marketing strategy but also the entire organizational strategy.

Today many of the most successful companies in the world have become so by designing the entire organization to serve consumers and stay close to them. These companies are committed to developing quality products and services and selling them at a price that gives consumers high value. In these companies, the marketing department, as well as design, engineering, production, human resources, finance, and other departments, focus on doing their jobs in ways that enhance the value of products to consumers. Some firms have found they can actually increase product quality and reduce costs at the same time, and they encourage employees throughout the company to seek ways to do so. Other firms first determine what consumers want and how much they are willing to pay for a product and then design, produce, and market the best-quality product they can for the price consumers are willing to pay.

Companies are making changes to serve consumers better for three major reasons. First, the dramatic success of Japanese companies, such as Toyota and Sony, that focus on providing consumers with value-laden products has spurred other companies to follow suit. In previous years, many U.S. companies could sell almost anything they were able to produce. Consumers accepted the level of quality of goods and services produced by U.S. companies as being as good as could be expected. However, as American consumers discovered the superior quality and lower prices of many Japanese products, they began to realize that many American products offered inferior value and shifted to purchasing foreign-made goods. Several U.S. companies had to redesign their organizations to serve consumers in order to survive and compete not only in the United States but also in world markets. Many have done so and are now world leaders in their industries.

The second major reason for the shift to focusing on consumers is the dramatic increase in the quality of consumer and marketing research. In the past, companies often did not have detailed information on the actual purchasers and users of their products. Although they conducted research to investigate new product concepts and to try to understand consumers, often this research was not continuous and did not identify the firm's actual customers. Today computer technology and scanners and other data sources have made it possible for companies to know personally who their customers are and the effects on those consumers of marketing strategy and changes in strategy. Both manufacturers and retailers can now carefully track consumer reactions to new products and services and evaluate marketing strategies better than ever before. Thus, companies are now better able to actually implement the marketing concept. Highlight 1.1 offers several examples of newer methods for researching consumers.

A third reason for the increased emphasis on consumers is the development of the Internet as a marketing tool. In the past, consumers received most of their information about products and services from traditional print and media advertising and shopped primarily in brick-and-mortar stores. While this is still the case for most purchases, marketers have recognized the potential for e-marketing to completely change the way consumers shop and purchase. This change could be a threat to traditional manufacturers and retailers unless they adapt their marketing strategies to include electronic commerce. This change is an opportunity for small companies and entrepreneurs, since the startup costs of marketing products and services are greatly reduced compared with traditional marketing methods. In either case, knowledge of consumers' shopping and purchasing patterns is needed to develop a successful e-marketing strategy, thus increasing the importance of consumer behavior research. Savvy marketers know that the Internet can be used to communicate vast amounts of information about products and product lines to consumers, to actually sell products and services directly to consumers, and to market to global consumers who could not be reached cost-effectively by traditional marketing methods. Finally, savvy marketers have also recognized that the Internet can be used to conduct marketing research studies and collect other useful information about consumers that can be used to develop effective marketing strategies.

In sum, many successful companies have recognized the importance of consumers and have sophisticated approaches and detailed data from which to develop organizational and marketing strategies. All of this should convince you that the consumer behavior course you are about to take is an important part of your business education. In the remainder of this chapter, we will discuss the nature of consumer behavior and the parties involved in studying and analyzing it. We will also investigate some relationships between consumer behavior and marketing strategy and the value of this course for a successful career. Although this text focuses on consumer behavior and marketing strategy, it should not be forgotten that employees in every business function should be involved in serving consumers. Highlight 1.2 discusses a method used by retailers to understand consumer shopping patterns.

What Is Consumer Behavior?

The American Marketing Association defines **consumer behavior** as "the dynamic interaction of affect and cognition, behavior, and the environment by which human beings conduct the exchange aspects of their lives."[1] In other words, consumer behavior involves the thoughts and feelings people experience and the actions they perform in consumption processes. It also includes all the things in the environment that influence these thoughts, feelings, and actions. These include comments from other consumers, advertisements, price information, packaging, product appearance, and many others. It is important to recognize from this definition that consumer behavior is dynamic, involves interactions, and involves exchanges.

Highlight 1.1

Digging Deeper into Consumers' Minds and Lives

Market researchers use a variety of techniques to learn about consumers. For example, focus groups, surveys, experiments, and scanner data studies have long helped marketers develop more effective strategies. However, a recent trend in market research is to dig deeper into consumers' minds and lives using a variety of anthropological techniques to better understand the deeper meaning of products and brands. Catherine DeThorne, ad agency Leo Burnett's director of planning, calls these techniques "getting in under the radar." Below is a sample of some of the types of research companies are doing.

- As Mary Flimin chops onions for risotto late one afternoon, a pair of video cameras and two market researchers stationed in a corner are recording her every move. Meg Armstrong and Joel Johnson, who represent a cookware company, want to see how a gourmet like Flimin cooks and what she likes. Hours later, Armstrong and Johnson review their observations. Even though Flimin said she often makes cakes and bakes with fresh fruit, Armstrong notes that "her baking dishes are stashed in the boondocks, so she doesn't bake much." This insight could not be captured by typical methods that rely on consumers to tell researchers what they do.
- Thomson Electronics hired E-lab to perform a study to find out how consumers mix listening to music with their daily lives. E-lab did a "beeper" study in which participants were instructed to write down what they were doing when they were

paged. Participants recorded where they were; what music, if any, was playing; who picked it; and their mood. Researchers also tailed people around their homes, noting where they kept their stereos and how their music collections were organized. The company was trying to find out how often people sit down to enjoy a CD as opposed to using it for background music. This information would help Thomson Electronics in its new-product decisions.
- Traditional focus groups often involve meetings among strangers that could inhibit consumers from saying what they really feel. To overcome this problem, ad agency Leo Burnett set up a meeting with six professional female friends in their late 30s and 40s at a coffee house called Urban Blend. While enjoying wine and crudités, the women discussed a Wells Fargo ad that touts its investments to woman-owned businesses. In one session, the women agreed that they would invest their money with this company if it were around the area. However, in a later session, some younger women felt the ad was pandering to them. Both of these insights are useful for the agency that handles advertising for the New York Stock Exchange and Morgan Stanley Dean Witter. Both sets of opinions will be considered when the agency creates ads targeted to either group.
- Before a Miramax movie opens in theaters, the previews are usually screened by groups of moviegoers around the country observed by psychiatrist Russ Ferstandig. As people watch the previews

Consumer Behavior Is Dynamic

Consumer behavior is *dynamic* because the thinking, feelings, and actions of individual consumers, targeted consumer groups, and society at large are constantly changing. For example, the Internet has changed the way people search for information about products and services. The fact that consumers and their environments are constantly changing highlights the importance of ongoing consumer research and analysis by marketers to keep abreast of important trends.

The dynamic nature of consumer behavior makes development of marketing strategies an exciting yet difficult task. Strategies that work at one time or in one market may fail miserably at other times or in other markets. Because product life cycles are

BETTER STRAPS THAN
A $300 PROM DRESS.

Courtesy of VF Corporation and The Hiebing Group.

and answer Ferstandig's questions, he watches their body language. Based on what he hears and sees, he may recommend that the Disney unit change previews to make them more compelling to audiences. He might suggest a short pause to let people catch up with a message or change the wording in a preview, such as taking out the word *comedy* in describing the movie *An Ideal Husband.*

• The MacManus Group uses a TV talk show format called "Just Ask a Woman" to encourage research participants to speak up in groups. In a project for Continental Airlines, 19 female business travelers gathered in a Manhattan loft set up like a talk show set. Cameras rolled, and two women with microphones encouraged the participants to stand up and share frustrations they encountered on the road—from bad airplane food to inefficient rental car services. It was as if Sally Jessy Raphael were on the set. As soon as the lights and cameras came on, the participants seemed to vie for the microphone.

• At Norman Thomas High School in Manhattan, Inez Cintron, 14, chats exuberantly with her girlfriends between classes. The topics: singer Lauryn Hill, Old Navy clothes, and the NBC hit *Friends.* Tru Pettigrew, a 30-year-old researcher for a company called Triple Dot, leans close. The trend hunter has dropped by the public high school to glean intelligence for Eastpak. He listens to the girls mix Spanish phrases into their English chatter—something new to Pettigrew that may result in Eastpak ads with "Spanglish." Pettigrew also is interested to hear that the teens, who preferred rival Jansport's packs, buy as many as eight backpacks to mix with their wardrobes. "That's a key piece of information," he says later.

Not everyone is cheering these modern market research methods. "It's kind of pathetic that people are willing to be subjects in order to help marketers get inside a certain group's head and sell, sell, sell," says Michael Jacobson of the Center for Science in the Public Interest. However, respondents are often paid—at least $100 by E-lab—for participating and are free to choose whether or not they want to be in the study.

Source: Melanie Wells, "New Ways to Get Into Our Heads," *USA Today,* March 2, 1999, pp. B1, B2. Copyright March 2, 1999. Reprinted with permission.

shorter than ever before, many companies have to innovate constantly to create superior value for customers and stay profitable. This involves creation of new products, new versions of existing products, new brands, and new strategies for them. For example, Mercedes-Benz has developed a more complete line of vehicles, including a sport utility vehicle, the ML 350, to try to reach more consumers. Compaq was the first company to offer low-price computers, and other manufacturers followed suit. However, one survey showed that the reason 50 percent of U.S. households don't have a computer is that they think they don't need one.[2] This highlights the fact that needs and wants change at different times for different consumer groups.

Highlight 1.2

Snooping on Shoppers to Increase Sales

Hundreds of companies nationwide are turning to electronic and infrared surveillance equipment to snoop on shoppers in their stores. Some even conduct old-fashioned stakeouts, complete with walkie-talkies, from catwalks in the stores. These companies are not trying to spot shoplifters. Rather, they are learning about shoppers' traffic patterns to change consumer buying habits.

Michael Newman/PhotoEdit, Inc.

Take Bashas's Markets, Inc., in Chandler, Arizona. A study showed that only 18 percent of the grocery store's customers ever went down the aisle with greeting cards, which are high-profit items. So George Fiscus, the store layout manager, moved the section, sandwiching it between the floral department and an aisle with peanut butter, jelly, and health foods that regularly drew 62 percent of the store's traffic. Nestled in their new home, the greeting cards showed a second-quarter sales jump of 40 percent.

Tracking consumers' every move is giving marketers both revealing statistical detail and new insights. The research efforts have also turned up some surprises:

- By peering from the catwalks at 1,600 shoppers, researchers for Marsh Supermarkets unearthed a troubling trend: People heavily shopped the periphery of the store—the produce, dairy, and meat sections—but frequently circumvented the core dry-goods section that takes up the bulk of store space. The Indiana store chain's inner aisles drew only 13 to 30 percent of traffic, while the periphery accounted for as much as 80 percent.

Consumer Behavior Involves Interactions

Consumer behavior involves *interactions* among people's thinking, feelings, and actions, and the environment. Thus marketers need to understand what products and brands mean to consumers, what consumers must do to purchase and use them, and what influences shopping, purchase, and consumption. The more marketers know about how these interactions influence individual consumers, target markets of similar consumers, and society at large, the better they can satisfy consumer needs and wants and create value for them. For example, one major change in society is the shrinking number of middle-income consumers and the increase in low- and high-income groups. How this change affects consumers' thoughts, feelings, and actions has important implications for marketing strategy. Some companies are changing their offerings to appeal to the growing markets and thus put less emphasis on the middle-income group. Gap Inc. expanded its upscale Banana Republic chain and its lower-end Old Navy stores to tap these two markets while keeping growth of middle-market Gap stores more limited.[3] It is likely that many consumers who buy clothes from Banana Republic versus Old Navy have different thoughts and feelings about their purchases and may have purchased them for different reasons and different occasions.

- VideOcart, Inc., a Chicago company that uses infrared sensors in store ceilings to track shopping carts, has spotted a lot of "dippers." These shoppers park their carts at the ends of aisles and then walk down, filling their arms with items from the shelves as they go. Marketers figure such shoppers probably buy less because they are limited by what they can carry.
- Certain departments draw huge numbers of people, but that doesn't guarantee proportionate sales, according to a study by the Food Marketing Institute trade group. By retracing the steps of 2,400 shoppers and checking what ended up in their grocery carts, the institute learned, for instance, that 77 percent of people walked through the bakery department, but only a third actually bought anything there.
- A study of Procter & Gamble products in Kmart stores found that sales rose sharply when items like coffee and toothpaste were placed outside their normal aisles on display racks. With no coupons or price cuts, sales of the newly located toothpaste rose as much as 119 percent over a three-week test period, whereas coffee sales soared more than 500 percent.

Although primarily a tool for retailers, traffic analysis is being used by consumer product companies as well. One traffic study showed that shoppers often zip through the snack aisle, spending only 42.7 seconds there, whereas they spend more than twice that in the coffee aisle. At a Kroger store in Atlanta, PepsiCo Inc.'s Frito-Lay unit tried to raise its sales by advertising its chips in the coffee aisle. Over jars of Nestea and Maxwell House, a red sign flashes, "America, Your Chip Has Come In," and suggests that shoppers pick up a bag of Doritos.

A study by New York City–based Envirosell Inc. determined that the first 30 feet inside a store entrance, the "decompression zone," should not be used to sell products. Most consumers need this space to get their bearings. They are uninterested in elaborate displays until they are past this zone. The company also determined that most shoppers, especially women, do not like to enter narrow aisles where they may be jostled from behind. Consequently, items in these aisles generally go unsold.

Paco Underhill, the founder of Envirosell Inc., advises storekeepers to keep stacks of shopping baskets at various locations within the store. It seems that only 34 percent of shoppers who don't have baskets actually purchase something, while 75 percent of shoppers with baskets buy some items.

Interestingly, a woman who shops with another woman spends twice as much time in the store than if she shops with a man. So Underhill suggests plenty of seating be available for men to relax and wait while their wives shop.

Consumer Behavior Involves Exchanges

Consumer behavior involves *exchanges* between human beings. In other words, people give up something of value to others and receive something in return. Much of consumer behavior involves people giving up money and other things to obtain products and services, that is, exchanges between buyers (consumers) and sellers (marketers). In fact, the role of marketing in society is to help create exchanges by formulating and implementing marketing strategies.

Approaches to
Consumer Behavior
Research

Consumer behavior is a complex phenomenon and an eclectic field. The majority of published research is done by marketing academics who vary greatly in their training, objectives, and methods. As shown in Exhibit 1.1, there are three major approaches to studying consumer behavior.

The interpretive approach is relatively new in the field and has become quite influential. It is based on theories and methods from cultural anthropology. This approach seeks to develop a deep understanding of consumption and its meanings.

Exhibit 1.1

Approaches to the Study of Consumer Behavior

Approaches	Core Disciplines	Primary Objectives	Primary Methods
Interpretive	Cultural anthropology	Understand consumption and its meanings	Long interviews Focus groups
Traditional	Psychology Sociology	Explain consumer decision making and behavior	Experiments Surveys
Marketing science	Economics Statistics	Predict consumer choice and behavior	Math-modeling Simulation

Studies use long interviews and focus groups to understand such things as what products and services mean to consumers and what consumers experience in purchasing and using them. Other studies might concern how advertising depicts women, how art and films reflect consumption meaning, or how possessions influence self-images. Although these studies typically are not designed to help marketers develop successful strategies, implications for strategy development can be inferred from them.

The traditional approach is based on theories and methods from cognitive, social, and behavioral psychology, as well as sociology. It seeks to develop theories and methods to explain consumer decision making and behavior. Studies involve experiments and surveys to test theories and develop insights into such things as consumer information processing, decision processes, and social influences on consumer behavior. This approach has had a profound impact on marketing thought, with some researchers focusing on theory testing and others on investigating the impact of marketing strategies on consumers.

The marketing science approach is based on theories and methods from economics and statistics. It commonly involves developing and testing mathematical models to predict the impact of marketing strategies on consumer choice and behavior. This approach has become a mainstay in the consumer packaged goods industry because it can handle large scanner data sets in an efficient manner to help solve marketing problems.

All three approaches have value and provide insights into consumer behavior and marketing strategy in different ways and at different levels of analysis. Insights from all three are integrated in this text, although the core of the book is based on the traditional approach.

It should also be noted that marketing practitioners spend millions of dollars each year to study consumers. These companies do their own research or hire marketing research firms, ad agencies, consulting firms, and academics to help them develop better marketing strategies to serve consumers. These companies may use any of the three approaches depending on the nature of the marketing problem or decision.

Uses of Consumer Behavior Research

As shown in Exhibit 1.2, there are three groups that use knowledge about consumer behavior and consumer behavior research. These include marketing organizations, government and political organizations, and consumers. Each group is interested in consumer behavior as it influences the consumer's interactions and exchanges with the other groups.

Exhibit 1.2

Relationships among Action-Oriented Groups Interested in Consumer Behavior

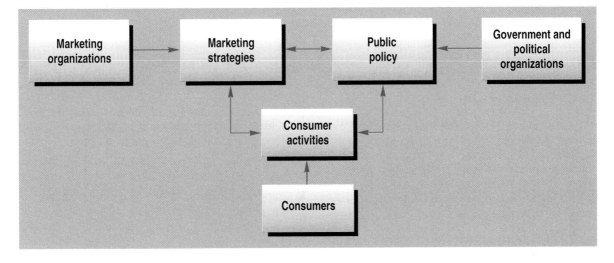

Nonprofit and government organizations can benefit from studying their consumers *Courtesy Jay Walter Thompson.*

The first group is marketing organizations, which include not only businesses attempting to sell products but also hospitals, museums, parks, law firms, universities, and other organizations that seek exchanges with consumers. Although the primary emphasis in this text is on exchanges between businesses and consumers, the ideas presented can also be used by other marketing organizations, such as the American Cancer Society, Yellowstone Park, or your college or university.

The second group in Exhibit 1.2 consists of various government and political organizations. These include government agencies such as the Federal Trade Commission and the Food and Drug Administration. The major concern of these organizations is monitoring and regulating exchanges between marketing organizations and consumers. This is accomplished through the development of public policies that affect marketing organizations and consumers. Political organizations include consumer activists such as Students Against Drunk Driving and various industry and trade organizations such as the American Marketing Association. These groups exert pressure on marketing organizations and consumers to behave in certain ways. For example, Highlight 1.3 shows the Code of Ethics of the American Marketing Association.

The third group interested in consumer behavior includes both consumers and organizational buyers who

Highlight 1.3

Code of Ethics of the American Marketing Association

Members of the American Marketing Association (AMA) are committed to ethical professional conduct. They have joined in subscribing to this Code of Ethics embracing the following topics:

Responsibilities of the Marketer   Marketers must accept responsibility for the consequences of their activities and make every effort to ensure that their decisions, recommendations, and actions function to identify, serve, and satisfy all relevant publics: customers, organizations, and society. Marketers' professional conduct must be guided by:

1. The basic rule of professional ethics: not knowingly to do harm;
2. The adherence to all applicable laws and regulations;
3. The accurate representation of their education, training, and experience; and
4. The active support, practice, and promotion of this Code of Ethics.

Honesty and Fairness   Marketers shall uphold and advance the integrity, honor, and dignity of the marketing profession by:

1. Being honest in serving consumers, clients, employees, suppliers, distributors, and the public;
2. Not knowingly participating in conflict of interest without prior notice to all parties involved; and

3. Establishing equitable fee schedules including the payment or receipt of usual, customary, and/or legal compensation or marketing exchanges.

Rights and Duties of Parties in the Marketing Exchange Process   Participants in the marketing exchange process should be able to expect that:

1. Products and services offered are safe and fit for their intended uses;
2. Communications about offered products and services are not deceptive;
3. All parties intend to discharge their obligations, financial and otherwise, in good faith; and
4. Appropriate internal methods exist for equitable adjustment and/or redress of grievances concerning purchases.

It is understood that the above would include, *but is not limited to,* the following responsibilities of the marketer:

In the area of product development and management

- Disclosure of all substantial risks associated with product or service usage;
- Identification of any product component substitution that might materially change the product or impact the buyer's purchase decision;
- Identification of extra cost-added features.

exchange resources for various goods and services. Their interest is in making exchanges that help them achieve their goals and in understanding their own behavior. Although the major concern of this text is with ultimate consumers, the logic presented here can also be applied in organizational markets; some examples of organizational buyer behavior are included later in the text.

Consumer Behavior's Role in Marketing Strategy

A **marketing strategy** is the design, implementation, and control of a plan to influence exchanges to achieve organizational objectives. In consumer markets, marketing strategies are typically designed to increase the chances that consumers will have favorable thoughts and feelings about particular products, services, and brands, and will try them and repeatedly purchase them. Also, marketing strategies are developed by retail stores, catalog retailers, e-tailers and other direct marketers to increase the chances that consumers will have favorable thoughts and feelings about purchasing from them and will actually do so. In addition, credit card companies, ATM companies, banks, and other organizations that make funds

In the area of promotions

- Avoidance of false and misleading advertising;
- Rejection of high-pressure manipulation or misleading sales tactics;
- Avoidance of sales promotions that use deception or manipulation.

In the area of distribution

- Not manipulating the availability of a product for purpose of exploitation;
- Not using coercion in the marketing channel;
- Not exerting undue influence over the resellers' choice to handle the product.

In the area of pricing

- Not engaging in price fixing;
- Not practicing predatory pricing;
- Disclosing the full price associated with any purchase.

In the area of marketing research

- Prohibiting selling or fund-raising under the guise of conducting research;
- Maintaining research integrity by avoiding misrepresentation and omission of pertinent research data;
- Treating outside clients and suppliers fairly.

Organizational Relationships   Make aware of how their behavior may influence or impact the behavior of others in organizational relationships. They should not demand, encourage, or apply coercion to obtain unethical behavior in their relationships with others, such as employees, suppliers, or customers.

1. Apply confidentiality and anonymity in professional relationships with regard to privileged information;
2. Meet their obligations and responsibilities in contracts and mutual agreements in a timely manner;
3. Avoid taking the work of others, in whole, or in part, and representing this work as their own or directly benefiting from it without compensation or consent of the originator or owner:
4. Avoid manipulation to take advantage of situations to maximize personal welfare in a way that unfairly deprives or damages the organization or others.

Any AMA member found to be in violation of any provision of this Code of Ethics may have his or her Association membership suspended or revoked.

Source: Reprinted by permission of the American Marketing Association.

available for purchases develop strategies to increase the chances that consumers will use their services. Marketing strategies involve developing and presenting marketing stimuli directed at selected target markets to influence what they think, how they feel, and what they do.

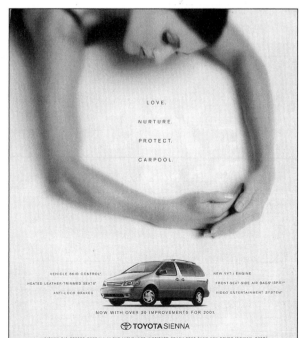

Of course, organizations develop strategies at many levels, from planning the future of large, multinational, multibusiness corporations like General Electric and Philip Morris down to planning a change in the strategy for a single brand/model or a single store. Although consumer behavior research is useful for all levels of strategic analysis, it is most commonly studied and applied at the brand and store levels. Also, published consumer behavior research most commonly focuses on North American markets. Although this book attempts to reflect the state of the art in terms of knowledge about consumer behavior, it will also go beyond these boundaries when possible.

Understanding consumer behavior has helped Toyota develop and market a number of successful vehicles   *Courtesy of Toyota Motor Sales, Inc. Photo of Sienna Car: Peggy Day; Photo of Woman: Howard Schatz.*

Exhibit 1.3

Some Marketing Strategy Questions Consumer Behavior Research Can Help Answer

1. Which consumers are likely to buy this product and our brand, what are they like, how are they different from consumers who don't buy, and how do we reach them?
2. What criteria are consumers likely to use to decide which products and brands to purchase? What will the consumer decision process entail, and what will influence it?
3. Is brand image, convenience, price, particular product attributes, or other criteria most important to consumers of this product?
4. What strategies should be used to encourage consumers to purchase our brand and not purchase those of competitors?
5. How do consumers process information about products, and how can this process be influenced to increase the chances that consumers will have a favorable impression of our brand?
6. What do consumers think and feel about our brand versus competitive brands? What can be done to improve their opinion of our brand?
7. How can we increase the chances that consumers will process information about our brand and come up with a favorable impression?
8. What behaviors do consumers have to perform to purchase and use this product and our brand? How can we increase the frequency with which consumers perform these behaviors? Are there opportunities to change the way consumers purchase and use this product that could give us a competitive advantage?
9. In what situations are consumers likely to purchase and use this product and our brand? How can the number of these situations be increased? What environmental factors influence purchase and use?
10. What price are consumers willing to pay for our product and still believe they are getting good value? Should sales promotions be used and, if so, which ones and how should they be timed?
11. What can we do to satisfy and even delight consumers with our brand so that they become loyal customers?
12. How can we delight consumers of our brand and also meet the needs of owners, employees, suppliers, channel members, society, and other stakeholders?

Exhibit 1.3 lists some marketing strategy questions that knowledge of consumer behavior and consumer behavior research can help answer. They can be addressed in formal consumer research, informal discussions with consumers, and intuition and thinking based on a sound understanding of consumer behavior principles.

It should be clear from Exhibit 1.3 that understanding consumers is a critical element in developing successful marketing strategies. Marketers have to analyze and understand not only consumers of their products and brands but also consumers of competitive offerings and the reasons they purchase competitive products. Understanding markets and developing and implementing superior strategies to attract and hold them profitably is the essence of marketing strategy. Highlight 1.4 discusses the use of consumer research to turn around a failing company.

Finally, it should be clear that marketing strategies, particularly as developed and implemented by successful companies, have a powerful force on consumers and society at large. We believe that marketing strategies not only adapt to consumer needs and wants but also change what consumers think and feel about themselves, about

▸ **High**light 1.4

Coach: Using Consumer Research to Turn Around a Business

Founded in 1941 in a SoHo loft in New York City, Coach built a reputation for quality leather purses in classic styles. By 1995, however, sales declines had CEO Lew Frankfurt well aware that the company was about to hit the wall. Upscale consumers preferred the offerings of companies like Louis Vuitton, Chanel, Gucci, and newcomer Kate Spade. Coach purses were viewed as conservative, traditional bags, the kind women carried to country clubs, rather than as fun, exciting, sexy, or modern.

To turn the company around, new designs using fabric, nylon, and lighter-weight leathers were selected to make the bags trendier. Instead of offering a new collection twice a year, Coach began offering a new collection every month. The company also redesigned its stores and expanded its distribution. It priced its bags at an average of about $200, making them an accessible luxury that appeals both to consumers who have to stretch their budgets to get one and to those who think nothing of spending $700 for Yves Saint Laurent's hot Mombasa bag.

Perhaps the most important change the company made was to select styles based on what consumers thought was cool rather than have designers decide what consumers *should* want. The company spends about $2 million a year on consumer surveys alone. A year before rolling out a product, Coach talks to hundreds of customers, asking for their opinions on every feature of a purse from comfort and strap length to style and color. It asks consumers to rank new designs against existing items. Coach test markets new products in a cross-section of stores around the country. This focus on consumers and understanding what they want sets the company apart in the fashion industry.

Using consumer research and focusing marketing efforts on what consumers want obviously paid off handsomely for Coach. Coach stores have annual sales per square foot of $865 compared to traditional retailers, like the Gap, which average $200 to $300. Coach's net income rose over 400 percent from 1999 to 2002.

Sources: LouAnn Lofton, "Coach's Success Story," Fool.com, June 12, 2003; Amy Tsao, "It's in the Bag for Coach," *Business-Week* Online, April 23, 2003; Julia Boorstin, "How Coach Got Hot," *Fortune,* October 28, 2002, pp. 131–134.

various marketing offerings, and about reasons and situations for purchase and use. This does not mean that marketing is unethical or an inappropriate activity. However, the power of marketing and the ability of consumer research and analysis to yield insight into consumer behavior should not be discounted or misused.

Credit card companies design marketing strategies to influence consumer behavior   *Dion Ogust/The Image Works.*

Back To...

Cyberconsumers: A Growing Group in the New Millennium

As noted earlier, Internet marketing enables marketers to establish one-on-one relationships with consumers and build consumer databases for conducting online consumer research. Successful brick-and-mortar stores like Wal-Mart and JC Penney, as well as point-and-click companies like Amazon.com and eBay, have improved their profitability by serving consumers well. Online consumer research can help these and other companies become even more profitable by answering the questions discussed below.

A first question an Internet marketer might research is whether people who want or need a product are also Internet users. In other words, does the target market have access to computers and a willingness and ability to shop and purchase through them? If not, and the likely growth of Internet use in the target market is small, other modes of distribution would seem more promising.

A second question for research is the size of the target market for the product or service and its geographic dispersion. If the market is small and widely dispersed, marketing on the Internet may make products available that consumers could not easily obtain otherwise.

A third question is whether buying the product or service through the Internet provides value to potential consumers. Surely, making airline reservations at any time of day or night is a convenience that many consumers value. Because Internet reservations save commissions that airlines would have to pay travel agents, airlines can offer even greater value by cutting fares purchased on the Internet. Because many airline travelers are highly educated and regular computer users, this service matches the market well. Similarly, a company like Peapod, which accepts orders and delivers groceries for a fee to busy households in its trading areas, provides value to its customers.

A fourth question is why consumers should buy through the Internet rather than more traditional modes of distribution. Although it can be a convenience, Internet marketers have disadvantages. Consumers cannot experience products firsthand as they can in retail stores. Many consumers are still fearful of giving out credit card information over the Internet, and many do not trust companies and products they do not know well. Internet marketers also have a disadvantage relative to stores, catalogs, and some other modes of purchase because consumers usually must seek them out rather than being contacted by the company. Unless the Internet marketer provides value through confidence, information, or the ability to obtain otherwise difficult-to-find items, the chances of success are limited. Consumer research can help Internet marketers understand their customers, satisfy their needs and wants, and create value for them. ❖

Summary   In this chapter, we argued that consumer behavior is an important topic in business education because achieving marketing objectives depends on knowing, serving, and influencing consumers. We discussed the nature of consumer behavior and the various groups interested in the topic. We also discussed the relationships between consumer behavior and marketing strategy. We hope that after reading this chapter you now appreciate the relevance and importance of a consumer behavior course for your business education. We also hope you will learn something about yourself by considering how the framework and information in our text apply to you as a potential marketing manager, a consumer, and a human being.

Key Terms and Concepts

consumer behavior   **4**
marketing concept   **5**
marketing strategy   **12**

Review and Discussion Questions

1. Why is consumer behavior an important course in business education?
2. Do you think marketing is a powerful force in society? Why or why not?
3. What is the role of consumer analysis in developing marketing strategies?
4. Offer three examples of situations in which a marketing strategy influenced your purchase behavior. Why did each succeed over competitive strategies?
5. Using Exhibit 1.3 as a takeoff point, discuss other questions and decisions in marketing strategy that could be affected by your study of consumer behavior.
6. Select a market segment of which you are *not* a member and, with classmates, discuss the kinds of information you would need to develop a strategy aimed at that segment.
7. Using a campus organization of interest (e.g., student government, professional fraternity, political interest group), discuss how a better understanding of the consumer behavior of students could help the organization improve its influence strategies.

Marketing Strategy in Action

Toyota

Of all the slogans kicked around Toyota, the key one is *kaizen,* which means "continuous improvement" in Japanese. While many other companies strive for dramatic breakthrough, Toyota keeps doing lots of little things better and better. In fact, in the first quarter of 2003, Toyota overtook Ford Motor Company to become the second largest automaker in the world. Ford had been the second largest since 1931.

Toyota simply is tops in quality, production, and efficiency. From its factories pour a wide range of cars, built with unequaled precision. Toyota turns out luxury sedans with Mercedes-Benz-like quality using *one-sixth* the labor Mercedes does. The company originated just-in-time production and remains its leading practitioner. It has close relationships with its suppliers and rigid engineering specifications for the products it purchases.

Toyota's worldwide leadership in the automotive industry was built on its competitive advantage across the supply chain. Between 1990 and 1996, Toyota reduced part defects by 84 percent, compared to 47 percent for the Big 3. It also reduced the ratio of inventories to sales by 35 percent versus 6 percent. These reduction advantages occurred despite the fact that the Big 3 relied on identical suppliers. A study by Jeff Dyer of The Wharton School of the University of Pennsylvania and Kentaro Nobeoka of Kobe University attributed Toyota's success partly to its implementation of bilateral and multilateral, knowledge-sharing routines with suppliers that result in superior interorganizational or network learning. Toyota uses six approaches to facilitate knowledge sharing: (1) a supplier association; (2) teams of consultants; (3) voluntary study groups; (4) problem-solving teams; (5) interfirm employee transfers; and (6) performance feedback and monitoring processes. This effort also involves intense levels of personal contact between Toyota and its suppliers.

Toyota pioneered quality circles, which involve workers in discussions of ways to improve their tasks and avoid what it calls the three Ds: the dangerous, dirty, and demanding aspects of factory work. The company has invested $770 million to improve worker housing, add dining halls, and build new recreational facilities. On the assembly line, quality is defined not as zero defects but, as another slogan puts it, "building the very best and giving the customer what she/he wants." Because each worker serves as the customer for the process just before hers, she becomes a quality control inspector. If a piece isn't installed properly when it reaches her, she won't accept it.

Toyota's engineering system allows it to take a new car design from concept to showroom in less than four years versus more than five years for U.S. companies and seven years for Mercedes. This cuts costs, allows quicker correction of mistakes, and keeps Toyota better abreast of market trends. Gains from speed feed on themselves. Toyota can get its advanced engineering and design done sooner because, as one manager puts it, "We are closer to the customer and thus have a shorter concept time." New products are assigned to a chief engineer who has complete responsibility and authority for the product from design and manufacturing through marketing and has direct contacts with both dealers and consumers. New-model bosses for U.S. companies seldom have such control and almost never have direct contact with dealers or consumers.

The 1999 Harbour Report, a study of automaker competencies in assembly, stamping, and powertrain operations, stated that the top assembly facility in North America (based on assembly hours per vehicle) is Toyota's plant in Cambridge, Ontario. In this plant, a Corolla is produced in 17.66 hours. Toyota was also rated number one in engine assembly, taking just 2.97 hours to produce an engine.

In Toyota's manufacturing system, parts and cars don't get built until orders come from dealers requesting them. In placing orders, dealers essentially reserve a portion of factory capacity. The system is so effective that rather than waiting several months for a new car, the customer can get a built-to-order car in a week to 10 days.

Toyota is the best carmaker in the world because it stays close to its customers. "We have learned that universal mass production is not enough," said the head of Toyota's Tokyo Design Center. "In the 21st century, you personalize things more to make them more reflective of individual needs."

In 1999, Toyota committed to a $13 billion investment through 2000 to become a genuinely global corporation without boundaries. In this way, it will be able to create worldwide manufacturing facilities that produce cars according to local demand. Its goal is to achieve a 10 to 15 percent global market share by 2010.

Why the drive toward customization of vehicles? Part of this is due to fierce competition that provides consumers with a multitude of choices. The Internet enables consumers to be more demanding and less compromising. They now have access to the lowest prices available for specific models of vehicles with all of the bells and whistles they desire. From the comfort of their homes, they are able to bypass dealers and still find the vehicle of their dreams.

Senior management at Toyota believes that *kaizen* is no longer enough. The senior vice president at the Toyota USA division, Douglas West, states that his division is committed to both creating and executing a new information system to drive the fastest, most efficient order-to-delivery system in the North American market. Toyota management has come to realize that *kaizen* alone can no longer predict business success. The sweeping changes taking place in the business environment can no longer rely on the *kaizen* philosophy of small, sustained improvements. In fact, one expert in the industry believes that "pursuing incremental improvements while rivals reinvent the industry is like fiddling while Rome burns." Competitive vitality can no longer be defined by continuous improvement alone.

Discussion Questions

1. In what ways is Toyota's new-product development system designed to serve customers?
2. In what ways is Toyota's manufacturing system designed to serve customers?
3. How does Toyota personalize its cars and trucks to meet individual consumer needs?
4. In its price ranges, how do you think Toyota cars stack up against the competition? (You can check out all of its models at **http://www.toyota.com**.)
5. How has the Internet changed the way consumers shop for and buy cars?

Sources: Alex Taylor III, "And It's Toyota by a Nose!" *Fortune*, June 9, 2003, p. 34; Marc Halpern, "Integrating the Supplier Chain, Toyota's U.S. Advantage," *Computer-Aided Engineering*, September, 1999, pp. 52–53; Gary S. Vasilash, "Making It: How the Automakers Measure Up," *Automotive Manufacturing and Production*, September 1999, pp. 70–71; Oren Harari, "Kaizen Is Not Enough," *Management Review*, September 1997, pp. 25–29; Alex Taylor III, "Why Toyota Keeps Getting Better and Better and Better," *Fortune*, November 19, 1990, pp. 66–77. Also see William Spindle, Larry Armstrong, and James B. Treece, "Toyota Retooled," *Business Week*, April 4, 1994, pp. 54–57; Edith Hill Updike, Keith Naughton, and Larry Armstrong, "I Think They Were Just Lying Low," *Business Week*, December 18, 1995, pp. 50–51; **http://www.toyota.com**.

2

A Framework for Consumer Analysis

Buying a Smith & Wesson: Good or Bad Idea?

Barbara Linton is 37, divorced, and the mother of two daughters, Joanne and Jenny, ages 7 and 9. A successful doctor, she makes more than $90,000 annually. She lives in her own home in a Chicago suburb with her children, who go to private schools.

Recently a number of robberies and burglaries have occurred close to her neighborhood. One of her friends was attacked in a mall parking lot and robbed. Barbara is concerned about her safety and that of her children and is considering buying a gun for home protection. However, she is worried about the safety of having a loaded gun in her home with the kids around.

Barbara's uncle owns a gun store and shooting club in her hometown near Minneapolis. She decides to visit him at the store and evaluate further the pros and cons of getting a gun on her next trip home.

After the 10 o'clock news report on another robbery in her area, Barbara decides to take the kids and fly home to see her family the following weekend. While there she goes to see her uncle at his shop.

"Hi, Uncle Al," she greets him. "How is the gun business?"

Uncle Al replies that the gun business is doing fine. He says the shooting club is also doing well and has lots of new members.

Barbara explains that she is thinking about buying a gun because of all the recent crime in her area. She also explains her concerns about the safety of having a gun around the house.

Uncle Al tells her he does not want to try to influence her decision. He believes people have to decide for themselves whether owning a gun is right for them. However, if they do choose to buy one, they need to learn how to load and fire it safely and effectively. He also says a gun lock can be put on the trigger housing to avoid problems with the children.

Barbara decides to buy a gun for her home. She asks her uncle to recommend the best model for her needs.

Uncle Al tells her he thinks a revolver is much simpler to operate and safer to handle

Mark Richards/PhotoEdit, Inc.

than an automatic. He recommends a Smith & Wesson Model 686 stainless-steel revolver with a 4-inch barrel and black rubber Pachmeyer grips for better handling. Although the Model 686 handles .357 caliber ammunition, .38 Special cartridges can also be used in it. He recommends using the .38s at first because they produce less recoil when fired, and then stepping up to the .357s when her skills develop because they have more stopping power.

Barbara and her uncle walk over to the shooting range with his Model 686. He explains how to load the revolver and how to shoot it in both single and double action. He also shows her a trigger lock and how to put it on the gun. Barbara loads the gun and tries it out at the range. She is surprised how easy it is to shoot and hit a silhouette target at 25 feet. She thinks the gun looks and feels good and would be right for her needs.

Her uncle cannot sell her one because she is no longer a resident of Minnesota, so she purchases a Model 686 when she returns to Chicago. She also buys rubber grips, two boxes of .38 Special cartridges, a Kolpin gun case, and a trigger lock for the gun. She joins an upscale shooting club to improve her skills and to meet other people who face the same problems she does. She now feels safer in her home.

What factors are involved in the purchases made by Barbara Linton? Many theories, models, and concepts have been borrowed from other fields and developed by marketing researchers in attempts to understand consumer behavior. In many cases, these ideas overlap and even compete with one another as useful descriptions of consumers. To date, no one approach is fully accepted, nor is it likely that a single, grand theory of consumer behavior can be devised that all researchers would agree on.

Nevertheless, in this chapter we present a framework for researching, analyzing, and understanding consumers to help marketers develop more effective strategies. The framework is a general one that can be used to analyze any consumer behavior issue facing marketers, from developing new products and services to improving strategies for existing products and services. It can be used to aid nonprofit organizations in developing exchanges with consumers, including donations and use

Exhibit 2.1

Three Elements for Consumer Analysis

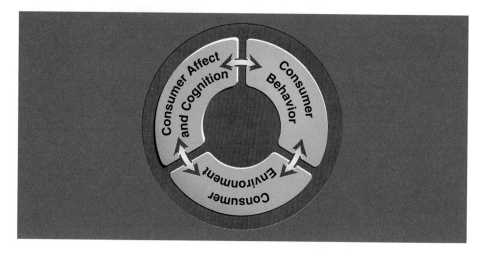

of nonprofit services, such as museums and libraries. The framework also provides the organizational structure for this book.

We begin the chapter by introducing three elements that should be researched and analyzed to develop effective marketing strategies: (1) consumer affect and cognition, (2) consumer behavior, and (3) consumer environments. Then we discuss the special relationships among these elements and the role of consumer research and analysis in developing marketing strategies. Next, we discuss marketing strategy—the stimuli placed in the environment to influence consumers. We conclude with a discussion of four levels of consumer analysis.

Three Elements for Consumer Analysis

Exhibit 2.1 presents three elements for consumer analysis and the relationships among them. Each element is critical for developing a complete understanding of consumers and selecting strategies to influence them.

Consumer Affect and Cognition

Consumer *affect* and *cognition* refer to two types of mental responses consumers exhibit toward stimuli and events in their environment. **Affect** refers to their feelings about stimuli and events, such as whether they like or dislike a product. **Cognition** refers to their thinking, such as their beliefs about a particular product.

Affective responses can be favorable or unfavorable and vary in intensity. For instance, affect includes relatively intense *emotions* such as love or anger, less strong *feeling states* such as satisfaction or frustration, *moods* such as boredom or relaxation, and milder overall *attitudes* such as liking McDonald's french fries or disliking Bic pens. Marketers typically develop strategies to create positive affect for their products and brands to increase the chances that consumers will buy them.

Cognition refers to the mental structures and processes involved in thinking, understanding, and interpreting stimuli and events. It includes the knowledge, meanings, and beliefs that consumers have developed from their experiences and stored in their memories. It also includes the processes associated with paying attention to and understanding stimuli and events, remembering past events, forming evaluations, and making

Highlight 2.1

Some Basic Questions about Consumer Affect and Cognition

Although many competing theories and ideas about consumer affect and cognition have been proposed, no single theory completely describes the workings of the consumer's mind. However, carefully studying and thinking about the information in Section 2 of this text should help you develop informed answers to questions about affect and cognition such as the following:

1. How do consumers interpret information about marketing stimuli such as products, stores, and advertising?

2. How do consumers choose from among alternative product classes, products, and brands?

3. How do consumers form evaluations of products and brands?

4. How does memory affect consumer decision making?

5. How do affect and cognition influence behavior and environments?

6. How do behavior and environments influence affect and cognition?

7. How do consumers interpret the benefits of marketing offerings?

8. Why are consumers more interested or involved in some products or brands than others?

9. How do marketing strategies influence consumers' affective and cognitive responses?

10. How do affective and cognitive responses influence each other?

purchasing decisions and choices. Although many aspects of cognition are conscious thinking processes, others are essentially automatic. Marketers often try to increase consumers' attention to products and their knowledge about them. For example, Volvo ads often feature detailed information about the safety features of the cars to increase consumers' knowledge and the chances that they will buy Volvos.

Section 2 of this text offers a detailed treatment of consumer affect and cognition and explains the importance of understanding them for developing marketing strategies. Highlight 2.1 offers a sample of the types of questions Section 2 is designed to answer.

Both affect and cognition are involved in the purchase and use of products   *(left)*
Myrleen Ferguson Cate/ PhotoEdit, Inc. (right)
John A. Coletti/Stock, Boston, LLC.

Highlight 2.2

Some Basic Questions about Consumer Behaviors

Although less attention has been given to studying overt behavior of consumers, many behavior influence techniques seem to be commonly used by marketing practitioners. Carefully studying and thinking about the information in Section 3 of this text should help you develop informed answers to questions about behavior such as these:

1. How do behavior approaches differ from affective and cognitive approaches to studying consumer behavior?

2. What is classical conditioning, and how is it used by marketers to influence consumer behavior?

3. What is operant conditioning, and how is it used by marketers to influence consumer behavior?

4. What is vicarious learning, and how is it used by marketers to influence consumer behavior?

5. What consumer behaviors are of interest to marketing management?

6. How much control does marketing have over consumers' behavior?

7. How do affect and cognition and environments affect behavior?

8. How does behavior influence affect and cognition and environments?

9. How can behavior theory be used by marketing managers?

10. Do the frequency and quality of consumer behavior vary by individuals, products, and situations?

Consumer Behavior

In this text, **behavior** refers to the physical actions of consumers that can be directly observed and measured by others. It is also called *overt behavior* to distinguish it from mental activities, such as thinking, that cannot be observed directly. Thus, a trip to The Gap at the mall involves behavior; deciding whether to go there is not an overt behavior because it cannot be observed by others. Examples of behaviors include shopping at stores or on the Internet, buying products, and using credit cards.

Behavior is critical for marketing strategy because only through behavior can sales be made and profits earned. Although many marketing strategies are designed to influence consumers' affect and cognition, these strategies must ultimately result in overt consumer behavior to have value for the company. Thus, it is critical for marketers to analyze, understand, and influence overt behavior. This can be done in many ways, including offering superior quality (Toyota), lower prices (Circuit City), greater convenience (Peapod online groceries), easier availability (Coke is sold in millions of stores and vending machines), and better service (Briggs & Stratton lawnmower engines are serviced at 25,000 locations). Marketers can also influence overt behavior by offering products, stores, and brands that are trendier (The Gap), sexier (Calvin Klein jeans), more popular (Nike), and more prestigious (Mont Blanc pens) than competitive offerings.

Section 3 of this text is devoted to overt consumer behavior. Highlight 2.2 offers a sample of the types of questions Section 3 is designed to answer to aid in developing successful marketing strategies.

Consumer Environment

The consumer **environment** refers to everything external to consumers that influences what they think, feel, and do. It includes social stimuli, such as the actions of

Lower prices can influence overt consumer behavior   *Tony Freeman/PhotoEdit, Inc.*

Consumer research can help marketers understand consumer affect and cognition, behavior, and environments   *Spencer Grant/PhotoEdit, Inc.*

others in cultures, subcultures, social classes, reference groups, and families, that influence consumers. It also includes other physical stimuli, such as stores, products, advertisements, and signs, that can change consumers' thoughts, feelings, and actions.

The consumer environment is important to marketing strategy because it is the medium in which stimuli are placed to influence consumers. For example, marketers run commercials during shows that their target markets watch to inform, persuade, and remind them to buy certain products and brands. Marketers can send free samples, coupons, catalogs, and advertisements by mail to get them into consumers' environments. Stores are located close to populated areas to get them in the proximity of consumers. Websites become part of a consumer's environment if they are contacted.

Section 4 of this text discusses the environment and its influence on consumers. Highlight 2.3 offers a sample of the types of questions Section 4 is designed to answer.

Relationships among Affect and Cognition, Behavior, and the Environment

In Exhibit 2.1 each of the three elements is connected by a two-headed arrow signifying that any of them can be either a cause or an effect of a change in one or more of the other element. For example, a consumer sees an ad for a new laundry detergent that promises to clean clothes better than Tide. This ad changes what the consumer thinks about the new brand and leads to a purchase of it. In this case, a change in the consumer's environment (the ad for the new detergent) led to a change in cognition (the consumer believed the new detergent was better), which led to a change in behavior (the consumer bought the new brand).

A change in laundry detergent purchase and use could come about in other ways. For example, a consumer receives a free sample of a new liquid detergent in the mail, tries it out, likes it, and then purchases it. In this case, a change in the consumer's environment (the free sample) led to a change in behavior (use and purchase), which led to a change in the consumer's affect and cognition (liking the new brand).

Another possibility is that a consumer is dissatisfied with his or her current brand of laundry detergent. On the next trip to the grocery store, the consumer inspects other brands and selects one that promises to get white clothes whiter. In this example, a change in affect and cognition (dissatisfaction) led to a change in the

---

▶ **High**light 2.3

Some Basic Questions about Consumer Environments

Environmental psychology seeks to extend knowledge about the relationships between environmental stimuli and human behavior. In consumer research, the major environmental factors examined have been concerned with the impact of various societal aspects. Carefully studying and thinking about the information in Section 4 of this text should help you develop informed answers to these questions about the environment:

1. In what physical environments do consumer behaviors occur?

2. How do environments influence consumers' affect and cognition and behavior?

3. How do consumer affect and cognition and behavior affect the environment?

4. What effect does culture have on consumers?

5. What effect does subculture have on consumers?

6. What effect does social class have on consumers?

7. What effect do reference groups have on consumers?

8. What effect do families have on consumers?

9. In what ways do consumers influence one another concerning marketing offerings?

10. How powerful are interpersonal influences on consumer behavior?

---

consumer's environment (inspecting other brands), which led to a change in behavior (purchase of a different brand).

Although changes can occur in other ways, these examples serve to illustrate our view of consumers, namely, that consumer processes not only involve a dynamic and interactive system but also represent a *reciprocal system*.[1] In a **reciprocal system,** any of the elements can be either a cause or an effect of a change at any particular time. Affect and cognition can change consumer behavior and environments. Behavior can change consumers' affect, cognition, and environments. Environments can change consumers' affect, cognition, and behavior.

There are five implications to viewing consumer processes as a reciprocal system involving affect and cognition, behavior, and the environment. First, any comprehensive analysis of consumers must consider all three elements and the relationships among them. Descriptions of consumers in terms of only one or two of the elements are incomplete. For example, to assume that affect and cognition always cause behavior and ignore the impact of the environment underestimates the dynamic nature of consumption processes. Similarly, to assume that the environment controls behavior without consideration of affect and cognition also gives an incomplete description. The development of marketing strategies should include an analysis of all three elements, their relationships, and the direction of causal change at particular times.

Second, any of the three elements may be the starting point for consumer analysis. Although we think that marketing strategists should start with an analysis of the specific overt behaviors consumers must perform to achieve marketing objectives, useful analyses could start with affect and cognition by researching what consumers think and feel about such things as the various brands of a product. Alternatively, the analysis could start with consumers' environments by examining changes in their worlds that could change their affect, cognition, and behavior. However, regardless of the starting point, all three elements and their relationships should be analyzed.

Exhibit 2.2

The Role of Consumer Research and Analysis in Marketing Strategy

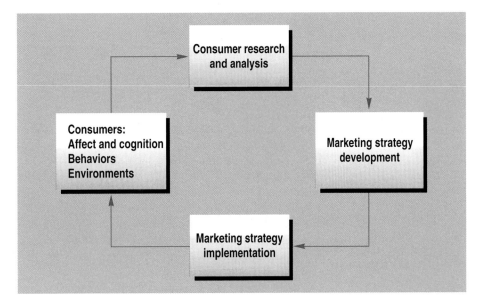

Third, because this view is dynamic, it recognizes that consumers can continuously change. Although some consumers may change little during a particular time period, others may change their affect, cognition, behavior, and environments frequently. Thus, keeping abreast of consumers involves continuous research to detect changes that could influence marketing strategies.

Fourth, although our example focused on a single consumer, consumer analysis can be applied at several levels. It can be used to analyze not only a single consumer but also groups of consumers that make up a target market—a larger group of consumers made up of all the purchasers of a product in an industry—or an entire society. Because marketing strategies can be applied at all of these levels, this approach is useful for all types of marketing issues, as discussed at the end of the chapter.

Finally, this framework for analyzing consumers highlights the importance of consumer research and analysis in developing marketing strategies. As shown in Exhibit 2.2, consumer research and analysis should be key activities for developing marketing strategies. Consumer research includes many types of studies, such as test marketing, advertising pretests, sales promotion effects, analysis of sales and market share data, pricing experiments, traffic and shopping patterns, surveys, and many others.

A logical sequence is to first research and analyze what consumers think, feel, and do relative to a company's offerings and those of competitors. In addition, an analysis of consumer environments is called for to see what factors are currently influencing them and what changes are occurring. Based on this research and analysis, a marketing strategy is developed that involves setting objectives, specifying an appropriate target market, and developing a marketing mix (product, promotion, price, place) to influence it. After the target market has been selected based on careful analysis of key differences in groups of consumers, marketing strategies involve placing stimuli in the enviroment that hopefully will become part of the target market's environment and ultimately influence its members' behavior.

Consumer research and analysis should not end when a strategy has been implemented, however. Rather, research should continue to investigate the effects of the strategy and whether it could be made more effective. For example, although AriZona Beverages implemented a successful strategy for selling its products, it tried to increase its market share by using squeezable sports bottles with a nozzle like the ones athletes use to guzzle on the run. Thus, marketing strategy should involve a continuous process of researching and analyzing consumers and developing, implementing, and continuously improving strategies.

Marketing Strategy   From a consumer analysis point of view, a **marketing strategy** is a set of stimuli placed in consumers' environments designed to influence their affect, cognition, and behavior. These stimuli include such things as products, brands, packaging, advertisements, coupons, stores, credit cards, price tags, salespeople's communications, and, in some cases, sounds (music), smells (perfume), and other sensory cues.

Exhibit 2.3 presents our complete framework, which we call the Wheel of Consumer Analysis. It is a wheel because it is constantly rotating with changes in consumers and in marketing strategy. Marketing strategy is treated as the hub of the wheel because it is a central marketing activity and is designed by marketing organizations to influence consumers.

Clearly, marketing strategies should be designed not only to influence consumers but also to be influenced by them. For example, if research shows that

Exhibit 2.3

The Wheel of Consumer Analysis

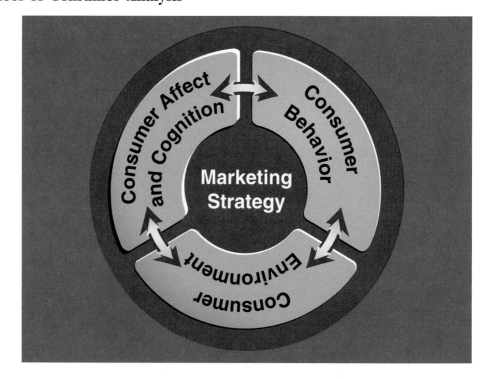

Highlight 2.4

Some Basic Questions about Marketing Strategy and Consumers

Consumers are the focal point in the development of successful marketing strategies. Marketing strategies both influence and are influenced by consumers' affect and cognition, behavior, and environment. Carefully studying and thinking about the information in Section 5 of this text should help you develop informed answers to questions about marketing strategies such as the following:

1. What are some effective ways to segment markets?
2. How can products be effectively positioned?
3. What are the relationships between product strategies and consumers?

4. What are the relationships between promotion strategies and consumers?
5. What are the relationships between channels of distribution and consumers?
6. What are the relationships between pricing strategies and consumers?
7. What consumer variables affect the success of a marketing strategy?
8. How can a firm develop brand-loyal consumers?
9. What is the role of consumer satisfaction in developing successful market offerings?
10. How does nonstore consumer behavior differ from behavior in stores?

consumers are disgusted (affect and cognition) with blatant advertisements for Calvin Klein jeans, the company may want to change its ads to better appeal to the market. If research shows that consumers in the target market do not shop (behavior) in stores where a company's product is featured, the distribution strategy may have to be changed. If research shows that consumers want to be able to get information from a company's website (environment) and none exists, the company may want to create one. Thus, marketing strategies should be developed, implemented, and changed based on consumer research and analysis.

Section 5 of this text is devoted to marketing strategy. Although the entire text focuses on applying consumer analysis to marketing strategy issues, Section 5 focuses specifically on market segmentation and each element of the marketing mix: product, promotion, price, and place (channels of distribution).[2] Highlight 2.4 offers a sample of the types of questions Section 5 is designed to answer.

Levels of Consumer Analysis

As noted, consumer research and analysis can be conducted at several different levels. The Wheel of Consumer Analysis is a flexible tool that can aid in understanding different societies, industries, market segments, or individual consumers. It can be used fruitfully by both marketing strategists and public policy officials to understand the dynamics that shape each of these levels.

Societies

Changes in what a society believes and how its members behave can be analyzed with the Wheel of Consumer Analysis. For example, a recent change in our society involves greater concern with health and fitness. How did this change occur? Surely, consumers were always concerned with living long, happy lives. A growing body of medical research indicated people could be healthier and live longer if they

Our society's emphasis on health and fitness can be accounted for by the Wheel of Consumer Analysis   *©1996 Weslo is a registered trademark of Icon Health & Fitness, Inc.*

ate properly and exercised regularly. This research may have changed attitudes of some consumers about their eating and exercise habits. As these consumers, particularly those on the West Coast, changed their attitudes and began living more healthful lifestyles, many other consumers copied these beliefs and behavior patterns. In addition, healthy, well-toned people are considered more attractive in our society. This belief may have accelerated the health and fitness movement. Also, because a variety of health-related industries, such as health foods, exercise equipment, and sports apparel, developed and promoted proper eating habits and regular exercise, consumers were increasingly exposed to the concept and benefits of an active lifestyle.

Of course, not everyone in society has changed his or her lifestyle, and some who did eventually reverted to less healthful habits. However, the brief discussion here shows changes in the environment (medical research reports), cognition and affect (beliefs about how to live longer and healthier), behavior (eating healthful foods and exercising), and marketing strategies (development and promotion of health foods, exercise equipment, and apparel products) that interacted to create this change in society in general. The Wheel of Consumer Analysis can account for these changes in our society and can also be applied to other societies to help explain their structures and practices.

Industries

The Wheel of Consumer Analysis can be used to analyze the relationships of a company and its competitors with consumers in specific industries. For example, consider the effects of health concerns on the beer industry. Lite beer from Miller took advantage of the health movement and created the market for reduced-calorie beer. Miller Brewing Company became the light-beer market leader by being the first to offer a product that was more consistent with a change occurring in society, and it also, through developing and marketing the product, helped accelerate the change. Thus, a change in consumer beliefs and behavior concerning calorie intake influenced a marketing strategy to introduce and spread the change in consumer beliefs and behaviors. The success of the product influenced competitors to also offer light beers, further changing demand for this product category.

However, another change in this industry is the concern with responsible drinking, which decreases demand for alcohol products in general. This change has led to the development and marketing of nonalcoholic beers and, for many consumers, abstinence from any alcoholic beverages. Consumer groups such as Mothers Against Drunk Driving and Students Against Drunk Driving have also influenced many members of society to reduce their alcohol consumption. Although being drunk and boisterous was considered acceptable behavior some years ago, many consumers no

The food industry has developed and marketed new products to respond to consumers' demand for faster food preparation   *Courtesy of the Quaker Oats Company (left) and Robert Bull (right).*

longer find it so. Similarly, smoking was at one time considered a sign of maturity and "coolness," whereas today fewer and fewer public places tolerate smoking.

At the industry level, changes in consumer cognition, affect, and behavior can threaten existing products and can also offer opportunities to develop products more consistent with new values and behaviors. Successful marketing strategies depend on analyzing consumer–product relationships not only for the company's products but for those of competitors, and creating an advantage over competitive offerings.

Market Segments

The Wheel of Consumer Analysis can be used to analyze groups of consumers who have some similarity in cognition, affect, behavior, and environment. Successful firms in an industry usually divide the total market into segments and try to appeal most strongly to one or more of them. For example, the emphasis on health encouraged many consumers to become involved in sports. However, specific shoes designed to play each sport effectively were not always available. Today consumers can find many varieties and styles of shoes for running, bicycling, soccer, basketball, and other sports. These shoes vary in design, features, and price ranges to appeal to groups of consumers that are similar in some ways.

Reebok, for example, developed its Blacktop shoe for young basketball players on urban outdoor courts. The shoe was a few ounces heavier than those of competitors, moderately priced, and designed for performance on asphalt and concrete. The shoe looked good, so it appealed to the 80 percent of consumers who buy athletic shoes solely for fashion, but it also was tough enough to stand up to rugged outdoor play. The shoe sold out in many stores in its first two months, and more than 2.2 million pairs were expected to be sold in its first year—a smashing marketing success.[3] Thus, by understanding the wants and preferences (cognition and affect) of urban youths (target market) for a good-looking, moderately priced, long-wearing shoe, promoted for regular guys who play basketball (behavior) on outdoor courts (environment), Reebok developed a successful marketing strategy.

Individual Consumers

Finally, the Wheel of Consumer Analysis can be used to analyze the consumption history, a single purchase, or some aspect of a purchase for a specific consumer. Lands' End, a catalog marketer, carefully analyzes individual consumers in terms of their previous purchasing history. The company can then target individual consumers with specialty catalogs of the types of merchandise previously bought. To understand Barbara Linton's purchase of a Smith & Wesson handgun, we need to consider her affect, behavior, cognition, and environment, discussed in the following case.

Back To...

Buying a Smith & Wesson

This case provides a simple description of the purchase of a gun and accessories. We hope it is written in such a manner that you can easily understand the sequence of events. However, imagine how difficult it would be to try to describe these events by considering *only* cognitive and affective *or* behavioral *or* environmental factors.

Cognitive and affective factors, such as Barbara's concern for her family's safety, her information processing and decision making to buy a gun, and her feelings of greater safety, are useful—but they alone could not explain what Barbara did and the environmental factors that influenced these thoughts and actions. Her overt behavior, such as visiting her uncle, trying the gun, and purchasing the gun and equipment, is also helpful, but is

incomplete for capturing the meaning of the behavior and the contexts in which these actions occurred. Environmental factors, such as the news reports on crimes, the proximity of the crimes to her neighborhood, the information from her uncle, the look and feel of the gun, the feedback from the environment from her shots hitting the target, and the time lapses and place changes between the events described, are necessary for understanding the case, but are quite sterile when discussed independently of Barbara's cognitive, affective, and behavioral events.

Thus, even for a simple description of a consumer purchase, all three elements—affect and cognition, behavior, and environment—work together to provide efficient, useful knowledge of consumer behavior. All three are also necessary for academic attempts to understand consumers and for managerial attempts to develop successful marketing strategies. Analysis of all three elements is superior to any one or two of the elements taken in isolation.

Finally, all three elements of the wheel are needed to understand not just a gun purchase by an individual consumer but also society's views and uses of guns, the gun industry, and various target markets for guns. All three elements are needed to analyze questions concerning the pros and cons of gun ownership in various societies, the relationships among gun buyers and various gun manufacturers and retailers in the industry, and relationships among the target markets for guns and various brands and models. Whether one is developing a marketing strategy to sell guns or legislation to stop the sale of guns, analysis of consumer affect and cognition, behavior, and environments is required for effective action.[4] ❖

Summary In this chapter, we presented our overall framework for the analysis of consumer behavior. We also described a general approach to developing marketing strategies intended to influence consumers' affect and cognition, behavior, and environments. We believe this framework can help you understand many of the complexities of consumer behavior. However, other concepts related to consumer behavior must be considered. Later in this text, we will present many of these concepts and discuss how they can be used to develop, select, and evaluate marketing strategies.

Key Terms and Concepts

affect **22**

behavior **23**

cognition **22**

environment **24**

marketing strategy **28**

reciprocal system **26**

Review and Discussion Questions

1. Explain consumer affect and cognition, behavior, and environment. Why do marketers need to consider all three in developing strategies?
2. Explain the relationship between consumer environments and marketing strategy.
3. Why must marketing strategies ultimately influence overt consumer behavior to be successful?
4. What are the implications of viewing consumer processes as a reciprocal system?
5. Explain four levels at which consumer analysis can be conducted. Offer one example of how consumer analysis could aid marketers at each level.
6. Offer three examples of how a change in a marketing strategy led to changes in your affect, cognition, behavior, and environment.
7. In considering your answer to question 6, do you think there was anything unethical in the marketing strategies?
8. ▼ Look up information on aging in the United States at the census website, **http://www.census.gov**. What changes are taking place in the age of the population in general and in racial, ethnic, and gender groups? For what levels of consumer analysis would this information be useful?

Marketing Strategy in Action

Starbucks

In 2003, Starbucks accomplished something that few companies ever do: It became a Fortune 500 company—a phenomenal achievement for a company that went public only 12 years earlier. The company had over 6,000 stores worldwide—all company owned, as Starbucks does not franchise its outlets—and planned to expand rapidly to over 10,000 stores.

Starbucks created not only a successful business but a thriving industry. When the company started its massive expansion in the early 1990s, the United States had about 200 coffeehouses. In 2003 there were over 14,000 coffeehouses, the majority of them not Starbucks but mom-and-pops that bloomed after the dawn of the $3 cup of coffee. According to a Starbucks executive, "We changed the way people live their lives, what they do when they get up in the morning, how they reward themselves, and where they meet. That's more important to me than just building a company."

More than 10 million coffee lovers spend an average of $3.60 at Starbucks weekly, and 10 percent of them come in twice a day. Starbucks has 7 percent of the U.S. coffee-drinking market and less than 1 percent abroad, suggesting ample room for growth. The coffee market is huge; coffee is the second most consumed drink in the world (water is first).

Starbucks' iced beverages, which offer larger profit margins than regular drip coffee, are big sellers in the South and Southwest. After making some adjustments, such as adding outdoor seating and couches to stores to better serve the needs of its customers, Atlanta locations have shown double-digit sales growth. Atlanta boasts 33 successful Starbucks, and plans for expansion are in the works. Plans for further expansion in cities with even more Starbucks stores, such as New York City and San Francisco, are also on the drawing board. Although 70 stores operate in New York City alone, it is estimated that growth there will continue until 200 stores are operating in the city! As for fears of market saturation, Starbucks has none. In fact, the java giant has two highly profitable outlets that face each other on Robson Street in Vancouver, British Columbia. Each store has more than $1 million in annual sales. International expansion is also taking place. In fact, the number one Starbucks in the world is located in Tokyo, and a total of 500 stores are slated to be operational in Asia in the next three years.

What is the secret of Starbucks' phenomenal success? According to Howard Schultz, chairman and CEO of Starbucks Corporation, the company's success is due to the experience created within the stores as well as the unsurpassed quality of the coffee. A steaming café au lait must be perfectly replicated, whether the store is in Seattle or New

Lauren Goodsmith/The Image Works.

York City. In a world filled with people leading busy, stressful lives, Schultz believes he has created a "third place" between home and work where people can go to get their own personal time out or to relax with friends.

Schultz also attributes his company's success to the 40,000 employees working worldwide. Starbucks' employee training program churns out "baristas" by educating 300 to 400 new hires per month in classes such as "Brewing the Perfect Cup at Home" and "Coffee Knowledge." Here they are taught to remind customers to purchase new beans weekly and that tap water might not be sufficient when brewing the perfect cup of coffee. They are also encouraged to share their feelings about coffee, selling, and working for Starbucks. Employees are also given guidelines to maintain and enhance self-esteem, to learn how to listen and acknowledge, and to know when to ask for help. E-mail, suggestion cards, and regular forms allow unsatisfied workers to communicate with headquarters. If the annual barista turnover of 60 percent, compared with 140 percent for hourly workers in the fast-food industry, is any indication of the quality of its training programs, Starbucks seems to have a handle on how to gain and maintain employee loyalty. What about the demographic makeup of the work force? About 80 percent of the employees are white, 85 percent have some education beyond high school, and the average age is 26.

The Starbucks success story is continuing into the 21st century as the company is quickly expanding into Europe and Asia. However, one question remains regarding the success of the company in countries already known for their coffee-making expertise: Will such Romans and Parisians care for Starbucks? Continued expansion and visibility has been created domestically as Starbucks has formed partnerships with companies such as United Airlines and Barnes & Noble Booksellers, both of which draw from the same type of knowledgeable customer.

More recently, Starbucks has opened several full-service dining establishments (Café Starbucks) in response to customers who want more at lunch and dinner. The menu offers full meals, breads, pastries, alcohol, and, of course, coffee. The company has also launched an Internet site that sells not only expensive coffee but also pricy kitchenware, home furnishings, and gourmet food. After some skepticism by analysts and a subsequent drop in share price, Schultz emphasized that "Every company must stick to its knitting, understand its core competency, know what the value proposition is for the customer, and do everything possible to get close to the customer. So you won't see us getting far afield from what we do now." As for the present, Starbucks is not likely to fall victim to a fad-driven society any time soon. The company seems to be doing just fine.

You can learn more about Starbucks at **http://www.starbucks.com**.

Discussion Questions

1. Based on the case information and your personal experiences, list at least five things you know about Starbucks. This list offers you some idea about your cognitions concerning the coffee shop chain.
2. List at least five things you like or dislike about Starbucks. This list gives you some idea of your affect for the coffee shops.
3. List at least five behaviors involved in buying a gourmet coffee drink from Starbucks. This list gives you an idea of the behaviors involved in a coffee purchase.
4. List at least five things Starbucks does in the environment to influence consumers' coffee purchases. This list gives you some idea of how the environment influences affect and cognition and behavior.
5. Review the Starbucks website at **http://www.starbucks.com**. Do you think the descriptions of specialty drinks increase sales? Why or why not?

Sources: Cora Daniels, "Mr. Coffee," *Fortune,* April 14, 2003, pp. 139–140; Benjamin Fulford, "Smell the Beans," *Forbes,* September 4, 2000, p. 56; Anonymous, "Interview with Howard Schultz: Sharing Success," *Executive Excellence,* November 1999, pp. 16–17; Nelson D. Schwartz, "Still Perking after All These Years," *Fortune,* May 24, 1999, pp. 203–210; Janice Matsumoto, "More Than Mocha—Café Starbucks," *Restaurants & Institutions,* October 1, 1998, p. 21; Naomi Weiss, "How Starbucks Impassions Workers to Drive Growth," *Workforce,* August 1998, pp. 60–64; Jennifer Reese, "Starbucks: Inside the Coffee Cult," *Fortune,* December 9, 1996, pp. 190–200.

two

Affect and Cognition and Marketing Strategy

3

Introduction to Affect and Cognition

"Everyday" Affect and Cognition: Greg Macklin Goes Shopping

Along with millions of other consumers, Greg Macklin makes a weekly trip to a local supermarket to buy groceries. On this sunny Saturday morning, Greg drives to the Giant supermarket with his three-year-old daughter, Angela. As he walks through the front doors of the store, Greg enters one of the most complex informational environments a consumer can face.

A supermarket is loaded with information. The average American grocery store stocks some 10,000 items, and some very large stores carry as many as 20,000. Large supermarkets offer many alternatives in each product category. For instance, one large store offers 18 brands of mustard in a variety of sizes. Moreover, most product packages contain lots of information. The average package of breakfast cereal, for example, contains some 250 individual pieces of information!

Despite this complexity, Greg (like most of us) feels no particular uneasiness about grocery shopping. He isn't particularly excited either, because this is familiar territory. During the next 45 minutes (the average time consumers spend in the store on a major shopping trip), Greg will process a great deal of information. He will make numerous decisions during the time it takes to fill his grocery cart. Most of his choices will be made easily and quickly, seemingly with little effort. Some choices, though, will involve noticeable cognition (thinking) and may require a few seconds. And a few choices may require substantial cognitive processing and several seconds, perhaps even minutes. How does Greg Macklin move through this complex informational environment so easily, buying several dozen products? The affective and cognitive processes that make this possible are the subject of this chapter.

Andy Sacks/Metty Images.

This apparently simple, everyday example of shopping for groceries actually involves rather complex interactions among various aspects of the supermarket environment, marketing strategies, Greg Macklin's behavior, and his affective and cognitive systems. In this chapter, we begin our examination of the affect and cognition portion of the Wheel of Consumer Analysis. We describe consumers' affective and cognitive systems, present a cognitive processing model of consumer decision making, and discuss the knowledge structures that consumers learn and store in memory. Our goal is to understand consumers' affective responses to their experiences, their cognitive interpretations of those experiences, and how these responses influence consumers' interpretations of new experiences and choice of behaviors to achieve their consumption goals.

Components of the Wheel of Consumer Analysis

In Chapter 2, you learned that consumer behavior situations such as Greg Macklin's grocery shopping trip can be analyzed in terms of four elements: behavior, environment, marketing strategies, and the internal factors of affect and cognition. We organized these four factors into a model called the Wheel of Consumer Analysis (see Exhibit 3.1). Because these factors interact and influence one another in a continuous, reciprocal manner, no factor can be fully understood in isolation. Therefore, we begin our analysis of affect and cognition by analyzing Greg Macklin's shopping trip in terms of the four elements in the wheel model.

Environment

What is the supermarket environment like? Well, on a Saturday morning, the market is likely to be *busy*, with many people *crowding* the aisles. The store is likely to be somewhat *noisy*. Because Greg is shopping with Angela, her *chattering* adds to the commotion. These social aspects of the environment will influence Greg's affect and cognition and his overt behavior. The store *layout*, the *width* of the aisles,

Exhibit 3.1

The Wheel of Consumer Analysis

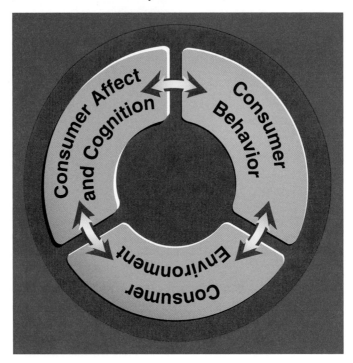

the special sale *signs* on the shelves, the product *displays* at the ends of the aisles and elsewhere in the store, the *lighting,* and other physical aspects of the super-market environment may also have an effect. Other environmental factors, such as the *temperature,* background *music* playing, and the *wobbly wheel* on his shopping cart, may have important effects on Greg's affect, cognition, and behavior.

Behavior

What kinds of behavior occur in this situation? Greg is engaged in a large number of behaviors, including *walking* down the aisles, *looking* at products on the shelves, *picking up* and *examining* packages, *talking* to Angela and a friend he met in the store, *steering* the wobbly cart, and so on. Although many of these behaviors may not seem to be of much interest to a marketing manager, some behaviors have impor-tant influences on Greg's affect and cognition and his eventual purchases. For exam-ple, unless Greg *walks* down the aisle containing breakfast cereals, he cannot *notice* and *buy* a package of Kellogg's Raisin Squares. Typically, marketers are most con-cerned about purchase behavior. In the supermarket environment, this means *pick-ing up* a package, *placing* it in the cart, and *paying* for it at the checkout counter.

Marketing Strategies

Much of the in-store environment Greg experiences is due to marketing strategy decisions made by the retailer and the manufacturers whose products the store carries. In fact, a grocery store is a good place to observe marketing strategies in action. The huge number of products sold in such stores requires an equally large number of marketing strategies. For instance, a firm's *distribution* strategy (place products only in upscale stores) determines whether that product is even present in a particular store. A variety *of pricing* strategies (reduced price on Oreo cookies) and *promotion* strategies (free samples of cheese) are evident in a supermarket environment. *Package designs* (easy-opening milk containers) and specific *product characteristics* (low-calorie frozen entrées) are also marketing strategies. Finally, specific environmental details such as *point-of-purchase displays* (a stack of Pepsi six-packs near the store entrance) are important aspects of marketing strategy. All of these marketing strategies are environmental stimuli that are meant to influence consumers' affect and cognition and their behavior.

Affect and Cognition

Greg's affective and cognitive systems were active in the supermarket environment. Indeed, consumers' affective and cognitive systems are active in every environment. However, only some of this internal activity is conscious, whereas a great deal of activity may occur with little awareness. For instance, Greg may *feel a bit angry* about getting a cart with a wobbly wheel. He also *pays attention* to certain aspects of the store environment and *ignores* other parts. Some products capture his *attention*, while others do not. He *interprets* a large amount of information in the store environment—from aisle signs to brand names to price tags to nutrition labels. In addition, he *evaluates* some of the products in terms of meeting his needs and those of his family. He *remembers* what products he still has on hand at home and what he has run out of and needs to replace. He *makes choices* from among some of the 10,000 to 20,000 items available in the store. In addition, he *makes decisions* about other specific behaviors: Should he go down aisle three or skip it this week? Should he stock up on canned peaches or buy just one can? Should he give Angela a cookie for being good? Should he take the wobbly cart back and get another one? Should he pay with cash or by check? Should he get paper or plastic bags?

Grocery shopping involves interactions among consumers' affective and cognitive systems, their behaviors, and the store environment *(left) Bob Daemmrich Photography, Inc./The Image Works; (right) Spencer Grant/Photo Researchers, Inc.*

In sum, Greg's grocery-purchasing behavior on this particular Saturday morning is a complex function of his social and physical environment, the marketing strategies designed to influence him, his own behavior, and the processes of his affective and cognitive systems. Each factor interacts with and reciprocally influences the others.

About 45 minutes after entering the Giant supermarket, Greg emerges with five bags of groceries containing 48 different products. Given our analysis of his shopping trip, we might be somewhat surprised to find he has a smile on his face and does not feel at all tired. In fact, he is already looking forward to his tennis match. How did Greg's affective and cognitive systems accomplish so much so quickly, with such apparent ease? How do we all perform similar feats while shopping?

Affect and Cognition as Psychological Responses

Affect and cognition are different types of psychological responses consumers can have in situations such as grocery shopping. **Affect** refers to feeling responses, whereas **cognition** consists of mental (thinking) responses. Consumers can have both affective and cognitive responses to any element in the Wheel of Consumer Analysis—the environment, behaviors, or even other affective and cognitive responses. Affect and cognition are produced by the affective and cognitive systems, respectively. Although the two systems are distinct, they are richly interconnected, and each system influences the other.[1]

In distinguishing affect from cognition, you can think of affect as something people *are* or something people *feel* (I *am* angry; Linda *is* in a good mood; Joe *feels* bored).[2] Because people experience affect in their bodies, affect seems to be a part of the person at the time she or he experiences it. In contrast, people *have* cognitions, thoughts, or beliefs (your mother *believes* Diet Pepsi is not fattening; Susan *knows* where the grocery store is; you *think* your interview suit is stylish). As mental states, cognitions are not usually felt in the body.

Types or Levels of Affective Responses

People can experience four broad types of affective responses: emotions, specific feelings, moods, and evaluations. Exhibit 3.2 identifies these affective responses and gives some examples of each type. Each type of affect can involve positive or negative responses. Feelings, for example, can be favorable (Joan was satisfied with

Exhibit 3.2

Types of Affective Responses

Type of Affective Response	Level or Physiological Arousal	Intensity or Strength of Feeling	Examples of Positive and Negative Affect
Emotions	Higher arousal and activation	Stronger	• Joy, love • Fear, guilt, anger
Specific feelings	↑	↑	• Warmth, appreciation, satisfaction • Disgust, sadness
Moods	↓	↓	• Alert, relaxed, calm • Blue, listless, bored
Evaluations	Lower arousal and activation	Weaker	• Like, good, favorable • Dislike, bad, unfavorable

her T-shirt) or unfavorable (John was disgusted with the service he received). Moods can be positive (relaxed) or negative (sad).

The four types of affect differ in the level of bodily arousal or the intensity with which they are experienced.[3] The stronger affective responses, including emotions such as fear or anger, may involve physiological responses (which are felt in the body) such as increased heart rate or blood pressure, perspiration, dry mouth, tears, rushes of adrenaline, or butterflies in the stomach. Specific feelings involve somewhat less intense physiological reactions (Jennifer was sad when she sold her old guitar). Moods, which involve lower levels of felt intensity, are rather diffuse affective states (Robert was bored by the long shopping trip).[4] Finally, evaluations of products or other concepts (I like Colgate toothpaste) often are fairly weak affective responses accompanied by low levels of arousal (sometimes one hardly feels anything at all).

The Affective System

Affective responses are produced by the affective system. Although researchers are still studying how the affective system operates, they generally agree on five basic characteristics.[5] One important property is that the affective system is *largely reactive*. That is, the affective system cannot plan, make decisions, or purposefully try to achieve some goal. Rather, a person's affective system usually responds immediately and automatically to significant aspects of the environment. An obvious example is color. Most people immediately have a positive affective response when they see a favorite color on a car or an item of clothing (see Highlight 3.1).

A related characteristic of the affective system is that people have *little direct control* over their affective responses. For instance, if you are insulted by a rude sales clerk, your affective system may immediately and automatically produce feelings of frustration and anger. However, people can have indirect control over their affective feelings by changing behavior that is triggering the affect or moving to another environment. For instance, you might complain about the rude clerk to the manager, which could reduce the negative affect you felt and create a new feeling of satisfaction. As another example, consumers who have negative affective reactions to a crowded clothing shop (feelings of discomfort, frustration, or even anger) might leave the store to shop in a less crowded environment, which stimulates more positive affective feelings.[6]

A third feature of the affective system is that affective responses are *felt physically* in the body. Consider the butterflies in the stomach associated with the excitement of making an important purchase, such as a new car or a house. These physical reactions can be powerful feelings. People's body movements often reflect their affective states (they smile when happy, frown when disturbed, clench fists when angry, sit up straight in anticipation, or slouch when bored) and communicate their emotional states to other people. Thus, successful salespeople read the body language of their prospects and adapt their sales presentations accordingly.

Fourth, the affective system can *respond to virtually any type of stimulus*. For instance, consumers can have an evaluative response to a physical object (I *love* my Sony stereo system) or a social situation (I *disliked* talking to the salesperson in the electronics store). People's affective systems can also respond to their own behaviors (I *enjoy* playing my stereo system). Finally, consumers' affective systems can respond to thoughts produced by their cognitive systems (I *like* to think about stereo systems).

The American Uncle Sam figure is used to convey symbolic meanings about products and services *Courtesy IRS website.*

Highlight 3.1

Automatic Affective Responses to Color

All living creatures have certain innate responses to the environment, and the response to color is one of the most important of these. The first thing people react to in evaluating an object (e.g., a product or building) is its color, and their automatic affective response can account for as much as 60 percent of their acceptance of the object. Your affective response to color can influence other emotions and feelings, as well as your cognitions and behaviors. Colors can attract or distract you; colors can make you feel good or bad; colors can draw you toward other people or repel you; colors can make you want to eat more or eat less.

A person's affective response to color involves automatic reactions of the eye, optic neurons, parts of the brain, and various glands. Consider people's responses to red. When the eye sees primary red, the pituitary gland (embedded in the brain) is stimulated to send out a chemical signal to the adrenal medullae (located above the kidneys), which secrete epinephrine or adrenaline that activates and arouses the body. People's emotions, such as anger or fear, are enhanced by this automatic reaction to red; this is why danger signals are usually red. Affective feelings of excitement are generated by red. Thus, cosmetics such as lipstick and rouge are based on red. In the presence of red, people also tend to eat more, which is why red is a popular color for restaurants.

People's affective systems have similar automatic reactions to other colors. For instance, a particular shade of vivid pink causes the brain to secrete norepinephrine, a chemical that inhibits the production of epinephrine. Thus, pink is a useful color for places where angry people must be confronted (a principal's office, certain areas of a prison, or the complaint center in a department store).

Yellow is the fastest color for the eye to see because the electrochemical reactions that produce vision work fastest in response to yellow stimulation.

Thus, yellow is an excellent color to command attention (traffic warning signals and Post-it Notes are examples). Placing a yellow car in the auto showroom will attract more attention from passing motorists than a car of a different color. Although many people think of yellow as cheerful and sunny, the yellow kitchen they often request may increase anxiety and shorten temper.

People's reactions to favorite colors tend to vary by socioeconomic status (income and education level). Lower-income people tend to like primary colors that are pure, simple, and intense. Primary colors can often be described in two words: "sky blue," "forest green." Upper-income people tend to prefer more complex colors that require three or more words for description ("a sort of gray-green with a little blue"). To lower-income people such colors seem "muddy" or washed out; simple colors that are bright and clean have a higher appeal for this group.

According to the experts, there are sex-based preferences for certain colors. The eye sees all colors as having either a yellow base or a blue base. Thus, red can be yellow-based (tomato red) or blue-based (raspberry). Men inherit a preference for yellow-based reds, whereas most women like blue-based reds. Thus, when women buy cosmetics that look good to themselves or their female friends, they usually gravitate toward the blue-based reds. However, most men tend to react more favorably to yellow-based red makeup.

Finally, blue is the stated favorite color of 80 percent of Americans. Blue is thought to be a calming color, but a very strong sky blue is much more calming than other shades. In its presence, the brain sends out some 11 tranquilizing chemicals to calm the body. Some hospitals use this color in the cardiac unit to calm fearful patients. In contrast, a very pale sky blue encourages fantasy and therefore might be a good color for the creative department in an ad agency.

Source: Adapted from Carlton Wagner, "Color Cues," *Marketing Insights*, Spring 1990, pp. 42–46.

Fifth, most affective responses are *learned*. Only a few basic affective responses, such as preferences for sweet tastes or negative reactions to loud, sudden noises, seem to be innate. Consumers learn some of their affective responses (evaluations or feelings) through classical conditioning processes (this topic is discussed later in the text). Consumers also acquire many affective responses through early socialization experiences as young children. Because affective responses are learned, they may vary widely across different cultures, subcultures, or other social groups. Thus, people's affective systems are likely to respond in rather different ways to the same stimulus.

What Is Cognition?

Human beings have evolved a highly sophisticated cognitive system that performs the higher mental processes of understanding, evaluating, planning, deciding, and thinking.[7]

- Understanding—Interpreting, or determining the meanings of specific aspects of one's environment.
- Evaluating—Judging whether an aspect of the environment, or one's own behavior, is good or bad, positive or negative, favorable or unfavorable.
- Planning—Determining how to solve a problem or reach a goal.
- Deciding—Comparing alternative solutions to a problem in terms of their relevant characteristics and selecting the best alternative.
- Thinking—The cognitive activity that occurs during all of these processes.

In this book, we use the term *cognition* broadly to refer to all these mental processes, as well as to the thoughts and meanings produced by the cognitive system.

A major function of people's cognitive systems is to interpret, make sense of, and understand significant aspects of their personal experiences. To help them do so, the cognitive system creates symbolic, subjective meanings that represent their personal interpretations of the stimuli they encounter; for instance, Greg Macklin made many cognitive interpretations during his shopping trip. Our cognitive systems are capable of interpreting virtually any aspect of the environment (That is one of the early Beatles' tunes). We can also interpret our behavior (Why did I buy that CD?) and our own affective states (Do I really like this sweater?). Cognitive interpretations can include the deeper, symbolic meanings of products and behaviors (Having a pager makes me feel in control). Finally, people can interpret the meanings of their own cognitions or beliefs (What does it mean that Hill's department store has "everyday low prices"?). Exhibit 3.3 lists some of the interpretations consumers' cognitive systems can create.

Exhibit 3.3

Types of Meanings Created by the Cognitive System

Cognitive interpretations of physical stimuli
This sweater is made of lamb's wool.
This car gets 28 miles per gallon.

Cognitive interpretations of social stimuli
The salesperson was helpful.
My friends think Pizza Hut is the best.

Cognitive interpretations of affective responses
I love Dove [ice cream] bars.
I feel guilty about not sending Mom a birthday card.
I feel mildly excited and interested in a new store.

Cognitive interpretations of symbolic meanings
This car is sexy.
This style of dress is appropriate for older women.
Wearing a Rolex watch means you are successful.

Cognitive interpretations of sensations
Colors on a box of breakfast cereal.
Sound of a soft-drink can being opened and poured.
Sweet taste of chocolate chip cookies.
Smell of your favorite cologne.
Feel of your favorite pair of jeans.

Cognitive interpretations of behaviors
I drink a lot of Diet Pepsi.
How to pay with a credit card.

A second function of our cognitive systems is to process (think about) these interpretations or meanings in carrying out cognitive tasks such as identifying goals and objectives, developing and evaluating alternative courses of action to meet those goals, choosing a course of action, and carrying out the behaviors. The amount and intensity of cognitive processing vary widely across situations, products, and consumers. Consumers are not always engaged in extensive cognitive activity. In fact, many behaviors and purchase decisions probably involve minimal cognitive processing.

Relationship between Affect and Cognition

The relationship between affect and cognition remains an issue in psychology.[8] Several researchers consider the affective and cognitive systems to be (at least somewhat) independent.[9] Others argue that affect is largely influenced by the cognitive system.[10] Still others argue that affect is the dominant system. We believe the two systems are highly interdependent. The affective and cognitive systems do involve different parts of the brain; however, these affective and cognitive areas are richly connected by neural pathways. Therefore, we must recognize that each system continuously influences the other.

Exhibit 3.4 illustrates how the two systems are related. Note that each system can respond independently to aspects of the environment, and each system can respond to the output of the other system. For instance, the affective responses (emotions, feelings, or moods) produced by the affective system in reaction to stimuli in the environment can be interpreted by the cognitive system (I wonder why I feel so happy; I don't like the insurance agent because she is too serious). These cognitive interpretations, in turn, may be used to make decisions (I won't buy insurance from this person).

Exhibit 3.4

The Relationship between the Affective and Cognitive Systems

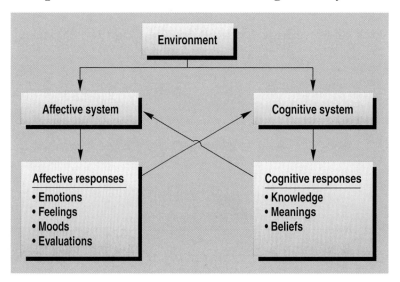

This ad portrays a sexual situation to convey the emotional benefits of the product   © *The Procter & Gamble Company. Used by permission.*

We also know that consumers' affective reactions to the environment can influence their cognition during decision making. For instance, if you go grocery shopping when you are in a good mood, you are likely to spend more money than if you are in a bad mood. The affect associated with being in a good mood influences cognitive processes during shopping so that you are more likely to think about the favorable qualities of things to buy. As another example, your cognitive interpretation of a TV commercial can be influenced by your affective reactions to the material in the preceding program.[11]

In contrast, consumers' cognitive interpretations of information in the environment can trigger affective reactions (Oh, is that a Honda Element? I like it). We know that people's affective systems can be influenced by their cognitive interpretations of their experiences in a situation.[12] For instance, if you interpret a salesperson's behavior as pushy, you probably will have a negative evaluation of the salesperson and you may even become angry. On the other hand, you probably will have a favorable affective response if you interpret the salesperson's behavior as helpful.

Marketing Implications

Both affect and cognition are important for understanding consumer behavior. Consider the cognitive and affective components of consumer satisfaction, a major goal of many marketing programs. Satisfaction has elements of both affect (feeling pleased, liking the product or service) and cognition (knowing why you like the product).[13] Likewise, a brand image includes knowledge and beliefs (cognitions) about brand attributes, the consequences of brand use, and appropriate consumption situations, as well as evaluations, feelings, and emotions (affective responses) associated with the brand.[14] Marketers need to understand both affective and cognitive responses to marketing strategies such as product design, advertisement, and store layout. For some marketing purposes, consumers' affective responses are more important; in other cases, cognition is key.

Affective responses are especially important for so-called feeling products.[15] These include certain foods (doughnuts, snacks, pizza), beverages (soft drinks, beer, wine), greeting cards, fragrances, skin care products, and sports cars that elicit strong affective reactions from consumers. For instance, consider consumers' affective responses to ice cream. For most people, eating ice cream is a highly sensory experience; they associate the product with affective feelings of happiness, fun, and excitement, as well as sensual pleasure. When Häagen-Dazs, the American maker of superpremium ice cream noted for its high butterfat content and intense flavors, expanded into Europe, the company promoted people's affective, sensual reactions to ice cream.[16] One British ad portrayed a seminude couple feeding ice cream to each other. The product was very successful in England, France, and Germany, where sales grew from $2 million to $30 million in just two years. In the remainder of this chapter, we focus on the cognitive system and the knowledge it creates. However, you should remember that the affective system operates continuously, and affective reactions can have powerful influences on decisions.

Using Metaphors to Communicate Affective and Cognitive Meaning

Because affect and cognition are so intimately interrelated, marketers should include both types of meaning in their marketing strategies. Paying careful attention to **metaphors** can help managers do so. Consider the basic metaphor "time is (like) money." People in Western societies may indirectly express this common metaphor in various ways:

- Can you *spend* some time with me?
- That will *save* time for us.
- I felt like I was *frozen* in time.
- He *squandered* his time on earth.

Current theory suggests that our minds operate by manipulating metaphors as we think, plan, and decide.[17] Metaphors represent one thing in terms of something else.[18] They have a standard form, "X is like Y," which enables consumers to proceed from the known (Y) to the unknown (X). For instance, the metaphor "time is like money" allows people to use their knowledge, beliefs, and emotions about money to help them understand time. People's thoughts and feelings about both time and money are structured by the deeper (more basic) metaphor of "resource" (time, like money, is a scarce and valuable resource). Thus, like money, time can be "spent" or "saved." Like money, time is something to be used carefully and wisely for important purposes. Like money, one should not waste time on frivolous endeavors. Highlight 3.2 gives another example of how metaphor influences consumers.

A metaphor can communicate both cognitive and affective meanings (thoughts and feelings) about a brand or a company. For this reason, metaphors are critical to effective marketing strategies. Marketers, whether they realize it or not, use many

- Should I read this ad carefully?
- Which friend should I consult?
- Which salesperson should I buy from?

Consumers use information to make such decisions. Of course, people's internal affective responses and their own behaviors constitute information that can influence their decisions. In addition, the environment is full of potential information. In a supermarket, for instance, marketing strategies such as a price tag, a coupon, sale signs in a store window, or a tasting demonstration of a new product provide information to consumers. If this information is to influence consumers' decisions, it must be *processed* (taken in, interpreted, and used) by their cognitive systems. To explain how the cognitive system processes information, researchers have developed **information-processing models.**[19] These models identify a sequence of cognitive processes in which each process transforms or modifies information and passes it on to the next process, where additional operations take place.[20] The decisions that underlie many human actions can be understood in terms of these cognitive processes.

Reduced to its essence, consumer decision making involves three important cognitive processes. First, consumers must *interpret* relevant information in the environment to create personal knowledge or meaning. Second, consumers must combine or *integrate* this knowledge to evaluate products or possible actions and to choose among alternative behaviors. Third, consumers must *retrieve product knowledge from memory* to use in integration and interpretation processes. All three cognitive processes are involved in any decision-making situation.

A Model of Consumer Decision Making

Exhibit 3.5 presents a general model of consumer decision making that highlights these cognitive processes of interpretation, integration, and product knowledge in memory. We provide an overview of this decision-making model here, and in subsequent chapters we discuss each element of the model in more detail.

Consumers must interpret or make sense of information in the environment around them. In the process, they create new knowledge, meanings, and beliefs about the environment and their places in it. **Interpretation processes** require exposure to information and involve two related cognitive processes: attention and comprehension. *Attention* governs how consumers select which information to interpret and which information to ignore. *Comprehension* refers to how consumers determine the subjective meanings of information and thus create personal knowledge and beliefs. We discuss exposure, attention, and comprehension processes in Chapter 5.

In this book, we use the terms **knowledge, meanings, and beliefs** interchangeably to refer to consumers' subjective understanding of information produced by interpretation processes. Exhibit 3.5 shows that knowledge, meanings, and beliefs may be stored in memory and later retrieved from memory (activated) and used in integration processes.[21] Later in the chapter, we discuss how consumers may organize these meanings and beliefs into *knowledge structures*.

Integration processes concern how consumers combine different types of knowledge (1) to form overall evaluations of products, other objects, and behaviors and (2) to make choices among alternative behaviors, such as a purchase. In the first instance, consumers combine knowledge and affective feelings about a product

Exhibit 3.5

Cognitive Processes in Consumer Decision Making

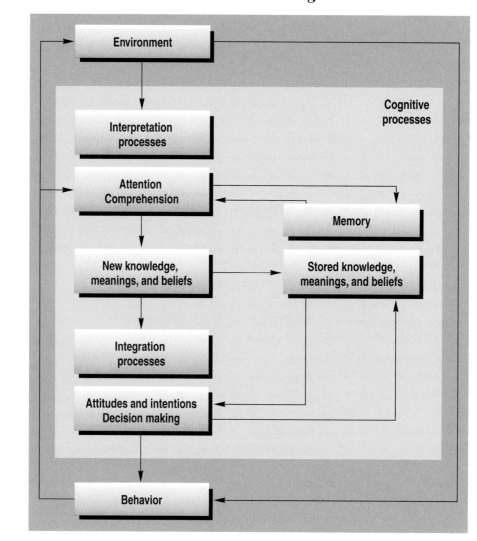

or a brand to form an overall evaluation or a *brand attitude* (I don't like Breyer's chocolate chip ice cream; Wrangler jeans are better than Levi's). We discuss attitudes and intentions in Chapter 6. Consumers also engage in integration processes when they combine knowledge with affective responses to choose a behavior (Should I shop at Sears or Penney's?). When consumers choose between different purchase behaviors, they form an *intention* or *plan* to buy (I intend to buy a new Bic pen this afternoon). Integration processes are also used to make choices among behaviors other than purchasing. For instance, a consumer might integrate knowledge in deciding when to go on a shopping trip, whether to pay with a check or a credit card, or whether to recommend a movie to a friend.

Product knowledge and involvement concern the various types of knowledge, meanings, and beliefs about products that are stored in consumers' memories. For example, consumers may have product knowledge about the characteristics or attributes of a brand of athletic shoe (air inserts in the heel), the outcomes of using the brand (I can run faster), or the ability of the brand to satisfy important goals and values (I will be fit). Product knowledge that is activated from memory has the potential to influence interpretation and integration processes. For example, consumers need a certain amount of knowledge about nutrition to interpret and understand the many health claims made by food companies. *Product involvement* refers to consumers' knowledge about the personal relevance of the products in their lives (nutrition information is important to my health goals). People's level of involvement with health issues will influence how much effort they exert in interpreting a nutritional message. We discuss product knowledge and involvement in Chapter 4.

In summary, Exhibit 3.5 shows that consumer decision making involves the two cognitive processes of interpretation and integration, both of which are influenced by product knowledge, meanings, and beliefs in memory. In Chapter 7, we discuss how all of these factors operate together in consumer decision making.

Additional Characteristics of the Cognitive System

Several aspects of the cognitive system influence decision making by consumers. **Activation,** for instance, refers to the process by which product knowledge is retrieved from memory for use in interpreting and integrating information. Activation of knowledge in memory is often automatic and largely unconscious (little or no conscious effort is involved).[22] Consumers typically experience activated knowledge as thoughts that "just come to mind." Daydreaming is a good example of activation; various bits of knowledge or meanings surface as a person's conscious mind drifts from one thought to another. Activation also operates when consumers intentionally try to recall certain bits of knowledge such as the location of a particular shop in the mall, the salesperson's name, or the price of that black T-shirt. People sometimes try to remember such things by giving themselves cues that might activate the desired knowledge (Let's see, I think her name begins with a *B*).

Another important characteristic of our cognitive systems (and also the affective system) is that much of its operations are **unconscious.** That is, much of our "thinking" occurs below the level of conscious awareness. Also, much of the knowledge, meanings, and beliefs that are activated from memory may not reach a conscious level. Some scientists suggest that as much as 90 to 95 percent of human mental activity is unconscious.[23] This means people usually are not aware of the interpretation or integration processes that occur more or less continuously in their brains, and often they are unaware of the output of those cognitive processes. Needless to say, these unconscious cognitive processes create a serious challenge for marketing researchers and managers who are trying to understand their consumers. Researchers are beginning to address this challenge with innovative interview methods such as ZMET and experimental procedures such as implicit learning.

The product knowledge in consumers' memories can be activated in various ways, most commonly by exposure to objects or events in the environment. Seeing the distinctive BMW grille, for example, may activate various meanings (sportiness or the idea that this is a rich person's car). Because marketers control certain aspects of the environment (ads, billboards, signs, and packaging), they have some influence on consumers' cognition. People's internal, affective states also can activate knowledge. For instance, positive knowledge and beliefs tend to be activated when a person is in a good mood, whereas more negative meanings are activated when the same person is in an unpleasant mood.

Finally, product knowledge in memory can be activated because it is linked to other activated meanings. Because meanings are associated in memory, activation of one meaning concept may trigger related concepts and activate those meanings as well. Consumers have little control over this process of **spreading activation,** which occurs unconsciously and automatically.[24] For instance, seeing a magazine ad for Jell-O may activate first the Jell-O name and then related knowledge and meanings such as *jiggly, tastes sweet, good for a quick dessert,* and the vague memory that Bill Cosby used to advertise it. Through spreading activation, various aspects of one's knowledge in memory can spring to mind during decision making.

Another important characteristic of the human cognitive system is its **limited capacity.** People can consciously consider only a small amount of knowledge at one time.[25] This suggests that the interpretation and integration processes during consumer decision making are fairly simple. For instance, it is unlikely that consumers consider more than a few characteristics of a brand in forming an attitude or intention to buy the brand. At the same time, we know people are able to handle rather complex tasks such as going to a restaurant or driving a car. This is because cognitive processes tend to become more automatic with experience. That is, over time, cognitive processes gradually become habitual and require less capacity and conscious control (less thinking is necessary).[26] Grocery shopping, for instance, is routine and cognitively easy for most consumers because many of the interpretation and integration processes involved in choosing food products have become automatic. Highlight 3.3 describes a common example of how **automatic processing** develops.

Marketing Implications

The simple model of consumer decision making just presented has many implications. Because the next several chapters cover this model in detail, only a few examples are given here.

Obviously, it is important for marketers to understand how consumers interpret their marketing strategies. For instance, marketers might have a sale to move a brand that is overstocked, but consumers might interpret the price decrease as an indication that product quality has dropped. Marketers also are highly interested in the knowledge, meanings, and beliefs that consumers have for their products, brands, stores, and so on.

The integration processes involved in forming brand attitudes (Do I like this brand?) and purchase intentions (Should I buy this brand?) are critical to understanding consumer behavior. Marketers need to know what types of product knowledge are used in integration processes and what knowledge is ignored. Because of the limited capacity of the cognitive system, marketers should expect consumers to consciously integrate relatively small amounts of knowledge when choosing brands to buy or stores to patronize.

Activation of product knowledge has many implications for marketing. For instance, the choice of a brand name can be highly important to the success of the product because of the various meanings the brand name can activate from consumers' memories. Jaguar is a good name for a sports car because it activates

High**light** 3.3

Increasing Automatic Cognitive Processing: Learning to Drive a Car

Practiced subjects can do what seems impossible to both the novice and the theorist. People can achieve dramatic improvements in skills with practice. For instance, consider your experience in learning to drive a car. When you first learned to drive, you probably couldn't drive and talk at the same time. The task of driving seemed difficult and was probably physically and mentally tiring. Today, if you are a skilled driver, you can probably drive in moderate traffic, listen to music on the radio, and carry on a conversation with a friend. Could you have done this when you first started driving? Probably then you kept the radio off. If anyone tried to talk to you, you ignored them or told them to shut up. Of course, even today you will probably stop talking if something unfamiliar occurs, such as an emergency situation on the road ahead. At least, we hope you do!

Learning to drive a car illustrates how cognitive processes (and associated behavior) become increasingly automatic as they are learned through practice. However, even highly automatic skills such as eating seem to require some cognitive capacity. Perhaps you like to munch on something while you study. You might snack on pretzels (as one of the authors does) or eat an apple while you read this chapter. But if you come upon a difficult passage that requires greater thought, you probably will stop chewing, or your hand holding the pretzel may pause in midair, while you interpret the meaning of what you are reading.

such meanings as *speed, agility, exotic, rare, beautiful, powerful,* and *graceful.*[27] Another implication is that marketers need to pay attention to differences among consumers because the same stimulus may activate different knowledge in different consumers. The cartoon in Highlight 3.4 illustrates this point.

Knowledge Stored in Memory

Exhibit 3.5 shows that consumers' knowledge in memory influences the cognitive processes involved in decision making. We will discuss consumers' product knowledge and involvement in the next chapter. In this section, we describe two broad types of knowledge that consumers create and discuss how this knowledge is organized in memory. We also discuss the cognitive learning processes by which consumers acquire knowledge.

Types of Knowledge

The human cognitive system can interpret virtually any type of information and thereby create knowledge, meanings, and beliefs.[28] Broadly speaking, people have two types of knowledge: (1) general knowledge about their environment and behaviors and (2) procedural knowledge about how to do things.[29]

General knowledge concerns people's interpretations of relevant information in their environments. For instance, consumers create general knowledge about product categories (compact disks, fast-food restaurants, mutual funds), stores (Sears, Wal-Mart, Kmart), particular behaviors (shopping in malls, eating ice cream, talking to salespeople), other people (one's best friend, the cute clerk at the 7-Eleven store on the corner, the professor for this course), and even themselves (I am shy, intelligent, and honest).

Highlight 3.4

Automatic Activation of Meanings from Memory

wareness of Activation. It is difficult to become aware of our own activation processes. You would have to pay special attention to what happens when you are exposed to an object, for instance, because most activation tends to be automatic and very rapid. Normally we are not conscious of the activation process that retrieves stored information from memory. The meanings just "come to mind."

© Bill Keane, Inc. Reprinted with special permission of King Feathers Syndicate.

General knowledge is stored in memory as *propositions* that link or connect two concepts:

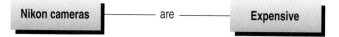

Most propositions are based on some personally relevant connection between the two concepts. For instance, your knowledge that a favorite clothing store is having a sale creates a simple proposition:

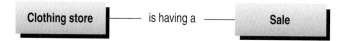

The connections or links in propositions are the key to understanding meaning. Knowledge or meaning exists when a concept in memory is linked to another concept via a proposition. Essentially, knowledge or meaning is defined by the connections between concepts. Consider how the meaning changes when the same two concepts are connected by a different type of association.

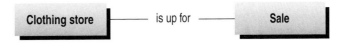

Consumers' general knowledge is either episodic or semantic.[30] *Episodic knowledge* concerns specific events in a person's life. For instance, "Yesterday I bought a Snickers candy bar from the vending machine" or "My last credit card bill had another mistake" are examples of episodic knowledge. Consumers also have general *semantic knowledge* about objects and events in the environment. For instance, your personal meanings and beliefs about Snickers candy bars—the peanuts, caramel, and calories it contains; the wrapper design; the aroma or taste—are part of your semantic knowledge. When activated from memory, the episodic and semantic components of general knowledge can influence consumers' decision making and overt behaviors.

Consumers also have **procedural knowledge** about how to do things.[31] Procedural knowledge is also stored in memory as a special type of "if . . . then . . ." proposition that links a concept or an event with an appropriate behavior.

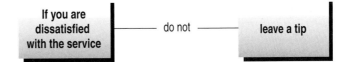

Other examples of procedural knowledge include "If the phone rings when you are busy, don't answer it," or "If a telemarketer presses you for a quick decision, say no and leave."

Over a lifetime of experience, consumers obtain a great amount of procedural knowledge, much of which is highly specific to particular situations. When activated from memory, this knowledge can directly and automatically influence a person's overt behavior. For instance, Susan has acquired the proposition: "If the price of clothing is reduced by 50 percent or more, I will consider buying it." If this procedural knowledge is activated when Susan sees a half-price sign in the jeans section, she is likely to stop and consider whether she wants a new pair of jeans.

Like general knowledge, people's procedural knowledge is relevant for many everyday situations. Consider the procedural knowledge consumers need to operate high-tech equipment such as computers, videocameras and VCRs, stereo receivers, and televisions. Many consumers think such products have become too complex and difficult to operate.[32] For instance, a recent survey found that only 3 percent of total TV viewing time is spent watching shows that have been recorded in advance. Apparently, many people do not have the appropriate procedural knowledge to use the timed recording feature on their VCRs. In recognition that relatively few consumers want and use all the features on their high-tech equipment,

As the market for sports shoes matured, Nike introduced many different types of shoes, requiring consumers to form more complex knowledge structures
Courtesy of Nike Inc.

some manufacturers are simplifying their products to reduce the procedural knowledge necessary to use them. For example, Philips, the giant Dutch electronics firm, developed a group of easy-to-use clock radios, VCRs, and tape players called Easy Line.[33]

Both general knowledge and procedural knowledge have important influences on consumers' behaviors. Consider the grocery shopping situation described at the beginning of this chapter. Various aspects of Greg Macklin's general and procedural knowledge were activated as he moved through the grocery store environment. This knowledge affected his interpretation and integration processes as he made numerous shopping decisions.

Structures of Knowledge

Consumers' general and procedural knowledge is organized to form structures of knowledge in memory. Our cognitive systems create **associative networks** that organize and link many types of knowledge together.[34] Exhibit 3.6 presents an associative network of knowledge for Nike running shoes. In this knowledge structure, the Nike concept is connected to various types of general knowledge, including episodic knowledge about past events (shopping at Wilson's) and semantic knowledge about the features of Nike shoes (their appearance, weight, and cushioning). Also included is knowledge of affective responses (memory of one's feelings after a hard run) and the interpretations of those affective feelings (relaxed and proud). This network of Nike knowledge also contains knowledge about appropriate behaviors (how to run lightly, wear cushioned socks) and related semantic knowledge about the consequences of these behaviors (avoid sore knees).

Part of this knowledge structure may be activated on certain occasions. For example, some knowledge may be activated by exposure to an athlete wearing Nike shoes

Exhibit 3.6

An Associative Network of Knowledge or Schema

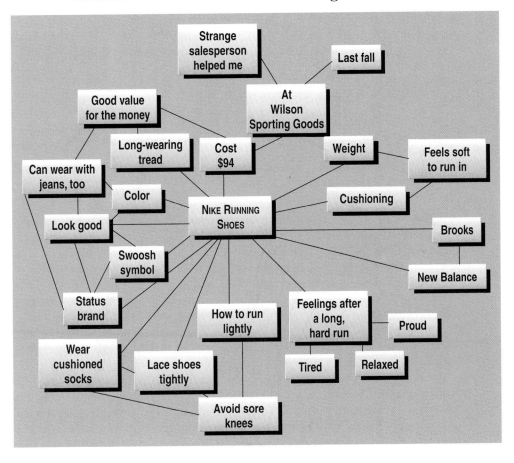

on TV or noticing the Nike swoosh symbol on a billboard ad. Other knowledge associated with Nike may be activated by experiencing the pleasant affective feelings of satisfaction and relaxation after a hard workout. Finally, some meanings associated with Nike may be activated through spreading activation as "activation energy" spreads from one meaning concept in the network to related meanings. Whatever Nike knowledge is activated during decision making has the potential to influence consumers' interpretation and integration processes at that time.

Types of Knowledge Structures

People have two types of knowledge structures: schemas and scripts. Each is an associated network of linked meanings, but **schemas** contain mostly episodic and semantic general knowledge, whereas **scripts** are organized networks of procedural knowledge. Both schemas and scripts can be activated in decision-making situations, and they can influence cognitive processes. The structure of knowledge in Exhibit 3.6

is a schema that represents one consumer's general knowledge about Nike running shoes.[35] Marketers should seek to understand consumers' schemas about brands, stores, and product categories.

When consumers experience common situations, such as eating in a fast-food restaurant, they learn what behaviors are appropriate in that situation. This procedural knowledge may be organized as a sequence of "if . . ., then . . ." propositions called a "script."[36] Following is an example of a simple script for eating in a fast-food restaurant:

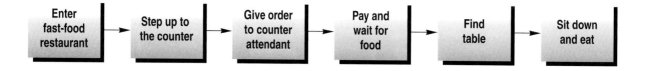

| Enter fast-food restaurant | → | Step up to the counter | → | Give order to counter attendant | → | Pay and wait for food | → | Find table | → | Sit down and eat |

As another example, consumers who frequently go to auctions may develop a generalized script containing procedural knowledge about how to register with the auctioneer before the sale starts, how to bid, when to use particular bidding tactics, how and when to pay for one's purchases, and so on. Their cognitive systems may organize this knowledge into a script. When activated in an auction situation, the script automatically guides and directs many (but not necessarily all) of the consumer's overt behaviors. Thus, consumers who have a well-developed script do not have to make conscious decisions about many auction-related behaviors because those behaviors are controlled by the script. Instead, they can focus their cognitive capacity on their bidding strategy.

Consumers, with lifetimes of experiences and learning, are likely to have a great many scripts about recurring situations in their lives. For instance, consumers may know how to acquire information about products and services from tests in *Consumer Reports,* from friends and acquaintances who are "experts," from the Internet, or from salespeople. Many consumers have scripts for how to access money to pay for purchases (by check, by credit card, or by getting a bank loan). Most consumers know how to shop for products in various types of stores (discount store, department store, boutique, from a catalog, via the Internet). Experienced consumers may have scripts for negotiating a purchase (from an automobile dealer, a seller at a flea market, an appliance salesperson). Exhibit 3.7 presents a simplified script for eating in a "fancy" restaurant.

Marketing Implications

To understand consumers' behavior, marketers need to know what product knowledge consumers have acquired and stored in memory. For instance, marketers may wish to determine how consumers organize a product category into product forms. (Do consumers see freeze-dried and instant coffee as separate product forms?) Marketers might want to know the contents of consumers' product schemas (see Exhibit 3.6 for some examples) or shopping scripts (associative networks of procedural knowledge regarding how to shop). In addition, marketers might need to know what types of knowledge are likely to be activated by particular marketing strategies. This may require a detailed analysis of the meanings that are activated

Exhibit 3.7

A Hypothetical Script of Appropriate Procedures for Dining at a "Fancy" Restaurant

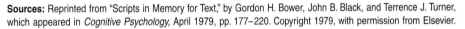

- Enter restaurant.
- Give reservation name to mâitre d'.
- Wait to be shown to table.
- Walk to table and sit down.
- Order drinks when waiter asks.
- Select dinner items from menu.
- Order meal when waiter returns.
- Drink drinks and talk until first course arrives.
- Eat soup or salad when it arrives.
- Eat main course when it arrives.
- Order dessert when finished with dinner.
- Eat dessert when it arrives.
- Talk until bill arrives.
- Examine bill for accuracy.
- Give waiter credit card to pay for bill.
- Add tip to credit card form and sign.
- Leave restaurant.

Sources: Reprinted from "Scripts in Memory for Text," by Gordon H. Bower, John B. Black, and Terrence J. Turner, which appeared in *Cognitive Psychology,* April 1979, pp. 177–220. Copyright 1979, with permission from Elsevier.

when consumers are exposed to a particular color of a car or a certain typeface for a print ad. In the next chapter, we examine consumers' product knowledge and involvement.

Cognitive Learning

How do consumers learn the general and procedural knowledge in their schema and script structures? In this text, we distinguish between two broad types of learning: behavioral and cognitive. Cognitive learning is discussed here; behavioral learning is discussed in Section 3.

Cognitive learning occurs when people interpret information in the environment and create new knowledge or meaning. Often these new meanings modify their existing knowledge structures in memory. Basically, consumers come into contact with information about products and services in three ways. Consumers can learn about products or services through *direct personal use experience*. Marketers use a variety of strategies, such as in-store trials and free samples, to give consumers direct experience with the product. Auto dealers encourage consumers to drive the car "around the block." Clothing stores provide changing rooms for customers to try on garments and mirrors to evaluate their appearance. Ice cream parlors offer free sample tastes, and bedding retailers nearly always set up beds so customers can lie down and experience the feel of a mattress before buying.

Cognitive learning can also occur through consumers' *vicarious product experiences*. That is, consumers can acquire knowledge indirectly by observing others using the product. Most vicarious observation probably occurs accidentally when consumers notice other people using a product or service (seeing people using rollerblades). Marketers can create vicarious product experiences for consumers through marketing strategies such as using in-store demonstrations or paying sports stars to wear certain clothes or shoes. Brands with higher market shares have an advantage over less popular brands because consumers are more likely to observe other people using a best-selling brand. Finally, much cognitive learning occurs

Exhibit 3.8

Three Types of Cognitive Learning

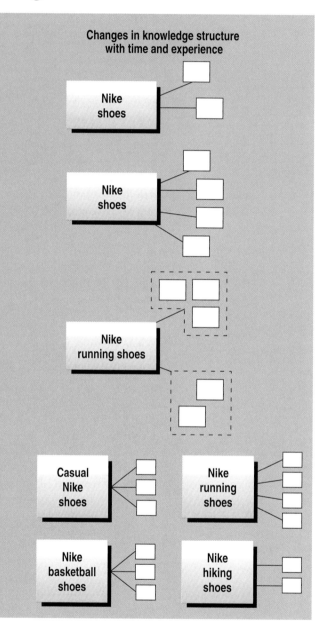

Type of cognitive learning

Changes in knowledge structure with time and experience

Accretion
Consumer begins to acquire knowledge, meanings, and beliefs about Nike shoes. With various experiences, new meanings are connected to the "Nike shoes" concept.

With additional experience, consumer continues to add new meanings and beliefs to the knowledge structure for Nike shoes.

Tuning
Consumer forms an overall meaning for entire knowledge structure that summarizes all the meanings and beliefs: "Nike shoes are running shoes." Sets of related meanings are combined to form "larger," more abstract meanings about cushioning and support, for example.

Restructuring
As more experience accumulates, consumer learns that Nike running shoes are highly variable, and not all Nike shoes are suitable for running. A restructuring of knowledge takes place. Separate knowledge structures, each with its own unique set of knowledge, meanings, and beliefs, are organized for the different types of Nike shoes that the consumer perceives.

when consumers *interpret product-related information* from the mass media (news stories, advertising, *Consumer Reports*, etc.) or from personal sources (friends and family).

Interpreting information about products and services can result in three types or levels of cognitive learning: accretion, tuning, and restructuring.[37] Exhibit 3.8

illustrates how these three types of cognitive learning can create and modify associative networks of knowledge. Marketers may develop strategies to influence each type of cognitive learning.

Accretion   Most cognitive learning probably occurs by **accretion.** As consumers interpret information about products and services, they add new knowledge, meanings, and beliefs to their existing knowledge structures: "Nike shoes are expensive," "Nike shoes have good cushioning" (see Exhibit 3.8). Much learning research has focused on how people form new items of knowledge through accretion learning. However, more complex types of cognitive learning that involve changes to the *structure* of the associative knowledge network can also occur.

Tuning   As consumers gain experience with a product, knowledge structures tend to become larger and more complex through accretion processes. At some point, consumers may adjust their knowledge structures to make them more accurate and more generalizable. Most knowledge structures undergo minor changes in meaning as consumers continue to process information from the environment. As shown in Exhibit 3.8, **tuning** can occur when parts of a knowledge structure are combined and given a new overall meaning. For instance, several characteristics of a Nike shoe (lacing pattern, insole, reinforced heel) might be interpreted to mean "good support for backpacking."

Restructuring   **Restructuring** involves the revision of the entire associative network of knowledge, which might include creation of entirely new meaning structures and/or reorganization of an old knowledge structure. Accretion, and sometimes tuning, can occur without much cognitive effort or awareness (essentially unconsciously and automatically). In contrast, restructuring usually involves extensive cognitive effort and substantial thinking and reasoning processes. Therefore, restructuring tends to be rare, occurring only when existing knowledge structures become excessively large and cumbersome (and possibly inaccurate). As illustrated in Exhibit 3.8, this may have happened in the athletic shoe market with the proliferation of specialized shoe models and styles introduced in the 1990s.

Sometimes the introduction of a new product that is quite different from current products can force consumers to restructure their existing product knowledge to accommodate the new product. For instance, many consumers had to restructure their knowledge about cooking techniques when they began using microwave ovens.

Changes in consumers' values can also precipitate a restructuring of consumers' product knowledge. For instance, the increasingly strong environmental values of the late 1980s may have led some consumers to restructure their knowledge about disposable diapers and aerosol containers. Highlight 3.5 describes changes in the credit card business that may require many consumers to tune or restructure their knowledge structures.

Marketing Implications   Many marketing implications are aimed at accretion learning. Marketers often present simple informational claims about their products (Crest has a tartar control ingredient) and hope that consumers will accurately

Highlight 3.5

Cognitive Learning about Credit Cards

Some people may think there is only one type of credit card, but in reality people can access their funds using many types of cards. As people learn more about types of cards, their knowledge structures will become more closely tuned to reality. As they learn even more, they may have to restructure their knowledge about the various ways they can use "plastic" to buy things. Here are the main types of credit cards available today.

• **Credit Cards.** Credit cards offer a convenient way to buy things now by borrowing the money and paying it back later. When thinking of credit cards, the typical consumer thinks of Visa (about 57 percent share) and MasterCard (about 25 percent share). Nearly all credit cards set a limit on how much can be borrowed and specify a minimum payment due each month, and many cards charge an annual fee. Credit cards charge relatively high interest compared with other borrowing methods; rates can be as high as 15 to 19 percent on the unpaid balance. Cash-back or reward cards have been introduced; Discover Card is a popular example. New card formats are being tried—the Discover Card-2-60 is actually a keychain too and, although as long as a normal card, it is not as wide.

• **Charge Cards.** American Express is the best-known charge card, traditionally targeted at well-heeled customers who pay their bills in full each month. With no preset spending limit, charge cards are particularly useful for business travelers who may incur very large business travel expenses from time to time. There is an annual fee for most cards; the Platinum card, for example, requires a $300 yearly fee. However, American Express recently introduced a no-fee Blue Card.

• **Stored Value Cards.** Usually issued in amounts ranging from $25 to $100, this card replaces cash. As the cards are swiped through telephones or computerized terminals the amount of the purchase is deducted. When their value is exhausted, either the cards are discarded or additional value can be added to them.

• **Debit Cards.** When using a debit card, the cost of a purchase is deducted instantaneously (sometimes within a day or two) from the cardholder's checking account.

• **Smart Cards.** This new type of card, embedded with a microchip, can perform many functions. Using information stored in its memory chip, the smart card can act as a credit card, an ATM card, a photo ID, a door key, and so forth. Acceptance of these cards is growing rapidly as new terminals are installed at merchants' places of business.

Sources: Stephen E. Frank, "Burned by the Masses, Cards Court the Elite," *The Wall Street Journal,* November 5, 1997, pp. B1, B13; American Express website at http://www.americanexpress.com; Visa website at http://www.corporate.visa.com; www.credit-land.com.

interpret the information and add this knowledge to their knowledge structures. In other cases, marketers may try to stimulate consumers to tune their knowledge structures (You need special Nike shoes for "back packing"). On rare occasions, marketers may wish to encourage consumers to restructure their knowledge (Actually, beef is just as healthful as chicken).

In sum, marketers need to monitor consumers' knowledge structures and manage that knowledge. Marketers need to consider what types of meanings they want consumers to form and provide the appropriate information for consumers to process. The next chapter presents several ideas for analyzing consumers' product knowledge.

Back To...

Greg Macklin Goes Shopping

To summarize what we have covered in this chapter and review the cognitive processing model, let's return to Greg Macklin doing his weekly grocery shopping. Consider what happened as Greg walked down the aisle containing breakfast cereal. We have divided this purchase occasion into smaller, discrete events and related each event to the appropriate part of our cognitive processing model. As you work through this example, consider how the various parts of the model fit together to help explain each event. (You may want to refer to Exhibit 3.5.) ❖

Environmental Behavioral Event	Cognitive and Affective Processes
• Greg noticed a bright orange shelf tag with an arrow and the words "Unadvertised Special."	Exposure to information and initial attention; slightly positive affective response
• The sign reminded him that the supply of breakfast cereal at his house was getting low.	Activation of stored knowledge
• He looked at the package more closely.	More attention
• He saw that the product was a Kellogg's cereal, Raisin Bran Crunch.	Simple comprehension—interaction with stored knowledge
• He thought that he likes most Kellogg's cereals and that his wife likes raisins.	Activation of additional stored knowledge about affective states
• He picked up a package and read "provides 11 essential vitamins and minerals."	Comprehension—interaction with activated knowledge
• As he turned the package around, he noticed more nutritional information. This reminded him of things he knows about nutrition.	Attention and more activated knowledge
• Greg quickly noticed that Raisin Bran Crunch has the standard 25 percent RDA of many vitamins and minerals and has no added salt. He understood what most of this nutritional information meant.	Attention and comprehension; interaction with activated knowledge
• Based on this information, Greg was favorably disposed toward Raisin Bran Crunch.	Integration and attitude formation with mildly positive affect
• He then looked at the price on the shelf—$2.99 for 18.2 ounces.	Attention and comprehension
• Greg considered all this information and decided to buy a package to see whether his wife would like it.	Integration processes: 　Form an intention to buy 　Purchase goal
• He tossed a package of Raisin Bran Crunch into the grocery cart and continued shopping.	Choice behavior
• When Greg got to the checkout counter, he paid for the cereal and the other products.	Purchase behavior

Packaging often includes a great deal of product information that consumers may process *Michael Newman/PhotoEdit, Inc.*

Summary   This chapter presented a number of concepts and ideas that will be used in later chapters. In particular, we introduced the important internal factors of affect and cognition and the affective and cognitive systems. We identified four types of affective responses ranging from emotions to specific feelings to moods to evaluations. We also described the cognitive system and the various types of meanings it constructs. We emphasized that these two systems are highly interrelated and the respective outputs of each can elicit responses from the other. We believe this interactive view is the most useful for understanding consumer behavior.

Next, we presented a model of the cognitive processes involved in consumer decision making. The model has three basic components—knowledge (also called meanings and beliefs) in memory—and two broad cognitive processes—interpretation and integration. An important feature of this model is the close reciprocal interaction between knowledge structures and the cognitive processes that both create and use this knowledge.

We discussed the content and organization of knowledge as associative networks or knowledge structures. We described how meaning concepts are linked to form propositions that represent general knowledge (episodic and semantic knowledge) and procedural knowledge (how to perform behaviors). Then we described two types of knowledge structures—schemas and scripts—that contain general and procedural knowledge, respectively. Schemas and scripts can be activated to guide cognitive processes and influence overt behaviors.

Key Terms and Concepts

accretion   **63**

activation   **53**

affect   **42**

associative network   **58**

attention   **51**

automatic processing   **54**

cognition   **42**

cognitive learning   **61**

comprehension   **51**

general knowledge   **55**

information-processing models   **51**

integration processes   **51**

interpretation processes   **51**

knowledge, meanings, and beliefs   **51**

limited capacity   **54**

metaphors   **48**

procedural knowledge   **57**

product knowledge and involvement   **53**

restructuring   **63**

schemas   **59**

scripts   **59**

spreading activation   **54**

tuning   **63**

unconscious   **53**

Review and Discussion Questions

1. Describe the four broad types of affective responses produced by the affective system, and give an example of each.
2. What is a cognition? Give an example that illustrates the distinction between information (stimuli) and cognition that represents the information.
3. How are the cognitive and affective systems different? How are they interrelated?
4. Consider a product such as an automobile or a perfume. Describe at least three types of meanings that consumers might construct to represent various aspects of the product. Discuss how marketers might try to influence each meaning.
5. Give an example of how a marketing strategy could cause spreading activation within a consumer's associative network of product knowledge.
6. What stores do you know that attempt to create a certain affective mood for customers? What things does the store do to create that mood? How does that mood interact and influence consumers' cognitions (beliefs and meanings)? How might that mood influence consumer behavior within the store, including purchase behavior?
7. Think of a purchase decision you recently made. Using this purchase decision as an example, list the main influence factors, your affective responses, your cognitions and your behaviors. Describe the reciprocal interactions that occurred among some of these factors. Describe how the three main cognitive processes (see Exhibit 3.5) occurred in your decision.
8. Using a topic that you know something about (e.g., basketball, movies, college), contrast your general and procedural knowledge, and discuss how they are related. Why might marketers be interested in each type of knowledge?
9. Highlight 3.5 describes how credit card companies have developed many types of cards by which consumers can access funds and make purchases. Companies like VISA, MasterCard, and American Express have targeted college students among many other segments. Visit the VISA website at **www.visa.com** and explore the different cards described there. Describe the types of cards VISA has available. Are some more appropriate than others for the student market? Do you think these cards would "fit" within a single knowledge structure about cards in general, or would they be separate schemas? Do you think consumers need separate scripts to use each type of card?

Marketing Strategy in Action

Barnes & Noble

For decades, bookstores were simply that—places that sold books. The typical mom-and-pop bookstore on the corner was small, quaint, sometimes a little musty, and bursting at the seams with books. It was a wonderful place to visit now and then, look around for a bit, find a book you like, and go home. Not inhospitable, but probably not somewhere you would want to while away an entire afternoon or evening. Today that old bookstore seems like a relic of a bygone era. Barnes & Noble's approach to book selling has revolutionized the entire industry.

Barnes & Noble has risen from rather ordinary beginnings to become the largest bookstore chain in the world. Founder and CEO Leonard Riggio began his empire by purchasing a struggling Manhattan bookstore in 1971. Riggio opened his first superstore, with 100,000 square feet of selling space, in New York in 1975. That store was so successful that he quickly opened more superstores throughout Manhattan and downtown Boston. The formula worked and the number of stores multiplied. In the early 1990s, the company began spreading the superstore concept throughout the United States. Today Barnes & Noble operates around 950 bookstores and another 426 video game and entertainment software stores. The company boasted sales of nearly $3.5 billion and operating profit of $232 million in 1999.

Riggio took a decidedly different approach to selling books. "Shopping is a form of entertainment," he says. "To customers, shopping is a social activity. They do it to mingle with others in a prosperous-feeling crowd, to see what's new, to enjoy the theatrical dazzle of the display, to treat themselves to something interesting or unexpected." Riggio made sure both the layout and operation of his stores provide customers with what they want. Barnes & Noble superstores are huge, yet clubby and inviting. They typically cover about 25,000 square feet (some are much bigger) and offer a selection of up to 150,000 titles, compared to 10,000 to 20,000 at the typical independent book seller. Books usually are discounted 20–30 percent. But a Barnes & Noble superstore is not defined merely by size and volume. The atmosphere is friendly, even somewhat luxurious—almost a cross between a public library and a den. There are large, overstuffed chairs; reading tables; background music; a coffee bar; bright lighting; and even well-maintained public restrooms. Bookstores used to discourage customers from reading in the store—spend more than a few minutes with a book and you would have expected an employee to tap you on the shoulder and suggest that you either buy the book or put it back. But Barnes & Noble actually wants you to pull a book or magazine off the shelf, grab a cup of coffee, flop down on a sofa, and make yourself at home. A company spokesperson explains, "The philosophy behind this is, the more customers we attract into the store and the longer they are encouraged to stay, the more books we sell." Many Barnes & Noble locations also offer a music section where the same philosophy applies. Customers are welcome to sit down with a pair of headphones and listen to a CD before they buy it.

Barnes & Noble also works to ensure that its superstores evolve into community meeting places. Each store or region is staffed with a public relations coordinator who works to bring events to the store. Live performances, readings, and book signings are common. Classes of elementary school kids are invited to come in and browse on a regular monthly basis. Stores even offer classes, book discussion groups, puppet shows, and story hours for children. The long store hours (9 AM to 11 PM) also provide a compelling lure. "For people who work all day, this is their leisure time," explains Lisa Herling, vice president for corporate communications. "Whether it's after a movie or after dinner, it's a destination location." Riggio puts it more succinctly: "If I get you for two hours, I've got you."

In 1995, a competitor with an entirely different value proposition emerged. **Amazon.com** began selling books over the Internet. Barnes & Noble countered two years later with **BarnesandNoble.com**, which tries to replicate the superstore experience on the Web. At the site you can participate in live chats with authors and listen to audio from one of the many archived book readings (featuring such renowned writers as Kurt Vonnegut, Susan Sontag, and Salmon Rushdie). Now the largest bookseller in the U.S., **BarnesandNoble.com** also offers free online courses through "Barnes & Noble University," where you can study subjects ranging from the humor of Shakespeare to overcoming shyness. You can even purchase a bag of Starbucks coffee and select the music you want to hear while you're browsing the site. Oh, yes, they do sell books on the site, too—750,000 titles—along with music, software, and posters. **BarnesandNoble.com** has attracted more than 5 million customers since 1997 and has emerged as the fourth-largest e-commerce site on the Web. Sales were up 4.5% in 2002 as were expectations that the venture would turn a positive cash flow soon.

Barnes & Noble's success comes not so much from *what* it is selling but *how* it is selling it. Both the brick-and-mortar stores and the online site provide customers with an atmosphere that turns book buying into a warm, friendly, inviting experience.

Discussion Questions

1. What affective responses do you think the Barnes & Noble environment creates? How might consumers' cognitive systems interpret these responses? From a marketing perspective, which is more important to Barnes & Noble—affect or cognition?
2. Rob goes to a Barnes & Noble location to hang out and meet people. Lisa goes only when she wants to purchase a specific book or

CD. Describe how their integration processes might convince them to choose Barnes & Noble over the myriad other options they have.

3. Many of the activities that take place at Barnes & Noble stores (or at **BarnesandNoble.com**) do not require a purchase. Participating in discussion groups and going to in-store performances are free. And obviously it doesn't cost anything to simply go in, sit in a chair, and read a book. So why do people buy? How do these free activities (behaviors) influence consumers' affect and cognition?

4. Create an associative network of your knowledge about Barnes & Noble. How did you acquire this knowledge? What might activate that knowledge structure? How can marketers activate your knowledge structure? What parts of your knowledge structure are most likely to influence your decision to visit a Barnes & Noble store? What parts are most likely to influence your decision to go to the **BarnesandNoble.com** website?

5. Describe a script for shopping at a bookstore. Think of a marketing strategy Barnes & Noble could try to influence a stage in this script.

6. ▼ Visit the Barnes & Noble website (**www.BarnesandNoble.com**). Do you have any suggestions for how to make the site more "sticky" (i.e., how to make visitors stay longer)?

Sources: Myron Magnet, "Let's Go for Growth," *Fortune,* March 7, 1994, pp. 60–72; Annette Foligno, "Barnes & Noble, Inc.," *Incentive,* August 1997, pp. 32–33; Chad Rubel, "Longer Closing Hours Are Here to Stay," *Marketing News,* January 2, 1995, pp. 22; Barnes & Noble 1999 annual report.

Consumers' Product Knowledge and Involvement

How Gillette Knows about Shaving

Every day more than 1 billion people around the world use one or more Gillette products, including razors and blades, batteries, and oral care appliances. And every working day at a Gillette plant in South Boston, some 200 men and women enter an aging building with a quaint sign, "World Shaving Headquarters." The men lather up their faces and begin to shave off the 0.015 of an inch their 10,000 whiskers grew in the previous 24 hours. This is one way Gillette learns about consumer reactions to its new products in the wet-shaving market. After shaving with a new prototype razor blade, each tester peers into a mirror and evaluates the razors of the future for such factors as "closeness of shave, sharpness of blade, smoothness of glide, and ease of handling." Then he punches his judgments into a computer for later analysis. In a nearby shower room, the women do similar product ratings after shaving their legs and under-

arms, or perhaps what Gillette calls the "bikini area."

Such research, supplemented by dozens of other marketing research studies, has helped Gillette churn out a nearly unprecedented stream of successful new products—as many as 20 per year. Each year from 1994 to 1999, Gillette derived at least 40 percent of its sales from products introduced in the previous five years.

Gillette's most important new product was the MACH 3 shaving system for men. The MACH 3 came along at the perfect time for Gillette. After witnessing double-digit growth throughout the early and mid-1990s, earnings and profit margins had begun to flatten by 1998, when the company rolled out the MACH 3. The first razor with three progressively aligned blades, the MACH 3 represented a major investment for Gillette (requiring five years of work, 35 patents, and an outlay of $1 billion for development and advertising costs). Despite a retail price of almost $7, the MACH 3 was an immediate winner. Within just six months of its introduction, it had become the best-selling razor on the shelves, with a market share of 17 percent. Global sales of the MACH 3 reached an estimated $1 billion in 1999.

Then, in 2002, Gillette introduced the MACH 3 Turbo, which incorporated several advances over the earlier MACH 3 model. Protected by 35 patents, the MACH 3 Turbo included new product attributes such as anti-friction blades, an ultra-soft protective skin guard, a new lubrication system, and an improved handle. These features provided new benefits to consumers.

In 2003, Gillette capitalized on the MACH 3 Turbo success by introducing a somewhat similar three-bladed razor for women called Venus. The company had made its first major effort to learn about the women's razor market in the early 1990s. Gillette spent nine months talking to women about what they needed from a razor. As a result, they learned that the handles of men's shavers tended to slip in the shower or bath, where women shave most often, and

that men's razors are difficult to maneuver over the curved surfaces of a woman's leg.

Based on that research, Gillette in 1992 created the Sensor for Women, a radically new razor with a broad, rigid handle designed for a comfortable, nonslip fit in the palm of a woman's hand and a lubricating strip impregnated with aloe to feel satiny on the skin. It shared the pivoting, twin-blade cartridge with the men's Sensor. The current Venus system draws many of its innovative attributes from the MACH 3 Turbo. For instance, the Venus model incorporates three blades positioned so each blade cuts progressively lower on the hair shaft, producing a closer shave. The Venus razor cartridge has soft protective cushions surrounding the blades and an oval shape with rounded corners for a smooth, comfortable shaving experience. The lubricating strip contains aloe and vitamin E to soften skin, and a blue strip fades with use to indicate when it is time to change the cartridge. You can check out Gillette's special women's shaving website at **www.gillettevenus.com**.

Sources: Adapted from Linda Grant, "Gillette Knows Shaving—and How to Turn Out Hot New Products," *Fortune,* October 14, 1996, pp. 207–210; James Heckman, "Razor Sharp: Adding Value, Making Noise With MACH 3 Intro," *Marketing News,* March 29, 1999, pp. E4, E13; Mark Maremont, "Gillette to Unveil Women's Version of MACH 3 Razor," *The Wall Street Journal,* December 2, 1999, p. B14; Gillette websites **www.gillette.com** and **www.gillettevenus.com**.

This description of Gillette's shaving business illustrates the importance of product attributes in marketing strategy and the need for marketers to understand what consumers think about product attributes and related benefits. In this chapter, we examine consumers' product knowledge and involvement, two important concepts in the affect and cognition portion of the Wheel of Consumer Analysis model. We begin by discussing four levels of product-related knowledge. Then we discuss consumers' knowledge about product attributes, benefits, and values. We show how these three types of meaning can be linked to form a simple associative network of knowledge called a *means–end chain.* Means–end chains provide a deep understanding of how consumers think and feel about products and brands. We also describe ZMET (the Zaltman Metaphor Elicitation Technique), which provides even deeper understanding of consumers by identifying the metaphors they use to think about products and brands. Next, we examine the important concept of consumers' interest in or involvement with products and other aspects of their environments. The means–end model is used to help explain consumers' feelings of involvement. We conclude by discussing how to analyze consumers' relationships with products and brands and how marketing strategies can influence consumers' involvement with products.

Levels of Product
Knowledge

Consumers have different **levels of product knowledge,** which they can use to interpret new information and make purchase choices.[1] Levels of knowledge are formed when people acquire separate meaning concepts (accretion process) and combine them into larger, more abstract categories of knowledge (tuning).[2] For instance, you might combine knowledge about the braking, acceleration, and cornering ability of an automobile to form a more inclusive concept that you call *handling*. Your knowledge of handling is at a higher, more abstract level because it includes these less abstract meanings.[3] Another example is the various types of bicycles that make up the overall bike category: racing, mountain, road bikes, city bikes. Each of these meaning categories can be separated into more specific knowledge categories (different types of road bikes or mountain bikes). Thus, a person's knowledge about bikes, mountain bikes, and types of mountain bikes may form an organized structure of bicycle knowledge at different levels.[4] Of course, people vary widely in the complexity of their knowledge structures about mountain bikes—and everything else.

No one level of knowledge captures all the possible meanings of an object, an event, or a behavior. Each level of meaning is useful for certain purposes, but not all purposes. Meanings at different levels of abstraction are related hierarchically in that more abstract meanings subsume (incorporate or include) meanings at lower levels. Thus, "responsiveness" for a tennis racquet subsumes the materials of its construction, the head shape, the type of strings, and so on. We use the concept of *levels of meaning* throughout the text to help us understand consumers' product knowledge. Consumers can have product knowledge at four levels—the product class, product form, brand, and model/features. Exhibit 4.1 gives examples of each level of product knowledge.

Exhibit 4.1

Levels of Product Knowledge

More Abstract			Less Abstract
Product Class	**Product Form**	**Brand**	**Model/Features**
Coffee	Ground	Folgers	1-pound can
	Whole bean	Starbucks	12-ounce bag, decaffinated
Automobiles	Sedan	Ford Taurus	Station wagon, with a/c and CD player
	Sports car	Mazda Miata	Leather seats, with a/c and 5 speeds
	Sports sedan	BMW	Model 325i, with a/c and automatic transmission
Pens	Ballpoint	Bic	$.99 model, red ink
	Roller ball	Pilot	$1.49 model, extra-fine tip
Beer	Imported	Heineken	Dark
	Light	Coors Lite	Kegs
	Low alcohol	Sharps	12-ounce cans

Skechers (the brand) produces many types (different models/features) of sports shoes (the product form). *Courtesy Skechers USA, Inc.*

Marketers are particularly interested in consumers' knowledge about *brands*. Most marketing strategies are brand oriented in that they are intended to make consumers aware of a brand, teach them about that brand, and influence them to buy it. Most marketing research focuses on consumers' knowledge of and beliefs about brands. Likewise, much of our discussion in this text will concern consumers' brand knowledge, even though we realize consumers know much more than that.

For some products, consumers can have knowledge about models, a more concrete level of product knowledge than brands. A *model* is a specific example of a brand that has one or more unique product features or attributes (Exhibit 4.1 gives several examples). For instance, Olympus digital cameras are available in several models; Coca-Cola comes in diet, caffeine-free, lemon-flavored, and other versions; and Ben & Jerry's ice cream is sold in many different flavors. The 325, 530, and 745 models of BMW automobiles vary in size, price, and exterior design and in distinctive features and options such as fancy wheels, automatic transmission systems, leather seats, navigation systems, and so on.

Going in a more abstract direction from the brand and model levels of knowledge, a *product form* is a broader category that includes several brands that are similar in some important way. Often the basis for a product form category is a physical characteristic that the brands share. For instance, freeze-dried, instant, ground, and whole-bean coffee are defined by their physical form. In some cases, certain product forms become so well established in consumers' minds that marketers can treat them as separate markets. Diet soft drinks, sports sedans, fast-food restaurants, and laptop computers are examples.

The *product class* is the broadest and most inclusive level of product knowledge and may include several product forms (and many brands and models within those categories). Coffee, cars, and soft drinks are examples. Concepts at the product class level may have relatively few characteristics in common (the various product forms of coffee are made from coffee beans). Marketing strategies to promote the entire product class can be effective for promoting brands with a high market share. For example, Frito-Lay might promote consumption of salty chip snacks (a product class that includes various types of potato, corn, and flavored chips). Because the company controls as much as a 60 percent market share, any increase in overall consumption of the product class is likely to benefit Frito-Lay more than its competitors.

Because consumers are likely to make separate purchase decisions at each level of knowledge, marketers need to understand how consumers organize their product knowledge in terms of these different levels.[5] For instance, a consumer might make a choice between alternative product classes (Should I buy a television or a stereo system?), different product forms (Should I purchase a large-screen TV or a plasma flat screen TV?), various brands (Should I buy an RCA or a Sony TV?), and alternative models (Should I choose a 32-inch RCA TV with stereo speakers or a 35-inch RCA set with surround sound?). All of these levels of product knowledge are relevant to the marketing manager, with the brand level of particular importance.

Consumers' Product Knowledge

Consumers can have three types of product knowledge: knowledge about the attributes or characteristics of products, the positive consequences or benefits of using products, and the values the product helps consumers satisfy or achieve (see Exhibit 4.2). Marketers should understand these three types or levels of consumers' product knowledge to develop effective marketing strategies.

Products as Bundles of Attributes

As the Gillette example demonstrates, marketers have many strategic options when it comes to product characteristics or attributes. Within the limits imposed by production capabilities and financial resources, marketing managers can add new attributes to a product ("Now, Diet 7UP contains 100% NutraSweet"), remove old attributes (caffeine-free Diet Pepsi), or modify existing attributes (in 1985, Coca-Cola managers modified the century-old secret recipe for Coke). Marketers can change brand attributes in an attempt to make their products more appealing to consumers. For instance, to give Liquid Tide its cleaning power, chemists at Procter & Gamble created a new molecule and included twice as many active ingredients as competitive brands. The 400,000 hours of research and development time seemed to pay off as Liquid Tide's initial sales skyrocketed.[6] Highlight 4.1 describes a new-model introduction based on a specific product attribute.

Perhaps because they are so interested in the physical characteristics of their products, marketers sometimes act as if consumers think about products and brands as *bundles of attributes*. Even the simplest products have several **attributes** (pencils have varying lead densities, softness of erasers, shapes, and colors). Of course, complex products such as automobiles and stereo receivers have a great many attributes. From a cognitive processing perspective, however, we might wonder if consumers really have knowledge in memory about all of these attributes and whether consumers actually activate and use this knowledge when deciding which products and brands to buy. Marketers need to know which product attributes are most important to consumers, what those attributes mean to consumers, and how consumers use this knowledge in cognitive processes such as comprehension and decision making.

Consumers can have knowledge about different types of product attributes.[7] *Concrete attributes* represent tangible, physical characteristics of a product, such as

This brand is promoting the functional consequences of its product attributes.
Courtesy of Campbell Soup Company.

Exhibit 4.2

Types of Product Knowledge

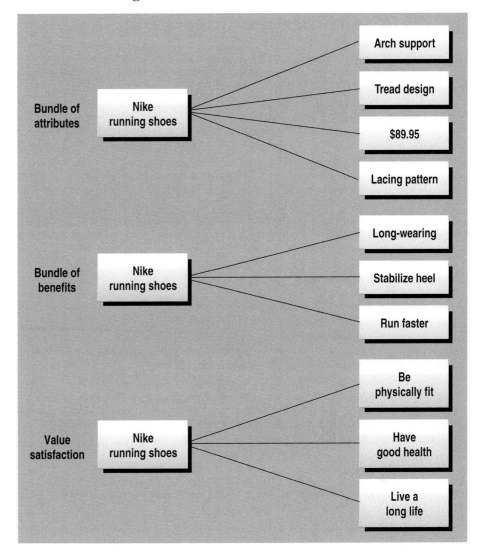

the type of fiber in a blanket or the front-seat legroom in a car.[8] *Abstract attributes* represents more subjective, intangible characteristics, such as the quality or warmth of a blanket or the stylishness or comfort of a car. Of course, consumers also have knowledge about their affective evaluations of each attribute (I don't like the itchiness of wool blankets; I love cookie dough ice cream).

Products as Bundles of Benefits

Marketers also recognize that consumers often think about products and brands in terms of their consequences rather than their attributes.[9] *Consequences* are the outcomes that occur when the product is purchased and used or consumed. For

Highlight 4.1

Reebok Adds a New Attribute

Reebok International hoped that adding a new attribute to its high-end running shoes would put it back in the running against arch-rival Nike. In 2000, Reebok introduced Smart Train, shoes that contain a built-in sensor and microchip that can accurately determine the distance you have run (or walked). The basic model of Smart Train shoes (which were scheduled to retail for $110) has a small L.C.D. readout on the tongue, which can display not only the distance traveled, but also your current pace, average pace, and calories burned—along with the time, day, and date. Reebok planned to sell an even more technologically advanced model for $250. The technology in those shoes would communicate with a wristwatch via radio waves. So runners could quickly glance at their wrists to get the information, rather than peering down at their shoes.

Does this technology make a difference to consumers? Many shoe innovations do not produce a noticeable benefit to the consumers, but runners who wear Smart Train clearly will be getting a feature not available in any other shoe. Now the question is whether consumers view this new attribute as relevant and valuable. Is knowing information about speed and pace important enough to enough runners to make this shoe a success in the market? Will runners find the shoe comfortable and supportive enough to wear?

Will people wearing the Smart Train feel higher status and receive positive recognition from others? Moreover, if people recognize such benefits, will they switch from their favorite brands and models to the Smart Train? Runners, like smokers, tend to stick with a brand or model they like once they find it.

Of course, as Reebok prepared for the rollout of the Smart Train, the company's competitors were not standing still. Nike developed a high-end model of cross-training shoe called Shox, which sells for $150. Shox feature foam "springs" in the heels, which Nike claims produce a "trampoline effect." Nike's promotion of the shoe revolved around one word—"Boing." The Adidas Equipment Ride sells for $120 and boasts of "heel to toe protection," including a specially designed heel that is supposed to reduce wear and tear on the foot and increase a runner's durability. Equipment Rides also come with reflective overlays that make the shoes highly visible from all angles at night—a big safety plus for those who run after dark.

As marketers continue to introduce new attributes into the sports shoe market, they should answer two critical questions: (1) What consequences do consumers think are provided by these attributes? (2) Are those consequences relevant to consumers? (It turns out that Smart Train was not a big success and the model was dropped.)

Source: Michael Marriot, "A Shoe That Will Give Runners and Walkers Instant Feedback," *New York Times,* September 21, 2000, p. G10; Michael McCarthy, "Nike Jumps to Show Off Shoe Shox Treatment, Promises Trampoline Effect," *USA Today*, October 17, 2000, p. 3B; Reebok website www.reebok.com

instance, a stereo system might be very loud, require assembly or repairs, or make the user feel proud. A facial cream might cause an allergic reaction or cost too much. Other consumers might think the buyer is either cool or outdated for buying a certain brand of jeans or sneakers.

Consumers can have knowledge about two types of product consequences: functional and psychosocial. **Functional consequences** are tangible outcomes of using a product that consumers experience rather directly. For instance, functional consequences include the immediate physiological outcomes of product use (eating a Big Mac satisfies your hunger; drinking a Pepsi eliminates your thirst). Functional consequences also include the physical, tangible performance outcomes of using or consuming a product—a hair blower dries your hair quickly, a car gets a certain number of miles per gallon, a toaster browns bread evenly, and an ink pen writes smoothly without skipping.

NEW! Natural RUFFLES® Potato Chips!

Ingredients by nature. Flavor by Ruffles

Enjoy great RUFFLES® brand taste with the benefits of all natural ingredients!

With NEW Natural RUFFLES® Potato Chips, we're bringing big flavor to smart snacking. Made with all natural ingredients, these chips feature the RUFFLES® brand taste you love, along with our classic crunch. And with no preservatives, no hydrogenated oils and nothing artificial, you get 100% RUFFLES® brand taste, naturally.

FIND ALL 7 NEW VARIETIES OF FRITO-LAY NATURAL SNACKS IN THE NATURAL SNACK SECTION OF YOUR SUPERMARKET.

Advertisement provided courtesy of Frito-Lay, Inc.

Psychosocial consequences refer to the psychological and social outcomes of product use. *Psychological consequences* of product use are internal, personal outcomes, such as how the product makes you feel. Most psychosocial consequences have an affective quality. For instance, using Matrix shampoo might make you feel more attractive, wearing Gap sportswear might make you feel more (or less) stylish, and eating an ice cream cone from Baskin-Robbins might make you feel rewarded. Consumers also may have knowledge about the *social consequences* of product use (My friends will like/respect/envy me if I buy a Sony stereo system; My mother will think I am a smart shopper if I buy this jacket on sale).

People's affective and cognitive systems interpret these consequences of product use and form knowledge and beliefs about these functional and psychosocial consequences in memory (see Exhibit 3.5 on page 52). People's affective systems may react to this knowledge as well. For instance, a consumer may feel negative affect (dissatisfaction) if a product needs repairs soon after it was bought. Or a consumer may experience positive feelings of pride and self-esteem if other people comment favorably on a new sweater. At a later time, both affective and cognitive knowledge may be activated from memory and used in other interpretation or integration processes.

Consumers can think about the positive and negative consequences of product use as possible benefits or potential risks. **Benefits** are the desirable consequences consumers seek when buying and using products and brands (I want a car with fast acceleration; I want a car with good mileage). Consumers can have both cognitive knowledge about benefits and affective responses to those benefits. Cognitive knowledge includes propositions linking the product to desired functional and psychosocial consequences (I want my home theater system to have excellent sound reproduction; If I wear that dress, people will notice me). Affective reactions to benefits include positive feelings associated with the desired consequence (I feel good when people notice me).

Consumers often think about products and brands as *bundles of benefits*[10] rather than bundles of attributes (see Exhibit 4.2). Therefore, marketers can divide consumers into subgroups or market segments according to their desires for certain product consequences, a process called *benefit segmentation*.[11] For example, some consumers of toothpaste seek appearance benefits (whiter teeth), whereas others are more interested in health benefits (preventing tooth decay).

Perceived risks concern the undesirable consequences that consumers want to avoid when they buy and use products. A variety of negative consequences might occur. Some consumers worry about the *physical risks* of product consumption (side effects of a cold remedy, injury on a bicycle, electric shock from a hair dryer). Other types of unpleasant consequences include *financial risk* (finding that the warranty doesn't cover fixing your microwave oven; buying new athletic shoes and finding them on sale the next day), *functional risk* (an aspirin product doesn't get rid of headaches very well; a motor oil additive doesn't really reduce engine wear), and *psychosocial risk* (My friends might think these sunglasses look weird on me; I won't feel confident wearing this dress). In sum, perceived risk includes consumers' knowledge or beliefs about unfavorable consequences, including the negative affective responses associated with these unpleasant consequences (unfavorable evaluations, bad feelings, and negative emotions).

The amount of perceived risk a consumer experiences is influenced by two things: (1) the degree of unpleasantness of the negative consequences and (2) the likelihood that these negative consequences will occur. In cases where consumers do not know about the potential for negative consequences (a side effect of a health remedy, a safety defect in a car), perceived risk will be low. In other cases, consumers may have unrealistic perceptions of product risks because they overestimate the likelihood of negative physical consequences. Highlight 4.2 describes some marketplace problems created by consumers' misperceptions of risk.

In a purchase decision, consumers consider the benefits and risks of each choice alternative by integrating information about positive and negative consequences (see Exhibit 3.5). Because consumers are unlikely to purchase products with high perceived risk, marketers try to manage consumers' perceptions of the negative consequences of product purchase and use. Lands' End, a successful mail-order and Internet company, tries to reduce consumers' perceptions of financial and performance risk by offering an unconditional, money-back-if-not-satisfied guarantee. A different marketing strategy is to intentionally activate knowledge about product risk to show how using a particular brand avoids the negative consequences. For instance, Micron Computers once ran advertising campaigns that were intended to generate doubt and anxiety among business executives by pointing out the negative consequences of not buying Micron computers—getting fired, for instance (see **www.buympc.com**). In one ad, a young executive is packing his office and reveals that he was fired because he did not select a Micron computer system.[12]

The other day, you hiked through terrain no one could find on a map.
So who's afraid of a mud splatter?

ERA, with its Active Stainfighter formula, tackles the laundry the way you tackle life. So we can even help get out those intimidating mud splatters. We figure, if you're going to be active, we'd better be too.

ERA

Work it out in the wash.

This ad emphasizes the benefits of using a product.
© *The Procter & Gamble Company. Used by permission.*

Products as Value Satisfiers

Consumers also have knowledge about the personal, symbolic values that products and brands help them satisfy or achieve (see Exhibit 4.2). **Values** are people's broad life goals (I want to be successful; I need security). Values often involve the emotional affect associated with such goals and needs (the strong feelings and emotions that accompany success). Recognizing when a value has been satisfied or a basic life goal has been achieved is an internal feeling that is somewhat intangible and subjective (I feel secure; I am respected by others; I am successful). In contrast, functional and psychosocial consequences are more tangible and are more obvious when they occur (I got compliments when I wore that silk shirt).

There are many ways to classify values.[13] One useful scheme identifies two types or levels of values: instrumental and terminal.[14] *Instrumental values* are preferred

Highlight 4.2

The Perception and Reality of Risk

Many people seem to believe consumer products should involve no risk and that attaining zero risk is possible. Yet, as we reduce significant risks in our environment, consumers seem to become ever more anxious about the imagined hazards of modern life. People are confused about perceived risks of products, partly because several of the major "hazards" of recent years turned out to be false alarms or were greatly exaggerated.

The Belgian Coca-Cola scare of 1999 is a recent example. At the time, Belgium was recovering from a major food contamination crisis. Countries across Europe and into Asia had banned imports of Belgian poultry, pork, eggs, and meat following the discovery that farmers had fed dioxin-contaminated grain to chickens, pigs, and cattle. In the wake of that incident, the country was again alarmed when a number of schoolchildren complained of nausea and vomiting after drinking some foul-smelling Coke. Coca-Cola probably made a tactical error by waiting a full week after the initial reports to issue a public response. In the meantime, damning newspaper headlines popped up all over Europe—from Sweden ("200 Poisoned by Coca-Cola") to Italy ("Alarm Across Europe for Coca-Cola Products")—as more and more consumers fell ill. Finally, the company admitted that the strange smell was caused by a bad batch of carbon dioxide and some chemicals that had gotten onto the outside of some cans. But it insisted that the product itself was not contaminated and should not have made anyone sick. Experts later attributed much of the illnesses to mass hysteria, caused largely by the climate of fear that lingered after the dioxin crisis.

In the United States, controversy has raged over genetically modified food. But the concern about such products appears somewhat selective. For example, McDonald's has asked suppliers to furnish only non-genetically modified potatoes; however, those potatoes eventually get fried in oil made from gene-altered corn and soybeans. Similarly, Frito-Lay no longer uses genetically modified corn in its chips, but its parent company, PepsiCo, still uses genetically modified corn syrup in soft drinks.

What would happen if consumers really knew *everything* that is in their food? In 2000 Kraft recalled millions of taco shells that may have contained genetically modified corn approved as animal feed but not yet okayed for human consumption. Yet there was no evidence that the corn would have been harmful to humans. Consider, however, the Food and Drug Administration guidelines for cornmeal (the primary ingredient in taco shells): Every 50 grams may legally contain one whole insect, 50 insect fragments, two rodent hairs, or one "rodent excretia fragment"—all "natural" materials. *Bon appetit!*

Sources: Holman W. Jenkins, Jr., "Business World: Eek! Attack of the Perfectly Harmless Tacos," *The Wall Street Journal*, October 4, 2000. p. A27; Anita Manning, "It's Hard to Avoid Modified Foods," *USA Today*, June 7, 2000, p. 6D; Kathleen Schmidt, "Coke's Crisis," *Marketing News*, September 27, 1999, pp. 1, 11; Henry Unger, "Illnesses in Coke Recall Found Psychsomatic," *The Atlanta Journal-Constitution*, April 1, 2000, p. F1.

modes of conduct. They are ways of behaving that have positive value for a person (having a good time, acting independent, showing self-reliance). *Terminal values*, on the other hand, are preferred states of being or broad psychological states (happy, at peace, successful). Both instrumental and terminal values (goals or needs) represent the most personal consequences people are trying to achieve in their lives. Exhibit 4.3 lists some of the values held by Americans.

Certain values, called *core values*, are central to people's self-concept—their knowledge about themselves. These core values are the key elements in a *self-schema*, an associative network of interrelated knowledge about oneself.[15] Besides values, self-schemas include knowledge of important life events (episodic memories), knowledge of one's own behavior, and beliefs and feelings about one's body (body image).[16] Consumers' core values have a major influence on their

Exhibit 4.3

Instrumental and Terminal Values of Americans

Instrumental Values (Preferred Modes of Behavior)	Terminal Values (Preferred End States of Being)
Competence Ambitious (hard working) Independent (self-reliant) Imaginative (creative) Capable (competent) Logical (rational) Courageous	**Social harmony** World at peace Equality (brotherhood) Freedom (independence) National security Salvation (eternal life)
Compassion Forgiving (pardon others) Helpful (work for others) Cheerful (joyful) Loving (affectionate)	**Personal gratification** Social recognition Comfortable life Pleasure (enjoyable life) Sense of accomplishment
Sociality Polite (courteous) Obedient (dutiful) Clean (neat, tidy)	**Self-actualization** Beauty (nature and arts) Wisdom (understanding) Inner harmony (no conflict) Self-respect (self-esteem) Sense of accomplishment
Integrity Responsible (reliable) Honest (sincere) Self-controlled	**Security** Taking care of family Salvation (eternal life)
	Love and affection Mature love (sexual and spiritual intimacy) True friendship (close companionship)
	Personal contentedness Happiness (contentment)

Sources: The values are Adapted with the permission of The Free Press, a division of Simon & Schuster Adult Publishing Group, from The Nature of Human Values by Milton Rokeach. Copyright © 1973 by The Free Press. Copyright © renewed 2001 by Sandra Ball-Rokeach. All rights reserved. The bold faced category labels for groupings of Rokeach's values shown are identified by Donald E. Vinson, J. Michael Munson, and Masao Nakanishi, "An Investigation of the Rokeach Value Survey for Consumer Research Applications," in *Advances in Consumer Research*, vol. 4, ed. W. D. Perreault (Atlanta, GA: Association for Consumer Research, 1977), pp. 247–52.

cognitive processes and choice behaviors; therefore, they are of particular interest to marketers. For instance, the growing core value of protecting the environment has created many new marketing opportunities. Thus, in the 1990s, McDonald's changed from polystyrene shell containers for its hamburgers to quilted paper wrappers.

Each type of knowledge—attributes, consequences, and values—also "contains" consumers' affective reactions to those concepts. However, because they represent especially important, personally relevant consequences, values often are associated with strong affective responses. Satisfying a value usually elicits positive affect (happiness, joy, satisfaction), whereas blocking a value produces negative affect (frustration, anger, disappointment). For many people, buying their first car satisfies the values of independence and freedom, and generates positive affective feelings of pride and satisfaction. On the other hand, your value of security is not satisfied (blocked) if your new bicycle lock is broken by a thief, which could create substantial negative affect (anger, frustration, fear).

In summary, consumers can have product knowledge about product attributes, consequences of product use, and personal values. Most marketing research focuses on one type of product knowledge—usually attributes or consequences, where the focus typically is on benefits rather than risks. Values are examined less frequently and usually in isolation. The problem is that studying only one type of knowledge gives marketers an incomplete understanding of consumers' product knowledge. They miss the critical connections among attributes, consequences, and values.

Means–End Chains of Product Knowledge

Consumers can combine the three types of product knowledge to form a simple associative network called a means–end chain.[17] A **means–end chain** links consumers' knowledge about product attributes with their knowledge about consequences and values.[18] The means–end perspective suggests that consumers think about product attributes subjectively in terms of personal consequences. (What is this attribute good for? What does this attribute do for me?) In other words, consumers see most product attributes as a *means to some end*. The end could be a consequence (a benefit or a risk) or a more abstract value.

A common representation of a means–end chain has four levels:[19]

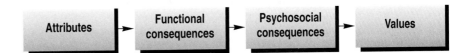

Exhibit 4.4 presents definitions of the four levels in the means–end chain and gives examples of each level. Sometimes the distinctions among the four levels can be a bit fuzzy. For instance, you might be uncertain whether "being with friends" is a psychosocial consequence or a value. Fortunately marketers don't have to worry about making such fine distinctions when using the means–end chain model to develop marketing strategies. The main point of the model is that consumers think in terms of personal consequences—at different levels. To represent that thinking, they create means–end knowledge structures linking tangible product attributes to functional and psychosocial consequences and, in turn, to more abstract and personal values and goals.

Because means–end chains represent consumers' personally relevant meanings for products and brands, they are unique to each consumer's background and personal interests. Thus, different consumers are likely to have different means–end chains for the same product or brand, although there usually are some similarities. And we should not be surprised to find that consumers' meanings for a product can be quite different from those of a marketing manager.

To summarize, the means–end chain model proposes that the meaning of a product attribute is given by its perceived consequences.[20] Consider two physical attributes Gillette designed into its popular MACH 3 Turbo razor: three thin, low-friction blades with a forward pivot design and an improved lubricating strip. These

Exhibit 4.4

A Means–End Chain Model of Consumers' Product Knowledge

Level of Abstraction	Examples		Explanation
Values	Self-esteem	Thrifty	Preferred end states of being and preferred modes of behavior.
Psychosocial consequences	Others notice me	I feel like a good shopper	Psychological (How do I feel?) and social (How do others feel about me?) consequences of product use.
Functional consequences	Excellent performance	Durable	Immediate, tangible consequences of product use. What does the product do? What functions does it perform?
Attributes	High price	Good-quality workmanship	Physical characteristics of product as well as more subjective, less tangible characteristics.

product attributes probably don't mean much to most consumers until they use the product and directly experience its consequences or else learn about them from advertising or from other consumers. Gillette's advertising was designed to communicate key product benefits in the hope that consumers would form the following means–end chains:

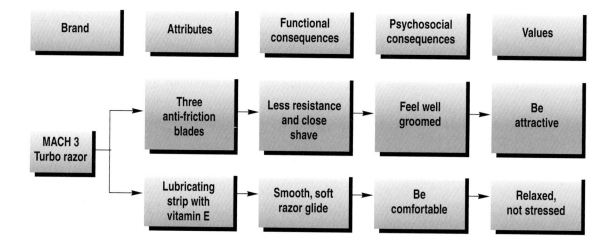

Examples of Means–End Chains

Exhibit 4.5 presents several means–end chains that represent one consumer's product knowledge for a product class (hair spray), a product form (flavored potato chips), and a brand (Scope mouthwash). This figure illustrates four important points about means–end chains. First, actual means–end chains vary considerably in the meanings they contain. Second, not every means–end chain leads to a value. In fact, the end of a means–end chain can be a consequence at any level of abstraction—from a functional consequence (This toothpaste will give me fresh breath) to a psychosocial consequence (My friends will like being close to me) to an instrumental value (I will be clean) to a value (I will be happy). In cases where product attributes have no connections to consequences, consumers do not know what the attribute is good for, and it probably will have little effect on their behavior. Third, some of the means–end chains in Exhibit 4.5 are incomplete, with "missing" levels of meanings. This illustrates that the actual product knowledge in consumers' means–end chains does not necessarily contain each of the four levels of product meaning shown in the idealized means–end chain model. Finally, although not shown in Exhibit 4.5, some product attributes may have multiple means–end chains, and these can be conflicting; that is, some attributes can lead to both positive and negative ends. For example, consider the means–end chains that may be associated with price. For a fairly

Exhibit 4.5

Examples of Means–End Chains

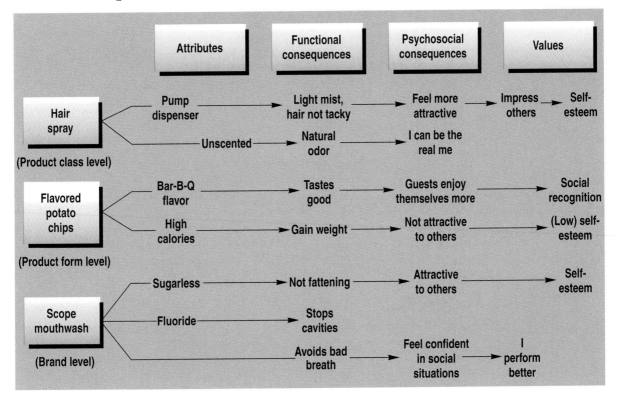

expensive product such as a watch, a higher price than a competitor's may have both positive and negative consequences (perceived benefits and risks). Consumers may have difficulty making purchase decisions that involve such conflicting meanings.

Identifying Consumers' Means–End Chains

Measuring means–end chains is best accomplished with one-on-one, personal interviews in which the researcher tries to understand a consumer's meanings for product attributes and consequences. The process involves two basic steps. First, the researcher must identify or elicit the product attributes that are most important to each consumer when he or she makes a purchase decision. Exhibit 4.6 describes three ways of identifying the most relevant attributes. The second step is an interview process called *laddering*, designed to reveal how the consumer links product attributes to more abstract consequences and values.[21] For each important attribute, the researcher asks the consumer a series of questions in the format "why is that important to you?" Exhibit 4.7 shows an example of a laddering interview. By identifying the means–end connections consumers make among product attributes,

---

Exhibit 4.6

Methods of Identifying Key Attributes Considered by Consumers

Direct elicitation

Researcher: Please tell me what characteristics you usually consider when deciding which brand of running shoe to buy.

Consumer: Let's see. I think about the cost, the high-tech features, the color and style, and the lacing pattern.

Free-sort task

Researcher: Here are several brands of running shoes. Assume that you are thinking of buying a pair of running shoes. I want you to sort these brands into groups so that the shoes in each pile are alike in some way important to you and are different from the shoes in the other piles.

or

Here are several brands of running shoes. I want you to sort them into groups using any basis you wish.

or

Now please describe what each pile means to you. Why are these brands together? How are these shoes different from those other shoes?

Consumer: Well, these shoes are all *high-tech* and *expensive*. Those are *cheaper* and have *fewer fancy features*. And these brands are in-between.

Triad task

Researcher: Here are three brands of running shoes. Assume that you were thinking of buying a pair of running shoes. In what important way are two of these similar and different from the third? Are there any other ways?

Consumer: "Hmmm. Well, these two shoes have *special construction features* to keep your heel stable and solid. This one doesn't. And these two have a *staggered lacing system,* while this one has a traditional lacing pattern."

Exhibit 4.7

Example of a Laddering Interview

Researcher:	You said that the lacing pattern in a running shoe is important to you in deciding what brand to buy. Why is that?
Consumer:	A staggered lacing pattern makes the shoe fit more snugly on my foot. **[physical attribute and functional consequence]**
Researcher:	Why is it important that the shoe fit more snugly on your foot?
Consumer:	Because it gives me better support. **[functional consequence]**
Researcher:	Why is better support important to you?
Consumer:	So I can run without worrying about injuring my feet. **[psychosocial consequence]**
Researcher:	Why is it important for you not to worry while running?
Consumer:	So I can relax and enjoy the run. **[psychosocial consequence]**
Researcher:	Why is it important that you can relax and enjoy the run?
Consumer:	Because it gets rid of tension I have built up at work. **[psychosocial consequence]**
Researcher:	Why is it important for you to get rid of tension from work?
Consumer:	So when I go back to work in the afternoon, I can perform better. **[value—achievement]**
Researcher:	Why is it important that you perform better?
Consumer:	I feel better about myself. **[value—self-esteem]**
Researcher:	Why is it important that you feel better about yourself?
Consumer:	It just is! **[the end!]**

consequences, and values, laddering helps managers understand what product attributes mean to the consumer. Marketing managers can then use the consumer insights gained from the means–end research to develop more effective marketing strategies. Effective marketing strategies connect the product to important psychosocial consequences and values, thus making the product personally relevant to consumers.

Marketing Implications

A basic advantage of means–end chain models is that they provide a deeper understanding of consumers' product knowledge than methods focusing only on attributes or benefits.[22] For instance, consider the following means–end chain for Liquid Tide laundry detergent:

This hypothetical consumer interprets the chemical attributes of Liquid Tide (special molecules) in terms of the more abstract attribute "cleaning power."

Cleaning power, in turn, is seen as providing the functional benefit of "cleaner clothes for the kids," which is seen as helping to achieve the instrumental value of "being a good parent," which finally leads to the terminal value of "feeling good about myself" or "self-esteem."

By identifying the sequence of connections between product-related meanings at different levels of abstraction, marketers can see more clearly what consumers really mean when they mention a product attribute or a consequence such as "cleaning power." Means–end chain analyses also identify the basic ends (values and goals) consumers seek when they buy and use certain products and brands, and this gives insight into consumers' deeper purchase motivations. Finally, means–end chains identify the consumer–product relationship—that is, they show how consumers relate product attributes to important aspects of their self-concepts. In sum, the more complete understanding of consumers' product knowledge provided by means–end analysis helps marketers devise more meaningful and effective advertising, pricing, distribution, and product strategies.

Sometimes companies begin with a desirable functional consequence that will appeal to many consumers, and have to learn what attributes consumers believe produce the desired outcome. Removing plaque on teeth is a desirable functional consequence, but how does one do it? Through its research, Gillette (marketers of Oral-B toothbrushes, the number one brand in the United States) learned that regular brushing did little to remove plaque from teeth. However, when a toothbrush reverses itself suddenly its bristles are "thrown out" a bit, and this action can dislodge bits of plaque. In partnership with Braun, a German appliance company it owns, Gillette developed an oscillating electronic toothbrush that easily produced such a motion. First-year sales were $700 million.[23]

Digging for Deeper Consumer Understanding

The means–end or laddering approach allows marketing managers to "dig" below consumers' surface knowledge about product attributes and functional consequences to their deeper meanings and beliefs about psychosocial consequences and value satisfactions. For many marketing problems, however, this is not deep enough.

Nearly every company has one or more key concepts, issues, or ideas at the very core of its business. For a soft-drink manufacturer, concepts such as "feeling good" or "refreshment" are the foundation of personal relevance for consumers. Managers need to understand what those concepts mean to consumers. Thus, a financial services company should know what consumers mean by "financial security" or "risky investment." A manufacturer of antibacterial soap needs to know the meaning of "being clean" or "germs" to consumers. A bank should know how its customers understand the "meaning of money."

Because such issues involve deep and unconscious meanings, standard consumer research methods such as questionnaire surveys, experiments, or even laddering cannot provide much insight or understanding. Therefore, many marketers have turned to qualitative research methods such as focus groups to obtain deep understanding. Focus groups can provide some useful insights into consumers' thinking, but are unable to dig really deeply into consumers' fundamental knowledge and meanings. An effective alternative approach, used by many companies, is ZMET (the Zaltman Metaphor Elicitation Technique), an innovative qualitative interview method developed by Professor Gerald Zaltman of the Harvard Business School.[24] More information about ZMET and its applications can be found on the website: **www.olsonzaltman.com**.

The ZMET Approach to Consumer Knowledge

As the name suggests, ZMET elicits metaphors from consumers that reveal their deep meanings (both cognitive and affective) about a topic. (You might review the metaphor discussion in Chapter 3.) Basically, consumers find pictures that express their thoughts and feelings about a topic, such as "going to the hospital," or "the role of peanut butter in your life," or "your experience of heartburn and indigestion." These pictures are metaphors for consumers' deeper thoughts and feelings. The ZMET interview is designed to guide consumers as they describe and explore the meaning of their picture metaphors, thus revealing those deeper cognitive and affective concepts.

The ZMET Interview

During a ZMET interview, trained interviewers spend about two hours with each consumer exploring the meaning of his or her pictures or visual metaphors. Several of the steps in ZMET are described below:[25]

- **The pre-interview instruction:** Several days before the interview, consumers are told to select six to eight pictures (from magazines or any other source) that express their thoughts and feelings about the topic or issue. For example, consumers might be asked to find pictures that express their thoughts and feelings about a *brand* such as Pepsi-Cola, an *idea* such as "the meaning of Donald Duck," or a *situation* such as "personal security when you travel on vacation."
- **Storytelling:** The first half of the ZMET interview is devoted to storytelling. Under the direction of trained interviewers, consumers "tell stories" about each picture that reveal the affective and cognitive meanings of that visual metaphor. Consumers seem quite willing to discuss the deep cognitive and affective meanings of their picture/metaphors.
- **Expand the frame:** The interviewer asks consumers to pretend that the (imaginary) frame around a picture is expanded in all directions so that more things come into view, "What people or things might come into the picture that would help me understand your thoughts and feelings about Donald Duck?" Consumers describe these new (metaphoric) images and their meaning. A consumer might say that Mickey Mouse would join Donald Duck in a picture, and the two of them would mingle with little kids, making them laugh.
- **Sensory images:** The interviewer elicits metaphors based on the other senses (not visual). Consumers are asked to describe a scent, sound, taste, and touch that would express their thoughts and feelings about the topic. For example, a consumer might say that the sound of a babbling brook expresses her utter relaxation as she enjoys a cold beer from a microbrewery.
- **Vignette:** Consumers are asked to create a short movie or one-act play that expresses their thoughts and feelings about the topic. Consumers are told to make a product or brand a character in the story. By treating the product or brand as though it were alive (metaphorically)—an entity that can think, feel, and act—consumers reveal deep meanings about the personality of the product and how they interact with it.
- **Digital image:** In the final step in a ZMET interview, consumers create a summary collage of the most meaningful pictures (metaphors) they brought to the interview. This can be done digitally by scanning the pictures into a computer and then manipulating them to create a collage. When done, the consumer narrates a detailed description of the image and its meaning.

By using ZMET to elicit metaphors and then probe their meanings in these steps, researchers are able to dig quite deeply into consumers' conscious and unconscious thoughts and feelings (both cognition and affect) about a topic. Often ZMET is able to uncover "knowledge that consumers do not know they know."[26]

Marketing Implications

The deep understanding and consumer insights gleaned from a ZMET study can stimulate managers' imaginations and guide their strategic thinking about a variety of marketing problems. For example, in a ZMET project about "going to the dentist," several consumers revealed that they felt "trapped" or "confined" at several stages on the "dentist journey." For some consumers, being in the dentist's chair has those qualities, but so does sitting in the waiting room before being ushered to the dentist's chair. In fact, anxiety and fear (for those consumers who experienced such feelings) was rather high in the waiting room environment. One implication of this study was to redesign waiting rooms (change the environment) to reduce anxiety (modify affective reactions), including using soft music, soothing colors, and other aspects of interior design. As another example of "being contained," several consumers expressed feelings of "release" and "joy" at being "freed" from the dentist's office when their visit was over. To express this feeling, one consumer brought an image of a young girl releasing a bunch of brightly colored balloons into the air. The company used that image in its advertising to communicate this meaning to potential new customers for its dentist referral service.

Involvement

Why do consumers care about some products and brands and not others? Why are consumers sometimes highly motivated to seek information about products, or to buy and use products in certain situations, while other consumers have no interest? Why did some loyal Coke drinkers make such a fuss when in 1985 Coca-Cola managers made a minor change in an inexpensive, simple, and seemingly unimportant soft-drink product (see Highlight 4.3)? These questions concern consumers' involvement, a key concept for understanding consumer behavior.

Involvement refers to consumers' perceptions of importance or personal relevance for an object, event, or activity.[27] Consumers who perceive that a product has personally relevant consequences are said to be involved with the product and to have a personal relationship with it. Involvement with a product or brand has both cognitive and affective aspects.[28] Cognitively, involvement includes means–end knowledge about important consequences produced by using the product (This CD would be fun to play at parties). Involvement also includes affect, such as product evaluations (I like the *David Letterman Show*). If product involvement is high, people may experience stronger affective responses such as emotions and strong feelings (I really love my Mazda). Although marketers often treat consumers' product involvement as either high or low, involvement actually can vary from quite low levels (little or no perceived relevance) to moderate (some perceived relevance) to very high levels (great perceived relevance).

Involvement is a motivational state that energizes and directs consumers' cognitive and affective processes and behaviors as they make decisions.[29] For instance, consumers who are involved with cameras are motivated to work harder at choosing which brand to buy. They may spend more time and effort shopping for cameras (visiting more stores, talking to more salespeople). They may interpret more

Highlight 4.3

Coca-Cola Learns about Consumer Involvement

In the spring of 1985, Coca-Cola Company shocked American consumers and other soft-drink manufacturers by announcing that the 99-year-old formula for Coke would be changed. The "new" Coke was a bit sweeter, and marketing research showed it was preferred to Pepsi-Cola. The original Coke formula was to be retired to a bank vault and never produced again.

What happened then was the beginning of Coca-Cola's lesson in consumer involvement. Outraged U.S. consumers complained bitterly to the Atlanta-based company about the loss of "a great American tradition." In Seattle, a group of strident loyalists calling themselves "Old Coke Drinkers of America" laid plans to file a class-action suit against Coca-Cola. They searched out shop owners, vending machine owners, and others willing to claim that the company's formula change had cost them business. Then, when June sales didn't pick up as expected, the bottlers also joined in the demand for the old Coke's return—and fast.

Although Coca-Cola had spent some $4 million in testing the new formula, it had missed one important factor: Millions of consumers had strong *emotional involvement* with the original Coke. They drank it as kids and still did as adults. Many consumers had a personal attachment to Coke. Says a Coke spokesperson, "We had taken away a little part of them and their past. They [consumers] said, 'You have no right to do that. Bring it back.'"

Coca-Cola had learned a costly lesson. Although consumers preferred the new taste in blind taste tests, Coca-Cola did not measure consumers' emotional reactions to removing the original Coke from the marketplace. Coca-Cola learned that a product is more than a production formula; extra meanings such as emotions and strong connections to self-image may also be present.

Although this "new Coke" situation happened some 20 years ago, its lessons about the power of consumers' involvement with a brand are still relevant today.

product information in the environment (read more ads and brochures). And they may spend more time and effort integrating this product information to evaluate brands and make a purchase choice.

Some researchers have used the term *felt involvement* to emphasize that involvement is a psychological state that consumers experience only at certain times and on certain occasions.[30] Consumers do not continually experience feelings of involvement, even for important products such as a car, a home, or special hobby equipment. Rather, people feel involved with such products only on certain occasions when the means–end knowledge about the personal relevance of those products is activated. As circumstances change, that means–end knowledge is no longer activated, and people's feelings of involvement fade (until another time).

Focus of Involvement

Marketers are most interested in understanding consumers' involvement with products and brands. But people also may be involved with other types of *physical objects* such as advertisements. During the 1990s, some people became quite involved with a series of ads for Taster's Choice coffee that portrayed flirtatious situations between a man and a woman. Consumers may be involved with other *people*—friends, relatives, lovers, perhaps even salespeople. People can also become involved with certain *environments* (their homes or backyards, amusement parks, the mountains, or the seashore). Some of these may be marketing environments—a clothing store the consumer especially likes, a particular shopping mall, or a favorite restaurant. Finally, people may be involved with specific *activities* or *behaviors* such as playing tennis, working, windsurfing, or reading. Some consumers become involved with marketing-related activities such as collecting coupons, shopping for new clothes, finding the cheapest prices in town, or bargaining with vendors at flea markets.

It is important that marketers clearly identify the focus of consumers' involvement. Marketers need to know exactly what it is that consumers consider to be personally relevant: a product or brand, an object, a behavior, an event, a situation, an environment, or several of these together. Highlight 4.4 describes some of the reasons consumers are involved with mountain biking. Since marketers are mostly interested in consumers' involvement with products and brands, this is our main focus in this chapter. In principle, however, marketers can analyze consumers' involvement with virtually anything (a store, a political candidate, a college course).

The Means–End Basis for Involvement

Means–end chains can help marketers understand consumers' feelings of personal relevance for a product because they clearly show how consumers' product knowledge is related to their knowledge about self.[31]

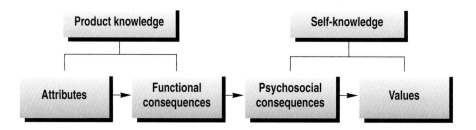

The level of product involvement a consumer experiences during decision making is determined by the type of means–end knowledge activated in the situation.[32] A consumer's level of involvement or self-relevance depends on two aspects of the means– end chains that are activated: the importance or self-relevance of the ends and the strength of connections between the product knowledge level and the self-knowledge level. Consumers who believe product attributes are strongly linked to important end goals or values will feel more involved with the product. In contrast, consumers who believe the product attributes lead only to functional consequences or product attributes are only weakly linked to important values will feel much less involved with the product. Consumers who believe the product attributes are not associated with any relevant consequences will experience little or no involvement with the product. We suspect that for ordinary consumer products such as soap, bread, toothpaste, or socks, most consumers experience low to moderate levels of involvement in the purchase decision.[33]

The affective system responds to the means–end knowledge that is activated in a decision situation.[34] This affect can vary from weak evaluations with little arousal (if relatively unimportant consequences are linked to the product) to highly charged affect such as emotions and strong feelings (when core values are related to the product).

Highlight 4.4

Why Are Some Consumers Involved in Mountain Biking?

When marketers consider the broad issue of consumer involvement, they should ask a fundamental question: Just what is it that consumers are involved with? The obvious answer is not always correct. For example, a recent ZMET study by one of the authors showed that consumers who were very highly involved with mountain biking (one person claimed, *"Mountain biking is my life!"*) were not involved for the same reasons. In fact, one consumer found the social subculture surrounding mountain biking to be more important than the bike itself:

> Biking is hanging out with friends and conversing about gears, injuries, favorite trails, training strategies, races coming up, and past races.

Some consumers were more interested in the thrill of riding as sport:

> The bike is one with you, with the speed and the exhilaration. You're going fast downhill, avoiding rocks and bumps, and you can't have a lapse in concentration, or you'll wreck. It's the competition of the sport, of overcoming the mountain.

Some consumers were primarily involved in racing activities. They were into racing and the thrill of competition, overcoming challenges, or just winning. Other equally involved mountain bikers were most interested in the feeling of freedom they get from mountain biking:

> A bicycle is a child's first form of freedom. It is one of your first true ways of breaking away from your house and going places.

Others were involved in mountain biking to get out into nature as a way to escape the stresses of daily life and have an uplifting, even spiritual experience:

> I'd go mountain biking in the wilderness and come upon this incredible vista. I'd suddenly realize that the universe is so big, and my problems are so minuscule in compar-

ison. The vista would just open up to me, and my problems would all go through it—and then they'd be gone.

Interestingly, many of the most involved bikers did not seem to be highly interested in their bike(s). Those consumers tended to see their bike as a means to an important end—such as a sense of achievement by winning races or spiritual balance through contact with nature. One person described the relationship with the bike this way:

> I love how I feel when I'm on my bike, more than I love my bike. I love what it can bring to me.

Other mountain bikers, however, were directly involved with their bikes. They knew a lot about their bikes and the various component parts, and how each attribute affected performance. These consumers had very elaborate means–end structures of product knowledge relating product attributes to functional consequences (performance) and values (achievement). In a sense, these consumers saw their bikes as an end in itself, and interacting with their bikes gave them important value satisfactions that other highly involved bikers did not find as interesting. Some consumers even formed very strong personal relationships with their favorite bike. As one consumer put it,

> My bike is an old friend. It's reliable. I know it. It's like a really comfortable pair of sneakers.

Not surprisingly, this group spent more money on their bikes, largely by continuously trying to improve their bikes (especially to make them lighter and stronger), compared to other involved consumers who tended not to spend a lot or tinker as much with their bikes.

Obviously consumers have very different ways of being involved with mountain biking and mountain bikes. The focus of their involvement influences how they will respond to marketing attempts to sell bikes and component parts.

Exhibit 4.8

A Basic Model of Consumer Product Involvement

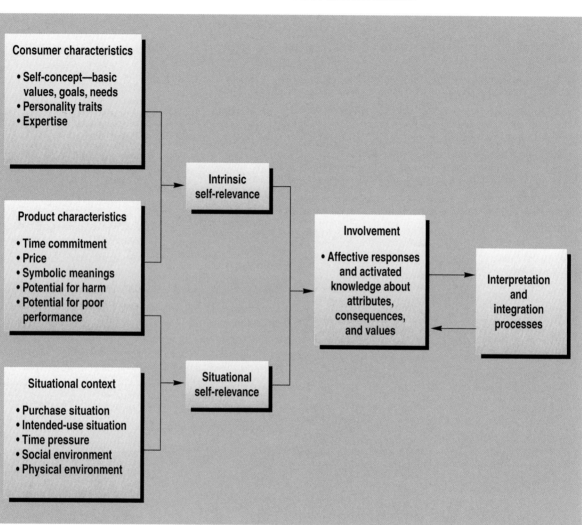

Sources: Adapted from Richard L. Celsi and Jerry C. Olson, "The Role of Involvement in Attention and Comprehension Processes," *Journal of Consumer Research,* September 1988, pp. 210–224. © 1988 Journal of Consumer Research. Reprinted with permission of the publisher, University of Chicago Press; and Peter H. Bloch and Marsha L. Richins, "A Theoretical Model for the Study of Product Importance Perceptions," *Journal of Marketing,* Summer 1983, pp. 69–81.

Factors Influencing Involvement

Exhibit 4.8 shows that a person's level of involvement is influenced by two sources of self-relevance: intrinsic and situational.[35] Each source can activate or generate means–end chains linking product attribute knowledge to personally relevant consequences and values.

Intrinsic self-relevance is based on consumers' means–end knowledge stored in memory.[36] Consumers acquire this means–end knowledge through their past

This ad seeks to enhance intrinsic involvement with the brand by focusing on the benefits of using the brand and the negative consequences of not using it. *Reprinted courtesy of GlaxoSmithKline.*

experiences with a product. As they use a product (or observe others using it), consumers learn that certain product attributes have consequences that help achieve important goals and values. For example, a consumer may learn that various attributes of a home entertainment system (surround sound, remote control, programmability) have favorable and unfavorable consequences (impress my friends, I can be comfortable and relaxed, too much trouble to use). Because this means–end knowledge is stored in memory, it is a potential *intrinsic* source of involvement. If this knowledge is activated, say, in a decision situation, the consumer will experience feelings of personal relevance or involvement with the product.

Exhibit 4.8 shows that intrinsic self-relevance is a function of both consumer and product characteristics, as is all means–end knowledge. Key consumer characteristics include people's values and life goals. Relevant product characteristics are the product attributes and the associated functional consequences (benefits and perceived risks). Perceived risks are important elements in product involvement, because consumers tend to feel more involved with products that might have serious negative consequences. Other product factors that may influence intrinsic sources of involvement include social visibility (Do people know you own the product?) and time commitment (Buying a refrigerator is involving because you are committed to your choice for a long time).

Situational self-relevance is determined by aspects of the immediate physical and social environment that activate important consequences and values, thus making products and brands seem self-relevant. For instance, a "50% Off" sign on fishing rods may activate self-relevant thoughts in a person interested in fishing (I can get a good deal on a new rod). Because many environmental factors change over time, situational self-relevance usually activates temporary means–end linkages between a product and important consequences or values. These connections between the product and personal consequences may disappear when the situation changes. For example, the person's involvement with buying this particular fishing rod may last only as long as the sale continues.

Aspects of the social environment can create situational self-relevance. For instance, shopping with others can make some consumers more self-conscious than shopping alone (I want to impress my friends with my sense of style). A chance observation in the physical environment, such as noticing a window display in a clothing store, may activate means–end knowledge about consequences that become associated with the clothing in the display (That sweater would be good to wear to the party next week). More general aspects of the physical environment can also influence situational self-relevance. The high temperatures on a summer day can make certain consequences more personally relevant and desirable (I need to take a break, cool off, or relax). In turn, this makes buying an ice cream cone or going to an air-conditioned movie theater more relevant and involving.

Exhibit 4.8 shows that consumers' overall level of involvement is always determined by a combination of intrinsic and situational self-relevance. Although intrinsic factors have the most influence on involvement in some cases, situational sources of involvement can have a major influence in many circumstances. Consider the common situation when a consumer's intrinsic self-relevance for a product is low (the product is not very important to one's self-concept). For instance, most people do not consider hot-water heaters to have much self-relevance. But if yours develops a leak, it becomes quite important to replace it quickly. The negative consequences of showering and washing in cold water are highly self-relevant. This means–end knowledge (which is activated only when your old water heater breaks) is a situational source of self-relevance with choosing and buying a new hot-water heater as quickly as possible. You are likely to experience this involvement and motivation only for the short time it takes to evaluate a few alternatives and make a quick purchase choice.

This example shows that marketers need to understand both the *focus* of consumers' involvement and the *sources* that create it. Even though most consumers are not personally involved with mundane products such as hot-water heaters, they can become temporarily involved with *the process of buying the product.* Having to replace a broken water heater (a situational source of involvement) makes people think about particular consequences of *purchase* that are important to them (paying money, the time and effort it takes to shop, the stress and hassle). The purchase situation also may activate product knowledge that is important during decision making (purchase price, speed of delivery, ease of installation) but that means–end knowledge is not relevant later, when the product is being used. Thus, involvement declines after the purchase, because most of the involvement the consumer experienced concerned the decision process, not the product itself.

This is not an isolated or rare example. Situational self-relevance always combines with consumers' intrinsic self-relevance to create the level of involvement consumers actually experience during decision making. This means consumers usually experience some level of involvement when making any purchase choice, even for relatively unimportant products. Even though intrinsic sources of involvement are low for many everyday consumer products (soap, bread, socks), situational sources (a sale or a coupon) can influence the level of involvement consumers feel. Thus, marketers can most easily influence consumers' product involvement by manipulating aspects of the environment that might function as sources of situational self-relevance.

Marketing Implications	Understanding consumers' product knowledge and involvement can help marketers understand the critical consumer–product relationship and develop more effective marketing strategies. A basic goal of many marketing strategies is to enhance consumers' product involvement by connecting products and services to consumers' goals and values.

Understanding the Key Reasons for Purchase

Marketers can use means–end analyses to identify the key attributes and consequences underlying a product purchase decision and to understand the meaning of those concepts to consumers. Restaurant decisions are a good example. Unlike people in cultures such as France, many Americans are not highly involved with food.

The fast-food industry's research suggests that the three most important factors in many consumers' decisions on where to eat are (1) time of day, (2) how long the customer wants to spend eating, and (3) price.[37] According to one expert, "We used to eat when the food was ready. Now we eat when *we* are ready." Often speed and convenience are critical consequences, not the food itself.

Rally's, a small chain of more than 400 restaurants, has developed marketing strategies to provide these desired consequences. The typical Rally's is small enough to be placed anywhere. A Rally's can be built for about $350,000, compared to more than $1 million for the average McDonald's. Rally's offers no customer seating. Food is ordered at walk-up or drive-through windows and eaten elsewhere. The drive-through line at a Rally's restaurant moves so rapidly that many customers are on their way within 45 seconds! Moreover, they pay only about $2 for a fully dressed burger, french fries, and a large Coke, about 85 cents less than the nearby McDonald's would charge. And the food? Actually, the food itself is not that important for many consumers. As one Rally's customer admitted, "The food is not very good here, but it's cheap, quick, and easy." By understanding what attributes and consequences customers really want, Rally's doubled sales and tripled profits from 1989 to 1990, whereas several competitors experienced stagnant growth or decline. For example, annual sales at an average Rally's ran about $1,300 per square foot compared to $400 at McDonald's.

Understanding the Consumer–Product Relationship

One of the most important concepts in this book concerns consumers' relationships with products and brands. Marketers need to understand the cognitive and affective aspects of these consumer–product relationships.[38] For instance, many Americans are highly involved with their autos, often treating them like pets (stroking, petting, grooming). For some consumers, the product–self relationship reflects a passionate level of intrinsic self-relevance. Such people love their cars and may engage in ritual forms of "worship" such as weekend cleaning and waxing. Teenagers who are "into" cars may link the general attributes of cars to important self-relevant consequences (self-respect, envy of peers, freedom). Highlight 4.5 illustrates how studying metaphors can give deep insight into the consumer–product relationship. A key task for marketing management is to manage this relationship.[39] Marketing strategies should be designed to create and maintain meaningful consumer–product relationships and modify those means–end relationships that are not optimal.[40]

If marketers can understand the consumer–product relationship, they may be able to segment the market in terms of consumers' intrinsic self-relevance.[41] For instance, some consumers may have positive means–end knowledge about a product category, whereas others may have favorable beliefs and feelings for a brand. Still other consumers may have favorable means–end knowledge about both the product category and the brand. Highlight 4.6 gives examples of the varying levels of brand loyalty in different product categories.

Researchers have identified four market segments with different levels of intrinsic self-relevance for a product category and brand.[42] Those with the strongest feelings are brand loyalists and routine brand buyers.

- *Brand loyalists* have strong affective ties to one favorite brand that they regularly buy. In addition, they perceive that the product category in general

Highlight 4.5

One Consumer's Relationship with His Mountain Bike

The ZMET process described earlier is one way to understand consumers' relationship with a product. In a series of ZMET interviews, young, highly involved mountain bikers revealed their thoughts and feelings (cognition and affect) about mountain biking and their mountain bikes. One person described his bike as follows:

> My mountain bike is like a cougar, well balanced, able to climb, able to control itself even on traitorous hills. It encourages me to push the limits. When I'm going to race, my bike almost says, "Now we're going to show people what we can do!"

This short statement contains several metaphoric expressions that reveal important and deep meanings for this person, even meanings that may be partially unconscious. Following is our interpretation of the key metaphors and metaphoric expressions in this short passage.

- **My bike is like a cougar.**
  Interpretation: My bike is sleek, fast, beautiful, powerful, and perhaps a bit dangerous.
- **My bike is well balanced.**
  Interpretation: My bike is stable, not easily tipped over.

- **My bike is able to control itself, even on treacherous hills.**
  Interpretation: My bike has a mind of its own; it knows what to do without much input from me. It can keep going even on difficult hilly terrain that looks friendly, but is really nasty and out to get us.
- **My bike encourages me to push the limits.**
  Interpretation: My bike is a force (a coach?) that is encouraging me to do my very best. . .and go for it.
- **My bike tells me, "Now we're going to show people what we can do!"**
  Interpretation: My bike is my partner in races—my bike works with me to do our very best.

Notice how these metaphors reveal this consumer's personal relationship with his bike. It almost seems as if the consumer considers the bike to be alive, which allows him to have a deeper and more meaningful relationship with the bike. Note also that these same metaphors serve as a vehicle for communicating those deep meanings to others. By studying consumers' metaphors, marketers can form a deeper understanding of how consumers think and feel about products and brands.

provides personally relevant consequences. Their intrinsic self-relevance includes positive means–end knowledge about both the brand and the product category, and leads them to experience high levels of involvement during decision making. They strive to buy the "best" brand for their needs. For instance, consumers often have strong brand loyalty for sports equipment such as tennis racquets or athletic shoes.

- *Routine brand buyers* have low intrinsic self-relevance for the product category, but they do have a favorite brand that they buy regularly (little brand switching). For the most part, their intrinsic self-relevance with a brand is not based on knowledge about the means–end consequences of product attributes. Instead, these consumers are interested in other types of consequences associated with regular brand purchase (it's easier to buy Colgate each time I need toothpaste). Such beliefs can lead to consistent purchase, but these consumers are not so interested in getting the "best" brand; a satisfactory one will do.

Highlight 4.6

Consumers' Relationships with Brands

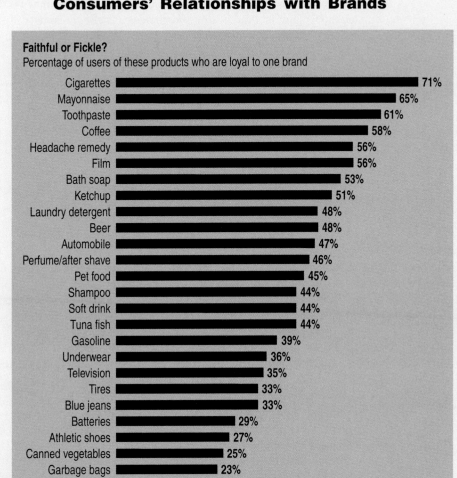

Faithful or Fickle?
Percentage of users of these products who are loyal to one brand

Product	Percentage
Cigarettes	71%
Mayonnaise	65%
Toothpaste	61%
Coffee	58%
Headache remedy	56%
Film	56%
Bath soap	53%
Ketchup	51%
Laundry detergent	48%
Beer	48%
Automobile	47%
Perfume/after shave	46%
Pet food	45%
Shampoo	44%
Soft drink	44%
Tuna fish	44%
Gasoline	39%
Underwear	36%
Television	35%
Tires	33%
Blue jeans	33%
Batteries	29%
Athletic shoes	27%
Canned vegetables	25%
Garbage bags	23%

Brand loyalty among consumers is a highly desirable goal for most marketers. Although brand loyalty seems to have eroded considerably over the past 30 years because of increased brand competition and extensive sales promotions (coupons and price reductions), it is not dead. A survey of some 2,000 customers found wide variations in brand loyalty across product classes (people who claimed to buy mostly the same brand).

Source: Wall Street Journal. Central Edition [Staff Produced Copy Only] Ronald Alsop, "Brand Loyalty is Rarely Blind Loyalty," *The Wall Street Journal,* October 19, 1989, pp. B1, B8. Copyright 1989 by Dow Jones & Co. Inc. Reproduced with permission of Dow Jones & Co. Inc. in the format Textbook via Copyright Clearance Center.

The other two segments have weaker levels of intrinsic self-relevance for a particular brand. Information seekers and brand switchers do not have especially positive means–end knowledge about a single, favorite brand.

- *Information seekers* have positive means–end knowledge about the product category, but no particular brand stands out as superior (you may be "into" skis, but you know many ski brands are good choices). These consumers use a lot of information to find a "good" brand. Over time, they tend to buy a variety of brands in the product category.
- *Brand switchers* have low intrinsic self-relevance for both the brand and the product category. They do not see that the brand or product category provides important consequences, and they have no interest in buying "the best." They have no special relationship with either the product category or specific brands. Such consumers tend to respond to environmental factors such as price deals or other short-term promotions that act as situational sources of involvement.

In sum, different marketing strategies are necessary to address the unique types of product knowledge, intrinsic self-relevance, and involvement of consumers in these four market segments.

Influencing Intrinsic Self-Relevance

If marketers can understand the means–end knowledge that makes up consumers' intrinsic self-relevance, they are better able to design product attributes that consumers will connect to important consequences and values.[43] A good example is Gillette's design of the MACH 3 Turbo razor, mentioned at the beginning of the chapter. Marketers also can try to strengthen consumers' intrinsic self-relevance for a given brand. Mazda once asked owners of Mazda cars to send in pictures of themselves with their cars, and some of the pictures were included in national magazine ads. This promotion was likely to activate and strengthen the intrinsic self-relevance of Mazda owners for their cars.

In the short run, it is difficult to modify consumers' intrinsic self-relevance for a product or brand. Over longer periods, though, consumers' means–end knowledge can be influenced by various marketing strategies, including advertising.[44] The outcome of this process is not completely predictable because many factors besides marketing strategy can modify consumers' means–end knowledge. For instance, consumers' direct experience of using a product or brand will have a strong impact on their means–end knowledge. If the actual product experience doesn't measure up to the image created by advertising, consumers are not likely to form the desired means–end meanings.

Influencing Situational Self-Relevance

Marketers use many strategies to create, modify, or maintain consumers' situational self-relevance, usually with the goal of encouraging a purchase. Semiannual clearance sales on summer or winter clothing are situational factors that may temporarily raise consumers' involvement with buying such products. Likewise, premiums such as stickers or small toys in cereal boxes or candy packages may temporarily increase children's involvement with a brand. Special pricing strategies, including rebates on new car models ("Get $1,000 back if you buy in the next two weeks"), may function as situational influences that create a temporary increase in involvement with buying the product.

Another source of situational self-relevance is to link a product to a social cause.[45] For instance, American Express once donated 1 cent from every purchase made with its card to refurbish the Statue of Liberty. In addition to making a total contribution of $1.7 million, American Express reaped lots of publicity and some new card applications. As other examples, Johnson & Johnson promotes Shelter Aid, a program that makes donations to shelters for battered women, while Avon Products sponsored a program in which its 415,000 U.S. Avon Ladies distributed 15 million brochures about breast cancer. Finally, if you buy enough wieners and bologna, Oscar Mayer will donate bats, uniforms, and scoreboards to kids' baseball teams.

Back To...

Gillette

Understanding consumers' product knowledge and consumer–product relationships requires that marketers examine the meanings by which consumers represent product attributes and link those meanings to higher-ordered meanings, such as the psychosocial consequences and values in consumers' self-schemas. A major reason for Gillette's successes is its ability to develop products with superior product attributes that consumers perceive as being linked to important, self-relevant psychosocial consequences and perhaps even personal values.

In this chapter, we considered the means–end chains consumers may have formed for the Gillette MACH 3 Turbo razor mentioned in the chapter opener. As another example, the wide-ribbed handle on the Gillette for Women Venus makes it easier to hold and control the razor, which leads to a smoother, closer shave with fewer cuts. In turn, women may feel more attractive, which gives them greater confidence in social situations and, finally, adds to their self-esteem. Companies like Gillette must identify and promote the desirable higher-ordered consequences linked to their products' attributes (and avoid attributes having negative consequences).

The means–end perspective is also useful for understanding consumers' intrinsic self-relevance for products and brands. It is likely that most consumers do not have intense levels of intrinsic self-relevance for any of these Gillette products. However, most consumers probably believe these products have a moderate degree of intrinsic self-relevance and certain market segments of consumers may experience higher levels of self-relevance. For example, because teens (both men and women) just beginning to shave may have higher levels of intrinsic self-relevance for razors and related products than do consumers in other market segments, they probably experience higher levels of involvement during purchase decision processes. Gillette might create special marketing strategies for such consumers.

Gillette's corporate policy is to market only those products that offer consumers significant improvements in shaving performance. That means avoiding putting superficial frills on existing products and calling them innovations—a practice recently retired CEO Alfred Zeien likened to "putting blue dots in the soap powder." For example, the MACH 3 Turbo is an improvement over the MACH 3 in that it has anti-friction blades and a better lubrication system, which combine to provide a

smoother, closer shave with fewer strokes. By continuing to provide such benefits for consumers, Gillette accounts for roughly one-third of the 20 billion razor blades sold annually around the world. ❖

Summary   In this chapter, we took a closer look at consumers' affective and cognitive responses to products. Consumers don't buy products to get attributes; rather, they think about products in terms of their desirable and undesirable consequences—benefits and perceived risks. By relating product attributes to their own personal and self-relevant consequences, values, goals, and needs, consumers form knowledge structures called means–end chains. The attributes of some products are strongly linked to important ends (consequences and values), whereas other products are only weakly associated with self-relevant consequences. These are sometimes called high- and low-involvement products, respectively. Consumers experience involvement as cognitive perceptions of importance and interest and affective feelings of arousal. Their feelings of involvement are determined by intrinsic self-relevance— the means–end knowledge stored in memory. Situational factors in the environment also influence the content of activated means–end chains and thereby affect the involvement consumers experience when choosing which products and brands to buy.

Key Terms and Concepts

attributes **74**
benefits **77**
functional consequences **76**
intrinsic self-relevance **92**
involvement **88**
levels of product knowledge **72**

means–end chain **81**
perceived risks **77**
psychosocial consequences **77**
situational self-relevance **93**
values **78**

Review and Discussion Questions

1. Select a product category and identify examples of product forms, brands, and models. Describe some of the attribute, consequence, and value meanings for each of these levels.
2. Analyze the possible meanings of mouthwash or deodorant in terms of positive (perceived benefits) and negative (perceived risks) consequences of use. Why are both types of meaning important?
3. Procter & Gamble Company (P&G) is one of the most admired marketing companies in the United States. P&G is known as an innovator of high-quality products with superior product attributes. Go to the P&G website at **www.pg.com/about_pg/science_tech/research_development/ innovations.jhtml** and check out the new-product ideas P&G is researching. Choose a new product and identify the key elements in the means–end chain

that P&G seems to have "designed into" the product. For instance, P&G recently introduced a new model of Crest toothpaste called MultiCare. A P&G spokesperson says, "In our research, consumers rated this the best Crest ever. Crest MultiCare delivers great protection, and the feeling it creates in your mouth, both during and after brushing, is really terrific." Crest MultiCare has a special foaming formula that delivers proven Crest protection against tartar and cavities and the acids that cause them, even in places that are hard to reach. Consumers also said that Crest MultiCare tastes great, freshens their breath, and leaves their mouths feeling clean long after brushing. (The main P&G website is **www.pg.com**. Explore the About P&G button for an overview of this interesting and innovative company.)

4. Define the concept of involvement and illustrate it by discussing products that, for you, would fall at various levels along an involvement continuum.

5. Consider the difference between consequences of possession and consequences of consumption as the basis for intrinsic self-relevance. What products are relevant to you for these two reasons? How does that influence your purchasing behavior?

6. Do you agree that most products have low to moderate levels of intrinsic self-relevance for most consumers? Why or why not?

7. Prepare one or two means–end chains for your choice of a major or an emphasis in marketing as part of your degree program. Do laddering of yourself to identify your means–end chains (see Exhibit 4.7). Label the attributes, consequences, and values that you identify.

8. Using the concept of means–end chains, discuss why different people might shop for athletic shoes at department stores, specialty athletic footwear shops, or discount stores. Why might the same consumer shop these stores on different occasions?

9. Discuss how a marketer of casual clothing for men and women can use consumers' product knowledge (means–end chains) and involvement to understand the consumer–product relationship.

10. Identify three ways marketers can influence consumers' situational self-relevance, and discuss how this will affect consumers' overall level of involvement. For what types of products are these strategies most suitable?

Marketing Strategy in Action

Nike

"Twenty-five years ago, Nike stuck its foot in the door of sports by providing better shoes for competitive athletes. Simple. All it took was a passion for sports, a few good ideas, and the will to make it happen. Today, much in the world has changed. Athletes are stronger and faster than ever. Competition is more intense than any time in history. When combined with advances in performance that technology can provide, the world frenzy for sports grows unabated.

Twenty-five years from now, no one knows what the world will be like. But we're thinking about it. We believe in it. We know that curiosity and a competitive spirit will be alive and well. We know that we will be there, helping athletes perform better. All it will take is a passion for sports, a few good ideas, and the will to make it happen. Over and over again."

With these words, Nike began its 1997 annual report and revealed the core values of this highly successful company. It all started quite humbly. In the 1960s young Philip Knight, CEO of Nike and former track star at the University of Oregon, partnered with his old track coach, William Bowerman, to sell running shoes to athletes. They drove to high school track meets and sold shoes out of the trunk of Knight's car. As it grew, the young company found itself perfectly timed to cash in on America's running craze in the 1970s. Nike sold $3 million in shoes in 1972, $270 million in 1980, and $1 billion in 1986.

It has not been all easy running for Nike. After its initial success in the 1970s, the company stumbled a bit in the mid-1980s. For one thing, demographic changes worked against Nike as the baby boomers pushed into their forties and felt less like running. Fewer people were taking up jogging, and those who did were doing fewer laps. Also, the market for running shoes had become highly segmented—a sure sign of a mature market—with many different models for every nuance of consumer need. In addition, price cutting was beginning to show its ugly head. Thus, Nike's unit sales of running shoes decreased 17 percent in 1984, and its market share declined in that year from 31 percent to 26 percent. The decline continued, and by 1987 Nike had only an 18.6 percent share of the market for athletic shoes, a market it had dominated just a few years earlier.

Another problem for Nike came along in the 1980s: competition. Reebok in particular created a new marketing orientation to selling sneakers based on fashion rather than performance, which Nike had emphasized (and still does). According to Reebok president Paul Fireman, "We go out to consumers and find out what they want. Other companies don't seem to do that." Fashion seemed to be what many consumers wanted in the mid-1980s. Reebok's soft-leather athletic shoes in fashion colors took the market by storm. Reebok sales increased from $84 million to $307 million in one year (1984 to 1985),

and Reebok took over the top spot from Nike in 1986. Perhaps consumers' interest in fashion should have been obvious by simple observation. Research showed that 70 to 80 percent of the shoes designed for basketball and aerobic exercise were actually used for casual street wear instead of the intended sports.

Nike fought back with technological features intended to enhance performance. In 1987, Nike introduced air inserts into the soles of its high-end shoes. The key model was the Air Jordan, the basketball shoe named after Michael Jordan, the superstar player for the Chicago Bulls. Nike also had the brilliant idea of producing its top-of-the-line models with a cutout in the sole so the consumer could actually see the attribute (encapsulated gas or "air") that provided the cushioning benefit.

Over the years, a key strategy for Nike has been to create shoes with special technical attributes (air inserts, stability reinforcement, lacing patterns) that would enhance performance. Knight also signed up star athletes to wear Nike shoes and serve as spokespersons, a strategy he used from the beginning. The most desirable spokesperson was what the company executives called "a Nike guy": a brilliant athlete with a competitive attitude and a somewhat rebellious demeanor. Michael Jordan became the Nike guy in the late 1980s. Nike spent very heavily on TV and print advertising to promote both Jordan and his shoe model. All this advertising was a rather unusual marketing strategy for the company that once eschewed mass advertising as unnecessary and somewhat demeaning, but the threat from Reebok loosened Knight's thinking about advertising. By the mid-1990s, some 35 ads later, Michael Jordan was the most popular athlete in the country.

Currently it is estimated Nike pays out more than $100 million a year to contract athletes to use and pitch Nike products. Nike spokespersons have included Andre Agassi in tennis, Alex Rodriguez in baseball, Carl Lewis and Michael Johnson in track and field, Bo Jackson for multisport shoes, and basketball players such as Kevin Garnett and Scottie Pippen. Nike adds new sports continuously, including mountain biking, climbing, and hiking. Nike made the plunge into golf by signing a five-year, $40 million contract with Tiger Woods. Woods not only wears Nike clothing and shoes and appears in commercials, but also switched to a Nike golf ball in 2000 and promptly won the U.S. Open tournament by a record margin. Later that year, Nike signed a new deal with Woods that pays him an estimated $100 million over five years. As usual, Nike also signed up women sports stars to wear and promote its products (the Nike website profiles several prominent female athletes, such as track and field star Marion Jones). Nike's print ads have portrayed women trying to excel in sports. A Nike ad in 1996 showed little girls imploring their parents for a ball, not a doll, for Christmas.

Nike faced a new set of challenges in the late 1990s. For one thing, the shoe market had changed. Many younger consumers eschewed athletic shoes in favor of hiking boots and more casual footwear. Plus, more teens began participating in nontraditional "extreme" sports like snowboarding and skateboarding. Nike did not have a product that successfully appealed to this segment of the shoe market. To a lot of teens, Nike had ceased to be cool. The company responded in 1999 by establishing a separate division called ACG (which stands for "all-conditions gear"). The ACG unit has designed a line of shoes and apparel that bears the distinctive ACG logo rather than the familiar Nike swoosh. Nike also added extreme athletes like snowboarder Mike Michalchuk to its roster of star endorsers.

A problem that Nike has found somewhat more difficult to solve is the controversy surrounding its overseas labor practices. In the mid-1990s, labor advocates and some members of Congress accused Nike of utilizing sweatshop labor in its plants in developing nations. Critics said some plants employed young children, paid substandard wages, and mistreated their employees. Protests sprang up in cities and on college campuses. In an attempt to quell the criticism, Nike created a new position for a vice president for corporate and social responsibility and hired a former Microsoft public relations guru to fill that role. Knight also personally promised to raise the minimum hiring age at its overseas plants, tighten air quality standards at those plants, and improve working conditions for foreign workers. To read more about what Nike has done in response to these charges of human rights abuses, check out its investor website (**www.nikebiz.com**).

Nonetheless, the flap has not completely subsided. In the spring of 2000, Nike was involved in well-publicized squabbles with two large universities over those schools' endorsement of the Worker Rights Consortium, an aggressive anti-sweatshop organization. Nike refused to renew a sports equipment contract worth $22 to $26 million with the University of Michigan, while Knight withdrew a $30 million donation he had made to the University of Oregon, his alma mater.

The opening statement to the 1997 annual report indicates Nike's commitment to sports. As a company, Nike is fascinated with the dedication and effort needed to excel in sports and the satisfaction such achievement provides the athlete. Nike goes beyond a concern with mere product attributes to focus on the personal benefits associated with using its products and the values satisfied by product use. Nike's advertising is designed to "make a connection" with the consumer, according to Dan Wieden, manager of Wieden & Kennedy, Nike's main advertising agency. Thus, Nike ads seldom pitch the product directly or talk about product attributes. In fact, some ads do not even mention the company's name, featuring instead only the swoosh logo. Most Nike ads seek to portray the core values of sport as Knight sees them (striving, effort, achievement, satisfaction). Most Nike ads activate these meanings and their associated emotions and moods, which then become linked to the product. Thus, for many consumers, Nike has an image that stands for performance, competition, achievement, and doing your personal best.

Despite its recent troubles, Nike is still a remarkable corporate success story. Philip Knight has transformed a simple sneaker into a set of symbolic meanings. Since the dark days of the 1980s, Nike has become one of the most powerful brand names in the world, in a category with Coke, Levi's, Disney, and Hallmark. Although overall sales dipped 8 percent in 1999 to $8.8 billion (with profits of $451 million), Nike's position atop the athletic footwear market is still secure, at least for now. By comparison, Nike's closest competitor, Reebok, recorded sales of just under $3 billion, with profits of $11 million, in 1999. Nike's worldwide shoe sales hit $5.2 billion (40 percent market share), while it raked in an additional $3.1 billion in sales of clothing and equipment. Of course, Nike has many viable competitors besides Reebok to worry about, including Adidas, Fila, and Converse. We can be sure the sneaker wars will continue.

Discussion Questions

1. Apparently there are two market segments of consumers for many product forms of athletic shoes: those who use the shoes to engage in the designated athletic activity and those who use the shoes primarily for casual wear and seldom engage in the athletic activity.
   a. Discuss the differences between these two segments in means–end chains, especially end goals, needs, and values for running, basketball, aerobics, or tennis shoes.
   b. Draw means–end chains to illustrate your ideas about how these two segments differ.
   c. What types of special difficulties does a marketer face in promoting its products to two market segments of consumers who use the product in very different ways?
2. Discuss your reaction to Nike's handling of the criticism of its overseas plants. In your opinion, what are Nike's ethical responsibilities in this situation?
3. Nike has expanded its product line well beyond the original running shoes. It now includes models for virtually every type of sport or physical activity. Visit the Nike website (**www.nike.com**) for a complete listing of the models it sells. Moreover, Nike continually introduces new models; on average, Nike introduces a new shoe style every day of the year. Discuss the pros and cons of this continual churn of new attributes and new products. How do you think consumers react to this?
4. Discuss Nike's typical advertising strategy in terms of the types of means–end connections it creates in consumers. Bring in an example of a current Nike ad to analyze and draw out the meaning connections you believe this ad is likely to create in a consumer.
5. Recently Nike abandoned the swoosh logo in its advertising and replaced it with the word *nike* in lowercase lettering. Why do you think Nike made this decision?
6. What do you think of Nike's attempt to reach the "alternative" market through its ACG unit? What barriers and opportunities exist? Should ACG deviate from Nike's traditional advertising strategy to reach these consumers?

7. Not everyone finds athletic shoes highly involving, but some people do. For example, kids who are "into shoes" often talk in staggering detail about the characteristics and benefits of the currently popular models. Identify some intrinsic and situational sources of involvement for athletic shoes, and describe some of the likely means–end chains for the most involved consumers. Discuss how Nike's advertising strategies might differ in marketing a shoe to highly involved and moderately involved consumers.

Sources: Nike investor website (**www.nikebiz.com**); Louise Lee, "Can Nike Still Do It?" *Business Week,* February 21, 2000, pp. 120–128; Bill Richards, "Nike Hires an Executive from Microsoft For New Post Focusing on Labor Policies," *The Wall Street Journal,* January 15, 1998, p. B14; David L. Marcus, "The Other Shoe Drops. Nike Strikes Its Critics," *U.S. News & World Report,* May 15, 2000, p. 43; Randall Lane, "You Are What You Wear," *Forbes,* October 14, 1996, pp. 42–46.

Attention and Comprehension

The Power of Advertising

I
n 1882, Harley Procter convinced the board of Procter & Gamble to give him $11,000 for an outdoor advertising campaign for Ivory Soap. The board was skeptical, but Procter's status as son of one of the founders probably helped the board see things his way. Soon after, Procter's ads for Ivory Soap started showing up on streetcars, fences, and storefronts, and in magazines. The ads boasted that Ivory Soap was "99 44/100 percent pure" and encouraged people to tell the company what they thought about the product. Before long, P&G's Cincinnati headquarters was deluged with responses from satisfied Ivory Soap users. Thus, a modern advertising giant was born.

For decades, P&G has been among the world's leading advertisers (its $1.7 billion in advertising spending in 1999 ranked second only to General Motors'). In 1933, P&G created the radio soap opera as a vehicle to promote its Oxydol brand laundry detergent. In a typical 15-minute program, the name Oxydol was mentioned about two dozen times. Within a year, sales of the product had doubled. In

the 1950s, P&G turned to television and was sponsoring 13 nationally televised soap operas by the middle of that decade. By the 1970s, characters from P&G ads had become pop culture icons. You may remember Mr. Whipple, who pleaded with shoppers not to squeeze the Charmin, or Rosie the waitress, who always had a roll of Bounty towels to clean up any spill. A 1985 survey showed that 93 percent of female shoppers recognized the smiling face of Mr. Clean, while only 56 percent could identify then Vice President George Bush.

Unquestionably, television has proven very successful for P&G. The company used primarily television to introduce consumers to new products like Crest toothpaste and Tide detergent, which are now cornerstones of the P&G empire. In the late 1980s, the company produced a series of TV ads that successfully repositioned Pringles potato chips as a cool brand for young people, giving the product a major boost after 20 years of sluggish sales.

P&G is very careful with its ad placement, taking pains to avoid controversial programming. For example, in 2000 it chose not to advertise in a syndicated show starring gay-bashing psychologist Dr. Laura Schlessinger. "We like to keep our brands out of controversy," says Robert Wehling, P&G's global marketing officer, "We just feel that a really controversial show is not a good environment for a brand message because, by its very nature, it divides the audience into *for* and *against*." Basically, it is a challenge to watch a few hours of television programming and not see an ad for some P&G product.

In 1997, P&G spent approximately $1.3 billion on TV advertising. But by 1999, P&G's television budget, although still massive, had fallen 16 percent to $1.1 billion as the company began to diversify its media mix. In 1999, the company increased magazine advertising by 17 percent, while newspaper ad spending nearly tripled. P&G has also explored direct-mail and Internet marketing. An example of this new, more varied approach was the 2000 introduction of Physique, a line of hair care products aimed at young women. In November 1999, P&G began its push for Physique by mailing out a half-million samples and launching a Physique website. If you e-mailed the website link to 10 other people, you were rewarded with a free bottle of shampoo. In December, ads for Physique began appearing on glasses and napkins at bars near college campuses. For example, some cocktail napkins featured a young man and woman in silhouette, with a caption reading, "New scientific evidence proves people with great hairstyles are less likely to go home alone." The goal was for students to see these ads just before holiday break so they would talk about the product when they went home to their families and friends. Only in January, a few weeks before the product was shipped to stores, did television ads begin to appear. The typical P&G brand spends 60 to 80 percent of its advertising budget on television. With Physique, it was well under 50 percent.

P&G vice president Mark Schar believes his company must better target its marketing pitches and that traditional TV advertising reaches too broad an audience. Wehling still believes in television for some products, but he thinks the Internet best suits others. "One example is Cover Girl," he says. "When a girl first starts using cosmetics, you'd like to have a robust website that she can go to that guides her every step of the way on how to deal with everything from skin cleansing to moisturizing." But at least one advertising agency executive isn't so sure. "The Internet and direct mail are good for select marketing, but P&G needs to move a lot of its products in mass," the exec says. "When an analysis is done carefully, they may find a need to do more TV, more traditional media, not less." What do you think?

Sources: Steve McClellan, "P&G Still TV's Best Friend?" *Broadcasting & Cable,* April 24, 2000, pp. 22–30; Emily Nelson, "P&G Peers Beyond TV to Reach Targets," *The Wall Street Journal,* July 6, 2000, p. B14; Jack Neff, "Marketers of the Century: Procter & Gamble," *Advertising Age,* December 13, 1999, pp. 24–25.
For more information on Procter & Gamble, visit its website, *www.pg.com.*

This example illustrates the importance to marketers of understanding consumers' exposure to marketing information as well as their attention to and comprehension of that information. The example also illustrates the powerful effects of television advertising. The Wheel of Consumer Analysis (see Exhibit 2.3) provides an overall perspective for understanding exposure, attention, and comprehension. Consumers' everyday environment contains a great deal of information, large parts of which are created through marketing strategies. For example, marketers modify consumers' environments by creating advertisements and placing them on TV. For the advertisements to be effective, consumers must come in contact with them. Exposure often occurs through consumers' own behaviors: They turn on the TV and switch to a favorite show. Once exposed, they must attend to and comprehend the advertisements (affective responses and cognitive interpretations).

In this chapter, we continue our examination of the affect and cognition portion of the Wheel of Consumer Analysis. We will consider the interpretation process, a key cognitive process in our general model of consumers' cognition shown in Exhibit 5.1. First, we examine how consumers become exposed to marketing information. Then we discuss attention processes by which consumers select certain information in the environment to be interpreted. Finally, we examine the comprehension processes by which consumers construct meanings to represent this information, organize those meanings into knowledge structures, and store them in memory. We emphasize the reciprocal interactions between attention and comprehension and consumers' knowledge, meanings, and beliefs in memory. Throughout the chapter, we discuss the implications of these interpretation processes for developing marketing strategy.

Although we discuss attention and comprehension separately, the boundary between the two processes is not very distinct. Rather, attention shades off into comprehension.[1] As interrelated processes of interpretation, attention and comprehension serve the same basic function of the cognitive system: to construct personal, subjective interpretations or meanings that make sense of the environment and one's own behaviors. Consumers then use this knowledge in subsequent interpretation and integration processes to guide their behaviors and help them get along in their environments.

Before beginning our analysis, we briefly review four important aspects of the cognitive system that influence how consumers interpret information (see Exhibit 5.1).

- Interpretation involves interactions between knowledge in memory and information from the environment. The incoming environmental information activates relevant knowledge in memory, which can be either schema or script knowledge structures.
- The activated knowledge influences which information consumers attend to and how they comprehend its meaning.
- Because their cognitive systems have a limited capacity, consumers can consciously attend to and comprehend only small amounts of information at a time.[2]
- Much attention and comprehension processing occurs quickly and automatically with little or no conscious awareness.[3] For instance, simple interpretations such as recognizing a familiar product (such as a Coca-Cola bottle) occur automatically and virtually instantly upon exposure, without any conscious awareness of the comprehension process. Automatic processing has the obvious advantage of keeping our limited cognitive capacity free for unfamiliar interpretation tasks that do require conscious thought.

Exhibit 5.1

Consumers' Cognitive Processes Involved in Interpretation

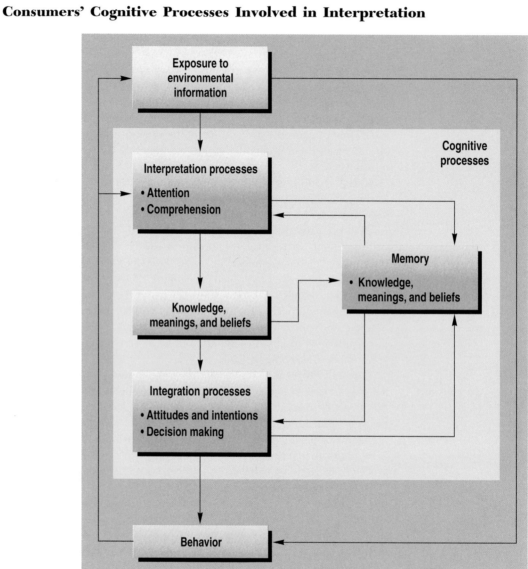

Although not a part of cognition in a strict sense, **exposure** to information is critical for consumers' interpretation processes. Consumers are exposed to information in the environment, including marketing strategies, primarily through their own behaviors. Thus, we can distinguish between two types of exposure to marketing information: purposive or **intentional exposure** and random or **accidental exposure.**

Consumers are exposed to some marketing information because of their own intentional, goal-directed *search behavior.* Typically, consumers search for relevant marketing information to help solve a purchasing problem. Before buying a camera, for instance, a consumer might read product evaluations of digital cameras in *Consumer Reports* or photography magazines or on Internet sites. Another consumer might ask a friend or a salesperson for advice about which brand of earphones to buy for her portable CD player.

Most investigations of consumer search behavior have found that levels of intentional exposure to marketing information are rather low. Before making a purchase, most consumers visit only one or two retail stores and consult very few salespersons and external sources of information.[4] This limited search may be surprising until you realize that most consumers already have substantial product-related knowledge, meanings, and beliefs stored in their memories. If they feel confident in their existing knowledge, or if they feel little involvement with the decision (low self-relevance), consumers have little motivation to engage in extensive search for information.

Marketing information is everywhere in the consumer-oriented environments of most industrialized countries. In the United States, advertisements for products and services are found in magazines and newspapers, on radio and TV, and on bus placards and bus-stop shelters—and they are increasing. Between 1967 and 1982, the total number of ads doubled; by 1997 that number had doubled again.[5] Billboards and signs promoting products, services, and retail stores are found along most highways. Stores contain a great deal of marketing information, including signs, point-of-purchase displays, and advertisements, in addition to information on packages. Consumers also receive product information from friends and relatives, from salespersons, and occasionally even from strangers. Of course, the Internet is a huge source of marketing information.

Typically, consumers are not exposed to these types of marketing information through intentional search behavior. Instead, most exposures are random or semirandom events that occur as consumers move through their environments and "accidentally" come into contact with marketing information. For instance, browsing ("just looking") in stores or on the Internet is a common source of accidental exposure to marketing information.[6] Consumers may discover new products, sales promotions, or new retail outlets when browsing. Some retailers design their store environments to encourage browsing and maximize the amount of time consumers spend in the store, which increases the likelihood they will be exposed to products and make a purchase. Website designers try to create "sticky" sites that encourage visitors to linger and explore the site more deeply.

Consumers seldom intentionally seek information about products or services when they watch television, yet they are accidentally exposed to many commercials during an evening of TV viewing at home. Highlight 5.1 describes other ways consumers may be exposed to TV ads outside the home. Because consumers probably don't feel very involved with most of the products promoted in these ads, their attention and comprehension processes are likely not extensive. Even so, simply increasing the accidental exposure can have a powerful effect on behaviors. For example, during the Persian Gulf War in early 1991, viewership of CNN skyrocketed to almost twice previous levels (exposure was up as much as 20 times in some time periods).[7] Advertisers on CNN such as 1-800-Flowers, a New York–based company that delivers flowers anywhere in the United States, and Sterling/Range Rover received large increases in accidental exposure to their ads, which also increased their business. For example, 1-800-Flowers' business on Valentine's Day is usually triple that of a normal day; but in 1991, orders increased 9 or 10 times to the point

Highlight 5.1

Measuring "Out-of-Home" Exposures to Television Advertising

The basic TV rating service by AC Nielsen measures couch potatoes—people sitting on their couches at home watching TV. Over the years, Nielsen has improved how it measures in-home exposure to television advertisements to include the use of "people meters," into which each TV viewer punches a personal code to show which household members are exposed. But in the United States, television is everywhere—in bars, airports, college dorms and fraternity/sorority houses, even in cars. Thus, the question is "How many people watch TV ads in environments where they may be exposed to ads?"

In 1993, ABC, NBC, and CBS commissioned Nielsen to conduct a study to answer this question. The study used a diary method in which viewers were asked to remember which programs they watched and where. Based on this research, Nielsen estimated that 28 million or so people received up to 25 percent of their TV viewing exposure out of the home, but those out-of-home exposures were not being counted in the regular TV ratings procedure.

Unmeasured viewers translate into lost advertising dollars, so some networks supplemented the Nielsen ratings with their own detailed research data. CNBC realized that its average viewer was educated, influential, and affluent—the kind of viewer advertisers covet. However, the network suspected that most of those viewers watched outside the home and thus remained uncounted by the Nielsen ratings. In 1998, CNBC surveyed *The Wall Street Journal* subscribers (whose annual median income is well over $100,000) and learned that 61 percent of them watched CNBC every day. Of those, 41 percent, or 700,000 people, watched CNBC outside the home. CNBC can use this information to show advertisers that the network reaches more people—and more affluent people—than it would appear based solely on the Nielsen estimates of exposure.

Nielsen is trying to make its methodology more thorough. It is testing a sensor, to be worn by survey participants, that would record any instance when the person was within audio range of a television. However, the sensor cannot measure whether people actually pay attention to a TV program or to specific advertisements. We might expect that people pay less attention to TV programs and the accompanying ads in many (but not all) out-of-home environments than they do at home.

Sources: Cyndee Miller, "Networks Rally around Study That Shows Strong Out-of-Home Ratings," *Marketing News,* April 26, 1993; Braden Phillips, "Diverse Auds Just Want to Be Shown the Money," *Variety,* April 26–May 2, 1999, p. 36.

where the company couldn't handle all the calls received. Exposure to marketing information can have powerful effects.

Selective Exposure to Information

As the amount of marketing information in the environment increases, consumers become more adept at avoiding exposure (some consumers intentionally avoid reading product test reports or talking with salespeople). Or consumers do not maintain accidental exposure to marketing information (some people automatically throw away most junk mail unopened). Such behaviors result in **selective exposure** to marketing information. Consider the problem marketers are having with consumers' selective exposure to TV commercials. In one simple study, college students observed family members watching TV. Only 47 percent of viewers watched all or almost all of the ads that appeared on ABC, NBC, and CBS, and about 10 percent left the room when the ads came on.[8]

Current technology enables consumers to control what ads they see on TV quite easily. Thanks to remote controls, viewers can turn off the sound or "surf" from one station to another during a commercial break. Consumers who have videocassette recorders can fast-forward past commercials on taped programs. In advertising circles, these practices are known as *zapping* and *zipping,* respectively. In homes with remote controls, the zapping (tune-out) factor has been estimated at about 10 percent for the average commercial. Some 20 percent of homes contain heavy zappers, who switch channels at the rate of one zap every two minutes. As remote controls have become ubiquitous, the situation has gotten worse. Advertisers, who pay media rates based on a full audience (currently $100,000 to $300,000 or more for 30 seconds of prime time on a major network), worry they are not getting their money's worth. One of their strategies to combat zapping is to develop commercials that are so engrossing that they won't be zapped.

Marketing Implications

Because of the crucial importance of exposure, marketers should develop specific strategies to enhance the probability that consumers will be exposed to their information and products. There are three ways to do this: facilitate intentional exposure, maximize accidental exposure, and maintain exposure.

In cases where consumers' exposure to marketing information is the result of intentional search, marketers should *facilitate intentional exposure* by making sure appropriate marketing information is available when and where consumers want it. For instance, to increase sales, International Business Machines Corporation trains its retail salespeople to answer consumers' technical questions on the spot so they don't have to wait while the salesperson looks up the answer. Consumers' search for information should be made as easy as possible. This requires that marketers anticipate consumers' needs for information and devise strategies to meet them. Some lumber companies cater to the novice do-it-yourself market by providing instructional brochures and in-store seminars on various building techniques, such as how to build a masonry wall or install a storm door. Putting relevant product information on the Internet certainly facilitates intentional exposure for some consumers.

Obviously marketers should try to place their information in environmental settings that *maximize accidental exposure* to the appropriate target groups of consumers. Certain types of retail outlets, such as convenience stores, ice cream shops, and fast-food restaurants, should be placed in locations where accidental exposure is high. High-traffic locations such as malls, busy intersections, and downtown locations are prime spots. Consider the Au Bon Pain cafés, a chain selling gourmet sandwiches, freshly squeezed orange juice, and fresh-baked French bread, muffins, and croissants.[9] Using a saturation distribution strategy, Au Bon Pain packed 16 stores into downtown Boston. Some stores were less than 100 yards apart; in fact, five outlets were inside Filene's department store. Besides being highly convenient for regular customers, the saturation strategy maximized the chances of accidental exposure. The thousands of busy commuters leaving Boston's South Station could hardly avoid walking by an Au Bon Pain café. Consumer awareness levels in Boston were high, although the company never advertised. "It's like having an outdoor billboard in every block; the stores themselves are a substitute for ads," according to a company spokesperson.

When it comes to gaining consumer exposure to its new products, few companies can surpass Disney.[10] Consider a movie like *Toy Story*. Disney exposed consumers (kids and adults) to information about *Toy Story* through the Disney channel, in Disney retail stores, in the Disney catalog, on the Disney website, and through powerful cross-promotions with partners such as Burger King. With all these resources, Disney computed that it can create 425 million potential exposures to any new project over a three-month period, and that figure does not include paid advertising or free publicity in the news media.

Most media strategies are intended to maximize accidental exposure to a firm's advertisements. Media planners must carefully select a mix of media (magazines, billboards, radio and TV programming) that maximize the chances the target segment will be exposed to the company's ads. Solving this very complex problem is crucial to the success of the company's communication strategy because the ads cannot have the intended impact if consumers do not see them. Besides inserting ads in the traditional media, companies attempt to increase accidental exposure by placing ads inside taxicabs, in sports stadiums, and on boats, buses, and blimps. Another marketing strategy involves placing several four-color ads (for noncompeting products) on grocery store shopping carts.[11] A big advantage of shopping cart ads is the much lower cost compared to the price of TV ads: $.50 per 1,000 exposures compared to about $10 to $20 per 1,000 exposures for network television. Advocates also claim this "reminder advertising" reaches consumers at the critical point when they make a purchase choice (an estimated 65 to 80 percent of brand buying decisions occur in the supermarket).

A long-standing strategy to increase accidental exposure to a brand is to get it into the movies, but many companies also try to place their brands in TV shows for even greater exposure.[12] Sometimes actors mention brand names on TV. Typically these exposures are not paid for; they are just part of the modern realism in television. For instance, on the long-running TV sitcom *Seinfeld*, Jerry's kitchen cabinets showed boxes of cereal in plain view. It is illegal for marketers to pay to place a product on TV unless the payment is disclosed, but it is OK to provide products free to be used as props. For instance, many TV shows clearly show the makes and models of automobiles. Marketers may hire a company that specializes in placing products in movies and on TV in the hope of exposing their brands to millions of viewers.

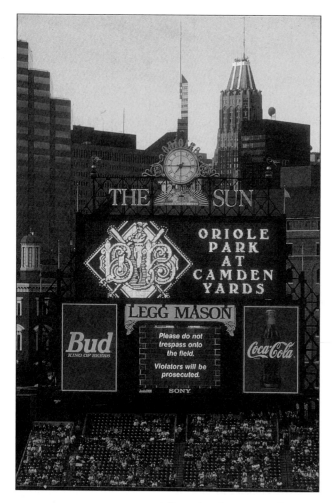

Marketers place ads in the environment to maximize the chances of accidental exposure *Lynn Fernandez/ The Image Works.*

A company's distribution strategy plays the key role in creating accidental exposure to products. Distribution is to products such as soft drinks, cigarettes, chewing gum, and potato chips what location is to fast-food restaurants—it's nearly everything.

Obviously, if the product is not on the grocery store shelves, at the checkout counter, or in the vending machine, the consumer cannot be exposed at the point of purchase, and sales will suffer.

Maximum exposure at the retail level is not desirable for all products, though. For instance, Burberry all-weather coats (with the distinctive plaid lining) or Bang & Olufsen stereo systems (made in Denmark) are sold only in a few exclusive, high-quality stores. Exposure is controlled by using a highly selective distribution strategy. Burberry, however, risks over-exposure due to the many unauthorized knock-offs of its iconic plaid colors that show up on clothes sold in discount and mass merchandising stores around the world. In sum, one of the most important functions of a company's distribution strategy is to create the *appropriate level of exposure* to the product.

Other marketing strategies are intended to *maintain exposure* once it has begun. Television advertisements, for instance, must generate enough attention and interest so that the consumer will maintain exposure for 30 seconds rather than zap the ad, turn to a magazine, or leave the room to get a snack. One tactic is to use distinctive sounds in TV commercials. For example, ads in a "Minds over Money" campaign for Shearson Lehman Brothers incorporated a buzzing, droning background sound that gradually grew louder every second, supposedly to represent the sound of a thought. Apparently the device did help maintain exposure to the ad because consumer awareness of the company increased by 50 percent over a three-year period.[13] As another example, IKEA, the Swedish furniture retailer, encourages browsing by providing lots of real-life furniture settings in its huge stores.[14] IKEA also provides baby sitting, restaurants, and snack bars that serve Swedish specialties at low prices. A key goal is to maximize the amount of time consumers spend in the store, which maintains their exposure to the products and increases the likelihood they will make a purchase.

Attention Processes

Once consumers are exposed to marketing information, whether accidentally or through their own intentional behaviors, the interpretation processes of attention and comprehension begin. In this section, we discuss attention, levels of attention, and factors affecting attention, and describe several marketing strategies that can influence consumers' attention.

What does it mean for a consumer to attend to a marketing stimulus such as a newspaper ad, a display in a store, or a clerk's sales pitch? First, **attention** implies selectivity.[15] Attending to certain information involves *selecting* it from a large set of information and ignoring other information. Consider the cognitive processes of shoppers in a crowded, noisy department store. They must selectively attend to conversations with salespersons, attend to certain products and brands, read labels and signs, and so on. At the same time, they must ignore other stimuli in the environment. Selective attention is highly influenced by the consumer's goals that are activated in the situation.

Attention also connotes awareness and consciousness. To attend to a stimulus usually means being *conscious* of it. Attention also suggests intensity and arousal.[16] Consumers must be somewhat *alert* and *aroused* to consciously attend to something, and their level of alertness influences how intensively they process the information. If you have ever tried to study when you were very tired, you know about the importance of arousal. If your level of arousal is very low, you might drift off to sleep while trying to read a text chapter (not this one, we hope!). When arousal is low, attention and comprehension suffer.

Variations in Attention

Attention processes vary along a continuum from a highly automatic, unconscious level called **preconscious attention** to a controlled, conscious level called **focal attention.**[17] As a consumer's interpretation processes shift from preconscious attention toward focal attention, greater cognitive capacity is needed, and the consumer gradually becomes more conscious of paying attention to a stimulus. At a focal level, attention is largely controlled by the consumer, who decides which stimuli to attend to and comprehend based on what goals are activated. As attention processes reach focal levels, comprehension begins to involve sense-making processes for constructing meaning. Exhibit 5.2 summarizes these differences in levels of attention.

As an example of these levels of attention, consider the shopping cart ads described earlier. How well do they work? ACTMEDIA, a dominant company in the industry, claims cart ads increased sales of advertised brands by an average of 8 percent. But other research found rather low levels of attention to these ads.[18] For instance, one study interviewed shoppers in stores with the cart ads. Only about 60 percent of these shoppers were aware of *ever* having seen any cart ads. Apparently the other 40 percent of shoppers did not attend to the ads beyond a preconscious level, even though they were exposed to the ads (they had many opportunities to see them). In addition, only 13 percent of the interviewed shoppers were aware of seeing any ads on that particular shopping occasion. Presumably these consumers processed the ads at relatively low levels of focal attention that produced some memory that an ad had been seen but not enough to make the consumers aware of the brand. Only 7 percent of the interviewed shoppers could name any brands advertised on their carts. Only these few consumers processed the ads at a sufficiently high level of focal attention to comprehend the brand names of the advertised brands and create a strong memory for them. In sum, these results question the effectiveness of shopping cart ads. In the crowded information environment of the supermarket, most consumers pay little attention to ads, even those on their grocery carts.

Exhibit 5.2

Levels of Attention

Preconscious attention	Focal attention
• Uses activated knowledge from long-term memory	• Uses activated knowledge from long-term memory
• No conscious awareness	• Conscious awareness
• Automatic process	• Controlled process
• Uses little or no cognitive capacity	• Uses some cognitive capacity
• More likely for familiar, frequently encountered concepts, with well-learned memory representations	• More likely for novel, unusual, infrequently encountered concepts, without well-learned memory representations
• More likely for concepts of low to moderate importance or involvement	• More likely for concepts of high importance or involvement

Most researchers assume that consumers' cognitive systems respond to all stimuli that receive some level of attention, whether preconscious or focal. The affective system also responds to attended stimuli, whether conscious or not. Affective responses can range from simple evaluations (good or bad) to strong feelings (disgust) to emotions (joy or anger). As interpretation processes move toward focal levels of attention, affective responses usually become more intense and consumers become more conscious of their affective states.

Factors Influencing Attention

Many factors can influence consumers' attention to marketing information. In this section, we discuss three particularly important influences: consumers' *general affective state*, consumers' *involvement* with the information, and the *prominence* of the information in the environment. We also discuss how marketers can try to increase consumers' attention to marketing information by influencing their involvement and by making the information more prominent.

Affective States   Consumers' affective arousal can influence their attention processes. As discussed earlier, low arousal reduces the amount and intensity of attention. In contrast, a state of high affective arousal is thought to narrow consumers' focus of attention and make attention more selective.[19] Some affective states that are responses to specific stimuli or situations are considered part of involvement. These are discussed in the next section. Other affective states, such as moods, are diffuse and general, and are not related to any particular stimulus. These affective states can also influence attention. For instance, consumers who are in a bad (or good) mood are more likely to notice negative (or positive) aspects of their environment.[20] Another example concerns whether consumers' general affective responses to happy and sad TV programs influence their cognitive reactions to the TV commercials shown on those programs.[21]

People's involvement with their pets helps attract attention to this ad
Courtesy of The Quaker Oats Company.

Involvement   The level of involvement a consumer feels is determined by the means–end chains activated from memory, related affective responses, and arousal level. Involvement is a motivational state that guides the selection of stimuli for focal attention and comprehension.[22] For instance, consumers who experience high involvement because of an intense need (Joe desperately needs a new pair of shoes for a wedding in two days) tend to focus their attention on marketing stimuli that are relevant to their needs (shoe ads and shoe stores).

People who find photography to be intrinsically self-relevant are more likely to notice and attend to ads for photo products. Or the situational self-relevance of actively considering the purchase of a new refrigerator influences consumers to notice and attend to ads and sales announcements for refrigerators. On occasion,

Highlight 5.2

Big Balloons Attract Both Attention and Controversy

Businesses love them, but town politicians are out to get those giant balloons shaped like goofy blue elephants, menacing King Kongs, and huge purple dinosaurs that fly from rooftops and parking areas to lure customers to stores, malls, and auto dealers. Balloons are proven attention-getters that can also drive sales. A Chrysler-Plymouth dealer in Minnesota claims that flying a clown Godzilla balloon over his dealership is a sure-fire boost to sales. Whenever the operator of a General Nutrition store in Texas flies a 30-foot parrot balloon, sales increase from 10 to 15 percent.

But hundreds of communities have banned the oversized balloons, calling them eyesores. One enterprising balloon business gets around the legal issue by renting balloons for the weekend, installing a balloon on Friday afternoon and removing it early Monday morning. By the time town officials notice the balloon, it is gone.

Balloons face other problems. A renegade blimp-like balloon in California became entangled in some overhead electrical wires, sparking a two-acre brush fire and knocking out power to homes and businesses. Then there are the vandals (arrows have been known to do in more than one balloon) and thieves. When a $3,000 inflated jack-o'-lantern balloon was stolen from the roof of the Nightmare Factory, a haunted house amusement in Austin, Texas, the owner estimated that the loss of the balloon cost him at least 2,000 customers. "It really underscored to me how important that pumpkin was in helping people find our place." Eventually that balloon was recovered and is back in place attracting the attention of potential customers.

Sources: Wall Street Journal. Central Edition [Staff Produced Copy Only] by Rodney Ho, "Retailers Love Big Balloons, but Others Try to Pop Them." *The Wall Street Journal,* October 7, 1997, pp. B1, B2. Copyright 1997 by Dow Jones & Co. Inc. Reproduced with permission of Dow Jones & Co. Inc. in the format Textbook via Copyright Clearance Center; Kristina Wells, "Ad Blimp Hits Wire, Starts Fire," Riverside Press-Enterprise, June 8, 2000, p. B4.

marketing strategies (contests, sales, price deals) can create a temporary state of involvement that influences consumers' attention to stimuli in that situation.

Sometimes marketers can take advantage of situational sources of self-relevance such as selling snow blowers after a big snow storm. For instance, a magazine called *Rx Being Well*, distributed to some 150,000 physicians' offices, bases its marketing strategy on the situational self-relevance of being in a doctor's office. The magazine is promoted to advertisers of health care products as an ideal medium to "reach consumers when they are most receptive. People in waiting rooms aren't just waiting. They're thinking about their health. . . . You'll be reaching consumers right before they go to drugstores or supermarkets with pharmacies where they'll see, remember, and buy your product."[23]

Environmental Prominence   The stimuli associated with marketing strategies can also influence consumers' attention. However, not every marketing stimulus is equally likely to activate relevant knowledge structures, receive attention, and be comprehended. In general, the most prominent marketing stimuli are most likely to attract attention; hence, marketers usually try to make their stimuli prominent features in the environment. For instance, some wine companies have created bright-blue bottles or unusually colorful labels to attract consumers' attention in the store. To capture consumers' attention, some radio and TV commercials are slightly louder than the surrounding program material, and the smells of baking products are exhausted from bakeries onto sidewalks or into malls. Highlight 5.2 describes how large balloons can influence attention and generate increased sales.

Marketing Implications

Marketers have developed many strategies to gain (or maintain) consumers' attention to their marketing information. Basically these strategies involve increasing consumers' involvement with the marketing information and/or making the marketing information more prominent in the environment. Influencing involvement requires attention to intrinsic and situational self-relevance.

Intrinsic Self-Relevance In the short run, marketers have little ability to influence consumers' intrinsic self-relevance for a product. Therefore, the usual strategy is to understand why consumers find the product to be self-relevant. First, marketers should identify, through research or guessing, the product consequences and values consumers consider most important. Then marketers should design strategies that will activate those meanings and link them to the product. The involvement thus produced should motivate consumers to attend to this information, interpret it more fully, and then act on it.

For instance, marketers of antiperspirants often emphasize qualities such as "stops odor" and "stops wetness"—rational and fairly tangible functional consequences of using the product. The marketers of Sure deodorant, however, identified two more self-relevant and emotionally motivating consequences of using their product: social confidence and avoiding embarrassment. In a long-running campaign, they communicated these psychosocial consequences with "Raise your

For many consumers, clothing and shoes are intrinsically self-relevant. The low prices also make such purchases situationally self-relevant *Courtesy of Payless ShoeSource Inc.*

hand if you're Sure" in ads that showed coatless consumers in social situations raising their arms and not being embarrassed by damp spots on their clothing. In a similar example, the marketers of Vaseline Intensive Care lotion identified a key consequence that was the basis of many consumers' intrinsic self-relevance with the hand lotion product category. While a competitor brand, Touch of Sweden, discussed its greaseless formula (an attribute), Vaseline marketers promoted skin restoration (a consequence). They communicated the implied psychosocial consequence of "looking younger" in ads showing dried-up leaves being rejuvenated with Intensive Care lotion.[24]

Situational Self-Relevance All marketing strategies involve creating or modifying aspects of consumers' environments. Some of these environmental stimuli may act as situational sources of self-relevance (a temporary association between a product and important self-relevant consequences). Situational self-relevance generates higher levels of involvement and motivation to attend to marketing information.[25] Consider consumers who receive a brochure in the mail describing a $1 million sweepstakes contest sponsored by a magazine publisher. This marketing information might generate feelings of excitement and perceptions of interest and personal relevance with the details of the contest. The resulting involvement could motivate consumers to maintain exposure and focus their attention on the marketing offer for magazine subscriptions that accompany the sweepstakes announcement.

Factors Affecting Environmental Prominence Marketers attempt to influence the prominence of their marketing information by designing bright, colorful, or unusual packages; developing novel advertising executions; or setting unique prices (having a sale on small items, all priced at 88 cents). Because they must attract the attention of consumers hurrying by the newsstand, magazine covers often feature

Vivid, unusual images give this display increased environmental prominence
Tony Freeman/Photo Edit, Inc.

photos known to have high attention value: pictures of celebrities, babies, or dogs, or pictures using that old standby, sex (attractive, seductively clothed models).

Vivid pictorial images can attract consumers' attention and help focus it on the product.[26] Nike, for instance, placed powerful graphic portrayals of athletes (wearing Nike clothes and shoes, of course) on large billboards. Window displays in retail stores attract the attention (and subsequent interest) of consumers who happen to pass by. Tiffany's, the famous New York jeweler, once used a window display showing construction of a giant doll, four times larger than the figures who were working on it. The doll had nothing to do with jewelry; it was intended to attract the attention of shoppers during the Christmas season.[27] Many stores use creative lighting to emphasize selected merchandise and thus attract and focus consumers' attention on their products. Mirrors are used in clothing shops and hair salons to focus consumers' attention on their appearance.

Novel or unusual stimuli that don't fit with consumers' expectations may be "selected" for additional attention (and comprehension processing to figure out what they are). For instance, a British ad agency created a dramatic stimulus to attract attention to the staying qualities of an adhesive called Araldite. The product was used to attach a car to a billboard along a major road into London. The caption read, "It also sticks handles to teapots."[28]

Even a novel placement of a print ad on a page can influence consumers' attention.[29] For instance, Sisley, a manufacturer and retailer of trendy clothing owned by Benetton, ran its print ads in an upside-down position on the back pages of magazines like *Elle* and *Outdoors*. Other marketers have experimented with ads placed sideways, in the center of a page surrounded by editorial content, or spanning the top half of two adjacent pages.

Marketers must be careful when using novel and unusual stimuli over long periods, because over time the prominence due to novelty wears off and fails to attract extra attention. For instance, placing a black-and-white ad in a magazine where all other ads are in color will capture consumers' attention only as long as few other black-and-white ads are present.

The strategy of trying to capture consumers' attention by making stimuli more prominent sometimes backfires. When many marketers are trying very hard to gain attention, consumers may tune out most of the stimuli, giving little thought to any of them. Consider the "miracle-mile" strips of fast-food restaurants, gas stations, and discount stores, each with a large sign, that line highways in many American cities. Individually, each sign is large, bright, colorful, and vivid. Together, the signs are cluttered, and none is particularly prominent in the environment. Consumers find it easy to ignore individual signs, and their attention (and comprehension) levels are likely to be low. Unfortunately, the typical marketing strategy is to make even larger and more garish signs in the hope of creating a slightly more prominent stimulus in the environment. The clutter gets worse, consumers' attention decreases further, and communities become outraged and pass ordinances limiting signs.

Sign clutter makes attention and comprehension difficult.
*Jeff Greenberg/
The Image Works.*

Clutter also affects print and television advertising (for example, too many commercials during program breaks). To cut the ad clutter found in most magazines, Whittle Communications limits the number of ads that can be put into its more than 40 magazines targeted at special audiences, including *GO* (Girls Only) for girls ages 11 to 14 and *in View* for college-age women.[30] In fact, some of the magazines have only one advertiser, thus maximizing possibilities of exposure and attention to that company's marketing messages.

Comprehension

Comprehension refers to the interpretation processes by which consumers understand or make sense of their own behaviors and relevant aspects of their environment. In this section we discuss the comprehension process, variations in comprehension, and the factors that influence comprehension. We conclude by discussing implications for marketing actions.

During comprehension, consumers construct meanings and form knowledge structures that represent relevant concepts, objects, behaviors, and events in their lives. As consumers focus their attention on specific environmental stimuli, salient knowledge structures (schemas and scripts) are activated from long-term memory. This knowledge provides a mental framework that guides and directs comprehension processing. Thus, new information in the environment is interpreted in terms of one's "old" knowledge activated from memory. Through cognitive learning processes (accretion or tuning, sometimes restructuring), these newly constructed meanings are incorporated into existing knowledge structures in memory. If, on future occasions, these modified knowledge structures are activated, they will influence the interpretation of new information, and so the comprehension process continues.

Variations in Comprehension

As shown in Exhibit 5.3, consumers' comprehension processes can vary in four important ways: (1) comprehension may be automatic or controlled, (2) it may produce more concrete or more abstract meanings, (3) it may produce few or many meanings, and (4) it may create weaker or stronger memories.

Automatic Processing   Like attention, most simple comprehension processes tend to be *unconscious* and *automatic*. For instance, most consumers around the world who see a can of Coca-Cola or a McDonald's restaurant immediately comprehend "Coke" or "McDonald's" without thinking about it. The direct recognition of familiar products is a simple comprehension process in which exposure to a familiar object automatically activates its relevant meanings from memory—perhaps its name and other associated knowledge.

In contrast, comprehending less familiar stimuli usually requires more conscious thought and control. Because consumers do not have well-developed knowledge structures for unfamiliar objects and events, exposure to completely unfamiliar stimuli is likely to activate knowledge structures that are only partially relevant at best. Consumers have to consciously construct the meanings of such information (or else intentionally ignore it). In such cases, comprehension is likely to be highly conscious and controlled and interpretations may be difficult and uncertain.

Level   The specific meanings that consumers construct to represent products and other marketing information in their environment depend on the **level of comprehension** that occurs during interpretation.[31] Comprehension can vary along a continuum from "shallow" to "deep."[32] *Shallow comprehension* produces meanings

Exhibit 5.3

Variations in Comprehension

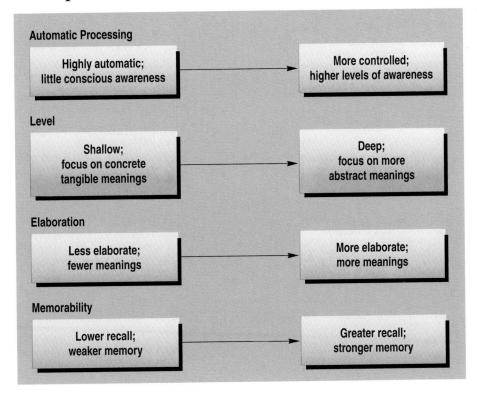

at a concrete, tangible level. For example, a consumer might interpret a product in terms of its product attributes (These running shoes are black, size 10, and made of leather and nylon).

In contrast, *deep comprehension* produces more abstract meanings that represent less tangible, more subjective, and more symbolic concepts. For instance, deep comprehension of product information might create meanings about the functional consequences of product use ("I can run faster in these shoes") or the psychosocial and value consequences ("I feel confident when I wear these shoes"). From a means–end perspective, deeper comprehension processes generate product-related meanings that are self-relevant, whereas shallow comprehension processes tend to produce meanings about product attributes.

Elaboration   Comprehension processes also vary in their extensiveness or elaboration.[33] The degree of **elaboration** during comprehension determines the amount of knowledge or the number of meanings produced, as well as the complexity of the interconnections between those meanings.[34] *Less elaborate* (simpler) *comprehension* produces relatively few meanings and requires little cognitive effort, conscious control, and cognitive capacity. *More elaborate comprehension* requires greater cognitive capacity, effort, and control of the thought processes. More elaborate comprehension produces a greater number of meanings that tend to be organized as more complex knowledge structures (schemas or scripts).

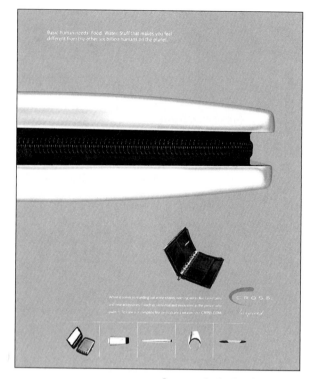

The unusual image attracts attention to this ad, while the copy encourages deeper and more elaborate comprehension
Courtesy of A. T. Cross Company.

Memorability   Both the level and elaboration of comprehension processes influence consumers' ability to remember the meanings created during comprehension.[35] Deeper comprehension creates more abstract, more self-relevant meanings that tend to be remembered better (higher levels of recall and recognition) than the more concrete meanings created by shallow comprehension processes. More elaborate comprehension creates greater numbers of meanings that tend to be well interconnected in knowledge structures. Memory is enhanced because the activation of one meaning can spread to other connected meanings and bring them to conscious awareness.[36]

In sum, marketing strategies that stimulate consumers to engage in deeper, more elaborate comprehension processes tend to produce meanings and knowledge that consumers remember better.

Inferences during Comprehension

When consumers engage in deeper, more elaborate comprehension processes, they create inferences. **Inferences** are interpretations that produce knowledge or beliefs that go beyond the information given.[37] For instance, some consumers might infer that a product is of good quality because it is advertised heavily on TV.[38] Highlight 5.3 concerns consumers' inferences about the Good Housekeeping seal.

Inferences play a large role in the construction of means–end chains.[39] By making inferences during comprehension, consumers can link meanings about the physical attributes of a product with more abstract meanings about its functional consequences and perhaps the psychosocial and value consequences of product use.

Inferences are heavily influenced by consumers' existing knowledge in memory.[40] If activated during comprehension, relevant knowledge provides a basis for forming inferences. For instance, consumers who believe that more expensive brands of chocolates are higher in quality than cheaper brands are likely to infer that Godiva chocolates are high quality when they learn that the chocolates cost more than $20 per pound.[41] As another example, incomplete or missing product information sometimes prompts consumers to form inferences to "fill in the blanks" based on their schemas of knowledge acquired from past experience.[42] For instance, consumers who are highly knowledgeable about clothing styles may be able to infer the country of origin and even the designer of a coat or dress merely by noticing a few details.

Consumers often use tangible, concrete product attributes as *cues* in making inferences about more abstract attributes, consequences, and values. In highly familiar situations, these inferences may be made automatically without much conscious awareness. For instance, some consumers draw inferences about the cleaning power of a powdered laundry detergent from its color: Blue and white granules seem to connote cleanliness. Or consumers might base inferences about product quality from physical characteristics of the package: The color, shape, and material of cologne bottles are important cues to quality inferences. As another example,

Highlight 5.3

Inferences about the Good Housekeeping Seal

The Good Housekeeping Seal of Approval has been around for more than 90 years. In 1997, the company updated the seal to make it look "more contemporary, more energetic, more bold, or radical," whereas others call it "a mistake—the type doesn't fit into the oval." Just what does the seal mean to consumers, and does anyone care?

The Good Housekeeping Seal is more than a stamp of approval for products—it is a legal warranty. *Good Housekeeping* magazine promises to provide a replacement or refund if any product bearing the seal is found to be defective within two years of purchase. With the new seal design, *Good Housekeeping* extended the warranty period from one year to two. The magazine delivers on this promise several hundred times a year.

To use the Seal, a company must first buy at least one page of black-and-white advertising in *Good Housekeeping* (the cost in 2003 was $195,425). Advertisers can use the Good Housekeeping seal in their ads and on their packages, free of charge, for a 12-month period. But first the product must meet the standards of the Good Housekeeping Institute, a product-testing lab founded in 1900 by *Good Housekeeping* magazine. With departments specializing in engineering, chemistry, beauty products, food, food appliances, nutrition, home care products, and textiles, the Institute can evaluate almost any product. The Institute is not a rubber stamp; it is quite careful in evaluating potential products and sometimes denies products for approval. (You can take a virtual tour of the Institute and see what types of product information it provides to consumers at **www.goodhousekeeping.com**.

Is it advantageous to have the Good Housekeeping seal on your product? Well, probably. First, most American consumers have been exposed to the Seal, either through ads or on packages. Good Housekeeping cites research showing that 95 percent of American women are familiar with the Seal, and almost all of them have positive feelings about it. As one of the product-testing organizations, the Seal has a rarefied status in consumer culture, having graced thousands of product packages since its inception in 1909. However, cultural changes in the American market may work against the Seal, because woman-dominated households that shop mainly in supermarkets are on the decline, and people in general may be relying less on brand-name products.

What is your opinion of the new Good Housekeeping seal? If consumers notice the Seal, what inferences do you think they will form? Does the Good Housekeeping Seal add value to a product?

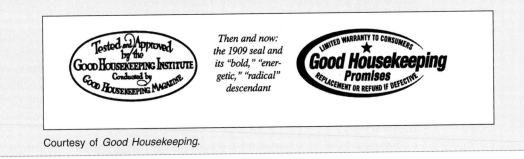

Then and now: the 1909 seal and its "bold," "energetic," "radical" descendant

Courtesy of *Good Housekeeping.*

Sources: Paul Lukas, "Marketing: In Which We Bash a Baby Seal," *Fortune,* September 8, 1997, pp. 36–37 © 1997 Time Inc. All rights reserved. The Good Housekeeping website at **www.goodhousekeeping.com**.

Hershey sells a premium-priced candy bar, Golden Almond, wrapped in gold foil, a packaging cue that implies quality to many consumers.

Marketers sometimes try to stimulate consumers to form inferences during comprehension. For example, Kellogg once used an advertising strategy for All-Bran with the headline "At last, some news about cancer you can live with." The ads repeated the National Cancer Institute's recommendation for increasing levels of fiber in the diet and then stated that "no cereal has more fiber" than All-Bran. Apparently Kellogg hoped consumers would make the inference that All-Bran's high-fiber product attribute leads to the desirable consequence of reduced risk of cancer. Many consumers might then form additional inferences that reduced risk of cancer helps them achieve the universal values of long life, health, and happiness. Such self-relevant consequences probably elicit favorable affective responses for most consumers.

Factors Influencing Comprehension

Many factors affect the depth and elaboration of comprehension that occurs when consumers interpret marketing information.[43] In this section, we examine three important influences: consumers' existing knowledge in memory, which affects their ability to comprehend; their involvement at the time of exposure, which affects their motivation to comprehend; and various aspects of the environment during exposure that affect their ability to comprehend.

Knowledge in Memory   Consumers' *ability to comprehend* marketing information is largely determined by their existing knowledge in memory. The particular knowledge, meanings, and beliefs that are activated in a given comprehension situation determine the level and elaborateness of the comprehended meanings produced.

Marketing researchers often discuss consumers' knowledge in terms of **expertise** or familiarity.[44] *Expert consumers* are quite familiar with a product category, product forms, and specific brands. They tend to possess substantial amounts of declarative and procedural knowledge organized in schemas and scripts. When parts of this knowledge are activated, these consumers are able to comprehend marketing information at relatively deep, elaborate levels.[45]

In contrast, *novice consumers* have little prior experience with the product or brand. They tend to have poorly organized knowledge structures containing relatively few, typically shallow meanings and beliefs. When parts of these knowledge structures are activated during exposure to marketing information, novices are able to comprehend the information only at superficial levels that produce relatively few concrete meanings. An example is the difficulty many consumers have in comprehending the instruction manuals that accompany many products. Novices find it difficult, if not impossible, to comprehend at a deep, elaborate level. To do so, they would have to increase their knowledge to approach that of an expert.

Marketers need to understand the existing knowledge structures of their target audience to develop effective marketing strategies that consumers can comprehend. For instance, S. C. Johnson Company, manufacturer of Raid and other bug killers, knows that most consumers have limited technical knowledge about how insecticides work. Instead of technical information, "the customer wants to see action."[46] The company's formulation for Raid bug spray allows consumers to immediately comprehend that the product works effectively: It attacks cockroaches' central nervous systems and drives them into a frenzy out onto the kitchen floor, where they race around in circles before they die.

Involvement   Consumers' involvement at the time of exposure has a major influence on their *motivation to comprehend* marketing information.[47] Consumers with high intrinsic self-relevance for certain products associate those products with personally relevant consequences and values that are central to their self-concept. The involvement experienced when such self-relevant knowledge structures are activated motivates these consumers to process the information in a more conscious, intensive, and controlled manner. For instance, consumers who feel highly involved tend to form deeper, more abstract meanings for the marketing information, creating more elaborate knowledge structures. In contrast, consumers who experience low levels of involvement when exposed to marketing information tend to find the information uninteresting and irrelevant. Because of their low motivation to interpret the information, their attention probably will be low and they are likely to produce few meanings (low elaboration) at a relatively shallow, concrete level. Their comprehension processes may produce only a simple identification response (Oh, this is a pair of socks).

Exposure Environment   Various aspects of the exposure situation or environment can affect consumers' *opportunity to comprehend* marketing information. These include factors such as time pressure, consumers' affective states (a good or bad mood), and distractions (noisy, pushing crowds). For instance, consumers who are in a hurry and under a lot of time pressure don't have much opportunity to process marketing information even if they are motivated to do so (high involvement).[48] In this situational environment, they are likely to engage in relatively shallow and nonelaborate comprehension processes.

Marketers can consider these environmental factors when designing their marketing strategies. Some retailers, for instance, have created a relaxed, slow-paced environment that encourages people to slow down and thoroughly absorb the information marketers make available. For instance, Ralph Lauren's Polo store in New York City is a special environment of glowing wood, antique furniture, oriental carpets, and warm lighting fixtures that simulates an elegant English manor. In addition, this environment helps create the desired images for the casually elegant clothing Lauren designs and sells.

Marketing Implications

To develop effective marketing strategies, marketers need to understand consumers' comprehension processes so they can design marketing information that will be interpreted appropriately. This requires consideration of the characteristics of the target consumers and the environment in which consumers are exposed to the information.[49]

Knowledge and Involvement   To encourage appropriate comprehension processing, marketers should design their messages to fit consumers' ability and motivation to comprehend (their knowledge structures and involvement). For instance, marketers of high-involvement products such as luxury cars usually want consumers to form deep, self-relevant meanings about their products. Many of the U.S. print ads for Saab, BMW, and Mercedes-Benz contain a great deal of information describing technical attributes and functional aspects of the cars. To comprehend this information at a deep, elaborate level, consumers must have fairly sophisticated knowledge about automobiles and sufficient involvement to motivate extensive comprehension processes.

For other types of products, however, marketers may not want consumers to engage in extensive comprehension processes. Sometimes marketers are interested in creating only simple, nonelaborate meanings about their products. For example, simple products (cologne or beer) tend to be promoted largely through *image advertising* that is not meant to be comprehended deeply or elaborately.[50] Consider the typical advertisement for cigarettes or soft drinks. Often these ads contain virtually no written information beyond a brief slogan such as "Come to Marlboro Country" or "Coke Is It." Most consumers probably comprehend such information in a nonelaborate way that produces an overall image and perhaps a general affective reaction, but not detailed means–end chains.[51] Other ads, such as billboards, act as reminders that are intended mainly to activate the brand name and keep it at a high level of "top-of-mind" awareness. In such cases, comprehension may be limited to simple brand recognition.

Remembering Memory and consumers' ability to recall meanings are important to marketers because consumers often do not make purchase decisions at the time of exposure, attention, and comprehension. Marketers usually want consumers to remember certain key meanings associated with their marketing strategies. Marketers hope consumers will remember the brand names and key attributes and benefits (main copy points) conveyed in their ads. Retailers want consumers to remember their names and locations, the types of merchandise they carry, and the dates of a big sale. Despite the millions spent each year on advertising and other marketing strategies, much marketing information is remembered poorly. For instance, few advertising slogans are accurately recalled from memory. And, even though some people can remember a slogan, many cannot associate it with the right brand name.[52] For instance, 60 percent of consumers recognized the slogan "Never Let Them See You Sweat," but only 4 percent correctly associated it with Dry Idea deodorant. Although 32 percent recognized "Cars That Make Sense," only 4 percent associated it with Hyundai. "America's Business Address" was recognized by 17 percent, but only 3 percent knew it was the slogan for Hilton hotels. Slogans have to be very heavily advertised to be remembered; a high scorer was General Electric's "We Bring Good Things to Life."

Miscomprehension of Marketing Information Research shows that a substantial amount of marketing (and other) information is miscomprehended in that consumers form inaccurate, confused, or inappropriate interpretations. In fact, most (perhaps all) marketing information is probably miscomprehended by at least some consumers (see Highlight 5.4).[53] The type of miscomprehension can vary from confusion over similar brand names to misinterpreting a product claim by forming an inaccurate means–end chain. It has been estimated that people may miscomprehend an average of 20 to 25 percent of the many different types of information they encounter, including ads, news reports, and so on.[54]

Although unethical marketers may intentionally create deceptive or misleading information that consumers miscomprehend, most professional marketers work hard to create marketing information that is understood correctly. For those who do not, the Federal Trade Commission has a program to identify and remove deceptive

▶ **High**light 5.4

Intentionally (?) Confusing Brand Names

Marketers guard their brand names jealously. Establishing a brand name in consumers' minds by making it familiar and meaningful usually requires a large financial investment. When another firm uses the same brand name or a similar one, companies believe their hard work and creative marketing strategies are being stolen. Lawsuits often result.

For example, in 1998 Polo Ralph Lauren Corporation filed a trademark infringement suit against Dallas-based Westchester Media, publisher of *Polo* magazine. For the first 22 years of its existence, *Polo* was dedicated to the sport of polo. However, Lauren became rankled when, in 1997, the magazine shifted its focus from sport to upscale fashion and lifestyle. Upon relaunch, the publisher mailed copies of the magazine to customers of Neiman Marcus, one of Polo Ralph Lauren's major retailers. Claudia Schiffer, who had previously modeled Ralph Lauren clothing, was pictured on the cover of an early issue. Lauren also may have been a bit irked to see the magazine's circulation

explode from less than 10,000 to about 250,000 following the redesign.

Lauren's company claimed it had trademarked the word *polo* in 1985 and that the magazine was unfairly trying to capitalize on Polo Ralph Lauren's carefully cultivated image and reputation. However, an attorney for the publisher argued, "No one can own *polo*. It's a generic term."

In July 1998, shortly after the lawsuit was filed, a federal judge ordered the publisher to place a disclaimer on the magazine stating that it was in no way affiliated with Polo Ralph Lauren. A year later, the court cemented that decision by issuing a permanent injunction to prevent the publisher from using the Polo name.

When trademarks and other elements of the marketing mix become similar to those of another company, ethical, economic, and competitive issues arise. Do you think the publishers of *Polo* magazine behaved unethically?

Sources: Wall Street Journal. Central Edition [Staff Produced Copy Only] by Wendy Bounds, "Polo Magazine Gets Whipped by Lauren." *The Wall Street Journal,* July 7, 1998, p. B10. Copyright 1998 by Dow Jones & Co. Inc. Reproduced with permission of Dow Jones & Co. Inc. in the format Textbook via Copyright Clearance Center; Reuters, "Lauren Wins Ruling Against Polo Magazine," *The New York Times,* August 6, 1999, p. C18.

marketing information and force a company to correct the false beliefs it creates.[55] For instance, in 1991, the Food and Drug Administration demanded that Procter & Gamble stop using "fresh" on the labels of Citrus Hill orange juice, a processed food.[56]

Exposure Environment   Many aspects of the environment in which exposure to marketing information occurs can influence consumers' comprehension processes. For instance, the type of store can affect how consumers comprehend the product and brands sold there. Thus, for some customers, a brand of jeans purchased in a "high-image" store like Saks or Bloomingdale's may have more positive meanings than the same brand bought at Sears or Kmart. Store characteristics such as size, exterior design, or interior decorations can activate networks of meanings that influence consumers' comprehension of the meanings of products and brands displayed there.

Another aspect of the exposure environment concerns the actual content and format of the marketing information.[57] Some information may be confusing, unclear, and hard to comprehend. For instance, the huge amounts of nutritional information on food product labels and in advertising claims are difficult for many consumers to comprehend in a meaningful way.[58]

Back To...

The Power of Advertising

When planning its advertising strategies, Procter & Gamble must consider the three processes within the broader interpretation process discussed in this chapter: exposure, attention, and comprehension. First, advertising, whether on TV or elsewhere, must have the potential for exposure to consumers. Most of P&G's advertising relies on accidental exposure—few consumers seek out the ads. P&G promoted Physique by placing ads on favorite television shows and also on cocktail napkins. Then, once exposed, consumers must give attention to the ad. To capture their attention, the ad should be vivid or interesting enough to stand out from the barrage of information consumers are hit with every day. For example, a newspaper ad for Tide detergent appearing around Mother's Day was designed to look like a big, colorful coupon, with the words "This coupon entitles you to sit back while someone else attempts to do the laundry." Finally, the ad must communicate self-relevant information about the product, such as showing how it meets consumers' needs and goals. Rarely does P&G advertising highlight only specific product attributes; rather, ads usually focus on a consequence of using a particular P&G brand (for example, using Pampers diapers facilitates a bond between mother and child).

A key challenge facing P&G is to figure out the optimal placement for its advertising. It was somewhat easier in the 1950s when many women, who did most of the family shopping, worked in the home and watched soap operas, many of which were sponsored by P&G. Today people are more active and are exposed to many different forms of media—television, radio, newspapers, and magazines, as well as the Internet. Changing times have forced P&G to become more aggressive, focused, and creative in its advertising efforts. Understanding exposure, attention, and comprehension will help P&G marketers promote their products appropriately to the consumer segments they most want to reach. ❖

Summary

In this chapter we discussed the behavioral process of *exposure,* by which consumers come into contact with marketing information. We also discussed the interrelated cognitive processes of *attention,* by which consumers select some of this marketing information for further processing, and *comprehension,* by which consumers interpret the meaning of this information.

Exposure to marketing information can occur by accident or as a result of an intentional search for information. Once exposure has occurred, the interpretation processes of attention and comprehension begin. For unfamiliar marketing information, these processes are likely to require some conscious thought. However, as consumers become more experienced in interpreting marketing stimuli, attention and comprehension processes require less cognitive capacity and conscious control and become more automatic. Attention varies from preconscious, automatic levels to focal levels where the comprehension begins. Comprehension varies in the depth of meanings produced (from concrete product attributes to abstract consequences and values) and in elaboration (few or many interrelated meanings). Both factors influence the memorability of the meanings created.

Attention and comprehension are strongly influenced by two internal factors: the knowledge structures activated in the exposure situation and the level of consumers' involvement. These respective factors influence consumers' ability and motivation to interpret the information.

In sum, designing and implementing successful marketing strategies—whether price, product, promotion, or distribution strategies—require that marketers consider three issues associated with these three processes:

1. How can I *maximize and/or maintain exposure* of the target segment of consumers to my marketing information?

2. How can I *capture and maintain the attention* of the target consumers?

3. How can I influence the target consumers to *comprehend* my marketing information *at the appropriate level of depth and elaboration?*

Key Terms and Concepts

accidental exposure   **108**
attention   **113**
comprehension   **120**
elaboration   **121**
expertise   **124**
exposure   **108**

focal attention   **114**
inferences   **122**
intentional exposure   **108**
level of comprehension   **120**
preconscious attention   **114**
selective exposure   **110**

Review and Discussion Questions

1. Describe the differences between accidental and intentional exposure to marketing information. Identify a product for which each type of exposure is most common, and discuss implications for developing effective marketing strategies.

2. Give an example of automatic attention and contrast it with an example of controlled attention. What implications does this distinction have for marketing strategy?

3. Media Dynamics has estimated that "the average adult in the U.S. (in 1993) was exposed to nearly 250 advertisements per day," not including myriad other messages on signs and billboards. (Others have proposed far higher estimates of more than 1,000 ads per day.) This exposure is important, but not as important as the number of choices consumers have to make in a day. Products and brands that can help simplify the decision process should be viewed favorably. Discuss how the interpretation processes of exposure, attention, and comprehension can influence consumers' purchase decisions.

4. Discuss the different types of knowledge and meanings that "shallow" and "deep" comprehension processes create. Can you relate these differences to different segments of consumers for the same product?

5. Review the differences in the knowledge and meanings produced by more and less elaborate comprehension processes. When should marketing activities encourage or discourage elaboration of knowledge and meaning?

6. Highlight 5.3 describes the Good Housekeeping seal. Visit the company website (**www.goodhousekeeping.com**) and read more about the seal and the Good Housekeeping Institute, which does product testing. Consider two market segments: (1) young married women in their twenties and early thirties, with young children; and (2) older married women in their forties and early fifties, with teenage children. Do you think these consumers will attend to the seal in product advertisements? What level of attention do you think is likely? What types of comprehension might these consumers have of the seal? Do you think the seal enhances the value of a product for these two types of consumers?

7. List some factors that could affect the inferences formed during comprehension of ads for packaged foods and for medical services. Give examples of marketing strategies you would recommend to influence the inferences that consumers form.

8. Consider an example of a marketing strategy that you think might result in some consumer miscomprehension. Describe why this miscomprehension occurs. Discuss the ethical issues involved. What could marketers (or public policymakers) do to reduce the chances of miscomprehension?

9. Discuss how interpretation processes (attention and comprehension) affect consumers' ability to recall marketing information. Illustrate your points with marketing examples.

10. Identify a recent brand extension and discuss how exposure, attention, and comprehension processes can influence the effectiveness of that brand extension.

Marketing Strategy in Action

Exposure, Attention, and Comprehension on the Internet

The Internet universe literally grows more cluttered by the minute. According to Network Solutions, Inc., which registers the vast majority of Web addresses around the world, about 10,000 new addresses are registered each day. That means by the time you finish reading this case, about 60 new domain names will have been gobbled up. With all the clutter on the Web, how have some firms been able to stand out and attract millions of customers?

First, there are some basics to which online firms must attend. These cost little more than some time and a little creativity. The first is creating a good site name. The name should be memorable (yahoo.com), easy to spell (ebay.com), and/or descriptive (wine.com—a wine retailer). And, yes, ideally it will have a *.com* extension. This is the most popular extension for e-commerce, and browsers, as a default, will automatically add a *.com* onto any address that is typed without an extension.

The second priority is to make sure the site comes up near the top of the list on any Web searches. If you use Lycos.com to perform a search for "used books," you get a list of more than 2.6 million websites. Studies have shown that most people will look only at the top 30 sites on the list, at most. If you are a used-book retailer and you show up as website #1,865,404 on the search list, there is a very good chance you will not attract a lot of business. A 1999 Jupiter Research study reveals that "searching on the Internet" is the most important activity, and Internet users find the information they are looking for by using search engines and Web directories. A good Web designer can write code that matches up well with search engine algorithms and results in a site that ranks high on search lists.

Virtually all popular websites have those basics down pat. So the third step is to reach out proactively to potential customers and bring them to your site. Many companies have turned to traditional advertising to gain exposure. Television advertising can be an effective option—albeit an expensive one. In late January 1999, hotjobs.com spent $2 million—half of its 1998 revenues—on one 30-second ad during the Super Bowl. According to CEO Richard Johnson, so many people tried to visit the site that the company's servers jammed. Johnson says the number of site hits was six times greater than in the month before. A quirky ad campaign may or may not help. Pets.com, now defunct, built its image around a wise-guy sock puppet. CNET, a hardware and software retailer, ran a series of television ads featuring cheesy music, low-budget sets, and unattractive actors. One such ad featured two men—one in a T-shirt that said "you," another in a T-shirt labeled "the right computer"—coming together and joining hands thanks to the efforts of another guy in a CNET T-shirt. The production quality was rudimentary enough that any sophomore film student could have produced it. The spots were so bad that they stood out from the slick, expensive commercials to which viewers were accustomed. Critics ripped the campaign to shreds, but CNET called it a success.

Other Internet firms have used sports sponsorships to increase visibility. CarsDirect.com, a highly rated site that allows consumers to purchase automobiles online, once purchased the naming rights to a NASCAR auto race (the CarsDirect.com 400). Lycos also has tried to make the most of NASCAR's increasing popularity. It spent hundreds of thousands of dollars to have its name and logo plastered all over the car of popular driver Johnny Benson. Meanwhile, online computer retailer Insight and furniture seller galleryfurniture.com each targeted football fans by purchasing the naming rights to college bowl games.

Of course, if you can reach consumers while they are in front of their computers rather than their television sets, you may stand an even better chance of getting them to your site. However, typical banner ads are inefficient, averaging click-through rates of only about 0.5 percent (only one of every 200 people exposed to the ad actually clicked on the ad). Too often, banner ads are just wallpaper; consumers may see them but they usually are not sufficiently stimulated to click-through. However, Michele Slack of the online advertising group Jupiter Communications believes banner ads can be useful if used correctly. "The novelty factor is wearing off," she says. But "when an ad is targeted well and the creative is good, click-through rates are much higher."

An alternative way to reach people who are already online is through partnerships. One of the most visible examples of such an alliance is the one between Yahoo! and Amazon.com. Let's say you're working on a project on the Great Depression and you want to see what kind of information is available online. If you go to Yahoo! and type in "Great Depression," you will not only be presented with a list of websites, but you will also see a link that will allow you to click to see a list of books on the Great Depression that are available through Amazon. Another example of a successful partnership was forged in 1998 between Rollingstone.com and the website building and hosting service Tripod. Every one of the 3,000 artist pages on Rollingstone.com contained a link to Tripod. The goal was to encourage fans to use Tripod's tools to build webpages dedicated to their favorite singers or bands. According to the research company Media Metrix, during the course of the alliance Tripod jumped from the Web's four-teenth most popular website to number eight. Alliances with nonvirtual companies are another option. In 2003, the Internet classified firm CareerBuilder kicked off a cross-promotional campaign with major Internet firms, including AOL and MSN.

A less subtle but nonetheless effective way to build traffic is to more or less pay people to visit your site. One study showed more than half of Internet consumers would be more likely to purchase from a site if they could participate in some sort of loyalty program. Hundreds of online merchants in more than 20 categories have signed up with a network program called ClickRewards. Customers making purchases at ClickRewards member sites receive frequent-flier miles or other types of benefits. Mypoints.com offers a similar incentive program in which customers are rewarded with air travel, gift certificates and discounts for shopping at member merchants. The search engine iwon.com was even more direct. It rewards one lucky visitor each weekday with a $10,000 prize. According to Forrester Research, companies in 2002 spent about $6 billion annually on online incentives and promotions.

Finally, some firms rely on e-mail to thoroughly mine their existing customer databases. The auction site Onsale (later merged with Egghead.com) proved just how successful e-mail can be. It sent out targeted e-mails to its customers based on their past bidding activities and previously stated interests. Click-through rates on these targeted e-mails averaged a remarkable 30 percent. E-mail marketing also holds promise for business-to-business firms. The Peppers and Rogers Group is a marketing firm that gives presentations around the United States. At the end of the presentations, people are invited to go to the company's website and sign up for their e-mail newsletter, *Inside 1 to 1*. The newsletter invites readers to visit the Peppers and Rogers website to learn more about various articles, promote their products and services, and participate in forums. *Inside 1 to 1* now boasts a subscriber base of 45,000, but the company estimates that about 200,000 people actually see it because subscribers forward it to their friends and colleagues. About 14,000 people visit the Peppers and Rogers site each week, with traffic often peaking immediately after the newsletter is sent.

As you can see, there is no one effective method for generating interest in a website. The same methods that have worked for some firms have failed for others. One certainty is that as the Internet grows and more people do business online, Internet firms will have to find ever more creative ways to expose customers to their sites and keep their attention once there.

Discussion Questions

1. Consider the e-mail campaigns discussed in the case. Why do you think these campaigns were successful? Discuss the attention processes that were at work. Do you see any potential drawbacks to this type of marketing?

2. During the 2000 Super Bowl, ABC invited viewers to visit its Enhanced TV website. Fans could play trivia, see replays, participate in polls and chat rooms, and view player statistics. The site received an estimated 1 million hits. Why? Frame your answer in terms of exposure, attention, and comprehension.

3. Think about your own Web surfing patterns. Write down the reasons you visit certain sites. Which of the marketing strategies discussed in the case do you find most (and least) influential?

4. Many online firms are competing in cyberspace with companies that already have a brick-and-mortar presence (e.g., Amazon.com versus Barnesandnoble.com). How can an Internet-only company gain exposure and attract the attention of consumers to draw business away from more established competitors?

Sources: Richard Cross and Molly Neal, "Marketing to the Mass of Marketers," *Direct Marketing,* February 2000, pp. 60–62, 75; Jennifer Lach, "Carrots in Cyberspace," *American Demographics,* May 1999, pp. 43–45; Martha L. Stone, "Classified Conundrum: Building Brand Names," *Editor & Publisher,* April 1999, pp. 18–19; Sarah Lorge, "Banner Ads vs. E-Mail Marketing," *Sales and Marketing Management,* August 1999, p. 18.

Attitudes and Intentions

The Gap

The Gap began in 1969 with a single store in San Francisco selling jeans and records. Fueled by heavy advertising, The Gap grew rapidly in the 1970s to 200 stores. In the process, The Gap became the epitome of "cool" by offering basic items such as T-shirts and jeans that looked like designer clothing, but without the arrogance. Although the company experienced a few bumps along the way, growth continued through the 1980s and most of the 1990s.

By 2000 there were 1,800 stores in Europe, North America, and Japan, including new stores such as GapKids and acquisitions such as Banana Republic. Ads were designed to communicate that Gap clothes fit with an individual's sense of style. A campaign in the early 1990s featured celebrities such as jazz great Miles Davis and neo-country singer k.d. lang mixing Gap fashions with their personal clothing. The message was clear: Gap clothes could be combined with anything from Armani sport coats to Grateful Dead headbands. Ads for The Gap and GapKids were "cool," and those symbolic meanings transferred to the clothes. Helped by clever

advertising and the quality and style of the clothes, The Gap gained acceptance by tots, teenagers, young adults, and graying baby boomers.

But successful products, brands, and companies often draw criticism, which can change consumers' attitudes and behaviors. The 1990s witnessed a backlash of ridicule and resentment toward The Gap, especially among teens and Generation Xers. TV shows like *Ellen* and *Saturday Night Live* lampooned The Gap's fashion and image. By the mid-90s, surveys found that The Gap name was losing some of its "cool" among young people. So in the latter part of the decade, the company countered with fashions and ad campaigns especially directed toward younger buyers in the hope that The Gap could regain some of its lost "coolness."

But in the late 1990s, that youth-based strategy led to another problem: Adults weren't buying at The Gap anymore. Gap stores were increasingly filled with

David Young-Wolff/PhotoEdit, Inc.

multipocketed cargo pants and other items that were more appropriate for teens than older consumers. CEO Millard Drexler admitted, "We got too young. We don't want to depend only on teenagers." In response, The Gap began to sell more business-casual clothing, like gabardine pants, woven shirts, and classic v-neck shirts, and it is offering those clothes in larger sizes to accommodate older adults' expanding waistlines. The advertising has changed, too. In the late 1990s, celebrities were out, along with the serious, youth-oriented ads and a more upbeat, colorful, mainstream appeal is in. A television campaign launched in 2000 featured rival "gangs" in khakis and jeans dancing to music from *West Side Story.* For the first time in years, The Gap showed multiple products in a single ad, intended to reinforce the notion that The Gap offers something fashionable for almost everyone, regardless of age. In 2003, celebrities were back as The Gap used iconic music stars Madonna and Missy Elliott to promote its corduroy jeans.

To further broaden its appeal, The Gap opened a handful of GapBody stores, which specialize in lingerie and personal care items, and experimented with selling maternity clothes on its website (**www.gap.com**). Some industry observers have speculated that we may even see Gap furniture and lifestyle stores in the near future. What do you think of The Gap's marketing strategies? Can The Gap be all things to all people? Can The Gap successfully market to adults while still being "cool" in the eyes of teens and college students?

Sources: Calmetta Coleman, "Gap Plans to Lure Back Mom and Dad with an Emphasis on Business Casual," *The Wall Street Journal,* May 12, 2000, p. B2; Alice Z. Cuneo, "Gap Brightens Color Palette in Ads Aimed at Mainstream," *Advertising Age,* March 20, 2000, pp. 3, 82; Christina Duff, "Bobby Short Wore Khakis—Who's He and Who Cares?" *The Wall Street Journal,* February 16, 1995, pp. A1, A6; The Gap's corporate website, **www.gapinc.com**.

This example illustrates the concept of consumers' attitudes, one of the most important concepts in the study of consumer behavior. Each year marketing managers like those at The Gap spend millions of dollars researching consumers' attitudes toward products and brands, and then spend many more millions trying to influence those attitudes through advertisements, sales promotions, and other types of persuasion. By influencing consumers' attitudes, marketers hope to influence their purchase behaviors. In this chapter, we examine two types of attitudes: attitudes toward objects and attitudes toward behaviors. We begin by defining the concept of *attitude* and discussing how people's salient beliefs lead to attitudes. Then we consider the information integration process by which attitudes toward objects are formed. Next, we discuss the information integration process that forms attitudes toward actions and influences people's intentions to

Highlight 6.1

A Brief History of the Study of Attitude

Attitude has been called "the most distinctive and indispensable concept in contemporary American social psychology." And it is one of the most important concepts marketers use to understand consumers. Over the years, researchers have tried a variety of approaches to studying attitudes in an attempt to provide a more complete understanding of behavior.

One of the earliest definitions of attitude was introduced by Thurstone in 1931. He viewed attitude as a fairly simple concept—the amount of *affect* a person has for or against an object. A few years later, Allport proposed a much broader definition: "Attitude is a mental and neural state of *readiness to respond,* organized through experience, and exerting a directive and/or dynamic influence on behavior."

Triandis and others combined three response types (thoughts, feelings, and actions) into the *tripartite* *model of attitude.* In this scheme, attitude was seen as consisting of three related components: *cognition* (knowledge about the object), *affect* (positive or negative evaluations of the object), and *conation* (intended or actual behavior toward the object). Later, Fishbein, like Thurstone, argued that it is most useful to consider attitude as a simple, unidimensional concept—the amount of affect a person feels for an object.

Today most researchers agree that the simple concept of an attitude proposed by Thurstone and Fishbein is the most useful. That is, attitude represents a person's favorable or unfavorable feelings toward the object in question. Beliefs (cognition) and intentions to behave (conation) are seen as related to attitude but are separate cognitive concepts, not part of attitude itself. This is the perspective we take in this book.

Sources: Adapted from Martin Fishbein, "An Overview of the Attitude Construct," in *A Look Back, A Look Ahead,* ed. G.B. Hafer (Chicago: American Marketing Association, 1980), pp. 1–19; Richard J. Lutz, "The Role of Attitude Theory in Marketing," in *Perspectives in Consumer Behavior,* 3rd ed., ed. H. H. Kassarjian and T. S. Robertson (Glenview, IL: Scott, Foresman, 1981), pp. 234–235.

perform behaviors. Finally, we examine the imperfect relationship between behavioral intentions and actual behaviors. Throughout, we identify implications of these concepts and processes for developing marketing strategies.

What Is an Attitude?

Attitude has been a key concept in psychology for more than a century, and at least 100 definitions and 500 measures of attitude have been proposed.[1] Although the dominant approach to attitudes has changed over the years (see Highlight 6.1), nearly all definitions of attitude have one thing in common: They refer to people's evaluations.[2] We define **attitude** as a person's *overall evaluation of a concept.*[3]

As you learned in Chapter 3, **evaluations** are *affective* responses, usually at relatively low levels of intensity and arousal (refer to Exhibit 3.2 on page 42). These evaluations can be created by both the affective and cognitive systems.[4] The affective system automatically produces affective responses—including emotions, feelings, moods, and evaluations or attitudes—as immediate, direct responses to certain stimuli. These favorable or unfavorable affective responses are generated without conscious, cognitive processing of information about the product. Then, through classical conditioning processes, these evaluations may become associated with a product or brand, thus creating an attitude.[5] We discuss this affective, noncognitive learning in Chapter 9.

In this chapter, however, we treat attitudes as affective evaluations created by the cognitive system. The cognitive processing model of consumer decision making (refer to Exhibit 3.5 on page 52) shows that an overall evaluation is formed when consumers integrate (combine) knowledge, meanings, or beliefs about the attitude concept. The goal of this **integration process** is to analyze the *personal relevance* of the concept and determine whether it is favorable or unfavorable: "What does this concept have to do with me? Is this a good or bad thing for me? Do I like or dislike this concept?" We assume consumers form an attitude toward each concept they interpret in terms of its personal relevance.

As shown in Exhibit 3.5, the evaluations produced by the attitude formation process may be stored in memory. Once an attitude has been formed and stored in memory, consumers do not have to engage in another integration process to construct another attitude when they need to evaluate the concept again. Instead, the existing attitude can be activated from memory and used as a basis for interpreting new information. Taste tests are a good example of how activated attitudes can influence consumers' judgments. Taste tests usually are conducted blind (tasters are not told what brands they are tasting) to avoid activating brand attitudes that would bias their taste judgments. Finally, an activated attitude can be integrated with other knowledge in decision making (we discuss how attitudes are used in decision processes in the next chapter).[6]

Whether a given attitude will affect interpretation or integration processes depends on its **accessibility** in memory or its *probability of activation*.[7] Many factors can influence the accessibility of attitudes, including salience or importance (more self-relevant attitudes are more easily activated), frequency of prior activation (attitudes that are activated more often are more accessible), and the strength of the association between a concept and its attitude (puppies tend to activate positive attitudes; zebras usually do not activate an attitude).[8] Marketers sometimes use cues to "prime" (partially activate) an attitude that is relevant to their strategies; consider the cute babies in ads for Michelin tires.[9]

Attitudes can be measured simply and directly by asking consumers to evaluate the concept of interest. For instance, marketing researchers might ask consumers to indicate their attitudes toward McDonald's french fries on three evaluative scales:

McDonald's French Fries

Extremely Unfavorable	-3 -2 -1 0 $+1$ $+2$ $+3$	Extremely Favorable
Dislike Very Much	-3 -2 -1 0 $+1$ $+2$ $+3$	Likes Very Much
Very Bad	-3 -2 -1 0 $+1$ $+2$ $+3$	Very Good

Consumers' overall attitudes toward McDonald's french fries (A_O) are indicated by the average of their ratings across the three evaluative scales. Attitudes can vary from *negative* (ratings of -3, -2, -1) through *neutral* (a rating of 0) to *positive* (ratings of $+1$, $+2$, or $+3$). Attitudes are not necessarily intense or extreme. On the contrary, many consumers have essentially neutral evaluations (neither favorable nor unfavorable) toward relatively unimportant, noninvolving concepts. A neutral evaluation is still an attitude, however, although probably a weakly held one.

Attitudes toward What?

Consumers' attitudes are always toward some concept. We are interested in two broad types of concepts: objects and behaviors. Consumers can have *attitudes toward various physical and social objects* (A_O indicates attitude toward the object), including products, brands, models, stores, and people (salesperson at the electronics store), as well as aspects of marketing strategy (a rebate from General

Motors; an ad for Wrigley's chewing gum). Consumers also can have attitudes toward intangible objects such as concepts and ideas (capitalism, a fair price for gasoline). A late 1990s survey of Americans' attitudes toward pollution and the environment found that compared to five years earlier, 76 percent were more concerned, 19 percent were less concerned, and 6 percent were unchanged. Consumers also can have *attitudes toward their own behaviors or actions* (A_{act} indicates attitude toward the act, action, or behavior), including their past actions (Why did I buy that sweater?) and future behaviors (I'm going to the mall tomorrow afternoon).

Levels of Attitude Concepts Consumers can have quite distinct attitudes toward variations of the same general concept. Exhibit 6.1 shows several attitude concepts that vary in their *levels of specificity,* even though all concepts are in the same product domain. For instance, Rich has a moderately positive attitude toward fast-food restaurants in general, but he has a highly favorable attitude toward one product form (hamburger restaurants). However, his attitude toward McDonald's, a specific brand of hamburger restaurant, is only slightly favorable (he likes Burger King better). Finally, his attitude toward a particular "model"—the McDonald's on the corner of Grant and Main—is somewhat negative (he had an unpleasant meal there).

Note that some attitude concepts are defined in terms of a particular behavioral and situational context (eating dinner with his children at the Grant Street McDonald's after a soccer game), whereas other concepts are more generic (McDonald's restaurants in general). Consumers could have different attitudes toward these concepts, and these attitudes might not be consistent with one another. Rich, for instance, has an unfavorable attitude toward eating lunch with his friends at the Grant Street McDonald's (he'd rather go to a full-service restaurant); however, he has a somewhat favorable attitude toward eating dinner there with his kids (it's easy and fast).

Note that although the same McDonald's "object" is present in each of these concepts, Rich's attitude toward that McDonald's is different in the two situations.[10] Because consumers are likely to have different attitudes toward different attitude concepts, *marketers must be sure to measure the attitude concept at the level of specificity most relevant to the marketing problem of interest.*

Marketing Implications

Marketers are highly interested in market share, a measure of purchasing behavior indicating the proportion of total sales in a product category (or product form) received by a brand. But marketers also need to attend to consumers' brand attitudes.

Brand Equity Brand attitude is a key aspect of brand equity. Brand equity concerns the value of the brand to the marketer and to the consumer.[11] From the marketer's perspective, brand equity implies greater profits, more cash flow, and greater market share. For instance, Marriott estimated that adding its name to Fairfield Inn increased occupancy rates by 15 percent (a tangible indicator of the value of the Marriott brand). In England, Hitachi and G.E. once co-owned a factory that made identical televisions for both companies.[12] The only differences were the brand name on the set and a $75 higher price for the Hitachi, reflecting the equity or value of the Hitachi brand.

From a consumer perspective, **brand equity** involves a strong, *positive brand attitude* (favorable evaluation of the brand) based on favorable *meanings and beliefs*

There is no other name in real estate that is as powerful as CENTURY 21.

You know when you walk through the door of a CENTURY 21 office. . .

that the agents in that office have been trained.

CENTURY 21 is rated the best. . .

at selling homes.

CENTURY 21. Rated number one.

This commercial tries to create favorable attitudes toward Century 21 by describing its positive attributes and consequences
Courtesy Century 21 Real Estate Corporation.

that are *accessible* in memory (easily activated).[13] These three factors create a strong, favorable *consumer–brand relationship*, one of the most important assets a company can own and the basis for brand equity. Highlight 6.2 presents more about the concept of brand equity.

Basically marketers can acquire brand equity in three ways: They can build it, borrow it, or buy it.[14] Companies can *build brand equity* by ensuring that the brand actually delivers positive consequences and by consistently advertising these important consequences. Consider the considerable brand equity built up over time by Campbell's soup, Green Giant vegetables, Mercedes-Benz automobiles, and Amazon.com. Anheuser-Busch created the Eagle brand of snack foods (including honey-roasted peanuts) and invested heavily in creating positive consumer attitudes (and brand equity) through advertising and sales promotions.

Companies can *borrow brand equity* by extending a positive brand name to other products. For example, the Coca-Cola line now includes Coca-Cola Classic, Coke, Diet Coke, Caffeine-Free Coke, Cherry, Lemon, and Vanilla Coke, and others. Tide no longer refers to only one type of detergent; the brand name has been extended to other products, and presumably some of Tide's original equity has been passed along, too. Consumer researchers are busy trying to determine if and how brand equity is transferred by brand-name extensions.[15] Some research shows that the success of a brand extension depends on the key meanings consumers associate with a brand name and whether those meanings are consistent or appropriate for the other product.[16]

Finally, a company can *buy brand equity* by purchasing brands that already have equity. For instance, the mergers and leveraged buyouts of the 1980s were partially

Exhibit 6.1

Levels of Specificity of an Attitude Concept

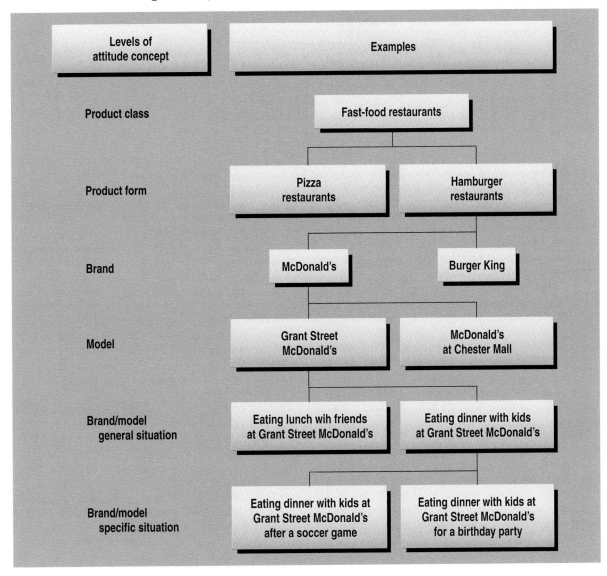

motivated by the desire to buy brands with strong equity. Thus, when Grand Metropolitan bought Pillsbury and Philip Morris bought Kraft, they acquired the equity of all the acquired brands.

Attitude Tracking Studies   Because many marketing strategies are intended to influence consumers' attitudes toward a brand, marketers can use measures of consumers' attitudes to indicate the success of those strategies. For instance, many companies regularly conduct large-scale attitude surveys, called *tracking studies*, to monitor consumers' brand attitudes over time. When these studies identify changes

Highlight 6.2

Building Brands

Corporations like McDonald's, Coca-Cola, and Procter & Gamble have spent years successfully developing and protecting their brands. However, in the 1990s a new breed of high-tech firm redefined the art of brand building. According to a 2000 survey by British consultant Interbrand, four of the five most valuable brands in the world are from the technology sector: Microsoft, IBM, Intel, and Nokia. The only old-line firm in the group is Coca-Cola. Furthermore, Internet firms like Yahoo! and Amazon.com are among the fastest-growing brands. These companies have accomplished overnight what used to take decades. How have they done it? Hint: It's more than just advertising.

Brand-building tactic 1: Give away the farm. Giving away free samples is not a new or particularly innovative strategy, but some high-tech firms have taken the concept of the freebie to a new level. America Online has taken great pains to make sure its diskettes and CD-ROMs are almost everywhere—in cereal boxes, alongside in-flight meals, on music CDs, even on the plastic bags that cover your morning newspaper. AOL believed it was difficult to simply explain to consumers the benefits of its services. Rather, it felt the best way to win over potential new customers was to let them try AOL free for a limited time and learn firsthand how it worked.

Brand-building tactic 2: Conduct public relations like a war. Sun Microsystems' effort to promote its Java software platform is an example of brilliant guerrilla marketing in action. For example, Java Beans is a Sun technology that allows for the development of reusable pieces of code. At one point, Sun learned that rival Microsoft planned a press conference to announce the introduction of a competing technology. The day before Microsoft's official rollout, Sun mailed bags of coffee beans to reporters. The bags contained a note asking, "Why is Microsoft so jittery?" and inviting reporters to a Java Beans seminar at a hotel next door to where the Microsoft announcement was taking place. According to Sun, more than 250 people attended to learn more about the company's Java Beans technology. Sun thus stole some of Microsoft's thunder while promoting its own product at the same time.

Brand-building tactic 3: Work the Web. Amazon has successfully spread its name all over the Web. Shortly after it opened its Internet "storefront" in 1995, Amazon received a request from a customer to create links from book recommendations on her website to Amazon. Not only did Amazon agree, but it also worked diligently to set up similar so-called "Associate" agreements with other websites. In exchange for posting an Amazon link on your site, you would receive from 5 to 15 percent of any revenue generated. By 1998, Amazon boasted more than 40,000 Associates.

Brand-building tactic 4: Make it funny. A number of Internet firms have capitalized on the irreverent spirit of the Web. Sun was one of the pioneers, publishing a comic book for software developers at the 1996 Internet World trade show. The comic book featured the bizarre-looking Java mascot, Duke, who pledged to "keep the Internet safe for everyone." Sun used humor to try to differentiate itself from Microsoft and its comparatively strait-laced image. Priceline.com produced a series of funny TV and radio ads featuring actor William Shatner "singing" about the virtues of saving money on Priceline. Yahoo! positioned itself as a fun, hip, slightly off-the-wall site, thanks to clever advertising and the memorable tag line "Do you Yahoo!?"

For these technology firms, the next challenge is to maintain the successful brand image they have built. Can they keep their brands relevant in the minds of consumers for decades, as Disney, Coca-Cola, and some other more traditional companies have done? For these older giants, the challenge is to figure out new, innovative methods of building brand equity as the rules of the game change more rapidly than ever before.

in consumer attitudes, marketers can adjust their marketing strategies, as The Gap did in the opening example.

One company that failed to track consumers' increasingly unfavorable attitudes was Howard Johnson's, one of the original restaurant chains in the United States. During the highway building boom in the 1950s and 1960s, HoJo's was known as a clean place with nice washrooms, predictable and wholesome food, and ice cream the kids would like. Consumers' attitudes were positive, and Howard Johnson's prospered. But over the next 20 years, HoJo's did not monitor customers' attitudes well, nor did it respond effectively to the strategies of competitors that were passing it by. For instance, Howard Johnson's used informal gauges of consumer attitudes, such as comment cards left on restaurant tables. Competitors such as Marriott, Denny's, and McDonald's ran sophisticated market tests that told them what customers liked and didn't like. Finally, after a long decline, Marriott bought out the once-powerful chain of Howard Johnson's restaurants.[17]

Attitudes toward Objects

In this section, we examine the information integration process by which consumers form **attitudes toward objects (A_O),** including products or brands. As shown in Exhibit 3.5, during the integration process, consumers combine some of their knowledge, meanings, and beliefs about a product or brand to form an overall evaluation. These considered beliefs may be formed by interpretation processes or activated from memory.

Salient Beliefs

Through their varied experiences, consumers acquire many beliefs about products, brands, and other objects in their environment. Exhibit 6.2 presents some of the beliefs one consumer has about Crest toothpaste. These beliefs constitute an associative network of linked meanings stored in memory. Because people's cognitive capacity is limited, only a few of these beliefs can be activated and consciously considered at once. The *activated beliefs* (highlighted in Exhibit 6.2) are called **salient beliefs.** Only the salient beliefs about an object (those that are activated at a particular time and in a specific context) create a person's attitude toward that object.[18] Thus, one key to understanding consumers' attitudes is to identify and understand the underlying set of salient beliefs.

In principle, consumers can have salient beliefs about any type and level of meaning associated with a product. For instance, consumers who possess complete means–end chains of product knowledge could activate beliefs about the product's attributes, its functional consequences, or the values achieved through using it. In addition, beliefs about other types of product-related meanings, such as country of origin, could be activated.[19] Salient beliefs could include tactile, olfactory, and visual images, as well as cognitive representations of the emotions and moods associated with using the product. If activated, any of these beliefs could influence a consumer's attitude toward a product.

Many factors influence which beliefs about an object will be activated in a situation and thus become salient determinants of A_O. They include prominent stimuli in the immediate environment (point-of-purchase displays, advertisements, package information), recent events, consumers' moods and emotional states, and consumers' values and goals activated in the situation.[20] For instance, noticing a price reduction sign for hiking boots may make price beliefs salient and therefore influential on A_O.

Exhibit 6.2

Relationship between Salient Beliefs about an Object and Attitude toward the Object

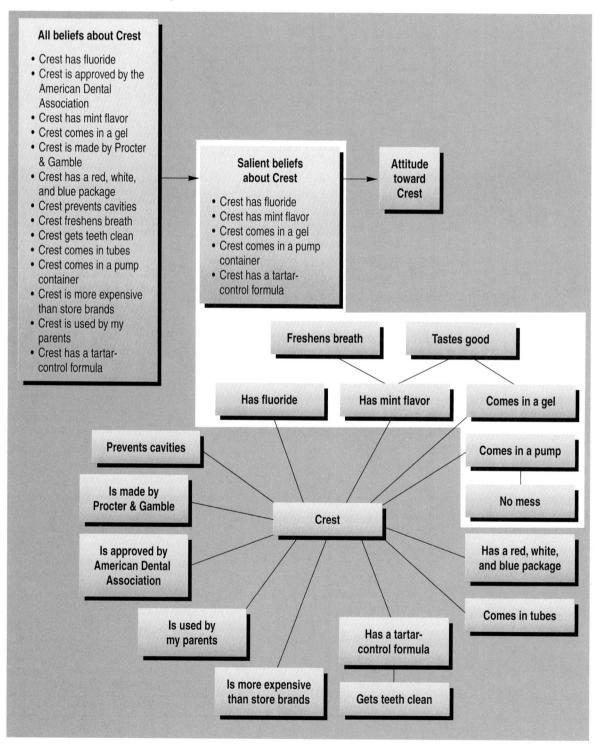

As smooth as silk. As fast as Tums.®

New Tums® Smooth Dissolve.™ Now Tums offers a silky new texture that dissolves fast, so it goes to work fast. Same good-for-you calcium. Very different texture.

This ad is intended to create new salient beliefs about product attributes and benefits *Reprinted courtesy of GlaxoSmithKline.*

Marketers may find that consumers' salient beliefs vary over time or situations for some products. That is, different sets of salient beliefs about a product may be activated in different situations or at different times.[21] For instance, a consumer who has just returned from the dentist is more likely to activate beliefs about tooth decay and cavities when thinking about which brand of toothpaste to buy. Variations in the set of salient beliefs over time and situations can produce changes in consumer attitudes depending on the situation, context, time, consumer's mood, and so forth. Consumers have more stable attitudes toward objects that have a stable set of salient beliefs. Normally, though, the amount of variation in salient beliefs and attitudes is not great for most objects.

The Multiattribute Attitude Model

A great deal of marketing research has focused on developing models for predicting the attitudes produced by this integration process. These are called **multiattribute attitude models** because they focus on consumers' beliefs about multiple product or brand attributes.[22] Of these, Martin Fishbein's model has been most influential in marketing.

The key proposition in Fishbein's theory is that the *evaluations of salient beliefs cause overall attitude.* Simply stated, people tend to like objects that are associated with "good" characteristics and dislike objects they believe have "bad" attributes. In Fishbein's multiattribute model, overall attitude toward an object is a function of two factors: the *strengths* of the salient beliefs associated with the object and the *evaluations* of those beliefs.[23] Formally, the model proposes that:

$$A_O = \sum_{i=1}^{n} b_i e_i$$

where

A_O = attitude toward the object

b_i = strength of the belief that the object has attribute i

e_i = evaluation of attribute i

n = number of salient beliefs about the object

This multiattribute attitude model accounts for the integration process by which product knowledge (the evaluations and strengths of salient beliefs) is combined to form an overall evaluation or attitude. The model, however, does not claim that consumers actually add up the products of belief strength and evaluation when forming attitudes toward objects. Rather, this and similar models attempt to predict the attitude produced by the integration process; they are not meant to describe the actual cognitive operations by which knowledge is integrated. In this book, we consider the multiattribute model to be a useful tool for investigating attitude formation and predicting attitudes.

Model Components   The two major elements of Fishbein's multiattribute model are the strengths and evaluations of the salient beliefs. Exhibit 6.3 illustrates how these components are combined to form attitudes toward two brands of soft drinks. This consumer has salient beliefs about three attributes for each brand. These beliefs vary in content, strength, and evaluation. The Fishbein model predicts that this consumer has a more favorable attitude toward 7UP than toward Diet Pepsi.

Belief strength (b_i) is the perceived probability of association between an object and its relevant attributes. Belief strength is measured by having consumers rate this probability of association for each of their salient beliefs, as shown here:

"How likely is it that 7UP has no caffeine?"
Extremely Unlikely   1 2 3 4 5 6 7 8 9 10   Extremely Likely

"How likely is it that 7UP is made from all natural ingredients?"
Extremely Unlikely   1 2 3 4 5 6 7 8 9 10   Extremely Likely

Consumers who are quite certain that 7UP has no caffeine would indicate a very strong belief strength, perhaps 9 or 10. Consumers who have only a moderately strong belief that 7UP is made from only natural ingredients might rate their belief strength as 6 or 7.

The strength of consumers' product or brand beliefs is affected by their past experiences with the object. Beliefs about product attributes or consequences tend

Exhibit 6.3

An Example of the Multiattribute Attitude Model

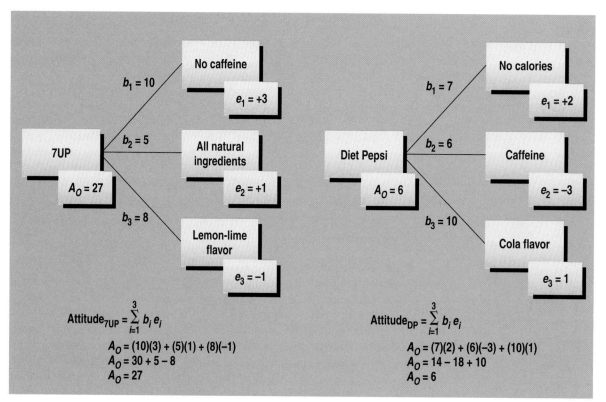

$$\text{Attitude}_{7UP} = \sum_{i=1}^{3} b_i e_i$$
$$A_O = (10)(3) + (5)(1) + (8)(-1)$$
$$A_O = 30 + 5 - 8$$
$$A_O = 27$$

$$\text{Attitude}_{DP} = \sum_{i=1}^{3} b_i e_i$$
$$A_O = (7)(2) + (6)(-3) + (10)(1)$$
$$A_O = 14 - 18 + 10$$
$$A_O = 6$$

to be stronger when based on actual use of the product. Beliefs that were formed indirectly from mass advertising or conversations with a salesperson tend to be weaker. For instance, consumers are more likely to form a strong belief that "7UP tastes good" if they actually drink a 7UP and experience its taste directly than if they read a product claim in an advertisement. Because they are stronger (and more likely to be activated), beliefs based on direct experience tend to have a greater impact on A_O.[24] Marketers therefore try to induce potential customers to actually use their products. They may distribute free samples; sell small, less expensive trial sizes; offer cents-off coupons; or have a no-obligation trial policy.

Fishbein argued that the typical number of salient beliefs about an attitude object is not likely to exceed seven to nine.[25] Given consumers' limited capacities for interpreting and integrating information, we might expect even fewer salient beliefs for many objects. In fact, when consumers have limited knowledge about low-involvement products, their brand attitudes might be based on very few salient beliefs, perhaps only one or two. In contrast, their attitudes toward more self-relevant products or brands are likely to be based on several salient beliefs.

Associated with each salient belief is a **belief evaluation (e_i)** that reflects how favorably the consumer perceives that attribute. Marketers measure the e_i component by having consumers indicate their evaluation of (favorability toward) each salient belief, as follows:

"7UP has no caffeine."

Very Bad -3 -2 -1 0 $+1$ $+2$ $+3$ Very Good

"7UP has all natural ingredients."

Very Bad -3 -2 -1 0 $+1$ $+2$ $+3$ Very Good

As shown in Exhibit 6.3, the evaluations of salient beliefs influence the overall A_O in proportion to the strength of each belief (b_i). Thus, strong beliefs about positive attributes have greater effects on A_O than do weak beliefs about equally positive attributes. Likewise, a negative e_i reduces the favorability of A_O in proportion to its b_i "weight."

As you learned in Chapter 4, consumers link beliefs to form means–end chains of product knowledge. Exhibit 6.4 presents means–end chains for three attributes of 7UP. Note that the evaluation of each product attribute is ultimately derived from the evaluation of the end consequence in its means–end chain. As shown in Exhibit 6.4, the evaluation of the end "flows down" the means–end chain to determine the evaluations of the less abstract consequences and attributes.[26] For instance, a person who positively evaluates the end "relaxation," an instrumental value, would tend to positively evaluate the functional consequence "I'm not jittery." In turn, the product attribute "no caffeine," which is perceived to lead to not being jittery and relaxation would have a positive evaluation. These evaluations would then influence the overall attitude, A_O, toward 7UP.

Consumers' evaluations of salient attributes are not necessarily fixed over time or constant across different situations.[27] For instance, consumers may change their minds about how good or bad an attribute is as they learn more about its higher-order consequences. Situational factors can also change the e_i components. In a different situation, some consumers may want to be stimulated (when getting up in the morning or working late at night to finish a project). If so, the now negative evaluation of the end value "relaxation" would flow down the means–end chain and create a *negative* evaluation of the "no caffeine" attribute, which in turn would

Exhibit 6.4

The Means–End Chain Basis for Attribute Evaluations

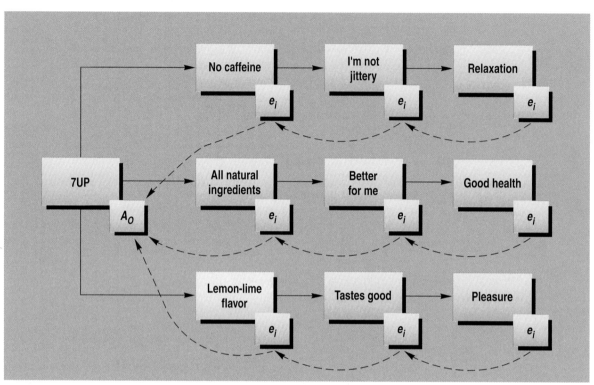

contribute to a less positive overall attitude toward 7UP (for that situation). In this situation, the consumer might have a more positive attitude toward Diet Pepsi, which does contain caffeine. This is yet another example of how the physical and social environment can influence consumers' affect and cognitions.

Marketing Implications

Marketers have been using multiattribute models to explore consumer behavior since the late 1960s. These models became popular because they have an intuitive appeal to researchers and managers and are relatively easy to use in research.[28] Not all of these models accurately reflect the basic Fishbein model, but most are adaptations of it. We will discuss a few of the many applications of these models next.

Understanding Your Customers The multiattribute model is useful for identifying which attributes are the most important (or most salient) to consumers. For instance, airline passengers love to complain about the lousy food served on planes.[29] Yet a survey found that only 40 percent of passengers rated good food and beverage service as important, whereas other attributes were mentioned as important much more frequently. These included convenient schedules (more than 90 percent), fast check-in (about 80 percent), comfortable seats (about 80 percent), and good on-time performance (about 85 percent). Perhaps airlines use such data to justify not improving the quality of the food they serve (airlines spend only about $4.25 per passenger on food). The relative importance of different attributes is likely to vary across market segments. For instance, three segments of the airline market—light travelers (1 or 2 trips per year), moderate travelers (3 to 9 trips per year), and frequent travelers (10 or more trips per year)—evaluated some attributes differently. Light travelers had greater concerns about safety and efficient baggage handling, whereas frequent travelers were more concerned with convenient schedules and frequent-flier programs.

Diagnosis of Marketing Strategies Although multiattribute models were developed to predict overall attitudes, marketers often use them to diagnose marketing strategies. By examining the salient beliefs that underlie attitudes toward various brands, marketers can learn how their strategies are performing and make adjustments to improve their effectiveness. For instance, in the value-conscious 1990s, marketers found that many consumers were more concerned with the quality and value of products relative to their prices.[30] It became fashionable once again to get a bargain, spend one's money wisely, and not overpay for quality. Many companies adjusted their strategies in light of these beliefs. Consider the motto of Wal-Mart, the world's largest retailer: "The low price on the brands you trust." Southwest Airlines combined low fares with friendly but bare-bones service to enhance consumers' value beliefs and oveall attitudes. Taco Bell reduced its operating costs enough to price several items on the menu less than $1 and create stronger beliefs about the value the fast-food restaurant provided.

Understanding Situational Influences Marketers can also use the multiattribute attitude model to examine the influence of situations. The relative salience of beliefs about certain product attributes may be greatly influenced by the situations in which the product is used. Situations vary in many ways, including time of day, consumer

The situation or context in which a product is used can have a significant influence on brand attitude.
Courtesy Schwinn Bicycle.

mood, environmental setting, weather, and hundreds of other variables. These situational characteristics affect which beliefs are activated from memory and influence attitudes toward the brands that might be purchased for use in those situations. For instance, one study of snack products found that beliefs about economy and taste were most important for three common snacking occasions: everyday desserts, watching TV in the evening, and kids' lunches.[31] However, when buying snacks for a children's party, beliefs about nutrition and convenience were most important. Such variations in salient beliefs can lead to different brand attitudes in these various situations.

Attitude-Change Strategies

The multiattribute model is a useful guide for devising strategies to change consumers' attitudes. Basically a marketer has four possible **attitude-change strategies:** (1) add a new salient belief about the attitude object—ideally, one with a positive e_i, (2) increase the strength of an existing positive belief, (3) improve the evaluation of a strongly held belief, or (4) make an existing favorable belief more salient.

Adding a new salient belief to the existing beliefs that consumers have about a product or brand is probably the most common attitude-change strategy.[32] Highlight 6.3 describes such a strategy in an antismoking campaign. Sometimes this strategy requires a physical change in the product. For instance, crunchy is an attribute now added to many food products.[33] Consider Honey Crunch Corn Flakes from Kellogg, French Toast Crunch from General Mills, and Cranberry Almond Crunch from Post. Candy is getting crunchier too—Reese's Crunchy Cookie Cups from Hershey and Nestlé's White Crunch. Even smooth Yoplait Yogurt (by General Mills) has a Crunchy Lite line containing nuts. People in general have positive attitudes toward "crunchy" and "crispy," which seem to be linked to feelings of freshness, fun, and stress relief. As one customer put it, "I don't know if it is the sound or what, but crunchy foods are satisfying."

Marketers can also try to change attitudes by *changing the strength of already salient beliefs.*[34] They can attempt to increase the strength of beliefs about positive attributes and consequences, or they can decrease the strength of beliefs about negative attributes and consequences. Papa John's pizza (**www.papajohns.com**) is outperforming the entire fast-food industry. Yet Papa John's costs a bit more than Little Caesar's, arrives no faster than Dominos, does not sell salads or sandwiches, and does not offer sit-down service.[35] Instead, Papa John's focuses on taste, as indicated by its corporate slogan, "Better ingredients, better pizza." It makes its own dough with purified water and its own sauce from fresh tomatoes, and uses only premium mozzarella cheese. Papa John's works hard to create strong consumer beliefs that its pizza tastes better, and apparently many consumers do believe. Many publications in markets around the country have rated Papa John's as the best-tasting pizza. In 1997, Papa John's was voted the best pizza chain in the United States.

Marketers can also try to change consumers' attitudes by *changing the evaluative aspect of an existing, strongly held belief* about a salient attribute. This requires constructing a new means–end chain by linking a more positive, higher-ordered consequence to that attribute. Cereal manufacturers such as Kellogg once tried to enhance consumers' attitudes by linking the food attribute of fiber to cancer prevention.

Consider how evaluations of beliefs about food attributes have changed (in the United States, at least) as their means–end meanings have evolved.[36] Attributes such as butterfat and egg yolks once were evaluated highly because they gave foods a rich, satisfying taste. But in the 1990s they became negative attributes, whereas

Highlight 6.3

Changing Teenagers' Attitudes toward Smoking

In recent years, many attempts have been made to convince teens of the dangers of smoking. One of the highest-profile efforts has been The Truth campaign from the American Legacy Association. You can see The Truth's approach firsthand at its website, **www.TheTruth.com**.

The Truth's edgy and brutally direct ads have created controversy and attracted national attention. For example, a TV spot featured an angry tobacco company executive ushering a young woman out of an office building while she loudly chastises him for his company's misleading marketing tactics. A magazine ad pictured a hand with bandaged fingers and asked readers to "Rip out the next cigarette ad you see because tobacco killed about 430,000 people last year and paper cuts didn't kill anybody" (interestingly, that ad ran in *Spin* magazine, which also accepts advertising dollars from tobacco companies). The Truth also has taken its campaign to the streets, filling part of an empty lot in Washington, DC, with 1,200 body bags, representing the number of people who die each day from tobacco-related illnesses. The Truth itself has become a cool "brand" among teens. During a summer-long promotional campaign in 2000, The Truth representatives gave away 150,000 baseball caps and T-shirts.

The ads are funded in part by money paid by tobacco companies as part of a 1998 agreement between the tobacco industry and 46 states. One stipulation of the agreement was that the ads should not "vilify" the tobacco companies. The definition of *vilify* was left open to interpretation. Does an ad that shows the Philip Morris headquarters in New York surrounded by body bags qualify as vilification? The tobacco industry has had little to say on the issue, although a Philip Morris spokesperson claims, "We're disappointed with some of the ads and the tone of the website. We don't think they accurately depict our company, our employees, and the way we do business." However, Mitch Zeller, executive vice president of the American Legacy Foundation, contends an in-your-face approach is the best way to reach teens: "Teenagers have a sense of immortality. They think the dangers don't apply to them. The body bags are designed to break through that kind of mindset."

Sources: Frank Santiago, "Body Bags Pile Up for Anti-Smoking Ads Aimed at Teens," *USA Today,* July 28, 2000, p. 3A; Chris Reidy, "Arnold Set to Fire Up Next Phase of Teen Antismoking Ads," *Boston Globe,* June 23, 2000, p. C3; Bob Moseley, "Can Magazines Handle TheTruth.com?" *Folio: The Magazine for Magazine Management,* August 2000, p. 17.

attributes such as low fats, once seen as rather undesirable, became more highly valued. For instance, Sealtest tried to link nonfat characteristics of "Sealtest Free" ice cream to important values such as health and fitness. Likewise, Kraft tried to link the key attributes of its fat-free line of salad dressings and mayonnaise (egg whites, skim milk, cellulose gel, and various gums) to important health consequences and values (lower risk of heart disease and longer life).

The final strategy for changing consumers' attitudes is to *make an existing favorable belief more salient,* usually by convincing consumers that the attribute is more self-relevant than it seemed. This strategy is similar to the previous one in that it attempts to link the attribute to valued consequences and values. Creating such means–end chains increases both the salience of consumers' beliefs about the attributes as well as the evaluations (e_i) of those beliefs. For example, the marketing strategies of sun care lotion manufacturers such as Bain de Soleil and Hawaiian Tropic emphasized the perceived risks of not using their lotions, which had a sunscreen attribute.[37] By linking the sunscreen attribute to important ends such as avoiding skin cancer and premature wrinkling, they sought to make the sunscreen attribute more salient (more self-relevant) for consumers. Such means–end chains should make sunscreen beliefs more likely to be activated and considered during decision making.

Attitudes toward Behavior

Consumers' attitudes have been studied intensively, but marketers tend to be more concerned about consumers' overt *behavior*, especially their purchase behavior. Thus, it is not surprising that a great deal of research has tried to establish the relationship between attitudes and behavior.[38] Based on the idea of consistency, you might expect attitudes toward an object (A_O) to be strongly related to behaviors toward the object. For instance, most market researchers believe, and operate under the assumption, that the more favorable a person's attitude toward a given product (or brand), the more likely the person is to buy or use that product (or brand).[39]

Thus, a marketing researcher might measure consumers' attitudes toward Pizza Hut and use the results to predict whether each person will purchase a pizza at

This ad uses a butterfly as metaphor for a person's metamorphosis to a state of self-esteem   *Self Esteem Clothing Back-to-School 2003 advertising compaign. Courtesy of Parker White.*

Exhibit 6.5

Relationships among Beliefs, Attitude, and Behaviors Regarding a Specific Object

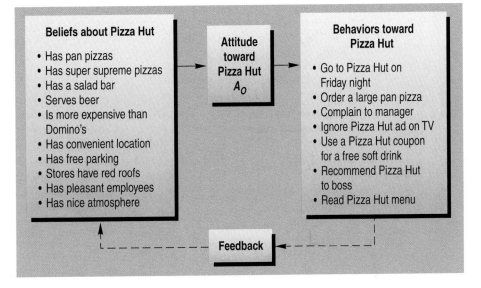

Pizza Hut within the next month. If this approach seems reasonable, you may be surprised to learn that consumers' attitudes toward an object often are not good predictors of their specific behaviors regarding that object. In fact, with a few notable exceptions, most research has found rather weak relationships between A_O and *specific* single behaviors.[40]

Exhibit 6.5 illustrates one problem with relating A_O to individual behaviors. The exhibit presents the relationships among a consumer's beliefs, attitude, and behaviors concerning a particular object: Pizza Hut. First, note that Judy, our consumer, has a *single overall attitude* toward Pizza Hut (in her case, a favorable A_O), which is based on her salient beliefs about Pizza Hut. For instance, she might go to Pizza Hut on Friday night and order a pizza, ignore a Pizza Hut ad on television, use a Pizza Hut coupon for a free soft drink, or recommend Pizza Hut to her boss. However, none of these specific behaviors is necessarily consistent with or even strongly related to her overall A_O, although some of them might be.

This does not mean consumers' attitudes are irrelevant to their behaviors. As shown in Exhibit 6.5, Judy's overall attitude (A_O) is related to the overall evaluative pattern of her behaviors (all of her behaviors regarding Pizza Hut taken together). However, it is not possible to predict with accuracy any specific behavior based on knowing a person's overall attitude toward the object of the behavior.

Although this proposition may seem strange, there are many examples of its validity. Consider that many consumers probably have positive attitudes toward Porsche cars, Rolex watches, and vacation homes, but most do not buy these products. Because favorable attitudes toward these products can be expressed in many different behaviors, it is difficult to predict which specific behavior will be performed. Consider three consumers who have generally favorable attitudes toward Porsches but do not own one. One consumer reads ads and test reports about

Porsches. The second consumer goes to showrooms to look at Porsches. The third consumer just daydreams about owning a Porsche. In sum, having a generally favorable (or unfavorable) attitude toward a product does not mean the consumer will perform every possible favorable (or unfavorable) behavior regarding that product. Marketers need a model that identifies the attitudinal factors that influence specific behaviors. Such a model is provided by Fishbein's theory of reasoned action.

The Theory of Reasoned Action

Fishbein recognized that people's attitudes toward an object may not be strongly or systematically related to their specific behaviors.[41] Rather, the immediate determinant of whether consumers will engage in a particular behavior is their *intention* to engage in that behavior. Fishbein modified and extended his multiattribute attitude model to relate consumers' beliefs and attitudes to their behavioral intentions. The entire model is presented in Exhibit 6.6.

The model is called a **theory of reasoned action** because it assumes that consumers *consciously consider* the consequences of the alternative behaviors under consideration and choose the one that leads to the most desirably consequences.[42] The outcome of this reasoned choice process is an intention to engage in the selected behavior. This behavioral intention is the single best predictor of actual behavior. In sum, the theory of reasoned action proposes that any reasonably complex, *voluntary* behavior (such as buying a pair of shoes) is determined by the person's *intention* to perform that behavior. The theory of reasoned action is not relevant for extremely simple or *involuntary* behaviors such as automatic eye blinking, turning your head at the sound of the telephone, or sneezing.

Formally, the theory of reasoned action can be presented as follows:

$$B \sim BI = A_{act}(w_1) + SN(w_2)$$

where

B = a specific behavior

BI = consumer's intention to engage in that behavior

A_{act} = consumer's attitude toward engaging in that behavior

SN = subjective norm regarding whether other people want the consumer to engage in that behavior

w_1 and w_2 = weights that reflect the relative influence of the A_{act} and SN components on BI

According to this theory, people tend to perform behaviors that are evaluated favorably and are popular with other people. They tend to refrain from behaviors that are regarded unfavorably and are unpopular with others.

Model Components   In this section, we describe and discuss each component of the theory of reasoned action, beginning with behavior.[43] Note that all the components of the model are defined in terms of a specific behavior, B.

Behaviors are specific actions directed at some target object (driving to the store, buying a swimsuit, looking for a lost Bic pen). Behaviors always occur in a situational context or environment and at a particular time (at home right now, in the grocery store this afternoon, or at an unspecified location in your town next week).[44] Marketers need to be clear about these aspects of the behavior of

Exhibit 6.6

The Theory of Reasoned Action

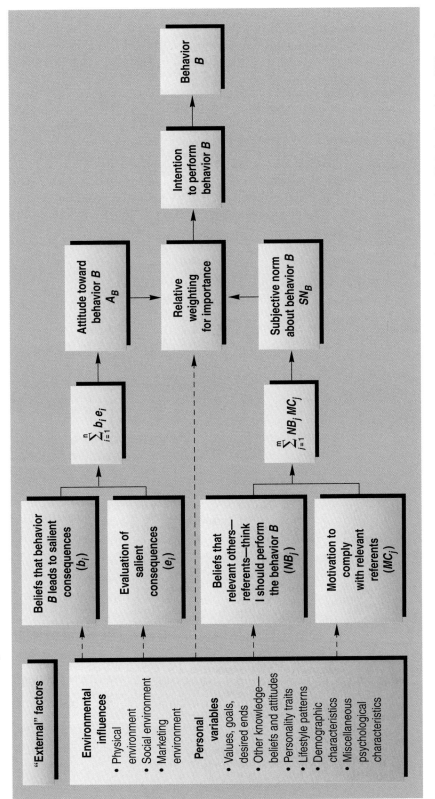

Source: Adapted from Martin Fishbein, "An Overview of the Attitude Construct," in *A Look Back, A Look Ahead*, ed. G. B. Hafer (Chicago: American Marketing Association, 1980), p. 8. Reprinted by permission of the American Marketing Association.

interest because the components of the theory of reasoned action must be defined and measured in terms of these specific features.

Basically a **behavioral intention (BI)** is a proposition connecting self and a future action: "I intend to go shopping this Saturday." One can think of an intention as a *plan* to engage in a specified behavior in order to reach a goal.[45] Behavioral intentions are created through a choice/decision process in which beliefs about two types of consequences—A_{act} and SN—are considered and integrated to evaluate alternative behaviors and select among them. Behavioral intentions vary in strength, which can be measured by having consumers rate the probability that they will perform the behavior of interest, shown as follows:

"All things considered, how likely are you to use newspaper coupons when buying groceries this week or next?"
Extremely Unlikely   1 2 3 4 5 6 7 8 9 10   Extremely Likely

As Exhibit 6.6 shows, the strengths and evaluations of a consumer's salient beliefs about the *functional* consequences of an action are combined $\left(\sum_{i=1}^{n} b_i e_i\right)$ to form an **attitude toward the behavior or action (A_{act})**. A_{act} reflects the consumer's overall evaluation of performing the behavior. Marketers measure the strengths and evaluations of the salient beliefs about the consequences of a behavior in the same way they measure beliefs about product attributes. Highlight 6.4 discusses these concepts.

A_{act} is quite different from A_O. Although both attitudes are based on an underlying set of salient beliefs, the beliefs are about somewhat different concepts. For instance, consider the following salient beliefs about "Chevrolet" (an object) and "buying a new Chevrolet this year" (a specific action involving the object):

Chevrolet (A_O)	Buying a New Chevrolet This Year (A_{act})
Moderately priced (+)	Gives me a mode of transportation (+)
Ordinary (−)	Will put me in financial difficulty (−)
Well built (+)	Will lead to high upkeep costs (−)
Dependable (+)	Will cost more now than later (−)
Easily serviced (+)	Will lead to high insurance rates (−)

Note that these salient beliefs have quite different evaluations. Thus, we should not be surprised to find that some consumers like Chevrolet in general (A_O) but have negative attitudes toward buying a Chevrolet this year (A_{act}).

It is possible for marketing strategies to have a differential impact on A_O and A_{act}. For instance, one study found that information about the store where a new product was sold affected consumers' attitudes toward purchasing the product (A_{act}) but did not influence their attitudes toward the product itself (A_O).[46] Marketers therefore must be careful to determine whether they are concerned with consumers' attitudes toward the object in general or some action regarding the object (such as buying it). Only attitudes toward behaviors are likely to be strongly related to specific behavioral intentions.

In addition, marketers must carefully identify the level of specificity most appropriate for the marketing problem. Attitudes at one level of specificity are not always consistently related to attitudes at other levels. For instance, Rick and Linda very

High light 6.4

Amazing Attitudes and Intentions toward Krispy Kreme Doughnuts

People begin lining up in the wee hours of the morning in darkness, some still in their pajamas. When dawn breaks and the ribbon is cut, they rush through the doors, screaming, "Krispy Kreme doughnuts, yowweeee!"

This scene has happened in cities all over North America and will happen again in the years to come. Why do some people have such intensely strong attitudes toward a simple and seemingly insignificant doughnut? Well, Krispy Kreme fans will tell you this is not an ordinary doughnut. The original glazed version is best served hot, and it tastes amazingly good (like a glazed fluffy cloud, according to one five-year-old).

Still, Krispy Kreme is relatively small, with 292 stores (in 2003) compared to 3,600 Dunkin' Donuts stores in the United States alone. Sales were $492 million in 2002, with earnings of $33 million and a very strong stock performance. Same-store sales are increasing, on average, by more than 11 percent per year, but there are some signs that sales in new stores are leveling off.

The brand Krispy Kreme is not as recognizable as Coke or McDonald's, but it is a very hot brand and enjoys highly positive attitudes. All types of people seem to have very positive attitudes toward Krispy Kreme (both A_O and A_{act}), as well as very strong behavioral intentions to buy and eat them.

Some analysts think attitudes toward Krispy Kreme are based on its association with the "American dream." From its beginnings as a regional icon in the South, Krispy Kreme went through some hard times before CEO Scott Livengood got control of the production processes. Another reason may be that even in hard times, with unemployment relatively high and military altercations around the globe, people still can enjoy the simple pleasure of an indulgent snack.

But there is more to it than that. Shrewd, if unconventional, marketing also has an influence. For instance, the company does very little advertising, relying instead on promotional strategies. For example, in 1996 Krispy Kreme once delivered several boxes of doughnuts to the *Today Show,* where they were eaten and commented on, garnering huge national exposure for the brand. Instead of spending huge sums on national advertising, the company gives away millions of doughnuts to charitable organizations that sell them for fund-raising projects. All of this creates exposure and goodwill that further enhances consumers' attitudes toward Krispy Kreme.

The big question is whether the highly positive attitudes and purchase intentions of many American consumers for Krispy Kreme can be maintained as new stores open. What do you think?

Source: Andy Serwer, "The Hole Story: How Krispy Kreme Became the Hottest Brand in America," *Fortune,* July 7, 2003, pp. 53–62. © 2003 Time Inc. All rights reserved. Reprinted by permission; website: **www.krispykreme.com**.

much like to go shopping (a general behavior) but avoid shopping on Saturdays when the malls are crowded (a more specific behavior).

The **subjective or social norm (SN)** component reflects consumers' perceptions of what other people want them to do. Consumers' salient *normative beliefs* (NB_j) regarding "doing what other people want me to do" and their *motivation to comply* with the expectations of these other people (MC_j) are combined $\left(\sum_{j=1}^{m} NB_j MC_j \right)$ to form *SN*. Along with A_{act}, *SN* affects consumers' behavioral intentions (BI).[47]

Measuring the strength of normative beliefs is similar to the belief-strength measures discussed earlier:

> **"Members of my family are in favor of my using coupons."**
> Extremely Unlikely   1 2 3 4 5 6 7 8 9 10   Extremely Likely

Motivation to comply is measured by asking consumers to rate how much they want to conform to other people's desires:

"Generally, how much do you want to do what your family wants you to?"
Not at All -3 -2 -1 0 $+1$ $+2$ $+3$ Very Much

The theory of reasoned action proposes that A_{act} and SN combine to affect behavioral intentions (BI) and that their relative influence varies from situation to situation. During the information integration process that creates BI, A_{act} and SN may be weighed differently (see Exhibit 6.6).[48] Some behaviors are primarily affected by the SN factor. For instance, intentions to wear a certain style of clothing to a party or to work are likely to be influenced more strongly by SN and the normative beliefs regarding "fitting in" than beliefs about the general consequences of wearing those clothes (A_{act}).[49] For other behaviors, normative influences are minimal, and consumers' intentions are determined largely by A_{act}. For instance, consumers' intentions to purchase Contac cold remedy are more likely to be affected by their salient beliefs about the functional consequences of using Contac and the resulting attitude toward buying it than by what other people expect them to do.

Marketing Implications

The situational context in which behavior occurs can have powerful influences on consumers' behavioral intentions. Consider a consumer named Brian, a 26-year-old assistant brand manager for General Foods. Last week, Brian had to decide whether to buy imported or domestic beer in two different situations. In the first situation, Brian was planning to drink a few beers at home over the weekend while watching sports on TV. In the other context, he was having a beer after work in a plush bar with a group of co-workers. The different sets of product-related and social beliefs activated in the two situations created different A_{act} and SN components. In the private at-home situation, Brian's product beliefs and A_{act} had the dominant effect on his intentions (he bought an inexpensive domestic beer). In the highly social bar situation, his normative beliefs and SN had the greater impact on his intentions (he bought an expensive imported beer).

To develop effective strategies, it is important to determine whether the A_{act} or SN component has the major influence on behavioral intentions (and thus on behavior). If the primary reason for a behavior (shopping, searching for information, buying a particular brand) is normative (you think others want you to), marketers need to emphasize that relevant normative influences such as friends, family, and co-workers approve of the behavior. Often this is done by portraying social influence situations in advertising. On the other hand, if intentions are influenced largely by A_{act} factors, the marketing strategy should attempt to create a set of salient beliefs about the positive consequences of the behavior, perhaps by demonstrating those outcomes in an advertisement. In sum, the theory of reasoned action identifies the types of cognitive and affective factors that underlie a consumer's intention to perform a specific behavior.

Although intentions determine most voluntary behaviors, measures of consumers' intentions may not be perfect indicators of the actual intentions that determine the behavior. In the following section, we discuss the problems of using intention measures to predict actual behaviors.

Intentions and
Behaviors

Predicting consumers' future behaviors, especially their purchase behavior (sales, to marketers), is a critical aspect of forecasting and marketing planning. According to the theory of reasoned action, predicting consumers' purchase behaviors is a matter of measuring their intentions to buy just before they make a purchase. In almost all cases, however, this would be impractical. When planning strategies, marketers need to make predictions of consumers' purchase and use behaviors weeks, months, or sometimes years in advance.

Unfortunately, predictions of specific behaviors based on intentions measured well before the behavior occurs usually are not very accurate. For instance, one survey found that only about 60 percent of people who intended to buy a car actually did so within a year.[50] And of those who claimed they did not intend to buy a car, 17 percent ended up buying one. Similar examples could be cited for other product categories (many with even less accuracy). This does not mean the theory of reasoned action is wrong in identifying intentions as an immediate influence on behavior. Rather, failures to predict the behavior of interest often lie with *how* and *when* intentions are measured.

To accurately predict behaviors, marketers should measure consumers' intentions at the same level of abstraction and specificity as the action, target, and time components of the behavior. Situation context also should be specified when it is important.

Exhibit 6.7 lists several factors that can weaken the relationship between measured behavioral intentions and the observed behaviors of interest. In situations where few of these factors operate, measured intentions should predict behavior quite well.

In a broad sense, *time* is the major factor that reduces the predictive accuracy of measured intentions. Consumers' intentions, like other cognitive factors, can and do change over time. The longer the intervening time period, the more unanticipated circumstances (such as exposure to the marketing strategies of competitive companies) can occur and change consumers' original purchase intentions. Thus, marketers must expect lower levels of predictive accuracy when intentions are measured long before the behavior occurs. However, unanticipated events can also occur during very short periods. An appliance manufacturer once asked consumers entering an appliance store what brand they intended to buy. Of those who specified a brand, only 20 percent walked out with it.[51] Apparently, events occurred in the store to change these consumers' beliefs, attitudes, intentions, and behavior.

Despite their less-than-perfect accuracy, measures of purchase intentions are often the best way to predict future purchase behavior. For instance, every three months United Airlines conducts a passenger survey measuring intentions to travel by air during the next three months. Obviously, many events in the ensuing time period can change consumers' beliefs, A_{act}, and SN about taking a personal or business trip by airline. To the extent that these unanticipated factors occur, the measured intentions will give less accurate predictions of future airline travel.

Finally, certain behaviors just cannot be accurately predicted from beliefs, attitudes, and intentions.[52] Obvious examples include nonvoluntary behaviors such as sneezing or getting sick. It also is difficult to predict purchase behaviors when the alternatives (brands) are very similar and the person has positive attitudes toward several of them. Finally, behaviors about which consumers have little knowledge and low levels of involvement are virtually impossible to predict because consumers have very few beliefs in memory on which to base attitudes and intentions. In such cases, consumers' measured intentions were probably created to answer the marketing researcher's question; such intentions are likely to be unstable and poor

Exhibit 6.7

Factors That Reduce or Weaken the Relationship between Measured Behavioral Intentions and Observed Behavior

Factor	Examples
Intervening time	As the time between measurement of intentions and observation of behavior increases, more factors can occur that act to modify or change the original intention so that it no longer corresponds to the observed behavior.
Different levels of specificity	The measured intention should be specified at the same level as the observed behavior, otherwise the relationship between them will be weakened. Suppose we measured Judy's intentions to wear jeans to class (in general). But we observed her behavior on a day when she made a class presentation and didn't think jeans were appropriate in that specific situation.
Unforeseen environmental event	Sam fully intended to buy Frito's chips this afternoon, but the store was sold out. Sam could not carry out the original intention and had to form a new intention on the spot to buy Ripple chips.
Unforeseen situational context	Sometimes the situational context the consumer had in mind when the intentions were measured was different from the situation at the time of behavior. In general, Peter has a negative intention to buy Andre champagne. However, when he had to prepare a holiday punch calling for eight bottles of champagne, Peter formed a positive intention to buy the inexpensive Andre brand.
Degree of voluntary control	Some behaviors are not under complete volitional control. Thus, intentions may not predict the observed behavior very accurately. For instance, Becky intended to go shopping on Saturday when she hoped to be recovered from a bout with the flu, but she was still sick and couldn't go.
Stability of intentions	Some intentions are quite stable. They are based on a well-developed structure of salient beliefs for A_{act} and *SN*. Other intentions are not stable, as they are founded on only a few weakly held beliefs that may be easily changed.
New information	Consumers may receive new information about the salient consequences of their behavior, which leads to changes in their beliefs and attitudes toward the act and/or in the subjective norm. These changes, in turn, change the intention. The original intention is no longer relevant to the behavior and does not predict the eventual behavior accurately.

predictors of eventual, actual behavior. In sum, before relying on measures of attitude and intentions to predict future behavior, marketers need to determine whether consumers can be expected to have well-formed beliefs, attitudes, and intentions toward those behaviors.

Back To...

The Gap

The Gap example illustrates how consumer attitudes develop and change over time. Understanding these trends can help marketers develop and evaluate marketing strategies. Measures of consumers' beliefs and attitudes can also be used to gauge the success of marketing strategies in solving a problem.

Measures of A_O (attitudes toward The Gap) and the related salient beliefs can identify problem areas needing attention. For instance, the negative consumer attitudes and the underlying beliefs, especially about product "coolness" and clothing styles, could suggest actions the company might take to enhance the favorability of consumers' attitudes toward Gap clothes.

For The Gap, it would also be important to understand the *SN* (subjective norm) component in the theory of reasoned action. The *SN* factor includes people's feelings about the coolness of Gap fashions. If the *SN* component becomes increasingly negative, The Gap should take remedial action. It is important to maintain strong behavioral intentions to shop at The Gap. Thus, the company should measure consumers' A_{act} and *SN* concerning shopping at The Gap, as well as their behavioral intentions to do so. ❖

Summary

We began this chapter by defining attitude as a consumer's overall evaluation of an object. We discussed how attitude objects vary in levels of abstraction and specificity. We then discussed consumers' attitudes toward objects, A_O, and described Fishbein's multiattribute model of how salient beliefs create A_O. We also discussed the theory of reasoned action, which identifies consumers' attitudes toward performing behaviors (A_{act}) and social influences (*SN*) as the basis for behavioral intentions (*BI*). Finally, we considered the problems of using measures of behavioral intentions to predict actual behaviors. Throughout, we discussed implications for marketers.

In this chapter, we identified consumers' activated knowledge, in the form of beliefs, as the basic factor underlying their attitudes, subjective norms, and intentions—and ultimately their behaviors. Moreover, we showed that these activated salient beliefs and the resulting attitudes and intentions are sensitive to situational factors in the environment, including marketing strategies. This provides another example of how cognition, environment, and behavior interact in a continuous, reciprocal process to create new behaviors, new cognitions (beliefs, attitudes, and intentions), and new environments.

Key Terms and Concepts

accessibility **136**
attitude **135**
attitude-change strategies **148**
attitudes toward objects (A_O) **141**
attitude toward the behavior
   or action (A_{act}) **154**
behavioral intention (BI) **154**
behaviors **152**
belief evaluation (e_i) **145**

belief strength (b_i) **144**
brand equity **137**
evaluation **135**
integration process **136**
multiattribute attitude models **143**
salient beliefs **141**
subjective or social norm (SN) **155**
theory of reasoned action **152**

Review and Discussion Questions

1. Define *attitude* and describe the two main ways consumers can acquire attitudes.
2. How do salient beliefs differ from other beliefs? How can marketers attempt to influence belief salience?
3. The Gap has been doing business for over 30 years. Over this time, with its stores, clothing products, and advertising, The Gap has built considerable brand equity. Discuss the types of brand equity The Gap has built among various consumer segments. Is The Gap vulnerable to losing this equity? What can The Gap do to protect its equity?
4. Consider a product category in which you make regular purchases (such as toothpaste or shampoo). How have your belief strengths and evaluations and brand attitudes changed over time? What factors or events contributed to those changes?
5. Using a product as an example, describe the key differences between A_O and A_{act}. Under what circumstances would marketers be more interested in each type of attitude?
6. Visit The Gap website at **www.gap.com**, and examine either the virtual style section or the current advertising section. Discuss the types of beliefs and attitudes you think this information would create. What effects might these beliefs and attitudes have on consumers' behavioral intentions? (Use the theory of reasoned action to guide your thinking and your answer.)
7. Use the example of The Gap to distinguish between the multiattribute attitude model and the theory of reasoned action. How could each model contribute to the development of a more effective marketing strategy for The Gap?
8. Discuss the problems in measuring behavioral intentions to (*a*) buy a new car, (*b*) buy a soda from a vending machine, and (*c*) save $250 per month toward the eventual purchase of a house. What factors could occur in each situation to make the measured intentions poor predictors of actual behavior?
9. How could marketers improve their predictions of behaviors in the situations described in question 8? Consider improvements in measurements, as well as alternative research or forecasting techniques.
10. Negative attitudes present a special challenge for marketing strategy. Consider how what you know about attitudes and intentions could help you address consumers who have a brand relationship described as "Don't like our brand; buy a competitor's brand."

Marketing Strategy in Action

Coca-Cola

Consumer attitudes are very Important to Coca-Cola, the world's largest marketer of soft drinks (2002 sales of $18 billion cases worldwide). Coca-Cola is perhaps the best-known brand name in the world. According to Warren Buffett, the largest holder of Coca-Cola stock, "This is fundamentally the best large business in the world. [The product] sells for a moderate price. It's universally liked. The per capita consumption goes up almost every year in every country. There is not another product like it."

Coca-Cola receives about 80 percent of its operating income ($8.6 billion in 1992) from overseas markets. Once a big American company with a substantial foreign market, Coca-Cola now is a huge international company with a substantial market in the United States. What are consumers' attitudes toward Coke in foreign markets? Consumers' attitudes toward the Coke brand and Coca-Cola company tend to be most favorable in countries whose culture differs considerably from America's. In many of these countries—especially those in the former communist world—Coke is an icon of American culture and a symbol of a market economy. For instance, Polish consumers' attitudes toward Coca-Cola were so positive that a crowd gathered and spontaneously broke into applause when the first Coke delivery truck came down the street. Brand attitudes like these are why Coca-Cola held a 45 percent share of the world market for soft drinks in 1992. (Although Coke and Pepsi are closely matched in the United States, Coke outsells Pepsi by a 4-to-1 margin elsewhere in the world.) Coca-Cola's goal was to achieve a 50 percent market share.

It seems consumers everywhere like the product (cola soft drinks) and the Coca-Cola brand. And those positive brand attitudes seem to influence consumers' behavior. In the United States, where attitudes toward the Coke brand are positive, the per capita consumption of Coke products in the early 1990s was 296. This means, on average, every person in the United States drank 296 8-ounce servings of Coca-Cola products per year! Could this level of consumption go even higher? Elsewhere around the world, there was substantial room for growth. In 1992, Austria had a per capita consumption of 150 Coke servings per year, compared to 83 in Hungary and only 8 in Romania. Consumption in Iceland was inexplicably high at 397 servings, and consumption was even higher in American Samoa at 500 servings per year.

Over the past 20 or so years, Coca-Cola has had many occasions to pay special attention to the attitudes of U.S. consumers. In July 1982, Coca-Cola did the unthinkable (at that time) and introduced a new brand called Diet Coke. Several executives feared "diluting" the Coca-Cola brand name and perhaps reducing favorable consumer attitudes toward the flagship brand. This did not occur, however. Diet Coke became one of the most successful new products of the 1980s.

By 1984 it had displaced 7UP to become the third most popular soft drink (after Coca-Cola and Pepsi). Thereafter the company rapidly introduced decaffeinated versions of Coca-Cola, Diet Coke, and Tab. But these successes were overshadowed by highly controversial marketing decision.

In the spring of 1985, chairman Roberto Goizueta announced a new brand with an improved taste, to be called "Coke." He also reported that the original Coca-Cola brand would be retired permanently. The original formula with its secret ingredient (Merchandise 7X) was to be locked in a bank vault in Atlanta, never to be used again. New Coke was to permanently replace the 99-year-old Coca-Cola brand. Goizueta called the new product the most significant soft-drink development in the company's history. Americans got their first taste of the new Coke in late April 1985. By July, the company reversed its earlier decision and announced that the original brand (and formula) was coming back under the brand name Coca-Cola Classic. New Coke was one of the most embarrassing new-product launches ever because the company failed to understand consumers' strong positive attitudes toward the original Coca-Cola brand.

The positive attitudes and beliefs that kept Coca-Cola consumers buying the brand over and over again are the basis of brand loyalty. Brand loyalty usually begins to develop when consumers acquire positive attitudes based on beliefs about desirable product attributes and functional benefits (Coca-Cola is sweet, carbonated, or refreshing). After the brand has been around for awhile, it can accumulate "extra" meanings through consumers' experiences in consuming the product. Some of these meanings can be highly emotional and self-relevant if the brand becomes associated with consumers' lifestyles and self-images.

In the case of Coca-Cola, many brand-loyal users associated the brand with fond memories of days gone by. When the company announced that it was replacing the original Coca-Cola brand, these consumers reacted as if they had lost an old friend. They inundated company headquarters with protests. One group in Seattle threatened to sue the company. Then, when June sales of new Coke didn't pick up, the company hastily brought back the original brand, renamed Coca-Cola Classic.

The decision to retire the old Coca-Cola formula had been very carefully researched. Managers thought they had covered every angle, especially taste characteristics. Coca-Cola had spent more than $4 million on many different taste tests of the new flavor, involving 200,000 consumers in some 25 cities. These tests revealed that more people preferred the new, sweeter flavor to the old (about 55 percent to 45 percent). But this research didn't measure everything. "All the time and money and skill poured into consumer research on the new

Coca-Cola could not measure or reveal the deep and abiding emotional attachment to original Coca-Cola," Donald Keough, president of Coca-Cola, said later. A company spokesperson put it this way: "We had taken away more than the product Coca-Cola. We had taken away a little part of them and their past. They said, 'You have no right to do that. Bring it back.' " So Coca-Cola did.

In 1994, Coke Classic was the leading brand in the United States with 20.4 percent market share (by volume); Pepsi had 17.8 percent; and New Coke, now called Coke II, had a tiny 0.1 percent. But Coca-Cola learned several valuable lessons from the New Coke fiasco, including the amount of equity associated with the Coke name.

The highly positive meanings and feelings many consumers have for Coca-Cola constitute its "brand equity." Brand equity concerns the meanings that attract consumers to the brand and underlie positive attitudes toward it. The 1985 fiasco with New Coke clearly showed that Coca-Cola has a powerful brand equity with its customers. Managers at Coca-Cola have used this equity to develop new brands, most of which have been successful. Most of these new brands are "line extensions," minor variations of the original brand. For instance, the Coca-Cola section of a supermarket shelf might include Coca-Cola Classic, Caffeine-Free Coca-Cola Classic, Diet Coke, Caffeine-Free Diet Coke, Cherry, Lemon, and Vanilla Coke, and others. In 1994 Coca-Cola managers introduced several flavor extensions of the Minute Maid orange soda brand along with a clear version of Tab. Managers intended these line extensions to leverage the brand equity in the Minute Maid and Tab brands and to defend against competitive new beverages such as Clearly Canadian and Snapple.

After this flurry of brand extensions, the broad strategy at Coca-Cola was to differentiate the entire product line without tainting the Coke icon or diminishing Coke's equity. Coca-Cola recognized a strong demand for different flavors of soft drinks and related beverages. In the decade from 1984 to 1994, teas and juices gained share, whereas regular and diet colas declined 6 percentage points, from approximately 64 percent in 1984 to about 58 percent in 1994. CEO Roberto Goizueta (now deceased) stated in the 1995 Coca-Cola annual report, "If the three keys to selling real estate are location, location, location, the three keys to selling consumer products are differentiation, differentiation, differentiation. Every marketing victory we have won has been the result of our total commitment to making our brands clearly distinctive from every other item on the grocery shelf." So instead of continuing to slap the Coke label on new products, the company introduced products with distinct brand names such as

Fruitopia, named a top 10 new product in its first year, and Surge, a soft drink with a slightly higher caffeine content.

In the 1990s, Coca-Cola managed brand equity and consumer attitudes with a variety of strategies. In 1995 it *acquired brand equity* by purchasing the Barq brand of root beer. Coca-Cola attempted to *create brand equity* through new-product development by launching a flotilla of new flavors for its Fruitopia and Nestea brands. It tried to *enhance brand equity* for Sprite by using more dynamic graphics on the package. Coca-Cola attempted to *borrow brand equity* through its sponsorship of the 1996 Summer Olympics, held in Atlanta (location of world headquarters). Finally, and most significantly, Coca-Cola attempted to *reactivate brand equity* by introducing new packages for Coke Classic that revived the vintage contour bottle. According to Goizueta, introducing the contour bottle throughout the world was the single most effective differentiation effort in the soft-drink industry for years.

Discussion Questions

1. Discuss the attitudes and related beliefs toward Coca-Cola of intensely brand-loyal consumers (perhaps like those who were upset by the New Coke in 1985). How might their attitudes and beliefs differ from those of less involved, less loyal consumers? What marketing implications would these differences have?

2. Do you think it possible for consumers to be loyal to more than one brand of soft drink? What about more than one brand of cola? Discuss the pros and cons of having several brands in a product category (as do Coca-Cola and Pepsi in the cola category). Compare the strategy of line extension to that of creating completely distinct brands for these products. What factors should marketers consider in making this important decision?

3. Many marketers made a distinction between customers and consumers. For instance, Coca-Cola sells cola syrup directly to its customers, the operators of bottling plants. The bottlers sell bottled Coke products to retailers, vending machine operators, restaurants, airlines, and so forth. Those organizations, in turn, sell Coca-Cola products to individual consumers who drink it. Discuss how the salient beliefs about Coke products might differ for customers and consumers. How might their attitudes toward Coke differ? Who should Coca-Cola pay more attention to—its customers or the consumer? Why?

4. Discuss Coca-Cola's various strategies for managing brand equity of its many products. For instance, what are the pros and cons of borrowing versus creating brand equity. Analyze Coke's attempt to "revive" brand equity by reintroducing the contour bottle around the world.

Sources: John Huey, "The World's Best Brand," *Fortune,* May 31, 1993, pp. 44–54; Anne B. Fisher, "Coke's Brand-Loyalty Lesson," *Fortune,* August, 5, 1985, pp. 44–46; Thomas Moore, "He Put the Kick Back into Coke," *Fortune,* October 26, 1987, pp. 46–56; Seth Lublove, "We Have a Big Pond to Play In," *Forbes,* September 13, 1993, pp. 216–224; Andrew Wallenstein, "Coca-Cola's Sweet Return to Glory Days," *Advertising Age,* April 17, 1995, p. 6. Copyright, Crain Communications, Inc., 1995; **www.cocacola.com**.

Consumer Decision Making

Buying a Used Car

Megan is a sophomore in college and has been working part-time at a local restaurant trying to earn enough money to buy a car. About a year ago her old 1985 Toyota, which she had been driving since high school, finally died. This last year was pretty tough for her—taking the bus, walking, relying on friends for rides. But last Saturday was Megan's lucky day! Her dad called that morning and said that if she wanted to buy a car, he was willing to help with the payments.

Megan was ecstatic. She immediately had visions of herself behind the wheel of that new Porsche Boxster she had seen in a magazine. But, alas, neither she nor her dad was made of money. Megan's resources were rather limited, and her dad was willing to contribute only about $150 toward the monthly payments, so she decided she would have to settle for something a little less spectacular. Thus, her search was on for a good, reliable used car.

Initially Megan wanted to purchase a car that was only one or two years old with low mileage. She called a couple of dealers Saturday afternoon to get an idea of prices. To her chagrin, most of those newer-model used cars were out of her price range. So she decided she would be content with a car that was four or five years old, assuming it was in good shape. First, though, she would check with her boyfriend, Dave.

Dave wasn't very enthusiastic. In his experience, most cars began needing more frequent repairs after four or five years. He thought Megan would be better off splurging on a newer-model car. Even though her payments might be higher, she would save herself time, money, and aggravation in the long run. Although Megan admitted Dave might have a point, she knew what her bank account looked like. She didn't want to have to endure the endless drudgery of waiting tables to be able to make the payments. Plus, her dad had said he preferred that she pay the car off in three years, so she was hesitant to stretch the payments out for a long period just to keep the monthly charges down. So Megan developed a complex plan to take all these factors into consideration. She would agree to payments of $300 per month for three years for any car less than three years old and would pay no more than $250 per month for three years for any car three years of age or older. If she couldn't find a good car that matched any of these requirements, she would consider stretching the payments out to four years, but no longer.

On Sunday morning, Megan eagerly picked up a copy of the local newspaper and began scanning the classifieds. Four cars that she really liked were probably within her price range. So, on Monday, she went with Dave to check them out. The first car they looked at was a privately owned, fire engine red Ford Mustang. It was four years old but had only 50,000 miles and looked beautiful. Moreover, the owner's asking price was very reasonable. But she and Dave noticed a few problems when they drove it. It hesitated a couple of times and made a strange knocking sound when going uphill. And what was that smell? Apparently, the owner had just moved from New York City, where he had driven the car around Manhattan every day—pretty tough conditions for a car. Megan regretfully decided that the Mustang wasn't for her.

On the way to the local Pontiac dealership to check out the second car, a Grand Am, Dave and Megan passed a billboard advertising a national used-car megastore. There was a franchise only about an hour away, so they would keep it in mind. At any rate, disappointment was in store at the Pontiac dealership. The Grand Am Megan coveted had been sold earlier that morning. But the salesperson showed her a one-year-old Sunfire instead. Dave hesitated. He informed Megan

that a friend of his just took her Sunfire into the shop for some engine work. To Megan, though, this one appeared perfect. It ran well, and the payments met her criteria—about $300 a month for three years. But there was something about this salesperson that she didn't trust. And Dave's story about his friend's car was a bit alarming. Megan loved the Sunfire, but she took the salesperson's card and said she would get back to him in a day or two.

The next day, Dave drove Megan to the big used-car franchise in a neighboring town. She had spoken with a friend Monday night who told her that this particular dealership had a good reputation and a huge selection and that people would come in from a couple of hours away just to see if they could find a deal there. Dave and Megan were looking around and spotted a five-year-old Chevrolet Malibu. The car had a good history and the payments were within range, but Megan didn't like the way the car looked. She found it kind of big and boxy—it looked like something her dad would drive. No, that wouldn't do. But also on the lot was a one-year-old Chevy Cavalier. It also test-drove well and looked sportier than the Malibu. If she stretched out the payments over four years, she would pay only $280 a month—well within her range. But Dave said he knew of a Chevy dealer back at school who might have a similar car at a better price. Maybe she wouldn't have to extend the payments to four years. So, again, Megan took the salesperson's card and told her that she'd be in touch.

On Wednesday, Dave and Megan went to the dealer Dave was telling her about. Unfortunately, the Cavaliers in stock were all several years old and didn't look or run as well as the one they had seen on Tuesday. However, the dealer had a four-year-old Dodge Avenger in stock. Payments were $270 a month over three years—a little more than Megan initially would have wanted to pay for a four-year-old car. However, the car had very few miles, seemed mechanically sound, and was bright purple—her favorite color. Megan paused a few moments to consider her decision. She hadn't even looked at all the cars on her list, so maybe she wasn't being thorough enough. But, for the price, she thought this Avenger was a steal. Plus, she had an important exam coming up later in the week and didn't want to waste any more time visiting dealerships. So she signed the papers and excitedly drove off the lot, confident she had made a wise decision. (As it turns out, Megan's dad was so impressed with her car-buying savvy that he agreed to chip in a few more dollars than expected to help cover the payments!)

Source: Inspired by Barbara Hayes-Roth, "Opportunities in Consumer Behavior," in *Advances in Consumer Research,* vol. 9, ed. Andrew A. Mitchell (Ann Arbor, MI: Association for Consumer Research, 1982) pp. 132–135. Reprinted with permission.

This example describes a complex purchase process that involves making several decisions. A **decision** involves a choice "between two or more alternative actions [or behaviors]."[1] *Decisions always require choices between different behaviors.* For instance, after examining the products in a vending machine, Joe chooses a Snickers candy bar instead of a package of Reese's Pieces. His choice was between the alternative actions of *buying Snickers* versus *buying Reese's Pieces.* Jill is trying to decide whether to see a particular movie. Her choice is really between the set of behaviors involved in *attending the movie* versus the behaviors involved in *staying home* (or going bowling, or whatever behavioral alternatives she was considering). In sum, even though marketers often refer to choices between objects (products, brands, stores), consumers actually choose between alternative *behaviors* concerning those objects (What should I *do*?).

Marketers are particularly interested in consumers' *purchase behaviors,* especially their choices of which brands to buy. Given the marketing orientation of this text, we emphasize consumers' purchase choices (Should I buy Levi's or Wrangler jeans?). It must be recognized, however, that consumers also make many decisions about nonpurchase behaviors. Sometimes these nonpurchase choices can influence consumers' purchase decisions (deciding to go for a walk or watch TV may expose consumers to marketing information about products). Sometimes these other behaviors are the targets of marketing strategies: "Come down to our store this afternoon for free coffee and doughnuts." Our analyses of purchase decisions can be generalized to these nonpurchase choices.

As shown in our model of consumer decision making in Exhibit 7.1, all aspects of affect and cognition are involved in consumer decision making, including knowledge, meanings, and beliefs activated from memory and attention and comprehension processes involved in interpreting new information in the environment.[2] The key process in **consumer decision making,** however, is the *integration process* by which knowledge is combined to *evaluate* two or more alternative behaviors and *select* one.[3] The outcome of this integration process is a **choice,** represented cognitively as a *behavioral intention (BI).* As you learned in the previous chapter, a

Exhibit 7.1

A Cognitive Processing Model of Consumer Decision Making

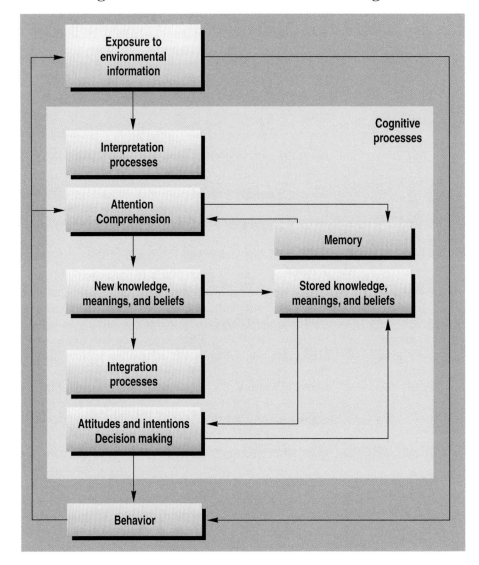

behavioral intention is a *plan* (sometimes called a *decision plan*) to engage in one or more behaviors.

We assume all voluntary behaviors are based on the intentions produced when consumers consciously choose from among alternative actions. Thus, decision-making processes occur even for the impulsive purchases that seem to underlie fads (see Highlight 7.1). This does not mean, however, that a conscious decision-making process necessarily occurs each time a purchase behavior is performed.[4] Some voluntary behaviors become habitual. They are based on intentions stored in memory that were formed by a past decision-making process. When activated, these

Highlight 7.1

Decision-Making Processes in Fads

Why do so many people suddenly get their eyebrows pierced, buy Pokemon cards, or wear super-baggy jeans? Understanding how fads start and end requires an understanding of the apparently "irrational" consumer decision making that underlies fad behavior.

Economists are bothered by fads given their assumption that consumer behavior is basically rational. The rationality is hard to reconcile with the herd psychology that drives fads in clothing, favored companies in the stock market, or the popularity of some recording artists (Britney Spears, 'N Sync).

Arguably the hottest fad of 2000 was the scooter. By no means are scooters new; they have been around since 1816. From the 1920s through the 1940s, they were available by mail order for a few dollars apiece. A lot of Depression-era kids made their own scooters by nailing a pair of roller skates to a milk crate. But the scooters of 2000 were much different, some reaching speeds of almost 70 miles per hour and selling for more than $200 apiece. The omnipresent Razor Scooter, designed in Germany around 1993, languished in obscurity for years until a Taiwanese company began to manufacture it. Suddenly, in 1999, sales of the Razor Scooter exploded in Japan. The craze quickly spread across the Pacific Ocean, to Australia and Hawaii, then on to California. In 1999, U.S. scooter sales were negligible. But from January through July 2000, Americans snapped up 600,000 scooters at a total price tag of $20 million, with sales nearly doubling each month beginning in March.

A theory of fads, proposed in 1992, suggests that people tend to imitate the actions of others when forced to make choices based on limited information about what is best, or what is appropriate. (This is called "vicarious learning" and is discussed in detail in Chapter 9.) These uncertain situations may spawn a "chain reaction" or "cascade of imitation" among consumers, which fuels the fad. Many purchase situations do involve a lot of uncertainty, such as new styles of clothing, music, furniture, or automobiles. Consumers seem to decide whether to buy such products by integrating their knowledge about the consequences of certain choice alternatives (which may be minimal) with their observations of what other consumers are choosing. Even if some consumers feel like saying *no* to a new product, a few *yes* responses by others may be enough to override their personal feelings and induce them to purchase and use the product. In turn, their *yes* behaviors can influence others to do the same, thus contributing to the cascade of imitation that fuels a fad.

Fads are very difficult to predict, but they can create major marketing opportunities for a company. Consider the popularity of sport utility vehicles among suburban car buyers, which began as a fad and turned into a trend. Most fads tend to be fragile, however. If a number of people begin to say *no*, the fad may end rather quickly (consider the relatively short-lived comebacks of cigar smoking and disco music). What fads are currently growing (or dying) in your area?

Sources: Cynthia Billhartz, "Scooters Are a Hoot," *St. Louis Post-Dispatch,* September 26, 2000, p. F1. Reprinted with permission of the St. Louis Post-Dispatch, copyright 2000; David Stipp, "Why People Often Act Like Sheep: The Theory of Fads," *Fortune,* October 14, 1996, pp. 49, 52.

previously formed intentions or decision plans automatically influence behavior; additional decision-making processes may not be necessary. Finally, some behaviors are not voluntary and are affected largely by environmental factors. For instance, product displays and aisle placements dictate how consumers move through stores. Decision making is not relevant in such cases.

In this chapter, we view consumer decision making as a problem-solving process. We begin with a general discussion of this perspective. Then we identify and describe the key elements in a problem-solving approach. Next, we discuss the problem-solving processes involved in purchase decisions. We identify three levels of problem-solving effort and describe several influences on problem-solving activities. We conclude by identifying several implications of consumer problem solving for marketing strategy.

Decision Making as Problem Solving

In treating consumer decision making as problem solving, we focus on consumers' goals (desired consequences or values in a means–end chain) that they seek to achieve or satisfy. A consumer perceives a "problem" because the desired consequences have not been attained (I am hungry. I need a reliable car. I want to lose weight.). Consumers make decisions about which behaviors to perform to achieve their goals and thus "solve the problem." In this sense, then, *consumer decision making is a goal-directed, problem-solving process.*

As the opening example illustrates, consumer problem solving is actually a continuous stream of interactions among environmental factors, cognitive and affective processes, and behavioral actions. Researchers can divide this stream into separate stages and subprocesses to simplify analysis and facilitate understanding. Exhibit 7.2 presents one such model of **problem solving** that identifies five basic stages or subprocesses. The first stage involves *problem recognition*. In the opening example, Megan's loss of her old car made her aware of a problem: She needed a new set of wheels. The next stage of the problem-solving process involves *searching for alternative solutions*.[5] (Megan called and visited dealers, talked to salespeople, and discussed the purchase with her boyfriend, Dave.) At the next stage, *alternatives are evaluated* and the most desirable action is *chosen*. (Megan evaluated cars as she found them during her search. In the end, she decided—formed a behavioral intention—to buy the Dodge Avenger.) In the next stage, *purchase*, the choice/intention is carried out. (Megan signed papers, made a down payment, and drove her car away.) Finally, the purchased product is *used*, and the consumer may *reevaluate* the wisdom of the decision. (Apparently Megan was quite satisfied with the car and with her problem-solving process, and so was her dad.)

In summary, this basic model indentifies several important activities involved in problem solving, beginning with problem recognition, which activates the initial motivation to engage in problem solving. Other activities include searching for information relevant to the problem, evaluating alternative actions, and choosing an action.

However, for several reasons, the generic model often provides an imperfect account of actual problem-solving processes such as those in the opening example. One reason is that *actual consumer problem solving seldom proceeds in a linear sequence* as portrayed in the generic model. For instance, Megan evaluated alternative cars as soon as she found them; she did not wait until she found all the alternatives.

Second, as emphasized in our Wheel of Consumer Analysis (refer to Exhibit 2.3 on page 28), *actual problem-solving processes involve multiple, continuous interactions among consumers' cognitive processes, their behaviors, and aspects of the physical and social environments.*[6] Such interactions occurred throughout Megan's problem-solving process. For instance, her cognitions (beliefs) changed as a function of environmental information she encountered, as when her boyfriend said the Sunfire had problems. The generic model does not easily handle these complex interactions.

Third, *most problem-solving processes actually involve multiple problems and multiple decisions.* Consider the number of separate decisions Megan made during the several days of her problem-solving process: Should I telephone the car dealers? Which ones? Should I drive to the car megastore? When should I go? Should I get

Exhibit 7.2

A Generic Model of Consumer Problem Solving

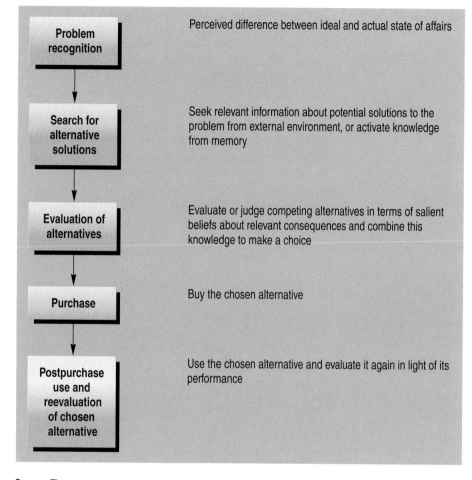

Problem recognition	Perceived difference between ideal and actual state of affairs
Search for alternative solutions	Seek relevant information about potential solutions to the problem from external environment, or activate knowledge from memory
Evaluation of alternatives	Evaluate or judge competing alternatives in terms of salient beliefs about relevant consequences and combine this knowledge to make a choice
Purchase	Buy the chosen alternative
Postpurchase use and reevaluation of chosen alternative	Use the chosen alternative and evaluate it again in light of its performance

Source: There are many sources for this general model. See, for example, James Engel, Roger D. Blackwell, and Paul W. Miniard, *Consumer Behavior,* 8th ed. (Hinsdale, IL: Dryden Press, 1995).

the Avenger? Actual problem-solving processes usually involve several choices that produce multiple behavioral intentions. Each intention is a step in an overall decision plan. The decision plan produces a sequence of purposive behaviors that consumers perform to achieve their desired goals (go to the car dealer, take a test drive, discuss things with Dave). The generic model implies that consumer problem solving involves a single decision, typically brand purchase choice, but this is seldom the case in reality.

Our cognitive processing model of consumer decision making, shown in Exhibit 7.1, is flexible enough to account for the nonlinear, continuous flow of interactions among behaviors, environments, and cognitions, and for the multiple decisions that occur in actual consumer problem-solving episodes. Moreover, it can help us understand how consumers process information during the important problem-solving stages of problem recognition, search for information, and evaluation of alternatives. Before using this model to analyze actual consumer decisions, however, we must discuss several elements of problem solving.

Elements of
Problem Solving

In this section, we describe three basic elements of problem solving: problem representation, integration processes, and decision plans. Later we discuss how these elements operate in consumer decision making.

Problem Representation

When faced with a choice, consumers must interpret or represent various aspects of the decision problem. This **problem representation** may include (1) an end goal, (2) a set of subgoals organized into a goal hierarchy, (3) relevant product knowledge, and (4) a set of simple rules or heuristics by which consumers search for, evaluate, and integrate this knowledge to make a choice. A problem representation serves as a *decision frame*, a perspective or frame of reference through which the decision maker views the problem and the alternatives to be evaluated.[7]

Often consumers' initial problem representations are not clear or well developed (Megan's wasn't). Nor are they fixed. In fact, the components of a problem representation often change during the decision-making process, as in the opening example. Marketers sometimes try to influence how consumers represent or frame a purchase choice.[8] For instance, consumers might be portrayed in advertisements as representing and then trying to solve a purchase problem in a particular way. Salespeople also try to influence consumers' problem representations by suggesting end goals (buy life insurance to assure your children's college education), imparting product knowledge (this special flash eliminates red eyes in the pictures), or suggesting choice rules (the more expensive coat is of higher quality).

The basic consequences, needs, or values that consumers want to achieve or satisfy are called **end goals.** They provide the focus for the entire problem-solving process. Some end goals represent more concrete, tangible consequences; other end goals are more abstract. For instance, a purchase decision to replace a bulb for a flashlight probably involves the simple end goal of obtaining a bulb that lights up—a simple functional consequence. Other product choices involve more abstract end goals such as desired psychosocial consequences of a product (a consumer wants to serve a wine that conveys her good taste to her guest). Finally, end goals such as instrumental and terminal values are even more abstract and general (a consumer chooses a car that makes him feel powerful or enhances his self-esteem). End goals also vary in evaluation. Some consumer decisions are oriented toward positive, desirable end goals, while others are focused on negative end goals—aversive consequences the consumer wishes to avoid.

This ad links the product/service to avoid a negative end goal.
Courtesy of WorldWide™
Sport Nutrition

Some end goals (e.g., being happy) are so general that consumers cannot act on them directly. For instance, most consumers cannot specify the decision plan of specific actions that will yield the best restaurant or avoid a "lemon" of a car. When consumers try to solve problems involving abstract end goals, they break down the general goal into several more specific subgoals. The end goal and its subgoals form a **goal hierarchy.** Forming a goal hierarchy is analogous to decomposing a complex problem into a series of simpler subproblems, each of which is dealt with separately. For most people, buying a new car requires at least one trip to a showroom, which generates the subproblems of which dealer(s) to visit and when to go shopping. Usually the consumer can generate a solution to the overall problem by solving the simpler subproblems in order.

Consumers' **relevant knowledge** in memory about the choice domain is an important element in problem solving.[9] Some knowledge may be acquired by interpreting information encountered in the environment during the problem-solving process. For instance, in the opening example, Megan learned a lot about cars, car dealers, and price ranges for cars. Other relevant knowledge may be activated from memory for use in integration processes.[10] The relevance of knowledge is determined by its means–end linkages to the currently active end goal. Parts of the activated knowledge may be combined in the integration processes by which consumers evaluate alternative behaviors (form A_{act}) and choose among them (form *BI*). Two types of knowledge are particularly important in problem solving: choice alternatives and choice criteria.

Choice Alternatives   **Choice alternatives** are the alternative behaviors that consumers consider in the problem-solving process. For purchase decisions, the choice alternatives are the different product classes, product forms, brands, or models the consumer considers buying. For other types of decisions, the choice alternatives may be different stores to visit, times of the day or week to go shopping, or methods of payment (cash, check, or credit card). Given their limited time, energy, and cognitive capacity, consumers seldom consider every possible choice alternative. Usually only a subset of all possible alternatives, called the **consideration set,** is evaluated.

Exhibit 7.3 illustrates how a manageable consideration set of brands can be constructed during the problem-solving process.[11] Some brands in the consideration set may be activated directly from memory; this group is called the *evoked set*.[12] For highly familiar decisions, consumers may not consider any brands beyond those in the evoked set. If consumers are confident they already know the important choice alternatives, they are not likely to search for additional ones. In other decisions, choice alternatives may be found through intentional search activities such as reading *Consumer Reports,* talking to knowledgeable friends, or finding brands while shopping.[13] Finally, consumers may learn of still other choice alternatives through accidental exposure to information in the environment, such as overhearing a conversation about a new brand, a new store or a sale. In the opening case, Megan learned about the car mega-dealer from a billboard ad, essentially by accident. However, the choice alternatives are generated, consumers form a consideration set of possible purchase options to be evaluated in the decision-making process.

To be successful, a brand must be included in the consideration sets of at least some consumers. For example, Kali Klena, marketing manager at Kellogg, flew from Milwaukee to Chicago even though a one-way flight cost between $34 and $186 and could take as long as three hours, including check-in time and transportation to and from the airports. Another choice alternative, the Amtrak train, took half that

Exhibit 7.3

Forming a Consideration Set of Brand Choice Alternatives

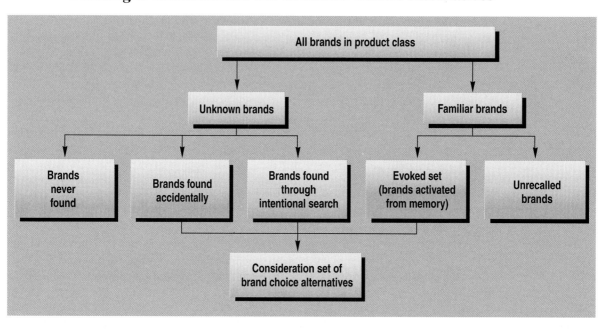

time and cost only $19. Ms. Klena didn't take the train because . . . well, she never thinks of taking the train. The train never entered her consideration set.

Marketers therefore develop strategies to increase the likelihood that a brand will be activated from consumers' memories and included in their evoked sets of choice alternatives. The activation potential of a brand, sometimes called its *top-of-mind awareness,* is influenced by many factors. One is the amount of past experience consumers have had in purchasing and using the brand. Consumers are much more likely to think of (activate) brands that they have used before. For this reason, popular brands with higher market shares have a distinct advantage. Because they are used by more consumers, these brands are more likely to be activated from memory and included in more consumers' consideration sets.[14] This increases the brands' probability of purchase, which in turn increases their activation potential, and so on. In contrast, unfamiliar and low-market-share brands are at a disadvantage because they are much less likely to be activated in consumers' evoked sets and thereby be considered as choice alternatives.

One marketing strategy to increase the activation potential of a brand is the repetitive and costly advertising campaigns devised by marketers of cigarettes, beer, soft drinks, and toothpaste (among others).[15] The heavy expenditures may be worthwhile because brands with high top-of-mind awareness are more likely to be included in the evoked set of choice alternatives that "come to mind" during problem-solving processes.

Finally, a company's distribution strategy can influence whether a brand is in consumers' consideration sets. Consider food products, for which an estimated 65 percent of decisions are made in the store. A key marketing strategy for such products

"*Lifetime guarantee? What do you think this is...
GM Goodwrench Service Plus!?*"

If it were, you'd get a lifetime guarantee on parts and labor.
Plus up-front pricing. Plus courtesy transportation.
For the select GM Goodwrench Service Plus dealer
near you, call 800 96 GM PLUS.

GM

**Goodwrench
Service**
Plus

The *Plus* means better.

www.gmgoodwrench.com   *See dealer for details of limited lifetime guarantee on select parts and labor.*   ©1997 GM Corp. All rights reserved.

A simple ad to increase top-of-mind awareness and get the brand into consumers' evoked sets   © 1997 GM Corp. All rights reserved.

is making sure the product is always on the shelf. This enhances the likelihood that consumers will encounter the brand at the time of the decision, which increases its chances of entering consumers' consideration sets and thus the probability of purchase.

Package design can influence both the consideration set and the choice decision. Package design can catch the consumer's attention in the store and increase the probability of considering the product further. Packaging also can communicate important information such as ingredients, the product's ease of use, and overall value, which may be integrated into the consumer's decision process.

Choice Criteria   As we described in Chapter 6, consumers' evaluations of the choice alternatives in the consideration set are based on their beliefs about the consequences of buying those products or brands. The specific consequences used to evaluate and choose among choice alternatives are called **choice criteria.** Virtually any type of product-related consequence can become a choice criterion in a brand-choice decision, including salient beliefs about functional consequences (product performance), psychosocial consequences (admiration of friends), or value consequences (a sense of achievement or self-esteem).[16] For most decisions, consumers probably have beliefs stored in memory about some of the relevant consequences of at least some choice alternatives in their consideration sets. If additional knowledge is desired, consumers may form a sub-goal of obtaining information about those choice alternatives. Achieving this subgoal may require intentional search behaviors such as visiting stores, reading *Consumer Reports,* or talking with knowledgeable friends. Information search may be motivated by consumers' uncertainty about appropriate choice criteria and/or choice alternatives.[17] In the opening case, Megan engaged in a substantial amount of intentional search to identify possible choice alternatives and form beliefs about appropriate choice criteria.

The probability that product knowledge is activated and used in the evaluation process is influenced strongly by the means–end relevance of that knowledge to the goal or subgoal being considered.[18] For instance, if the dominant end goal is self-esteem, beliefs about product consequences that are perceived as helping to achieve self-esteem are most likely to be used as choice criteria. Differences in the purchase context, such as buying a sweater for yourself versus buying one as a gift, may activate different end goals (being perceived as stylish versus being perceived as generous). These end goals, in turn, may activate different choice criteria (fashionable design versus expensive looking).

As we discussed in earlier chapters, marketers often place prominent stimuli in the immediate decision environment to activate certain choice criteria from consumers' memories. For instance, special price tags activate beliefs about price consequences (saving money). Prominent labels on food packages, such as "sugar-free" or "low sodium," enhance the likelihood that the consequences associated with

Some meetings leave you with a sense of wonder.

This one can leave you with a sense of security.

A new life has just come into yours. How do you provide security that lasts far into the future for your newborn? That's where meeting with one of our agents can help. Northwestern Mutual Life has consistently been rated "the most financially sound life insurance company" in a FORTUNE® magazine survey. Which means that, no matter what happens to you, tomorrow's dreams can still come true.

Have you heard from The Quiet Company?

Northwestern Mutual Life®

©1996 The Northwestern Mutual Life Insurance Company, Milwaukee, Wisconsin · www.NorthwesternMutual.com/planning

This ad links choice criteria for buying life insurance from Northwestern Mutual Life to consumers' goals and values
Courtesy Northwestern Mutual Life Insurance Company, Milwaukee, Wisconsin.

those attributes (good health) will be used as choice criteria. Finally, salespeople often emphasize certain product benefits in their sales pitches, which increases the likelihood that beliefs about those consequences will be used as choice criteria.

Not every activated belief about product or brand consequences is necessarily used as a choice criterion. Only *discriminant consequences*—consequences that are perceived to differ across choice alternatives—can be used as choice criteria.[19] Beliefs about common or very similar consequences of the choice alternatives do not discriminate among alternative actions. To present an obvious example, if all the soft drinks in a vending machine contain caffeine, the consequences of caffeine (stimulation) cannot be used as a choice criterion for deciding which brand to buy. However, if a different set of choice alternatives (brands that vary in caffeine content) is being considered, caffeine content may be a choice criterion. This is an important point. The choice criteria that are relevant (activated) for a decision depend, in part, on the particular set of choice alternatives under consideration.[20] Highlight 7.2 discusses other influences on choice criteria that are used in the decision-making process.

Consumers' choice criteria also vary in evaluation. Some choice criteria are perceived as positive, desirable consequences (more horsepower or leather seats) and elicit positive affective responses. Other choice criteria, such as price, may be thought about in negative terms as unpleasant consequences or perceived risks to be avoided.[21] To avoid rejection, marketers may try to reduce perceived risk by assuring consumers of product quality or by offering warranties and guarantees.[22] Consumers tend to reject choice alternatives perceived to have negative consequences unless the alternatives also have several positive consequences. For example, many Americans treat caffeine as a negative choice criterion. The popularity of this choice criterion was influenced by basic changes in societal values about health and by 7UP's no-caffeine marketing strategy: "Never had it, never will." Other soft-drink manufacturers responded to consumers' increasing use of this negative choice criterion by introducing their own brands of caffeine-free soft drinks.[23] Consumers who perceive that a choice involves both positive and negative consequences may be motivated to search for information to resolve the conflict between the benefits and risks of the decision.[24]

Integration Processes

The integration processes involved in problem solving perform two essential tasks: The choice alternatives must be evaluated in terms of the choice criteria, and then one of the alternatives must be selected.[25] Two types of integration procedures can account for these evaluation and choice processes: formal integration strategies and simpler procedures called *heuristics*.

Highlight 7.2

Marketing a New Choice Criterion for Restaurant Decisions

Transmedia Network Inc. has come up with an innovative strategy called IDine to serve customers with a reward/discount program when they buy restaurant meals. IDine has two options, IDine *Prime* and IDine *Choice*. Between the two programs, Transmedia has built a customer base of more than 2.5 million.

Consumers in IDine *Prime* pay a $49 annual fee and are then eligible for 20 percent discounts at any of 10,000 restaurants across the United States. Members can visit the IDine website (**www.idine.com**) to find participating restaurants in their area. All they have to do after their meal is pay with a registered credit card. Their monthly credit card statement will show the charges made at the participating restaurant, along with credits totaling 20 percent of those charges.

Transmedia began to offer programs like IDine *Prime* in the mid-1990s. Initially it worked well, but customers eventually became frustrated with high restaurant turnover and the scarcity of participating restaurants in suburban areas. Customers also wanted more than just dining discounts. So to supplement IDine *Prime,* Transmedia launched the Internet-based

IDine *Choice* program. IDine *Choice* allows customers to collect and redeem IDine points, much like a frequent-flier program. Participating restaurants looking to drum up business during off-hours can post an incentive on the IDine website. Then customers can log onto the site to search for restaurants in their area that are offering enticing rewards. On average, consumers earn $20 in IDine points when they spend $100 at a restaurant. They can redeem those points for free dining at participating restaurants or exchange them for frequent-flier miles with American Airlines. Restaurants participating in IDine *Choice* pay only when a consumer takes advantage of an incentive. In addition, restaurants can update their incentives instantly, offering bigger incentives when traffic is low and smaller incentives (or no incentives) when traffic is high.

Some are skeptical whether IDine *Choice* can succeed in the long run. During peak dining hours, there is a little reason for restaurants to offer incentives. Do you think the lure of IDine points is strong enough to make consumers change their eating habits and decide to dine during off-peak hours?

Sources: Anonymous,"Transmedia Comes Back to the Table," *Credit Card Management*, September 2000, pp. 12–14. Reprinted with permission. IDine website (**www.idine.com**).

Exhibit 7.4 presents several formal models of the integration processes involved in evaluating and choosing among choice alternatives. The key distinction is between compensatory and noncompensatory approaches.

Compensatory integration processes combine all the salient beliefs about the consequences of the choice alternatives to form an overall evaluation or attitude (A_{act}) toward each behavioral alternative. The multiattribute attitude model ($A_{act} = \Sigma b_i e_i$) is a compensatory model, so called because a negative consequence (expensive) can be compensated for or balanced by a positive consequence (high status). It is important to recognize that consumers do not necessarily integrate large numbers of beliefs in their evaluation processes. In fact, given their limited cognitive capacity, the number of choice criteria consumers can consider at one time may be quite restricted, perhaps as few as one or two. Although the multiattribute attitude model accounts for how the choice alternatives are evaluated, it does not specify how the consumer chooses which behavior to perform. Most marketers assume consumers select the alternative with the most positive A_{act}. Other *choice rules* are possible, however. For instance, consumers might choose the first alternative they find with a positive A_{act}.

Exhibit 7.4

Formal Models of Information Integration Processes in Choice

Compensatory processes	
Multiattribute model	A perceived weakness or negative evaluation on one criterion can be compensated for by a positive evaluation on another criterion. Separate evaluations for each choice criterion are combined (added or averaged) to form an overall evaluation of each alternative. Then the highest-rated alternative is chosen.
Noncompensatory processes	
Conjunctive	Consumer establishes a minimum acceptable level for each choice criterion. Accept an alternative only if every criterion equals or exceeds the minimum cutoff level.
Disjunctive	Consumer establishes acceptable standards for each criterion. A product is acceptable if it exceeds the minimum level on at least one criterion.
Lexicographic	Consumer ranks choice criteria from most to least important. Choose the best alternative on the most important criterion. If tie occurs, select best alternative on second most important criterion, and so on.
Elimination by aspects	Consumer establishes minimum cutoffs for each choice criterion. Select one criterion and eliminate all alternatives that do not exceed the cutoff level. Continue eliminating alternatives until one alternative remains. Choose it.
Combination processes	Mix of compensatory and noncompensatory processes, combined or "constructed" on the spot to adapt to environmental factors.

Source: *Information Processing Theory of Consumer Choice,* by James R. Bettman, © 1979. Adapted by permission of Pearson Education, Inc., Upper Saddle River, NJ.

Exhibit 7.4 also describes several types of **noncompensatory integration processes.** They are noncompensatory because the salient beliefs about the positive and negative consequences of the choice alternatives do not balance or compensate for each other. For example, applying the *conjunctive* choice rule requires that an alternative be rejected if any *one* of its consequences does not surpass a minimum threshold level of acceptability. Thus, Edie might reject a particular model of Reebok aerobic shoe if it has one negative consequence (too expensive), even though it has several other positive consequences (good support, comfortable, stylish colors). As another example, applying a *lexicographic* integration strategy might require consideration of only one choice criterion, which makes a compensatory

LEAN BEEF IS NEARLY AS LEAN AS CHICKEN. BET THAT REALLY FRUSTRATES CHICKENS, AFTER ALL THE RUNNING AROUND THEY DO.

IT MAY BE SURPRISING, BUT LEAN BEEF HAS ONLY ONE MORE GRAM OF SATURATED FAT THAN A SKINLESS CHICKEN BREAST. AND SIX TIMES MORE ZINC, THREE TIMES MORE IRON AND EIGHT TIMES MORE VITAMIN B12. GO FIGURE.

www.BeefItsWhatsForDinner.com

Marketers try to reduce the perceived risk associated with their product   *Courtesy of the Cattlemen's Beef Board.*

process impossible. Tina might evaluate a pair of dress shoes favorably and buy them because they are superior to the other alternatives on the most important consequence (the color matches her outfit exactly), whereas other, even unfavorable consequences are not considered (not durable and slightly uncomfortable).

Research suggests consumers do not seem to follow any single rule or strategy in evaluating and choosing from among alternatives.[26] For one thing, they probably do not have sufficient cognitive capacity to simultaneously integrate several beliefs about many alternatives. Compensatory integration processes are especially likely to exceed cognitive capacity limits.[27] Moreover, many problem-solving tasks do not involve a single choice to which a single integration rule could be applied. Instead, consumers make multiple choices in most purchase situations (choices of information sources to examine, stores to visit, product forms or brands to buy, methods of payment). Each choice is a distinct subproblem that requires separate integration processes.

Rather than a single integration strategy, consumers are likely to use a combination of processes in many problem-solving situations.[28] A noncompensatory strategy might be used to quickly reduce the choice alternatives to a manageable number by rejecting those that lack one or two key criteria (a conjunctive strategy). For example, Bill might reject all restaurants that do not have a salad bar. Then the remaining brands in his consideration set (perhaps only two or three restaurants) could be evaluated on several choice criteria (price level, variety, atmosphere) using a more strenuous compensatory strategy.

Another issue is whether consumers have complete integration rules stored in memory ready to be activated and applied to the relevant product beliefs. Current research suggests instead that most integration processes are *constructed* at the time they are needed to fit the current situation. This suggests that rather than following fixed strategies, consumers' integration processes are relatively simple, very flexible, and easily adapted to varying decision situations.[29] These simple integration "rules" are called *heuristics*.

Basically, **heuristics** are simple "if . . ., then . . ." propositions that connect an event with an appropriate action. Because they are applied to only a few bits and pieces of knowledge at a time, heuristics are highly adaptive to specific environmental situations and are not likely to exceed cognitive capacity limits.[30] Heuristics may be stored in memory like miniature scripts that are applied fairly automatically to information encountered in the environment. Or they may be constructed on the spot in response to the immediate environment.

Exhibit 7.5 presents examples of three types of heuristics that are particularly important in problem solving. *Search heuristics* are simple procedures for seeking information relevant to a goal. Some consumers have a simple search rule for buying any small durable product such as a radio or a kitchen appliance: Read the product tests in *Consumer Reports*. *Evaluation heuristics* are procedures for evaluating

Exhibit 7.5

Examples of Consumer Heuristics

Search heuristics	Examples
• Store selection • Sources of information • Source credibility	If you are buying stereo equipment, always go to Sam's Hi-Fi. If you want to know which alternatives are worth searching for, read the test reports in *Consumer Reports*. If a magazine accepts advertisements from the tested products, don't believe its product tests.

Evaluation heuristics	Examples
• Key criteria • Negative criteria • Significant differences	If comparing processed foods, examine sodium content. If a salient consequence is negative (high sodium content), give this choice criterion extra weight in the integration process. If alternatives are similar on a salient consequence (all low sodium), ignore that choice criterion.

Choice heuristics	Examples
For familiar, frequently purchased products:	**If choosing among familiar products, . . .**
• Works best	Choose the product that you think works best—that provides the best level of performance on the most relevant functional consequences.
• Affect referral	Choose the alternative you like the best (select the alternative with most favorable attitude).
• Bought last	Select the alternative you used last, if it was satisfactory.
• Important person	Choose the alternative that some "important" person (spouse, child, friend) likes.
• Price-based rule	Buy the least expensive alternative (or buy the most expensive, depending on your beliefs about the relationship of price to product quality).
• Promotion rule	Choose an alternative for which you have a coupon or that you can get at a price reduction (seasonal sale, promotional rebate, special price reduction).
For new, unfamiliar products:	**If choosing among unfamiliar products . . .**
• Wait and see	Don't buy any software until someone you know has used it for at least a month and recommends it. Don't buy a new car (computer, etc.) until the second model year.
• Expert consultant	Find an expert or more knowledgeable person, have him or her evaluate the alternatives in terms of your goals, then buy the alternative the expert selects.

Source: Adapted from "An Examination of Consumer Decision Making for a Common Repeat Purchase Product," by Wayne D. Hoyer, in *Journal of Consumer Research,* December 1984, pp. 822–829. Copyright 1984 Journal of Consumer Research. Reprinted with permission of the publisher, University of Chicago Press.

THERE'S USED.

THEN THERE'S **BRAND SPANKIN' USED.**

8-YEAR/80,000-MILE LIMITED WARRANTY
125-POINT INSPECTION
3.9% APR
24-HOUR ROADSIDE ASSISTANCE
CARFAX REPORT
CAR RENTAL ALLOWANCE

CHRYSLER CERTIFIED PRE-OWNED FIVE STAR ●●●●●

This ad emphasizes one choice criterion in the decision-making process: "brand new" Courtesy of DaimlerChrysler Corporation. Photographed by Clint Clemens and Troy Woods.

and weighting beliefs in terms of the current goal being addressed in the problem-solving process. Dieting consumers may have a heuristic that identifies the most important choice criteria for food: low in calories and the resulting consequence of losing weight. *Choice heuristics* are simple procedures for comparing evaluations of alternative actions in order to choose one. A simple choice heuristic is to select the alternative you bought last time if it was satisfactory; another is to rely on an expert's advice.

Decision Plans

The process of identifying, evaluating, and choosing among alternatives during problem solving produces a **decision plan** made up of one or more behavioral intentions. Decision plans vary in their specificity and complexity.[31] Specific decision plans concern intentions to perform particular behaviors in highly defined situations: "This afternoon Jim intends to go to Penney's and buy a blue cotton sweater to go with his new slacks." Other decision plans involve rather general intentions: "Paula intends to shop for a new car sometime soon." Some decision plans contain a simple intention to perform a single behavior: "Andy intends to buy a large tube of Aim toothpaste." In contrast, more complex decision plans involve a set of intentions to perform a series of behaviors: "Val intends to go to Bloomingdale's and Macy's, browse through their sportswear departments, and look for a lightweight jacket."

Having a decision plan increases the likelihood that the intended behaviors will be performed. However, as we discussed in Chapter 6, behavioral intentions are not always carried out. For instance, a purchase intention may be blocked or modified if environmental circumstances make it difficult to accomplish the decision plan. Perhaps the problem-solving process will recycle and a new decision plan might be developed: "Andy found that the store was sold out of large tubes of Aim, so he decided to buy two medium-size tubes." Sometimes unanticipated events identify additional choice alternatives or change consumers' beliefs about appropriate choice criteria; this could lead to a revised decision plan: "While reading the paper, Val learned that Saks was having a 25 percent-off sale on lightweight jackets, so she decided to shop there first instead of Bloomingdale's."

Problem-Solving Processes in Purchase Decisions

The amount of cognitive and behavioral effort consumers put into their problem-solving processes is highly variable. Problem-solving effort varies from virtually none (a decision plan is activated from memory and carried out automatically) to very extensive. For convenience, marketers have divided this continuum into three levels of problem-solving activity: extensive, limited, and routinized or habitual.[32]

Relatively few consumer choice problems require **extensive decision making.** Extensive decision making usually involves a substantial amount of search behavior to identify choice alternatives and learn the appropriate choice criteria with which to evaluate them. Extensive decision making also involves several choice decisions and substantial cognitive and behavioral effort. Finally, it is likely to take rather long periods—such as Megan's decision to buy a used car in the opening example or purchasing your first sound system.

Many consumers' choice problems require **limited decision making.** The amount of problem-solving effort in limited decision making ranges from low to moderate. Compared to extensive decision making, limited decision making involves less search for information. Fewer choice alternatives are considered, and less integration processing is required. Choices involving limited decision making usually are carried out fairly quickly, with moderate levels of cognitive and behavioral effort.

For still other problems, consumers' choice behavior is habitual or routine. **Routinized choice behavior,** such as buying another Pepsi from the vending machine down the hall or purchasing a package of gum at the checkout counter, occurs relatively automatically with little or no apparent cognitive processing. Compared to the other levels, routinized choice behavior requires very little cognitive capacity or conscious control. Basically, a previously learned decision plan is activated from memory and carried out relatively automatically to produce the purchase behavior.

The amount of effort consumers exert in problem solving tends to decrease over time as they learn more about a product and gain experience in making decisions. With repeated decisions, product and brand knowledge becomes organized into means–end structures and becomes more clearly related to consumers' goals. Consumers also learn new productions and heuristics, which become organized into scripts or decision plans stored in memory.[33] When activated, these heuristics and decision scripts automatically affect purchase-related behaviors. Running down to the convenience store for a loaf of bread or stopping to fill up the car's tank at a favorite gas station are well-developed decision plans that require little cognitive effort.

As another example of routinized choice behavior, consider the study of 120 consumers who were observed shopping and buying laundry detergent in three chain grocery stores.[34] Most consumers examined very few packages of detergent. In fact, 72 percent looked at only one package and only 11 percent looked at more than two. An even lower number of packages were physically picked up: 83 percent of the consumers picked up only one package, and only 4 percent picked up more than two. Obviously most of these consumers did not engage in much in-store problem-solving activity for this product.

Finally, consumers took an average of 13 seconds after they entered the aisle to make their detergent choices. Given that the detergent section spanned an entire aisle and several seconds were required to walk to the appropriate area, it is obvious these typical consumers were making an extremely quick choice involving minimal cognitive and behavioral effort. The majority of consumers in this study were engaged in routinized choice behavior. They were merely carrying out a simple decision plan; for example, find the large size of Tide and buy it.

Influences on Consumers' Problem-Solving Activities

The level of consumers' problem-solving effort in making brand purchase decisions is influenced by environmental factors as well as the cognitive (knowledge) and affective responses activated during the problem-solving process. We discuss three aspects of this activated knowledge and affect that have direct effects on problem solving: (1) consumers' goals; (2) their knowledge about choice alternatives and choice criteria, as well as heuristics for using this knowledge; and (3) their level of involvement. Following the discussion of these affective and cognitive factors, we examine several environmental influences on consumer problem solving.

Exhibit 7.6

Types of Purchase End Goals and Related Problem-Solving Processes

Dominant End Goal	Basic Purchase Motivation	Examples
Optimize satisfaction	Seek maximum positive consequences	Buy dinner at the best restaurant in town
Prevention	Avoid potential unpleasant consequences	Buy rustproofing for a new car
Resolve conflict	Seek satisfactory balance of positive and negative consequences	Buy a moderately expensive car of very good quality
Escape	Reduce or escape from current aversive circumstances	Buy a shampoo to get rid of dandruff
Maintenance (satisfaction)	Maintain satisfaction of basic need with minimal effort	Buy bread at the nearest convenience store

Sources: Adapted from Geraldine Fennell, "Motivation Research Revisited," *Journal of Advertising Research,* June 1975, pp. 23–28; J. Paul Peter and Lawrence X. Tarpey, Sr., "A Comparative Analysis of Three Consumer Decision Strategies," *Journal of Consumer Research,* June 1975, pp. 29–37. Copyright 1975 Journal of Consumer Research. Reprinted by permission of the publisher, University of Chicago Press.

Effects of End Goals

The particular end goals consumers are striving to achieve have a powerful effect on the problem-solving process. Exhibit 7.6 presents five broad end goals that lead to quite different problem-solving processes. For instance, consumers who have an *optimizing* end goal are likely to expend substantial effort searching for the best possible alternative. In contrast, consumers with a *satisfaction/maintenance* end goal are likely to engage in minimal search behavior. In yet other decisions, consumers may have conflicting end goals that must be resolved in the problem-solving process.

In general, marketers have relatively little direct influence over consumers' abstract end goals, such as basic values. However, marketers can try to influence less abstract end goals, such as desired functional or psychosocial consequences, through promotional strategies. Perhaps the major implication for marketers is to identify the dominant goals in consumers' problem representations and design product and promotion strategies that link product attributes to those goals.[35]

Effects of Goal Hierarchies

Consumers' goal hierarchies for a problem have a powerful influence on problem-solving processes. If consumers have a well-defined goal hierarchy stored in memory, it may be activated and the associated decision plan carried out automatically.[36] Even if a complete decision plan is not available, a general goal hierarchy provides a useful structure for developing an effective decision plan without a great deal of problem-solving effort.

In contrast, consumers who have little past experience will not have well-developed goal hierarchies. Their problem solving is likely to proceed haltingly, by trial and error. Consider first-time buyers of relatively important products such as televisions, sports equipment, cars, and houses. These consumers must construct a goal hierarchy (a series of subgoals that seem related to the end goal) and develop a decision plan to achieve each subgoal (as Megan had to do in the opening example). In these types of decisions, marketers are likely to find confused or frustrated consumers who use general "strategies" such as wandering around various stores in a mall hoping to accidentally run into something that will satisfy their end goals.

Another reason for browsing without a specific decision plan in mind is that the consumer feels involved with a particular product class or form and likes to associate with it. Consumers who are very interested in music may enjoy browsing in record shops. Some consumers are involved with a particular store or set of stores in a mall or a shopping area in town. Perhaps the atmosphere of these stores is exciting and stimulating, which provides part of the attraction. In sum, browsing can and usually does serve multiple goals, needs, and values for different consumers.

Effects of Involvement and Knowledge

Consumers' problem-solving processes are greatly affected by the amount of product knowledge they have acquired through their past experiences and by their level of involvement with the product and/or the choice process. The activated knowledge about goals, choice alternatives and choice criteria, and heuristics affects consumers' ability to create an effective decision plan. Consumers' involvement with the product or decision affects their motivation to engage in the problem-solving process. Exhibit 7.7 summarizes how different combinations of product knowledge and involvement influence specific elements of consumers' problem representations and the overall problem-solving process. Marketers should determine the levels of knowledge and involvement of their target customers and develop strategies consistent with the types of problem solving described in Exhibit 7.7. Highlight 7.3 describes how Procter & Gamble responded to consumers who were engaged in routinized problem solving (low knowledge and involvement) because of too many choices.

Environmental Effects

Environmental factors can affect consumer decision making by disrupting the ongoing flow of the problem-solving process. Four types of disruptive events, or **interrupts,** have been identified.[37] First, interrupts can occur when *unexpected information* (inconsistent with established knowledge structures) is encountered in the environment. For instance, carrying out a decision plan or script may be interrupted when you unexpectedly find that aspects of the physical or social environment have changed: A store has been remodeled and departments have been moved around, a rejected brand now has a new attribute, or your friends now favor a different night spot. Such environmental interrupts may cause the consumer to take conscious control of the problem-solving process, identify a new end goal, develop a new goal hierarchy, and construct a different decision plan. A 1997 strike at United Parcel Service (UPS) created a dramatic interrupt for many businesses. As many as 90 million parcels were not picked up from small retailers and manufacturers during the 15-day strike. Many UPS customers vowed to diversify their shipping business in the future, allowing the U.S. Postal Service and FedEx to capture some of UPS's customers.[38]

Exhibit 7.7

Effects of Involvement and Product Knowledge on Consumers' Problem-Solving Processes

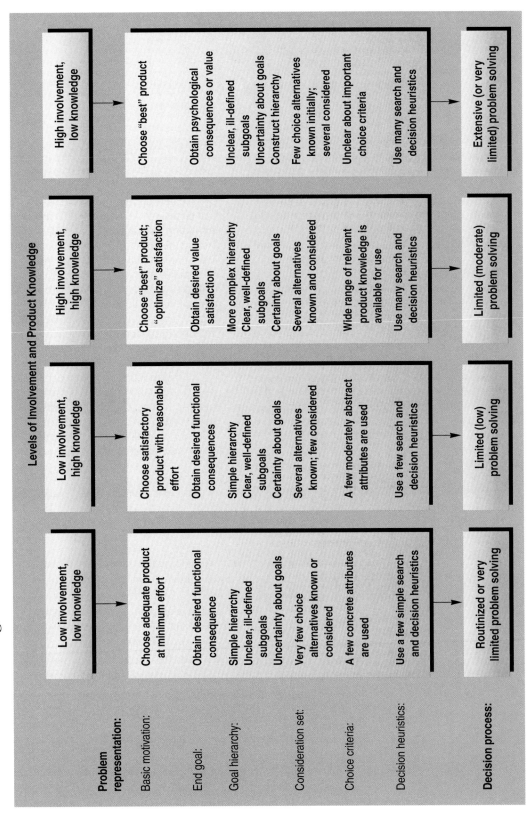

Problem representation:	Levels of Involvement and Product Knowledge			
	Low involvement, low knowledge	Low involvement, high knowledge	High involvement, high knowledge	High involvement, low knowledge
Basic motivation:	Choose adequate product at minimum effort	Choose satisfactory product with reasonable effort	Choose "best" product; "optimize" satisfaction	Choose "best" product
End goal:	Obtain desired functional consequence	Obtain desired functional consequences	Obtain desired value satisfaction	Obtain psychological consequences or value
Goal hierarchy:	Simple hierarchy Unclear, ill-defined subgoals Uncertainty about goals	Simple hierarchy Clear, well-defined subgoals Certainty about goals	More complex hierarchy Clear, well-defined subgoals Certainty about goals	Unclear, ill-defined subgoals Uncertainty about goals Construct hierarchy
Consideration set:	Very few choice alternatives known or considered	Several alternatives known; few considered	Several alternatives known and considered	Few choice alternatives known initially; several considered
Choice criteria:	A few concrete attributes are used	A few moderately abstract attributes are used	Wide range of relevant product knowledge is available for use	Unclear about important choice criteria
Decision heuristics:	Use a few simple search and decision heuristics	Use a few search and decision heuristics	Use many search and decision heuristics	Use many search and decision heuristics
Decision process:	Routinized or very limited problem solving	Limited (low) problem solving	Limited (moderate) problem solving	Extensive (or very limited) problem solving

183

Highlight 7.3

P&G's Simplifying Solutions to the Proliferation of Consumer Choice

Years ago, more people took their time while shopping, browsing among the merchandise, and deliberating about their choices; but consumer decision making changed. Browsing time in 1996 was down by 25 percent compared to 1991. On an average grocery shopping trip in 1996, consumers spent an average of just 21 minutes to buy 18 of the approximately 30,000 items available in a supermarket. Many consumers do not bother to check the prices—they just want to buy the same products at the same prices each week.

Perhaps these habitual decision-making processes are reactions to the proliferation of choices they face in the supermarkets and elsewhere. In addition to the many brands in each product category, it seems that each brand comes in dozens of model variations and sizes. Each of these choice alternatives is being marketed with promotions, advertising, package design, and so forth. In the late 1980s, Procter & Gamble, perhaps the top consumer goods company in the world, made as many as 50 price changes per day across 110 brands, offered 440 sales promotions each year,

and constantly tinkered with the package size, color, and contents. "We were confusing [consumers]," admitted P&G president and COO, Durk Jager.

With this recognition, P&G began to overhaul many of its sales and marketing activities. By 1997, P&G had eliminated 25 percent of its products by selling off some brands (Lava soap and Aleve pain reliever) and cutting the number of alternatives in its other product lines. For instance, P&G halved the variations of Head & Shoulders shampoo from 30 to 15. When P&G learned that most mothers did not want boy and girl diapers, it began selling only unisex diapers. The simplification process will continue. By 2000, P&G cut out another 20 percent of its products.

Why did P&G take such seemingly drastic action? According to Jager, "Consumers were drowning in far too many products." Although consumers may like variety, "too much meaningless variety" is not good. Offering too many choices complicates consumer decision making and might backfire on a company. A company that simplifies consumers' decision making may create substantial goodwill and greater sales.

Source: Wall Street Journal. Central Edition [Staff Produced Copy Only]. Raju Narisetti, "P&G, Seeing Shoppers Were Being Confused, Overhauls Marketing," *The Wall Street Journal,* January 15, 1997, pp. A1, A8. Copyright 1997 by Dow Jones & Co Inc. Reproduced with permission of Dow Jones & Co Inc. in the format textbook via copyright clearance center.

Second, *prominent environmental stimuli* can interrupt a problem-solving process. Many marketing strategies are intended to interrupt consumers' ongoing problem solving. For instance, a large in-store display for Oreo cookies, "as advertised" shelf tags, or the announcement of a sales promotion ("Attention, Kmart shoppers. In aisle 3B we are offering . . .") may interrupt an ongoing problem-solving process as well as activate new knowledge or goals from memory.

Third, *affective states* such as moods (feeling bored) and physiological events (feeling hungry, sleepy, or thirsty) can interrupt an ongoing problem-solving process.[39] For instance, feeling tired during a shopping trip might activate new goals and start a different problem-solving process (find a comfortable place to sit down and have a soda or cup of coffee). Getting into a bad mood can terminate a problem-solving process.

Fourth, *conflicts* that arise during the course of purchase decision making can interrupt the problem-solving process (see Highlight 7.4). *Goal conflict* occurs when consumers recognize the presence of incompatible goals.[40] Goal conflict may occur when consumers discover that alternatives cannot be found to satisfy incompatible goals. For instance, Susan may experience an *approach–approach conflict* in choosing between a new camera and a new stereo receiver because each product leads to

Highlight 7.4

Goal Conflict during Decision Making

For years, fur coats were symbols of fashion, wealth, and elegance. But thanks to a highly publicized antifur movement, fur sales tumbled 50 percent in the late 1980s. In 2000, however, as the economy boomed and antifur activists became less visible, fur made a comeback. It appears that consumers are torn between the positives (looking good and staying warm) and the negatives (public scorn and concern for animal welfare) associated with wearing fur.

In the 1990s, the group People for the Ethical Treatment of Animals was in the forefront of a very effective and creative campaign to discourage people from wearing fur. Antifur activists appealed to consumers' sense of humanity by graphically exposing the often inhumane ways in which animal pelts are harvested (for example, anal electrocutions of minks). Celebrities became involved in the cause, many posing without clothes in ads that stated, "I'd rather go naked than wear fur." Some activists took a more personal approach, dousing fur wearers on the street with fake blood. Wearing fur soon became almost unconscionable. In London, department stores began to stow their furs away in massive refrigerators because no one would buy them. Consumers who already owned fur coats (but wouldn't wear them) paid to have them stored in large warehouses. Furriers everywhere went out of business.

But slowly and quietly, fur made a comeback. In 1999, fur sales rose 10 percent from the previous year, while 220 designers used fur in their collections, five times more than in 1995. In one week in New York City in 2000, Oscar de la Renta, Tommy Hilfiger, Marc Jacobs, and rapper-turned-designer Sean "Puffy" Combs all featured fur at their fashion shows.

Why the fur revival? The good economic times helped, making it possible for more consumers to afford fur. Also, the antifur movement may have become less of a chic cause than it was a decade earlier. Furthermore, it is now easier for designers to use fur that doesn't look like fur by incorporating it into blended fabrics. In this less natural-looking form, fur is perhaps more acceptable. But clearly, many are still uneasy when confronted with the harsh reality that fur comes from dead animals. When designer John Galliano mounted a fox's head on a garment, it became worldwide news. Similarly, singer Mary J. Blige generated controversy by sporting a coat festooned with rabbit claws. Designer Katayone Adeli was planning to use fur in her collection, but she was shocked when she saw the pelts. Instead, she opted for fake fur.

The conflict some consumers experience in deciding whether to buy and wear fur is not unique. Many other consumer decisions involve similar conflicts and uncertainties.

Source: Valli Herman-Cohen, "Commentary: The Fur Fury; Is PETA Driven by Animal Rights or Resentment of the Rich," *Los Angeles Times,* February 18, 2000, p. E1; Emma Brockes, Jess Carter-Morley, and Laura Craik, "This Time It's For Real," *The Guardian,* February 10, 2000, p. 2.2.

a desirable goal (creativity and relaxation, respectively), but neither product can satisfy both goals. *Avoidance–avoidance conflicts* occur when consumers must choose between two alternatives with different negative consequences. For instance, Sam is trying to decide whether to buy a new mountain bike. He doesn't want to be embarrassed by continuing to ride his old bike, but he doesn't want to spend money on a new one, either. Finally, *approach–avoidance conflicts* occur when consumers consider both the positive and negative consequences of a purchase or action. For instance, Paul is trying to decide about a new personal CD player that is on sale for a very low price (positive outcome), but he is afraid the quality may be low (negative outcome). Highlight 7.4 describes goal conflict in a common decision.

The effects of *interrupts* on consumers' problem-solving processes depend on how consumers interpret (comprehend) the interrupting event. In general, consumers tend to resume an interrupted problem-solving task, especially if it is important or involving.[41] In other cases, an interrupting event can change the problem-solving

This ad links the product to an end goal of optimizing satisfaction
Courtesy of Carushka Inc.

process. For instance, an interrupt may activate new end goals that require a new problem-solving process. Interrupt events (such as learning about a new product attribute) may activate knowledge structures that suggest new decision criteria. In other cases, a choice heuristic may be activated by the interrupt (a friend recommends a brand, and you decide to take her advice). Finally, an especially strong interrupt, such as losing your job, may block the current problem-solving process (choosing a new car), and the process may not resume. In sum, the effects of interrupts depend on how the consumer interprets them. For instance, is your hunger severe enough to interrupt your shopping for new jeans, or can you skip lunch today? Does this new brand of hairstyling spray seem worth trying, or should you pass it up? Do you care that your friend thinks these shoes look ridiculous?

Implications for Marketing Strategy

To develop effective marketing strategies, marketers need to know the types of problem-solving processes their customers use to make purchase decisions. As shown in Exhibit 7.7, these processes can vary widely. Marketers that target several consumer segments, each with different problem-solving processes, may have to develop multiple strategies to influence the different decision outcomes. In the following sections we consider some general implications for marketing strategies for routinized choice behavior and limited and extensive decision making.

Routinized Choice Behavior   Much consumer choice behavior is routinized. When consumers think they know all they need to know about a product category, they are not motivated to search for new information. Their choice behavior is based on a learned decision plan stored in memory. In such cases, the appropriate market strategy depends on the strength of the brand's position in the market.

Marketers of established brands with substantial market shares must maintain their brands in the evoked sets of a significant segment of consumers. Because consumers in this situation engage in little or no research, marketers have minimal opportunities to interject their brands into consumers' consideration sets during problem solving. Thus, it is important that a brand be included in the choice alternatives activated at the beginning of the problem-solving process. In general, the more automatic the choice behavior becomes, the more difficult it is for marketers to interrupt and influence the choice.

Marketers of new brands or brands with a low market share must somehow interrupt consumers' automatic problem-solving processes. They may develop strategies of producing prominent environmental stimuli such as large or unusual store displays, create strong package graphics that stand out on the shelf, give away free samples, or run sales promotions (buy one, get one free).[42] Such strategies are intended to catch consumers' attention and interrupt their routine choice behaviors.

The goal is to jolt consumers into a more conscious and controlled level of limited decision making that includes the new brand in the consideration set.

Finally, marketers of leading brands such as Doritos snack chips, Snickers candy bars, Budweiser beer, and Dell computers may *want* consumers to follow a routine choice process. Because these brands already have a high market share, they are in the evoked sets of many buyers. It is important for these marketers to avoid marketing-related environmental interrupts such as stockouts, which could jolt consumers into a limited decision-making process and lead them to try a competitor's brand. One critical aspect of the overall marketing strategy for such brands is an efficient distribution system to keep the brands fully stocked and available (in a prominent shelf/display position) whenever consumers are in a choice situation. Frito-Lay, manufacturer of Fritos, Ruffles potato chips, and many other snack products, has developed a superb distribution system partly for this reason. Marketers of industrial products attempt to make their buyers' decision-making processes more routine by computerizing and automating the order process.

Limited Decision Making   Most consumer decisions involve limited problem-solving effort. Because most consumers already have a lot of information about the product from previous experiences, the basic marketing strategy here is to make additional pieces of information available to consumers when and where they need them. Advertisements to increase top-of-mind awareness may help get a brand into the evoked set of choice alternatives at the beginning of the decision process. This is important because most consumers are not likely to search extensively for other alternatives. Moreover, it is critical that the brand be perceived to possess the few key choice criteria used in the evaluation process. Advertisements that capture consumer's attention and communicate favorable beliefs about salient attributes and consequences of the brand may be able to create that knowledge. Finally, because consumers are giving some conscious thought to the decision, successful interrupts are not as difficult as they are with routinized problem solving. Marketers may try to design a store environment that stimulates impulsive purchases, a type of limited decision making.[43]

Buying a beverage at the supermarket may be either a routinized choice or limited decision making
David Young-Wolff/PhotoEdit, Inc.

Extensive Decision Making   Compared to more common routinized choices and limited decision making, relatively few consumer decisions involve extensive problem solving. However, when consumers do engage in extensive decision making, marketers must recognize and satisfy their special needs for information. In extensive decision-making situations where their knowledge is low, consumers need information about everything—including which end goals are important, how to organize goal hierarchies, which choice alternatives are relevant, what choice criteria are appropriate, and so on. Motivated consumers may seek such information from many sources. For instance, a 1997 survey by Wirthlin Worldwide, a marketing research firm, found that more than two-thirds of consumers who were planning vacations sought advice from family and friends, about one-third consulted travel guidebooks, and 27 percent spoke with travel agents.[44] About 11 percent got information from travel channels on TV, and 17 percent found relevant information through the Internet. Marketers should strive to make the necessary information available in a format and at a level that consumers can understand and use in the

High**light** 7.5

Using the Internet to Simplify the Car Buying Process

Buying a new car usually involves haggling with a salesperson over prices and options. Many consumers find this process uncomfortable, even offensive. According to one study, nearly 40 percent of consumers prefer one-price shopping. Fortunately for those people, there are alternatives that reduce or eliminate the aversive consequences of negotiating with an auto dealer.

You can now buy a new vehicle entirely through the Internet. Let's say you are shopping for a Ford Explorer. You can visit DealerNet (**www.dealernet. com**) to compare the Explorer to, say, the Nissan Pathfinder or Jeep Cherokee on price, safety, and fuel economy. Then you can click over to Edmund Publications (**www.edmund.com/edweb**) to get the current invoice price (what the dealer pays the manufacturer). From there, you can visit **Autoweb.com**, where you type in the model, color, and options you want and receive a quote from a local dealer. From there, it is up to you to contact the dealer and finish the transaction. Or you can take that quote to another dealer and try to bargain for an even better price. If you are extremely averse to car dealers, you don't have to deal with them at all. AutobytelDIRECT (**www.autobytel.com**) will contact a dealer and negotiate a price for you. If you want, they can even arrange to have the vehicle delivered to your home so you never have to set foot on a dealer's lot! Is it worth it? Possibly. According to a J. D. Power & Associates survey, Internet shoppers saved an average of $500 on new-car purchases compared to those who visited the showroom.

Of course, buying a vehicle on the Internet is not for everyone—in 1999 only 1 percent of auto sales were made via the Web—but the Internet can be a valuable resource nonetheless. J. D. Power & Associates says 60 percent of car buyers now use the Internet for research and price comparisons. Even the National Automobile Dealers of America has begun to post invoice prices on its website (**www.nada.org**). So even if you feel the need to kick the tires and lift the hood before you make a purchase, you can still use the Web to collect a lot of information, which will put you in a position of strength when negotiating with a salesperson.

Sources: David Welch, "Car Dealers Say: Follow That Mouse," *Business Week,* April 10, 2000, pp. 106–110; Lindsay Chappel, "Consumers Say They Like to Dicker," *Automotive News,* January 24, 2000, p. 136; Karl Ritzler, "Buying a Car Online: Click the Tires," *Atlanta Journal-Constitution,* June 18, 2000, p. P1.

Buying a new or used car involves extensive decision making for most consumers
Michael Newman/ PhotoEdit, Inc.

problem-solving process.[45] Highlight 7.5 describes how some companies provide special information to consumers buying new cars.

Because consumers intentionally seek product information during extensive decision making, interrupting their problem-solving processes with a brand promotion is relatively easy. Informational displays at the point of purchase—for instance, displays of mattresses that are cut apart to show construction details—or presentations by salespeople can be effective sources of information. Complex sales materials such as brochures and product specifications may be effective, along with high-information advertisements. Consumers in extensive problem-solving situations will attend to relevant information, and they are motivated to comprehend it. Marketers may take advantage of consumers' receptivity to information by offering free samples, coupons, or easy trial (take it home and try it for a couple of days) to help consumers gain knowledge about their brands.

Back To...

Buying a Used Car

In this chapter, we examined a number of concepts that can help us understand Megan's rather complex problem-solving process. Her decision to buy a used car involved fairly extensive problem-solving activities, including a substantial amount of search behavior and quite a bit of cognitive activity in evaluating alternative actions. As you review her decisions, note that her choice alternatives and choice criteria were greatly influenced by the information she encountered in the environment because she had very little knowledge about cars stored in memory. Note also that her goal hierarchy and decision plan were constructed through trial and error during the problem-solving process. This example also reveals the continuous, reciprocal interactions that occur among affect and cognition, behavior, environment, and marketing strategy. Many extensive and limited decision-making processes are similar to Megan's experiences, although probably less complex. In contrast, habitual choice behavior involves little or no problem solving and little effort. Because the decisions were made in the past and stored in memory, purchase behaviors are generated automatically when the decision plan is activated. Thus, environmental factors have less chance to interrupt and influence the purchase process. ❖

Summary   In this chapter, we examined consumers' decision-making processes as they choose between alternative behaviors. Our primary focus was on purchase choices of products and brands. We treated decision making as a problem-solving process in which the consumer's cognitive representation of the problem is key to understanding the process. Problem representation involves end goals, a goal hierarchy, activated product knowledge, and choice rules and heuristics. For many consumer decisions, the problem representation involves several interrelated subproblems, each with its own set of subgoals, organized as a goal hierarchy. Consumers use simple decision rules called heuristics for finding, evaluating, and integrating beliefs about the alternatives relevant for each subgoal in a goal hierarchy. The entire set of decisions produces a series of behavioral intentions or a decision plan.

We also saw that consumers' problem-solving processes vary widely. Some purchase choices require very extensive problem-solving efforts, while other purchases are made virtually automatically in a highly routinized manner. Many purchases involve limited decision making that falls somewhere between these two extremes. We described how consumers' end goals, goal hierarchies, product knowledge, and involvement affect the problem-solving process. Then we discussed how various aspects of the decision environment affect the problem-solving process. We concluded by drawing implications of these concepts for marketing strategy.

Key Terms and Concepts

Review and Discussion Questions

1. Give two examples to illustrate the idea that decision choices are always between alternative behaviors.

2. Describe the problem-solving approach to consumer decision making, and discuss why it is a useful perspective.

3. Identify three ways choice alternatives can enter the consideration set. Describe a marketing strategy you could use to get your brand into consumers' consideration sets for each situation. Why do products or brands not in the consideration sets have a low probability of being purchased?

4. Describe the components of a problem representation. Give an example of how marketers can influence consumers' problem representations.

5. Give an example of how two different "frames" for the same purchase decision can lead to different problem-solving processes. How do these differences relate to consumer–product relationships discussed earlier?

6. Think of a purchase decision from your own experience in which you had a well-developed goal hierarchy. Describe how that affected your problem-solving processes. Then select a decision in which you did not have a well-developed goal hierarchy and describe how it affected your problem-solving processes.

7. Assume the role of a product manager (product management team) for a product about which target consumers have a fairly high level of product knowledge. Consider how each of the formal integration processes would result in different responses to your product and how you could adjust marketing strategy to deal with these differences.

8. Give at least two examples of how a marketing manager could use the various types of interrupts discussed in this chapter to increase the likelihood of purchase of his or her product.

9. Discuss how consumers' involvement and their activated product knowledge affect the problem-solving processes during purchase decisions for products like a new automobile, an oil change, a cold remedy, and health insurance.

10. Relate the examples of decision heuristics shown in Exhibit 7.5 to the concept of involvement. When are these heuristics likely to be useful to the consumer? Under what conditions might they be dysfunctional?

Marketing Strategy in Action

Hallmark Cards

It is one of the least likely businesses ever invented. However, Hallmark and its main competitors—American Greetings and Gibson Greetings, plus an assortment of so-called alternative card companies—make a good living selling sentiment to American consumers. In fact, a greeting card is one of the most profitable things that can be made with paper and ink. Consider the "Three Little Angels" card, Hallmark's best-selling Christmas card ever, which has sold more than 37 million units and brought in more than $22 million during the 24 years it has been produced.

Messages of congratulations and good cheer have been exchanged for centuries, but not until recent times have they taken the form of greeting cards. The first greeting cards were Christmas cards, invented in 1843 by a British businessman too busy to write his traditional Christmas letter. By the 1870s, expensive Christmas cards were quite popular among wealthy Americans. Joyce C. Hall and Jacob Sapirstein (founders of Hallmark and American Greetings, respectively) are regarded as the architects of the modern-day greeting card industry. (You can review the history of Hallmark at **www.hallmark.com/** and American Greetings at **americangreetings.com/**.) Hall and Sapirstein transformed a turn-of-the-century fad for picture postcards into a social custom in which consumers buy and send cards to convey their feelings and sentiments about birthdays, weddings, births and deaths, graduations, and so on. Today's consumer can buy a greeting card to signify virtually any situation and circumstance you can imagine (and some you can't imagine). Sending greeting cards is so popular in the United States that greeting cards constitute as much as 50 percent of the volume of first-class mail.

The business Joyce Hall started in 1910 has grown into Hallmark Cards, Inc., a $4 billion worldwide organization headquartered in Kansas City, Missouri. Hallmark publishes greeting cards in more than 30 languages and distributes them in more than 30 countries. An estimated 3.5 billion Hallmark cards are available in the United States alone. The company produces 11,000 new card designs and 8,000 reused designs each year. In addition, Hallmark markets thousands of related items such as gift wrap, party goods, Christmas ornaments, jigsaw puzzles, ribbon, and writing paper. Hallmark also owns Binney & Smith, maker of Crayola crayons; Revell-Monogram, the world's largest maker of plastic model kits; and Hallmark Entertainment, producer of family-oriented television programming.

Hallmark's Traditional Products and Brands

Consumers consistently rank the Hallmark brand name among the top 10 quality brands in any category. The company markets greeting cards under a number of different brand names, including:

- Ambassador. A Hallmark tradebrand for mass merchandise retailers such as grocery stores, drugstores, and discount stores. It is sold in more than 22,000 locations.
- Warm Wishes. A line of 99-cent cards designed to help Hallmark compete against discount card retailers.
- Shoebox Greetings. A collection of witty, irreverent greeting cards designed to compete with the so-called alternative cards. These cards reflect today's lifestyles, with topics ranging from male–female relationships to pregnancy, and from stress in the workplace to congratulating a co-worker on a promotion.
- Mahogany. A greeting card line created specifically for African American consumers. The designs and messages celebrate African American heritage, tradition, and culture.
- Hallmark en Español. A card line for Hispanic consumers with bilingual (Spanish and English) messages and culturally specific captions. This line contains cards for dates important to Hispanic consumers.
- The Tree of Life. A line of cards for Jewish consumers for holidays such as Passover, Rosh Hashanah, and Hannukah.
- Hallmark Business Expressions. Customized cards created to help business clients form lasting relationships with their customers and employees. Hallmark has designed custom cards for the New York Yankees, NASA, Radio Shack, and State Farm Insurance.
- The company also offers Hallmark Keepsake Ornaments and Party Express party products, such as matching printed plates, table covers, and decorations appropriate for specific occasions.

The Hallmark brand is closely identified with approximately 8,000 independently owned card specialty stores—including 5,000 Hallmark Gold Crown stores. The Hallmark and Shoebox brands, along with exclusive Hallmark Keepsake Ornaments, are available exclusively at the Gold Crown stores. Hallmark-branded products are also available at an additional 39,000 mass merchandise outlets.

Today Hallmark sells much more than greeting cards

Hallmark Online

Hallmark launched its website in 1996. Initially the site contained corporate information and soon expanded to allow consumers to send their own e-cards (some for free, some for a charge). However, the company that really prospered from the increased use of e-cards was not Hallmark but a newcomer, Blue Mountain Arts (**www.bluemountain.com**). Blue Mountain offered free e-cards and became one of the Internet's most popular sites. In September 1999 it attracted more than 9 million visitors, ranking it 18th on Media Metric's list of the top 50 websites. American Greetings also reported a surge in activity on its site thanks in large part to an alliance with America Online.

In the summer of 1999, Hallmark responded with a relaunch of its consumer website (the Web address is now listed on the back of all of Hallmark's traditional paper cards). Visitors can choose from a collection of about 600 free e-cards, which are unique to the website (not available in stores). In fact, the e-cards are created by a separate team of designers. Customers can also purchase gifts and send flowers at the Hallmark site. There is even a service that will e-mail you a reminder of upcoming holidays, birthdays, anniversaries, and so forth. The notice is intended to stimulate problem recognition and a subsequent problem-solving session to select an appropriate greeting card (hopefully, a Hallmark card). Hallmark reported its 1999 Web traffic increased 200 percent, with Web sales jumping up 600 percent.

The Marketing Problem

Distribution is a key element of Hallmark's marketing strategy: putting its products where consumers can easily access them and make purchase decisions. Nationwide, Hallmark personal expression products are found in more than 47,000 retail outlets. In the mid-1980s, Hallmark emphasized the Hallmark Gold Crown stores as the place to buy high-quality greeting cards and receive special services. To buy the exclusive high-end Hallmark card and other products, consumers first had to decide to go to a Hallmark card shop. This strategy of dedicated Hallmark stores seemed to work well for many years, but by the mid- to late 1990s it was in serious question. Between 1990 and 2000, Hallmark's overall market share in the United States declined from 50 percent to about 40 percent.

Historically, about 75 percent of Hallmark's top-of-the-line cards were sold in the specialty shops. This was fine as long as many consumers chose to shop at those locations. But as distribution of greeting cards to mass merchandisers and other locations (airports and bus stations) increased—and as the Internet grew in popularity—consumers' shopping behavior changed. Fewer consumers were deciding to go to a card specialty store first—let alone a Hallmark store—to shop for cards. Many time-starved customers found it easier to buy cards at stores they already frequented (grocery stores, discount chains, drugstores) or to send a free card via e-mail rather than make a special trip to a Hallmark store. Specialty card shops once accounted for nearly 65 percent of greeting card sales but that figure fell to less than 33 percent by the late 1990s. Also, mass merchandisers were selling an increased number of cards. Although Hallmark produces its Ambassador and Warm Wishes lines of cards for sale in these outlets, it did not sell its top-of- the-line cards there.

How should Hallmark distribute its many brands if sales at dedicated card stores continue to fall? Should Hallmark develop distribution deals to begin selling its upscale cards to the mass merchandisers, even at the risk of alienating the owners/operators of the Hallmark Gold Crown shops? Will its current Web strategy prove effective in the long run? Solving these difficult marketing problems requires understanding many aspects of consumer decision making and problem solving. But Hallmark has a major asset: its name. The Hallmark brand has considerable equity and a strong reputation for quality and integrity, particularly among older consumers.

Discussion Questions

1. Why do so many consumers continue to buy and send greeting cards instead of writing a letter, sending an e-mail, or making a phone call? Discuss your answer in terms of the means–end framework.

2. The "typical" decision-making process for buying a Hallmark card is likely to vary in different situations. Think about three different occasions for buying a card: a birthday, a graduation, and a wedding. How would consumer knowledge and involvement vary across these situations? Discuss how problem recognition, search, and evaluation might differ. What types or level of decision making would you expect in each situation?

3. Understanding how and why consumers make store choices (i.e., buying a card in a Wal-Mart rather than in a Hallmark Gold Crown store) is particularly important to Hallmark. Discuss how store choice interacts with and influences choices of Hallmark products and brands.

4. Do you think Hallmark should modify its in-store distribution strategy? What about its Web strategy? What assumptions do you make about consumer decision making that lead you to this recommendation?

5. Marketing research estimates men account for only 15 to 20 percent of greeting card purchases in the United States. Furthermore, young consumers and those over 50 don't buy as many cards as those in middle age. Why do you think this is so? What can Hallmark do to reach these two segments?

Sources: Kipp Cheng, "Hallmark.com Revamps Consumer-Targeted Site," *Adweek,* May 24, 1999, p. 46; Michael Hartnett, "The New Card Game: Playing Catch-Up," *Supermarket Business,* March 15, 2000, pp. 67, 74; Matt Hamblen, "Greeting Card Rivals Tap Tech to Stay on Top," *Computerworld,* March 1, 1999, pp. 1, 97.

three

Behavior and Marketing Strategy

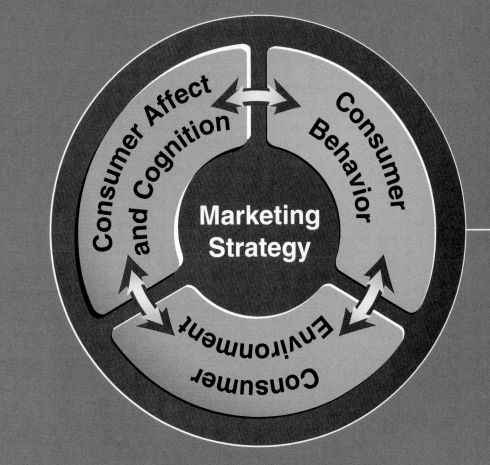

8

Introduction to Behavior

Lands' End Inlet Store

"I have to run over to Walgreen's to pick up Angie's medicine," said Kari Jardine to her husband, Andy. "Do you want to go with me?"

"Sure," Andy responded. "I'd like to pick up some magazines for my flight to New York tomorrow."

On the way, the Jardines chatted about the recent snowfall and how much they enjoyed Christmas and New Year's, although both agreed they were glad the holidays were over. It was nice to get back to a more normal routine without all the hassle of shopping in crowded malls for Christmas gifts.

The snowplows had left large mounds of snow in the parking lot at the strip mall where the drugstore was located. Once in the store, Kari went back to the pharmacy to pick up the prescription, and Andy went to the magazine rack in the front of the store. Andy pulled out $10 from his wallet and purchased copies of *Golf Digest* and *Sports Illustrated* and two

Peppermint Patties to munch on during the drive home.

As they walked out of Walgreen's, Andy suggested that rather than go right home, they take a few minutes to look in the Lands' End Inlet store two doors down. "I saw a cranberry golf sweater in the Lands' End catalog that I liked. Maybe it will be in the store and I could try it on."

"That would be fine with me," replied Kari. "I could look for a new spring coat. I don't have to be at work until noon."

The sweater Andy was interested in was in the store. He tried it on and liked it. He remembered the normal price was $56, but the sale catalog price was $39. The outlet store price was $38.50. He decided to purchase it and saw another sweater he liked. The other sweater was a black wool cardigan, marked down from $70 to $56. Although a little reluctant to purchase the other sweater because it was more expensive and wasn't much different from a green sweater he had received for Christmas, he decided to purchase it too. After all, he deserved it, and he could return the green sweater to Marshall Field's.

Wayne Scarberry/The Image Works.

Kari found a three-quarter-length, sand-colored, lightweight parka and was trying it on. "What do you think?" she asked Andy as he walked toward her, sweaters dangling over his arm.

"How much is it?" he asked.

"Let's see. It's $56 marked down from $70," Kari answered. "What did you find?"

After agreeing that the coat and sweaters were good buys, the Jardines went to the checkout counter in the center of the store. "Did you find everything you need today?" asked the salesclerk.

"Yes, and we're ready to check out," stated Kari.

"Fine," said the salesclerk, checking the price tags and ringing up the merchandise. "Well, let's see. The sweaters are an additional 30 percent off today. So that's $11.55 off one and $16.80 off the other.

"See this symbol?" the salesclerk said, pointing to a small black ship's steering wheel stamped on the coat's price tag. "That means it's 60 percent off, which will save you . . . $35.40."

The Jardines looked at each other and smiled. "Wow! You mean we're saving 50 or 60 bucks on this stuff?" exclaimed Andy.

"That's right," said the salesclerk, handing them their Visa card receipt and the bag of clothes. "We'll have more spring clothes in the next week or two. Be sure to stop back and look for those big markdowns."

Driving home, the Jardines figured out how much they had saved from the normal retail price. The total at retail was $196, and they paid $94.24, which included the 5 percent state sales tax. They felt good about their stop at the Lands' End Inlet. Andy decided to keep the green sweater he had gotten for Christmas since they had gotten such a good deal on the two new sweaters. He enjoyed eating his candy.

You can learn more about Lands' End products at **www.landsend.com**.

What overt consumer behaviors were performed in this trip to Lands' End Inlet? The Wheel of Consumer Analysis now turns from affect and cognition to behavior, that is, from what consumers feel and think to what they actually do. This section provides an overview of overt consumer behaviors and marketing strategies designed to influence them. In this chapter, we discuss the nature of overt consumer behavior and why it is important to marketing. We develop and explain a general model of overt consumer behavior for use in designing marketing strategies. In Chapter 9, we explain the basic tools marketers use to influence those behaviors. These tools include classical conditioning, operant conditioning, and vicarious learning or modeling. Once you understand the behaviors marketers want consumers to perform from this chapter and the tools marketers use to influence these behaviors from the next chapter, you are ready to explore how marketers can develop comprehensive strategies to influence overt consumer behaviors by systematically employing these tools; this is the focus of Chapter 10.

What Is Overt Consumer Behavior?

The term *consumer behavior* means many things. In some cases, it refers to a field of study or a college course. In others, it refers to what consumers think, feel, and do, and everything that influences them. However, **overt consumer behavior** has a specific meaning. It refers to *the observable and measurable responses or actions of consumers.* Thus, overt behavior is distinct from affect and cognition because it is external and can be observed directly rather than being an internal psychological process that must be inferred.

The fact that *overt behavior* refers to external actions that are observable leads many analysts to think it is a simple phenomenon. For example, marketers frequently refer to purchasing behavior, shopping behavior, or usage behavior as though they were simple acts. However, each is a complex set of actions that require consumers to do many things. For example, to purchase even a simple product like a jar of Jif peanut butter or a Bic pen at a 7-Eleven store, a consumer must perform a multitude of complex actions. Also, because overt behavior is so obvious and prevalent, many analysts may think it is uninteresting or unworthy of study.

One problem in studying overt consumer behavior is determining the appropriate level of analysis. Overt consumer behavior can be analyzed fruitfully at the level of a momentary movement of a few muscles or a single finger to the lifetime usage of products. When designing computer keyboards, finger movements are critical for marketers who are trying to develop more comfortable and efficient products. When forecasting demand for Pampers, it is important to know not only expected birth rates but also frequency of diaper changes and the number of years the product is used per child.

Another problem in studying overt behavior is deciding whether individual consumers or the entire world market is the appropriate level. When selling a car, a salesperson is concerned with getting an individual consumer to sign a contract and pay for the car. In forecasting world demand for cars, current sales and trends in usage in world markets must be analyzed.

A third problem is that the linkages between overt behavior and affect and cognition are not well developed at a theoretical level. The way in which mental events (affect and cognition) can cause physical actions (overt behavior) is poorly understood.

In spite of these problems, understanding overt consumer behavior is an important part of consumer analysis and developing marketing strategies.

The Importance of Overt Consumer Behavior

Although overt behavior is complex, it is a critical component of consumer analysis. The success of marketing strategies depends on maintaining and changing overt consumer behavior, not just influencing affect and cognition. There are at least three reasons this is important. First, although in many cases influencing affect and cognition leads to overt behavior, this linkage often does not hold. Consumers often have favorable attitudes about products but do not buy them, and favorable attitudes about stores, but do not shop there. As discussed in Chapter 6, even specific measures of behavioral intentions are frequently poor predictors of overt behavior.

Second, as discussed in Chapter 2, behavior precedes and causes affect and cognition in some cases. For example, suppose a consumer tries out a friend's Titleist

983K driver at a driving range. Perhaps little thought was given to evaluating or buying the club beforehand. However, as the golf ball sails 260 yards, the consumer is awed by the club's performance, decides to buy one, goes into the pro shop, and plunks down $500. It seems likely that the successful behavior of hitting the ball well was an important determinant of purchase rather than just the small amount of prepurchase affect and cognition. For low-price, low-involvement products like a new candy bar, consumers often try them first and then decide whether they like them and will buy them again.

Third, most marketing strategies cannot succeed without influencing overt consumer behavior. Although some intermediate strategies may focus on changing recall or recognition of ads or products, in most cases marketing strategies are designed to ultimately maintain or increase the sales of particular products, services, or stores. This is usually accomplished by (1) increasing the frequency of purchase and use by existing customers, (2) maintaining purchase and use levels of existing customers and increasing purchase and use by new customers, or (3) increasing purchase and use by both existing and new customers. These can happen only by influencing overt consumer behavior.

There is no question that many marketing practitioners are acutely concerned with overt consumer behavior. Many marketing research techniques are designed to assess overt shopping behavior in stores and product purchase and use patterns, and many strategies are designed to increase these behaviors.

A Model of Overt Consumer Behavior

Traditional views of the purchase or adoption process in marketing treat it as a series or chain of cognitive events followed by a single overt behavior, usually called *adoption* or *purchase*. Consider the models of the adoption process as it is commonly treated in marketing (Exhibit 8.1). These models are consistent with the view that *cognitive variables* (awareness, comprehension, interest, evaluation, conviction, etc.) are the main concern of marketing and the primary controllers of behavior. According to this view, the marketing task is to change these cognitive variables and move consumers through each stage until a purchase is made.

Although the models in Exhibit 8.1 are valuable, adoption or purchase can also be analyzed as a *sequence of behaviors*. From this perspective, marketing managers usually want to increase the frequency of these behaviors, and they design strategies and tactics for doing so. Although strategies and tactics to change affective and cognitive processes such as attention, knowledge or attitude may be useful intermediate steps, they must ultimately change behavior to be profitable for marketers.

Exhibit 8.2 offers a model of a behavior sequence that occurs in the purchase of many consumer goods. Before discussing each of these stages, several qualifications should be noted. First, although we suggest that this is a logical sequence, consumers commonly perform many other combinations of behavior. For example, an unplanned (impulse) purchase of Twix cookie bars could start at the store contact stage. Not every purchase follows the sequence shown in Exhibit 8.2, and not every purchase requires that all of these behaviors be performed. However, the model is useful for categorizing a variety of marketing strategies in terms of the behaviors they are designed to influence.

Second, the model in Exhibit 8.2 is intended to illustrate only one type of behavior sequence for retail purchases; similar models could be developed for other types of purchases, such as mail-order, phone, Internet, or catalog-showroom exchanges. Further, the sequences involved with other behaviors of interest to

Exhibit 8.1

Traditional Models of the Adoption/Purchase Process

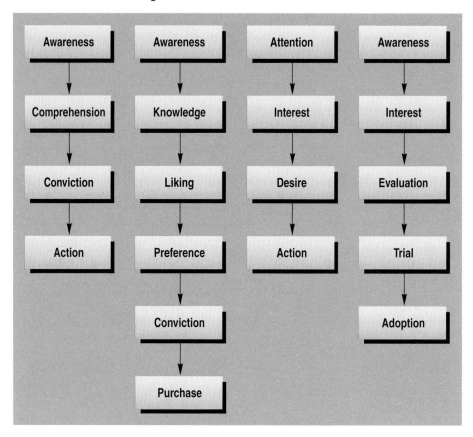

consumer analysis, such as voting, physician care, banking, or consumer education, could be modeled in much the same way. We believe that any attempt to influence behavior should include an analysis of the behavior sequence that is necessary or desired. Unfortunately, many marketing managers do not consider exactly what behaviors are involved in the actions they are attempting to get consumers to perform.

Third, the time it takes for a consumer to perform these behaviors depends on a variety of factors. Different products, consumers, and situations may affect not only the total time to complete the process but also the time lags between stages. For example, an avid water skier purchasing a Mastercraft powerboat likely will spend more time per stage, and more time will elapse between stages, than a consumer purchasing a Timex quartz watch.

Fourth, members of the channel of distribution usually vary in their emphasis on encouraging particular behaviors. Retailers may be more concerned with increasing store contact than with purchase of a particular brand; manufacturers are less concerned with the particular store patronized but attempt to increase brand purchase; credit card companies may be less concerned with particular store or product contacts as long as their credit card is accepted and used. However,

Exhibit 8.2

A Common Behavior Sequence for a Retail Store Consumer Goods Purchase

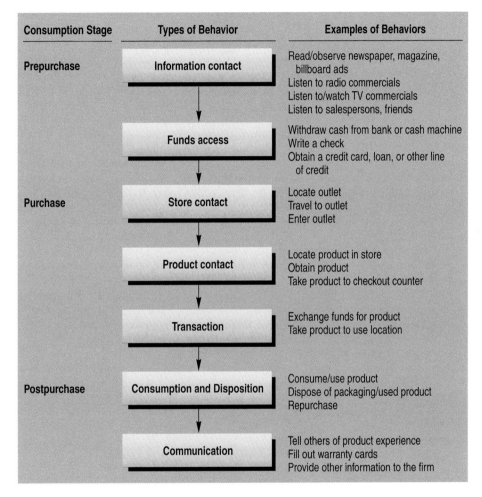

Consumption Stage	Types of Behavior	Examples of Behaviors
Prepurchase	**Information contact**	Read/observe newspaper, magazine, billboard ads Listen to radio commercials Listen to/watch TV commercials Listen to salespersons, friends
	Funds access	Withdraw cash from bank or cash machine Write a check Obtain a credit card, loan, or other line of credit
Purchase	**Store contact**	Locate outlet Travel to outlet Enter outlet
	Product contact	Locate product in store Obtain product Take product to checkout counter
	Transaction	Exchange funds for product Take product to use location
Postpurchase	**Consumption and Disposition**	Consume/use product Dispose of packaging/used product Repurchase
	Communication	Tell others of product experience Fill out warranty cards Provide other information to the firm

although emphasis may vary, all three of these behaviors are common in a retail exchange, and all three organizations can benefit from the others' efforts. Highlight 8.1 discusses a creative strategy for influencing consumers' purchasing behavior that involves a discount card company and restaurants.

Finally, the seven categories of the consumer behavior chain in Exhibit 8.2 deserve comment. Although we believe these are logical and useful categories of behavior, other labels or breakdowns could also be useful. For instance, this behavior chain could be carefully broken down into individual actions of each muscle in the consumer's body, and research could be conducted at that level. However, given the lack of knowledge concerning overt consumer behavior, the levels in Exhibit 8.2 are a useful starting point. With these qualifications, we now turn to a discussion of each type of behavior and some marketing strategies currently employed to increase the probability of one or more of them.

Highlight 8.1

Increasing Restaurant Patronage with a Transmedia Card

Transmedia Network Inc. came up with an innovative strategy to serve consumers profitably with a discount card for restaurant meals. Here's how it works. Transmedia offers cash advances to restaurants that in turn give Transmedia twice the cash amount in credits for meals. For example, Transmedia offers $5,000 for $10,000 worth of restaurant credits. It then offers its cardholders a 25 percent discount on meals (before tax and tip) eaten at restaurants that honor its cards. Usually it takes about six months for a group of cardholders to use all the $10,000 credit at a particular restaurant. After giving cardholders the 25 percent discount, Transmedia still gets $7,500 for its initial $5,000 cash advance.

Restaurants deal with Transmedia because they benefit from the quick cash, and the additional business is still profitable. Restaurants have high fixed costs, but variable costs of food and service are only about 30 percent of the price of a meal. So if a check is $100, the restaurant gets $50 from Transmedia, the cost of the meal is about $30, and the restaurant makes $20. The cards help restaurants fill unused capacity and are a big help to new restaurants trying to build clientele.

Consumers benefit from lower prices, but Transmedia initially had trouble getting them to sign up. Even after advertising and offering free cards, consumers initially didn't believe the company could deliver such good deals. In Transmedia's first directory, published in 1985, 41 restaurants were listed and only 225 consumers signed up. By 1995, 5,500 restaurants worldwide were on board and nearly 600,000 consumers had discount cards. Transmedia's revenue grew to $65.5 million in 1995, with net income of more than $4 million. It charges consumers $50 for its card.

Transmedia's success has attracted competitors such as In Good Taste, Dining à la Card, and Dinner On Us Club. However, its biggest problem is keeping restaurants on its list. Restaurants often sign up when they're new or need quick cash, but then drop Transmedia when their cash position improves. Also, 70 percent of Transmedia's charges are in the New York metropolitan area.

Overall, this strategy increases the probability of consumers purchasing meals in specific restaurants and is profitable for Transmedia, the restaurants, and consumers who dine out a lot.

Sources: Nikhil Hutheesing, "Keeping the Seats Warm," *Forbes,* January 1, 1996, pp. 62–63; Richard S. Teitelbaum, "Good Food Cheap? Pick a Card!" *Fortune,* March 18, 1996, p. 133.

Information Contact

A common early stage in the purchase sequence, called **information contact,** occurs when consumers come into contact with information, either intentionally or accidentally, about products, stores, or brands. This stage includes behaviors such as reading or observing newspaper, magazine, and billboard ads; surfing company and other sites on the Web; listening to radio commercials; watching TV commercials; and talking to salespeople and friends. At this point, the practical problem for marketers is to increase the probability that consumers will observe and attend to the information and that this will increase the probability of other behaviors.

Not only do marketers seek to provide consumers with information, but consumers also search for information about products, brands, stores, and prices.[1] Marketing managers for brands with low market shares usually want to increase overall search behavior because it may increase the probability of switching to their firm's brands.

Managers of high-market-share brands may try to discourage external search behaviors because the behavior may result in a shift to another brand. For example,

Not all consumer purchases are from retail stores; some are made through electronic media
Frank Siteman/ PhotoEdit, Inc.

Heinz has a major share of the market for ketchup and does not want consumers to search for information concerning different brands. Ads showing Heinz as the thicker, richer ketchup while depicting other brands as thin and unsavory may discourage loyal consumers from searching for an alternative. They may also help attract non-Heinz purchasers by demonstrating the negative consequences of using another brand.

The extent of a consumer's search depends on many factors, such as those listed in Exhibit 8.3. In general, empirical research has shown that

1. Consumers tend to engage in more search when purchasing higher-priced, more visible, and more complex products—that is, products that intrinsically create greater perceived risk.

2. Search is also influenced by individual factors such as the perceived benefits of search (e.g., enjoyment), self-confidence, purchase role, demographic aspects of the consumer, and product knowledge already possessed.

3. Search efforts tend to be further influenced by factors in the marketplace (such as store distribution) and by situational factors (such as time pressure impinging on the shopper).[2]

Information search can be extensive for some products
Bonnie Kanan/ PhotoEdit, Inc.

From a public policy standpoint, information search is encouraged to develop more knowledgeable consumers.[3] However, there are differences in the effort required by consumers to obtain information from different sources and in the believability of the information. For example, Exhibit 8.4 illustrates five common sources of information and rates them on the dimensions of effort required and believability. This model predicts that internal sources (stores experiences) and personal sources (friends and relatives) are commonly used because they are easiest to access and most believable. Marketing sources (advertising) would also be commonly used because they are readily available. However, marketing sources are not as believable because advertisers have something to gain from the transaction. Finally, public sources (*Consumer Reports* and other impartial studies) and experiential sources (personally examining or testing the product) are less likely to be used, at least in this early stage, because more effort is required to obtain information from these sources.

Information search could also be broken down into a sequence of basic behaviors. However, the main marketing task is to increase the probability that the target market will come into contact with product, brand, or store information and pay attention to it.

Numerous marketing strategies are directed at bringing about these attentive behaviors. For example, media scheduling, message content and layout, color and

Exhibit 8.3

Factors Affecting Information Search by Consumers

Influencing Factor	Increasing the Influencing Factor Causes Search to:
I. Market characteristics	
A. Number of alternatives	Increase
B. Price range	Increase
C. Store concentration	Increase
D. Information availability	Increase
1. Advertising	
2. Point of purchase	
3. Sales personnel	
4. Packaging	
5. Experienced consumers	
6. Independent sources	
II. Product characteristics	
A. Price	Increase
B. Differentiation	Increase
C. Positive products	Increase
III. Consumer characteristics	
A. Learning and experience	Decrease
B. Shopping orientation	Mixed
C. Social status	Increase
D. Age and household life cycle	Mixed
E. Product involvement	Mixed
F. Perceived risk	Increase
IV. Situational characteristics	
A. Time availability	Increase
B. Purchase for self	Decrease
C. Pleasant surroundings	Increase
D. Social surroundings	Mixed
E. Physical/mental energy	Increase

Sources: Reprinted from Del I. Hawkins, Kenneth A. Coney, and Roger Best, Jr., *Consumer Behavior: Implications for Marketing Strategy,* 8th ed., 2001, Irwin/McGraw-Hill p. 544. Reproduced with permission from The McGraw-Hill Companies.

Exhibit 8.4

A Comparison of Information Sources

Source	Effort Required	Believability
Internal (stored experiences in memory)	Low	High
Personal (friends, relatives)	Low	High
Marketing (advertising)	Low	Low
Public (*Consumer Reports*, other studies)	High	High
Experiential (examining or testing product)	High	High

Highlight 8.2

Encouraging Information Contact for Magazine Subscriptions

Including subscription cards in magazines is a useful marketing tactic because the cards are available while the magazine is being read and enjoyed. These cards make it convenient for readers of the magazine (the likely target market for future issues) to renew a subscription or start a new one.

Traditionally, magazine marketers have bound subscription cards to the magazines. One drawback to such "bind-in" cards is that readers often simply ignore them. Because the cards are bound to the issue, readers leaf through the entire magazine without giving the card (or the idea of starting or renewing a subscription) any consideration.

An alternative method of including subscription cards in magazines is to place them between the pages, unbound. These are called "blow-in" cards. When magazines are being read or carried, blow-in cards frequently fall out. Consumers usually pick up the cards and examine them for at least a moment. In other words, the probability of information contact increases when blow-in rather than bind-in cards are used. It is not surprising, then, that blow-in cards are more effective than bind-in cards at generating subscription renewals.

humor in advertising, and repetition all involve presenting stimuli to increase the probability that potential consumers will attend to relevant cues. In addition, *fear appeals* are used to bring about attentive behaviors and to vicariously stimulate emotions by exposing the observers to possible aversive consequences of certain conditions (inadequate insurance, faulty tires and batteries, the absence of smoke alarms, not flossing regularly).

Strategies such as contests and prizes bring about attentive behavior and promise rewards for engaging in certain actions that bring the consumer into closer contact with the product or point of purchase. Finally, ads that show models receiving social approval and satisfaction from purchasing a product provide stimuli that can move the consumer closer to purchase by stimulating the "buying mood." Highlight 8.2 discusses a strategy for encouraging information contact for magazine subscriptions.

Funds Access

Current views of marketing emphasize exchange as the key concept for understanding the field. However, relatively little attention has been given to *what consumers exchange* in the marketing process. Although time and effort costs are involved, money is the primary medium of consumer exchange. The consumer must access this medium in one form or another before an exchange can occur, engaging is what is known as **funds access.** The primary marketing issues at this stage are (1) the methods consumers use to pay for particular purchases and (2) the marketing strategies to increase the probability that consumers will access funds for purchase.

ATMs provide one means of funds access, a bank withdrawal of cash *James Marshall/The Image Works.*

For many purchases, consumers carry cash, checks, or credit cards
David Young-Wolff/ PhotoEdit, Inc.

Consumers can pay for a product offering in a variety of ways. These include cash in pocket; bank withdrawal of cash; writing a check; using credit cards such as Visa, MasterCard, and American Express; opening a store charge account; using debit cards; and drawing on other lines of credit, such as bank loans and GMAC financing. Another issue concerns the *effort* the consumer exerts to obtain the actual funds that are spent or used to repay loans. Funds obtained from tax refunds, stock sales and dividends, gambling winnings, awards, or regular paychecks may be valued differently by the consumer and spent in different ways. Some retailers encourage the purchase of big-ticket items by offering interest-free loans for a few months while consumers are waiting for their tax refunds.

A variety of other strategies can increase the probability that consumers will access funds for purchases. For example, JC Penney offers a small gift to anyone who fills out a Penney's credit card application. The probability of purchasing at Penney's increases when a consumer has a credit card because cash may not always be available. Other strategies include locating ATMs in malls, instituting liberal credit terms and check-cashing policies, and accepting a variety of credit cards. Deferred payment plans and layaway plans that allow the consumer additional time to raise the required funds help stores avoid lost sales. Gift certificates are also used to presell merchandise and provide consumers with another source of funds that is restricted for particular purchases. All of these strategies have a common goal: to increase the probability of an exchange by increasing the probability of accessing funds.

Other strategies can be employed to increase certain types of purchases. For example, a store could offer a small discount for using cash to avoid the costs of paying credit card fees. An analysis of the conditions surrounding particular purchases may lead to other successful tactics. For example, many major home appliances are purchased only when both partners in a household are present, and a necessary condition is that they can obtain funds. One tactic for an appliance store might be to offer a small gift to any couple that comes to the store with their checkbook or approved credit card. Thus, the appropriate contingencies are prearranged for an appliance sale. Any number of other tactics (such as offering rebates) could be used in conjunction with this tactic to further increase the probability of purchase. Highlight 8.3 discusses a strategy used by credit card issuers to encourage consumers to obtain and use their credit cards for funds access.

Store Contact

Although catalog, telephone-order, and Internet purchases are important, most consumer goods purchases are still made in retail stores. Thus, a major task of retailers is to get consumers into the store where purchases can occur. **Store contact** includes (1) locating the outlet, (2) traveling to the outlet, and (3) entering the outlet.

The nature of consumers in their roles as shoppers affects the probability of store contact. Some consumers may enjoy shopping and spend many hours looking in stores. To others, shopping may be drudgery. Some shoppers may be primarily

⊷ **High**light 8.3

Rewards for Credit Cards

For most of their lives, Harlan and Beverly Ness, both 56, made little use of Visa or MasterCard. But this spring they decorated and furnished their Florida condominium with a Northwest Visa. Their motivation: free airline tickets.

Until last year, Stuart Feldstein would have written a check for his son's tuition and housing at the University of Tennessee. Instead, he charged the $13,000 on his GM Gold Card. His motivation: a $650 rebate toward the purchase of a General Motors car or truck. "It's my car fund," says Feldstein of Budd Lake, New Jersey.

The Nesses and Feldstein are foot soldiers in a revolution in the way consumers use credit cards. You can fill your car with gas, buy lunch at a fast-food restaurant, mail a package at the post office, take a cab, see a doctor, pick up milk at the supermarket, and go to a movie—all with a credit card.

"You don't have to carry cash, you don't have to write a check, and you get a record at the end of the month," says Philip Purcell, CEO of Dean Witter Discover.

In one recent year, total credit card charges soared 25 percent—to $421.9 billion from $338.6 billion the year before—the biggest percentage increase since 1984. Revolving credit card balances make up 28 percent of all consumer installment debt, and credit card debt is growing faster than consumer debt in general. This means that some people are using cards instead of bank loans or store credit. Igniting the plastic explosion are rebates on merchandise ranging from cars to computers, wider acceptance of cards by business, and new technology that makes credit card use faster than writing a check.

The industry's greatest growth is in rebate cards, thanks to the stunning success of the GM Card. In just 20 months it had 9 million cardholders in the United States and another 2 million in Canada. Cardholders get 5 percent rebates on purchases to spend on GM vehicles—up to $500 a year. The card also encourages consumers to transfer balances from other cards and earn GM rebates. That helped make it the fastest-growing credit card ever. Ford, Shell Oil, and GE Rewards are just some of the other companies that offered reward cards. However, Ford dropped its card because it often discounted its most popular model, which would have sold well anyway.

As reward cards grow in popularity, consumer advocates warn that they can be costly. "If you charge a lot and if you pay in full each month—which are the two big ifs—you can get something for nothing. But most people don't pay in full and end up racking up all that interest," says Ruth Susswein of consumer group Bankcard Holders of America. About 70 percent of cardholders carry balances from month to month. They should ignore rebates and get low-interest cards, Susswein says.

Card companies also have begun to form partnerships with universities. One example is Bank One Corp.'s alliance with the University of Tennessee's Visa "affinity" credit card, which is adorned with the university's picture and logo. The university benefits by receiving a small percentage from every transaction charged. But the credit card companies are the real winners. They now have access to the lucrative, credit-hungry student population. After securing this segment, the bank can market other products, such as car loans, first mortgages, and debt-consolidation loans.

Regardless of the type of card, charging is expected to soar. "Consumers like convenience and they'll pay for it," says one analyst.

Sources: Marcia Vickers, "Big Cards on Campus," *Business Week,* September 20, 1999, pp. 136–138; Anne Willette, "Rewards Are a Big Part of New Appeal," *USA Today,* May 11, 1994, pp. 1B, 2B. Copyright 1994, *USA Today.* Reprinted with permission.

price oriented and favor particular low-price outlets. Others may seek a high level of service or unique products and stores that express their individuality. These differences are important dimensions of designing market segmentation strategies for stores.

Attractive architecture can increase store contact
Pascal Quittemelle/Stock, Boston, LLC.

Outdoor signs can increase store contact
John Coletti/Stock, Boston, LLC.

Many strategies are designed to increase the probability of store contact. For example, consider the methods used to increase the probability that shoppers will be able to locate a particular outlet. Selecting convenient locations in high-traffic areas with ample parking has been very successful for many retailers, such as 7-Eleven convenience stores and Denny's restaurants.

A major advantage for retailers locating in shopping malls is the increase in consumers' ability to find the outlet as well as the additional shopping traffic created by the presence of the other stores. Yellow Pages, newspaper, and other ads frequently include maps and information numbers to aid shoppers in locating an outlet. Outdoor signs and logos (such as Domino's Pizza's distinctive sign) are well known. One recreational vehicle dealer close to Columbus, Ohio, used an interesting approach to aid potential customers in locating the dealership. The dealer's TV ads consisted of the actual scenery, landmarks, and road signs people would see when traveling to the dealership. Every turn was shown, as were directional signs on the highway, to help potential customers find the outlet.

Other tactics are used to get potential customers to the vicinity of stores or malls. For example, carnivals in mall parking lots, free fashion shows or other mall entertainment, and visits by celebrities such as Santa Claus, the Easter Bunny, Sesame Street characters, and soap opera actors are used to draw consumers to the mall. Further, mall directories and information booths help shoppers find particular stores.

Finally, tactics are used to get the potential customer physically into the store. Advertised sales, sale signs in store windows, door prizes, loss leaders, sounds (such as popular music), and smells (such as fresh popcorn) are commonly employed. A variety of other in-store issues are discussed later in the text, particularly in Chapter 19.

Hopefully product contact leads to a transaction and consumption
David Young-Wolff/ PhotoEdit, Inc.

Product Contact

Whereas a major concern of retailers is increasing and maintaining selective store patronage, manufacturers are primarily concerned with selective demand—purchase of their particular brands and models. Many of the methods employed

Cents-off coupons
encourage product contact
*Jeff Greenberg/
PhotoEdit, Inc.*

to accomplish such **product contact** involve **push strategies** such as trade discounts and incentives to enhance retailers' selling efforts. For example, offering retailers a free case of Tide liquid detergent for every 10 cases purchased can be a powerful incentive for them to feature liquid Tide in newspaper ads, put it in prominent displays, and even sell it at a lower price while maintaining or increasing profit margins. Many approaches also involve **pull strategies,** such as cents-off coupons, to encourage the consumer to purchase the manufacturer's brand.

Once potential buyers are in the store, three behaviors are usually necessary for a purchase to occur: (1) locate the product or brand in the store, (2) physically obtain the product or brand, and (3) take the product or brand to the point of exchange (e.g., the checkout counter).

Products must be easily located. Store directories, end-of-aisle and other displays, in-store signs, information booths, and helpful store personnel all help consumers move into visual contact with products. While consumers are in the store, their visual contact with the many other available products increases the probability of purchase.

One interesting tactic employed by a major chain involves a variation of "blue-light specials." Blue-light specials were pioneered by Kmart. These tactics offer shoppers in the store the opportunity to purchase products at special prices when a blue light is flashing at a particular location. Usually, the sale item is one that is low-priced and sold at its normal location. A variation of this tactic moves the sale merchandise and blue light to a location in the store where high-priced or high-margin items are located. This brings the blue-light shoppers to the vicinity of such products and into visual contact with them—which increases the probability of making these more-profitable sales. This has been reported to be very successful.

Physically coming into contact with a product provides an extremely important source of stimuli and possible consequences that influence whether a purchase will occur. Attractive, eye-catching packaging and other aspects of product appearance influence the stimuli attended to by the consumer. Trying the product in the store can also affect purchase probabilities.

The behavior of sales personnel can also affect the contingencies at the point of purchase. For example, consider salespeople who are overly aggressive and use high-pressure tactics. One way for consumers to remove the aversive treatment is to purchase the product—and some consumers do this rather than walk away.

Salespeople can also change the contingencies for purchasing versus not purchasing. For example, one of our associates told us of his experience in selling furniture to ambivalent customers who stated their intention to "go home and think it over." Once the potential buyer leaves the store, the probability of a sale is reduced. Our associate, however, changed the contingencies for leaving. Potential buyers who wanted to think it over were told, "If you buy now, the price is $150. If you go home and come back later, the price will be the original $175." Although we are not advocating this specific practice, we do want to stress that salespeople can modify the behavior of potential buyers.

A number of tactics are used to get potential buyers to the checkout or payment location. For example, checkout counters are commonly placed next to the

A positive purchase experience increases the probability of repurchase at the same store   *Elena Rooraid/PhotoEdit, Inc.*

exit, and parking vouchers are usually validated at this location. Also, salespeople frequently escort the buyer to the checkout, where they may help arrange financing.

Transaction

In a macro sense, *facilitating exchanges* is viewed as the primary objective of marketing. In a micro sense, this involves **transactions** in which consumers' funds are exchanged for products and services. Many marketing strategies involve removing obstacles to transactions. The credit methods discussed earlier are examples. So is the use of express checkout lanes and electronic scanners to decrease the time consumers must wait in line. (Some consumers will leave a store without making a purchase if checkout lines are too long.) Credit card companies offer prompt purchase approvals to decrease the chances a sale will be missed because of a long wait.

Because the behavior of checkout personnel has long been recognized as an important influence on purchase, these personnel are often trained to be friendly and efficient. McDonald's personnel frequently offer *prompts* in an attempt to increase the total amount of purchase. Regardless of the food order, prompts for additional food are offered: "Would you like some fresh, hot french fries with that?" or "How about some McDonald's cookies today?" Because these are very low-cost tactics, few incremental sales are required to make them profitable.

Positive consequences are critical elements in obtaining transactions. Tactics such as rebates, friendly treatment and compliments by store personnel, and contest tickets may increase the probability of purchase and repurchase. The quality and value of the product or service itself are also important. These may involve functional, experiential, and psychosocial benefits.

Consumption and Disposition

While **consumption** and use would seem to be very simple behaviors to delineate, they are not because of the vast differences in the natures of various products and services. For example, compare typical behaviors involved in the purchase of nondurables such as a burger and fries versus a durable such as an automobile. The burger and fries are likely to be consumed rather quickly and the packing disposed of properly. Certain strategies can increase the probability that consumption will be relatively quick, such as seats in a restaurant that are comfortable for only a short time. As a result, current customers do not take up space for too long that could be used for new customers. Prompts are often used to encourage proper disposal of packaging, such as "thank you" signs on refuse containers.

In contrast, an automobile purchase usually involves several years of consumption or use. In addition, periodic service is required, and additional complementary products such as gas must be purchased. Finally, an automobile may be disposed of in several ways (selling it, junking it, or trading it in on another model). At present, little is known about the process by which consumers dispose of durable goods.

Consumption of this product could last for several years, with limited options for disposition   *Superstock.*

Regardless of the type of product, however, a primary marketing concern is increasing the probability of repurchase. For nondurable packaged goods, commonly employed tactics include the use of in- or on-package coupons to encourage the consumer to repurchase the same brand. (Many consumers frequently use coupons and take pride in the money they save.) In addition, proof-of-purchase seals have often been used to encourage consumers to purchase the same brand repeatedly, thereby obtaining enough seals to receive "free" gifts. Gold Medal flour has long used this tactic, and Pampers diapers ran a promotion in which a coupon for a free box of diapers was sent to buyers who mailed in three proof-of-purchase seals.

For durable goods, proper instructions on the care and use of the product may be useful because they help the consumer receive full product benefits. In addition, high-quality service and maintenance provided by the seller can help to develop long-term client relationships.

Communication

A final set of behaviors that marketers attempt to increase involves **communication.** Marketers want consumers to communicate with two basic audiences: They want consumers to (1) provide the company with marketing information and (2) tell other potential consumers about the product and encourage them to purchase it. Consumers can communicate with the company or other consumers about products, brands, or stores at any time, not just at the end of the purchase sequence. We discuss this behavior here because consumers who have purchased and used a product are likely to be more knowledgeable about it and more influential in telling other consumers about it.

From Consumers to Marketers   Marketers typically want at least three types of information from consumers. First, they want *information about the consumer* to investigate the quality of their marketing strategy and the success of market segmentation. Warranty cards are commonly used for this. These cards commonly ask about consumer demographics, what magazines consumers read, where they obtained information about the product, where they purchased it, and what competing brands they own or have tried. Free gifts are sometimes offered to encourage

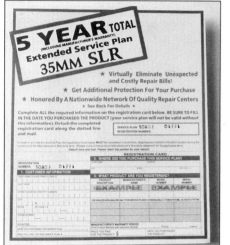

Extended service plans offer marketers a source of information about their consumers and product performance *Michael Newman/PhotoEdit, Inc.*

consumers to return warranty cards—as well as subtle threats that the warranty will be canceled if the card is not filled out and returned promptly.

A second type of information sought from consumers is the *names of other potential buyers* of the product. Some firms and organizations offer awards for the names of several potential buyers and a larger award if any of the prospects actually makes a purchase. Finally, marketers seek consumer information about *defective products*. Money-back or other guarantees that require the consumer to contact the store or company provide this information and also reduce the risk of loss to the consumer. For example, General Mills offers "a prompt adjustment of equal value" if the consumer is dissatisfied with Cheerios.

From Consumers to Consumers   Marketers also want consumers to tell their friends and others about the product. A product that is effective and performs well may encourage this behavior. However, other tactics can also encourage it. Tupperware parties have long been used to take advantage of the fact that consumers respond favorably to information from their friends and to create an environment that heavily encourages purchase. This approach has been so successful that, during the first 25 years of its existence, Tupperware doubled its sales and earnings every 5 years.

Newly opened bars and lounges frequently offer customers free drinks to encourage them not only to return but also to tell others about the place and to bring their friends. Word-of-mouth communication is the primary way such establishments become popular. Health clubs, such as Bally Total Fitness or Golds Gym run promotions in which members who bring in new customers get special rates for themselves as well as for their friends. One cable TV company ran a promotion in which any subscriber who got a friend to purchase the service received $10. Such tactics increase not only communication but also other behaviors in the purchase sequence. Finally, consumers often learn purchase and use behaviors through observing others perform them, as discussed in the next chapter.

Marketing Implications

The model of overt consumer behavior has several implications for marketers. First, marketing managers need to consider carefully precisely what behaviors are necessary for consumers to purchase and use particular products and brands and have clear implications for offering products in appropriate outlets. Also, it provides a starting point for thinking and analyzing precisely what behaviors a marketing strategy is designed to influence. Depending on whether the marketer is a brand manager, store manager, or credit card company marketer, the desired responses vary. However, each type of behavior listed in the model can be further broken down for more detailed analysis. A model for influencing these behaviors is discussed later in this section.

Second, it should be clear from the discussion that marketing strategies and tactics are designed to alter overt consumer behavior by changing one or more aspects of the environment. In some cases, intermediate steps include increasing cognitive activity about the offering and developing positive affect prior to the desired behaviors. These could involve providing information about competitive offerings that highlight the superiority of a company's products. For example, Cadillac ran a series of humorous ads depicting Mercedes-Benz owners as driving underpowered cars; the Cadillac has a 275 horsepower engine compared to the Mercedes 215 horsepower. These ads require consumers to process the comparative information and are designed to increase affect for Cadillac relative to Mercedes and lead to a brand switch. However, many purchases are made on a routine or habitual basis without excessive cognitive activity, including some car purchases from customers who are dealer and brand loyal. Also, many car ads offer little product information but rely on peripheral cues to develop positive affect designed to build brand equity and lead to overt purchase behavior. The frequency and quantity of cognitive activity and affect development for various purchases are not fully understood. However, high-involvement purchases typically involve greater affect and cognition than do low-involvement products. They also typically involve more overt behavior.

Back To...

Lands' End Inlet Store

This case discusses a simple shopping trip and mentions a variety of behaviors. Although the story does not detail every behavior, such as those necessary to get ready to go shopping and drive the car to the strip mall, there is sufficient information that we can understand what occurred. Let's examine Andy Jardine's actions in terms of the types of behaviors discussed in the chapter and evaluate the value of the behavioral sequence model. A list of events and types of behavior follows.

From this brief description, we get a good idea of what behaviors were performed and consider some marketing strategies to increase desired behaviors. For example, if the Lands' End store had a large sign close to the front door or in the front window that explained the discounts available, perhaps the Jardines would have purchased more products. (The store had such a sign, but it is in the back of the store where consumers may not readily see it.) Thus, the behavioral sequence model helps explain behaviors, isolate them into manageable parts, and allow the analysis of tactics and strategies to increase desired behaviors.

This case illustrates a second point discussed in the chapter: Consumer behaviors do not always follow the exact sequence laid out in Exhibit 8.2. For example, communication can occur in any stage of the process. Also, more than one product is often purchased on a single shopping trip, which can lead to differences from the exact sequence laid out in Exhibit 8.2.

However, the general model, the categories of behavior listed, and the level of analysis seem useful for understanding the behaviors. In addition, if the probability that the Jardines will return to the Lands' End Inlet is increased by providing the good deals, their behavior has been positively reinforced;

Event	Type of Behavior
Is offered shopping opportunity	Information contact
Responds verbally to offer	Communication
Drives to drugstore	Store contact
Enters drugstore	Store contact
Locates magazines and candy	Product contact
Obtains products	Product contact
Takes $10 from wallet	Funds access
Exchanges money for products	Transaction
Suggests going to outlet store	Communication
Walks to and enters outlet store	Store contact
Locates and tries on sweaters	Product contact
Discusses Kari's coat	Communication
Takes out Visa card	Funds access
Exchanges funds for products	Transaction
Is offered information by salesclerk	Information contact
Purchases sweaters and coat	Transaction
Is offered more salesclerk information	Information contact
Takes products home	Transaction
Eats candy on the way home	Consumption

the fact that Andy exclaimed about the savings suggests such reinforcement.

A third point concerns the limitations of the behavioral approach for understanding consumer behavior and developing marketing strategies. For one thing, the analysis has not considered what the Jardines were thinking and feeling during this shopping episode. For example, we certainly know something about Andy from the descriptions of what he remembered, what he decided, his reluctance to purchase, his feeling that he deserved the other sweater, and that he felt good about the purchases. In addition, a more detailed description of the major environmental stimuli would allow a deeper understanding of the shopping episode. Thus, although studying overt behavior can provide valuable insights for designing effective marketing strategies, it is also necessary to study consumers' affect and cognition as well as environmental factors. ❖

Summary   This chapter introduced the topic of overt consumer behavior and discussed its importance to marketing. A sequential model of overt consumer behavior was developed for used in analyzing and increasing responses. The model listed the following seven behaviors: information contact, funds access, store contact, product contact, transaction, consumption and disposition, and communication. Each was discussed in terms of a variety of marketing strategies and tactics used to increase the chances that the behavior will occur or that the frequency of it will increase. In some situations and for some products, these behaviors may be rather automatic and require little cognitive activity. Others entail considerable cognitive activity and affect development prior to, during, and after purchase and consumption.

Key Terms and Concepts

communication   **209**
consumption   **208**
funds access   **203**
information contact   **200**
overt consumer behavior   **196**

product contact   **207**
pull strategies   **207**
push strategies   **207**
store contact   **204**
transactions   **208**

Review and Discussion Questions

1. Describe the differences between traditional models of the adoption process (for example, awareness, interest, evaluation, trial, adoption) and the behavior sequence presented in Exhibit 8.2.
2. What advantages do you see in the use of the behavior sequence model for marketing researchers and for marketing managers?
3. Use the behavior sequence model to describe recent purchases of a product and of a service.
4. Consider the challenges presented by the information search stage of the behavior sequence for each of the following: (*a*) a leading brand, (*b*) a new brand, and (*c*) an existing low-share brand.
5. Give some examples of marketing strategies aimed at addressing the funds access problems of college seniors.
6. Visit several local supermarkets and note examples of push and pull strategies used to increase product contact for grocery items. Share these observations with your class.
7. List at least three examples of situations in which marketing efforts have been instrumental in changing your consumption or disposal behavior for products you have purchased.
8. Assume the role of a marketing manager for each of the purchases you described in response to question 3. Which behaviors would you want to change?
9. Suggest strategies for decreasing the frequency of postholiday merchandise returns to a department store.

Marketing Strategy in Action

Peapod Online Grocery—2003

The online grocery business turned out to be a lot tougher than analysts thought a few years ago. Many of the early online grocers, including Webvan, ShopLink, StreamLine, Kozmo, Homeruns, and PDQuick, went bankrupt and out of business. At one time, Webvan had 46 percent of the online grocery business, but it still wasn't profitable enough to survive. The new business model for online grocers is to be part of an existing brick-and-mortar chain. Large grocery chains, like Safeway and Albertson's, are experiencing sales growth in their online business but have yet to turn a profit. Jupiter Research estimates that online grocery sales will be over $5 billion by 2007, about 1 percent of all grocery sales, while it expects more than 5 percent of all retail sales to be online by then. A few years ago, optimistic analysts estimated online grocery sales would be 10 to 20 times that by 2005, but it didn't work out that way.

One of the few online grocers to survive in 2003 is Peapod, the first online grocer, started by brothers Andrew and Thomas Parkinson in 1990. However, even Peapod was failing until 2001 when Dutch grocery giant Royal Ahold purchased controlling interest in the company for $73 million. Peapod operates in five markets, mainly by closely affiliating itself with Ahold-owned grocery chains. Peapod by Giant is in the Washington, DC, area, while Peapod by Stop and Shop runs in Boston, New York, and Connecticut. The exception is Chicago, where Peapod operates without an affiliation with a local grocery chain. Peapod executives claim the company is growing by 25 percent annually and has 130,000 customers, and all of its markets except Connecticut are profitable. Average order size is up to $143 from $106 three years earlier.

The online grocery business seemed like a sure winner in the 1990s. Dual-income families strapped for time could simply go online to do their grocery shopping. They had about the same choices of products that they would have had if they went to a brick-and-mortar grocery, about 20,000 SKUs (stockkeeping units). They could browse the "aisles" on their home computers and place orders via computer, fax, or telephone. The orders were filled at affiliated stores and delivered to their homes in a 90-minute window, saving them time and effort and simplifying their daily lives. For all of this convenience, consumers were willing to pay a monthly fee and a fee per order for packaging, shipping, and delivery. Since most of the products purchased were well-known branded items, consumers faced little risk in

Peapod.com web page reprinted with permission.

buying their traditional foodstuffs. Even perishables like produce and meat could be counted on to be high quality, and if consumers were concerned, they could make a quick trip to a brick-and-mortar grocery for these selections. However, while all of this sounded good, most consumers didn't change their grocery shopping habits to take advantage of the online alternative.

Currently analysts do not expect the online grocery industry to take off in the near future, if ever. Miles Cook of Bain & Company estimates that only 8 to 10 percent of U.S. consumers will find ordering groceries online appealing, but only about 1 percent will ever do so. He concludes: "This is going to remain a niche offering in a few markets. It's not going to be a national mainstream offering." Jupiter Media Metrix analyst Ken Cassar concludes that "The moral of the story is that the ability to build a better mousetrap must be measured against consumers' willingness to buy it."

Discussion Questions

1. What behaviors are involved in online grocery shopping? How does online grocery shopping compare with traditional shopping in terms of behavioral effort?

2. What types of consumers are likely to value online grocery shopping from Peapod?

3. Overall, what do you think about the idea of online grocery shopping? How does it compare with simply eating in restaurants and avoiding grocery shopping and cooking altogether?

Sources: Rob Kaiser, "Peapod Still Blooms Without Chain Help, No Local Stores to Reduce Costs," SiliconInvestor.com, May 27, 2003; Keith Regan, "Online Grocery Still a War of Attrition," EcommerceTimes.com, March 15, 2002; Greg Sandoval, "Online Grocers Take Stock," CNETNews.com, July 13, 2001.

Conditioning and Learning Processes

Lottery Games: Powerball and Mega Millions

About 51 percent of American consumers buy at least one lottery ticket every year, according to the North American Association of State and Provincial Lotteries. Lotteries are legal in 38 states and there are hundreds of lotteries in foreign countries, some of which have been running for several centuries. State lotteries started out as biannual events, but it was soon apparent that more frequent lotteries and instant-winning scratch cards would increase sales. For example, the Arizona Lottery reached a record $322.3 million in fiscal year 2003 and was supplemented with a record $159.2 million in sales of scratch tickets. Overall, these sales added at least $94.5 million to the state coffers.

In the United States, lotteries were traditionally operated state by state, and jackpots seldom reached over $5 to $10 million. However, since lottery ticket sales grow dramatically when jackpots get large, several consortia started running multistate lotteries.

Powerball, based in Iowa, was formed in 1988 and is played in 24 states plus Washington, DC, and the U.S. Virgin Islands. Mega Millions, launched in 1995 as the Big Game, has 10 states in its consortium. Powerball states tend to have smaller populations (except for California), while Mega Millions boasts more populous states, including New York, Illinois, and Massachusetts. Powerball has about 82 million players and Mega Millions about 95.6 million.

Some of the largest individual prizes to date include a $363 million Mega Millions prize that was shared by two people and a Powerball prize of $250 million also shared by two people. By state, some of the largest winners were in West Virginia ($315 million), Indiana ($296 million), Massachusetts ($197 million), Wisconsin ($195 million), and New Jersey ($265 million).

Lottery winners typically have choices of how they will receive their winnings, either as a lump sum or as an annuity over a period of years. For example, Bernadette Geitka won a Mega Millions jackpot worth $183 million. However, to receive the full amount she

State lottery cards
AP/Wide World Photos.

would have had to take a percentage of it each year for 26 years. Instead, she opted for a lump sum payment of $112 million. The $112 million netted out to $76 million after taxes were paid.

"Almost everyone takes the up-front payment," says Joe Maloney, a spokesperson for the Multi-State Lottery Association, which oversees the Powerball game. However, he argues that financially the annuity is the better choice. "If you were to win $100 million, the cash option might be about $59 million," he estimates. "Taxes get taken out right away, so you start with just over $40 million. There's no way you're going to get a high enough annual return every year to build that up to $100 million over the life of the annuity." Apparently most winners are more than happy to have just $40 million to spend!

One problem for lotteries is that players often need constant prodding to keep them interested until the jackpots get large. Both Powerball and Mega Millions start at $10 million but need about a $100 million jackpot to get consumers really excited about buying tickets. Many lotteries use consumer research, including surveys, penetration studies, and focus groups, to keep their sales booming. Lottery officials have learned, for instance, that tickets are often impulse items. So they cover convenience stores with banners, place lottery tickets and displays near other impulse items like candy, and use clever TV ads to keep consumers buying. Scratch tickets were also an innovation to get consumers to play more regularly; even relatively small winnings from scratchers keep consumers playing.

So what are the odds of winning a lottery? The odds of winning a large one-state lottery are about 6 million to 1, while the odds of winning a large multistate lottery as Bernadette Geitka did are 135 million to 1. For comparison, the odds of being hit by lightning are about 400,000 to 1.

Sources: Gordon T. Anderson, "Lottery Fever: $400 Million and Counting," CNNmoney.com, July 3, 2003; "State Lottery Ticket Sales Reach Record $322 Million," azcentral.com, July 3, 2003; "As Jackpot Grows, So Do Lottery Sales," Charlotte.com, June 17, 2003.

What accounts for the success of lottery games? This chapter deals with two types of conditioning and one type of learning. The two types of conditioning are classical and operant, and the learning discussion focuses on vicarious learning.[1] Traditionally these topics have focused primarily on influencing overt behavior. However, they are also useful for conditioning affect, and cognitive theories are useful for explaining why they are effective. The chapter first discusses classical conditioning and then turns to operant conditioning and vicarious learning.

Classical Conditioning

Many of you have likely heard of Pavlov's experiments in which he conditioned a dog to salivate at the sound of a bell. Pavlov did this by first pairing the sound of the bell with sprays of meat powder for a number of trials. Eventually he eliminated the meat powder, and the dog would salivate to the sound of the bell alone. Pavlov's research provides the basis for classical conditioning.

In general, **classical conditioning** is a process by which a neutral stimulus becomes capable of eliciting a response because it was repeatedly paired with a stimulus that naturally causes the response. Stimuli that cause responses naturally are called *unconditioned stimuli* (the meat powder in the Pavlov experiments); the response that occurs naturally in its presence is called an *unconditioned response* (salivation in the Pavlov experiments). When the neutral stimulus can cause a similar response through repeated pairings, it becomes a conditioned stimulus. When it does cause the response, the response is then called a *conditioned response*. This process is shown in Exhibit 9.1, and four points should be noted.

First, classical conditioning can be accomplished not only with unconditioned stimuli but also with previously conditioned stimuli. For example, most of us are previously conditioned to the sound of a doorbell ringing and will look up almost automatically on hearing it. This previously conditioned stimulus has been used in the beginning of Avon TV commercials to attract consumers' attention to the ad itself as well as to Avon's services.

Second, classically conditioned behaviors are controlled by stimuli that occur *before* the behavior. For example, in Pavlov's experiment, the meat powder and bell were presented before salivation occurred.

Third, the behaviors influenced by classical conditioning are assumed to be under the control of the autonomic nervous system. This system controls the so-called smooth muscles. Thus, the behaviors are assumed to be involuntary and not under the conscious control of the individual.

Last, and perhaps most important for consumer behavior and marketing strategy, affective responses often follow the principles of classical conditioning.[2] For example, when a new product for which people have neutral feelings is repeatedly advertised during exciting sports events (such as the Super Bowl), it is possible for the product to eventually generate excitement on its own solely through the repeated pairings with the exciting events. Similarly, an unknown political candidate may come to elicit patriotic feelings in voters simply by having patriotic music constantly playing in the background of his or her political commercials. A number of

This cute ad could condition affect to Healthtex clothes for kids   *Courtesy The Martin Agency.*

Exhibit 9.1

The Process of Classical Conditioning

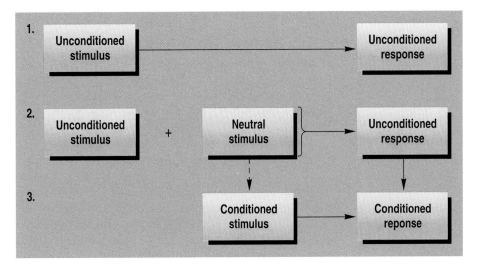

Affect for Volkswagen cars may be conditioned by this attention-getting ad
Bill Cash Photography © 2001; © Steve Casimiro, Courtesy of Getty Images.[TM]

firms currently use stimuli in commercials and ads that are designed to generate emotions.

Because it can account for many of the responses that environmental stimuli elicit from individuals, classical conditioning has important implications for marketing and consumer behavior. Through this process, a particular stimulus can come to evoke positive, negative, or neutral feelings. Consequently, classical conditioning can influence an individual to work to obtain, to avoid, or to be indifferent to a wide variety of products and services.

Consider product-related stimuli. External stimuli that elicit positive emotions can be paired with the product so that the product itself elicits positive affect. Behavior may then be triggered that brings the potential consumer into closer contact with the product. "Closer contact" refers to a general relationship between a person's behavior and a given stimulus (e.g., a product). For example, if a product elicits positive affect, an individual exposed to it is more apt to behave positively toward it than if negative emotions are elicited. Attending behavior is also apt to be a function of classically conditioned affect. Stimuli that elicit stronger emotional responses (either positive or negative) are, at least over a considerable range, likely to receive more attention from an individual than stimuli that are affectively neutral. To the degree that attending behavior is necessary for product purchase or other product-related behavior, classical conditioning influences whether consumers come into contact with products.

Similarly, stimuli may produce certain general emotional responses, such as relaxation, excitement, nostalgia, or some other emotion likely to increase the probability of a desired behavior (such as product purchase). Radio and TV ads often use famous broadcasters whose voices have been paired with exciting sports events for years. These voices may elicit excitement as a result of this frequent pairing. Repeated pairings of these voices with advertised products can result in feelings of excitement associated with the products.

Music, sexy voices and bodies, and other stimuli are used in similar ways. For example, magazine ads for Calvin Klein's Obsession perfume featured a naked woman being kissed by three men. Such stimuli may influence behavior without conditioning simply by drawing attention to the ad. Of course, the attention-generating properties of the stimulus itself probably developed through previous conditioning that occurs "naturally" in society.

The use of telephones ringing or sirens in the backgrounds of radio and TV ads and the presence of famous celebrities are common examples of how stimuli that are irrelevant to the content of an ad or the function of the product are used to increase attention paid to the ad itself. For example, Michael Jordan and Tiger Woods have been featured in commercials for Nike and other products. In this context, one of the major resources organizations use to market their products is made available through previous classical conditioning of consumers.

Stimuli at or near the point of purchase also serve the goals of marketers through the stimuli's ability to elicit behaviors. Christmas music in a toy department is a good example. Although no data are available to support the point, we suspect that carols are useful for eliciting the emotions labeled the "Christmas spirit." Once these feelings have been elicited, we suspect (and retailers seem to share our suspicions) that people are more apt to purchase gifts for loved ones. In other words, Christmas carols are useful for generating emotions that are compatible with purchasing gifts.

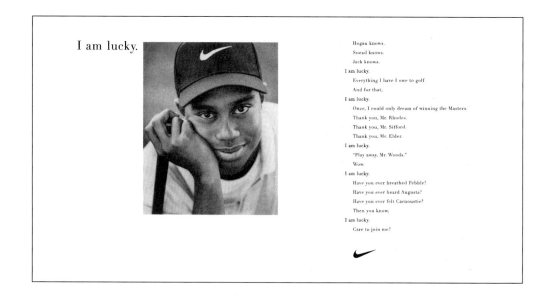

The presence of Tiger Woods in ads may condition affect to the advertised brand
Courtesy Nike, Inc.

Consumer Research on Classical Conditioning

A number of consumer research studies have investigated classical conditioning. The authors of one program of research state, "There are enough demonstrations in our literature to accept the fact of classical conditioning of consumers' attitudes toward consumption objects."[3] Others have argued that classical conditioning may be most useful in marketing in low-involvement situations:

> Consumer involvement is low when the products have only minor quality differences from one another. . . . This is especially the case in saturated markets with mature products. It is exactly in these markets that product differentiation by means of emotional conditioning is the preferred strategy of influencing consumers.[4]

Because most products are mature and many markets are saturated, classical conditioning is likely to be a useful strategy for low-involvement purchases. However, classical conditioning can also be useful for high-involvement situations, such as the purchase of athletic shoes by teenagers. Marketers of brands such as Nike, Adidas, and Fila seem well aware that the presence of superstar athletes in their commercials performing exciting slam dunks and fast breaks can condition positive affect to their products and lead to increased sales. Automobile companies seem well aware that the presence of attractive models, exciting locations, and popular background music can influence purchase through classical conditioning.[5]

Marketing Implications

The use of classical conditioning as a marketing tool has several implications. First, classical conditioning directs attention to the presentation of stimuli that, because of previous conditioning, elicit affect in consumers. In some cases, these feelings are likely to increase the probability of certain behaviors and/or decrease the probability of other behaviors. Second, in many cases, marketers may find it useful to condition responses to stimuli. By repeatedly pairing Tiger Woods, an exciting golfer and sports personality, with Rolex watches and Nike golf clothes, these products may generate greater excitement and increased purchases. Exhibit 9.2 summarizes a number of marketing tactics consistent with classical conditioning principles.

Operant Conditioning   **Operant conditioning** is the process of altering the probability of a behavior being emitted by changing the consequences of the behavior. It differs from classical conditioning in at least two important ways. First, whereas classical conditioning is concerned with involuntary responses, operant conditioning deals with behaviors that are usually assumed to be under the conscious control of the individual. By *conscious control*, behaviorists mean under the control of the skeletal nervous system that governs the "striped" muscles; they are not stating that behaviors are under the control of cognitions. Second, although classically conditioned behaviors are *elicited* by stimuli that occur *before* the response, operant behaviors are *emitted* because of consequences that occur *after* the behavior.

In any given situation, at any given time, there is a certain probability that an individual will emit a particular behavior. If all of the possible behaviors are arranged in descending order of probability of occurrence, the result is a **response hierarchy.** Operant conditioning has occurred when the probability that an

Exhibit 9.2

Some Marketing Tactics Consistent with Classical Conditioning Principles

Conditioning Responses to New Stimuli		
Unconditioned or Previously Conditioned Stimulus	**Conditioned Stimulus**	**Examples**
Exciting event	A product or theme song	New product advertised during the Super Bowl
Patriotic events or music	A product or person	Patriotic music as background in commercials
Use of Familiar Stimuli to Elicit Responses		
Conditioned Stimulus	**Conditioned Response(s)**	**Examples**
Popular music	Relaxation, excitement, "goodwill"	Christmas music in retail stores
Familar voices	Excitement, attention	Famous sportscaster or movie star narrating a commercial
Sexy voices, bodies	Excitement, attention, arousal	Calvin Klein commercials and many others
Familiar cues	Excitement, attention, anxiety	Sirens sounding, telephones or doorbells ringing in commercials
Familiar social cues	Feelings of friendship and love	Television ads depicting calls from family or close friends

individual will emit a behavior is altered by changing the events or consequences that follow the behavior.

Some events or consequences increase the frequency with which a given behavior is likely to be repeated. For example, if a reward, such as a cash rebate, is given at the time of purchase, it may increase the probability that a shopper will purchase in the same store in the future. In this case, because the reward increases the probability of the behavior being repeated, it is called **positive reinforcement.** Positive reinforcement is likely the most common type of consequence marketers use to influence consumer behavior. In general, the greater the amount of the reward and the sooner it is received after the behavior, the more likely the behavior will be reinforced and the consumer will perform similar behaviors in the future. For example, a $1 coupon for Tropicana orange juice, would likely increase the probability of purchase of juice and lead to future purchases of this product than would a 50-cent coupon. Similarly, if the coupon is redeemable at the time of purchase, it will likely be more effective than a mail-in coupon for which the consumer has to wait for the reward.

The frequency of consumer behavior can also be increased by removing aversive stimuli. This is called **negative reinforcement.** For example, if a consumer

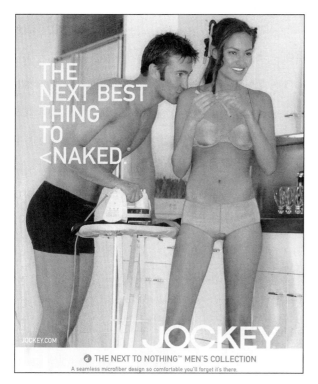

This Jockey ad illustrates the use of attractive people to elicit a conditioned response © *Jockey International, Inc. World rights reserved.*

purchases a product to get a salesperson to quit pressuring him or her, the consumer may be negatively reinforced. That is, by performing the behavior of purchasing, the aversive stimuli (the actions of the pushy salesperson) are removed. In the future, when confronted with pushy salespeople, operant conditioning would predict that the consumer will be more likely to purchase again.

Sometimes operant techniques are used to decrease the probability of a response. If the environment is arranged so that a particular response results in neutral consequences, over a period of time that response will diminish in frequency. This process is referred to as **extinction.** For example, at one time the A&P grocery chain was the largest retailer in the world. However, one mistake it made was to overstock its own brands (which had higher profit margins) and understock nationally branded merchandise. Consumers who were loyal to a number of nationally branded products often could not obtain them at an A&P store. Eventually many consumers quit shopping at A&P, partially because they could not obtain their favorite brands. Thus, A&P inadvertently used extinction on its own customers.

If a response is followed by a noxious or aversive event, the frequency of the response is also likely to decrease. The term **punishment** is usually used to describe this process.[6] For example, suppose you went to a clothing store and the salespeople were rude to you. Wouldn't this decrease the chances that you would go back there? Punishment is often confused with negative reinforcement, but they are distinctly different concepts. Exhibit 9.3 presents a summary of the four methods of operant conditioning.

A good deal could positively reinforce purchase from the same store   *Chris Brown/Stock, Boston, LLC.*

Exhibit 9.3

Operant Conditioning Methods

Operation Performed after Behavior	Name	Effect
Present positive consequences	**Positive reinforcement**	Increases the probability of behavior
Remove aversive consequences	**Negative reinforcement**	Increases the probability of behavior
Neutral consequences occur	**Extinction**	Decreases the probability of behavior
Present aversive consequences	**Punishment**	Decreases the probability of behavior

Credit card stimuli can influence consumer behavior
David Young-Wolff/ PhotoEdit, Inc.

There are a number of other important ideas about operant conditioning. We discuss three—reinforcement schedules, shaping, and discriminative stimuli—that have major implications for designing marketing strategies to influence consumers' behavior.

Reinforcement Schedules

A number of different **reinforcement schedules** can be employed. For example, it is possible to arrange conditions so a positive reinforcer is administered after every desired behavior. This is called a **continuous reinforcement schedule.** Marketers usually try to keep the quality of their products and services constant so that they will be continuously reinforcing with every purchase, but this is difficult to do. For example, frequent product recalls for automobiles indicate a failure to maintain product quality. Services such as airlines may be unable to control contingencies such as bad weather; overbooked, canceled, and late flights; and unfriendly employees, which can make flights nonreinforcing. Because sporting events may be boring or the home team may get beaten, they may not be continuously reinforcing for some consumers.

Conditions can also be arranged so that every second, third, or tenth time the behavior is performed, it is reinforced. This is called a **fixed ratio schedule.** Similarly, it is possible to have a reinforcer follow a desired behavior *on an average* of, say, one-half, one-third, or one-fourth the time the behavior occurs, but not necessarily every second, third, or fourth time. This is called a **variable ratio schedule.** The various state lotteries are examples of prizes awarded on variable ratio schedules.

The variable ratio schedules are of particular interest because they produce high rates of behavior that are reasonably resistant to extinction. Gambling devices are good examples. Slot machines are very effective in producing high rates of response, even under conditions that often result in substantial financial losses. This property of the ratio schedule is particularly important for marketers because it suggests that a great deal of desired behavior can be developed and maintained with relatively small,

A different car for each day of the week could be reinforcing for some consumers *Courtesy Washington State Lottery; Agency: McCann-Erickson, Seattle.*

infrequent rewards. Deslauriers and Everett found that by giving a free token for riding a bus on a variable ratio schedule, the same amount of bus riding could be obtained as when rewards were given on a continuous schedule.[7] Thus, for approximately one-third the cost of the continuous schedule, the same amount of behavior was sustained.[8]

Numerous other examples of the use of variable ratio schedules can be found in marketing practices. In addition to state lotteries, common examples include sweepstakes, contests, and door prizes, in which individuals must behave in a certain way to be eligible for a prize. Highlight 9.1 discusses the use of variable ratio schedules for selling Pepsi and Mountain Dew products.

Shaping

Another operant conditioning concept that has important implications for marketing and consumer behavior is **shaping.** Shaping is important because, given consumers'

Could shaping be used to help consumers learn this behavior? *Joe McBride/Getty Images.*

Highlight 9.1

Using Variable Ratio Schedules to Increase Pepsi Purchases

PepsiCo ran an "Unlock the Great Taste and Win" sweepstakes. The grand prizes in the contest were two Lamborghini sports cars with an estimated retail value of $215,000 each. Other prizes included Kawasaki jet skis, compact vending machines, vacations, and sterling silver key chains.

Although consumers could receive two game chances without purchases by writing the company, most game chances were distributed through purchase of Pepsi and Mountain Dew products. Here's how it worked. With purchases of multipacks—12-, 20-, or 24-can packages—consumers had a chance to receive a free, inexpensive key chain. Behind the key chain package was notification of any major prize won. However, only one out of two multipacks contained the key chain and chance of winning. Thus, on average, consumers would have to purchase two multipacks to get a chance at the major prizes. PepsiCo used a variable ratio schedule to allocate prize chances to increase the probability that consumers would purchase several multipacks.

Some bottle caps on 2-liter, 3-liter, and 16-ounce nonreturnable bottles also contained chances to win,

but no key chain. Also, the odds of winning were better when consumers bought the more expensive multipacks. For example, the odds of winning the grand prizes from a multipack purchase were 1 in 18,444,000, whereas the odds of winning the grand prizes from a bottle purchase were 1 in 113,118,597. In addition, only by purchasing multipacks could a consumer win the sterling silver key chains valued at $50; the bottle purchases allowed winning only a brass key chain valued at $10. All prizes were awarded on variable ratio schedules.

Overall, variable ratio schedules were used to allocate the chances to win prizes as well as the prizes themselves. By offering the chances to win and the inexpensive key chains on a variable ratio schedule, PepsiCo increased the probability of consumers making more than one purchase. Also, the cost of the key chains was only half what it would have been if every multipack contained one. Offering major prizes on a variable ratio schedule is likely the only way expensive products can be used as reinforcers for purchase of inexpensive products and still be profitable. To learn more about Pepsi, visit its website at **www.pepsi.com**.

existing response hierarchies, the probability that they will make a particular desired response may be very small. In general, shaping involves a process of arranging conditions that change the probabilities of certain behaviors *not as ends in themselves but to increase the probabilities of other behaviors.* Usually shaping involves the positive reinforcement of successive approximations of the desired behavior or of behaviors that must be performed before the desired response can be emitted.

Many firms employ marketing activities that are roughly analogous to shaping. For example, loss leaders and other special deals are used to reward individuals for coming to a store. Once customers are in the store, the probability that they will make other desired responses (such as purchasing full-priced items) is much greater than when they are not in the store. Carnivals held in shopping center or auto dealer parking lots may be viewed as attempts to shape behavior because consumers are more likely to come in and purchase when they are already in the parking lot than when they are at home. Similarly, free trial periods may be employed to make it more likely the user will have contact with the product so that he or she can experience the product's reinforcing properties. Real estate companies that offer free trips to look over resort property are employing a shaping tactic, as are casinos that offer free trips to gamblers. In both cases, moving people to the place of purchase (or place of gambling) increases the probability that these behaviors will be performed.

Shaping is not confined to a one-step process; it can be used to influence several stages in a purchase sequence. For example, suppose a car dealer wants to shape an automobile purchase. Free coffee and doughnuts are offered to anyone who comes to the dealership. Five dollars in cash is offered to any licensed driver who test-drives a car. A $500 rebate is offered to anyone who purchases a car. This example demonstrates not only how operant principles can be used in a multistep process but also how they can be used in a high-involvement purchase situation.

Discriminative Stimuli

It is important to distinguish between the reinforcement and discriminative functions played by stimuli in the operant model. So far in this section, we have focused on the reinforcing function. However, the *mere presence or absence of certain stimuli* can serve to change the probabilities of behavior. These are called **discriminative stimuli.**

Discriminative stimuli are often said to "set the occasion" for behaviors. This means discriminative stimuli can be presented before a behavior and can influence whether the behavior occurs. In fact, discriminative stimuli allow operant conditioners to account for the effects or antecedents to behavior on changing behavior. (As you recall, reinforcers and other consequences always occur *after* the behavior.) For example, suppose Pizza Hut runs an ad that offers a free quart of Pepsi with every large pizza purchased. This offer may increase the probability of purchasing a large pizza from Pizza Hut. However, the offer itself is not a reinforcer since it is offered *before* the behavior. Rather, the offer is a discriminative stimulus.

Many marketing stimuli are discriminative. Store signs ("50 percent off sale") and store logos (Wal-Mart's sign, Target's Bullseye) or distinctive brand marks (the Nike swoosh, the Levi's tag, the Polo insignia) are examples of discriminative stimuli. Previous experiences have perhaps taught consumers that purchase behavior will be rewarded when the distinctive symbol is present and will not be rewarded when the symbol is absent. For example, many consumers purchase Ralph Lauren shirts, jackets, and shorts that have the embroidered polo player symbol on them and avoid other Ralph Lauren apparel that does not have this symbol. A number of competitors have tried to copy the polo player symbol because of its power as a discriminative stimulus. Clearly, much of marketing strategy involves developing discriminative stimuli that increase certain behaviors.

Marketing Implications

Many marketing strategies and tactics are consistent with operant conditioning principles. If these are carefully designed, they can be quite effective in influencing consumer behavior. Many marketing tactics involve giving rewards after a purchase to increase its probability in the future. These rewards include rebates, contest tickets, bonuses, prizes, in-package coupons, and courteous thanks from salespeople. Although most strategies involve keeping product and service quality on a continuous reinforcement schedule, other types of rewards can be offered on a partial reinforcement schedule. Shaping is used to develop earlier behaviors in a purchase sequence to increase the chances of later behaviors. Finally, many store and brand symbols and logos have become discriminative stimuli for some consumers. Exhibit 9.4 summarizes a number of these tactics.

Vicarious Learning | **Vicarious learning** refers to processes by which people change their behaviors because they observed the actions of other people and the consequences that occurred. In general, people tend to imitate the behavior of others when they see

Exhibit 9.4

Some Marketing Tactics Consistent with Operant Conditioning Principles

Continuous Reinforcement Schedules	
Desired Behavior	**Reward Given Following Behavior**
Product purchase	Manufacturers' rebates; in-package coupons; contest tickets
Store visits	Discounts; door prizes; store coupons

Partial Reinforcement Schedules	
Product purchase	Prizes for every second, third, etc. purchase
	Prizes to some fraction of people who purchase
Store or restaurant patronage	Cash or free meal after 10 purchases

Shaping		
Behavior	**Consequences**	**Final Response Desired**
Obtaining a credit card	Prize; low initial interest rate	Expenditures using card
Trip to mall or store	Events or entertainment	Purchases in mall or store
Entry into store	Door prizes	Purchases in store
Product trial	Free samples; cash or other reward for trial	Purchase of product

Discriminative Stimuli		
Desired Behavior	**Reward Signal**	**Examples**
Brand purchase	Distinctive brandmarks	Nautica sailboat; Nike swoosh
Store visit	Ads; store window signs; store logos	"50 Percent Off Sale"; "Clearance Sale"; McDonald's golden arches

it leads to positive consequences and to avoid performing the behavior of others when they see that negative consequences occur.

Vicarious learning is also called *modeling*. Overt modeling involves consumers actually observing the model, such as seeing a salesperson demonstrating a Hoover vacuum cleaner in a store (live modeling) or seeing a commercial that depicts this behavior (symbolic modeling).

Exhibit 9.5 shows the vicarious learning process. Many advertisements and TV commercials show models buying and using products and receiving positive consequences for doing so. Advil commercials have shown people suffering from arthritis pain but smiling and enjoying activities after they take the product. Toothpaste and deodorant commercials frequently show people being accepted and admired after using particular brands of these products.

Uses of Vicarious Learning in Marketing Strategy

There are three major uses of vicarious learning or modeling in marketing strategy. First, modeling can be used to help observers *acquire one or more new response*

For some consumers, these are discriminative stimuli *(shots of Mercedes logo, IBM logo, Kellogg's Corn Flakes box) Michael Newman/PhotoEdit; (Best Buy logo) Tim Boyle/Getty Images; (Evian water bottle label) Markow Tatiana/CORBIS SYGMA.*

patterns that previously did not exist in their behavioral repertoires. Second, modeling can be used to *decrease* or *inhibit undesired behaviors*. Third, modeling can lead to *response facilitation*, whereby the behavior of others "serves merely as discriminative stimuli for the observer in facilitating the occurrence of previously learned responses."[9]

Developing New Responses   Modeling can be used to develop new responses that previously were not in the consumer's behavioral repertoire.[10] Consider the videocassette machines used in a variety of department and other stores to

Exhibit 9.5

The Vicarious Learning Process

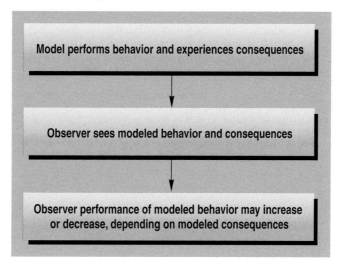

Model performs behavior and experiences consequences

↓

Observer sees modeled behavior and consequences

↓

Observer performance of modeled behavior may increase or decrease, depending on modeled consequences

Overt modeling: demonstrating new behaviors
Alan Carey/The Image Works.

demonstrate use of a product. Sears has long used this method to demonstrate the appropriate and safe use of its chain saws. The appropriate uses of Berkeley fishing equipment and Olt duck calls are also demonstrated in this way. New behaviors are also frequently modeled in TV commercials. For example, insurance is traditionally purchased from an agent either at the agent's office or in the consumer's home, not in retail stores. Sears used a modeling strategy when it began in-store sales of Allstate insurance. Basically, the TV commercial shows a family coming to the Sears store and dropping off its old insurance policy for comparisons with Allstate rates. After a pleasant shopping trip, the family returns and is told that Allstate can provide a better deal, thus modeling the positive consequences of the new behavior. Similarly, Arm & Hammer baking soda ads showed new uses of the product as a carpet and refrigerator freshener and portrayed the models being complimented on the freshness of their homes. WD-40 lubricant ads also model new uses of the product.

Inhibiting Undesired Responses Modeling can also be used to decrease the probability of undesired behaviors. Because of the ethical and practical problems involved in using punishment to influence consumer behavior, we have given little attention to ways of reducing the frequency of undesired responses. Such problems are far less prevalent when aversive consequences are administered to models rather than to actual consumers, however. Thus, vicarious learning may be one of the few approaches that can be used to reduce the frequency of unwanted elements in the behavioral repertoire of a potential or present customer.

It is well known from the modeling literature that, under appropriate conditions, observers who see a model experience aversive outcomes following a particular act will reduce their tendency to exhibit that behavior. Similarly, vicarious learning can employ extinction to reduce the frequency of behavior.

Consider the following examples. Hefty bags have been advertised on TV using a modeling approach. Various family members are shown taking out the trash in "bargain bags." Of course, the bargain bag breaks and garbage is spewed all over the driveway. This is a very annoying experience! The frustrated family member is then told about Hefty bags, uses them successfully, and is socially reinforced for doing so. Head and Shoulders shampoo commercials have shown people initially being found attractive by members of the opposite sex but then being rejected when the models scratch their heads, indicating they may have dandruff. Following the use of the advertised product, the model is shown being happily greeted by an attractive member of the opposite sex.

A common use of this type of modeling is in public service advertising. Many behaviors considered socially undesirable can be modeled and shown to have aversive consequences. These behaviors include littering, smoking, driving drunk, using drugs, overeating, wasting energy, and polluting. One commercial, for example, showed a drunken driver being caught, taken to court, and given a considerable fine and jail sentence for his behavior.

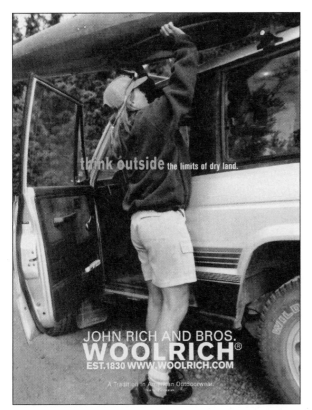

Response facilitation: modeling the types of people and occasions for wearing Woolrich clothes
Courtesy of Woolrich Incorporated.

Response Facilitation   In addition to developing new behaviors and inhibiting undesired ones, modeling can be used to facilitate the occurrence of desired behaviors that are currently in the consumer's repertoire. Modeling has been used extensively in advertising not only to illustrate the uses of a product but also to show what types of people use it and in what settings. Because many of these uses involve behaviors consumers already perform, the model's function is merely to *facilitate these responses* by depicting positive consequences for using the product appropriately. For example, Nyquil ads show adult cold sufferers using the product before going to bed and then sleeping comfortably. This technique also appears frequently in advertising for high-status products. Such ads do not demonstrate any new behaviors but show the positive consequences of using the product. A series of Lowenbrau ads stressing the use of this beer for very special occasions is a good example.

It is also possible to influence emotional behavior through a vicarious learning approach. Bandura noted that many emotional behaviors can be acquired through observations of others as well as through direct classical conditioning:

> Vicarious emotional conditioning results from observing others experience positive or negative emotional effects in conjunction with particular stimulus events. Both direct and vicarious conditioning processes are governed by the same basic principles of associative learning, but they differ in the force of the emotional arousal. In the direct prototype, the learner himself is the recipient of pain- or pleasure-producing stimulation, whereas in vicarious forms somebody else experiences the reinforcing stimulation and his affective expressions, in turn, serve as the arousal stimuli for the observer.[11]

To the degree that positive emotions toward a product are desired, vicarious emotional conditioning may also be useful for the design of effective advertisements.

Factors Influencing Modeling Effectiveness

There is no question that watching a model perform a behavior often increases the likelihood that the observer will also perform the behavior. It is well established in the psychological literature that in many situations, modeling is effective in changing behavior, as illustrated in Highlight 9.2. However, certain factors have been found to increase the likelihood that vicarious learning will occur. These factors can be divided into three groups: (1) model and modeled behavior characteristics, (2) observer characteristics, and (3) characteristics of modeled consequences.

Model and Modeled Behavior Characteristics   Several personal characteristics of observed models influence the probability that an observer will imitate the modeled behavior.[12] Models who are found to be attractive may be sought out, whereas less attractive models may be ignored. Models who are perceived to be credible and successful exert greater influence than those who are not. In addition,

High light 9.2

Do Professional Models Make Women Feel Bad about Their Appearance?

Many cues in our culture may communicate to women and young girls that being thin and fit is a prerequisite to being considered attractive in our society. Professional models, such as Kate Moss, Naomi Campbell, Claudia Schiffer, and Cindy Crawford, and many TV and movie stars who appear in commercials and ads and grace the covers of magazines usually appear to be tall, thin, and fit. In fact, many modeling agencies will not hire fashion models unless they are at least 5′7″ tall. Pictures of the models' bodies are often computer generated and computer enhanced to appear thinner and more shapely. Even Barbie dolls may be a problem; if Barbie were life-size, she would be 5′9″ tall and have measurements of 36-18-33.

Critics argue that these images have negative effects on many women and girls. Some suggest that eating disorders and self-esteem problems have resulted;

90 percent of the 8 million Americans with severe eating disorders are women. One study of 803 women found that, in 1985, 30 percent were dissatisfied with their appearance, whereas in 1995, 48 percent were dissatisfied. Increasingly, women believe there are two standards to serve: thinness and looking fit, according to the study's author. Overall, 46 percent were dissatisfied with their weight; 40 percent with their muscle tone; 47 percent with their hips, buttocks, thighs, and legs; 51 percent with their waists and stomachs; and 25 percent with their chests, shoulders, and arms.

Do you think models used in ads and commercials have negative effects on women's body images? Do you think this causes problems like eating disorders and low self-esteem? Is it appropriate to use computer-enhanced models to sell fashions, exercise clothing and equipment, and cosmetic surgery?

Sources: Ingeborg Majer O'Sickey, "*Barbie Magazine* and the Aesthetic Commodification of Girls' Bodies," in *On Fashion,* ed. Sheri Benstock and Suzanne Ferris (New Brunswick, NJ: Rutgers University Press), pp. 21–40; Nanci Hellmich, "Looking Thin and Fit Weighs on More Women," *USA Today,* September 25, 1995, p. 1D; Craig Thompson and Diana L. Haytko, "Speaking of Fashion: Consumers' Use of Fashion Discourses and the Appropriation of Countervailing Cultural Meanings," *Journal of Consumer Research,* June 1997, pp. 15–22.

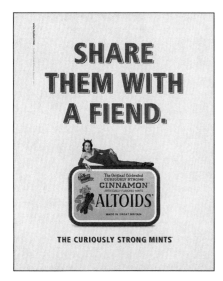

Modeling an appropriate occasion for product usage
Courtesy Callard & Bowser–Suchard Inc.

high-status and competent models are more influential in determining modeling success.

Observers are also influenced by the manner in which the modeled behavior is performed. If the sequence of the modeled behavior is detailed very carefully and vividly, modeling effects tend to increase. The rate of learning also depends on the salience and complexity of the modeled behaviors. Interestingly, models who display a bit of apprehension and difficulty and yet complete the task are more effective than models displaying no struggle or difficulty. A reason for this was suggested by Manz and Sims:

It appears that an observer can identify more with a model who struggles and overcomes the difficulties of a threatening task than a model who apparently has no problem. A model who is seen as possessing substantially greater abilities may not be considered a reasonable reference point for the observer. However, experts who display little difficulty in completing a task (e.g., professional athletes) may serve as ideals to be emulated in nonthreatening situations.[13]

Another factor that influences the effectiveness of models is the perceived similarity of the model to the observer. This finding supports the common practices of using models similar to people in the target market in commercials and attempting

Highlight 9.3

Diffusion of Innovations: A Modeling Process?

Modeling plays a prime role in spreading new ideas, products, and social practices within a society or from one society to another. Successful diffusion of innovations follows a common pattern: (1) New products and behaviors are introduced by prominent examples, (2) the product/behavior is adopted at a rapidly accelerating rate, and (3) adoption then either stabilizes or declines, depending on the product/behavior's functional role. The general pattern of diffusion is similar, but the mode of transmission, the speed and extent of adoption, and the life span of innovations vary for different products and forms of behavior.

Modeling affects adoption of innovations in several different ways. It instructs people in new styles of behavior through social, pictorial, or verbal displays. Some observers are initially reluctant to buy new products or embark on new undertakings that involve risks until they see the advantages gained by earlier adopters. Modeled benefits accelerate diffusion by weakening the restraints of more cautious, later adopters. As acceptance spreads, the new gains further social support. Models not only exemplify and legitimize innovations, they also serve as advocates for products by encouraging others to adopt them.

Source: Adapted from Albert Bandura, *Social Learning Theory* (Englewood Cliffs, NJ: Prentice-Hall, 1977) pp. 50–51. Copyright 1977. Reprinted by permission of Pearson Education, Inc., Upper Saddle River, NJ.

to increase similarities between customers and salespeople when hiring and assigning sales personnel. Many advertisers take advantage of these characteristics in developing commercials. These characteristics may also influence whether modeling aids in the diffusion of new products, an issue discussed in Highlight 9.3.

Characteristics of Observers   Any number of individual-difference variables in observers can be expected to mediate successful modeling. For example, individual differences in cognitive processing as well as in physical ability to perform a modeled behavior may affect the process. Bandura suggests that in many cases observers who are dependent, lack confidence and self-esteem, and have been frequently rewarded for imitative behavior are especially prone to adopt the behavior of successful models.[14] However, perceptive and confident people readily emulate idealized models who demonstrate highly useful behaviors.

Perhaps most important is the value the observer places on the consequences of the modeled behavior. For example, if consumers value the social approval obtained by a model in the Grecian Formula (hair coloring) commercial, they are more likely to purchase and use the product.

Characteristics of Modeled Consequences   Just as operant conditioning places importance on the consequences of behavior, so does vicarious learning. Of course, in vicarious learning, the observer does not experience the consequences directly. Thus, a major advantage of vicarious learning for consumers is that they can learn effective purchase and use behavior while avoiding negative consequences.

Research has demonstrated that positively reinforcing a model's behavior is a key factor in facilitating vicarious learning. In terms of consumer behavior, much fruitful research could be done on identifying appropriate reinforcers for various types of products. Currently, however, little is known about what types of positive consequences would be most effective to model. Similarly, for modeling applications that seek to decrease undesired behaviors, the most effective types of negative consequences to model in commercials are unknown. Although it has been demonstrated that modeling is useful in deterring smoking,[15] reducing drinking,[16] reducing uncooperative behavior of children,[17] and reducing energy consumption,[18] many other areas of consumer behavior are unexplored.

Marketing Implications

Vicarious learning or modeling has many implications for marketing strategies designed to influence consumer behavior. First, modeling can be helpful in developing information contact behaviors. For example, TV commercials could show consumers how to contact a company's webpage to get more information about products. The commercials could also show consumers how to order products from the Internet or by phone. Second, modeling can be used to increase store contact and product contact behaviors by demonstrating how consumers can get to a store or mall or find products. Commercials could also show consumers enjoying the shopping experience at the store and enthusiastically looking over products. Third, modeling can be used to influence funds access and transactions, such as the commercials for Master Debit Cards that showed a consumer using one to complete a transaction in time to make a flight, while another consumer who was writing a check missed the flight. Fourth, modeling can help to influence consumption by demonstrating how a product can be used safely and effectively. Infomercials for fishing tackle like the Banjo Minnow show how to rig it and how it catches many species of fish. Multi-task woodworking equipment infomercials show how to set the machine up for different jobs and the excellent results it obtains. Modeling can also be used to affect disposition by showing consumers safe ways to dispose of hazardous products like motor oil or paint. Finally, modeling can affect communication by showing ads in which consumers tell others about how good a product is and encouraging them to buy it.

In sum, advertisements and commercials commonly use modeling to influence consumer behavior. By carefully analyzing the salient characteristics of the models and modeled behaviors, the target consumers, and the consequences depicted in ads, marketers can increase advertising effectiveness. Exhibit 9.6 summarizes some uses of modeling to influence consumer behavior.

Exhibit 9.6

Some Applications of Modeling to Influence Consumer Behavior

Modeling Employed	Desired Response
Instructor, expert, salesperson using product (in ads or at point of purchase)	Using product in correct, technically competent way
Models in ads asking questions at point of purchase	Asking questions at point of purchase that highlight product advantages
Models in ads receiving positive reinforcement for product purchase or use	Trying product; increasing product purchase and use
Models in ads receiving no reinforcement or receiving punishment for performing undesired behaviors	Extinction or decrease in undesired behaviors
Models in ads (similar to target market), using product in novel, enjoyable ways	Using product in new ways

Back To...

Lottery Games: Powerball and Mega Millions

As discussed in this chapter, operant conditioning offers a number of insights into the success of state lottery games. First, the fact that more consumers buy lottery tickets when the jackpot is large is consistent with the idea that the greater the reinforcement, the higher the probability of the desired behavior.

Second, although lotteries started out as biannual events, lottery officials soon recognized that more frequent games and instant-winning scratch cards could increase overall lottery revenue. This is consistent with the idea that the sooner after the behavior the reinforcement is given, the more likely the behavior is to occur and be repeated.

Third, the prizes in lottery games are given on a variable ratio schedule, a powerful tactic for influencing and maintaining behavior. Even though the odds of winning are very small, some players continue to buy tickets for every game. Critics of lotteries state that poorer people buy the most tickets, spend a larger fraction of their incomes on the games than do others, and may spend money on tickets instead of on food for their children.

Fourth, the fact that lottery-ticket purchase behavior has to be prodded is consistent with the concept of extinction. That is, the behavior of consumers who repeatedly buy lottery tickets and consistently fail to win anything decreases and may terminate in the absence of any reinforcement. Thus, lottery games that offer a number of prizes can reinforce more players. Even occasional, relatively small amounts of cash won on scratch tickets can keep consumers playing over a number of years or even a lifetime. Some critics argue that lottery games encourage some consumers to become compulsive gamblers.

In sum, operant conditioning can account for the success of lotteries. However, cognitive, affective, and environmental theories do so as well, and they add insights into the processes involved. For example, cognitive approaches might explain why consumers quit playing instant-cash games after a few weeks. Perhaps consumers purchased some tickets and didn't win, and extinction occurred. However, after a few weeks, consumers may have seen or heard of some winners and believe most of the big prizes have already been won. Thus, they think their chances of winning are not as good as when the game first started, so they quit buying. Overall, the combination of cognitive, affective, behavior, and environmental theories offers the best account for the success of lotteries and of consumer behavior in general. ❖

Summary   This chapter provided an overview of conditioning and vicarious learning. Both classical and operant conditioning were discussed. Classical conditioning is a process by which a neutral stimulus becomes capable of eliciting a response when repeatedly paired with a stimulus that naturally causes the response. Marketers use classical conditioning to create favorable affect for products and stores and increase the chances that consumers will perform desired behaviors. Operant conditioning deals with influencing behavior with both antecedents and consequences. The antecedents to behavior that influence it are called discriminative stimuli. The consequences of behaviors are arranged to either increase or decrease the behaviors in the future. The chapter also discussed vicarious learning or modeling, a process by which an individual changes a behavior by watching others perform it and observing the consequences of it. Conditioning and modeling processes are commonly used in developing marketing strategies to influence consumer behavior.

Key Terms and Concepts

classical conditioning   **218**
continuous reinforcement schedule   **224**
discriminative stimulus   **227**
extinction   **223**
fixed ratio schedule   **224**
negative reinforcement   **222**
operant conditioning   **221**

positive reinforcement   **222**
punishment   **223**
reinforcement schedule   **224**
response hierarchy   **221**
shaping   **225**
variable ratio schedule   **224**
vicarious learning   **227**

Review and Discussion Questions

1. Describe classical conditioning and identify three responses in your own behaviors that are the result of classical conditioning.
2. Under what conditions would the use of classical conditioning be likely to produce positive results as part of marketing strategy?
3. What are the major differences between classical and operant conditioning?
4. Describe operant conditioning and identify three responses in your own behaviors that are the result of operant conditioning.
5. Review each of the four types of manipulations of consequences that can be used to change the probabilities of a behavior under operant conditioning. Give marketing examples for each.
6. Why are variable ratio reinforcement schedules of greater interest to marketing managers than other types of reinforcement schedules?
7. Define *shaping* and explain why it is an essential part of many marketing conditioning strategies.
8. Examine the marketing strategies used to sell fast-food hamburgers and automobiles. Identify specific examples of classical conditioning, operant conditioning, shaping, and discriminative stimuli for each product type.
9. Describe the steps in the modeling process necessary to change behavior.
10. What are the three major uses of modeling in marketing strategy?
11. Why might a marketing organization use symbolic rather than live overt modeling? Give examples to illustrate your points.

Marketing Strategy in Action

Rollerblade Inc.

In 2002, in-line skating ranked third among the most popular sports for children ages 6 to 17, behind basketball and soccer, according to the Sporting Goods Manufacturers Association. About 7.5 million youths skate an average of over 25 times per year. This is quite a change from 1980, when Minneapolis-based Rollerblade Inc. introduced its first in-line roller skate.

Rollerblade's founder, Scott Olson, was a hockey player with the Winnipeg Jets' farm teams who envisioned a roller skate with the action of an ice skate that hockey players and skiers could use to train during the off-season. At first, the plan was to use modern materials to construct a model based on an 18-century design. However, Olson discovered a similar in-line skate already on the market and purchased the patent from Chicago Roller Skate Company. Olson and his brother, Brennan, perfected the design using a plastic molded ski-type boot atop a blade of polyurethane wheels. Their first sales were to Olson's teammates as well as a few to sporting goods stores. Thus began the sport of blading.

Although they generally cost twice as much as conventional roller skates, in-line skates are purchased for two reasons. First, they are faster and therefore more exciting to use than conventional skates. Second, they provide skaters with a better aerobic workout, requiring the use of more muscles. However, it is more difficult to learn how to use in-line skates because they require greater balance and their faster speeds may cause more severe injuries if a skater falls.

By 1986, wholesale sales of in-line skates had risen to $3.5 million. Recognizing an opportunity to get in on a growing market, a number of companies began producing competitive products. First Team Sports, Inc., also based in Minneapolis, started manufacturing its Ultra-Wheels brand skates, which included the first in-line skates for children. Roller Derby Skate Corporation in Litchfield, Illinois, a manufacturer of standard roller skates since 1936, produced an in-line skate with a toe-stopper for those accustomed to conventional skates (Rollerblades had a rubber stopper located on the heel). The ice skate manufacturer Bauer entered the market with a skate that had a leather rather than plastic boot.

Rollerblade Inc.'s sales increased when it expanded its target market. At first, the product was targeted to hockey players, who were 95 percent male and 18 to 25 years old. However, by broadening the target to include 18-to-35-year-old males and females, the company increased sales considerably.

By 1990, industry wholesale sales of in-line roller skates topped $50 million, which almost equaled sales in the conventional roller skate business. Rollerblade Inc. maintained a 66 percent market share, First Team Sports had 22 percent, Bauer had 5 percent, Roller Derby had 3 percent, and other competitors combined had the remaining 4 percent. Rollerblade could have done even better, but it could not fill store orders for several months because it ran out of inventory early in the year. By 1998 there were 30 million in-line skaters, although growth in the number of skaters was slowing down; skate boarding was taking off as a cool alternative.

The fierce competition in the industry involved not only product features but also marketing elements. Companies rushed to sign celebrities to promote their products. Competitors also moved into new retail markets, including discount and department stores. Rollerblade expanded its market by selling to Macy's and Nordstrom.

Although the name Rollerblades may become a generic term for this type of skate, the company's management will have to work hard to maintain its market lead. "We have been pioneers and continue to maintain an edge," a company spokesperson said. "You only get one shot at pioneering a new sport, and that's exciting."

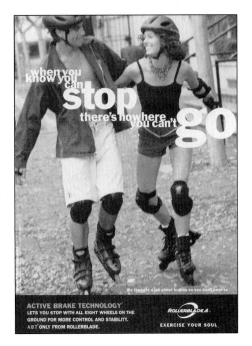

Courtesy Rollerblade, Inc.

Discussion Questions

1. What role do you think modeling could have played in the diffusion of this innovation? (See Highlight 9.3.)

2. How could you use modeling to teach a friend how to use Rollerblades?

3. If you were designing a commercial for Rollerblades to be used for an in-store videotape demonstration, how would you design the commercial to take advantage of your knowledge of modeling?

Sources: "Innovator Tries to Protect Its Lead," *The New York Times*, August 7, 1990, pp. C1, C6; Lois Therrian, "Rollerblade Is Skating in Heavier Traffic," *Business Week,* June 24, 1991, pp. 115–116; Linda Kanamine, "In-Line Skating Revolutionizes Fitness Craze," *USA Today,* July 15, 1994, pp. 1C–2C; Zina Moukheiber, "Later, Skater," *Forbes,* November 29, 1999, pp. 108–110; **http://www.rollerblades.com**.

Influencing Consumer Behaviors

What Were These Marketers Trying to Do?

Ralston-Purina ran a promotion for six of its children's cereals aimed at adults. Inside 11 million boxes of cereal with names like Freakies and Ghostbusters, Ralston-Purina included tiny models of sports cars. Ten of the boxes contained a scale-model red Corvette that could be redeemed for the real thing: a new Chevrolet Corvette. Citicorp offered gifts tied to the amount charged on its credit cards. For $500 charged on its Visa card, consumers got free golf balls or a travel clock; for $8,000 in charges, they received a round-trip airline ticket to anywhere in the United States.

General Mills inserted a single $1 bill into every 20th box of its Cheerios cereal. The promotion involved giving away $1 million.

PepsiCo offered chances to win cash and prizes in its "Count the Wins" baseball game. Numbers were printed inside specially marked cans and bottle caps of Pepsi. If the number matched the total number of wins by the Milwaukee Brewers on specific dates, the holder qualified for drawings for $10,000 and $30,000. In addition, there were a number of instant prizes, including $1,000, two tickets to a Brewers game, and 2-liter bottles of any Pepsi product.

American TV of Madison, Wisconsin, offered 100 pounds of beefsteak to those who purchased specially marked items. Some items with prices as low as $69 still qualified for the steak bonus.

What types of strategies were these marketers using? In Chapter 8, we described some basic types of consumer behaviors that marketers try to influence. In Chapter 9, we explained the basic behavioral tools marketers use to do so. In this chapter, we go beyond describing consumer behaviors and explaining marketing tools and focus on developing marketing strategies to influence consumer behaviors. First, we develop a typology of different types of strategies that marketers use to influence consumers. Then we illustrate marketing strategies for influencing consumer behavior in two areas of marketing: sales promotion and social marketing. Finally, we present a general model for developing, implementing, and evaluating the effectiveness of a consumer behavior influence strategy. With the knowledge gained in the first two chapters of this section, this chapter offers a framework for developing successful marketing strategies to influence consumer affect, cognition, and, ultimately, behavior.

Consumer Behavior Influence Strategies

Exhibit 10.1 presents a model of how marketers can influence overt consumer behaviors. First, marketers obtain information on consumers' affect, cognition, and behavior relative to the product, service, store, brand, or model of concern through consumer research. Based on this information and managerial judgment, various marketing mix stimuli are designed or changed and are implemented by placing them in the environment. These stimuli include such things as products, brand marks, packaging, advertisements and commercials, price tags, coupons, store signs and logos, and many others. These stimuli are designed to influence consumers in one or more ways. Often they are designed to influence consumers' affect and cognition in positive ways to increase the chances of overt behavior. In other cases, they are designed to influence behavior somewhat directly without a complete analysis of affective and cognitive responses. Measuring changes in consumers' affect, cognitions, and behaviors results in feedback in the form of consumer research data, as well as sales and market share information. These help marketers evaluate the success of the strategy and provide new input into the strategy development process. Based on this information, the process continues as marketing mix stimuli are reworked to further influence consumers.

Exhibit 10.1

Approaches to Influencing Overt Consumer Behaviors

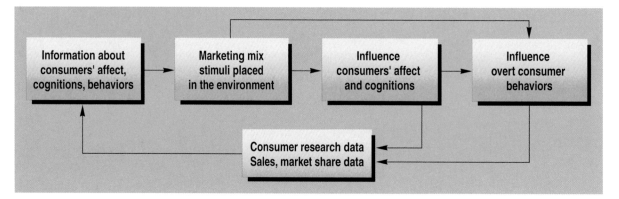

The model in Exhibit 10.1 is completely consistent with the Wheel of Consumer Analysis because consumers' affect, cognitions, and behaviors lead to changes in the environment (marketing strategy elements), which can lead to changes in consumers' affect, cognitions, and behaviors, which lead to further changes in the environment. It again demonstrates the dynamic nature of consumer behavior and marketing strategy.

It is important to recognize that influencing overt consumer behavior is most critical. If consumers only change what they think and feel but do nothing, no exchanges occur, no sales are made, and no profits are earned. Thus, although changing consumer affect and cognition are frequently useful and important steps in influencing overt consumer behavior, they are often only intermediate steps in the influence process. Consumers must perform one or more overt behaviors, such as store contacts, product contacts, transactions, consumption, or communication, so that marketing strategies can benefit organizations. Also, products and brands cannot satisfy consumer needs and wants unless some behavior occurs, such as buying and using them.

Marketers usually want to maintain a particular level of overt consumer behaviors or increase the level. If market share is at an optimal level such that increasing it would be unprofitable, marketers will likely try to maintain the level. However, in most cases, marketers try to increase the number of consumers who purchase an offering and/or increase the frequency of purchase by current buyers. In some cases, organizations try to decrease behavior, such as reducing the joint behaviors of driving and drinking.

Exhibit 10.2 presents four strategies designed to influence overt consumer behavior. For affective strategies, marketing mix elements are designed to influence consumers' affective responses in order to influence overt consumer behaviors. For example, for many years Michelin tire ads have featured a cute baby sitting in a floating tire to generate warm feelings and attention to the importance of safe tires when driving with children.

Exhibit 10.2

Strategies Designed to Influence Overt Consumer Behaviors

Type of Strategy	Description of Strategy	Strategic Focus	Sample Strategies	Ultimate Objective of Strategy
Affective	Strategies designed to influence consumers' affective responses	Consumers' emotions, moods, feelings, evaluations	Classically conditioning emotions to products	Influence overt consumer behaviors
Cognitive	Strategies designed to influence consumers' cognitive responses	Consumers' knowledge, meanings, beliefs	Providing information highlighting competitive advantages	Influence overt consumer behaviors
Behavioral	Strategies designed to influence consumers' behavioral responses	Consumers' overt behaviors	Positive reinforcement; modeling desired behaviors	Influence overt consumer behaviors
Combined	Strategies designed to influence multiple consumer responses	More than one of the above	Information about product benefits with emotional tie-ins and rebates	Influence overt consumer behaviors

Lands' End catalogs include extensive product information to influence cognition—a cognitive strategy
Bill Aron/PhotoEdit, Inc.

In the second strategy, marketing mix elements are designed to influence consumers' cognitions in order to influence consumer behaviors. Lands' End catalogs include extensive product information to help consumers decide whether particular garments are right for them.

In the third strategy, marketing mix elements are designed to influence consumers' overt behaviors somewhat directly. This does not mean consumers do not think about or feel anything when they experience antecedents or consequences of their behaviors. However, it does suggest that, in some cases, information processing is relatively automatic and little conscious information processing occurs. Many consumer behaviors are habitual and involve little decision making. Many marketing strategies are designed to influence these behaviors without a complete analysis of affect and cognition, such as coupons and other sales promotion tactics.

Finally, as is common in practice, various marketing mix stimuli are used to influence some combination of consumers' affect, cognitions, and behaviors in order to influence other consumer behaviors. For example, a Target ad featured a color picture of a Little Tikes Playhouse with two cute kids enjoying it, a product description, an age range of 1.5 to 4, the words "assembly required," and a sale price of $98.88. This ad was trying to influence affect from the cute kids enjoying the playhouse; cognition in terms of product and price information; and the behaviors of store contact, product contact, transaction, and consumption.

In sum, marketing strategies are designed to ultimately influence overt consumer behavior. These strategies should be designed with a precise understanding of the behaviors they are intended to influence, as well as whether affect and cognition are also to be influenced in important ways. In the next section, we discuss two areas of marketing—sales promotion and social marketing—that have focused on influencing behavior somewhat directly.

Sales Promotion

One area of consumer research that has recognized the value of analyzing overt behaviors is sales promotion. Leading experts define **sales promotion** as "an action-focused marketing event whose purpose is to have a direct impact on the behavior of a firm's customers."[1] Two points are noteworthy in this definition.

First, the firm's customers may be channel members, such as retailers, in which case the promotion is called a **trade promotion.** Trade promotions, such as advertising or display allowances, are used by companies to push products through the channel to consumers. Alternatively, the firm's customers may be final consumers, in which case the promotions are called **consumer promotions.** Consumer promotions, such as coupons and free samples, are used by manufacturers and retailers to persuade consumers to purchase products and visit retail outlets. In one recent year, overall expenditures on promotion were divided 44.3 percent on trade promotions, 30.6 percent on advertising, and 25.1 percent on consumer promotions.

Second, most consumer promotions are designed to influence the probability of purchase or other desired behaviors without necessarily changing prepurchase consumer attitudes about a brand. If the promotion is for a new brand, then purchase and use may lead to favorable postpurchase attitudes and future purchases. If purchase is for an existing brand, consumers with a neutral or slightly positive attitude may use the promotion to reduce purchase risk and try the brand. For consumers who already purchase a brand, a promotion may be an added incentive to remain loyal.

This text is concerned primarily with consumer promotions and their influence on consumer behavior. There are many types of consumer promotions; the following list covers most of them.[2]

1. *Sampling.* Consumers are offered regular or trial sizes of the product either free or at a nominal price. For example, Hershey Foods handed out 750,000 candy bars on 170 college campuses.

2. *Price deals.* Consumers are given discounts from the product's regular price. For example, Coke and Pepsi are frequently available at discounted prices.

3. *Bonus packs.* Bonus packs consist of additional amounts of the product that a company gives to buyers of the product. For example, Gillette occasionally adds a few extra blades to its blade packs without increasing the price. Bonus packs are discussed in Highlight 10.1.

4. *Rebates and refunds.* Consumers, either at purchase or by mail, are given cash reimbursements for purchasing products. For example, consumers are often offered rebates for purchasing Chrysler or Ford automobiles.

5. *Sweepstakes and contests.* Consumers are offered chances to win cash and/or prizes through either chance selection or games of skill. For example, Marriott Hotels teamed up with Hertz Rent-A-Car in a scratch-card sweepstakes that offered more than $90 million in prizes.

6. *Premiums.* A premium is a reward or gift that comes from purchasing a product. For example, Procter & Gamble offered a free package of Diaperene baby wash-cloths with the purchase of any size Pampers.

7. *Coupons.* Consumers are offered cents-off or added-value incentives for purchasing specific products. For example, Lenscrafters offered newspaper coupons for $20 off the purchase of contact lenses from its stores.

These basic types of consumer promotions are often used in combination to increase the probability of desired behaviors. For example, P&G offered a $1-off coupon plus a premium coupon for a free Duncan Hines cake mix for purchasing

Highlight 10.1

Consumer Reactions to Bonus Packs

Bonus packs are frequently used consumer promotions. You can walk down the health and beauty aids aisles of any discount store and see all sorts of products claiming "25% more free" or "4 ounces free." These package labels are designed to attract shoppers' attention and ultimately get consumers to buy the products. Some shoppers, when presented with bonus packs, will buy them rather than another brand or buy more than planned, knowing that the larger size will be offered for a limited time only. Others are rewarded for continuing to buy their regular brands when they are promoted as bonus packs.

Marketers can track bonus pack sales easily to determine the effectiveness of promotions and their impact on market share. But how do bonus packs influence consumer cognitions? A study of hair shampoo found that 43 percent of respondents said they would switch for "20% more free," but 90 percent said that "25% more free" would get them to switch brands.

Marketers commonly use three ways to present bonus pack information: "units free," "percent free," and "percent more free." "Units free" simply tells the consumer how many extra ounces or pieces are included in the package at no additional cost. The "percent free" format presents the free amount as a percentage of bonus size, whereas "percent more free" presents the free amount as a percentage of the smaller, regular size. Consumers apparently have a preference for how this information is presented as 91 percent of the respondents in the survey indicated a clear preference for the "percent more free" format over the "percent free" format. They believed that "more" was better, and preferred the "percent more free" wording, even when the actual amount of free product was greater in the "percent free" format. In addition, 73 percent of respondents preferred the "percent more free" format to "ounces free."

When questioned as to who they thought was paying for the "free" product, 75 percent of all respondents believed the consumer was either directly or indirectly paying for the extra amount offered in bonus packs. Interestingly, those who switched for a bonus pack believed that the manufacturer incurred the cost of the extra product, whereas those who did not switch believed the consumer paid. Nearly half the respondents surveyed said the amount of free product it would take to get them to switch depended on the type of product.

The University of New Haven studied consumer reactions to Vaseline Intensive Care Lotion bonus pack promotions. Results from the study showed that perceived value and liking for the Vaseline brand were positively associated with purchasing decisions. Also, the perception by the consumer that bonus packs were in limited supply led to increased purchasing. The study also determined that the tendency of consumers to buy more than they need (stockpile) is positively related to perceived value of the product, skepticism of the bonus quantity, and age of the consumer. Older customers are more likely to stockpile. Perhaps, older consumers have more money with which to buy multiple packs, or are more value conscious than their younger counterparts. It was also noted that consumers who "buy only when about to run out of the product" are not the ideal target customer for bonus pack promotions. Why? Because when these buyers purchase a bonus pack, their purchase cycle for the product is lengthened till they consume the additional amount of product.

How do you react to bonus packs? Will you switch brands of shampoo, deodorant, or toothpaste to get an extra amount free? Do you make careful decisions about whether to accept a bonus pack deal versus your regular brand or do you just go for it? How much thinking do you do in the grocery store when presented a different brand of coffee with an extra "2 ounces free" before making a coffee purchase?

Sources: Beng Soo Ong, "Determinants of Purchase Intentions and Stock-Piling Tendency of Bonus Packs," *American Business Review*, January, 1999, pp. 57–64; Larry J. Seibert, "What Consumers Think about Bonus Pack Sales Promotions," *Marketing News*, February 17, 1997, p. 9. Reprinted by permission of the American Marketing Association.

any size Folgers coffee. Recently many consumer promotions have featured coupons plus a promise to make donations to specific charities for every coupon or refund certificate redeemed. For example, Hartz Mountain offered a $1 coupon on its flea and tick repellent, plus a 50-cent donation to the Better Health for Pets Program.

Consumer promotions can be used to influence behavior in a variety of ways. Next, we discuss four aspects of behavior that promotions are designed to affect.

Purchase Probability

Most consumer promotions are designed to increase the probability that consumers will purchase a particular brand or combination of products. However, a firm may hope to achieve any number of subgoals when running a promotion. The primary goal may be to get consumers to try a new product. For example, Hershey offered a free package of Reese's Crunchy Peanut Butter Cups with the purchase of any other Reese's candy product to attempt to induce trial of the new product. Kellogg offered a coupon for an 18-ounce box of its popular corn flakes with the purchase of its Kellogg's Mini Buns. Some car dealers offer special discounts for first-time buyers.

A second subgoal of consumer promotions is to position a brand or company in the minds of consumers to encourage them to purchase and continue to purchase the company's brand. In this case, the promotion is designed to maintain or change consumers' affect, cognitions, and behaviors. One way of doing so is to use frequent promotions to obtain a competitive price on a brand that is positioned as a high-priced, high-quality product. In this way, the lower price has less chance of leading consumers to believe the product is of lower quality than competitive brands. For example, Kellogg frequently offers coupons and premiums on its market-leading cereals.

Another use of promotion for positioning purposes is to offer to make contributions to charity for each coupon or refund certificate redeemed by consumers. This tactic may increase consumer perceptions of the firm's societal commitment. Consumers who are socially and ecologically concerned may then switch to that

Some ads involve attempts to influence purchase timing. Some attempt to influence purchase quantity *(left) Courtesy Pizza Hut, Inc.; (right) Courtesy of The Quaker Oats Company.*

company's brands. In addition to the Hartz Mountain example already noted, many other companies use this type of promotion. Post Alpha Bits offered a 50-cent coupon and promised to make an unspecified donation to Hospitals for Children for each coupon redeemed. Chef Boyardee Pizza Mix offered a 20-cent coupon and promised to make a 25-cent donation to Adam Walsh Resource Centers for each coupon redeemed. Krunchers Potato Chips offered a 25-cent coupon and promised to make a contribution to the Better Homes Foundation. Procter & Gamble offered a 50-cent refund for a number of its soap products and promised a $1 contribution to Keep America Beautiful, Inc., for each refund certificate redeemed.

A third subgoal of consumer promotions is to obtain a brand switch. Consumer promotions may lead to brand switches by making the purchase of a brand more attractive than purchase of the usual brand at full price.

A final goal of consumer promotions is to develop brand loyalty. Because some consumers tend to purchase products based on coupons and other promotions, frequent deals on particular brands may keep them relatively loyal to the firm's brands. Companies, such as Kellogg and P&G, that have broad product lines and a number of top-selling products frequently offer a variety of consumer promotions for their products. Even deal-prone consumers may remain loyal through a long succession of coupons and other deals.

Purchase Quantity

A number of consumer promotions are designed not only to influence purchase of a brand but also to influence the number or size of units purchased. For example, Quaker Oats offered a 70-cent coupon for purchasing two bottles of Gatorade. Best Foods offered a $1 coupon for purchasing two 18-ounce or larger jars of Skippy peanut butter. P&G offered $2, $5, and $8 refunds for purchasing 1, 2, and 3 gallons of Tide, Cheer, Era, or Solo liquid laundry detergent. A free Mennen Speed Stick deodorant was offered with the purchase of two at the regular price. Such promotions may increase the amount of a company's product that consumers purchase and may increase brand loyalty. However, consumers who already are loyal to particular brands may simply stock up on them during a promotion and wait until the next promotion to purchase again. Some consumers prefer to purchase products only when they can get a deal on them. U.S. car manufacturers have unintentionally conditioned many consumers to wait for rebates rather than buy a car without one.

Purchase Timing

Consumer promotions can also be used to influence the time at which consumers purchase. For example, special discounts can be offered to encourage consumers to eat at particular restaurants on nights when business is slow. Pizza Hut often offers discounts and special family prices for Monday or Tuesday nights. Other retail stores have special sales on specific dates to encourage purchases at that time. Services such as airlines and telephone companies offer special rates to encourage consumers to use them at specific times and dates to even out demand. One trend in the use of coupons shortens the redemption period to encourage consumers to purchase sooner. Finally, most sweepstakes and contests are of relatively short duration to encourage consumers to enter the contest by purchasing the product promptly.

Purchase Location

Consumer promotions can also be used to influence the location or vendor of particular products. Retail stores and retail chains offer their own coupons, contests, and other deals to encourage consumers to shop at their outlets. For example, one grocery chain offered $20 worth of beef if a consumer was selected at a specific store and was found to have a beef product in his or her shopping cart. Some retail chains, such as Wal-Mart, have a standing offer to meet any other store's price on a product if the Wal-Mart price is higher. Such promotions and tactics can build store traffic and encourage store loyalty, as discussed in Highlight 10.2.

Effectiveness of Sales Promotions

There is little question that promotions effectively influence consumer behavior. However, which promotion tools are generally most effective for achieving particular behavioral changes is not fully understood. One study compared four consumer promotion tools—coupons, rebates, sweepstakes, and premiums—for their impact on various consumer purchase behaviors.[3] These behaviors included purchasing a product consumers said they didn't need, purchasing a product they had never tried before, purchasing a different brand than they regularly used, purchasing more than usual, purchasing sooner than usual, and purchasing later than usual.

➤ **High**light 10.2

Amoco's Big Summer Fill-up

Amoco Oil Company ran a promotion designed to build store loyalty to Amoco filling stations. The promotion required consumers to fill up (a minimum of 8 gallons) at an Amoco station 10 times and get a promotion card punched by an attendant. This all had to be done within a specified three-month period. After 10 fill-ups, consumers could mail the card to the "Amoco Fill-up" address and receive coupons for $1 off on their next five fill-ups.

Consider the possible outcomes of this promotion. If consumers complied with all the requirements and used the five coupons, they made 15 trips to an Amoco station and made 15 purchases of 8 gallons or more. This is a considerable amount of behavior and sales to generate for the company for a relatively small $5 reward. In addition, because Amoco gas is more expensive than gas at discount stations, the consumer may not have saved money. If a consumer averaged buying 10 gallons at a time and paid 5 cents more a gallon for Amoco gas, in 15 trips, he or she spent an additional $7.50 to save $5. However, Amoco gas is of excellent quality and may give the consumer savings

in better gas mileage, and the consumer's car may run better by using it. Thus, the promotion could get consumers in the habit of going to an Amoco station and lead to loyalty. The superior product could also contribute to this loyalty.

The promotion card also stated that it would take six to eight weeks to receive the coupons. If the consumer continued to use Amoco in the meantime, the company continued to make full-price sales. If the consumer went to other stations during the waiting period, receipt of the coupons could bring them back to Amoco, giving the company a second chance to develop loyalty.

If consumers did not fill up 10 times in three months, they did not qualify for the promotion. However, in making a point of trying to go to an Amoco station, the consumer might also have developed a loyalty to it. In this case, Amoco developed a loyal customer but did not have to pay the promotion value to do so. Overall, this promotion strategy would appear to be one that was well designed and capable of building long-term loyal customers. To learn more about Amoco, visit its website at **www.amoco.com**.

Exhibit 10.3 presents the results of that study. In general, consumers reported that coupons were the most effective promotion for changing these behaviors. More than 70 percent reported they purchased a product they had never tried before because of a coupon, and more than 75 percent said they purchased a different brand than they regularly used because of a coupon. Of the four promotion tools, coupons are the most commonly available and easiest to use.

Rebates and premiums were both shown to be effective in changing consumer behavior in this study, but less so than coupons. The study found that the larger the rebate, the greater effort consumers would expend to obtain the product. Finally, although some consumers also reported that sweepstakes influenced them, such promotions were the least effective overall. The study also found that changes in behavior varied by the type of product and characteristics of the consumers. For example, for products such as shampoo, coffee, batteries, toothpaste, and personal appliances, promotions could persuade the majority of consumers to try a different brand. However, for products such as alcoholic beverages, automobiles, motor oil, pet food, and floor coverings, consumers reported that promotions would not persuade them to switch brands. In terms of consumer characteristics, consumers who are more affluent, educated, and older are more likely to participate in consumer promotions, according to this study.

In sum, promotions can influence consumer behavior, although many factors alter their effectiveness. It seems likely that the greater the reward, the less effort

Exhibit 10.3

Promotion Effects on Consumer Behavior

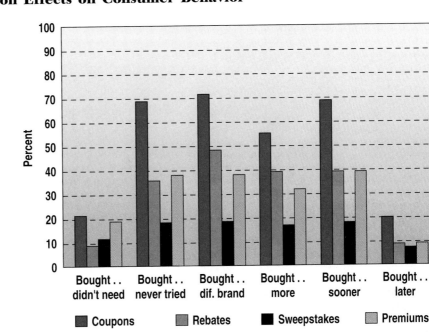

Source: "Study: Some Promotions Change Consumer Behavior," *Marketing News,* October 15, 1990, p. 12. Reprinted with permission of the American Marketing Association.

required to obtain it, and the sooner it is obtained after the behavior, the more likely the promotion will be influential. However, further research on consumer promotions is needed to better understand the affective, cognitive, behavioral, and environmental factors that influence their effectiveness.

Social Marketing

Social marketing is "the application of commercial marketing technologies to the analysis, planning, execution, and evaluation of programs designed to influence the voluntary behavior of target audiences in order to improve their personal welfare and that of their society."4 Unlike commercial marketing, which benefits consumers as a means to achieving the organization's objectives, the end goal of social marketing is to benefit the target audience or the broader society. Social marketing is typically concerned with influencing and changing consumers' overt behavior, but can also be used to influence affect and cognitions as an intermediate step. For example, social marketing could be used to increase the self-esteem of laid-off workers or to help calm traumatized mental patients so they can function more effectively in society. As with commercial marketing, social marketing can be applied at the individual, household, target market, or societal levels.

Increasing Desired Behaviors

Social marketing can increase many types of behaviors. For example, research has shown that various incentives can increase the probability that parents will take their children in for dental and health care. In addition, prompts can be used to increase parental discussion of a child's problems with health care providers. Providing

A social marketing ad designed to influence consumer behavior   *Rhoda Sidney/Stock, Boston, LLC.*

feedback and chances to win prizes can help increase seatbelt usage, which could save thousands of lives each year. Small incentives can also increase the use of carpools, which could help save natural resources and reduce air pollution. Providing information to grocery shoppers concerning the amount of fat and fiber in products and offering alternatives can influence the purchase of more nutritious foods.

Decreasing Undesired Behaviors

Many types of undesired consumer behaviors also can be decreased through social marketing programs. For example, various types of interventions can decrease smoking, drunken and other unsafe driving, dropping out of school, illegal drug use, and teenage pregnancy. Although no program has been totally effective, the importance of these problems makes even small changes very valuable in improving individuals' lives and society in general.[5]

Some famous ad campaigns were designed to decrease undesired behaviors.[6] These ads were developed by the Ad Council of the United States and participating ad agencies. For example, "Just Say No" was designed by DDB Needham Worldwide to decrease the use of illicit drugs; "Help Stop AIDS. Use a condom" was designed by Scali, McCabe, Sloves, Inc., to decrease the frequency of unprotected sex; "Take time out. Don't take it out on your kid" was designed by Lintas: Campbell-Ewald to decrease physical abuse of children. A stronger focus on such problems from a consumer behavior perspective could provide even better approaches to solving them.

A Strategic Model for Influencing Consumer Behaviors

Marketing managers develop strategies to accomplish particular objectives. Often these objectives deal with maintaining or increasing sales or market share by a particular amount or percentage, subject to a budget constraint. To accomplish these objectives, managers focus on influencing consumers' affect, cognitions, and behaviors. Influencing these factors can involve both long-term and short-term strategies. For example, building brand equity—consumers' beliefs about positive product attributes and favorable consequences of brand use—is usually a long-term strategy designed to influence long-term sales and the ability to charge higher prices. Brands like Harley-Davidson, Titleist, and Sony have developed high brand equity and market share by influencing consumers' affective and cognitive responses, which had led to long-term purchase and use behaviors. Stores like The Gap and Wal-Mart also develop store images and store equity to influence consumers to shop at their stores. American Express has developed a prestige image for its credit cards to influence consumers to use them.

In other cases, marketing managers use strategies to influence consumers in the short run, but at the same time they hope these consumers will also become long-term, loyal customers. Many of the sales promotion tactics discussed in this chapter are designed to increase sales quickly for a short period of time.

Exhibit 10.4

Steps in Developing Consumer Behavior Influence Strategies

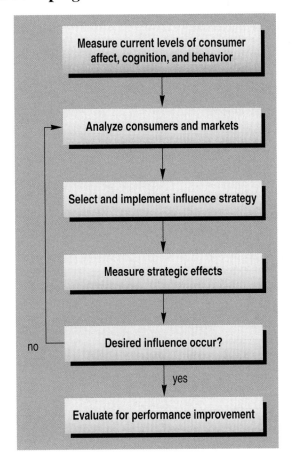

Regardless of whether the strategy is for the short or long run, managers need to understand consumers' affect, cognitions, and behaviors to develop strategies to influence them. Exhibit 10.4 presents a general model managers can use to help them develop successful influence strategies.

Measure Current Levels of Consumer Affect, Cognition, and Behavior

To design successful strategies, marketers should first know what consumers think, feel, and do about a company's products, stores, or other offerings. Marketers should know the same things about competitive offerings. In other words, consumers' affect, cognitions, and behaviors should be measured to form the basis for successful strategies. A number of ways to measure various affective and cognitive responses were discussed in Section 2 of the book; Exhibit 10.5 lists some ways to measure overt consumer behaviors. As shown, for each of the seven types of behavior identified, there are a variety of ways to measure them. Although all of these methods are commonly used in marketing and consumer research, they are not

Exhibit 10.5

Examples of Methods Used to Measure Overt Consumer Behaviors

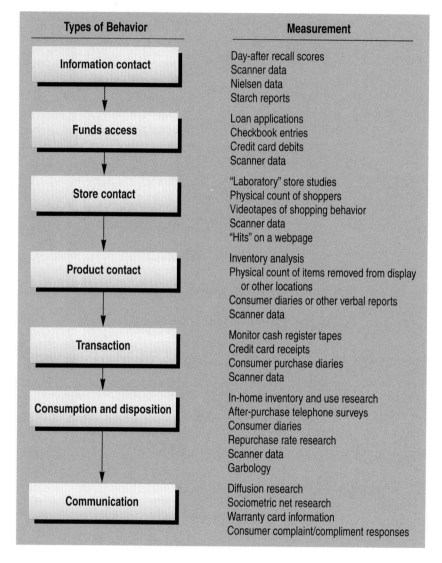

Types of Behavior	Measurement
Information contact	Day-after recall scores Scanner data Nielsen data Starch reports
Funds access	Loan applications Checkbook entries Credit card debits Scanner data
Store contact	"Laboratory" store studies Physical count of shoppers Videotapes of shopping behavior Scanner data "Hits" on a webpage
Product contact	Inventory analysis Physical count of items removed from display or other locations Consumer diaries or other verbal reports Scanner data
Transaction	Monitor cash register tapes Credit card receipts Consumer purchase diaries Scanner data
Consumption and disposition	In-home inventory and use research After-purchase telephone surveys Consumer diaries Repurchase rate research Scanner data Garbology
Communication	Diffusion research Sociometric net research Warranty card information Consumer complaint/compliment responses

always used sequentially to investigate all the behaviors consumers must perform to purchase and use products correctly.

One approach that allows for monitoring a number of stages in a purchase sequence is the **scanner cable method,** available from research companies such as Information Resources, Inc. (IRI), and Nielsen Marketing Research USA. IRI's research systems are used by many leading companies, including General Foods, Procter & Gamble, General Mills, and Frito-Lay. The systems are designed to predict which products will be successful and which ads work best to sell them. They have been expanded from use in grocery stores to include drugstores and mass merchandisers. IRI has constructed consumer panels in a number of cities and

Consumers use a BehaviorScan–coded ID card when shopping in the markets covered by the scanner network *Robert Bull.*

monitors households nationwide. It monitors purchases in grocery stores in many markets ranging from big cities to small towns.

Panel members provide information about the size of their families, their income, their marital status, how many TVs they own, what types of newspapers and magazines they read, and who does most of the shopping. IRI provides a special bar-coded identification card that shoppers present to the cashier when they pay for products in grocery stores, drugstores, and other stores. By passing the card over the scanner or entering the digits manually into the register, the cashier records everything each shopper has purchased. One executive at Frito-Lay, which used IRI's services for the introduction of Sun Chips snacks, concluded, "The beauty of scanner data is that we get a complete description of a household from the panel and can match it with purchasing patterns. We know exactly who's out there buying our product and that helps us design marketing and advertising plans accordingly."[7]

A number of behaviors in the purchase sequence can be monitored and influenced using scanner methods. For example, information contact can be influenced because media habits of households are monitored, and commercials can be changed until contact occurs. Funds access can be monitored on the cash register tape by recording prices and the method of payment. Because every purchase in the store is recorded, store contact, product contact, and transaction information are available, as well as the dates and times of these behaviors. As such, the effectiveness of various sales promotions and other marketing strategies on specific consumer behaviors can be determined. Successful promotions can be offered again to encourage store and brand loyalty. Because the time between purchases can be determined, information on consumption and usage rates is also available.

There are two reasons to start strategy development by measuring consumers' affect, cognitions, and behavior. First, these measures provide baseline data for determining the effectiveness of the influence strategy after it has been implemented. A **baseline** is the level of consumers' responses prior to implementation of a new strategy. Second, these measures help identify opportunities and threats in the market. For example, if consumers know more about a competitive retail chain, like it better, and shop there more frequently, strategies must be developed to increase these responses for the company's stores. Hopefully, the research also identifies the reasons consumers shop at the competitive chain so that a strategy can be developed to increase their acceptance of and purchases at the company's stores.

Analyze Consumers and Markets

After collecting baseline data, the next step is to analyze the information by evaluating consumer responses from various current and potential markets. Consumers may not purchase a product for many reasons, and consumer research is designed to uncover the reasons. Perhaps they do not know about the product, do not like it, or do not know where to buy it. Perhaps they purchase a competitive product with which they are highly satisfied. The strategies that are appropriate depend on the levels of consumers' affective, cognitive, and behavioral responses to the company's products relative to competitive products.

For existing products, marketers often seek strategies to attract consumers away from competitive products. There are many strategies for doing so, including developing advertising to highlight benefits superior to competitive offerings, developing more convenient packaging, lowering prices through sales promotions, or expanding distribution outlets. Strategies for existing products may also focus on increasing purchases by current users. These strategies involve finding new uses for a product, new occasions for its use, or decreasing the cost of using it. Finally, strategies for existing products involve expanding markets geographically, such as seeking global markets where opportunities may be better because there are so many consumers who are nonusers, competition is weaker, or the product has strong affective appeal. For example, many American products and brands are well liked and sought out by consumers in some global markets. However, failure to analyze global consumers can lead to poor strategies, as discussed in Highlight 10.3.

For new products, strategies often focus on affect and cognition to create favorable behavioral responses. Consumers are informed about the nature of a new product, its benefits, and where it can be purchased to increase the probability that they will buy it. Creating positive affect is part of the process. For example, when JCPenney developed its Diahann Carroll line of women's clothes and its Nefertiti Collection of African prints, it sought to create positive affect for its stores with African-American women consumers. In other cases, marketers focus more on behavioral responses initially for new products. For example, free samples of a new soap or toothpaste are mailed to consumers to generate trial.

Select and Implement Influence Strategy

Based on the consumer and market analyses, a strategy to influence consumer responses is selected and implemented. The strategy may involve any or all of the marketing mix elements and may be designed to accomplish both short-term and long-term objectives. For example, many sales promotions have short-term objectives of generating sales to new customers that hopefully lead to long-term loyalty. Advertising campaigns may increase short-term sales but are often designed to create long-term brand equity and deep meanings for consumers that will also lead to long-term loyalty. Most product strategies involving changes in quality, packaging, or branding include long-term objectives, as do strategies involving new or different

Highlight 10.3

American Appliance Makers Misjudge European Consumers

In the late 1980s, the U.S. market for refrigerators and other major appliances was mature. But in western Europe, barely 20 percent of households had clothes dryers versus some 70 percent in the United States. In Europe there are dozens of appliance makers, nearly all ripe for consolidation, whereas in the United States four producers control 90 percent of the market. Europe, then, should have been a golden opportunity for U.S. appliance makers Whirlpool Corporation and Maytag.

In 1989, archrivals Whirlpool and Maytag leaped across the Atlantic. Maytag bought Britain's Hoover for about $320 million, and Whirlpool paid $960 million for the appliance unit of Dutch electronics giant Philips and spent another $500 million to retool its plants.

But the invasion fizzled. In 1995, Maytag sold its European operations to an Italian appliance maker, booking a $135 million loss. Whirlpool continued in the market, but experienced flat sales and declining earnings per share. Where did these companies go wrong?

In part, these companies misjudged European consumers. American consumers often want the lowest price and when appliances wear out, they buy new ones. However, many Europeans still think of appliances as investments. They will pay more and expect to get more in finish, durability, and appearance. Also, American households often put their washer and dryer in the garage or basement or tuck it away in a closet, where noise and appearance don't matter. However, many Europeans live in smaller houses and often put their laundry equipment in their kitchens, where noise and looks matter greatly.

Apparently, the failure to properly analyze consumers in European markets led to unsuccessful market entry strategies. Although there were many factors that made the market an attractive opportunity, failure to understand consumers' affect, cognition, and behavior led to a huge loss for Maytag and a marginal position for Whirlpool in European markets. Whirlpool has designed a new strategy involving three pan-European brands—Bauknecht for the affluent, Whirlpool for the middle market, and Ingis for the low end. Only time will tell if this strategy shows a better understanding of consumers and markets.

To learn more about these companies, visit their websites at **www.maytag.com** and **www.whirlpool.com**.

distribution methods. Pricing strategies most often incorporate short-term changes to influence sales, but long-term strategies are also used. Keeping prices high relative to competition over many years can create an image of distinctiveness or quality, whereas charging low prices for many years can create the perception of value for the money. For example, when Toyota introduced new models of the Camry, Celica, and Paseo, it cut prices by $700 to $1,000 to positively influence consumer value perceptions.

Measure Strategic Effects

After implementing the strategy, its effects must be measured to see whether and how much it influenced consumers' affect, cognition, and behavior and whether it did so enough to achieve objectives. If not, considerable analysis and evaluation need to be done to determine why the strategy failed. This is a complicated problem because influence strategies fail for a number of reasons:

1. *Faulty objectives.* The objectives were set too high and consumers were more resistant to influence than anticipated. In this case, the objectives have to be reconsidered.

By conditioning affect, marketers can influence behavioral responses. *AP/Wide World Photos.*

2. *Faulty strategy.* The objectives were appropriate but the strategy was faulty. In this case, the strategy can be improved and reimplemented or a new strategy developed and implemented.

3. *Faulty implementation.* The objectives and strategy were appropriate, but the strategy was poorly implemented. In this case, the strategy can be reimplemented more effectively if it is still viable or a new strategy can be developed and implemented.

4. *Faulty measurement.* Either the baseline or strategic effects measures were faulty. In this case, measurement needs to be improved and the same or a new strategy developed and implemented.

5. *Unanticipated competitive reactions or consumer changes.* The objectives were appropriate and the strategy was appropriate and implemented well, but competitors developed and implemented better strategies or consumers changed in unanticipated ways. In this case, a new strategy is likely needed.

6. *Combination.* Two or more of the above occurred. In this case, a complete audit of the strategy development system is likely needed.

Sorting out the reasons a strategy failed is obviously a difficult yet critical task if a company is to be successful. Without knowledge of why a strategy failed, managers have a difficult time improving their new strategies.

If the strategy is successful in achieving desired changes in consumer responses, the company probably did a good job of consumer analysis and strategy development and implementation. However, there could still be important problems in the process. Objectives may have been set too low, measurement may have overestimated the responses, or competition may have made a major strategic error that helped the company. Thus, not only the effects but also the process of developing consumer behaviors that influence strategies need to be frequently evaluated.

Evaluate for Performance Improvement

Regardless of how successful a particular marketing strategy is, there is often room for improvement. Developing and implementing strategies to influence consumer behavior is a dynamic process that requires constant monitoring of the company's and competitors' ongoing strategies, developing new strategies, and anticipating competitors' new strategies. Other environmental changes that influence consumers should also be analyzed and evaluated.

Marketing Implications

Marketers ultimately need to influence consumers' overt behavior to achieve organizational objectives such as sales, market share, and profits. This is sometimes done by first influencing consumers' affect and cognition. In other cases, marketers focus on intermediate behaviors that lead to the desired behaviors of purchase and use or focus on the desired behaviors somewhat directly. Regardless, it is useful to follow a sequential process for developing successful strategies that allows success or failure to be measured. The model discussed in this part of the chapter is one approach to help marketers do so. Although marketers often develop strategies with particular objectives in mind, commonly used approaches are frequently somewhat ad hoc and do not always allow for detailed analyses and evaluations of consumers' responses to a chosen strategy. The model presented here provides a general framework for overcoming this problem. Although using this approach requires considerable consumer research, such research could help develop better strategies. Even if only a few types of affective, cognitive, and behavioral responses are identified and analyzed, marketers could have a better system for developing and evaluating their strategies. Of course, the costs and benefits of detailed consumer analysis have to be assessed in deciding how much time and money to expend.

Back To...

What Were These Marketers Trying to Do?

What were these marketers trying to do? Clearly they were trying to influence consumer behavior by changing the consequences of the behavior. Both Ralston-Purina and General Mills were trying to get consumers to buy their cereals, and PepsiCo was trying to get consumers to buy its soft drinks. Note that although consumers would have to do some amount of information processing to purchase these products, the promotions were designed to get them to *buy* the products, not to change their attitudes or beliefs about them. Perhaps purchase and use would then lead consumers to remember how good the products were or change their attitudes about the products' taste or quality. However, such changes in cognition would likely come after the desired change in purchase and use behavior.

Citicorp was also trying to influence consumer behavior by getting consumers to charge more on their credit cards. American TV was trying to get consumers to come to its retail stores and make purchases, including those with the free-steak offer. As with the manufacturers previously discussed, this credit card company and this retailer were not trying to change what consumers thought or felt about their services or stores; rather, they were trying to influence consumer behavior by changing the consequences. Of course, this in turn might change consumers' cognition about these marketers and their products and services.

Further, depending on the success of such promotions, these marketers and their competitors might continue to offer them or come up with new promotion approaches, which are evidenced in the environment. Thus, while the focus of this chapter (and Section 2) is on behavior, analysis of the reciprocal inter-actions among affect and cognition, behavior, and the environment is still required for complete understanding of consumer behavior.

Finally, after completing this section of the text, you should have new insights into the use of promotions such as those discussed in this chapter. ❖

Summary
This chapter discussed a general approach to influencing overt consumer behaviors. Marketers accomplish this by changing the environment to influence consumers' affective and cognitive responses as intermediate steps or by focusing on behavioral responses somewhat directly. Two areas of marketing that have focused on overt consumer behavior—sales promotion and social marketing—were discussed. Finally, the chapter presented model of the steps in developing consumer behavior influence strategies and offered guidelines for using the model effectively.

Key Terms and Concepts

baseline **253**	scanner cable method **252**
consumer promotion **243**	social marketing **249**
sales promotion **242**	trade promotion **243**

Review and Discussion Questions

1. This chapter argues that influencing overt consumer behavior is more critical for marketers than influencing only affect and cognition. Do you agree? Why or why not?
2. Offer one example of each of the seven types of sales promotion listed in the chapter. How many of these have influenced your consumer behavior? Which ones do you prefer?
3. Offer one example of a situation where a sales promotion could affect your purchase probability, purchase quantity, purchase timing, or purchase location.
4. What factors do you think influence whether consumers respond to a social marketing campaign to donate blood to the Red Cross?
5. What factors do you think influence whether consumers respond to a social marketing campaign to reduce drunken or other unsafe driving?
6. List everything you know (cognition), feel (affect), and do (behavior) concerning Crest toothpaste. How could marketers identify your level of each of these factors?
7. In reviewing Exhibit 10.5, which methods do you think are best for measuring the effects of a marketing strategy?
8. Why is it so difficult to determine the reasons for a strategic failure to influence consumers?
9. If a consumer behavior influence strategy met its objectives, can the marketer conclude that everything was done as effectively as possible? Why or why not?

Marketing Strategy in Action

Cub Foods

In 2003, Cub Foods, had 78 corporate and 30 franchised stores. The chain built its success by focusing on its primary market: families of four or five individuals with adults ages 24 to early 40s who are informed, value-conscious consumers—consumers like Leslie Wells.

Leslie Wells's recent expedition to the new Cub Foods store in Melrose Park, Illinois, was no ordinary trip to the grocery store. "You go crazy," says Wells, sounding a little shell-shocked. Overwhelmed by Cub's vast selection, tables of samples, and discounts as high as 30 percent, Wells spent $76 on groceries—$36 more than she had planned. Wells fell prey to what a Cub executive calls "the wow factors": a shopping frenzy brought on by low prices and clever marketing. That's the reaction Cub's super warehouse stores strive for—and often get.

Cub Foods has been a leader in shaking up the food industry and forcing many conventional supermarkets to lower prices, increase services, or, in some cases, go out of business. With Cub and other super warehouse stores springing up across the country, shopping habits are changing too. Some shoppers must drive 50 miles or more to a Cub store instead of going to the nearest neighborhood supermarket and bag their own groceries at Cub Foods. Their payoff is that they find almost everything they need under one roof, and most of it is cheaper than at competing supermarkets. Cub's low prices, smart marketing, and sheer size encourage shoppers to spend far more than they do in the average supermarket.

The difference between Cub and most supermarkets is obvious the minute a shopper walks through Cub's doors. The entry aisle, called a "power alley" by some, is lined two stories high with specials, such as bean coffee at $2 a pound and half-price apple juice. Above, the ceiling joists and girders are exposed, giving "the subliminal feeling of all the spaciousness up there. It suggests there's massive buying going on that translates in a shopper's mind that there's tremendous savings going on as well," says Paul Suneson, director of marketing research for Cub's parent, SUPERVALU Inc., the nation's largest food wholesaler.

Cub's wider-than-usual shopping carts, which are intended to suggest expansive buying, fit easily through the wide aisles, which channel shoppers toward high-profit impulse foods. The whole store exudes a seductive, horn-of-plenty feeling. Cub customers typically buy in volume and spend four times the supermarket average per shopping trip. The average Cub store has sales quadruple the volume of conventional stores.

Cub Foods has a simple approach to grocery retailing: low prices, made possible by rigidly controlled costs and high-volume sales; exceptionally high quality for produce and meats—the items people build shopping trips around; and immense variety. It's all packaged in clean stores that are twice as big as most warehouse outlets and four times as big as most supermarkets. A Cub store stocks between 35,000 and 49,000 items, double the selection of conventional stores, mixing staples with luxury, ethnic, and hard-to-find foods. This leads to overwhelming displays: 88 kinds of hot dogs and dinner sausages, 12 brands of Mexican food, and fresh meats and produce by the ton.

The store distributes maps to guide shoppers. But without a map or a specific destination, a shopper is subliminally led around by the arrangement of the aisles. The power alley spills into the produce department. From there the aisles lead to highly profitable perimeter departments: meat, fish, bakery, and frozen foods. The deli comes before fresh meat because Cub wants shoppers to do their impulse buying before their budgets are depleted on essentials.

Overall, Cub's gross margin—the difference between what it pays for its goods and what it sells them for—is 14 percent, six to eight points less than most conventional stores. However, because Cub relies mostly on word-of-mouth advertising, its ad budgets are 25 percent less than those of other chains.

Courtesy SUPERVALU.

Discussion Questions

1. List at least five marketing tactics Cub Foods employs in its stores to increase the probability of purchases.

2. What accounts for Cub's success in generating such large sales per customer and per store?

3. Given Cub's lower prices, quality merchandise, excellent location, and superior assortment, offer reasons that many consumers in its trading areas refuse to shop there.

Sources: Supervalu.com, July 2003; "Shopping Day," WEEK.com, March 2002; Michael Garry, "Cub Embraces Non-Foods," *Progressive Grocer,* December 1991, pp. 45–48; Steve Weiner and Betsy Morris, "Bigger, Shrewder and Cheaper Cub Leads Food Stores into the Future," *The Wall Street Journal,* August 26, 1985, p. 17.

four

The Environment and Marketing Strategy

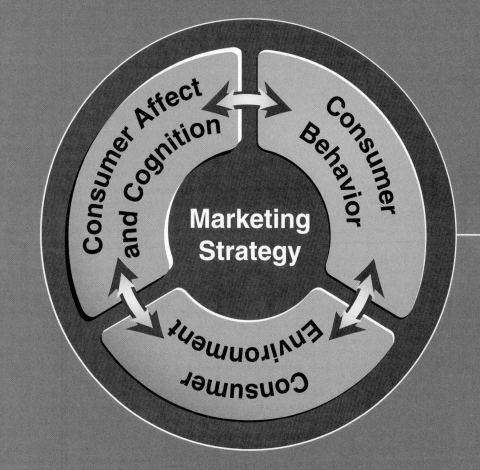

11

Introduction to the Environment

Megaresorts in Las Vegas

The wave of expansion in Las Vegas in the late 1990s was amazing, even by that city's own flamboyant standards. Despite flat tourism growth, hotel and casino owners tried to outdo one another in a spectacular game of architectural one-upmanship, adding 12,500 hotel rooms in 1999 (incidentally, that's just slightly fewer than the total number of rooms in the entire city of Milwaukee). In May 1999, actress Sophia Loren smashed a bottle against the side of a gondola to mark the opening of The Venetian, a 3,000-suite resort that replicates the romance of Old World Italy, complete with canal rides and Renaissance paintings. If Italy isn't your thing, perhaps you could visit the Paris–Las Vegas Casino Resort, opened in September 1999. It features eight French restaurants; a "Parisian" boulevard complete with street performers; and, of course, the obligatory 540-foot reproduction of the Eiffel Tower.

One of the most successful new megaresorts is Mandalay Bay, literally an oasis in the middle of the Las Vegas desert. Also opened in 1999, the $1 billion, 3,700-room hotel is designed to resemble a South Seas paradise. The palm trees out front, the live macaws in the lobby, and the huge aquarium are just the beginning. Mandalay Bay's 11-acre tropical water park includes a sand-and-surf beach with six-foot artificial waves. You can unwind with a deep-tissue massage or a "volcanic dust body treatment" in the resort's luxurious 30,000-square-foot spa. Plus, you may find intricate floral and animal prints in your room.

Mandalay Bay also features a wide range of dining options. Las Vegas casinos used to be known primarily for their free buffets, where you could gorge yourself on huge slabs of prime rib until your left ventricle cried out for mercy. Today the fare is more upscale and varied, designed to appeal not only to visitors but also to Las Vegas natives in search of a fine dining experience. Famed restaurateur Wolfgang Puck explains, "People want to eat where the locals do." Mandalay Bay features

The circular diagram shows: Consumer Affect and Cognition, Consumer Behavior, Consumer Environment, and Marketing Strategy at the center.

Dave G. Houser/CORBIS

15 restaurants, including Puck's Trattoria de Lupo, featuring Italian cuisine and architecture. Eat at Chef Carlie Palmer's famed Aureole and marvel at the four-story-tall wine tower. Other themed restaurants serve up Mexican, Chinese, and Russian fare.

The entertainment venues within Mandalay Bay have made it into an event destination as well as a vacation spot. Luciano Pavarotti has performed in the 12,000-seat Events Center. In September 1999, tickets were going at $3,500 apiece for a championship boxing match in the Conference Center. The House of Blues has been a hot spot for performers like B.B. King and Dwight Yoakam.

The hotel rooms ooze luxury. The average room is 500 square feet, with floor-to-ceiling windows, a separate soaking tub and shower, and a 27-inch TV. The more opulent suites are downright enormous—up to 6,670 square feet. If you are willing to spend $200 a night or more, you can stay in Las Vegas' first five-star hotel, The Four Seasons, up on the 38th and 39th floors.

In case you were wondering, Mandalay Bay does have a casino—a huge one. It contains 2,400 slot/video poker machines, 122 table games, and a poker room. However, the casino is not really the centerpiece of the resort. Las Vegas hotels used to be laid out in an "X" pattern, with the casino in the middle, so to go practically anywhere inside the hotel you had to walk through the casino. That is not the situation in newer megaresorts like Mandalay Bay. For example, while spending per room in Las Vegas rose from $333 in 1996 to $360 in 1999, gambling revenue per room fell from $193 to $181 over the same period.

Today not everyone goes to Las Vegas (or Atlantic City) to gamble. In the 1990s, six states legalized riverboat gambling. There also are an increasing number of casinos all over the country operated by Native American tribes. You can even gamble online. In the face of this competition, Las Vegas resort operators have expanded their offerings. The casinos, while still very popular, are now just one part of an increasingly diverse Las Vegas experience.

Sources: Joshua Levine, "Las Vegas' New Tables," *Forbes,* December 27, 1999, pp. 304–306; John Deiner, "Face Off," *Washington Post,* July 16, 1999, p. E2; Mandalay Bay website, **www.mandalaybay.com.**

This example describes several aspects of the physical and social environment that can influence people's behaviors, cognitions, and affective responses. This chapter provides an overview of these environmental influences and presents a framework for thinking about environmental influences on consumers that is useful for creating effective marketing strategies.

We begin by discussing several ways of thinking about the environment. Next, we identify three environments—social, physical, and marketing—and review the key dimensions of each. Then we discuss the related concept of situations and show how marketers can analyze environmental factors in terms of situations. Finally, we discuss five marketing-related situations: information acquisition, shopping, purchasing, consumption, and disposition.

The Environment

The **environment** refers to all the physical and social characteristics of a consumer's external world, including physical objects (products and stores), spatial relationships (locations of stores and products in stores), and the social behavior of other people (who is around and what they are doing). As part of the Wheel of Consumer Analysis (see Exhibit 2.3), the environment can influence consumers' affective and cognitive responses and their behavior. For instance, consumers respond to a new store by interpreting features of this environment and deciding what behaviors to perform to accomplish their shopping goals.

Marketers are especially interested in the interpreted environment, sometimes called the *functional* (or *perceived*) *environment,* because this is what influences consumers' actions.[1] Because each consumer has a unique set of knowledge, meanings, and beliefs, the perceived or functional environment that each consumer experiences will be somewhat different. Marketers, however, are seldom interested in the idiosyncratic perceptions of individual consumers; rather, they seek to understand the consensus interpretations of the environment shared by groups of consumers. Fortunately, marketers can usually identify target market segments of consumers who share common cultural backgrounds and have similar interpretations. For example, large groups of American consumers probably have similar perceptions of shopping malls, credit cards, or fast-food restaurants and therefore use them in similar ways.

The environment can be analyzed at two levels: macro and micro. Marketers need to determine which level of environmental analysis is relevant for a marketing problem and design their research and marketing strategies appropriately. The *macro environment* includes large-scale, broad environmental factors such as the climate, economic conditions, the political system, and the general landscape (seashore, mountains, prairie). These macro environmental factors have a general influence on behavior, such as when the state of the economy influences aggregate purchases of homes, automobiles, and stocks. Highlight 11.1 describes how a change in the macro environment can create and eliminate marketing opportunities.

The *micro environment* refers to the more tangible physical and social aspects of a person's immediate surroundings—the dirty floor in a store, a talkative salesperson, the hot weather today, or the people in one's family or household. Such small-scale factors can have a direct influence on consumers' specific behaviors, thoughts, and feelings. For instance, people tend not to linger in dirty, crowded stores; during a heat wave, consumers may wait until evening to go shopping; you get frustrated and angry in a slow-moving checkout line when you want to get home to prepare dinner.[2] Highlight 11.2 gives an example of how the micro environment can influence consumers' behavior.

Highlight 11.1

Dress (casually) for Success

The 1990s saw the advent of "casual Fridays" as companies large and small relaxed their dress codes to allow employees to leave their business suits at home and dress more comfortably. Today even "casual Friday" has become a thing of the past, replaced by the casual workweek in many companies.

The Society for Human Resource Management says 87 percent of employers allowed casual dress at least once a week in 2000—up from 24 percent in 1992. Forty-four percent of businesses had a full-time casual-dress policy. Even old-line Wall Street firms like J.P. Morgan and Goldman Sachs have gotten into the act. A tight job market has helped fuel these changes. In one study, 80 percent of employees said a casual-dress policy is their most valued perk, and companies have been forced to adjust their dress codes to help attract the best candidates. The Silicon Valley dot-com culture, in which suits and ties are virtually unheard of, helped popularize the corporate dressing-down trend.

Not even law firms are exempt. To keep pace with their more casually dressed clients, attorneys have adjusted their wardrobes accordingly. A partner in a San Francisco firm believes if he wore a suit on a visit to a client, "I'd look like I'm selling toner." At Yahoo! the only time the in-house attorneys are seen in suits and ties is on Halloween.

The casual-dress trend has had a major effect on clothing manufacturers. From 1998 to 1999, tie sales dropped more than 3 percent while suit sales were off 10 percent. In response, upscale designers like Giorgio Armani and Hugo Boss have created lines of golf apparel suitable for the office. Nordstrom offers cashmere jacket sweaters that can cost as much as a nice suit. Lands' End has created an entire business-casual catalog, with recommended attire for both men and women. However, not all clothing manufacturers have bought into the trend. A coalition of menswear manufacturers has attempted to convince companies to institute "dress-up Thursdays" to help spur sales of formal business attire.

The casual workplace is not without critics. One woman was harsh in her assessment of her co-workers' appearance. "They look like they're here to do the floors or move furniture," she says. "You wonder what the clients think." Indeed, evidence suggests dressing down may promote slacking off. In one study, nearly half of companies instituting a casual workweek saw an increase in absenteeism and tardiness, while 30 percent saw a rise in "flirtatious behavior." Furthermore, some women and minorities believe a casual-dress policy puts them at a disadvantage. They argue that formal business attire helps them to be taken seriously by their white male colleagues.

Sources: San Francisco Chronicle (1865–) [Staff produced copy only] "Dressing Down/Lawyers Shedding Suits and Ties to Match Casual Look of Their Dot-Com Clients," by Harriet Chang. *San Francisco Chronicle,* September 7, 2000, p. A15, Copyright 2000 by San Francisco Chronicle. Reproduced with permission of San Francisco Chronicle in the format Textbook via Copyright Clearance Center; "The New Dress for Success," Julia King, *Computerworld,* May 8, 2000. Copyright © 2000 by Computerworld, Inc. Framingham, MA 01701. All rights reserved. Reprinted with permission.

Aspects of the Environment

As noted in Chapter 2, the environment has two aspects or dimensions: the social and the physical. Through their marketing programs (building a new store, training sales people), managers have direct control over certain aspects of the social and physical environments. But marketers have little or no control over large parts of the social and physical environments. Both the controllable and uncontrollable aspects of the social and physical environments can influence consumers' overt behaviors as well as their affective and cognitive responses.

The Social Environment

Broadly defined, the *social environment* includes all social interactions between and among people. Consumers can interact with other people either directly (you discuss

Highlight 11.2

Weather Effects on Sales

How cold does it have to be for men in Chicago to start shopping for coats? Why, on a rainy day in Florida, do people in Miami hit the stores in droves while their neighbors across the state in St. Petersburg stay home? Retailers are paying increased attention to the weather and trying to learn more about its effect on sales.

Our calendar is divided neatly into four seasons, but consumers do not necessarily behave in accordance with what the calendar says. The first cool, fall-like days following a long summer will spark an increase in sales of antifreeze, wiper blades, and fire logs—and that is the case whether those first chilly days occur in early September or mid October. Similarly, a late spring delays the purchase of gardening supplies and suntan lotion. Consumers also adjust their shopping patterns during extended stretches of extreme weather. For example, during the nationwide heat wave in June 1999, factory shipments of central air conditioners and air-source heat pumps hit an all-time high. A key strategy for stores is to have the appropriate products available at the appropriate times.

It is very risky to make plans for this year based on last year's weather because weather repeats itself from year to year only about one-third of the time. So rather than relying solely on historical data, more firms are turning to professional forecasters for help. Strategic Weather Services is one company that tries to help businesses match availability to consumer demand. Strategic Weather's clients include Wal-Mart, Kmart, and Sears. Sears, for example, ordered a long-range forecast for some of its key cities almost a year in advance. The forecasts suggested cooler-than-normal weather on the West Coast and warmer temperatures in the Southeast. Sears responded by removing some coats from a distribution center in Georgia and sending them to Los Angeles. The result was increased coat sales out west and fewer markdowns in the Southeast.

In case you were wondering about the questions posed above, men in Chicago generally don't start buying coats until the thermometer drops below 41 degrees Fahrenheit. And when it rains in Florida, the large senior citizen population of St. Petersburg chooses to stay out of the weather, while in Miami younger people shop because they can't go to the beach or the pool. Such precise, geographically specific knowledge can help a retailer gain an important competitive advantage.

Sources: Teri Agins and Kathryn Kranhold, "Retailing: Coat Peddlers Are Using Forecasters to Beat the Heat," *The Wall Street Journal,* February 18, 1999, p. B1; Chris Cawthorn, "A Weather Eye on Nonfoods," *Supermarket Business,* May 1999, pp. 149–152; Robert Mader, "A/C Shipments on Record Pace," *Contractor,* September 1999, pp. 1, 20.

sports equipment or clothes with a friend, talk to a salesperson) or vicariously (you watch your father negotiate a car price, observe the clothing other people are wearing). People can learn from both direct and vicarious social interactions.

It is useful to distinguish between macro and micro levels of the social environment. The **macro social environment** refers to the indirect and vicarious social interactions among very large groups of people. Researchers have studied three macro social environments—culture, subculture, and social class—that have broad and powerful influences on the values, beliefs, attitudes, emotions, and behaviors of individual consumers in those groups. For instance, a marketer might find that consumers in different subcultures or social classes have quite different means–end chains concerning a product, which indicates they are likely to respond differently to marketing strategies. Such differences make macro social environments useful for market segmentation.

The **micro social environment** includes face-to-face social interactions among smaller groups of people such as families and reference groups. These direct social interactions can have strong influences on consumers' knowledge and feelings about

Face-to-face interaction with a salesclerk is a common example of a micro social environment *Jeff Greenberg/The Image Works.*

products, stores, or ads and on their consumption behavior. For instance, people learn acceptable and appropriate behaviors and acquire many of their values, beliefs, and attitudes through direct social interaction with their families and reference groups. The influence of families, moreover, can continue for years as some adult consumers purchase the same brands, patronize the same stores, and shop in the same way their parents once did.

Families and reference groups are influenced by the macro social environments of culture, subculture, and social class. Exhibit 11.1 illustrates the flow of social influence from the macro environments of culture, subculture, and social class to the micro environments of reference groups and family, and then on to the individual consumer. We discuss these social influences at length in Chapters 12, 13, and 14.

The hierarchical relationships portrayed in Exhibit 11.1 can help us understand how various levels of the social environment can influence consumers. For instance, consumers in different subcultures may have the same cultural values but reflect them in different ways. Likewise, consumers in different social classes may attempt to satisfy a subcultural value in different ways. Consider how people can satisfy the common American value of achievement. A person living in a rural subculture might fulfill this value by going to agriculture school, earning a degree, and becoming an excellent farmer. In an urban subculture, a person with the same achievement value might go to law school after college, earn a degree, and become a successful attorney. Similarly, the social class of an individual can influence the college decision (a local community college, a large state school, or an internationally famous university). In turn, these macro social influences are filtered by a person's family situation (parents' expectations and financial support) and reference groups (where one's friends are going to college). In sum, although many individuals may share the same cultural values, their methods of achieving these values may differ considerably, depending on their macro and micro social environments. This suggests that people in different social environments are likely to use different means to reach essentially the same ends.

Exhibit 11.1 also identifies other social entities involved in transferring meanings, values, and behavior norms from the macro social environment to individual

Exhibit 11.1

Flows of Influence in the Social Environment

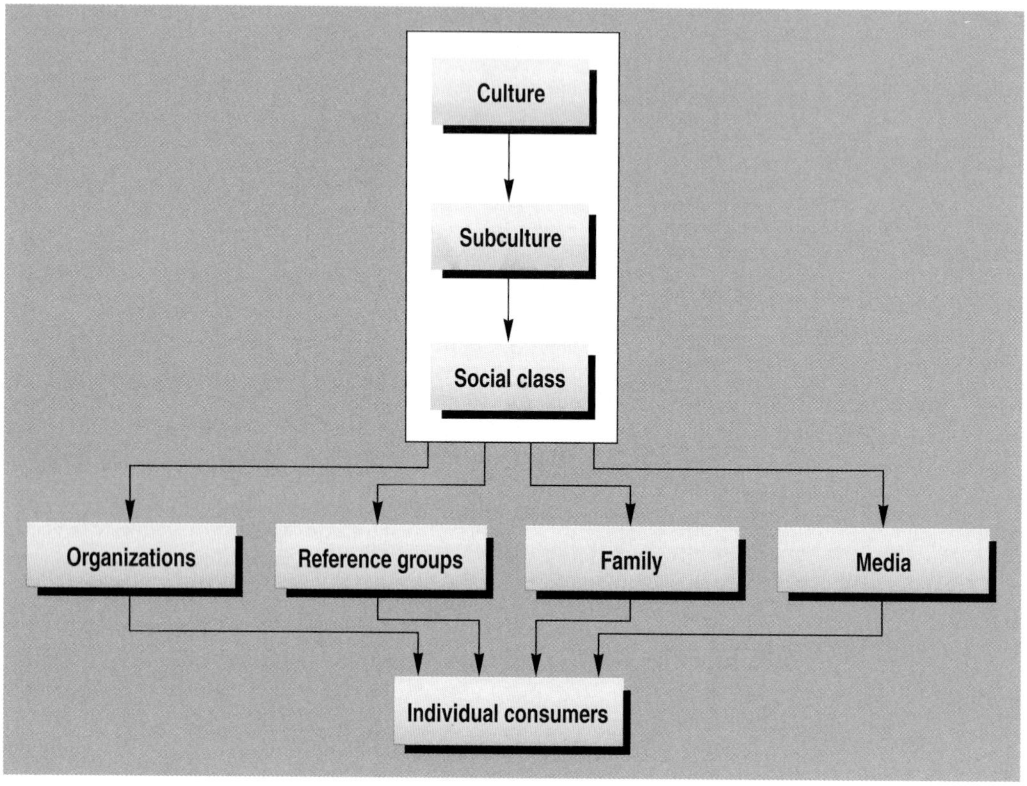

consumers. These include media such as TV programs, newspapers, magazines, movies, literature, and music, as well as other organizations such as religious and educational institutions, police and the courts, and government. Organizations also include business firms that develop marketing strategies to influence individual customers.

The Physical Environment

The **physical environment** includes all the nonhuman, physical aspects of the field in which consumer behavior occurs.[3] Virtually any aspect of the physical environment can affect consumer behavior. The physical environment can be divided into spatial and nonspatial elements. Spatial elements include physical objects of all types (including product and brands), as well as countries, cities, stores, and interior design. Nonspatial elements include intangible factors such as temperature, humidity, illumination, noise level, and time. Marketers need to understand how various aspects of the physical environment influence consumers' affect, cognitions, and behaviors. In this section we discuss three factors in the nonspatial environment: time, weather, and lighting.

Time   Time has a great effect on consumer behavior.[4] For instance, behaviors are influenced by the time of day (stores tend to be more crowded during the lunch hour), the day of the week (Mondays are often slow days for restaurants), the day of the month (sales may drop off just before the last of the month and pick up again

ON THE TWELFTH DAY OF CHRISTMAS
MY TRUE LOVE FINALLY GOT TO THE POINT.

Lavish the ones you love with some of our luscious indulgences and you'll definitely be
giving them something to sing about. For the Godiva boutique nearest you, call 1 800 9-GODIVA.
Or visit us on the Internet at www.godiva.com. On AOL (keyword: GODIVA)

New York   Paris   GODIVA   Tokyo   Brussels
Chocolatier

The time of year, such as the Christmas holiday season, can have a major influence on purchase behavior
Courtesy Godiva Chocolatier, Inc.; Illustrator Chelsey McLaren.

after the first, when paychecks arrive), and the season of the year (during the pre-Christmas holiday season, people's shopping behaviors are quite different from other times of the year).

As another example of the effects of time, consider that the Daylight Saving Time Coalition once petitioned Congress to increase daylight saving time by seven weeks per year. Advocates of this change included the management of 7-Eleven convenience stores, who believed more women would stop at its stores on the way home from work if it were still light outside. The company estimated this extra daylight would increase sales by $30 million. Another advocate of this change was the Barbeque Industry Association. Reasoning that people would cook out more if it were light during the dinner hour, this association predicted an increase in sales of charcoal briquettes of 15 percent ($56 million) and of 13 percent ($15 million) for starter fluid. Golfers were expected to play 4 million more rounds and buy an additional $7 million worth of clubs and balls, and tennis buffs could get in 9.8 million more hours of outdoor play and spend another $7 million on equipment. Thus, what might seem a minor change in time could well have considerable impact on consumer behavior.[5]

Weather   Many firms have recognized that weather influences consumer behavior (see Highlight 11.2). Obviously earmuffs, gloves, and heavy coats are winter products, and most suntan lotions, air conditioners, and bathing suits are sold during the summer. Some firms are paying even closer attention to the weather, not just for a season but on a daily basis. For example, Campbell Soup Company bases some of its spot radio advertising on weather reports. Whenever a storm is forecast, Campbell's ads urge listeners to stock up on soup before the weather worsens; after the storm hits, the ad copy changes to tell people to relax indoors and warm themselves with soup. Although research on the relationships between weather and consumer behavior is in its early stages, the weather has proven an important influence on affect (such as moods), as well as on cognitions and purchase behavior.[6]

Lighting   Considerable evidence reveals that lighting affects behavior. It has been found that people work better in brighter rooms, but workers find direct overhead lighting unpleasant. In business meetings, people who intend to make themselves heard sit under or near lights, whereas those who intend to be quiet often sit in darker areas. Intimate candlelight may draw people together; bright floodrights can cause people to hurry past a location. Overall, lighting may affect the way people work and interact with others, their overall comfort, and even their mental and physical health.[7]

Although it seems likely that lighting could affect consumers' moods, anxiety levels, willingness to shop, and purchase behavior, little research is available on this topic. However, one discussion of lighting in retail stores and malls suggested specialized lighting systems increased sales dramatically. Pillowtex Corporation used tiny spotlights attached to glass shelves, rather than overhead lighting, for illumination in its showroom at the Dallas World Trade Center. The corporation attributed one-third of its $3 million-plus annual sales to this lighting approach.[8]

Marketing Implications

Although marketing managers cannot control much of the environment, they can influence certain aspects of the environment. Actually, every marketing strategy created by a marketing manager involves changing some aspect of the social and physical environments. For example, aspects of the physical environment are changed by promotion strategies (a magazine ad, a billboard along the highway), product strategies (a new squeeze bottle for Crest toothpaste, a styling change in the Ford Taurus), distribution strategies (the location of a Burger King, a product display in a store), and even pricing strategies (a sale sign in a window, a price tag on a sweater).

Other marketing strategies modify aspects of the social environment. For instance, Lexus trains its salespeople to be less aggressive and less pushy with customers. A health club encourages members to invite a friend for a free workout. Wal-Mart stations an employee at the store entrance to smile and welcome customers to the store.

These environmental factors are created through marketing strategies and are designed to influence consumer affect, cognitions, and behaviors. In this sense, marketers can be seen as environmental managers.[9]

Situations

Because a huge number of elements make up the social and physical environment, marketers may find it difficult to identify the most important environmental influences on consumers' affect, cognitions, and behaviors. It can be easier to analyze the influences of the environment in the context of specific *situations*.[10] A situation is neither the tangible physical environment (a checkout counter, a storefront, your living room, the temperature today, a landscape) nor the objective features of the social environment (the number of people in a store, the time of day).[11] Rather, *a situation is defined by a person who is acting in an environment for some purpose.* A situation occurs over a period of time that can be very short (buying a soda in a vending machine), somewhat longer (eating lunch), or quite protracted (buying a house). The person's goals define a situation's beginning (goal activation or problem recognition), middle (working to achieve the goal), and end (achieving the goal). Thus, a **situation** involves *a sequence of goal-directed behaviors, along with affective and cognitive responses and the various environments in which they occur.* For instance, going to the mall to look for a CD is a shopping situation, whereas having lunch with your best friend is a consumption situation. This view of situations as a series of goal-directed interactions among the environment, affect and cognitions, and behavior is fully consistent with the Wheel of Consumer Analysis.

Situations vary in complexity. Some situations take place within a single physical and social environment, and involve simple goals, relatively few behaviors, and few affective and cognitive responses. Examples of relatively simple consumption-related situations include buying stamps at the post office, bargaining with a salesperson over the price of a stereo system, or discussing a spring break trip with friends over dinner. Other consumer situations are more complex. Complex situations may take place in multiple physical and social environments, involve several (perhaps conflicting) goals, and require many different behaviors and cognitive and affective responses. Shopping for a new winter coat at the mall is an example of a more complex situation.

Many consumer behavior situations are common and *recurring*. For instance, American consumers frequently buy gas for their cars, watch TV in the evening, shop for new clothes, rent videos, and go to grocery stores. As their experiences accumulate over time, consumers form clear goals, develop consistent problem representations for these recurring situations, and learn appropriate behaviors to solve the problem. Thereafter, when the problem situation occurs again, appropriate knowledge schemas and scripts may be activated from memory to influence consumers' behavioral, affective, and cognitive responses in that environment/situation. To the extent that people tend to form approximately the same interpretations for common consumer-related situations, their behaviors will also tend to be similar. When common reactions occur, marketers can develop marketing strategies that should affect consumers in a target segment in similar ways.

In contrast, consumers may not have clear goals or relevant knowledge when faced with new or unfamiliar situations. They may have to consciously interpret and integrate information to determine their goals, identify salient environmental factors, and choose appropriate behaviors. Marketers should develop strategies to help consumers cope with unfamiliar situations. For instance, life insurance salespeople are trained to help consumers recognize their situation by defining their goals (college education for children, retirement plans, pay off mortgage) and identifying key environmental considerations (children's ages, time to retirement, current savings). Then, in the context of that situation, the salesperson can demonstrate the self-relevance of life insurance.

Analyzing Situations

A powerful approach to understanding environmental influences is to analyze the situations in which the consumer experiences the environment. Marketers should understand the physical and social environments in terms of the perspectives of the consumers who experience them.[12] To analyze a situation, marketers should first determine the major goals that define the situation for their target customers.[13] Then they should identify the key aspects of the social and physical environments in the situation, including marketing strategies that might affect the consumer. Finally, marketers should attempt to understand consumers' affective, cognitive, and behavioral responses to these environmental characteristics.

Marketers can learn about personal consumption situations by asking consumers to describe the major occasions when they consume the product. A study conducted by one of the authors provides an example of such an analysis. We asked several candy users to describe the major situations when they ate candy. One young woman, a college freshman, identified three major consumption situations that she described in terms of her own goals, feelings, and behaviors:

Situation 1. Hungry—in a rush.

Environment: hectic; many other people around; between classes at the university.

Goal: satisfy hunger and get energy.

Affect/cognition: feeling hungry, stressed, and tense.

Behavior: snack on candy between and during classes.

Situation 2. Lazy—relaxed.

Environment: quiet, alone at home in evening.

Goal: relax so I can concentrate on work.

Affect/cognition: feeling relaxed and calm, but alert.

Behavior: snack on candy while reading or studying.

Situation 3. Calm—at lunch.

Environment: calm; alone in kitchen at lunchtime.

Goal: I need a reward.

Affect/cognition: happy to be home after hectic class schedule; starting to calm down.

Behavior: eat candy for dessert.

These three consumption situations occurred in three different environments, and each situation involved somewhat different goals, affective and cognitive states, and behaviors. Different products are likely to appeal to the consumer in these situations.

Marketing strategies are seldom based on an analysis of a single consumer. Marketers are interested in identifying situations that large numbers of consumers experience similarly. Then managers can develop marketing strategies (special products, prices, or advertising campaigns) for these consumption situations. For instance, a study of fast-food restaurants identified four consensual use situations: lunch on a weekday, a snack during a shopping trip, an evening meal when rushed for time, and an evening meal with family when not rushed for time.[14] The authors found that different choice criteria were used in these situations (speed of service was more important at lunch; menu variety was more important in the evening when not rushed). Moreover, certain restaurants (different environments) were considered more appropriate for certain situations. Finally, even if the same fast-food restaurant was patronized in these different situations, consumers' behaviors and affective and cognitive reactions in those situations could be quite different (rushed/not rushed, relaxed/not relaxed).

Generic Consumer Situations

In this section, we consider five generic consumer situations: information acquisition, shopping, purchase, consumption, and disposition (see Exhibit 11.2). These broadly defined situations are relevant for most products. Marketers can analyze these situations to identify consumers' behavioral goals, relevant affect and cognitions, and the key environmental factors, and can then develop marketing a strategies to change, facilitate, or maintain the key behaviors.

Information Acquisition Situations The **information acquisition situation** includes the environments where consumers acquire information relevant to a problem-solving goal such as a brand or store choice. An information acquisition situation may contain social factors (word-of-mouth communications from friends, persuasion attempts by a salesperson) and physical stimuli (prominent signs in a store, labels on a product package) that can influence consumers' affect, cognitions, and behaviors. As you learned in Chapter 5, such information may be acquired accidentally, as consumers randomly come across information in their environments, or intentionally, as they consciously seek information relevant to their current goals.

Marketers have considerable control over many aspects of consumers' information environments, especially the advertising, sales promotion, and personal selling elements of the promotion mix. Marketers can place signs in stores and on the front windows of shops, send direct-mail material about their products to consumers, and place ads on TV, in magazines, and on billboards.[15] They can add information to packages and labels or provide salespeople with special information to convey to customers.[16] Other

Exhibit 11.2

Five Generic Consumer Situations

Situations	Generic Behaviors	Specific Behaviors and Environments
Information acquisition	Information contact Communication	Reading a billboard while driving Discussing running shoes with a friend at a weekend race Watching a TV commercial at home
Shopping	Store contact Product contact	Window-shopping in a mall Browsing through an L. L. Bean catalog in a restaurant Comparing brands of shirts in a store
Purchase	Funds access Transaction	Obtaining a Visa card at a bank Paying at the counter at Starbucks Calling in an order to Lands' End from home
Consumption	Use	Eating a taco at Taco Bell Using a refrigerator for 15 years
Disposition	Disposal	Recycling aluminum cans Throwing away a hot dog wrapper at a hockey game

aspects of consumers' information environments are not under marketers' direct control. For example, marketers can try to generate publicity and new articles about their product or encourage consumers to tell other consumers about it. However, they may not be successful in creating this environmental information.

Two especially important generic behaviors in information acquisition situations are *information contact* and *communication*. Because approximately two-thirds of retail purchases are based on decisions made in the store, contact with marketing information in a store can have a significant influence on consumer behaviors. Various marketing actions are designed to facilitate information contact. For instance, A&P supermarkets (among others) allow ads on shopping carts.[17] Pepsi-Cola has experimented with putting multicolored ads on paper grocery bags.

Modern technology allows marketers to direct information at precisely defined target groups. Many grocery stores have electronic coupon dispensers connected to the checkout scanners that issue different coupons depending on what products a consumer buys. For instance, people buying peanut butter might receive a coupon for bread, or customers who buy Folgers coffee might receive a coupon for Maxwell House. Other marketing strategies are designed to facilitate information contact at the point of purchase. An example is the interactive computer display developed for Clarion Cosmetics. By answering a few simple questions, consumers can receive information about which Clarion products are best for their skin color and tone.[18]

Communicating with customers, usually via salespeople, is an important marketing strategy for many companies. For example, Toyota, manufacturer of the Lexus luxury car, intensively trains its salespeople about all aspects of the car.[19] Thus, Lexus salespeople spend an average of 90 minutes presenting a car to each potential customer, much more than the industry average. Service after the sale is extremely important for all auto manufacturers and dealers. Consumers' top complaint with auto service is having to bring the car back because the problem was not fixed properly the first time. Research showed that Lexus consumers believed this was largely because of poor communication in that their problems were not adequately explained to the mechanics doing the work. So, when Lexus buyers come to the dealers for service, they speak directly to the diagnostic experts who will examine their cars. Owners can even stay during the diagnosis to make sure the problems are clearly communicated to the mechanics.

Shopping Situations   The **shopping situation** includes the physical, spatial, and social characteristics of places where consumers shop for products and services. Shopping behavior can occur in a variety of environments, such as in boutiques, department and discount stores, malls, and pedestrian-only retail areas being developed in many cities, in the home (via catalogs, television home shopping programs, or the Internet), at flea markets and auctions, and so on. In retail environments alone, a huge number of physical factors—including store design and layout, lighting and display fixtures, colors, the overall size of the store, and miscellaneous other factors (such as temperature and noise level)—may affect consumers' behaviors (the length of time they stay in the store) and their cognitions and affective states (moods or feelings of involvement with shopping).

Shopping situations also include the merchandise (the particular products and brands) displayed in stores, catalogs, and on the Internet. One innovation in car selling is the auto center in which a dealer combines several franchises under one roof. Customers can examine dozens of makes and models in one shopping trip, much like shopping for a new dress or business suit at a large department store.

In addition, the shopping environment includes social factors such as how many salespeople and checkout personnel are in the store, how store personnel act toward customers, the presence of friends or relatives accompanying the consumer, the degree of crowding, and the types of other people found there. All these aspects of the shopping environment can influence consumers' behaviors, cognitions, and affective responses. For instance, many people dislike going to an auto showroom where they fear being "attacked" by hungry salespeople. At a Lexus dealership, no sales-people are in sight.[20] Instead, consumers are greeted by a receptionist behind a marble desk. Without interruption, they can learn more about Lexus offerings by studying the "media wall" consisting of videos and print materials. Only on request will the receptionist call a sales representative to talk to the consumer.

Of the many behaviors affected by the shopping environment, two are particularly important: store contact and product contact. *Store contact* is critical for retailing success, and many marketing strategies are intended to get consumers to come to the store. Giving away a free CD to the first 100 people to show up at an electronics store on a Saturday morning is an example of such a strategy.

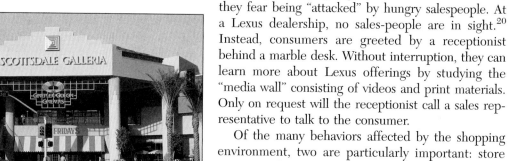

By locating at the entrance to a popular mall, TGI Friday's increases the probability of store contact
John Elk/Stock, Boston, LLC.

Location is another critical environmental influence on store contact for many types of stores; for example, fast-food restaurants and convenience food stores need to be located in high-traffic locations. (Highlight 11.3 describes an unusual strategy to increase store contact behavior over the Internet.) As another example, consider the location strategy of Sunglass Hut of America, which operates some 200 small

Highlight 11.3

Customer Service Online

Online shopping offers consumers a tremendous amount of freedom and independence. But how much independence is too much? The quality of customer service across the Web is quite uneven, and the

CORBIS Royalty Free

effects are tangible. A Jupiter Communications survey found that more than one-quarter of online shoppers were dissatisfied, while a Forrester Research Inc. study revealed that more than two-thirds of consumers who drop items into an online shopping cart don't complete their purchase.

Some websites have taken bold (and expensive) steps to give their sites a more human touch. The hardware retailer HomeTownStores.com added a new personal greeter service. Each one of the 14,000 daily visitors to the site was welcomed by a live chat operator. Customers with questions did not have to send an e-mail and wait for a response. They could ask their greeter and get a response almost immediately. Within a month, sales had risen 30 percent and the site's monthly e-mail volume had dropped from thousands to just a few dozen.

Cameraworld.com has also benefited from an investment in customer service. It added Internet voice capability to its site, allowing a customer to speak directly to a sales representative while viewing the site. The company claims 25 percent of its visitors who used the voice service bought something, compared to only 3 percent of its customers overall.

Customer service innovations like these are not cheap. The software alone can cost up to $500,000, not including maintenance and installation. Of course, that doesn't include the cost of hiring and training the employees required to make it all work. Another online hardware store, HomeWarehouse.com, was estimated to spend $2.5 million on customer service during the 1999 holiday season alone.

At many sites, however, customers are still largely on their own. In November 1999, a reporter from *Advertising Age* went undercover to learn about the quality of customer service at 21 of the largest online retail sites. The results were mixed. For example, the writer (posing as a fan of director Stanley Kubrick) sent an email to the movie and music retailer CDNow asking for movie recommendations. Within a few hours, a representative responded with a detailed list of films from Kubrick and other directors that the customer might enjoy. The Gap, in response to a request for a hypoallergenic holiday gift, took a few days but eventually responded with a comprehensive list of options. L. L. Bean and Lands' End requested more information, then came back within a day with some suggestions. Other retailers were less helpful. KBToys.com and JCPenney acknowledged the e-mails, but failed on their promises to provide an answer within 24 to 48 hours. Seven sites (a full one-third of the sample) didn't respond at all. That group included Internet pioneers Amazon.com and eToys (now defunct), along with department store giants Bloomingdale's, Macy's, and Nordstrom.

Clearly, online retailers are trying to figure out the appropriate level and form of customer service. As in a brick-and-mortar outlet, what some consumers find helpful, others might find annoying or distracting. However, it seems apparent that the online sites that thrive will be those that take the extra step to provide customers with the personalized help they need.

Sources: Thomas J. Mullaney, "Needed: The Human Touch," *Business Week e.biz,* December 13, 1999, pp. E53–54; Polina Shklyanoy, "E-tailers Lack Customer Care," *Advertising Age,* November 29, 1999, p. 65.

kiosks selling high-quality sunglasses for \$35 to \$200.[21] Their locations in the well-traveled aisles of shopping centers, malls, and airports facilitate store contact. Their marketing strategy also addresses information acquisition by facilitating communication with the customer. Each Hut is staffed with well-trained, knowledgeable salespeople who are able to tell customers why they should pay \$80 or more for a pair of sunglasses.

The location of smaller boutique-type stores (candy, natural foods, gifts) in shopping malls can have a critical effect on store contact behaviors. A desirable location is close to the entrance of one of the large, popular anchor stores, usually department stores, found at the ends or middle of the mall. These anchor stores draw many consumers, and the smaller stores benefit from the traffic flowing past their doors. The importance of location within the mall was clearly shown during the recession of the early 1990s.[22] When some retailers, such as Bonwit Teller and B. Altman, filed for bankruptcy, The Mall at Short Hills, an upscale mall in New Jersey, lost two of its four anchor stores. Immediately the surrounding smaller stores at the mall also began having difficulties. Such changes in mall shopping environments can initiate a cycle of reciprocal effects on behaviors, affect and cognitions, and the environment. As more stores fail, a mall accumulates more empty, boarded-up stores, the shopping environment further deteriorates, and consumers become concerned and begin staying away.

Product contact is another important behavior affected by environmental characteristics of the shopping situation. Consider how the probability of product contact is reduced in very large stores (too many competing products), or if shoppers are discouraged from lingering in a store by overcrowding (too many other shoppers), or if sales personnel are overly aggressive (driving off some customers). Some stores use restful music, warm color schemes, and low-key salespeople to encourage shoppers to linger, thus enhancing the probability of product contact. In large self-service stores, signs are hung from the ceilings to identify product locations. To facilitate product contact, Hallmark redesigned its product displays using colored strips to identify different types of greeting cards and help customers find the right cards quickly.[23] In sum, retailers try to make the shopping environment attractive, informative, and easy to use.[24]

Another goal of store design is to make the shopping environment more fun and exciting so that consumers will spend more time in the store and be more likely to make contact with the merchandise. Highlight 11.4 describes an example of modifying the in-store environment to make shopping less stressful.

Although the retail store environment is important, other types of shopping environments are becoming significant. These include shopping at home by telephone, by mail, or via the Internet (see Highlight 11.5). Obviously, the environment at home is dramatically different from the in-store shopping environment. Other shopping environments are relevant for some products, including garage sales, flea markets and swap meets, auctions, sidewalk sales, and private sales of merchandise by individuals and street vendors. In some cities, you can avoid shopping situations entirely by hiring someone else to shop for you.[25]

Purchasing Situations   The **purchasing situation** includes the social and physical stimuli present in the environment where the consumer makes the purchase. Consider the differences in the purchasing environment for buying fresh vegetables

High light 11.4

The Checkout Line of the Future

In 2000, an IBM television commercial showed a young man strolling through a store, furtively stuffing items in his pockets. On his way out the door, he is confronted by a security guard who, instead of nailing the guy for shoplifting, proceeds to hand him a receipt and send him happily on his way. Is automatic checkout just a fantasy? Perhaps for now. But developments in technology seem to indicate that the days of the traditional checkout line may be numbered. People are looking for faster ways to accomplish the purchase transaction.

The relative speed of Internet shopping has helped to lower customers' tolerance for long waits in stores. Just 57 percent of shoppers say they are satisfied with the speed of their shopping experience. Furthermore, 83 percent of women and 91 percent of men say they have stopped shopping at a given store because of long lines. Retailers are aware of this trend and are looking for ways to speed up the checkout process.

So-called smart packaging may be the way of the future. Massachusetts Institute of Technology's AutoID Center has joined forces with Procter & Gamble and other consumer products companies in an effort to perfect a universal standard for a smart-packaging technology. In a smart-packaging system, products are marked with what amounts to a high-tech bar code that emits a signal. A computer at the store's exit picks up the signal and automatically rings up the purchase. Smart packaging not only would eliminate long cash register lines but would also serve as a deterrent to shoplifting and counterfeiting. Similar smart shelving would allow stores to better control their inventory. Inventory data would be sent via the Internet to store managers, manufacturers, and distributors so they would know automatically when a new shipment is needed.

Some major retailers are already moving forward with their own innovations. Kmart has spent $100 million on checkout line improvements, including cash registers that can be moved around the store. Wal-Mart employs a corporate checkout team that spends hours poring over videotapes of checkout lines and coming up with ways to make things move along more quickly. Wal-Mart's "line buster" service is designed to eliminate long lines. If employees see checkout lines beginning to stack up, they will break out hand-held computers, scan the items in your cart, and give you a card that contains the total amount of the purchase. To check out, all you have to do is give the card to the cashier, who will simply swipe it through a reader to officially ring up the sale. Some Wal-Mart locations even feature self-checkout stations where you can scan and bag your purchases yourself. The system will automatically charge your credit card and provide you with a receipt.

Sources: Wall Street Journal. Central Edition [Staff Produced Copy Only] by Emily Nelson, "Big Retailers try to Speed Up Checkout Lines," *Wall Street Journal,* March 13, 2000, pp. B1, B6. Copyright 2000 by Dow Jones & Co. Inc. Reproduced with permission of Dow Jones & Co. Inc. in the format Textbook via Copyright Clearance Center; Joshua Macht, "Mortar Combat," *Inc.,* September 14, 2000, pp. 102–110.

at a supermarket versus at an outdoor farmers' market. In some cases the purchasing environment is similar to the shopping environment, but they are seldom identical. In most self-service stores, for instance, consumers pay for the products they have selected at a checkout counter at the front of the store or at one of several cash register locations around the store.

In some stores, the purchasing environment is designed to be quite distinct from the shopping environment. For instance, the central checkout counter at one trendy music store was designed to look like a giant piano keyboard with black and white keys. In other retail environments, such as an automobile dealership, the purchasing environment may be a separate room used exclusively for the purchase transaction. This is where the salesperson and customer(s) retire to negotiate the final details of the purchase and write the check.

Highlight 11.5

The Shopping Environment on the Web versus in the Store

Many Americans love to shop, but where? E-commerce is definitely growing, but Internet purchases remain a very small segment of the total retail market. Internet sales approached $30 billion in 2000, a 75 percent jump from 1999. But they still accounted for only 4 percent of the $750 billion in overall retail sales. In theory, it is possible to sit at your computer and purchase everything you could ever possibly need. So why do consumers still make an average of three shopping trips per week, a number that has remained steady for several years?

Many Internet shoppers struggle with the technology. Imagine visiting a retail store at the mall, spending time flipping through CDs, browsing through books, and perusing the clothing racks. You load yourself down with merchandise and trudge up to the cash register, only to find that it is broken. Furthermore, it is the only register in the store, so after all that time you can't complete the purchase. There is nothing you can do but put down your merchandise and walk out. Would you ever come back to that store? Probably not. Incidents like this are almost unheard of in the brick-and-mortar world, but they are still all too common in the virtual world. In 2000, as many as 44 percent of online shoppers experienced technical failures at checkout. Of those, 28 percent said they would never buy from that site again, while 10 percent claimed they would cease shopping online altogether.

Many consumers also seem willing to trade the perceived convenience of online shopping for the experience of shopping in a store. Consider Christmas shopping. Malls are crowded, parking is a pain, and tempers can be short. But people go to the stores anyway, in part to experience the sights and sounds of the holiday—the lights, the music, seeing the children on Santa's lap, etc. Similarly, when buying a designer suit or dress, part of the allure for some is strolling through an elegant, well-decorated store, receiving personalized attention from a sales associate, and feeling somewhat "above" the less wealthy consumers who cannot afford such an experience. Do you get these same deep feelings and cognitions from Internet shopping? Probably not.

Internet sites are trying their best to make the e-commerce experience more enjoyable. Companies like Amazon.com have revamped and simplified their sites, replacing the tabs that used to clutter the top of the welcome page and deleting a lot of the clutter (graphics, links, and promotional text). Newer Net shoppers are less willing to tolerate confusion and technical glitches. No longer is the Internet a male-dominated domain, populated mainly by well-educated techies who want to buy stuff on the Web just because it seems cool. Half of new users in 2000 had incomes below $50,000, while 35 percent had high school degrees or less. As e-commerce reaches the mainstream, customer service, reliable checkouts, and no-hassle returns (many of the same factors that drive success for traditional brick-and-mortar stores) will become increasingly important.

Sources: Wendy Zellner, "Wooing the Newbies," *Business Week,* May 15, 2000, pp. EB116–EB120; Alison Stein Wellner, "A New Cure for Shoppus Interruptus," *American Demographics,* August 2000, pp. 44–47; Lester C. Thurow, "Internet's Altering Retail, But We Still Crave Human Contact. 5,000 More Years of Shopping," *Boston Globe,* February 22, 2000, p. D4.

Sometimes the shopping environment intrudes into the purchasing environment. For instance, checkout lines at grocery stores usually include displays of products such as magazines, gum and candy items, film, and cigarettes to stimulate impulse purchases. The information acquisition and purchase environments also may overlap. For instance, A&P, a chain of some 1,200 grocery stores, once experimented with showing ads on TV monitors placed at the checkout aisle, but many consumers complained that this type of information contact was too intrusive. Besides, few customers left the line to get a product that was advertised.

Marketers are particularly interested in influencing two behaviors in purchasing situations: *funds access* and the *final transaction*. For instance, most grocery stores and other retail stores have streamlined the transaction procedures in the purchasing situation by installing scanner equipment to speed up the checkout process. Sotheby's, the world-famous auction house for fine art, found that the extreme escalation of art prices in the late 1980s had created a funds access problem for customers. Buyers did not have the large sums of cash (millions, in some cases) necessary to buy fine works of art, so Sotheby's instituted a credit policy by which it would lend up to one-half the cost of artwork, using the other works of art owned by the borrower as collateral.

Consumption Situations   The **consumption situation** includes the social and physical factors present in the environments where consumers actually use or consume the products and services they have bought. Obviously consumption behaviors (and related cognitive and affective processes such as enjoyment, satisfaction, or frustration) are most relevant in such situations.[26] Consider how clean, tidy, well-lighted, and attractively decorated consumption environments in full-service and fast-food restaurants, pubs and bars, nightclubs and discos, and ice cream parlors can enhance consumers' enjoyment of the purchased products. For such businesses, the design of the consumption environment may be critical to consumers' satisfaction with their purchases.

Consider the consumption environment in two bars at the Minneapolis and Detroit airports.[27] Host International, a division of Marriott Corporation, recreated the Cheers bar from the famous TV show of the same name, including Sam's Red Sox jersey framed on the wall, the wooden Indian statue inside the door, and the Wurlitzer jukebox. In addition, two familiar patrons are perched at the bar: replicas of Norm and Cliff. Now many of these Cheers bars are found in other U.S. airports.

For products such as appliances, clothing, cars, and furniture, marketers have almost no direct control over the consumption environment. These products are taken from the retail environment and consumed elsewhere (usually in consumers' homes). Moreover, for many of these products, the consumption situation involves multiple consumption behaviors over long periods (most people own and use a car or a microwave oven for several years). In some cases, the consumption environment changes during the useful life of the product, and this can affect consumption-related cognitive and affective responses (satisfaction) and behaviors (repairs and services). Perhaps the best marketers can do in these consumption situations is to monitor consumers' satisfaction levels and behaviors over the lifetime of the product.

In other cases, however, marketers have much control over the consumption environment. For instance, many service businesses, such as hairstylists, dentists and doctors, and hotels and motels, have total control over the consumption environment because consumption of these products and services occurs on the seller's premises. Obvious examples are golf courses, ski resorts, and theme parks such as Euro Disneyland outside Paris and Disney World in Florida, where the consumption environment is a major part of the product/service consumers buy. Disney Enterprises goes to great lengths to ensure that the consumption environment is perfect. The opening example of megaresorts in Las Vegas concerns the consumption environment as a major attraction.

Disney World very carefully controls the consumption environment because it is largely what consumers are buying   *AP/Wide World Photos.*

Design of the consumption environment can also be critical in the restaurant industry.[28] The Rainbow Room in New York serves halibut in gold-colored foil to enhance the theatricality of the dining experience. Highly decorated theme restaurants are popular in many U.S. cities. A restaurant in Salt Lake City replicates an 18th-century French farmhouse, down to ponds with geese and swans, peacocks roaming the grounds, servers in period costumes, and dried herbs and flowers hanging from the beamed ceilings. An entrepreneur in Chicago created a series of offbeat restaurants where the consumption environment was as important as the food. One spot, R. J. Grunts, offered a burger and health food menu served by blue jean–clad waitpersons, with mystical, New Age music playing in the background.

Not all consumption environments are successful. A singles-type restaurant called Not So Great Gritzbe's had a sign reading "Eat and Get Out." The walls were decorated with Tums and Alka-Seltzer ads, and the food critic awards were crossed out. Although the media were intrigued, consumers became worried and the restaurant closed.

Disposition Situations   For certain products, marketers may need to consider other types of environmental situations. For instance, the **disposition situation** is highly relevant for some businesses; used-car lots and used-clothing stores are obvious examples. Here the key behavior of interest is *disposal* of products. Many people simply throw away unwanted products or give them to charity. Others sell their unwanted products at flea markets, garage sales, and swap meets. These situations offer interesting environments for study.[29] Disposition situations are relevant for public policy issues, too.

In many countries, including the United States, consumers are developing stronger values of quality, cost consciousness, and concern for the natural environment that in turn are fueling interest in used products and recycling of waste. Thus, the markets for recycled goods and used products (furniture, appliances, clothing, housewares) are likely to increase, and we can expect entrepreneurs to develop strategies to serve these markets.

Marketing Implications

Marketers need to identify the key social and physical environmental features of the information acquisition, shopping, purchasing, consumption, and disposition situations for their products. They also need to understand consumers' affective, cognitive, and behavioral responses to these environmental factors. For example, some aspects of these environments may block behaviors crucial for the marketing success of the firm's product. Marketing strategies can be developed that modify the environment to stimulate, facilitate, and reinforce the desired behaviors. If funds access is a problem for consumers, the company might introduce debit cards, accept regular credit cards, or offer charge accounts. If consumers are becoming increasingly discouraged with the shopping environment in many cities (noisy streets, difficult parking, crowded stores, fear of crime), clever marketers are likely to introduce alternative shopping environments, such as home shopping opportunities through the mail or by telephone. For instance, a home delivery service for groceries is available in San Francisco and other cities. Strong growth for such businesses is forecast into the 2000s.

Back To...

Megaresorts in Las Vegas

The megaresorts in Las Vegas are extraordinary physical and social environments designed to appeal to many types of consumers besides gamblers. Families and conventioneers are two primary target markets. Vegas has long offered sporting events and lavish entertainment to draw adults and conventioneers to the gambling tables. The megaresorts hope to attract families with theme parks for the kids, evening entertainment for the parents, and a fantasy environment for everyone. Each property offers many entertainment situations such as luxurious rooms, elaborate pools, exciting celebrity entertainers, laser light shows, theme parks and amusement rides, excellent restaurants, and various gambling activities (slot machines, card games, roulette).

In 1999, 34 million visitors came to Las Vegas (up from 18 million 10 years earlier and just slightly less than the number who visited Orlando, Florida, home of Disney World). The crowds created a unique social environment and opportunities for many other businesses. For example, Belz Corporation opened a sprawling shopping complex consisting of 150 factory outlet stores. Even the famous Guggenheim Museum in New York explored the possibility of opening a branch museum on the Vegas strip next to The Venetian megaresort.

The megaresorts in Las Vegas need to understand various situations in developing their marketing strategies. The consumption situation is most obvious. In addition to traditional gambling activities, these megaresorts offer customers an elaborate, fantastic physical environment, plus a wide range of entertainment. These properties of the consumption environment help keep customers at the property and close to the gambling tables.

The information contact situation is relevant for making consumers aware of the resorts and their attributes. In the 1990s, many Las Vegas resorts aired TV ads in California (where 25 percent of Las Vegas' visitors are from) that portrayed families enjoying the theme parks and eating delicious dinners. More recently, the focus of Las Vegas advertising shifted to adults who come to Vegas to party. ❖

Summary   This chapter presented an overview of environmental influences on consumer behavior. We identified three basic types of environments: social, physical, and marketing. The social environment includes the effects on consumer behavior of culture, subculture, social class, reference group, and family. The physical environment includes the effects of both spatial and nonspatial factors. The marketing environment includes all stimuli associated with marketing strategies that influence consumers' affect, cognitions, and behaviors either directly or indirectly.

Next, we discussed the important concept of situations, which involves the continuous interaction over time of consumers' affective and cognitive responses and behaviors with one or more environmental settings. We identified five generic situations most relevant for consumer research: information acquisition, shopping, purchasing, consumption, and disposition. We discussed the important social and physical aspects of the environments in those situations, as well as the key behaviors of interest. A basic premise of the chapter was that marketing strategies must not only be adapted to changing environmental conditions but also play an important role in creating the environment.

Key Terms and Concepts

consumption situation **279**	micro social environment **266**
disposition situation **280**	physical environment **268**
environment **264**	purchasing situation **276**
information acquisition situation **272**	shopping situation **274**
macro social environment **266**	situation **270**

Review and Discussion Questions

1. Go to the Mirage home page at **http://themirage.com/** and explore the various environments at this hotel, including a volcano that erupts every few minutes, a tropical rain forest, a giant aquarium with live sharks, gourmet restaurants, waterfalls and connected lagoons, a spa, a European-style shopping boulevard, Siegfried & Roy's jungle habitat for white tigers, a pool for Atlantic bottlenose dolphins, and more than 3,000 deluxe rooms and suites. Describe how these environments might appeal to consumers in different market segments. How might these environments influence consumers' behaviors (stay at the Mirage and gamble there)?

2. Consider the distinction between macro and micro environments for grocery shopping. Which of these is more important for marketing strategy?

3. Contrast the two approaches marketers can take to analyze environmental effects: considering the direct effects of specific environmental factors versus considering environmental factors in the context of situations. Under what circumstances might each of these two approaches be more appropriate?

4. Use the situation of shopping for a personal CD player to describe the relationships between the physical and social environments. Point out those aspects that marketers could control.

5. What is a situation? Use examples from your own recent purchases to show how situations differ from environments.

6. Are environmental factors more important as influences for new or recurring situations? Why?

7. Use the Wheel of Consumer Analysis to describe how affect, cognitions, and behaviors interact with environmental factors in a textbook purchase situation.

8. How can marketers use situational analysis to segment markets? Identify some product categories in which the approach has been used to the advantage of the marketing organization.

9. For each of the five generic marketing situations, identify uncontrollable and controllable factors that should be considered in the development of marketing strategies.

Marketing Strategy in Action

America's Movie Theaters

The price of admission to many of America's movie theaters sometimes buys an experience sensible people would pay to avoid. The blackened and musty carpet in the lobby could be a relic from the silent-screen era. The $1.50 bucket of popcorn—that's the small size—holds 10 cents' worth of corn covered with a strange liquid, perhaps derived from petroleum. Beneath the broken seats, sticky coats of spilled soda varnish the floor. The screen is tiny, the sound is tinny, and the audience is rude. Oh, and one more thing: The picture stinks.

Many theater owners bought into the business at low prices after antitrust rulings forced the major Hollywood studios, which had previously owned the leading theater chains, to give up their movie houses. The new owners got a great deal. They owned the only show in town (sometimes literally), and the studios promoted the movies. As the easy profits rolled in, many exhibitors lost contact with their customers. They milked the business and let their theaters deteriorate.

But the success of videocassette rentals and cable TV during the early 1980s converted many moviegoers to stay-at-homers. These changes forced exhibitors to recognize their folly. By 1985, theaters were no longer the only show in town. Attendance dropped 12 percent over 1984 figures. The $5 billion-a-year American movie theater industry was fighting for survival.

This put the theater owners in a bind. To regain the loyalty of their customers, they needed to pour money into refurbishing, rebuilding, and restoring the glamor of moviegoing. But at the same time, they were being hurt by the new competing technologies.

To survive during these changes, exhibitors developed a couple of temporarily successful strategies. One was to develop their lobby concession stands as a source of revenues. To keep some of their customers, many theaters kept ticket prices fairly low—the average price in 2002 was about $6.00—a price that lagged behind inflation. Once inside, though, moviegoers were a captive market for the popcorn, soda, and candy sold at markups of 500 percent or more. A well-run concession stand generated at least $1 of sales and as much as 75 cents of profit per ticket buyer. Exhibitors found they could survive by charging ever more outrageous prices for popcorn.

What brands of candy were in the typical concession stand? Usually it was a strange mix of oversized boxes that included very few of the best-selling brands in the United States. Theaters tended to stock candy brands like Milk Duds, Sno Caps, and Jujyfruits, hardly big sellers on the outside. The exception was Snickers, the number one brand in the United States, which was present in most concession stands. Do moviegoers have different tastes than the rest of the population? No, of course not. The movie house operators preferred these brands because they were more profitable. With limited space available, the operators stocked the brands with the highest profit margins.

The profits from concession sales can be considerable. For instance, in 1985 a tub of popcorn that cost 30 cents was sold for about $2—a markup of 567 percent. A soft drink (often a Coke) that cost the theater 10 cents might have sold for 75 cents—a 650 percent markup. Candy produced a much smaller profit, with markups of about 180 percent. On average, about 40 percent of the $850 million in annual concession sales came from popcorn, another 40 percent from soft drinks, and only about 20 percent from everything else. Critics claim that by sticking to the most profitable brands, theater owners are missing an opportunity to increase overall candy sales by stocking more popular brands. As it stands now, only about one-third of moviegoers buy anything from the concession stand.

The other strategy was the multiscreen theater. During the 1980s, exhibitors began chopping up their grand old theaters into smaller ones that many moviegoers have come to hate. Individual exhibitors did great, though (as long as they were the only theaters in town). A theater with four screens, about the national average, is four times as likely to book a hit picture; the exhibitor then shows the hit in the largest room and less popular movies in smaller theaters. In the 1990s, the trend to multiscreen theaters gave way to the construction of multiplexes—theaters with 20+ screens (often with stadium seating) around a central core with restaurants, game rooms, and elaborate concession stands.

But at a macro level, huge multiplexes may not be what the industry needs. There simply aren't enough movies doing business at any one time to fill 20 screens. By the end of the 1990s, all four publicly traded theater chains in the United States were losing money and watching their stock prices plummet. Ticket sales were slowly edging upward, from about 900 million in 1970 to just under 1.5 billion in 1999. However, when you factor in the growing population, that translates into a 15 percent per capita decline in moviegoing (and a per capita decline of 73 percent from 1950). As a writer for *Variety* said, "Filmgoing used to be a part of the social fabric. Now it is an impulse purchase."

Marketers that understand their customers can gain an advantage. Many people believe that movie theaters are competing with the DVD player and VCR. But Madelyn Fenton, director of marketing for American Multi-Cinema in Los Angeles, says that DVDs and VCRs have actually helped movie theaters by addicting some people to certain actors, directors, or movie genres. Fenton claims that the real consumer decision is whether to stay home or go out. Most people have limited free time and many ways to spend it. Movie theaters need to make the "going out to a movie experience" more positive than the "stay-at-home experience." One way to do that is to offer a better experience when going to a movie.

Howard Lichtman of Cineplex Odeon Corporation, operator of 3,000 screens in North America, emphasizes the movie experience: "People at home can pop popcorn and dim the light. They can even line up the chairs in their living rooms in a row. But watching a movie at home is not the same as going to a movie theater." Lichtman considers the real threat to moviegoing to be other forms of entertainment outside the home, such as going out to dinner or going to the ballet. The look of Odeon theaters around the country shares a certain art deco glamor, but an Odeon theater in Des Moines and one in Los Angeles may have different features to appeal to local interests. For instance, the Cineplex Odeon Carnegie Hall theater shows a lot of "art movies:" That theater also contains a stylish café serving coffees, bottled waters, and a wide assortment of fancy pastries. The café and foods appeal to people who attend "art movies" because they like to discuss the movie before and after they see it.

Another exhibitor says, "We have to upgrade the quality of the moviegoing experience." His newest theaters have granite-floored lobbies with painted murals, spacious auditoriums, and first-rate sound and projection. The higher construction costs paid off in more customers at higher-than-average ticket prices and a splendid $1.35-per-ticket take at the concession stand.

In areas with lots of competition, theater chains are increasingly attempting to differentiate themselves by modifying the moviegoing environment. For instance, AMC in Los Angeles has tried to develop an advantage over its competition by offering patrons something more than popcorn and Goobers at a concession stand. Many of their theaters contain a café offering premovie and postmovie taste treats such as crab cakes, salads, gourmet pizza, croissant sandwiches, and egg rolls. So, instead of going to dinner and a movie, consumers can go to dinner in a movie theater.

To make the movie experience more convenient (by cutting down on standing-in-line time), AMC allows customers to purchase tickets online or phone- ahead and buy with their credit cards. In some theaters, AMC has installed self-serve dispensers of tickets and vouchers for the concession stand. AMC has tried some other marketing ideas to encourage moviegoing. It has a MovieWatcher program targeted at the frequent moviegoer. Members get points for every movie they attend that qualify them for prizes, including posters and special movie screenings. "We are trying to develop a loyal customer base," says AMC's Fenton. Check out its website (**www.amctheatres.com**) to learn more about the AMC theater experience.

Of course, despite the recent trends and experiments with modifying the movie environment, there are still plenty of grungy movie theaters with the same old concession stands. Perhaps the bottom line is that the concession stand is very important to theater profits whether it sells Milk Duds and popcorn or cappuccino and cheesecake.

Discussion Questions

1. The VCR is a physical aspect of the marketing environment that has affected moviegoing behavior in the United States. Compare and contrast the consumption situations of watching a movie in a theater versus seeing the same movie at home on your DVD player or VCR. Discuss the reciprocal interactions among environment, behavior, and cognitive and affective responses. What long-term effects do you think the in-home VCR environments will have on moviegoing? What can movie theaters do to improve the situation?

2. What macroenvironmental factors might affect moviegoing behavior (both decrease and increase)? Consider their impacts on different market segments. What marketing implications does your analysis have for theater owners or movie companies?

3. Analyze the information acquisition, purchasing, and consumption environments of different movie theaters in your local area. What recommendations do you have for changing these environments to increase sales and profits?

4. Analyze the effects of the consumption situation at movie theaters on consumers' purchase of snacks at the concession stand. What could theater owners do to change the purchasing and consumption environments in their theaters to encourage higher levels of snack consumption and greater sales at concession stands?

Sources: Motion Picture Association of America website (**www.mpaa.org**); anonymous, "Business: Apocalypse Now," *The Economist,* January 15, 2000, p. 70; Cyndee Miller, "Theaters Give 'Em More Than Goobers to Win Back Viewers," *Marketing News,* October 1, 1990, pp. 1, 6; March Magiera, "Theater Chains Applaud Fall Promotions," *Advertising Age,* September 16, 1991, p. 27; Alex Ben Block, "Those Peculiar Candies That Star at the Movies," *Forbes,* May 19, 1986, pp. 174–176; Stratford P. Sherman, "Back to the Future," *Fortune,* January 20, 1986, pp. 909–914.

12

Cultural and Cross-Cultural Influences

McDonald's . . . All Around the World

Practically anywhere you go in the United States you will find a McDonald's, whether you are in a big city, a college town, or some backwater burg in the middle of nowhere. By 1994, there was one McDonald's for every 25,000 people in the United States, and the company was finding it very difficult to open new restaurants without cannibalizing sales from an existing restaurant. So instead, McDonald's has turned increasingly to overseas markets.

Today McDonald's derives slightly more than 50 percent of its operating income and an estimated 90 percent of its growth from its foreign operations.

Managers must decide where to build new restaurants and how many to build. James Cantalupo, president of McDonald's international division, uses a simple formula based on a country's population and per capita income to roughly estimate the number of stores that can be profitable in a country:

$$\frac{\text{Population of country X}}{\text{\# of people per U.S. McDonald's}}$$

$$\times \frac{\text{Country X per capita income}}{\text{U.S. per capita income}}$$

$$= \text{Potential penetration of McDonald's in country X}$$

This formula suggests the world could handle at least another 48,000 McDonald's restaurants. Another perspective in this issue is gained by realizing that each day, 46 million customers walk through the doors of 30,000 McDonald's restaurants around the globe. Despite this volume, McDonald's serves less than 1 percent of the world's population on any given day. Thus, even though McDonald's is the largest and best-known global food service retailer, it still has enormous potential for growth in the global market.

It may be difficult for the average American (who may take McDonald's for granted) to appreciate what a McDonald's restaurant means to consumers in foreign countries. According to Tim Fenton, former head of

McDonald's in Poland, "It's hard for Americans to understand, but McDonald's is almost heaven-sent to these people. It's some of the best food around. The service is quick and people smile. You don't have to pay to use the bathroom. There's air conditioning. The place isn't filled with smoke. We tell you what's in the food. And we want you to bring the kids."

In addition, McDonald's carries considerable cultural meaning that many consumers value. Many people around the world see McDonald's as a quintessential American product, along with Levi's, Coke, and Marlboro. These important cultural meanings influence consumers' behavior toward McDonald's in the international marketplace.

McDonald's walks a fine line between a global and a local strategy. In many ways, McDonald's seems "global." It sells its major food products (the Quarter Pounder and Big Mac burgers, fries, Coke, and milk shakes) nearly everywhere in a standard form. It also goes to great lengths to maintain the quality and consistency of its key products (beef patties, fries, and buns are uniform worldwide). Also, McDonald's works hard to create its global vision of high quality and consistency around the world by training its personnel. Many McDonald's employees have received degrees in "Hamburgerology" at McDonald's Hamburger University in Oak Brook Illinois. HU provides instruction to restaurant personnel in 23 languages and awarded its 50,000th degree in 1995.

Despite its global approach, McDonald's also makes many adaptations to local customs, tastes, and norms. Details of the store decor often reflect local sensitivities and culture. Sometimes McDonald's must adapt to legal and regulatory constraints on certain marketing strategies and actions. For instance, Germany does not allow special promotions like "buy one, get one free." McDonald's sometimes makes even more significant adaptations to local tastes. For example, menu items vary somewhat from one country to another. Favorite foods may be featured along with the standard McDonald's fare: salads with shrimp in Germany, veggie burgers in Holland, black-currant shakes in Poland. Beer is available in some European countries. Occasionally even the names of standard McDonald's products are different. "Quarter Pounder" is an English measurement term that means little in countries using the metric system. In many European and Asian McDonald's, this worldwide favorite is known as McRoyal or Hamburger Royal.

How can McDonald's be sensitive to local customs while maintaining its core service and product quality? The company learns and reflects the local culture by hiring as many locals as possible. McDonald's employees often fly in from headquarters to help develop new markets. But nearly all of them go back after a period and turn the operation over to locals with more intimate knowledge of the local culture and customs. For example, Tim Fenton went to Poland in 1992 with a team of 50 experts from the United States, Russia, Great Britain, and Germany. By 1994, all jobs except Fenton's had been taken over by Polish nationals (he too left eventually).

Sources: Chuck Hutchcraft, "After Bombing, McDonald's Says Enough Already," *Restaurants & Institutions,* June 1, 2000, p. 20; James L. Watson, "China's Big Mac Attack," *Foreign Affairs,* May/June 2000, pp. 120–134; for more information on McDonald's international operations, visit the company's website (**www.mcdonalds.com**) and click on "Country Sites."

This brief summary of McDonald's complex global operations points to the importance of culture in understanding consumer behavior. To develop effective strategies, marketers need to identify important aspects of culture and understand how they affect consumers. In this chapter, we examine the topic of culture and consider its influence on consumers' affect, cognitions, and behaviors. We also describe some important characteristics of American culture and discuss the implications of cultural analysis for developing marketing strategies. Then we present a model of the cultural process that shows how cultural meaning is transferred by marketing strategies to products and how consumers then acquire those meanings for themselves. Finally, we discuss cross-cultural (international) differences and their implications for developing global marketing strategies.

What Is Culture?

As the broadest aspect of the macro social environment, culture has a pervasive influence on consumers. Yet despite increasing research attention, culture remains difficult for marketers to understand. Dozens of definitions have confused researchers about what "culture" is or how culture works to influence consumers.[1] Fortunately, recent theoretical developments help clarify the concept of culture and how it affects people.[2] We treat **culture** as the meanings that are shared by most people in a social group. In a broad sense, cultural meanings include common affective reactions, typical cognitions (beliefs), and characteristic patterns of behavior. Each society establishes its own vision of the world and constructs that cultural world by creating and using meanings to represent important cultural distinctions.

Marketers should consider several issues when analyzing culture. First, cultural meaning can be analyzed at different levels. Often culture is analyzed at the macro level of an entire society or country (Canada, France, Poland, Kenya, or Australia). However, because culture is the meanings shared among a group of people (of any size), marketers can also analyze the cultural meanings of subcultures (African Americans, the elderly, people who live in New England) or social classes (middle versus working class). We discuss subcultures and social class in Chapter 13. Marketers can even analyze the shared cultural meanings of smaller groups such as a reference group (people who live on the same dormitory floor, members of a sorority or a street gang, or a group of co-workers) or family (people in one's nuclear or extended family). We discuss reference groups and family influences in Chapter 14.

The cultural meaning of the bald eagle is shared by most American consumers
Courtesy The United States Postal Service.

A second issue, the concept of shared or common meaning, is critical to understanding culture. In Section Two we examined psychological meaning—the personal, mental representations of objects, events, and behaviors stored in the memories of individual consumers. In this chapter we consider **cultural meaning** at a macro social level. *A meaning is cultural if many people in a social group share* *the same basic meaning*. These cultural meanings are somewhat fuzzy in that all people in a social group are not likely to have exactly the same meaning for any object or activity (What is an old person, an environmentally safe product, or a good bargain?). Fortunately, meanings have to be only "close enough" to be treated as shared or common.

Third, cultural meanings are created by people. Anthropologists often say that cultural meanings are constructed or negotiated by people in a group through their social interactions. The *construction of cultural meaning* is more obvious at the level of smaller groups. Consider the social meanings of clothing fads among college students—what look is cool this semester? At the macro societal level, cultural institutions such as government, religious and educational organizations, and business firms also are involved in constructing cultural meaning.

Fourth, cultural meanings are constantly in motion and can be subject to rapid changes. In the early days of the consumption society in 18th-century England, for instance, the cultural changes in people's values, perceptions, and behaviors were so dramatic that one observer believed a kind of madness had taken over society. Later in this chapter, we examine the processes by which cultural meanings move about in society, partly through marketing strategies.

A final issue is that social groups differ in the amount of freedom people have to adopt and use certain cultural meanings. North American and European societies afford people a great deal of freedom to select cultural meanings and use them to create a desired self-identity. In most other societies (China, India, Saudi Arabia), people have relatively less (but increasing) freedom to do so.

In the following sections we discuss two useful perspectives for understanding cultural meaning. Marketers can examine the *content* of a culture, or marketers can treat culture as a *process*.[3]

The Content of Culture

The usual approach in marketing is to analyze culture in terms of its major attributes or its content.[4] Marketers typically focus on identifying the dominant values of a society, but culture is more than values.[5] The **content of culture** includes the beliefs, attitudes, goals, and values held by most people in a society, as well as the meanings of characteristic behaviors, rules, customs, and norms that most people follow. The content of culture also includes meanings of the significant aspects of the social and physical environment, including the major social institutions in a society (political parties, religions, chambers of commerce) and the typical physical objects (products, tools, buildings) used by people in that society.

The goal of cultural analysis is to understand the cultural meanings of these concepts from the point of view of the consumers who create and use them.[6] For example, many Americans have similar affective or emotional responses to the raising of the American flag (patriotic feelings), a 50-percent-off sale (interest or excitement), or accidentally breaking a vase in a store (anxiety or guilt). Affective responses may vary across cultures. Many Americans and Northern Europeans would become angry or frustrated if kept waiting for 15 minutes in a checkout line, whereas people in other societies may not have a negative affective reaction.

Behaviors also can have important cultural meanings. For instance, the meaning of shaking hands when greeting someone (welcome or friendliness) is shared by many peoples of the world, although in some cultures people bow or kiss instead. Protesters in America or other countries who burn the American flag are communicating disapproval or hatred through their behaviors. Some

affection

The shopping environment can be quite different in the cultures of the United States and Tunisia *(left) Chuck Keeler/Getty Images; (right) Lorne Resnick/ Getty Images.*

consumption-related behaviors have a cultural meaning that is unique to particular societies. For instance, the bargaining behaviors that are common (and expected) among shoppers in the open market bazaars of Northern Africa indicate a skilled and shrewd consumer. But in the United States, such bargaining behaviors are not appropriate for shopping in Kmart or Wal-Mart and would be considered naive or rude.

Aspects of the social environment can have rich cultural meanings. For instance, the cultural meanings of shopping for a new sweater at a self-service discount store may be quite different from shopping in an upscale department store with attentive personal service from salespeople. Likewise, the physical or material environment—including the landscape, the buildings, the weather, and specific objects such as products—can have significant cultural meaning. For instance, objects such as wedding rings and new cars have cultural meaning for many consumers. All societies have certain objects that symbolize key cultural meanings. Consider the shared meanings that many Americans associate with the flag, the Statue of Liberty, or the bald eagle (pride, freedom, individualism).

Finally, marketing strategies may have shared cultural meanings. People's reactions to advertising, for instance, tend to be culturally specific.[7] In the United States, many advertising appeals are straightforward and direct, but consumers in other societies may consider such appeals blunt or even offensive. Foreigners consider many U.S. ads to be overly emotional, even schmaltzy. Thus, a McDonald's ad that featured a young man with Down syndrome who found a job and happiness at McDonald's was a tearjerker for Americans but was booed and jeered at the International Advertising Film Festival in Cannes. The British tend to be embarrassed by a direct sell; their ads are noted for self-deprecating humor. In contrast, the French rarely use humor but prefer stylish and rather indirect appeals, which Americans may find surrealistic. For example, a French ad (also shown in North

America) showed a lion and a tawny-haired woman crawling up opposite sides of a mountain; at the peak, the woman outroars the lion for a bottle of Perrier. Most Japanese consumers prefer ads in which affective mood and emotional tone are emphasized over facts. Although some Japanese ads travel well to other cultures, many are not understood outside Japan.[8] As a final example, marketing strategies such as pricing or distribution have cultural meanings that can differ across societies. Many U.S. consumers have positive reactions to frequent sales promotions such as discounting, sales, and coupons, but consumers in other cultures may have more negative meanings (Is something wrong with this product?).

In sum, marketers need to understand the cultural meanings of their products and brands. For instance, an analysis of beverage products focused on the status and age meanings carried in various beverage products; milk, for example, is seen as weak and appropriate for younger people, whereas wine is considered sophisticated and for mature adults.[9] As we will see later, consumers seek to acquire certain cultural meanings in products and use them to create a desirable personal identity.

Measuring the Content of Culture

Marketers have used many procedures to measure cultural content, including content analysis, ethnographic fieldwork, and measures of values. Some of these methods are different from the more traditional approaches common in consumer research (surveys, telephone interviews, focus groups).[10] Although all these techniques identify important meanings shared by people, they do not show how consumers perceive products to be related to those meanings. Means–end chains are useful for that purpose.

Content Analysis   The content of culture can often be read from the material objects produced by the social group. For instance, consumer researchers have examined comic books to gain insights into the dominant values in a culture.[11] Other researchers have examined a historical record of print advertisements to see how American values and women's roles have changed during the past 90 years.[12]

Ethnographic Fieldwork   Marketers have begun to use ethnographic methods (adapted from anthropology) to study culture.[13] These procedures involve detailed and prolonged observation of consumers' emotional responses, cognitions, and behaviors during their ordinary daily lives. Based on this rich and detailed data, researchers interpret or infer the values and key meanings of the culture. Unlike anthropologists who might live in the studied society for months or years, consumer researchers tend to make their observations more quickly. Using a combination of direct observations, interviews, and video and audio recordings, researchers have examined consumer behavior at flea markets and swap meets.[14] To understand what brands and products kids were using, toy company Mattel once commissioned a global study in a dozen countries, including the United States and China, in which it recorded everything kids had hanging on their bedroom walls.[15]

Measures of Values   Marketers also use procedures to directly measure the dominant cultural values in a society. A popular approach is the Rokeach Value Survey in which consumers rank order 36 general values in terms of their importance.

PAIN FEELS SO MUCH BETTER THAN GUILT.

Are you the kind of athlete who measures your workouts by how sore you feel the next day? If you'd rather make it to the gym than make excuses, you are Russell material. Just like the 200 NCAA® Division I and 15 Major League Baseball® teams we outfit.

ARE YOU RUSSELL ATHLETIC MATERIAL?

www.russellathletic.com | ©2000 Russell Athletic, a division of Russell Corporation

Many Americans continue to hold the core values of physical fitness and attractive appearance   *Courtesy of Russell Athletic, a division of Russell Corporation.*

Kahle's List of Values asks consumers to rank order nine person-oriented values. Marketers can then use these data to segment consumers in terms of their dominant value orientation.[16]

Various commercial techniques regularly survey large, representative samples of consumers in the United States and Europe. For instance, the Yankelovich MONITOR tracks more than 50 social trends (and value changes) and reports on their significance for consumer marketing (see **www. yankelovich.com/monitor**). Recent Yankelovich surveys showed that U.S. consumers ranked the value of privacy as their number two concern, right behind safety. Levelor, manufacturer of window blinds, addressed this consumer value by developing the UltraDark™ blind with superior light control that provides exceptional privacy.[17] Another commercial method called VALS (Values and Lifestyles) identifies segments of consumers with different sets of end values. VALS has been widely adapted by advertising agencies to help them better understand their target customers.

The Core Values of American Culture

A typical marketing analysis of cultural content begins by identifying the core values of the social group. **Core values** are the abstract end goals that people strive to achieve in their lives. Knowing the core values held by people in a society can help marketers understand the basis for the customer-- product relationship for those consumers. For instance, many Americans value mastery and being in control of their lives and the environment. The fascination with lawns (control of nature), remote controls (control over TV exposure), and time management systems (control over time) seem to reflect this value. This value persists even though most people realize that some things (nature) cannot be closely managed and controlled. Exhibit 12.1 presents several basic core values shared by many Americans.

Changing Values in America

The constant changes in American cultural values can affect the success of a company's marketing strategies. As consumers' values change, their means–end connections with existing products and brands also change, which can change the important consumer–product relationship.

Changes in values can create problems (as well as opportunities) for marketers. For instance, BMW was probably the ultimate yuppie (young urban professional) status symbol in the 1980s, but sales dropped as the economy cooled in the 1990s and people's perceptions of the BMW image changed. After the consumption excesses of the 1980s, many consumers had become less materialistic and more concerned about social issues such as protection of the environment. By the late- 1990s, people's values regarding luxury had shifted again and sales of BMW, Mercedes,

Exhibit 12.1

Core Values in America

Value	General Feature	Relevance to Consumer Behavior
Achievement and success	Hard work is good; success flows from hard work	Acts as a justification for acquisition of goods ("You deserve it")
Activity	Keeping busy is healthy and natural	Stimulates interest in products that save time and enhance leisure-time activities
Efficiency and practicality	Admiration of things that solve problems (e.g., save time and effort)	Stimulates purchase of products that function well and save time
Progress	People can improve themselves; tomorrow should be better	Stimulates desire for new products that fulfill unsatisfied needs; acceptance of products that claim to be "new" or "improved"
Material comfort	"The good life"	Fosters acceptance of convenience and luxury products that make life more enjoyable
Individualism	Being one's self (e.g., self-reliance, self-interest, and self-esteem)	Stimulates acceptance of customized or unique products that enable a person to "express his or her own personality"
Freedom	Freedom of choice	Fosters interest in wide product lines and differentiated products
External conformity	Uniformity of observable behavior; desire to be accepted	Stimulates interest in products that are used or owned by others in the same social group
Humanitarianism	Caring for others, particularly the underdog	Stimulates patronage of firms that compete with market leaders
Youthfulness	A state of mind that stresses being young at heart of appearing young	Stimulates acceptance of products that provide the illusion of maintaining or fostering youth
Fitness and health	Caring about one's body, including the desire to be physically fit and healthy	Stimulates acceptance of food products, activities, and equipment perceived to maintain or increase physical fitness

Source: Excerpt from Leon G. Schiffman and Leslie Lazar Kanuk, *Consumer Behavior,* 4th ed., p. 424. © 1991. Reprinted by permission of Pearson Education, Inc., Upper Saddle River, NJ.

and Porsche were up sharply. Highlight 12.1 presents examples of corporate responses to changing environmental values.

Changes in cultural values can create new marketing opportunities, too. For instance, chicken restaurants saw significant growth as American consumers turned away from burgers to products seen as more healthful. Increasing health values have led many restaurants to add new "healthy or heart-conscious" items (with reduced levels of fat, sugar, and cholesterol) to their menus.

Changes in cultural values are usually accompanied by changes in behavior. For instance, the values of convenience and saving time led to increases in home shopping

Highlight 12.1

Online Privacy: A Growing Cultural Concern

As the Internet and e-commerce have expanded, consumers have become increasingly concerned with online privacy. Some highly publicized breaches of privacy have heightened awareness of the issue.

Leading Internet advertising firm DoubleClick drew the ire of consumers, state's attorneys general, and the Federal Trade Commission in 2000, when it was revealed the company had planned to link specific names and addresses with information it had collected on Web surfing behavior. Privacy advocates also raised their eyebrows at a start-up firm called Predictive Networks, which created software capable of following consumers around the Internet and building profiles of them based on the sites they visit. Predictive Networks could then use that information to deliver targeted advertising and news to consumers. Even e-mail has proven susceptible. Alibris, which sells rare books online, pleaded guilty to intercepting e-mail messages intended for Amazon.com.

Companies have a variety of ways to track you when you visit their sites:

- *Cookies* are data files placed on your hard drive, usually the first time you visit a site. Every time you return to the site, the cookie is activated so the site can "remember" what kinds of information and products you have looked at previously.
- *Virtual ID cards* include your computer's IP address, the type of operating system installed, and the name of the browser you use. Your browser sends an ID card each time you request information from a website.
- *Advertisements* can be stored on a site other than the one you are looking at. If you click on such an advertisement, the site where that ad is actually stored can place a cookie on your hard drive and track your activity.
- *Web bugs* are not used often, but they are powerful. They allow your activity to be tracked by sites other than the one you are visiting. If a company has a strategic partner, it might want to use a Web bug to allow that partner to verify certain information about site traffic.

It will be interesting to see whether lawmakers will take a hands-off approach, or enact new privacy laws that will limit the ways companies can gather and use consumer information.

Sources: Andrea Petersen, "A Privacy Firestorm at DoubleClick," *The Wall Street Journal,* February 23, 2000, pp. B1, B4; Julia Angwin, "A Plan to Track Web Use Stirs Privacy Concern," *The Wall Street Journal,* May 1, 2000, pp. B1, B18; Jeffrey L. Seglin, "Dot.Con; As Competition Heats Up, Ethics, Morals, and Manners Get Lost in Cyberspace," *Forbes ASAP,* February 21, 2000, p. 135.

behaviors, including use of mail catalogs, TV shopping channels, and Internet shopping. Marketers often talk about behavior in terms of lifestyles: typical ways in which people live their lives to achieve important end goals or values. Exhibit 12.2 lists several important lifestyle trends in American society along with an example of how each may affect marketing strategies. Marketers should monitor these cultural changes and adjust their marketing strategies as necessary.

Culture as a Process

Understanding the content of culture is useful for designing effective marketing strategies, but we can also think about culture as a *process*. Exhibit 12.3 presents a model of the cultural process in a highly developed consumer society.[18] The model shows that cultural meaning is present in three "locations": in the social and physical environments, in products and services, and in individual consumers. The **cultural process** describes how this cultural meaning is moved about or transferred between these locations by the actions of organizations (business, government, religion, education) and by individuals in the society. There are two ways meaning is transferred in a consumption-oriented society. First, marketing strategies are designed to move

Exhibit 12.2

Lifestyle Trends in America

Trends	Impact on Marketing Strategies
Control of time	Americans increasingly value their time and seek greater control of its use.
Component lifestyles	Consumer behavior is becoming more individualistic because of the wider array of available choices.
Culture of convenience	With the rising number of two-income households, consumers are spending more on services to have more free time for themselves.
Growth of home shopping	Consumers want more time for themselves and are frustrated by waiting in checkout lines.
Shopping habits of the sexes to converge	Men continue to do more of the shopping, and working women take on many male shopping habits.
Home entertainment	The VCR, DVD, and large-screen TV are behind the boom in home entertainment, which brought about increased purchases of take-out food and changes in the nature of home furnishings and appliances.
Casual dress	There has been a widespread interest in more casual fashions.
Spread of the diversified diet	Americans are eating differently (e.g., concern with fat content, greater fish consumption).
Self-imposed prohibition of alcohol	The trend has been toward "lighter" drinks (e.g., vodka, "lite" beer) as well as a decline in the overall consumption of alcohol.
Lightest drink of all—water	Some people consider bottled or sparkling water to be chic; some are concerned about the quality of their tap water.
Bifurcation of product markets	There is a growing distance between upscale and downscale markets, and companies caught in the middle may fare poorly.
Product and service quality are more important, if not everything	Products falling below acceptable quality standards will be treated mercilessly.
Heightened importance of visuals in advertising and marketing	With the cable TV revolution, the imperative for advertisers is to make the message seen, not heard.
Fragmentation of media markets	As new sources of programming emerge, loyalty to network TV fades.
New employee benefits for two-income families	More employers will offer flexible work hours, job sharing, and day care services.
Growing appeal of work at home	Workers will want to work at home on their own computers.
Older Americans—the next entrepreneurs	Older people want to work past the traditional retirement age and have the resources to invest in their own businesses.
Young Americans—a new kind of conservative	Although 18- to 29-year-olds are socially liberal, they are economically and politically conservative.
Public relations—tough times ahead for business	Business does not receive the credit it deserves for the creation of new jobs because people remain suspicious about how business operates.

Source: Adapted from "31 Major Trends Shaping the Future of American Business," *The Public Pulse* 2, no. 1.

Exhibit 12.3

A Model of the Cultural Process

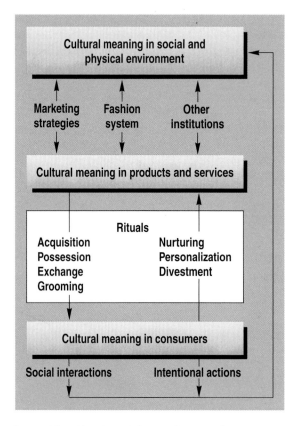

Source: Adapted from Grant McCracken, "Culture and Consumption: A Theoretical Account of the Structure and Movement of the Cultural Meaning of Consumer Goods," *Journal of Consumer Research,* June 1986, pp. 71–84. Copyright 1986 Journal of Consumer Research. Reprinted with permission of the publisher, University of Chicago Press.

cultural meanings from the physical and social environments into products and services in an attempt to make them attractive to consumers. Second, consumers actively seek to acquire these cultural meanings in products to establish a desirable personal identity or self-concept.

Moving Cultural Meanings into Products

Advertising has been the most closely studied method of transferring cultural meaning from the physical and social environments into products.[19] From a cultural process perspective, advertising can be seen as a funnel through which cultural meaning is poured into consumer goods.[20] Essentially, advertisers must decide what cultural meanings they want their products to have and then create ads that communicate those cultural meanings, often using symbols (whether words or images) to stand for the desired cultural meanings.[21]

A *symbol* is something (a word, image, or object) that stands for or signifies something else (the desired cultural meaning). For instance, to communicate cool, refreshing, summertime meanings, Nestlé Nestea showed a person falling, fully clothed, into a cool swimming pool. The long-running "Heartbeat of America" campaign for Chevrolet showed various symbols of small-town American life to represent traditional American values such as simplicity, family, patriotism, and friendship. Some animals have distinctive symbolic meanings that marketers can associate with products (the bull in Merrill Lynch ads, the bald eagle in ads for the U.S. Postal Service's Express Mail service, the ram for Dodge "ram tough" trucks). Names can convey cultural meaning that enhances the value of the product. For instance, Urban Decay, marketer of funky nail polishes, used such names for its colors as Oil Slick, Gash, Uzi, Rust, and Pallor. Highlight 12.2 describes another cultural symbol used in advertising.

Although advertising may be the most obvious marketing mechanism for moving meanings into products, other aspects of marketing strategy are involved as well. Consider pricing strategies. Discount stores such as Kmart and Wal-Mart use low prices to establish the meaning of their stores. For many consumers, high prices have desirable cultural meanings that can be transferred to certain products (Mercedes-Benz cars, Rolex watches, Chivas Regal Scotch, European clothing designers) to create a luxurious, high-status, high-quality image. Different price endings ($14.87 versus $14.99 versus $15.00) also may communicate specific cultural meanings.[22]

Japanese automobile companies intentionally design the product attributes of their cars to communicate important cultural meanings. For instance, the design of the automobile interior (leather versus cloth seats, analog versus digital gauges, wood versus plastic dash) as well as the locations of the controls and how they look and feel when one operates them can transfer cultural meaning to the product. Even distribution strategies can influence the transfer of meaning. The limited distribution of Burberry trench coats and related products in better clothing stores enhances their image.

Other factors besides marketing strategies can influence the transfer of meaning from the cultural world into products.[23] For instance, journalists who report the results of product tests of cars, stereo systems, or ski equipment are moving meaning into the products. The so-called fashion system, including designers, reporters, opinion leaders, and celebrities, transfers fashion-related meanings into clothing, cooking, and home furnishing products.[24] Consumer advocates such as Ralph Nader (who convinced people that the Chevrolet Corvair was unsafe) or government agencies such as the Consumer Product Safety Commission (which required warning labels telling people not to step on the top level of a stepladder) are involved in transferring meanings to products.

Cultural Meanings in Products

Products, stores, and brands express cultural or symbolic meaning.[25] For instance, certain brands have meanings concerning the sex and age groups for which they are appropriate: Virginia Slims are for women, Camels are for men; Rollerblades and T-shirts are for young people, gardening tools and laxatives are for older people. Some products embody cultural meanings, such as the Cooperstown Collection of high-quality reproductions of baseball team jerseys, jackets, and hats, including defunct teams such as the Washington Senators.[26] Buying and using such products make their cultural meanings tangible and visible, and communicate those meanings to others.

The cultural meanings of products are likely to vary across different societies. For instance, most societies have favorite foods that represent important meanings in that culture, but not in others—Danes love eel, Mexicans love chilies, Irish love Guinness, French love cheese, Americans love hamburgers.

Highlight 12.2

The Cultural Meanings in Products and Brands: "The Jolly Green Giant"

People are often unaware of the cultural origins of everyday objects in their environments, even if they sense the fundamental meanings of these objects. Consider the Jolly Green Giant, the symbol of Green Giant Company, canners of vegetables in the Le Sueur Valley of Minnesota. In print and TV ads, the smiling Giant stands, hands on hips, towering over the entire valley and looking down on the happy, elfin workers harvesting the succulent produce below. His body is green, and he is dressed entirely in green leaves. Perhaps you noticed the Giant doesn't move (think of the consequences for the elves) or say much beyond the obligatory "Ho, ho, ho!" at the end of each ad. In 1925 Leo Burnett, a Chicago advertising agency, adapted the Green Giant from an illustration in a book of Grimm's fairy tales. The giant in that original illustration was white, wore a bearskin cloak, and bore an intimidating scowl.

What is the cultural meaning of the Jolly Green Giant? Is the Jolly Green Giant only an easy-to-remember brand symbol, or could it be something more? From a cultural perspective, the Jolly Green Giant can be seen as a modern manifestation of ancient European fertility symbols that represented the spirit of vegetation.

Figures clothed in leaves have deep cultural meanings that date back hundreds of years. Sir James George Fraser described many of these symbolic figures in his masterwork *The Golden Bough.* In many early European cultures, people celebrated the rites of spring by honoring the spirits of the sacred trees or plants. By the nineteenth century, this ritual had become personalized; a person from each rural community dressed in leaves or flowers. For instance, the gypsies of Transylvania and Romania had Green George, a boy "covered from top to toe in green leaves and blossoms." In Bavaria (southern Germany), the leaf person was Quack; in England, it was Jack in the Green; in Switzerland, it was the Whitsuntide Lout. Other popular names for the fertility symbol were the Leaf King, the Grass King, the May King, and the Queen of May.

Even as recently as 100 years ago, fertility figures representing the spirit of vegetation were found in many parts of Eastern Europe, Germany, and England. Although details of the costume and ritual varied from place to place, the overall concept and representation of the central figure were consistent. A youthful person was dressed in leaves and other vegetation. Sometimes the person was symbolically dunked into a pond or stream. Thus were the spirits of fertility and water honored, and the community was assured continued supplies of water and forage.

Clearly these fertility figures are similar to the Jolly Green Giant. Is this just a coincidence, or does the obvious symbolism of such a figure still convey compelling meanings to the sophisticated citizens of the modern world? Did the creative staff at Leo Burnett intentionally appropriate an ancient fertility symbol, or did the idea emerge from their collective unconscious? And how did the meanings of a giant get added to the equation? Whatever the answers, the Jolly Green Giant seems to represent deep symbolic cultural meanings that are partially responsible for the success of the product.

Can you think of other examples of ancient cultural symbols used in modern advertising? How about the Keebler elves? What about the genielike Mr. Clean (called Mr. Proper in Germany and Austria) or Red Devil tools? Do you remember the white knight of Ajax fame who rode in with lance at the ready and blasted the dirt out of people's laundry?

Sources: Greg Hassell,"Ho, Ho, Ho Is Back, and It's Not Santa," *Houston Chronicle,* August 18, 1999, p. 1; Tom E. Sullenberger, "Ajax Meets the Jolly Green Giant: Some Observations on the Use of Folklore and Myth in American Mass Marketing," *Journal of American Folklore* 87 (1974), pp. 53–65.

Of course, not all people in a social group perceive a product, brand, or activity to have the same cultural meaning. For example, some teenagers may begin to smoke Marlboros to gain the positive cultural meanings they perceive in the act of smoking and in the brand. Other teens may reject smoking to avoid gaining the negative meanings they perceive in that action.

Holidays such as Thanksgiving and birthdays usually involve rituals that maintain the cultural meanings of those important events
(left) Chuck Savage/CORBIS; (right) George Shelley/CORBIS.

Some of the cultural meanings in products are obvious to anyone who is familiar with that culture, but other meanings are hidden. Nearly everyone can recognize the basic cultural meanings in different styles of clothing (jeans and a sweatshirt versus a business suit), makes of automobiles (Mercedes-Benz versus Ford versus Honda), types of stores (JCPenney versus Wal-Mart versus Nordstrom or Saks). But other, less obvious cultural meanings in products may not be fully recognized by consumers or marketers. For instance, you may not realize the important meanings of a stereo or a bicycle until it is broken or stolen. A research study interviewed consumers whose houses had been burglarized to learn the most significant meanings of the missing possessions.[27]

Many companies know little about the symbolic cultural meanings of their products. This was the case in 1985 when Coca-Cola Company changed the taste attributes of Coca-Cola to make it slightly sweeter with less of a bite.[28] When it introduced new Coke, the company was surprised by an immediate flurry of protests from customers. Millions of consumers had consumed Coca-Cola as kids and had strong cultural meanings for (and emotional ties to) the original product. These consumers resented its removal from the marketplace, and some brought lawsuits against the company. In response, Coca-Cola quickly reintroduced the original product under the brand name Coca-Cola Classic. (The Marketing Strategy in Action in Chapter 6 reviews this situation.)

Finally, many products contain *personal meanings* in addition to cultural meanings. Personal meanings are moved into products by the actions of individual consumers. Although these meanings tend to be idiosyncratic and unique to each consumer, they are important as a source of intrinsic self-relevance that can affect consumers' involvement with the product.

Moving Cultural Meanings from Products into Consumers

The cultural process model identifies rituals as ways of moving meanings from the product to the consumer. **Rituals** are *symbolic actions performed by consumers to create, affirm, evoke, or revise certain cultural meanings.*[29] For instance, the consumption rituals performed on Thanksgiving Day by American families who feast on turkey and all the trimmings affirm their ability to provide abundantly for their needs.

Not all rituals are formal ceremonies such as a special dinner, a graduation, or a wedding. Rather, many rituals are common aspects of everyday life, although people usually do not recognize their behavior as ritualistic. Consumer researchers have begun to investigate the role of rituals in consumer behavior, but our knowledge is still limited.[30] We discuss five consumption-related rituals involved in the movement of meaning between product and consumer: the actions associated with acquisition, possession, exchange, grooming, and divestment.[31] Future research is likely to reveal other ritualistic behaviors that consumers perform to obtain cultural meanings in products.

Acquisition Rituals   Some of the cultural meanings in products are transferred to consumers through the simple *acquisition rituals* of purchasing and consuming the product. For instance, buying and eating an ice cream cone is necessary to receive the meanings the product contains (fun, relaxation, a reward for hard work, a treat or pick-me-up). Other acquisition behaviors have ritualistic qualities that are important for meaning transfer. For example, collectors who are interested in possessing scarce or unique products (antiques, stamps or coins, beer cans, and so on) may perform special search rituals when they go out on "the hunt," including wearing special lucky clothes.

The *bargaining rituals* involved in negotiating the price of an automobile, stereo system, or some object at a garage sale can help transfer important meanings to the buyer (I got a good deal). Consider how an avid plate collector in his early sixties describes the meanings conveyed by bidding rituals at an auction or a flea market:

> There's no Alcoholics Anonymous for collectors. You just get bit by the bug and that's it. The beauty and craftsmanship of some of these things are amazing. They were made by people who cared. There's nothing like getting ahold of them for yourself. Especially if you get it for a song and you sing it yourself. It's not *getting* a great deal, it's *knowing* that you've got a great deal that makes for the thrill. It's even better if you had to bid against someone for it.[32]

In sum, the acquisition rituals performed in obtaining products (purchase, search, bargaining, bidding) can help move meanings to the buyer.

Possession Rituals   *Possession rituals* help consumers acquire the meanings in products. For instance, the new owners of a house (or apartment) might invite friends and relatives to a housewarming party to admire their dwelling and formally establish its meanings. Many consumers perform similar ritualistic displays of a new purchase (a car, clothing, stereo system) to show off the new possession, solicit the admiration of their friends, and gain reassurance that they made a good purchase.

Other possession rituals involve moving personal meaning from the customer into the product. For instance, *product nurturing rituals* put personal meaning into the product (washing your car each Saturday, organizing your CD collection, tuning your bicycle, working in your garden).[33] Later these meanings can be moved back to the consumer, where they are experienced and enjoyed as satisfaction or pride. These possession rituals help create strong, involving relationships between products and consumers.

Personalizing rituals serve a similar function. Many people who buy a used car or a previously owned house perform ritualistic actions to remove meanings left over from the previous owner and move new meanings of their own into the product.

Grooming rituals such as blow drying one's hair are rituals that transfer positive meanings such as beauty and self-confidence into the consumer
Robert Llewellyn/CORBIS.

For instance, consumers will purchase special accessories for their new or used cars to personalize them (new floor mats, better radio, different wheels and/or tires, custom stripes). Repainting, wallpapering, or installing carpeting are rituals that personalize a house to "make it your own."

Exchange Rituals Certain meanings can be transferred to consumers through *exchange rituals* such as giving gifts.[34] For instance, giving wine or flowers to your host or hostess on arriving at a formal dinner party is a ritual that transfers cultural meanings (thanks, graciousness, generosity).

People often select gifts for anniversaries, birthdays, or important holidays such as Christmas that contain special cultural meanings to be transferred to the receiver. For instance, giving a nice watch, luggage, or a new car to a college graduate might be intended to convey cultural meanings of achievement, adult status, or independence. Parents often give their children gifts that are intended to transfer very particular cultural meanings (a puppy represents responsibility; a bike represents freedom; a computer conveys the importance of learning and mastery).

Grooming Rituals Certain cultural meanings are perishable in that they tend to fade over time. For instance, personal care products such as shampoo, mouthwash, and deodorants and beauty products (cosmetics, skin care) contain a variety of cultural meanings (attractive, sexy, confident, influence over others). But when transferred to consumers through use, these meanings are not permanent. Such meanings must be continually renewed by drawing them out of a product each time it is used. *Grooming rituals* involve particular ways of using personal care and beauty products that coax these cultural meanings out of the product and transfer them to the consumer. Many people engage in rather elaborate grooming rituals to obtain these meanings (see Highlight 12.3). What types of grooming rituals do you perform when getting ready to go out?

Divestment Rituals Consumers perform *divestment rituals* to remove meaning from products. Certain products (items of clothing, a house, a car or motorcycle, a favorite piece of sports equipment) can contain considerable amounts of personal meaning. These meanings may be the basis for a strong customer–product relationship. For instance, products can acquire such personal meaning through long periods of use or because they symbolize important meanings (a chair may be a family heirloom).

Often consumers believe that some of the personal meanings must be removed before such products can be sold or even thrown away. Thus, for instance, a consumer may wash or dry-clean a favorite item of clothing that she plans to give away or donate to charity to remove some of the personal meanings in the product. A consumer may remove certain highly personal parts of his house (a special chandelier), car (a special radio), or motorcycle (a custom seat) before selling it.

In certain cases, the personal meaning in the product is so intense that the consumer cannot part with the object. Thus, people hang onto old cars, clothes, or furniture that have sentimental personal meaning. One study found that certain consumers had become highly attached to their Levi's jeans and kept them for years, some as long as 20 or 30 years.[35] These consumers associated many salient

Highlight 12.3

Grooming Rituals

What are the symbolic, and perhaps unconscious, meanings associated with consumers' personal grooming rituals? One study found that hair care activities dominated the grooming behavior of the young adults (18 to 25 years old) in the sample. Most of these consumers shampooed their hair nearly every day, and many felt frustrated and emotional about this activity. For instance, one 20-year-old woman said, "Fixing my hair is the most difficult. I spend hours— actually hours—doing my hair. It drives me crazy!"

Because many of the meanings associated with hair care were thought to be relatively unconscious, direct questioning could not be used to tap into these deeper, more symbolic meanings; consumers might just offer rationalizations for their behavior. So the researcher showed male and female consumers pictures of a young man using a blow dryer and a young woman in curlers applying makeup. Each consumer was asked to write a detailed history about the person in the picture. Their stories give some insights into the meanings of these grooming rituals.

For many consumers, hair grooming with the blow dryer seemed to symbolize an active, take-charge personality who is preparing to go on the "social prowl." For example, one 20-year-old man said, "Jim is supposed to stay home and study tonight, but he's getting ready to go out, anyway. He's hoping to meet some hot chicks, and he wants his hair to look just right."

Symbolic meanings about work and success were prominent in other stories, as the following excerpt from a 21-year-old woman's story illustrates: "Susan is getting ready for her first presentation, and she's very nervous. If it goes well, maybe her boss will help with a down payment on a new car."

What do you think are some of the deeper reasons for women using makeup? Why are more and more companies in the beauty industry now focusing on cosmetics for men (including eye cremes, face powder, and clear vitamin E for lips)? Uncovering consumers' deep symbolic meanings for certain products can be quite difficult. However, the knowledge can give marketers useful insights into consumers' reactions to their products.

Sources: Adapted with permission from Dennis W. Rook, "The Ritual Dimension of Consumer Behavior," *Journal of Consumer Research,* December 1985, pp. 251–264, Copyright 1985 Journal of Consumer Research. Reprinted with permission of the publisher, University of Chicago Press; Chris Bynum, "Saving Face," *New Orleans Times-Picayune,* April 18, 2000, p. F1. Copyright 2003 The Times-Picayune Publishing Co. All rights reserved.

meanings with Levi's jeans, including the confidence they felt when wearing the product and the feeling that Levi's were appropriate in many social situations. Other consumers talked about their Levi's as an old friend who had accompanied them on many adventures and valued the jeans for the memories they contained. If divestment rituals are unable to remove these meanings, consumers may keep such objects forever, or at least until the personal meanings have become less intense.

Cultural Meanings in Consumers

Consumers buy products as a way to acquire cultural meanings to use in establishing their self-identities. Consider the sports fan who buys a team hat or jacket. Major League Baseball Properties, a licensing and marketing organization, sells authentic jerseys from the New York Yankees (about $175) and the 1919 Chicago Black Sox ($245) to middle-aged fans who want to identify with their favorite teams, present and past.[36] Or consumers might buy Ben and Jerry's Rain Forest Crunch ice cream (made from nuts grown in the Amazon rain forest) or Tide detergent sold in packages made from recycled materials to acquire the ecological values represented by these products. People buy such products to move important cultural meanings into themselves and to communicate these meanings to others. In this sense, consumers can use products to partially create their self-concept or self-identity.

Americans have a lot of freedom to create different selves through their choices of lifestyles, environments, and products. Self-construction activity is especially intense during the teenage and young adult years. Young people try different social roles and self-identities, and often purchase products to gain meanings related to these roles. Thus, teenage rebellions against parents' values and lifestyles usually involve the purchase and consumption of certain products. As most people become more mature with age, their self-concepts become more stable (sometimes even rigid), and their interest in self-change lessens. Of course, changes, even radical changes, in self-concept are still possible, but they are increasingly rare. Even so, consumers still use the cultural meanings in products to maintain and fine-tune their current self-identities.

Although products can transfer useful meanings to consumers, goods cannot provide all the meanings consumers need to construct healthy self-concepts.[37] People obtain self-relevant meanings from many other sources, including work, family, religious experiences, and various social activities. Often the meanings gained through these activities are more self-relevant and more satisfying than those obtained through product consumption.

Unfortunately, especially in highly developed consumption societies, many people consume products in an attempt to acquire important life meanings. Some of these consumers may engage in almost pathological levels of consumption as they desperately purchase products seeking to acquire cultural meanings with which to construct a satisfactory self-concept. Such consumers can end up heavily in debt and very unsatisfied.

Most people have favorite possessions filled with very important, self-relevant meanings. People have high levels of involvement with such objects. Researchers have begun to study these cherished objects to understand consumer–product relationships.[38] For instance, elderly people tend to feel strong attachments to objects such as photographs or furniture that remind them of past events,[39] whereas younger consumers tend to value objects that allow them to be active in self-relevant ways (sports or hobby equipment, work-related objects such as books or computers). Marketers need to understand these consumer–product relationships to develop effective strategies.

Moving Meanings to the Cultural Environment

The cultural process model in Exhibit 12.3 shows that the meanings consumers acquire can be transferred to the broad cultural environment through people's social behavior. In a society consisting of many individuals living and working together, culture (shared meaning) is created by the actions of those people. Much of the movement of meaning to the cultural environment is an automatic consequence of the daily social interactions among people. Sometimes, however, people intentionally try to create new cultural meanings in an attempt to change society. For instance, various interest groups in society (punks, "greens" or environmental activists, gay rights activists) try to influence others to adopt new cultural meanings. Consumer interest groups have similar goals.

In sum, Exhibit 12.3 portrays the cultural process as a *continuous and reciprocal movement of meaning* between the overall cultural environment, organizations, and individuals in the society. As with the Wheel of Consumer Analysis, the influences are bidirectional in that the meanings can flow in both directions.

Marketing Implications

Managing Cultural Meaning

The cultural process model suggests that a basic marketing task is management of the cultural meanings of the brand or product.[40] The shared cultural meanings of a brand are a large part of its economic value, or its *brand equity*.[41] Managing brand meanings requires that marketers identify the brand meanings shared by consumers and monitor changes in those meanings. Means–end analysis and ZMET interviews are useful for this purpose. Marketing strategies might be directed at maintaining positive brand meanings or creating new meanings. These strategies would have to select appropriate meanings from the cultural environment and move or transfer them into products and brands.

Although marketers usually think cultural meanings are fixed and are not affected much by a company's actions, marketing strategies do influence the overall cultural environment. A conspicuous example is the proliferation of marketing stimuli in the physical environment (signs, billboards, media advertisements). Less obvious is how the huge volume of marketing strategies affects our social environment and the shared meanings of modern life.[42]

Using Celebrity Endorsers in Ads

A popular advertising strategy in North America and Japan for moving cultural meanings into products and brands is to have celebrities endorse the product.[43] Among the celebrities who have appeared in ads are musician Ray Charles (Pepsi), Cher and the ballet dancer Mikhail Baryshnikov (cologne), golfer Tiger Woods (Buick), Cindy Crawford (Omega watches), basketball star Michael Jordan (Nike), actor Mr. T (1-800-Collect), Tommy LaSorda (diet aid), and politicians Ann Richards and Mario Cuomo (Doritos).

From a cultural perspective, celebrities are cultural objects with specific cultural meanings. In developing an effective celebrity endorsement strategy, marketers must be careful to select a celebrity who has appropriate meanings consistent with the overall marketing strategy (the intended meanings) for the product. Musicians

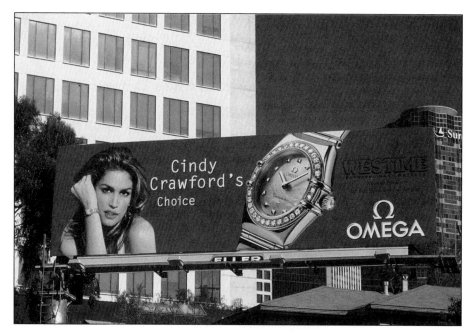

Celebrities can transfer positive meaning to a product *Gary Conner/ PhotoEdit, Inc.*

such as Elton John and Sting (for Coke) or Britney Spears (for Pepsi) have distinctive cultural images based on their records, live performances, and video appearances, which enhance their appeal as celebrity spokespersons. Some celebrities, such as Madonna, have shrewdly re-created their images (and their cultural meaning) over time as the appeal of one set of cultural meanings wanes. Interestingly, celebrities who have been typecast (something most actors complain about) are more likely to have shared cultural meanings that can be associated with a product—Sylvester Stallone, for instance. Actress Meryl Streep, for example, may not be a desirable spokesperson because she has played such a wide variety of roles that she does not have a clear set of cultural meanings.

Sometimes the cultural meanings of celebrity spokespersons are related to their credibility and expertise concerning a product. For instance, Cher and Elizabeth Taylor promoted their own perfume brands, while Phil and Steve Mahre, the twin American ski racers, promoted K2 skis. In other cases, the celebrity's cultural meanings are not logically linked to the product, but the marketer hopes the general meanings of the celebrity as a credible and trustworthy person will help transfer important meanings to the product. Highlight 12.4 discusses some issues in using celebrities to promote one's products.

Marketers need to understand more about how celebrities transfer meaning to the product. What happens to the cultural meanings of celebrities who are disgraced (Ben Johnson is caught using steroids, Kobe Bryant is charged with sexual assault), fall from public favor (an actor plays poorly in several films), retire from public life (Michael Jordan stops playing basketball, Ingmar Bergman stops making films), or return to fame and favor as their celebrity status is partially renewed (Bob Dylan or Mickey Rooney)? How can marketers use such celebrities in transferring cultural meanings to their products and brands? Do consumers gain the meanings embodied by a celebrity merely by purchasing the endorsed brand, or are ritualistic behaviors necessary?

Although it is popular to criticize the North American and European fascination with celebrities as trivial and shallow, celebrities represent important cultural meanings that many consumers find personally relevant. By purchasing and using the product endorsed by the celebrity, consumers can obtain some of those meanings and use them in constructing a satisfying self-concept.

Helping Consumers Obtain Cultural Meanings

By understanding the role of rituals in consumer behavior, marketers can devise rituals that help transfer important cultural meanings from products to the customer. For instance, a real estate firm might develop an elaborate purchase ritual, perhaps including an exchange of gifts on the purchase occasion, to verify the transfer of the house, alongside its meanings, to the buyer. Some upscale clothing stores perform elaborate shopping and buying rituals for their affluent customers, including showing them to a private room, serving coffee or wine, and presenting a selection of clothes. When dining in a fine restaurant, people participate in many rituals that transfer special meanings, including being seated by the maitre d', talking to the wine steward, using various types of silverware and glasses, eating each course separately, and so on.

Finally, consider the strategies used by Nissan to create rituals for American buyers that help transfer meanings about its Infinity luxury car to consumers.[44] Dealers were supposed to gently welcome customers in Japanese style as honored guests

Highlight 12.4

Celebrity Endorsers

Many marketers use celebrity spokespersons to promote their products. Perhaps the world's hottest pitchman in 2001 was golf superstar Tiger Woods. According to one marketing expert, "There were three people for whom the American public has broad, powerful association: Bill Cosby, Colin Powell, and Michael Jordan. Now there are four." Woods' 1999 income totaled $47 million—and his golf winnings accounted for only a small fraction of that. When Woods became a professional in 1996, he signed a $40 million contract with Nike based on his tremendous success as an amateur. Over the next four years, Nike's relatively meager golf revenue grew from $100 million to $250 million. In May 2000, Nike owned 1.3 percent of the $1.5 billion golf ball market. By July, after Woods had won three major tournaments, Nike's share had jumped to 2.3 percent. Later that year, Nike rewarded Woods with a five-year contract extension worth $100 million, the richest deal ever for an active athlete. Woods also has lucrative deals with American Express, Wheaties, Rolex, and EA Sports, among others. There is even a seemingly incongruous agreement with Buick, which hopes the young, dynamic Woods can help change its cars' stodgy image and attract younger buyers. (The average Buick owner is 67 years old.)

Part of what makes stars like Woods so appealing to marketers is wholesome image and seemingly universal appeal. But the problem with celebrity endorsers is that they are indeed human. Some get in trouble with the law (consider Kobe Bryant or Mike Tyson) or have flamboyant personalities that limit their mainstream marketability (Dennis Rodman). One option is to use dead celebrities. For example, actor-dancer Fred Astaire has posthumously pitched vacuum cleaners, dance instruction videos, and condoms, while Marilyn Monroe has recently pushed perfume. Or a company can utilize inanimate "celebrities," as MCI did with Bugs Bunny and his Looney Tunes pals.

Among female stars, a very popular endorser is probably supermodel Cindy Crawford who has been seen in ads for Pepsi, Revlon, Kellogg, Omega watches, and FosterGrant sunglasses. Crawford's association with FosterGrant in 1999 helped revive a once hugely popular brand name as retailers' FosterGrant sales leaped anywhere from 15 percent to 100 percent from 1998 to 1999. Do you think Crawford and Tiger Woods will be able to remain such hot commodities for years to come? Is there a risk they could become oversaturated?

Sources: Becky Ebenkamp, "Fostering a Grant Tradition," *Brandweek,* January 24, 2000, pp. 26–29; Michael Bamberger, "Mining Woods for Gold," *Sports Illustrated,* September 25, 2000, p. 27; Becky Yerak, "Woods Gives Marketing Its $1 Billion Man," *Detroit News,* August 10, 2000, p. A1.

(not aggressively descend on the "mooches," a derogatory term for a naive customer used by some American car salespeople). Tea or coffee was to be offered, served on fine Japanese china. Each Infinity dealership was to have a special shoki-screened contemplation room where consumers could sit quietly with the car, "meditating" about their purchase and the consumer–product relationship. These rituals helped reinforce the low-pressure, relaxed meanings Nissan wanted to develop about the Infinity approach to car selling.

Cross-Cultural Influences

Foreign markets have become quite important for many businesses, including the U.S. film industry. Because domestic ticket sales were flat over the past decade (about 1 billion tickets per year), film companies have looked to foreign markets for growth. In 1996, U.S. film studios received from 35 to 50 percent of their total revenues from foreign markets.[45] Thus U.S. companies are under pressure to develop films that appeal to both U.S. and foreign consumers.

To develop strategies that are effective in different cultures, marketers have to understand the differences in cultural meanings in different societies. In this section, we examine **cross-cultural differences** in meanings and consider how they affect consumers in different societies. We also discuss how marketers can treat cross-cultural differences in developing international marketing strategies.

Cross-cultural differences do not always coincide with national borders. This is obvious in many countries where cultural differences among internal social groups are as great as between separate nations. Consider the former Soviet Union (with 15 republics and many large cultural differences), Belgium (two language cultures—Flemish and French), Canada (two language cultures—English and French), and Switzerland (German-, French-, Italian-, and Swiss-speaking regions). Understanding the cultural influences in such regions requires an analysis of subcultures, discussed in Chapter 13.

Likewise, national borders do not always demarcate clear cross-cultural differences. For instance, many people living on either side of the long Canadian–U.S. border share similar cultural characteristics (French-speaking Quebec is an exception). Likewise, people in southern Austria and northern Italy, or northern France and southern Belgium, share many similarities.

Cross-Cultural Differences

Marketers must consider cross-cultural differences when developing marketing strategies for foreign markets. We discuss a few of these differences here.

Differences in Consumption Culture   The level of consumption orientation in different markets is an important cross-cultural factor that companies should consider when developing international marketing strategies. Obviously, a large part of U.S. culture involves consumption activities. Many other areas of the world—including Canada, most Western European countries, and Japan—also have strong consumer cultures. Even in relatively poor countries, significant segments of society may have a developing consumer culture. For instance, India, Mexico, and many South American countries have a large middle class of consumers that can consume at significant levels. The Asian countries of the so-called Pacific Rim have a rapidly growing middle class with substantial spending power.

In much of the world, however, people have less opportunity to participate in a consumption culture. For instance, the ordinary citizens of many Eastern European countries, the former Soviet Union, China, and most Third World countries do not have sufficient purchasing power to consume at high levels, nor are these societies able to produce goods in sufficient number and variety to meet the consumption needs of their people.

Self-Concept   People in different cultures may have strikingly different concepts of themselves and how they should relate to other people.[46] Consider the differences between the vision of an independent self typical in North America and Western Europe and the concept of self as highly interrelated with others that is more common in Japan, India, Africa, South America, and even some southern European cultures.

Americans, with their strong individualistic orientation, tend to think of self in terms of personal abilities and traits that enable people to achieve the ideals of independence from others, freedom of choice, and personal achievement. In contrast, the Japanese tend to value a self that is sensitive to the needs of others, fits into the group, and contributes positively to the harmonious interdependence among the group members. These cross-cultural differences in self-concept are likely to affect how people in those cultures interpret product meanings and use products to achieve important ends in their lives. For example, Japanese gift-giving behavior is strongly affected by the socially oriented self-concept.

Especially when they return from trips abroad, the Japanese feel a rather strong social (cultural) obligation to bring souvenir gifts to the folks back home. This type of gift giving is called *omiyage*.[47] Friends, parents, siblings, and relatives are the typical recipients. A quick study of *omiyage* among Japanese tourists at the Los Angeles airport revealed 83 percent had bought *omiyage*, spending an average of $566 on such items compared to $581 on personal items. The number of people bought for was high (by American standards); 45 percent of Japanese tourists bought *omiyage* gifts for 15 or more people. Interestingly, although nearly 80 percent of the tourists mentioned that *omiyage* was a strong social norm in Japan, only 7 percent claimed to enjoy buying *omiyage*. Most treated it as a necessary chore. As for marketing strategies, it is important to know that the packaging and wrapping of *omiyage* gifts has important cultural meaning, partly because gifts are seldom opened in front of the giver. The appearance of the package is highly valued by Japanese consumers.

Aspects of American culture—jeans, music, and Coca-Cola—are a part of many cultures around the world   *Georg Gerster/Photo Researchers, Inc.*

The meanings of the end values or goals found in means–end research are likely to be quite different in different cultures, as are the means to achieve them. Consider the value of self-esteem or "satisfaction with self." North Americans, for instance, might satisfy self-esteem needs by acting in ways that represent their independence and autonomy from the group. But for the Japanese, cooperation with a group is an act that affirms the self. In Japan, giving in to the group is not a sign of weakness (as it might be interpreted in North America); rather, it reflects tolerance, self-control, flexibility, and maturity, all aspects of a positive self-image for most Japanese. In contrast, stating one's personal position and trying to get one's way (acts valued in America as "standing up for what one believes") may be thought childish and weak by the Japanese.

Similar Cross-Cultural Changes   It is becoming more common to find similar cultural changes occurring in many societies around the world at about the same time. For instance, the social roles for women in North American society have changed considerably over the past 20 years. As more women worked outside the home, their values, goals, beliefs, and behaviors have changed.[48] Similar changes have occurred around the world. Today's women in America and Europe, and increasingly in Japan and other countries, want more egalitarian marriages. They want their husbands to share in the housework and nurturing of children, and they want to establish a personal identity outside the family unit. These common cross-cultural changes have created similar marketing opportunities in many societies (for convenience products and time-saving services).

Everywhere people want more leisure and more free time. Even in Japan, where up to 60 percent of workers spend Saturdays on the job, are beginning to loosen up and relax a bit.[49] Although the traditional Japanese values of hard work, dedication, and respect for the established order are still dominant, some Japanese, especially among the young, are starting to see certain aspects of Western culture and lifestyles as preferable to their own.[50] For instance, as the Japanese become more consumption oriented and price conscious, the number of malls and discount stores is increasing rapidly.[51]

Materialism *Materialism* has been defined as the "importance a consumer attaches to worldly possessions."[52] Consumers with this value tend to acquire many possessions, which they see as important for achieving happiness, self-esteem, or social recognition (all prominent values in American culture). Although researchers disagree about its exact definition, **materialism** is a multidimensional value including *possessiveness, envy* (displeasure at someone else possessing something), and *nongenerosity* (unwillingness to give or share possessions).[53] Another study points to four dimensions of materialism: Possessions are symbols of success or achievement (prominent American values), sources of pleasure, sources of happiness, and representations of indulgence and luxury.[54] Materialistic values underlie the development of a mass consumption society, as we saw in the opening example, and in turn are stimulated by increasing consumption opportunities.

The United States is usually considered the most materialistic culture in the world. But a few studies suggest that Americans may not be more materialistic than European societies. For instance, one study found that consumers in the Netherlands had about the same level of general materialism as American consumers.[55] But interestingly, the Dutch consumers were more possessive than the Americans. Perhaps it is not accidental that the Dutch have no garage sales and flea markets are rare. Whereas U.S. consumers seem to replace old products with new ones fairly readily, the Dutch seem to form stronger relationships with their possessions.

Marketing Implications Marketers must determine which cross-cultural differences are relevant to their situations. A sensitivity to and tolerance for cross-cultural differences in meaning is a highly desirable trait for international marketing managers. Most international companies also hire managers from the local culture because they bring an intimate knowledge of the indigenous cultural meanings to strategic decision making.

Although cross-cultural differences can be large and distinctive, in some cases people seem to have rather similar values and consumer–product relationships. Some analysts see the entire world as moving toward an "Americanized" culture, although this is a controversial idea. (Highlight 12.5 discusses some examples of the exporting of American popular culture.) To the extent that common cultural meanings are becoming similar across societies, marketers should be able to develop successful strategies that are global in scope.

Developing International Marketing Strategies

Cross-cultural differences provide difficult challenges for international marketers. Even something that seems simple, such as translating a brand or model name into another language, can cause problems. When Coca-Cola was introduced in China in the 1920s, the translated meaning of the brand name was "bite the wax tadpole!"

Highlight 12.5

MTV around the World

In August 1999, 200,000 screaming young people packed Moscow's Red Square for an MTV concert featuring the Red Hot Chili Peppers. When MTV was founded in 1981, such a scene would have been unimaginable. However, the cable network has been remarkably successful in spreading music and popular culture to almost all corners of the planet.

At any given time, an estimated 2 million people are watching MTV, and 1.2 million of those viewers are located outside the U.S. The network predicts that overseas operations could provide more than half of its operating profit by 2006. However, breaking into international markets has not been without pitfalls. When MTV launched its first international channel in Europe in 1987, the MTV European kids saw wasn't all that different from the American version. The network sent a single feed, with English-speaking DJs, to all of Europe. It did not go over particularly well. MTV learned that each country had different tastes and that superstars with universal appeal, like Madonna and Michael Jackson, were the exception rather than the rule. According to MTV Networks' chairman Tom Freston, "We were going for the most shallow layer of what united viewers and brought them together." Today MTV delivers five feeds to Europe: one for the United Kingdom and Ireland; another for Germany, Austria, and Switzerland; one for Italy; one for Scandinavia; and a more general fifth feed for France, Greece, Belgium, and several other nations.

MTV has applied this formula around the world, with 22 different feeds customized for various markets. Although much of the programming is locally produced and up to 70 percent of the videos in most markets feature local music, MTV's omnipresence allows it to market celebrities and products on a worldwide scale. According to Latino entertainer Jennifer Lopez, an MTV favorite who has created a line of cosmetics and jeans, "The exposure that I get on MTV, and MTV internationally . . . I mean, you can't buy that kind of advertising." Corporations are noticing, too. Sales at Mexican Levi Strauss stores jumped 30 percent following a promotion advertised solely on MTV in Mexico. When liquor distributor Allied-Domecq wanted to boost flagging sales of Kahlua in Asia, it launched a major advertising push on MTV and became sole sponsor of *MTV Party Zone,* a dance show broadcast throughout the continent. The results? Brand awareness of Kahlua among adults age 30 and younger skyrocketed from 15 to 50 percent and sales tripled in some markets, despite the Asian economic crisis. Hollywood film studio MGM went a step further, forging a multimillion-dollar global partnership with MTV to promote the James Bond movie *The World is Not Enough.* MTV channels in Europe, Asia, Latin America, and the United States all featured programming, contests, and giveaways tied in with the film. An MGM executive remarked, "We were never able to do this before on a global basis."

MTV has its critics, of course, but it vehemently disagrees that it is spreading a homogeneous pop culture around the world. Instead, MTV claims the key to its international success is its local appeal. Perhaps both positions are true. In the future, we can expect to see more global corporations taking advantage of the network's influence among young consumers worldwide. In the words of a Compaq executive, "When you want to reach that audience, you can really only go with MTV."

Source: Brett Pulley and Andrew Tanzer, "Summer's Gemstone," *Forbes,* February 21, 2000, pp. 107–111.

Sales were not good, and the symbols were later changed to mean "happiness in the mouth." American Motors' Matador brand had problems in Puerto Rico because *matador* means "killer." Ford Motor Company changed the name of the Comet to Caliente when it introduced this car in Mexico. The low sales levels were understood when marketers realized that *caliente* is slang for "streetwalker." Sunbeam Corporation introduced its mist-producing hair curling iron in the German market under the name Mist-Stick, which translated meant "manure wand."[56]

American companies are not the only ones that have difficulty translating brand names. Chinese marketers had to seek help to find better brand names for several products they hoped to export, including "Double Happiness" bras, "Pansy" men's underwear, and "White Elephant" batteries.[57]

The above meanings illustrate how cross-cultural differences in language and related meanings can strongly affect the success of a marketing strategy. However, although differences in cultures can often be identified, marketers do not agree on how to treat these differences. There are at least three overall approaches, which we discuss next. First, a firm can adapt its marketing strategy to the characteristics of each culture. Second, a firm can standardize its marketing strategy across a variety of cultures. Arguments over which of these is the preferred strategy have been raging for more than 20 years in the literature on marketing and consumer behavior. Third, a firm can use a marketing strategy to change the culture.

Adapting Strategy to Culture

The traditional view of international marketing is that each local culture should be carefully researched for important differences from the domestic market. Differences in consumer needs, wants, preferences, attitudes, and values, as well as in shopping, purchasing, and consumption behaviors, should be carefully examined. The marketing strategy should then be tailored to fit the specific values and behaviors of the culture.

The *adaptation* approach advocates modifying the product, the promotion mix, or any other aspect of the marketing strategy to appeal to local cultures.[58] Black & Decker, for example, had to modify its hand tools because electrical outlets and voltages vary in different parts of the world. Philip Morris had to alter its ads for Marlboro cigarettes in Britain because the government believed British children are so impressed with American cowboys that they might be moved to take up smoking. Nestlé modified the taste of its Nescafé coffee and the promotions for it in the adjoining countries of France and Switzerland to accommodate different preferences in each nation.[59]

Standardizing Strategy across Cultures

This approach is often called **global marketing.** It argues for marketing a product in essentially the same way everywhere in the world. It is not a new idea; Coca-Cola has used this basic approach, called "one sight, one sound, one sell," for more than 40 years. Other companies, such as Eastman Kodak, Gillette, and Timex, have marketed standard products in essentially the same way for several decades.

Opinions of global marketing have varied over the past decade, but many marketers are beginning to treat the standardized approach more seriously. One of its major advocates is Professor Theodore Levitt of Harvard Business School. Levitt argues that because of increased world travel and worldwide telecommunications capabilities, consumers the world over are thinking and shopping increasingly alike. Tastes, preferences, and motivations of people in different cultures are becoming more homogeneous.[60] Thus, a common brand name, packaging, and communication strategy can be used successfully for many products. For example, given the international popularity of the *Dallas* TV show, actress Victoria Principal sold Jhirmack shampoo all over the world. Similarly, Victor Kiam sold his Remington shavers using the same pitch in 15 languages. Sales of Remington shavers went up 60 percent in Britain and 140 percent in Australia using this approach. Playtex marketed its WoW bra in 12 countries using the same advertising appeal.

Ads for Benetton emphasize the diversity of its customers
Courtesy of United Colors of Benetton. Photo: James Mollison.

One advantage of the standardized approach is that it can be much less expensive in terms of advertising and other marketing costs.[61] Executives at Coca-Cola once estimated that they save more than $8 million a year in the cost of thinking up new imagery. Texas Instruments runs the same ads throughout Europe rather than having individual ad campaigns for each country, and it estimates its savings at $30,000 per commercial. Playtex produced standardized ads for 12 countries for $250,000, whereas the average cost of producing a single Playtex ad for the United States was $100,000.[62]

Apparently a global (standardized) marketing approach can work well for some products. However, many marketers have severely criticized the global marketing approach.[63] We believe two issues cloud the debate between advocates of adapting versus standardizing international marketing approaches. First is the question of the nature of the product and how standardized the global approach is. For example, advocates of standardizing recognized that Black & Decker had to modify its products to suit local electrical outlets and voltages; yet they would argue the basic meaning and use of such products are becoming similar across cultures. If so, the same type of promotion campaign should work in different cultures.

Second, and perhaps more important, is the question of whether advocates of the standardizing approach are focusing on a long-term trend toward similarity across cultures or are suggesting that cultures are nearly identical today. Unlike the detractors of this approach, we believe that most advocates of global marketing have identified a long-term trend of increasing global homogeneity along many, but not necessarily all, dimensions. We also believe advocates are suggesting that marketers should be aware of this trend and adapt to it when appropriate. Thus, in essence, both sides are arguing that marketers should adapt to cultural trends, and there seems to be little disagreement between the two positions at this level.

Changing the Culture   The first approach we discussed argues for adapting marketing strategy to local cultures. The second approach argues that cross-cultural differences are decreasing and in some cases can be ignored. The third approach suggests that marketing strategies can be developed to influence the culture directly. As the cultural process model in Exhibit 12.3 shows, marketing does not simply adapt to consumers' changing cultural values and behaviors; marketing is also an active part of the cultural process.[64]

Marketing strategies both change and are changed by culture. For example, one long-run strategy may be to attempt to change cultural values and behaviors. Some years ago, Nestlé marketed vigorously to convince mothers in some Third World countries to change from breast-feeding to using the company's baby formula product. The campaign was very successful in persuading mothers that breast-feeding was not as healthful for their children as the company's formula, and it dramatically changed their feeding practices. Unfortunately, because of poor water sanitation and improper formula preparation, infant mortalities increased. Thus, the preference for and practice of breast-feeding had to be reinstilled in those countries, which was done successfully. This company changed cultural preferences and behaviors—and then changed them back—in a relatively short time.

Marketing Implications: The European Union

Marketers in the United States and elsewhere are adjusting to the **European Union (EU).** On January 1, 1993, the EU became a common market of approximately 325 million people. Originally a union of 12 European countries, the EU has grown as countries such as Sweden and Austria have joined (more members are expected). Creating the EU involved many changes, including reducing the technical barriers that have separated countries in Europe. Customs clearances and import duties are removed so goods and people can move freely across the borders, various regulations are standardized (size of trucks, tax levies), and legal requirements are becoming more similar.

Despite these changes, the considerable cross-cultural differences among the EU countries will not disappear. Perhaps the vision of a single European market (in terms of common cultural meanings) is premature. Each society is likely to retain its own language, tastes, cultural meanings, customs and rituals, and probably its own currency for some time into the future. In fact, some experts believe the economic union may accentuate existing cross-cultural differences. (Highlight 12.6 describes cross-cultural differences in driving habits.) More extreme forecasts predict a return to the Europe of "cultural regions" that existed before the nation–states of today were created. Examples of this possibility are the hostilities in Bosnia, the disintegration of the Soviet Union, and the difficulties in integrating eastern and western Germany. Everyone agrees, though, that marketers cannot look at Europe in the same way.

Marketing to the 113 million households in these diverse markets will take agile management. It will be difficult to develop standardized marketing strategies to sell products in all countries in Europe. Although some products may lend themselves to standardized strategies, others will require careful adaptation to local cultures.

Consider the problems faced by Sara Lee Company, a $12 billion food and consumer products company based in Chicago, as it studied its various European markets.[65] Sara Lee's European operation has a best-selling herbal bath soap in Great Britain called Radox, but it has not tried to sell it in other countries because of connotations with the name. Some European consumers confuse Radox with the bug killer Raid, and others think of Radox as something with a half-life and unsuitable to put on your skin. A similar situation exists for Sanex, a Spanish soap, promoted

High**light** 12.6

Cross-Cultural Driving Habits

Although some people still believe Europe will become one culture with the arrival of economic unity, the large and important cultural differences among the European countries will not go away. In fact, cross-cultural differences may intensify. Nowhere are Europe's rich cultural differences more clearly revealed than in people's behaviors behind the wheel of a car or the handlebars of a motorbike.

Cultural stereotypes probably have some basis in fact. The British and Japanese will wait patiently in traffic for hours, whereas Germans may become upset if held up for even a few minutes. In some countries it is an insult to be passed, and the polite drivers in the United Kingdom pull over to let speedier cars by. Many French and Italian drivers share a certain disdain for authority and the laws of the road. Germans may be somewhat aggressive and impatient, as the stereotype goes, but they follow the traffic rules. For instance, speed restrictions now found on many sections of the autobahn are followed rather strictly. But once that spot is passed, many German drivers take this to mean "go as fast as the car is capable." This can surprise the sedate British driver of an old Volkswagen, who can be very quickly overtaken by a huge Mercedes-Benz traveling at 130 mph.

In the safety-conscious Nordic countries, driving tests are difficult and sobriety is strictly enforced. Drivers in Norway and Finland tend to be competent and relatively placid. Enforcement of traffic laws is strict, with some fines contingent on one's income. The Swedes drive with their lights on at all times, day and night, as if anticipating the three-month winter night. In contrast, southern Europeans seem to have a more casual attitude toward the laws and driving speed, and reflect a greater propensity to take risks. In Greece, for instance, one can be surprised by a large truck traveling at high speeds down the center of a narrow mountain road. The many shrines along Greek roads give evidence of the gruesome toll.

Italian cities offer an exciting driving experience where aggressive jockeying for position in heavy traffic reminds many of a Grand Prix race. In Italy, a tiny Fiat 126 was spotted speeding recklessly down a steep mountain road. Several high-spirited teenagers were actually standing out of the tiny car's sunroof, waving wildly and laughing. Closer inspection revealed the driver was also out of the sunroof, standing on the dashboard and negotiating the mountain road with his bare feet on the steering wheel.

Will the new unified Europe create a new breed of driver with a standardized temperament? For driving, the values of the culture concerning life and death, and the macho values associated with the male ego, seem to be the key considerations. These end values seem likely to continue to vary considerably across European societies.

Source: Adapted from Tony Lewin, "What Drives Macho Mad?" *The European,* June 21, 1991, p. 17 (Elan section). Reprinted with permission of the author.

nearly everywhere in Europe but England. To the English, Sanex comes across as "sanitary," which connotes inappropriate meanings. The company faces similar problems in transferring popular U.S. brands, such as Hanes, L'Eggs, and Sara Lee, to European countries. For example, L'Eggs translates to *les oeufs* in French, which might not work very well.

But Sara Lee is developing pan-European marketing strategies for some of its products. For instance, its coffee brand, Douwe Egberts, was sold in seven countries in 1989 using various brand names. Sara Lee standardized the product's package sizes and color to emphasize the brand name and emblem. It used one standard television commercial, shown everywhere in Europe, that portrayed the coffee as a congenial drink that binds families together. Sara Lee managers hope the brand will eventually develop a true European identity.

Back To...

McDonald's . . . All Around the World

In the early 1980s, many experts believed McDonald's was too big and cumbersome to prosper in a mature economy. However, McDonald's has proven the critics wrong by operating a complex service business all around the world.

McDonald's elicits many different meanings in cultures around the globe. To many people in the United States today, McDonald's represents convenience and value. But in other nations—especially in Eastern Europe and in developing regions—McDonald's may represent much more. For many consumers, McDonald's golden arches symbolize America and the all the meanings that go with it: freedom, economic prosperity, achievement, and material comfort.

In the United States, eating at a McDonald's is a fairly routine experience, but in some nations consumers have developed rather unique consumption rituals that indicate McDonald's is indeed something special. When the first McDonald's opened in Moscow in 1990, people patiently waited in line for two hours to get in the door. Young couples dressed up and went there on dates. In China, when rural residents visit Beijing, they often don't consider their trip complete without a meal at McDonald's. They even keep their McDonald's cups and napkins as souvenirs of their meal.

McDonald's international success is based on its skill at adapting to the local culture while retaining the symbolic cultural meanings its restaurants already possess. Thus, while much of the menu is standard around the world, McDonald's is willing to offer some of the local favorite foods mentioned in the introduction. It also hires locals as managers and employees.

In some cases, McDonald's actually influences cultural change. In China, kids almost never ate out until the first McDonald's opened—and when they did eat out, they certainly didn't order their own food. Today Chinese children routinely march up to the McDonald's counter and place their orders. Also until recently, people in East Asia rarely paid much attention to birthdays. But thanks partly to McDonald's promotional efforts that include cake, gifts, and exclusive use of a special Ronald Room for the celebration, birthdays are now a significant event.

Of course, not all meanings attached to McDonald's are positive. In the both the United States and overseas, some regard the golden arches as a symbol of unhealthy, fatty food. In a partial response, McDonald's appointed a worldwide nutrition director in 2003 to encourage customers to eat smart. ❖

Summary   In this chapter, we examined the influences of culture and cross-cultural factors on consumers' affective responses and cognitions, behaviors and the physical and social environment. We defined culture as the meanings shared by people in a society (or in a social group) and discussed how marketers can study the content of culture. We identified several important values and lifestyle trends in American culture and drew some implications for marketing strategies. We presented a model of the cultural process by which cultural meaning is moved between different locations—especially from the environment to products and on from products to consumers. Then we examined the influences of cross-cultural differences on consumers. Finally, we discussed how marketers might use this knowledge to develop effective international marketing strategies.

Key Terms and Concepts

content of culture	**289**		culture	**288**
core values	**292**		European Union (EU)	**313**
cross-cultural differences	**307**		global marketing	**311**
cultural meaning	**288**		materialism	**309**
cultural process	**294**		rituals	**299**

Review and Discussion Questions

1. Define *culture* and contrast two approaches to cultural analysis: the content of the culture versus the cultural process.
2. Identify a major change in cultural values that seems to be occurring in your society (choose one not discussed in the book). Discuss its likely effects on consumers' affect, cognitions, and behaviors and on the social and physical environment.
3. Select a product of your choice and discuss two implications of your analysis in question 2 for developing marketing strategies for that product.
4. Briefly describe one example of a price, product, and distribution strategy that moves cultural meaning into the product (do not use examples cited in the text).
5. Select a print ad and analyze it as a mechanism for moving cultural meaning into the product.
6. Choose a popular celebrity endorser and analyze the meanings being transferred to the product endorsed.
7. Select a holiday other than Christmas—for example, Thanksgiving or Independence Day. Discuss the major cultural values reflected in this holiday celebration. What rituals did your family perform for this holiday, and how did they create meaning?
8. Think about what you do when getting ready to go out. Try to identify some grooming rituals you perform that involve certain products. How do you use some particular product (blow dryer, cologne, shampoo)? What implications might these rituals have for marketing this product?
9. Describe how possession rituals can transfer meaning from products to consumers.
10. Describe a personal experience in which you performed a divestment ritual. What personal meanings did you remove through the ritual?
11. Discuss how the three main approaches to dealing with cross-cultural factors in international marketing could be applied to the marketing of a soft drink such as Pepsi-Cola. Describe one problem with each approach. Which do you recommend?

Marketing Strategy in Action

Sony

In just over a half-century, Sony Corporation has gone from a 10-person engineering research group operating out of a bombed-out department store to one of the largest, most complex, and best-known companies in the world. Sony co-founders Masaru Ibuka and Akio Morita met while serving on Japan's Wartime Research Committee during World War II. After the war, in 1946, the pair got back together and formed Tokyo Telecommunications Engineering Corporation to repair radios and build shortwave radio adapters. The first breakthrough product came in 1950, when the company produced Japan's first tape recorder, which proved very popular in music schools and in courtrooms as a replacement for stenographers.

In 1953, Morita came to the United States and signed an agreement to gain access to Western Electric's patent for the transistor. Although Western Electric (Bell Laboratory's parent company) suggested Morita and Ibuka use the transistor to make hearing aids, they decided instead to use it in radios. In 1955, Tokyo Telecommunications Engineering Corporation marketed the TR-55, Japan's first transistor radio, and the rest, as they say, is history. Soon thereafter, Morita rechristened the company as Sony, a name he felt conveyed youthful energy and could be easily recognized outside Japan.

Today Sony is almost everywhere. Its businesses include electronics, computer equipment, music, movies, games, and even life insurance. It employs 190,000 people worldwide and does business on six continents. In 1999, Sony racked up sales of $63 billion; 31 percent of those sales came from Japan, 30 percent from the United States, and 22 percent from Europe. (To visit some of Sony's country-specific websites, go to **www.sony.com** and click on "Global Sites.")

Perhaps Sony's most famous product is the Walkman. Created in 1979, the Walkman capitalized on what some perceived as the start of a global trend toward individualism. From a technological standpoint, the Walkman was fairly unspectacular, even by 1979 standards, but Sony's marketing efforts successfully focused on the freedom and independence the Walkman provided. One ad depicted three pairs of shoes sitting next to a Walkman with the tag line "Why man learned to walk." By 2000 more than 250 million Walkmans had been sold worldwide, but Sony was concerned. Studies had shown that Generation Y (ages 14 to 24) viewed the Walkman as stodgy and outdated. So Sony launched a $30 million advertising and marketing campaign to reposition the product in the United States. The star of the new ads was Plato, a cool, Walkman-wearing space creature. The choice of a nonhuman character was no accident according to Ron Boire, head of Sony's U.S. personal-mobile products group. He wanted a character that would appeal to the broadest possible range of ethnic groups—thus, the space creature. Boire explains, "An alien is no one, so an alien is everyone."

Sony's current vision, however, extends far beyond the Walkman: to become a leader in broadband technologies. Sony looks forward to a day when all of its products—televisions, DVDs, telephones, game machines, computers, and so on—can communicate with one another and connect with the Web on a personal network. A Sony executive provides an example of such technology in action: "Say you are watching TV in the den, and your kids are playing their music way too loud upstairs," he says. "You could use your TV remote to call up an onscreen control panel that would let you turn down your kids' stereo, all without having to get up from your recliner."

Sony sees its new PlayStation2 filling a major role in the Internet of the future. In March 2000, Sony introduced the PlayStation2 in Japan and sold 1 million units within a week. *Newsweek* featured the PlayStation2 on its cover that spring, even though it wasn't offered in the United States until later in the year. Most consumers probably bought PlayStation2 to play video games, but its potential goes far beyond that. It is actually powerful enough to be adapted to guide a ballistic missile. Sony envisions consumers turning to the PlayStation2 for not only games but also movies, music, online shopping, and any other kind of digital entertainment currently imaginable. Ken Kutaragi, president of Sony Computer Entertainment, predicts the PlayStation2 will someday become as valuable as the PC is today: "A lot of people always assumed the PC would be the machine to control your home network. But the PC is a narrowband device that . . . has been retrofitted to play videogames and interactive 3-D graphics. The PlayStation2 is designed from the ground up to be a broadband device."

The PlayStation2 also reflects a changing attitude within Sony regarding partnerships with other companies. Toshiba helped Sony design the Emotion Engine, which powers the PlayStation2. In previous years, these kinds of alliances were the exception rather than the rule with Sony. Sony was perceived as arrogant because it rarely cooperated with other companies, preferring to develop and popularize new technologies on its own. Recently, however, that has changed. Sony has worked with U.S.-based Palm to develop a new hand-held organizer with multimedia capabilities, cooperated with Intel to create a set of standards for home networks, and launched a joint venture with Cablevision to build a broadband network in the New York metropolitan area. Nevertheless, some critics believe Sony remains too insular, looking on from the sidelines while other companies join forces to create entertainment powerhouses. Sony has no alliances with U.S. cable or television networks, raising some doubts about its ability to fully develop its home Internet services. Sony has talked with other music companies about possible joint ventures, but nothing has come to fruition.

Unlike many U.S.-based multinationals, Tokyo-based Sony traditionally has marketed itself on a regional rather than a global basis. For example, Sony has almost 50 different country-specific websites from which consumers can order products. However, there are signs that strategy may be changing, at least to some degree. Sony launched **www.Sonystyle.com**, a website that is the company's primary online outlet for selling movies, music, and electronic products. Sony also plans to provide product service and support on the site, and eventually software upgrades as well. The current main website (**www.sony.com**) is mainly a source for corporate and investor information. Also, in 1997 Sony embarked on a worldwide ad campaign designed to make itself and its products more relevant in the eyes of younger consumers. Ironically, much of Sony's future growth may come from its own backyard. The primary buyers of electronic and digital products are ages 15 to 40. It is estimated that by 2010, two-thirds of the people in the world in that age bracket will live in Asia. Tokyo is already a powerful influence on Asian culture. Asia's most popular youth magazines are published in Tokyo, and most of the music Asian young people listen to comes from Tokyo. So part of Sony's challenge is to continue to grow on a global scale while paying close attention to the burgeoning market at home.

Immediately following World War II and for some years thereafter, the label "Made in Japan" connoted cheap, shoddy, imitation products. Today, for many people, that same label stands for excellence and innovation. Certainly Sony can take much of the credit for that transformation. Now the question is whether Sony's products and marketing efforts can keep pace (or set the pace) in the upcoming age of digital convergence.

Discussion Questions

1. Identify and discuss some of the cultural meanings for Sony possessed by consumers in your country. Discuss how these cultural meanings were developed and how they influence consumers' behaviors (and affect and cognition). What is the role of marketing strategies in creating and maintaining (or modifying) these cultural meanings?

2. It is often stated that the world is becoming smaller because today people can communicate relatively easily across time and distance. Discuss whether that has been beneficial for Sony. What are some marketing challenges it presents?

3. What do you think about Sony's tradition of region-specific or nation-specific marketing? Would Sony be better served by working to create a more uniform global image?

4. What kinds of factors do you think Sony considers when deciding how to market its products in various countries? How might its American marketing efforts differ from those in Japan or Europe?

5. Describe the benefits Sony gets from some of the international alliances mentioned in this case study. Do you believe Sony needs to become more aggressive in forming such partnerships?

Sources: Brent Schlender, "Sony Plays to Win," *Fortune,* May 1, 2000, pp. 142–157; Evan Ramstad, "Backpacks with Speakers? Electronics Makers Court Jaded Gen Y—Big Ad Budget, Little Alien: Walkman's Plan for Reeling in the Ears of Wired Youths," *The Wall Street Journal,* May 18, 2000, p. B1; Janet Pinkerton, "Sony Founded on Friendship, Ambition," *Dealerscope,* January 2000, p. 16.

Subculture and Social Class

Mountain Dew

Although the can design has changed a lot, Mountain Dew looks and tastes basically the same today as it did 35 years ago. However, the people who drink Mountain Dew now are radically different. PepsiCo, Mountain Dew's parent company, has been very successful in its efforts to market the soft drink to a whole new generation of consumers—so successful that in 1999, Mountain Dew passed Diet Coke to become the third most popular soft-drink brand in the United States (after Coca-Cola and Pepsi-Cola), with a 7.2 percent share of the $58 billion soft-drink market.

Mountain Dew began as a regional brand before PepsiCo purchased it in 1964. Until the 1980s, it was proud of its image as a "hillbilly" drink; in fact, Mountain Dew marketers referred to their product as "zero-proof hillbilly moonshine." Vintage Mountain Dew cans and bottles featured a bearded mountaineer, with a pig at his feet, firing a shotgun in the general direction of an outhouse! In a long-running ad campaign, Mountain Dew bragged that it would "tickle your innards."

Today that backwoods image is long gone. The soft drink's recent success is based on its ability to connect to active young people—primarily males. Mountain Dew's advertising and promotions are directed toward teenagers, with a secondary market of 20- to 39-year-olds. In 1995, PepsiCo launched the "Do the Dew" campaign. Commercials featured cool teens on mountain bikes, skateboards, and snowboards, all the while (of course) enjoying the refreshing taste of Mountain Dew. The campaign continues in that same vein today. "The brand is all about exhilaration and energy," according to Scott Moffit, director of marketing for Mountain Dew. "We have a very crystal-clear, vivid positioning."

Indeed, so-called "extreme" sports are a major part of the Mountain Dew lifestyle and image. The soft drink has sponsored ESPN's X Games and NBC's Gravity Games, and has attached its name to events at numerous skate parks around the United States. It even has its own team of extreme athletes competing in

Courtesy of Mountain Dew.

skateboarding, BMX racing, freestyle skiing, and other nontraditional sports.

You can also find Mountain Dew associated with more mainstream events like the Super Bowl and the NCAA basketball tournament, although the brand's marketers are careful that the advertising you see in connection with these high-profile events cultivates the same active, youthful, cutting-edge Mountain Dew image. Mountain Dew does not want young people to think it has "sold out." As one executive says, marketing to a more mainstream audience is fine, but "We don't want to do it in a way that makes our core customers question us."

Now the challenge for Mountain Dew is to explore other growth markets without losing its core group of drinkers. Latino and African American youth have traditionally favored Mountain Dew's archrival, Sprite (manufactured by Coca-Cola). Moffit admits ethnic consumers generally don't care much about extreme sports, so Mountain Dew is hoping music will prove a more inviting lure. In addition to rolling out a series of ads featuring popular hip-hop artist Busta Rhymes, it sponsored the "Dew Pirate Radio Tour" in 22 cities during the summer of 2000. The tour was a party on wheels, with club DJs mixing fast-paced urban beats in the shadow of a brightly colored Mountain Dew van. On the Mountain Dew website (**www.mountaindew.com**), you can listen to music not only from alternative artists like Staind and The Mighty, Mighty Bosstones but also hip-hop stars like Sisqo and Wu-Tang Clan.

Sources: Theresa Howard, "Being True to Dew," *Brandweek,* April 24, 2000, pp. 28–31; Greg Johnson, "Mountain Dew Hits New Heights to Help Pepsi Grab a New Generation," *Los Angeles Times,* October 9, 1999, pp. C1, C7; **www.mountaindew.com**.

This example illustrates the marketing importance of a major subculture in the United States (and many other countries, too) and how changing demographic characteristics can affect marketing strategy. In this chapter, we discuss two aspects of the macro social environment: subcultures and social class. In Chapter 11 you learned that culture, subculture, and social class are three levels of the macro social environment. The size of these social groups is a key distinction.

Culture is usually analyzed at the level of a country or an entire society; subcultures are segments of the society. Social class can be considered a special subculture defined in terms of social status. Subcultures and social classes are cultural groups in that their members share common cultural meanings; however, both are part of the larger society and thus are influenced by the overall culture. Thus, we would not expect middle-class Germans to have the same meanings, behaviors, and lifestyles as middle-class Americans. Social class and subcultures are useful for segmenting markets, understanding the shared cultural meanings of large groups of consumers, and developing targeted marketing strategies.

We begin the chapter by discussing the concept of subcultures. Next, we describe several important subcultures found in the United States (and elsewhere in the world) and draw implications for marketing strategy. Then we examine the concept of social class by describing the social class structure of U.S. society.

Subcultures

Subcultures are distinctive groups of people in a society that share common cultural meanings for affective and cognitive responses (emotional reactions, beliefs, values, and goals), behaviors (customs, scripts and rituals, behavioral norms), and environmental factors (living conditions, geographic location, important objects). Although most subcultures share some cultural meanings with the overall society and/or other subcultures, some of a subculture's meanings must be unique. Highlight 13.1 describes a distinctive subculture.

Major demographic changes occurring in the United States and other countries make the analysis of subcultures more important than ever. For instance, the U.S. population is aging (in 2000, the median age was 36, three years older than in 1990).[1] Also, many societies are becoming more culturally diverse, partly through increased immigration of people from other cultures. About 20 percent of Americans were members of minority groups in the early 1980s; by 2010, this will climb to about 30 percent. The overall culture in the United States is influenced by these different subcultural groups, each with unique perspectives and cultural meanings. To understand this diversity, marketers identify subcultures and try to develop marketing strategies to address their needs.

Marketers have used a variety of mostly demographic characteristics to identify subcultures. Exhibit 13.1 lists several demographic characteristics used to classify people into subgroups and gives examples of subcultures. These subcultures are not mutually exclusive; a person can simultaneously be black, middle class, a male, and a resident of the northwestern United States with a moderate income. Marketers can combine demographic distinctions to identify smaller and more narrowly defined subcultures (affluent black consumers living in the South).

Analyzing Subcultures

As with culture, subcultures can be analyzed at different levels. Subcultural analysis is often done in stages. First, a broad subculture is identified based on some general demographic characteristics (black Americans, elderly Japanese, middle-income Italians). Then, depending on the marketing purpose, this broad group can

Highlight 13.1

A "Not-so-Hidden" Subculture

The gay subculture has demographics that marketers would normally find attractive. The estimated 20 million homosexuals in the United States are, on average, younger, more affluent, and better educated than the average American, and represent a $514 billion market. The average income in gay households is more than $55,000, while 70 percent have at least a college education. Moreover, 89 percent of gays say they are more likely to buy a product if advertising is targeted to them. Historically many companies have been reluctant to market specifically to gays; however, that is changing.

Corporations have feared that by appealing to gays, they risked a backlash from conservative groups and homophobic consumers. Indeed, Disney was the target of a boycott when it sponsored an all-gay day at its theme parks and began to offer benefits for domestic partners of gay employees. However, mainstream America generally seems to have become more tolerant of the gay lifestyle. Hollywood stars like Ellen DeGeneres have "come out," Congress has openly debated the legalization of gay marriages, and it is increasingly common to see gay characters in prime time network television shows.

As part of this trend, more companies are taking steps to appeal directly to gay consumers. Some have taken a subtle approach. Subaru hired openly lesbian tennis star Martina Navratilova as a corporate spokesperson. The carmaker's ads have also featured license plates that would probably pass unnoticed by most people but are designed to catch the attention of the gay audience. For example, one plate read "XENA LVR" (Xena Lover), a reference to a television character with a huge lesbian following. Furniture maker Mitchell Gold ran a pink-framed ad in the *New York Times* that showed two men on a couch with a little girl nearby and the tag line "A kid deserves to feel at home." Even IBM got into the act with an ad showing two businessmen and the words "We're not your typical Mom & Pop operation."

Other companies have taken an even more forthright approach. Breweries and distilleries have aggressively pursued the gay dollar for years, running scores of print ads in gay publications like *Advocate* and *Out*. United Airlines launched a print campaign as part of its stated quest to become the "official airline" of the gay community. Another avenue for reaching the gay community is the Internet. That is especially true for baby boomers and older people who traditionally don't read many gay-oriented magazines and newspapers. According to a Greenfield Online study, 65 percent of gay Internet users go online more than once a day, and 71 percent of them make online purchases. Some of the website **Gay.com**'s clients have included TBS Superstation, General Motors, Saturn, and eBay.

Coming on board next may be large consumer products companies. Currently most of those that advertise in gay publications and on gay websites are targeting disposable income, pushing high-ticket or luxury items. But in the words of one magazine executive, "Advertisers don't seem to realize that gay people wash their clothes."

Sources: Michael Adams, "Promophobia," *Incentive,* September 1999, pp. 88–90; Rachel X. Weissman, "Gay Market Power," *American Demographics,* June 1999, pp. 32–34; Jennifer Gilbert, "Ad Spending Booming for Gay-Oriented Sites," *Advertising Age,* December 6, 1999, p. 58.

be further segmented into subsubcultures based on other demographic characteristics (affluent, middle-income, or poor Americans; elderly Japanese who are healthy versus those who are ill; middle-income Italians living in large cities or those in small towns). If deemed necessary, the segmentation process could continue, creating ever smaller and more precisely defined subcultures.

Careful research and thoughtful analysis are necessary to develop a clear understanding of subcultures. Consider the confusion about so-called yuppies (young urban professionals). Originally a narrow subcultural group, yuppies gradually came

Exhibit 13.1

Types of Subcultures

Demographic Characteristic	Examples of Subcultures
Age	Adolescents, young adults, middle aged, elderly
Religion	Jewish, Catholic, Mormon, Buddhist, Muslim
Race	Black, Caucasian, Asian
Income level	Affluent, middle income, poor, destitute
Nationality	French, Malaysian, Australian, Canadian
Gender	Female, male
Family type	Single parent, divorced/no kids, two parents/kids
Occupation	Mechanic, accountant, priest, professor, clerk
Geographic region	New England, Southwest, Midwest
Community	Rural, small town, suburb, city

to mean rich, selfish youths and, because of intense media attention through the 1980s, became virtually synonymous with the baby boomer generation. However, the best estimates counted only about 4 million yuppies, a mere 5 percent of the baby boomers.[2]

Subculture analysis can follow the same approach as cultural analysis, discussed in Chapter 12. Typically marketers examine the *content of the subculture* by describing the cultural meanings shared by members of the subculture (especially their values and lifestyles). It is much less common for marketers to examine the *cultural processes* by which cultural meanings "move" from the external world of the subculture to products and services on to the people in the subculture.

In analyzing a subculture, marketers seek to identify the typical characteristics, meanings, a1nd behavioral tendencies shared by people in those groups. Despite sharing some qualities, however, most subcultures are quite diverse. The media tend to characterize members of a subculture in the same way (blacks are poor ghetto residents; elderly people are doddering and ill), but this can be a major mistake in developing marketing strategies. Members of a black or elderly subculture are quite different. For example, marketers have identified a subgroup of "young" elderly people, called "Opals," who think and act younger than their years, have money to spend, and are healthy enough to do so.[3] In sum, it is difficult to identify a "typical" person in a subculture.

The task for marketers is to determine what level of analysis is appropriate for the problem (how fine should the distinctions be?) and develop marketing strategies for that level. Consider Maybelline's strategy in developing the cosmetic line Shades of You for women with dark skin.[4] The company recognized that women of color (mostly blacks and darker-skinned Hispanics) have different skin tones and thus need different cosmetics. For instance, blacks have about 35 different skin colors compared to about 18 for whites. Maybelline spent considerable effort and money developing the proper formulas for 12 shades of liquid makeup and 8 blushes. Sold in drugstores and supermarkets at the lower end of the price scale, the product was almost immediately a hit with dark-skinned women.

Some marketers create products specifically for subcultural groups such as this line of cosmetics for African American consumers *Reprinted with permission of Maybelline, Inc.*

Geographic Subcultures

Americans like to think of their country as a melting pot, but the mass American market is a myth for many product categories.[5] In different parts of the United States, the physical environment (topography, climate, natural resources) and social environment (economics, population demographics, lifestyles) are quite different, and these factors affect the culture and buying behavior.[6] In reality the United States is a polycultural nation, a mosaic of submarkets and subcultures. In some ways, Boston and Houston are as different as Hamburg (Germany) and Milan (Italy).

Marketers may find it easier to accept Europe and Latin America as separate cultural regions than to recognize Arizona, Texas, and Louisiana as different markets. For example, product ownership varies widely across the nation. Consumers in California own a much higher percentage of foreign cars than their counterparts in the Midwest or South. Very few brands enjoy uniform sales across the country. Many national brands get 40 to 80 percent of their sales in a core region, but they are specialty brands (with lower market shares) in other areas of the country. In the mid-1980s, for instance, Ford pickups were the favorite in a number of northwestern states, whereas Chevy pickups dominated in many southern states.[7] Wonder Bread sells best in New York (for reasons unknown), whereas snack nuts sell best in Portland, Maine. Seattle leads in sales of "healthy" foods such as Cheerios and is also tops in Hershey's chocolate bars. Coping with this diversity requires attention to regional subcultures.

There are many ways to analyze the United States in terms of **geographic subcultures.** In one creative approach, Joel Garreau divided the North American continent into nine geographic areas that he labeled the "nine nations" of North America.[8] U.S. marketers concentrate on the eight areas shown in Exhibit 13.2. Garreau argued that a variety of environmental factors—including economic, social, cultural, political, topographical, and natural resource factors—combine to form these nine areas. The exhibit also summarizes the "personalities" of these areas.

Despite criticisms, this framework may be useful for some products and services in developing specific marketing strategies to appeal to consumers in each area. For example, preferences for and consumption of various beverages vary dramatically in different geographic areas of the United States, and analysis of cultural differences in these regions may help determine which beverages can be marketed most effectively.[9]

Borderland Regions   As we emphasized in Chapter 12, cultural and subcultural differences do not always coincide with national (or other artificial) boundaries. Consider the so-called borderlands along the 2,000-mile border between Mexico and the United States.[10] About 5.2 million people (35 percent Hispanic) live in 25 borderland counties in California, New Mexico, Arizona, and Texas that have grown about 30 percent since 1980. Another 3 million people live on the Mexico

Exhibit 13.2

Eight "Nations" of the United States

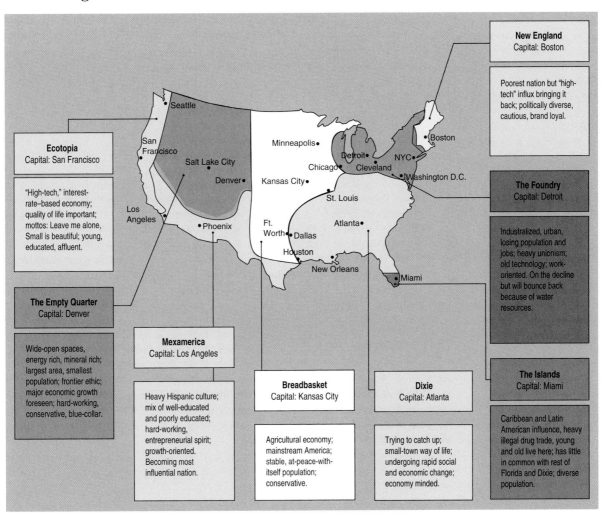

New England
Capital: Boston

Poorest nation but "high-tech" influx bringing it back; politically diverse, cautious, brand loyal.

Ecotopia
Capital: San Francisco

"High-tech," interest-rate–based economy; quality of life important; mottos: Leave me alone, Small is beautiful; young, educated, affluent.

The Foundry
Capital: Detroit

Industrialized, urban, losing population and jobs; heavy unionism; old technology; work-oriented. On the decline but will bounce back because of water resources.

The Empty Quarter
Capital: Denver

Wide-open spaces, energy rich, mineral rich; largest area, smallest population; frontier ethic; major economic growth foreseen; hard-working, conservative, blue-collar.

Mexamerica
Capital: Los Angeles

Heavy Hispanic culture; mix of well-educated and poorly educated; hard-working, entrepreneurial spirit; growth-oriented. Becoming most influential nation.

Breadbasket
Capital: Kansas City

Agricultural economy; mainstream America; stable, at-peace-with-itself population; conservative.

Dixie
Capital: Atlanta

Trying to catch up; small-town way of life; undergoing rapid social and economic change; economy minded.

The Islands
Capital: Miami

Caribbean and Latin American influence, heavy illegal drug trade, young and old live here; has little in common with rest of Florida and Dixie; diverse population.

Source: Map from *The Nine Nations of North America.* Copyright © 1980 by Joel Garreau.

side. The borderlands constitute a geographic subculture with significant marketing potential.

Consider the area called *Los Dos Laredos* (the two Laredos): Laredo, Texas, and Nuevo Laredo, Mexico. Although separated by the Rio Grande River, residents on both sides give little thought to the border as they freely cross the bridges to shop, work, and enjoy themselves. A bank official puts it this way: "We're not the United States and we're not Mexico. We're different. We think we gather the best of both cultures." According to one citizen, "We're more like Minneapolis and Saint Paul than the U.S. and Mexico, because we are the same people."

The borderlands are an important regional market even though the overall demographics are downscale (people have lower-than-average incomes). The U.S. side is swelled by thousands of Mexican citizens who cross the border to work and spend their pesos. Although some shopping areas are bordertown tacky, Laredo's new retailing centers contain chain stores like Wal-Mart, Sam's Club, and HEB of California. Successful marketing strategies recognize the Hispanic culture as the major influence in the borderlands. For instance, many of the signs and store names are in Spanish, prices are often given in both pesos and dollars, and most stores accept either currency. Because Hispanic families tend to be large, grocery stores usually stock big sizes, including 50-pound sacks of rice.

Age Subcultures

Age groups can also be analyzed as subcultures because they often have distinctive values and behaviors. However, marketers must be cautious about segmenting consumers based on their actual age. Many adult American consumers think of themselves as 10 to 15 years younger than they really are.[11] Thus, their behaviors, affect, and cognitions are more related to their psychological age than to their chronological age. Consider this statement from an 89-year-old woman: "I might be 89 years old, but I feel good. I feel like I could fly the coop. I do. I feel younger, like I'm 45 or 50. I want to doll up, and I like to fuss. . . . I don't know I'm old. I feel like I'm going to live a long time." This suggests marketers should analyze subjective or "cognitive age" (the age one thinks of oneself as being) rather than chronological or actual age. Many different **age subcultures** can be identified and analyzed, but we will discuss only three here: teens, baby boomers, and the mature market.

The Teen Market   The American teenage population has been gaining affluence while fluctuating in size.[12] In the mid-1980s, there were about 26 million people in the United States ages 13 to 19. This number decreased to about 25 million in the mid-1990s and increased to about 27 million by 2000. Teens are important not only because they have a major influence on household purchases but also because of their own discretionary purchasing power. Teenagers spent more than $115 billion in 2000.

Several studies have found that teenagers do a large portion of the grocery shopping for the family: Estimates are that from 49 to 61 percent of teenage girls and 26 to 33 percent of teenage boys frequently perform this task. In addition, about 60 percent of teens help make the supermarket shopping list, and 40 percent select some of the brands to be purchased. It is no wonder that brand-name food marketers advertise in magazines such as *Seventeen*.

Brand loyalty has also been found to form early among teenage shoppers. In a survey of women ages 20 to 34, at least 30 percent said they made a brand decision as a teenager and continued to use the brand to the present. Sixty-four percent said they looked for specific brands when they were teenagers. Thus, a final reason this market is so important for many products and services is the potential to develop brand loyalty that may last a lifetime. However, marketing certain products to teens, such as R-rated films, is highly controversial, as Highlight 13.2 describes. Highlight 13.3 describes the importance of the Internet for teenagers.

Baby Boomers   **Baby boomers** are people born between 1946 and 1964. In 2000, there were about 80 million people in this group—roughly a third of the U.S. population. Boomers are in their early 40s to late 50s and in their prime earning

Highlight 13.2

The Movie Industry Targets Kids

For years the Motion Picture Association of America has operated with a rating system designed to protect kids from violent, sexually explicit, or otherwise inappropriate movies. However, some critics say the way in which the industry has marketed its movies has undermined its own rating system.

For example, children under 17 cannot attend R-rated films unless accompanied by an adult. Nonetheless, Sony's Columbia Pictures tried unsuccessfully to advertise the R-rated Bruce Willis film *The Fifth Element* on the kids' cable network Nickelodeon. In an attempt to publicize its R-rated science fiction movie *Mimic,* Disney's Miramax unit gave away promotional posters to the Boy Scouts and a Boys and Girls Club in the Kansas City area. In addition, a study by the Parents' Television Council revealed that during a three-week span in 2000, 83 percent of movie commercials aired on network television between 8 and 9 PM (the prime family viewing hour) were for R-rated films.

Studios have even included kids in their market research. Columbia Tristar sounded out a group of 50 children ages 9 to 11 about their thoughts on a sequel to *I Know What You Did Last Summer,* a film featuring a serial killer who slashes victims with an ice hook. MGM/United Artists screened commercials for the R-rated thriller *Disturbing Behavior* before a group of four hundred 12- to 20-year-olds. The research results showed their favorite scene was one in which a woman smashes her head into a mirror.

Moreover, it isn't just R-rated films about which critics are upset. A PG-13 rating serves as a warning to parents that a movie may contain violence or language that may be unsuitable for children under 13. However, some studios have created toy tie-ins to promote their PG-13 films. These toy tie-ins reach children as young as 4 years of age.

The studios admit their critics make some valid points, but they argue there are two sides to the story. For instance, the firm that conducted the research for the *I Know What You Did Last Summer* sequel says that it made economic sense to interview 9-, 10-, and 11-year-olds because kids that age made up a large portion of the audience for the original movie. Furthermore, industry executives maintain it is impossible to make sure young children don't see any advertising for R-rated films. Plus, they say some films, despite their R-ratings, are quite suitable for young audiences. They point specifically to the World War II movie *Saving Private Ryan,* starring Tom Hanks, and *Amistad,* which deals with the brutality of the American slave trade.

Do you believe the movie industry has behaved ethically in the way it has promoted its films to kids? Or are executives overstepping their bounds? Should some kind of mandatory restrictions be in place to protect children from advertising for potentially inappropriate films?

Sources: Glenn Simpson, Bruce Orwell, and Jill Carroll, "Studios Concede Bad Judgment on Ads," *The Wall Street Journal,* September 28, 2000, p. B14; Doreen Carvajal, " 'R' Films Tested on Youths; Memos Reveal Marketing Ploys Involving Kids as Young as 9," *Denver Post,* September 27, 2000, p. A-1; Greg Schneider, "Studios Make Limited Vow on Violence; Guidelines Received Coolly on Hill," *Washington Post,* September 28, 2000, p. A-1.

and spending years. The baby boomer market is the largest and most affluent in history and will have a major economic impact for the next 40 years.[13] In 1997, the boomer age group spent more than $1.5 trillion. Over the next decade or so, baby boomers will account for about half of all discretionary spending.[14]

Although the baby boomer subculture is extremely diverse, some general characteristics have been identified. The group is characterized as having a blend of "me-generation" and old-fashioned family values and as strongly influencing the values of other groups.[15] A study by the Cadwell Davis Partners ad agency found that many people who aren't baby boomers feel as if they are. Baby boomers emphasize health and exercise, and have reduced their consumption of cigarettes, coffee, and

This ad is intended to appeal to teens and young adults
Courtesy of J. Crew.

strong alcoholic beverages. Forty-six percent of this market has completed college and two-thirds of baby boomer wives work, compared with about half the wives in the rest of the population. In terms of products, this group emphasizes quality and is far less concerned with bargain hunting than their parents were.

Baby boomers have a strong impact on markets for housing, cars, food, clothing, cosmetics, and financial services. For instance, nearly one-fourth of boomers are single, creating strong markets for vacations and convenience packaged goods. In addition, although they are having fewer children per household, the sheer size of the boomer group led to an increase in births in the 1990s—a "baby boom echo." Boomers who are new parents are especially attractive to marketers. Given the large incomes and small family sizes of this group, spending per child is likely to be the largest in history. Markets for children's products have expanded accordingly. Toy sales, for example, are expected to increase more than twice as fast as the population of children for whom they are intended. Other markets, such as child care services and computer software for tots, may double in the next few years.

The baby boomer market, then, is the most lucrative and challenging marketers have ever seen. Many firms have designed new products and redesigned and repositioned old ones for this market. Wheaties used to appeal to kids as "the breakfast of champions"; now it is promoted to adults with such slogans as "what the big boys eat." Commercials for Snickers candy bars show adults rather than children eating this candy for a snack. Crest and other brands have introduced toothpaste formulas to fight plaque, an adult problem. Levi Strauss has redesigned its jeans to give a little extra room in the seat to accommodate "booming boomer bodies." Even Clearasil, traditionally an antiacne medication for teenagers, has developed Clearasil Adult Care to appeal to the growing number of baby boomer adults with skin problems.

The Mature Market As America ages (similar trends are occurring in other industrialized countries such as Japan and most European nations), marketers have recognized the economic importance of the mature market, defined as consumers over age 55.[16] Because the mature market is quite diverse, marketers often consider smaller subcultural groups based on narrower age ranges, such as older (55 to 64), elderly (65 to 74), aged (75 to 84), and very old (85 and over). The mature market is one of the most rapidly growing subcultures in American society. In 2000 there were 35 million consumers over 65, up from 30 million in 1987. Nearly 80 percent of the current U.S. population is expected to live until their late 70s. At present, about one in four Americans is older than 50; by 2020, about one-third will be. Between now and 2020, the number of people age 50 or older will increase by 74 percent (as baby boomers continue to age), whereas the number

Highlight 13.3

Reaching the Internet Subculture

For almost as long as people have been buying and selling things, consumers have relied heavily on word of mouth to help them decide what to purchase. Today word of mouth has gone high-tech. Many companies have recognized that young people tend to be very cynical about slick, well-packaged advertising campaigns. So they are going online with "grassroots" campaigns designed to get kids to talk to one another about how cool their products are.

On the surface it is a relatively simple concept. Firms search Internet chat rooms and special-interest bulletin boards in search of kids who are into movies, music, shoes, or whatever the company is selling. They then offer these young people free products—CDs, posters, or movie tickets—to get them to talk up specific products online. The low-budget 1999 movie *The Blair Witch Project* demonstrated how effective so-called viral marketing could be. Made for just $35,000, *Blair Witch* took in more than $250 million in box office receipts worldwide, thanks in large part to an elaborate website and tons of positive comments made in chat rooms by young people who had been treated to screenings of the movie.

Electric Artists charges $40,000 per month to recruit cyber spokespeople. Its clients have included Imagine Entertainment, Paramount Pictures, and Wenner Media (publisher of *Rolling Stone* magazine). For example, in 2000, Wenner Media wanted to create a buzz about an upcoming *Rolling Stone* issue that featured the pop band 'N Sync on the cover. It retained Electric Artists to e-mail images of the cover to 100,000 teenagers. Within days, 3,000 of those young fans had pasted the cover onto their own websites.

These efforts are most likely to be successful for things kids like to talk about—primarily movies and music. But even some apparel makers have gotten into the act. Timberland has hired a team of youngsters to stop by music and television chat rooms and chime in with "I just saw the hottest apparel online . . . "

Internet patter campaigns are not without questions. Often it is difficult to track how successful such campaigns really are, and they may not work with all products. For example, one company that recruits cyber pitchfolk rejected a six-figure offer from Mazda because they didn't think Mazda was "cool" enough to benefit from this kind of Internet word of mouth. Finally, how long will it be until teens begin to cast a cynical eye at these pitches, and dismiss them as just another form of slick marketing?

Sources: Peter Kafka, "Talk is Cheap," *Forbes,* April 17, 2000, p. 150; Michael McCarthy, "The Blair Web Project," *Brandweek,* November 15, 1999, pp. 56–60.

under age 50 will increase by only 1 percent.[17] In 2020, there could be as many as 58 million elderly (over 65) or as few as 48 million, according to the U.S. Census Bureau. The exact number of older Americans expected in 2020 is hard to predict; it all depends on the mortality rate, especially gains made against specific diseases such as heart ailments, cancer, and stroke.

The next century will see huge increases in demand for products and services for older consumers, including adult day care; home health care; prescription and over-the-counter drugs; medical care of all types; and foods low in cholesterol, sugar, salt, and calories. Other nonhealth-related products include planned vacation travel, restaurants, recreational vehicles, and hotels and motels. Recognizing that extended families will be larger, theme parks such as Six Flags–Great America created packages for grandparents, parents, and grandkids as a group. Older people are better educated than previous generations, which creates increased demand for educational programs, books, and news.

Traditionally marketers have ignored the mature market, perhaps because it was assumed to have low purchasing power. However, in addition to its sheer size, the

Targeting the mature market
Courtesy Leo Burnett/Singapore; Art Director: Andrew Bell; Copywriter: Martin Lee; Photographer: Paul Torcello.

economic character of this market deserves careful consideration. Although many members of this group no longer work, they often have considerable discretionary income. Unlike younger groups, members of mature markets are usually free of most of the financial burdens associated with child rearing, mortgages, and furnishing a household. Given these differences, per capita discretionary income is higher for the mature group than for any other age group—about 50 percent of the nation's total.[18]

It is also important to recognize how the mature market is changing. In 1985, only 9 percent of the elderly had a college degree and only 44 percent had graduated from high school. By 1995, the share of older people with college educations rose to more than 12 percent, and at least one-fourth had some college. The mature market is becoming more educated and thus has greater incomes. Increases in income will also come about because many of those in tomorrow's mature market will benefit from pension and retirement plans.

Finally, because many people in the mature market subculture are retired, they have more time to enjoy entertainment and leisure activities. Although this market historically has spent more money on food for home consumption than away-from-home consumption, restaurants now cater to them with senior citizen discounts, early-bird dinners, and menus designed for the tastes and requirements of older people.

The elderly represent a significant market for skin care products, vitamins and minerals, health and beauty aids, and medications that ease pain and promote the performance of everyday activities. In addition, they are a significant market for condominiums in the Sunbelt states, time-share arrangements, travel and vacations, cultural activities, and luxury items given as gifts to their children and grandchildren. Overall, then, the mature market subculture represents an excellent marketing opportunity that will become even better in the future.[19]

Developing marketing strategies that appeal to consumers in the mature market is more difficult than it looks.[20] Few companies are experts at it. Many marketers have inaccurate perceptions of this large and diverse group, including persistent images of frail, stubborn, and indigent people who, if not confined to bed, are tottering around on canes. Yet only 5 percent of Americans over 65 are institutionalized. People are staying healthy and active much later into their lives than ever before.

Some ads are beginning to use themes and models that older consumers can identify with. No longer depicted as weak and doddery, older people are shown doing the things they do in real life: working, playing tennis, falling in love, and buying cars. McDonald's, for instance, was a forerunner in this style with its "Golden Years" spots that showed an elderly man and woman meeting for lunch at McDonald's and an elderly man on his first day of work at McDonald's.

Ethnic Subcultures

In the past two decades, the ethnic makeup in the United States has changed dramatically.[21] In 1980 one of every five Americans was a member of a minority group. In 1990 one in four Americans claimed to have either Hispanic, Asian, African, or Native American ancestry. The increases were unequal across **ethnic subcultures** because of different immigration patterns and birth rates. For instance, the Asian subculture grew 80 percent during the 1980s, compared to increases of 4.4 percent in the white population, 14 percent for blacks, and 39 percent for Hispanics. Increases in these minority subcultures are expected to continue so that by 2010 about one-third of American children will be black, Hispanic, or Asian.[22]

Marketers must recognize that ethnic diversity is not distributed equally across the United States.[23] The most ethnically diverse regions in the country are in the Southwest and the South; the least diverse are in the Midwest, where the proportion of whites may exceed 90 percent. The most ethnically diverse county in the nation is San Francisco, with approximately equal proportions of whites, blacks, Hispanics, and Asians. New York City and Los Angeles are highly diverse cities. Following we discuss the three major ethnic subcultures in the United States: black, Hispanic, and Asian.

The Black Subculture   The black or African American subculture is the largest minority group in the United States, with some 35 million people and about 8.4 million families (about 12 percent of the total population), a market worth about $500 billion annually.[24] African Americans are a highly diverse group. Although many black Americans are poor, two-thirds are not. More than 26 percent of black families had incomes exceeding $50,000 in 1997, up from 18 percent in 1980. However, 17 percent of black families were very poor (incomes less than $5,000) in 1997. Although the 17 million relatively poor blacks concentrated in densely populated urban centers are more visible in the media, 8 million blacks live in suburban neighborhoods.

Economic conditions for blacks vary considerably in different metropolitan areas. For example, about one-fourth of blacks in Washington, DC, are affluent, compared to only 1 in 25 in Miami. In San Francisco, 1 in 10 blacks is affluent and more than half are middle class. Middle-class blacks may have more in common with middle-class whites and Asians than lower-class blacks. The diversity in the African American subculture suggests marketers should further segment the black market based on factors such as income, social class, or geographic region. Highlight 13.4 presents an example of such a subsubculture.

Highlight 13.4

Targeting African Americans on the Web

Much has been made of the so-called "digital divide." Indeed, the percentage of whites using the Internet is significantly higher than the percentage of African Americans who are online. But a closer look at those numbers tells a somewhat different story. African Americans are going online at a rate twice that of the general population. Moreover, 30 percent of African Americans plan to make purchases online, compared to 21 percent of the general population. The increasing number of sites targeted toward the African American audience is evidence that the Internet community is taking notice.

BlackVoices.com is one of the pioneering African American–oriented sites. It features news, book reviews, chat rooms, and entertainment, along with an extensive listing of job opportunities.

BlackPlanet.com aims to create a virtual community of African Americans. It was founded in September 1999, and within four months had built a base of 200,000 registered users. BlackPlanet quickly attracted some big-name advertisers, including Bell-South, General Motors, and the United States Army. According to founder Omar Wasow, "Most African American sites are designed to connect you to information, while our goal has always been connecting people to other people." BlackPlanet does this by providing its members with e-mail accounts, personal webpages, games, and forums. Membership in 2003 was nearly 10 million.

Africana.com is a somewhat more highbrow site focusing on education. Founded by Harvard professor Henry Louis Gates, Jr., a preeminent African American intellectual, Africana.com offers lesson plans for teachers, African news, links to dozens of African radio stations, and noted guest columnists like Nigerian Nobel Prize winner Wole Soyinka and Harvard law professor Charles Ogletree. From its inception in January 1999, Africana.com has not accepted banner advertising (which Gates believed would detract from the site's content and dilute its brand image), opting instead to sell "sponsorships" similar to those found on public television. In September 2000, Gates sold Africana.com to Time Warner, a move that will quite possibly result in Africana.com forming collaborations with other Time Warner media outlets like CNN and *Time* magazine.

These are just a few of an increasing number of sites aimed at African Americans. But with so many sites serving such a relatively limited—albeit economically powerful—audience, how many can survive long term? Scott Mills, CEO of **BET.com** (a partnership between Black Entertainment Television, Microsoft, USA Networks, and News Corporation) is skeptical. "How many of the sites are going to be large, successful, viable? Three, at best," Mills predicts.

Sources: Roger O. Crockett, "Attention Must Be Paid," *Business Week e.biz,* February 7, 2000, p. EB 16; Daniel Golden, "Web Site That Unites Blacks Is Big Ambition of Henry Louis Gates," *The Wall Street Journal,* February 17, 2000, pp. A1, A8; anonymous, "Market Profile: Wasow Directs Movement of BlackPlanet," *Advertising Age,* February 28, 2000, p. 56; Davis Kirkpatrick, "Co-founders of Africana.com Sell Venture to Time Warner," *The New York Times,* September 7, 2000, p. 2.

Increasingly, marketers are targeting African Americans with special products and marketing strategies. For example, Tyco, Hasbro, and Mattel are all marketing "ethnically correct" dolls designed for the black market (10 percent of U.S. children under 10 are black).[25] Mattel's dolls, Shani (Swahili for "marvelous") and her two friends, Asha and Nicelle, have different skin tones, hairstyles, and facial features that reflect the diversity of black women. Some marketing strategies directed at the black subculture have been highly controversial. In 1991, G. Heileman Brewing Company succumbed to public pressure and canceled plans to market a high-alcohol malt beer, "PowerMaster," to low-income, inner-city black consumers.[26]

The Hispanic Subculture   According to recent statistics, approximately 37.4 million Hispanics live in the United States (about 12 percent of the total population).[27] Hispanics are people with Spanish-speaking ancestry from such places as Mexico (at 66 percent, by far the largest group in the United States), Puerto Rico, Cuba, and various countries in Central and South America. When combined into a single subculture, Hispanic people account for more than $390 billion in purchasing power.

Hispanics are distributed unequally across the United States, with most living in the border states of Texas, California, Arizona, and New Mexico (each state has a Hispanic population exceeding 500,000). The top six Hispanic U.S. cities are New York (mostly Puerto Ricans and Dominicans); Miami (Cubans); Los Angeles, Houston, and San Antonio (Mexicans); and Chicago (a mix of all). In these regions, the Hispanic subculture has a significant effect on the overall culture.

The Hispanic subculture is diverse, and reaching Hispanic consumers efficiently and effectively can be difficult. Some Hispanics are third- or fourth-generation U.S. citizens and are well assimilated into American culture; they can be reached by traditional U.S. media (TV, radio, and magazines). Other Hispanics retain much of their original culture and may speak mostly or only Spanish. To oversimply, marketers can identify three broad segments (subgroups) in the Hispanic subculture: only Spanish speaking; bilingual, favoring Spanish; and bilingual, but favoring English.

Using Spanish in ads can be an effective way to reach all three groups. Recently developed Spanish-language media (special TV channels, newspapers, and magazines) make it easier than ever to reach the Hispanic market.[28] For instance, the magazine *La Familia de Hoy* is targeted at Hispanic women who speak English as a second language and have children at home. Several large companies have placed ads in Spanish in the magazine, including Procter & Gamble, American Airlines, Kraft, AT&T, and Kinney Shoes. Successful advertising campaigns tend to use large, colorful ads that combine the "American dream" with the traditional values of the Hispanic extended family.

Many companies would like to develop marketing strategies targeted at the Hispanic market, but getting good information about Hispanic needs, values, and beliefs is difficult. Companies must decide whether to develop one general

Gillette can place these two ads in English and Spanish-language magazines directed at Hispanic consumers *(both) The Gillette Company.*

marketing strategy for all Hispanics or adapt the strategy for each segment of the Hispanic subculture. Coors, for instance, opts for the adaptive, tailor-made approach, showing ads with a rodeo theme in Houston but not in Miami. Goya Foods developed different products for Miami (Cubans prefer black beans) and New York (Puerto Ricans like red beans).

Marketing to domestic subcultures requires a careful analysis of consumers' affect, cognitions, and behaviors.[29] For example, a telephone company once tried to target the Hispanic market by employing Puerto Rican actors. In the ad, the wife said to her husband, "Run downstairs and phone Mary. Tell her we'll be a little late." However, this commercial ignored Hispanic values and behaviors. For one thing, Hispanic wives seldom order their husbands around; for another, few Hispanics would find it necessary to phone if they are going to be late, because being late is expected. Similarly, Coors ads featuring the slogan "Taste the high country" were not effective with Mexican Americans, who could not identify with mountain life. The Spanish-language Coors ads were modified to suggest that mountains were a good source of beer, but one did not need to live in the mountains to enjoy it. The new slogan in its English translation became "Take the beer from the high country and bring it to your high country—wherever it may be."[30]

Asian Subculture   Although only about 4.2 percent of the population in 2000, Asian Americans are among the most rapidly increasing ethnic group in the United States.[31] The population of people with Asian ancestry increased 80 percent in the 1980s (largely because of increased immigration), growing from 3.8 million in 1980 to about 7 million in 1989 to about 11.9 million in 2000, and have a purchasing power of about $110 billion. Asian Americans are concentrated in a few areas of the country, where they have an important influence on the overall culture. Most Asians (56 percent) live in the West, particularly in California (13 percent of Californians were Asian in 2000). Asian Americans are highly urbanized, with 93 percent living in cities (three-quarters of the 3 million Californian Asians live in the Los Angeles basin or the San Francisco Bay area).

The Asian subculture in these regions requires special marketing attention for many companies. Grocery stores in Koreatown in Los Angeles stock large bags of rice near the checkout counter (where stores in middle America put the charcoal). Understanding how Asian American consumers make purchase decisions is critical to the success of many products. One study found that country of origin and length of time in this country are critical factors in how Asian consumers make purchase decisions.[32] For instance, Vietnamese Americans are more likely to adhere to the cultural model in which the man makes the decision for any large purchase, whereas women in Japanese households tend to have more influence on their husbands.

Asian Americans are a prime market because they are more affluent than any other racial or ethnic group. In 1997 the median income of an Asian American household was $43,200, compared to $38,800 for whites, $24,900 for Hispanics, and $23,900 for African Americans. Asian income levels are high for two reasons. First, the education level is high (35 percent of adults have completed four or more years of college, compared to 22 percent of white Americans). Second, more Asian Americans live in married-couple households with two wage earners.

It is tempting to think of Asian Americans (and other minority subcultures) as a single, homogeneous market, but this subculture is highly diverse. Some Asians are well integrated in American culture, whereas others live in Asian communities and maintain much of their original culture, including their languages. Because Asian people come from several distinctive cultural backgrounds—Japan, China, Southeast Asia, and the Pacific Islands—many marketers further segment the Asian community into subcultures based on language or nationality.[33] MCI, for instance, developed such effective print ads targeted at recent immigrants from Hong Kong and Taiwan that the company had to hire additional Chinese-speaking operators to handle the influx of calls. Implementing such targeted marketing strategies is possible in communities where specialized media (newspapers, magazines, radio) can reach Asian subcultures.

Gender as a Subculture

Despite the modern tendency to downplay differences between men and women, there is ample evidence that men and women differ in important respects other than physically. For instance, women may process information differently than men and seem more "generous, more nurturing, and less dominating than men."[34] For some marketing purposes, gender differences may be significant enough to consider the two sexes as separate subcultures. For instance, research has found that women treat possessions differently than men do. Some men see ownership and possession of products as a way to dominate and exert power over others, discriminate themselves from others (status differentiation), and even engage in subtle forms of aggression over others. Women, in contrast, tend to value possessions that can enhance personal and social relationships. Compared to most men, most women seem to value caring over controlling, sharing over selfishness, and cooperating over dominating. Many marketers may find it useful to develop different marketing strategies for the male and female subcultures.

In the late 1990s, more marketers began to see women as a distinctive subculture and key market segment. Women control approximately 60 percent of U.S. wealth and influence more than 80 percent of all purchases. Moreover, some 25 percent of working women bring home bigger paychecks than their husbands. This led Tom Peters, well-known business author, to declare, "Women are opportunity No. 1."[35] In some markets, the changes during the past quarter-century have been dramatic. For example, women constituted only about 1 percent of all business travelers in 1970, but they accounted for roughly 50 percent by 1997. Recently executives were surprised to find that 60 percent of customers at a do-it-yourself building supplies chain were women and about two-thirds of PC purchases for the home were made by women. Today women either make or greatly influence most purchasing decisions, and companies that do not recognize this are headed for trouble. In response, the Westin hotel chain has developed strong marketing relationships with women by including irons and full-length mirrors in the rooms and conveying a respectful attitude in the restaurants (ask the woman to taste the wine), among other things.[36]

Champion seeks women customers with specially designed products and targeted advertising
Courtesy Champion Woman.

Income as a Subculture

It is possible to consider level of income as a subculture, because people at different income levels tend to have quite different values, behaviors, and lifestyles. Typically, however, income is used to further segment a subculture defined on some other characteristic (age, ethnic group, region). Many myths and misconceptions about income distribution in the United States can confuse marketers. For instance, if you think lower-income households are dominated by minorities, you are wrong; most poor Americans are white. Affluence doesn't necessarily increase with age, either.

Marketers often divide American households into three income categories: *downscale* (under $25,000 income per year), *upscale* (over $50,000 per year), and *middle income* ($25,000 to 50,000 per year).[37] Demographic characteristics of these income groups illustrate one reason to stay in college and graduate: There is a very strong relationship between college education and income level. Nearly half of upscale adults have completed four years of college, but only 10 percent of downscale adults have done so. Nearly half (46 percent) of American households are downscale. Although the upscale subculture constitutes an excellent market for high-quality luxury goods, only one in five households falls into this category. The mass market is downscale, which partially accounts for the huge success of discount retailers such as Wal-Mart. Some American marketers have found that the downscale market can be very profitable. Highlight 13.5 presents another strategic approach to income segments.

Acculturation Processes

A process of acculturation begins when a person from one culture moves to a different culture or subculture to live and work. **Acculturation** refers to how people in one culture or subculture understand and adapt to the meanings (values, beliefs, behaviors, rituals, lifestyles) of another culture or subculture.[38] **Consumer acculturation** refers to how people acquire the ability and cultural knowledge to be skilled consumers in different cultures or subcultures.

Acculturation processes are important in the modern world. Many societies face the problem of assimilating large numbers of immigrants from rather different cultural backgrounds into the host culture. For instance, in the United States, the Hispanic and Asian subcultures grew rapidly during the 1990s.

Acculturation is also important for people who move to different regions within the same country and must adapt to different subcultural meanings. In the United States, one out of six Americans moves each year.[39] However, two-thirds of these move within the same county (the median distance moved is only 6 miles), and the subcultural changes in most of these moves are probably minor. In contrast, about 10 percent of Americans move to a different region of the country (most of these people are college graduates), and they are likely to face some acculturation problems as they learn a new regional subculture. Finally, acculturation is important for marketing managers, who must try to understand the cultural meanings of consumers in societies and subcultures different than their own.

The degree to which immigrants, movers, and marketers become acculturated into a new culture or subculture depends on their level of **cultural interpenetration,** the amount and type of social interactions they have with people in the host culture.[40] Social contact with people in other subcultures can occur through direct, personal experience at work, while shopping, or in living arrangements.

▶ **High**light 13.5

Income as a Subculture: Two-Tier Marketing

Did you know that there are two different types of Winnie-the-Pooh (the cute stuffed bear friend of Christopher Robin in the classic books by A. A. Milne)? The Walt Disney Company, which owns the rights to Milne's characters, carefully markets Pooh to two different income segments. The original line-drawn figure of Pooh that appears on fine china, pewter spoons, and pricey kids' stationery is sold in upscale specialty shops and fine department stores such as Nordstrom. Another Pooh, a plump, cartoonlike bear wearing a red T-shirt, adorns plastic key chains and bedsheets and appears in animated videos. These products are sold in Wal-Mart stores and discount drugstores. Only in Disney's own stores do the two Poohs appear together.

Disney is not an aberration; many other marketers are adopting a similar "two-tiered" strategy. This is because the middle class that once seemed to include almost everyone is not growing in numbers or in purchasing power. In contrast, the two extremes of the income distribution are growing. Over the past 20 years, real incomes of the wealthiest fifth of the population increased by 21 percent, whereas wages for the lower 60 percent have stagnated or even dropped. These changes make it attractive for a company to adopt either an upscale or downscale approach to marketing, although a few companies, like Disney, can target both income segments. Lester Thurow, an economist at M.I.T., put it this way: "The $4 restaurant meal is doing all right, and the $50 meal is doing all right. The $20 meal is in trouble."

In the past, many of America's biggest brands focused on the middle market. For example, Levi's and Ivory soap seemed to reflect the idea that a reasonably good product, properly packaged and promoted, could be sold to almost anyone. But this approach no longer seems to work in many categories. Take the automobile market, for instance. The income trends discussed above mean that fewer people can afford a new car (especially since the median price of a car increased by 22 percent in constant dollars just during the 1990s). In 1997, the wealthiest 20 percent of the population accounted for more than half of all new car sales, up from 40 percent in 1980. This helps explain why the market for low-mileage used cars was booming in the mid-1990s. Many folks wanted to buy a nice, high-quality product, but couldn't afford the cost of buying new. Nearly new was affordable.

Source: "Two-Tier Marketing," from the March 17, 1997 cover story of *Business Week*, n3518 p. 82(7). Copyright 1997 by The McGraw-Hill Companies, Inc. Reprinted with permission from David Leonhardt.

Social experiences also may be indirect or vicarious, as in observing other people from a distance or on television. Some Americans may lack a cultural understanding of people in other societies and subcultures because much of their social contact with such people has been shallow and indirect. Many Americans learn about other cultures and subcultures largely through vicarious observation of subcultural portrayals in the mass media (movies, television programs, books, news media). When people have the opportunity for deeper cultural interpenetration (through work experiences or living in proximity to other types of people), they tend to become more thoroughly acculturated.

When people come into contact with a new culture or subculture, they may go through **four stages of acculturation** corresponding to four levels of cultural interpenetration.[41] In the *honeymoon stage,* people are fascinated by the exotic foreign culture or subculture. Because cultural interpenetration is shallow and superficial, little acculturation occurs. Tourists traveling to various regions of the United States may experience this stage.

If cultural interpenetration increases, people may enter a *rejection stage,* where they recognize that many of their old behaviors and meanings may be inadequate

The models in this ad could represent either working-class or middle-class consumers   *Courtesy Cigna Corporation.*

for acting in the new subculture. Some people may develop hostile attitudes toward the new subculture and reject its key values and meanings. Cultural conflicts tend to be maximal in this stage.

If cultural interpenetration continues and deepens, people may reach the *tolerance stage.* As they learn more cultural meanings and behaviors, they may begin to appreciate the new subculture, and cultural conflict will decrease.

Finally, in the *integration stage,* adjustment to the subculture is adequate, although acculturation need not be complete or total. At this stage, people are able to function satisfactorily in the new culture or subculture, which is viewed as an alternative way of life and is valued for its good qualities.

Consider the acculturation problem faced by immigrants who come to the United States with their own cultural meanings and values and must adapt to the different cultural meanings of American society. One study of immigrants from India found that transitional objects such as Indian clothing, jewelry, special furniture, movies, photographs, and music were highly valued as reminders of their home culture.[42] Educated immigrants may tend to become more acculturated because their high education levels lead to greater cultural interpenetration. Many Hispanics tend to maintain their cultural values and traditions, and full acculturation may take three or four generations. But even long-term resident Hispanic Americans, Asian Americans, or African Americans may never completely incorporate all of the values, meanings, and behaviors of mainstream American culture.

An important aspect of the acculturation process is proficiency in the language of the new culture. Ability to speak English obviously influences the level of cultural interpenetration that an immigrant can achieve in the United States. For instance, Hispanic immigrants who live and work in Spanish-speaking neighborhoods, surrounded by similar people, may penetrate little into American society and may become only partially acculturated. Immigrants with more education are more likely to speak English and can obtain better jobs, which in turn allows for greater cultural penetration and enables them to become more completely acculturated. Interestingly, immigrants who join families already living in the United States tend to be more passive and penetrate less deeply into American culture than the more innovative family members who were the first to come to the United States.

Social Class

An expert in social class research has made the following observations:

> There are no two ways about it: Social class is a difficult idea. Sociologists, in whose discipline the concept emerged, are not of one mind about its value and validity. Consumer researchers, to whose field its use has spread, display confusion about when and how to apply it. The American public is noticeably uncomfortable with the realities about life that it reflects. All who try to measure it have trouble. Studying it rigorously and imaginatively can be monstrously expensive. Yet, all these difficulties notwithstanding, the proposition still holds: Social class is worth troubling over for the insights it offers on the marketplace behavior of the nation's consumers.[43]

We agree with these observations concerning both the problems and the value of social class analysis. For our purposes in this text, **social class** refers to a

Exhibit 13.3

Social Class Groups for Consumer Analysis

Upper Americans (14 percent of population). This group consists of the upper-upper, lower-upper, and upper-middle classes. They have common goals and are differentiated mainly by income. This group has many different lifestyles, which might be labeled postpreppy, conventional, intellectual, and political, among others. The class remains the segment of our society in which quality merchandise is most prized, special attention is paid to prestige brands, and the self-image ideal is "spending with good taste." Self-expression is more prized than in previous generations, and neighborhood remains important. Depending on income and priorities, theater; books; investment in art; European travel; household help; club memberships for tennis, golf, and swimming; and prestige schooling for children remain high-consumption priorities.

Middle class (32 percent of population). These consumers definitely want to "do the right thing" and buy "what's popular." They have always been concerned with fashion and following recommendations of "experts" in print media. Increased earnings result in better living, which means a "nicer neighborhood on the better side of town with good schools." It also means spending more on "worthwhile experiences" for children, including winter ski trips, college educations, and shopping for better brands of clothes at more expensive stores. Appearance of home is important because guests may visit and pass judgment. This group emulates upper Americans, which distinguishes it from the working class. It also enjoys trips to Las Vegas and physical activity. Deferred gratification may still be an ideal, but it is not so often practiced.

Working class (38 percent of population). Working-class Americans are "family folk" depending heavily on relatives for economic and emotional support, such as tips on job opportunities, advice on purchases, and help in times of trouble. The emphasis on family ties is only one sign of how much more limited and different working-class horizons are socially, psychologically, and geographically compared to those of the middle class. In almost every respect, a parochial view characterizes this blue-collar world. This group has changed little in values and behaviors despite rising incomes in some cases. For them, "keeping up with the times" focuses on the mechanical and recreational, and, thus, ease of labor and leisure is what they continue to pursue.

Lower Americans (16 percent of population). The men and women of lower America are no exception to the rule that diversities and uniformities in values and consumption goals are to be found at each social level. Some members of this world, as has been publicized, are prone to every form of instant gratification known to humankind when the money is available. But others are dedicated to resisting worldly temptations as they struggle toward what some believe will be a "heavenly reward" for their earthly sacrifices.

Source: Excerpted from Richard P. Coleman, "The Continuing Significance of Social Class to Marketing," *Journal of Consumer Research*, December 1983, pp. 265–280. Copyright 1983 Journal of Consumer Research. Reprinted with permission of the publisher, University of Chicago Press.

national status hierarchy by which groups and individuals are distinguished in terms of esteem and prestige. Coleman recommends that four social class groups be used for consumer analysis in the United States: *upper, middle, working,* and *lower class.* Exhibit 13.3 describes these groups and identifies some marketing implications for each.

Identification with each social class is influenced most strongly by one's level of education and occupation (including income as a measure of work success). But social class is also affected by social skills, status aspirations, community participation, family history, cultural level, recreational habits, physical appearance, and social acceptance by a particular class. Thus, social class is a composite of many personal and social attributes rather than a single characteristic such as income or education. The four social classes can be considered as large subcultures because their members share many cultural meanings and behaviors.

Although the members of each social class share distinct values and behavior patterns to some degree, each of the four major groups can be further differentiated. Although there are a number of similarities in values and behaviors within groups in a given class, vast differences can exist in family situations and income levels among subgroups.

For instance, families in each social class can be further classified as relatively overprivileged, average, or underprivileged.[44] *Overprivileged* families in each social class are usually those with incomes 25 to 30 percent above the median for the class, and therefore have "extra" money to seek better forms of the life preferred by the class. However, because these families continue to share values, behaviors, and associations with other members of the class, they typically do not move to a higher social class. The *average* families are those in the middle-income range who can afford the kind of house, car, apparel, food, furniture, and appliances expected by their social class peers. Finally, the *underprivileged* families have incomes that fall at least 15 percent below the class midpoint and therefore must scrimp and sacrifice to be able to purchase the appropriate products for that class.

Social class and relative standing within a class are important sources of consumers' beliefs, values, and behaviours.[45] Most of the people an individual interacts with on a day-to-day basis are likely to be members of that person's social class. Family, peer groups, and friends at work, school, and in the neighborhood are all likely to be of the same social class. These people teach the individual appropriate values for the class as well as behaviors that are acceptable to it. This process can occur either through direct instruction ("You don't have a chance anymore unless you go to college") or vicariously (an individual sees neighborhood friends going to college, graduating, and purchasing new cars).

At a conceptual level, social classes are useful for investigating the process by which consumers develop their characteristic beliefs, values, and behavior patterns. For example, the upper class may well be socially secure and not find it necessary or desirable to purchase the most expensive brands to impress other people. Middle-class people, on the other hand, often engage in such conspicuous consumption. As Highlight 13.6 shows, even homeless people (perhaps the lowest social class in American society) engage in consumption behavior.

Social Class versus Income

The social class concept aids in understanding consumer values and behavior; it is also useful for market segmentation and prediction of consumer behavior. However, there has long been a controversy as to whether social class or income is the better variable for use in consumer analysis. Advocates of each position muster a number of arguments for the superiority of their favorite variable and point out a variety of methodological and conceptual problems with the other one.

Recently consumer researchers have recognized that each variable has its advantages and disadvantages, and the choice among using social class, income, or a combination of the two depends on the product and the situation. For example, Charles Shaninger offers the following tentative generalizations:[46]

1. Social class is more relevant than income for areas of consumer behavior that do not involve high dollar expenditures but do reflect underlying differences in lifestyle, values, or homemaker roles not captured by income (e.g., using imported

Highlight 13.6

The Lowest Social Class? The Homeless in America

For a variety of reasons, homeless men and women crowded many American cities during the 1980s and 1990s. Estimates in 2000 of the homeless population were 3 million and the number was rising. Without a home and seldom with a job, the homeless are at the bottom of the social class hierarchy. However, despite their very low socioeconomic status, homeless people are consumers. They exert considerable physical and cognitive effort performing various consumption behaviors: finding a place to sleep, getting food, acquiring simple possessions (warm clothing), and keeping their meager possessions safe. In a real sense, these consumption activities constitute a full-time job.

One intensive study of the homeless learned much about this distinctive subculture or social class. For instance, most homeless individuals have a few possessions—a shopping cart is very desirable. Some of their possessions are scavenged from trash cans or abandoned cars and buildings, and some are purchased (hot meals are especially valued). Often individuals exchange possessions using barter. Some homeless people earn a small income doing odd jobs or, most frequently, by recycling (selling empty bottles or scrap metals). Others work sporadically as day laborers or, for example, by washing car windows at intersections.

Maslow's needs hierarchy identifies the basic needs of homeless people: food, water, shelter, and security. By definition, all homeless people lack a house or an apartment, but some do have housing of their own. These can range from vacant buildings or abandoned automobiles to makeshift (self-constructed) shelters on vacant lots built from abandoned building materials to partially protected areas such as bridges and tunnels that provide useful shelter.

The consumer product most often purchased by homeless people is food. But food can also be obtained from charitable shelters, by finding "road-kill" meat, and by scavenging food from dumpsters. Some homeless people become skilled at scavenging food, for instance, by checking the dumpsters of fast-food restaurants soon after closing.

Clothing is particularly important in the winter, and homeless people try to accumulate layers of clothing to provide protection from the cold. Multiple layers of clothing also offer protection from violence such as beatings or rape. Clothing is often scavenged, although charity distribution centers can be a good source.

Another need is personal hygiene and health care. Satisfying these needs is difficult for homeless people, partly because of their restricted access to water. Homeless people find it difficult to wash themselves and their clothes. Shelters are useful for these purposes. Of course, virtually no homeless individuals have any health insurance. Thus, they are likely to seek medical attention from emergency rooms or free clinics. One homeless person deliberately got arrested when he was depressed or sick to get medical attention in jail.

Finally, various sorts of tools are important possessions for many homeless people. Shopping carts are useful to carry their possessions (to keep them from being stolen). Tools that aid in scavenging parts from cars or buildings (screwdrivers, flashlights, tire irons) are valued.

Source: Ronald Paul Hill and Mark Stamey, "The Homeless in America: An Examination of Possessions and Consumption Behaviors," *Journal of Consumer Research,* December 1990, pp. 303–321; www.nscahh.com.

or domestic wines). Social class is superior for both method and place of purchase of highly visible, symbolic, and expensive objects such as living room furniture.

2. Income is generally appropriate for understanding purchases of major kitchen and laundry appliances and products that require substantial expenditures but are not status symbols within the class.

3. The combination of social class and income is generally superior for product classes that are highly visible, serve as symbols of social class or status within the class, and require either moderate or substantial expenditure (such as clothing, automobiles, and television sets).

In sum, determining whether social class, income, a combination of these, or other variables are most useful in a particular situation requires a careful analysis of the relationships between the product and the consumer. In other words, consumer affect and cognitions, behaviors, and the environment must all be analyzed to develop appropriate marketing strategies.

Back To...

Mountain Dew

The Mountain Dew example illustrates how one company effectively positioned its product to the youth subculture. The teen market is expected to grow at a rate twice that of the general population through 2010. Moreover, many marketers believe young people are becoming increasingly brand loyal. So it is quite possible that Mountain Dew will reap the rewards of its current marketing success for years to come.

Consumers in different age categories, such as teenagers versus baby boomers, early 40s to late 50s, are likely to have rather different values, cultural meanings, and behavior patterns. Partly this is because people in these age categories grew up in different decades with very different cultural experiences. However, each broad subcultural segment is itself actually quite diverse. Therefore, marketers may have to use other variables to identify narrower and more precise segments. For example, the age categories could be further broken down into ethnic, geographic, religious, or community subgroups. It is very likely, for instance, that the cultural values and behavioral norms of young blacks differ somewhat from those of young whites or Hispanics. Marketers could also look at different social classes within

the teenage group. Here again we would expect to see major differences in the product perceptions, values, and behavior patterns of upper-, middle-, and lower-class teens.

The opening example shows how Mountain Dew recognized the differences in the teenage market. While extreme sports helped bring in a certain segment of the youth subculture, Mountain Dew recognized the need to attract more Hispanics and African Americans—thus, the addition of hip-hop stars and urban music to the Mountain Dew marketing effort. Perhaps a new challenge will be to convince more young females to "Do the Dew."

Teens of today are very different from teens of 50, 25, or even 10 years ago. For one thing, many are plugged into the information superhighway, where accessing bulletin boards, sending e-mail, and surfing the Internet are common. Thus, teens are likely to be prime targets for high-tech marketing communications—a fact not lost on Mountain Dew's parent, PepsiCo, which has formed a marketing partnership with the popular Internet search engine Yahoo! Also, teens are much more comfortable with diversity than their predecessors (by 2010, nearly one in three teens will belong to a minority). Many teens are experienced shoppers, partly because they have been shopping for years to help out in single-parent and dual-income families. Thus, today's teens are more seasoned and marketing-savvy consumers than previous generations, and therefore require different marketing strategies. Although the Mountain Dew example focused on implications for advertising and product positioning, subcultural factors also have important implications for other aspects of marketing strategy, including product development, pricing, and distribution. ❖

Summary

This chapter discussed two macro social influences on consumers' behaviors, cognitions, and affective responses: subculture and social class. These social factors influence how people think, feel, and behave relative to their physical, social, and marketing environments. We discussed subcultural influences in terms of geographic area, age, ethnic group, and other factors. Social class influences were discussed in terms of their roles both in explaining consumer behavior and as a strategic tool.

Key Terms and Concepts

acculturation **336**
age subcultures **326**
baby boomers **326**
consumer acculturation **336**
cultural interpenetration **336**

ethnic subcultures **331**
four stages of acculturation **337**
geographic subcultures **324**
social class **338**
subcultures **321**

Review and Discussion Questions

1. Discuss how subcultures and social class influence how consumers learn cultural meanings (values, behaviors, lifestyles). Give a specific example.
2. Check out the Nike webpage devoted to women's sports and sports equipment at **www.nike.com/nikegoddess**. Discuss how Nike seems to understand women as a subculture and how that approach has directed its marketing strategies. Contrast your analysis of Nike with a competitor such as Reebok (**www.reebok.com**).
3. What ethical factors should a marketer consider in developing marketing strategies targeted at particular subcultures or social classes? (What is your reaction to selling fortified wine to homeless people, cigarettes to Hispanics, or diet plans to overweight people?)
4. Are college students a subculture? Why or why not? How could a marketer use knowledge about this group to develop marketing strategy?
5. Identify the age subcultures among members of your own family (or neighborhood). How do these cultural differences affect the consumption behaviors of these people for foods, personal care products, and clothing?
6. Define the concept of *social class*. What are the major social class groups in the United States (or your home country)? What are the major social class groups in the immediate community where you live? How did you recognize these social class groupings?

7. Select two product classes (such as foods, beverages, clothing, automobiles, furniture). How might each social class you identified in question 6 respond to marketing strategies for these products?

8. Think of a subculture not discussed in the text and briefly describe it. Discuss marketing implications for this subculture. What product categories would be most relevant for this cultural group?

9. Discuss the acculturation process in terms of what might happen if you came into contact with a different subculture (say, you moved to a different area of the country or city).

10. Discuss the concept of *cultural interpenetration* in terms of the acculturation of immigrant populations in your country. What marketing opportunities do you see in this situation?

Marketing Strategy in Action

Abercrombie & Fitch

As you stroll into the store, you are greeted by blaring music, racy photos, and a cooler-than-cool "sales force" that doesn't actually try to sell you anything. And if you're over 25, there is a decent chance you are the oldest person in the place. To borrow a phrase from another company's marketing compaign, Abercrombie & Fitch is definitely not your father's clothing store—although, interestingly, it may have been your grandfather's.

A&F is one of a handful of retail chains that has done a masterful job of appealing to fashion-conscious teens and college students. The challenge for A&F, The Gap, J. Crew, and others is how to remain relevant to the notoriously fickle youth subculture.

Founded in 1892, A&F was originally an outlet for camping gear. Early in its history, in fact, it outfitted former U.S. president Theodore Roosevelt's African safaris. Later it established a niche selling conservative menswear to an older clientele, but eventually sales plummeted and A&F filed for bankruptcy. The Limited purchased the chain in 1988 and four years later hired Michael Jeffries to oversee A&F operations. Jeffries wanted to shift the company's focus away from, as he describes it, the "70 to death" demographic toward a much younger and faster-growing group: consumers between ages 14 and 24. The tweed suits came off the racks, replaced by jeans and T-shirts. It worked. By the time The Limited spun off A&F in 1998, the company was already a hit. Sales exploded from $165 million in 1994 to $1.6 billion in 2002. The number of stores jumped from 36 in 1992 to 340 in 2003 (plus 167 Abercrombie stores and 112 Hollister Company stores). A 1999 survey showed A&F to be the sixth coolest brand in the world among kids, outranking Levi's and Nintendo. In the summer of 1999, A&F's spot in the pantheon of youth culture was solidified in a hit pop song by the group LFO, who sang about how much they liked girls who "look like Abercrombie and Fitch."

A&F and its direct competitors are appealing to the so-called "echo boom" generation—people born between 1977 and 1994. It is estimated that by 2010, the United States will have 34 million people between ages 12 and 19. And, unlike previous generations, most of these youths have money to spend. In 1998 the average teen earned almost $80 per week, and because most live at home and have few financial responsibilities, much of that money goes toward clothing.

At an A&F store, there is no such thing as a minor detail. According to an analyst at Goldman, Sachs, & Co, "they are very single-minded and very driven. Everything they do is directed to making sure they are truly representative of the lifestyle of their core college-age consumer." A&F unabashedly admits it hires employees based less on skill than on how they look and act. In fact, because A&F believes young people don't like being told what to buy, the sales staff doesn't actually offer sales help. Their job is to greet customers, walk around, and look beautiful. "We're not interested in salespeople or clerks," declared Lonnie Fogel, director of investor relations. "We're interested in finding people who represent the brand's lifestyle . . . who portray the image of the brand." And management makes certain employees don't deviate from that image. For example, employees can wear only certain kinds of shirts with certain styles of pants. And black shoes are completely forbidden because the company believes they project an undesirable urban street image.

A&F's reach is not limited to its storefront. It is one of only a handful of clothing companies that have successfully targeted young buyers via catalogs. Alloy and the very hip Delia's also have a large catalog customer base. But A&F's publication, the *Quarterly,* is more than just a catalog. It has become required reading for people who consider themselves cool. The catalog is filled with erotic photographs of scantily clad co-eds and buff frat boys cavorting on the beach or caught in compromising positions. The Christmas 1999 catalog included a fake interview with a mall Santa purported to be a pedophile, along with sex advice from a renowned porn star. Older folks—including the Michigan attorney general—expressed their concern, and A&F agreed to distribute the publication only to people over 18. But one can assume the controversy and eatablishment outrage probably made the catalog (and the brand) all the more appealing to A&F's younger clientele.

How does any company remain popular and keep up with what fashions young people consider cool? It's not easy. Thanks to the Internet and MTV, the concept of "fashionable" has become a constantly moving target. Wet Seal is a company that specializes in "club" clothing. Its president, Ed Thomas says, "The market is all about change. You have to constantly reinvent yourself to attract people to your store and that's constantly a challenge." The Limited, A&F's former sister chain, was once hailed for its skill at keeping pace with youth fashion trends. But somewhere along the line it lost its touch. In 1998, a $40 million operating loss forced The Limited to close stores. A&F is trying to keep pace with its customers by filling its merchandising and design staffs with people right out of college—young people who already live the A&F lifestyle. Plus, the company employs a team of "field editors," college students from all over the United States who provide weekly reports on the latest fashion and lifestyle trends.

Despite A&F's success, it does not have a monopoly on the youth market. Some elements of that subculture don't find the A&F lifestyle or clothing appealing. "A lot of my friends think Abercrombie's kind of silly, between the way they advertise with magazines and their high prices," says Erik Lappinen, a high school senior from New Jersey. Another New Jersey high school student, Kristen Ricciardi, agrees:

"I'd rather buy the same clothes from The Gap or American Eagle and not have the company's name on my shirt." Gap, Inc.'s Old Navy stores, with their $8 T-shirts and $25 cargo pants, appeal to those who want to keep pace with fashion but won't pay A&F's prices. Of course, there are some young people who want to get as far away as possible from the A&F lifestyle and sense of fashion. At the 270-store Hot Topic chain, you can buy patent leather military boots, hair dye, vinyl pants, and even jewelry for your pierced tongue.

Why have A&F and other companies been so successful marketing to teens and college students? It is largely because they appeal to a sense of belonging that is especially important to people in this age group. "These young people want to be with one another," says the 55-year-old Jeffries. "That is totally different. My generation grew up as loners." So while the definition of what is fashionable may vary from person to person, most young people do feel social pressure to wear clothes and live a lifestyle that others in their peer group consider cool.

Of course, there is a catch-22: How cool is too cool? Airwalk initially marketed its shoes to teens who were part of a more alternative subculture. But eventually so many people were wearing Airwalks that the brand was perceived as mainstream and therefore not appropriate footwear for someone truly avant-garde. Now the company is trying to reshape its image to become more relevant to those in its original target market. So, somewhat paradoxically, while young people seek social acceptance, they also want to retain some sense of individuality. As one teen said about A&F, "No one wants to admit they shop at a store because it's cool."

In sum, it is a never-ending battle for companies like A&F. Cultural tastes change, fashions change, established competitors redouble their efforts, and new competitors spring up seemingly out of nowhere. To remain a major player in the youth clothing market for the long haul requires an intelligent marketing strategy and an accurate feel for the ever-changing lifestyles of young consumers.

Discussion Questions

1. Companies like J. Crew (**www.jcrew.com**) and Banana Republic (**www.bananarepublic.com**) are targeting many of the same consumers as Abercrombie & Fitch. Visit their websites and discuss how their marketing strategies differ from those of A&F. Would you suggest any changes in these strategies that would allow these two companies to better position themselves in the minds of consumers?

2. The success of specialty clothing stores has come at the expense of large department stores like Sears and JCPenney. What can department stores do to make themselves more relevant to the youth subculture?

3. Check out the Hot Topic website (**www.hottopic.com**). Compare the submarkets (subsubcultures) Hot Topic is aiming for with those of Abercrombie & Fitch. Identify the behaviors, affective responses, and cognitions most important in shopping at each store.

4. How can A&F guard against becoming too mainstream and experiencing a customer backlash? Do you believe it is possible for A&F to remain popular with young shoppers for a span of many years?

5. Both A&F and The Gap are trying to use their brand names to market clothing to different age groups. For example, A&F has opened a chain of children's stores called abercrombie (lowercase "a"), while Gap, Inc., has had success with GapKids and BabyGap, Check out **www.abercrombiekids.com** and discuss the advantages and potential disadvantages of such a diversification strategy.

Sources: Lauren Goldstein, "The Alpha Teenager," *Fortune,* December 20, 1999, pp. 201–204; Rebecca Quick, "Is Ever-So-Hip Abercrombie & Fitch Losing Its Edge with Teens?" *The Wall Street Journal,* February 22, 2000, pp. B1, B4; Abigail Goldman, "Store Most Likely to Succeed: A&F," *Los Angeles Times,* April 3, 1999, p. 3; Stephanie Stoughton, "Listening to the 'Echo Boom,'" *Washington Post,* March 6, 1999, pp. E1, E3; **www. abercrombie.com.**

Reference Groups and Family

Chuck E. Cheese

Kids are big business. Children 12 and younger, directly or indirectly, account for $700 billion in spending in the United States each year. Furthermore, their numbers have been growing. In 2000, the number of elementary school–age kids in the United States numbered an estimated 36 million, about three times the number of youngsters in that age bracket in the 1980s. As you might expect, companies are paying more and more attention to these young consumers and their parents. One of the most successful youth marketers has been CEC Entertainment, parent company of Chuck E. Cheese Pizza.

The first Chuck E. Cheese opened in San Jose, California, in 1977, founded by Nolan Bushnell, who also founded the pioneering video game company Atari. By 2003, CEC Entertainment operated 455 Chuck E. Cheese restaurants in 47 states and three countries. Revenue in 2003 was $602 million, up 19 percent from 2000.

To describe Chuck E. Cheese as a restaurant seems rather inadequate, even though food and drink sales account for 70 percent of the company's revenue. It's almost like an indoor amusement park, with ball pits, rides, video games, and prizes. A new addition to many restaurants is "Studio C," a high-energy, interactive stage show starring the company's mouse mascot, Chuck E. Cheese. Oh, yes, about that mouse . . . kids love him! A 2000 survey found that among boys and girls between ages 6 and 8, Chuck E. Cheese is more popular than Winnie the Pooh, Bugs Bunny, or even his rodent cousin Mickey Mouse.

Birthday parties account for 12 to 15 percent of Chuck E. Cheese's business. In the words of one analyst, Chuck E. Cheese has transformed the birthday party "from Mommy's nightmare into Mommy's dream." With more and more single-parent families and households in which both parents work, fewer people have the time or energy to organize birthday parties for their kids. Many parents find it much

*Marjorie Farrell/
The Image Works.*

easier to simply outsource the party to Chuck E. Cheese. For a flat fee, the restaurant will provide dinner, soda, and even the birthday cake. And, of course, kids have access to all the fun and games.

Although Chuck E. Cheese is a destination spot for kids, the company works hard to make sure its restaurants also provide a suitable environment for parents. Although kids can exercise tremendous influence on the choice of a family dining spot, parents are the gatekeepers who ultimately make the final decision. In recent years, Chuck E. Cheese has upgraded its menu with better-quality pizza and an enhanced salad bar. It is also working to provide more seating for adults. At least one Chuck E. Cheese, near Detroit, even serves beer. The formula appears to be working. The average Chuck E. Cheese customer visits between five and seven times per year, and families spend an average of $9 per person each visit.

Chuck E. Cheese isn't the only restaurant that targets the youth subculture. Peter Piper installs cutting-edge video and simulator games to attract a slightly older crowd, while Rainforest Café boasts an interactive environment and plenty of at-table activities. Jeepers! has puppet shows and make-believe stores and doctor's offices. Even more traditional chains like Denny's, Friendly's, and T.G.I. Friday's have studied ways to better serve children and families.

Nor is the kid-oriented marketing restricted to the restaurant market. The market for children's grooming products in the United States has reached $3 billion annually. Fashion retailer Gap, Inc., has enjoyed success with its BabyGap and GapKids stores. Even big-name designers of adult clothing have gotten into the act, creating clothing for kids 3 to 5 years old—for example, a $250 black motorcycle jacket from Versace and a $150 cocktail dress from Nicole Miller.

Sources: C. Dickinson Waters, "Chuck E. Cheese Evolution on Main Street Gets an A-Plus Wall Street Rating," *Nation's Restaurant News,* April 3, 2000, pp. 11, 88; Carol Casper, "Babes in Toyland," *Restaurant Business,* October 15, 1998, pp. 61–62; **www.chuckecheese.com.**

This example shows how changes in the American family can affect marketing strategies targeted at kids or adults who buy for kids. In making these purchasing decisions, mothers and fathers influence each other's affective responses, cognitions, and behaviors. These decisions are also influenced by other people in the social environment, including relatives, friends, and peers (both kids and adults are highly influenced by peer groups). In this chapter, we discuss two types of social influences: reference groups and family.

Reference groups and family are aspects of the micro social environment for consumers. Social interactions with reference groups and family are often direct and face to face, which can have immediate influences on consumers' cognitive, affective, and behavioral responses to marketing strategies.[1] For instance, the social environment created when two friends shop together can influence each person's shopping experience, decision processes, and overall satisfaction with a purchase. As you learned in Chapter 11 (see Exhibit 11.2), reference groups and family are important in transmitting (moving) cultural meanings in the overall society, subcultures, and social class to individual consumers. For all these reasons, reference groups and family have significant implications for marketing strategies.

Reference Groups

Individuals may be involved in many different types of groups. A **group** consists of two or more people who interact with each other to accomplish some goal. Important groups include families, close personal friends, co-workers, formal social groups (Kiwanis, professional associations), leisure or hobby groups (a bowling team), and neighbors. Some of these groups may become reference groups.

A **reference group** involves one or more people whom someone uses as a basis for comparison or point of reference in forming affective and cognitive responses and performing behaviors. Reference groups can be of any size (from one person to hundreds of people) and may be tangible (actual people) or intangible and symbolic (successful business executives or sports heroes). People's reference groups (and single referent persons) may be from the same or other social classes, subcultures, and even cultures. Exhibit 14.1 lists several types of reference groups and their key distinguishing characteristics. These distinctions can be combined to better describe specific groups. For example, your immediate co-workers constitute a formal, primary, membership group. Although these distinctions can be useful, most consumer research has focused on two primary, informal groups: peers and family. Issues of major importance to marketing concerning reference group influence include the following:

1. What types of influence do reference groups exert on individuals?
2. How does reference group influence vary across products and brands?
3. How can marketers use the concept of reference groups to develop effective marketing strategies?

Exhibit 14.1

Types of Reference Groups

Type of Reference Group	Key Distinctions and Characteristics
Formal/informal	Formal reference groups have a clearly specified structure; informal groups do not.
Primary/secondary	Primary reference groups involve direct, face-to-face interactions; secondary groups do not.
Membership	People become formal members of membership reference groups.
Aspirational	People aspire to join or emulate aspirational reference groups.
Dissociative	People seek to avoid or reject dissociative reference groups.

Analyzing Reference Groups

Reference groups are cultural groups in that members share certain common cultural meanings. For instance, peer groups of college students tend to develop specific meanings and behavior norms about appropriate clothing (I am an Abercrombie & Fitch person.), and peer groups of teenage boys may share certain meanings about what types of athletic shoes are hot. These reference groups can influence the affective and cognitive responses of consumers as well as their purchase and consumption behavior (What should I wear today?).

Marketers try to determine the content of the shared meanings of various reference groups (the common values, beliefs, behavioral norms, and so on). Then they select certain reference groups to associate with or promote their products. But marketers seldom examine the social processes by which reference groups move cultural meaning to products and from products to the consumer.

Reference groups can have both positive and negative effects on consumers. Many social groups incorporate desirable, positive cultural meanings and become *associative* reference groups that consumers want to emulate or be affiliated with. Other social groups embody unfavorable or distasteful meanings and serve as a negative point of reference that people want to avoid; they become *dissociative* reference groups.

Types of Reference Group Influence

Most people are members of several primary informal groups and a few formal, membership groups (church, civic, and professional associations). In addition, people are aware of many other secondary groups, both formal and informal. Why do people use some of these groups as a reference group and not others? And how do these reference groups influence consumers' affect, cognitions, and behaviors? Basically, people identify and affiliate with particular reference groups for three reasons: to gain useful knowledge, to obtain rewards or avoid punishments, and to acquire meanings for constructing, modifying, or maintaining their self-concepts. These goals reflect three types of reference group influence: informational, utilitarian, and value-expressive.

Informational reference group influence transmits useful information to consumers about themselves, other people, or aspects of the physical environment such as products, services, and stores. This information may be conveyed directly— either verbally or by direct demonstration. For instance, a consumer trying to decide on a purchase of running shoes or stereo equipment might seek the advice of friends who are knowledgeable about those categories. A person who is trying to learn to play tennis might ask friends to demonstrate how to serve or hit a backhand shot.

Consumers tend to be more influenced by reference groups if the information is perceived as reliable and relevant to the problem at hand and the information source is perceived to be trustworthy.[2] Reference sources can be a single person, such as when the late Dave Thomas expounded on the merits of Wendy's hamburgers. Highly credible reference groups are more likely to have informational influence on consumers. Thus, some marketers hire recognized experts to endorse a product and tell consumers why it is good.

Information can also be obtained indirectly through vicarious observation. For instance, an avid fisher may carefully note the types of equipment famous bass fishers are using in a fishing tournament or on TV fishing shows. This is common behavior; many golfers, skiers, mountain climbers, and other sports enthusiasts engage in similar vicarious observations of products used by their reference groups. This is why Nike hired basketball star Michael Jordan (obviously an expert) to wear Air Jordan basketball shoes.

Information can be transmitted from reference groups to consumers in three ways. Sometimes consumers intentionally seek informational influence to reduce the perceived risk of making a decision or to help them learn how to perform certain behaviors. Thus, most beginning sky divers listen very carefully to their new reference group of experienced skydiving instructors as they present information about how to pack a parachute or how to land correctly. Consumers who buy a new computer may seek information provided by a reference group of more experienced users who can help them learn how to use the product effectively.

In other cases information is accidentally transmitted, such as when someone overhears reference group members talking about a product or observes members of a reference group using the product. A third way information may be transferred to the consumer is when reference group members initiate the process. This can occur with enthusiastic reference group members who seek to proselytize for an activity and gain new members. For example, rollerbladers might try to persuade others to take up the sport. Marketers might use a strategy of getting current customers to create new customers (bring along a friend for dinner and get your meal for half the price).

Utilitarian reference group influence on consumers' behaviors (and affect and cognitions) occurs when the reference group controls important rewards and punishments. Consumers usually will comply with the desires of a reference group if (1) they believe the group can control rewards and punishments, (2) the behavior is visible or known to the group, and (3) they are motivated to obtain rewards or avoid punishments.

In some work groups (a formal, membership reference group), people are expected to wear formal business suits, whereas other work groups encourage very casual dress (jeans and T-shirts in some Silicon Valley, California, companies). Rewards and punishments may be tangible (raises, bonuses, being fired), or psychological, and social consequences may occur (admiring looks or snide remarks behind your back). Peer groups often administer such psychosocial rewards and punishments for adherence to and violations of the reference group code. Consider how your own peer reference group in college influences your dress behavior. Marketers use these factors by showing such sanctions in TV commercials (people recoiling from offensive body odor, bad breath, or dandruff flakes on someone's shoulder).

Value-expressive reference group influence can affect people's self-concepts. As cultural units, reference groups both contain and create cultural meanings (beliefs, values, goals, behavioral norms, lifestyles). As you learned in Chapter 12, people constantly seek desirable cultural meanings to use in constructing, enhancing, or maintaining their self-concepts. By identifying and affiliating with certain reference groups that express these desired meanings, consumers can draw out some of these meanings and use them in their own self-construction projects.

One group of people who buy Harley-Davidson motorcycles and associated products consists of middle- and upper-middle-class professional people (including doctors, dentists, lawyers, and professors). Derisively called RUBS (rich urban bikers) or weekend warriors by hard-core Harley owners (the tattooed and bearded Outlaws or pseudo-Outlaws), many of these consumers treat the radical, hard-core Harley owners as an aspirational reference group (very few RUBS will ever become hard-core bikers).[3]

The hard-core Harley bikers express several desirable meanings and values for the RUBS (and probably convey negative meanings to nonbikers). By identifying to

Reference groups share
value-expressive products
Leland Bobbe/Getty Images.

some extent with the hard-core biker as an aspirational reference group, RUBS can gain some of these important meanings, including feelings of freedom (from work and family), freedom of spirit, radical independence, patriotism (Harleys are built in the United States), and a feeling of belonging to a unique group. Perhaps some RUBS are also able to inspire a bit of the fear and awe (among nonbikers or owners of other brands) that the hard-core bikers relish.

These reference group meanings can influence affect, cognitions, and behaviors, including purchases of biker clothing and bike accessories. Harley-Davidson recognizes these value-expressive desires and needs, and markets (often through licensing) a variety of products to satisfy them, including black leather jackets, "colors" (clothing with insignias and biker logos), many biking accessories, and even a Harley-Davidson brand of beer.

In summary, all three types of reference group influence can be accomplished by a single reference group. For instance, as a reference group for the weekend biker, hard-core Harley-Davidson bikers can be a source of information (through magazines and observation), rewards and punishments (waving back or haughtily ignoring the RUBS on the road), and subcultural meanings that express one's values.

Reference Group Influence on Products and Brands

Reference groups do not influence all product and brand purchases to the same degree. Based on research, reference group influence on product and brand decisions is thought to vary on at least two dimensions.[4] The first dimension concerns the degree to which the product or brand is a necessity or a luxury. A *necessity* is owned by virtually everyone (a flashlight), whereas a *luxury* is owned only by consumers in particular groups (a sailboat). The second dimension is the degree to which the object in question is conspicuous or known by other people.[5] A *public good* is one that other people are aware an individual owns and uses, one for which they can identify the brand with little or no difficulty (a car). A *private good* is used

Exhibit 14.2

Effects of Public–Private and Luxury–Necessity Dimensions on Reference Group Influence for Product and Brand Choice

	Necessity	Luxury

Public	**Public necessities**
	
	Reference group influence
	    Product: Weak
	    Brand: Strong
	Examples: Wristwatch, automobile,
	    man's suit
		Public luxuries
		
		Reference group influence
		    Product: Strong
		    Brand: Strong
		Examples: Golf clubs, snow skis,
		    sailboat

Private	**Private necessities**
	
	Reference group influence
	    Product: Weak
	    Brand: Weak
	Examples: Mattress, floor
	    lamp, refrigerator
		Private luxuries
		
		Reference group influence
		    Product: Strong
		    Brand: Weak
		Examples: Plasma TV, trash
		    compactor, ice maker

Source: Adapted from William O. Bearden and Michael J. Etzel, "Reference Group Influences on Product and Brand Purchase Decisions," *Journal of Consumer Research*, September 1982, p. 185. Copyright 1982 Journal of Consumer Research. Reprinted with permission of the publisher, University of Chicago Press.

at home or in private so that other people (outside the immediate family) would be unaware of its possession or use (a hair dryer).

Combining these two dimensions produces the matrix shown in Exhibit 14.2. This exhibit suggests that reference group influence will vary depending on whether the products and brands are public necessities, private necessities, public luxuries, or private luxuries. Consider wristwatches, which are public necessities. Because everyone can see whether a person is wearing a wristwatch, the *brand* may be susceptible to reference group influence. However, because the product class is owned and used by most people, there is likely to be little reference group influence on whether one should purchase a watch.[6]

Reference Groups and Marketing Strategy

We have seen that reference groups are an important influence on consumers. Not only do members of primary informal groups affect consumer knowledge, attitudes, and values, but they also affect the purchase of specific products and brands, and even the selection of stores in which purchases are made. In some cases, an analysis of primary informal group influences can be used to develop marketing strategies. For example, in industrial marketing, a careful analysis of the group influence dynamics among the various people who have a role in a purchase decision may be useful for determining appropriate marketing approaches.[7] Similarly, peer group influence is a major asset of firms that sell in-home to groups, as in the case of Tupperware parties. In such instances, many individuals conform to the norms of the group by purchasing a few items. Occasionally marketers try to stimulate reference group influence (a health club offers you two months' service free if you get a friend to sign up for a one-year membership).

Salespeople may attempt to create a reference group influence by describing how a customer is similar to previous purchasers of the product (There was a couple in here last week much like you. They bought the JVC speakers). Salespeople could describe themselves as a reference group (Oh, your two children go to East High School? My kids go there, too. We bought them a Dell PC to help them with their science projects).

Finally, soliciting experts to aid in the direct sale of products can be a successful strategy for some firms. For example, a consumer's dentist is likely to be a highly influential reference individual, particularly for products related to dental care.[8] Thus, the manufacturer of the Water Pik might offer gifts to dentists for encouraging patients to use the product. The company could keep track of a dentist's sales by having consumers list their dentists on the warranty cards for products. Of course, experts can also have an adverse impact on the sales of a new product if they convey negative information.[9]

For most mass-marketed products, a detailed analysis of the interactions of specific primary informal groups is impractical. Instead, marketers tend to portray both primary informal and aspirational groups in advertising:

> Reference group concepts have been used by advertisers in their efforts to persuade consumers to purchase products and brands. Portraying products being consumed in socially pleasant situations, the use of prominent/attractive people endorsing products, and the use of obvious group members as spokespersons in advertising are all evidence that marketers and advertisers make substantial use of potential reference group influence on consumer behavior in the development of their communications. Alluding to reference groups in persuasive attempts to market products and brands demonstrates the belief that reference groups expose people to behavior and lifestyles, influence self-concept development, contribute to the formation of values and attitudes, and generate pressure for conformity to group norms.[10]

There are many examples of the use of reference group concepts in advertising. Pepsi has featured popular stars such as Beyoncé and Faith Hill and popular athletes such as Sammy Sosa and Jeff Gordon, with whom many young people may identify. For many years Converse, Puma, Nike, and other running shoe companies spent a large portion of their promotion budgets on giveaways to successful athletes, as well as on hiring these athletes to wear and recommend their brands. The popular series of Miller Lite advertisements featuring well-known retired athletes appealed to baby boomers who followed the careers of these personalities and considered some of them heroes to be emulated. Highlight 14.1 describes the reference group appeal used by Pfizer.

Family   Most consumer behavior research takes the individual consumer as the unit of analysis. The usual goal is to describe and understand how individuals make purchase decisions so that marketing strategies can be developed to more effectively influence this process. The area of family research is an exception: It views the family as the unit of analysis.[11]

Actually, marketers are interested in both families and households. The distinction between a family and a household is important.[12] The U.S. Census Bureau defines a housing unit as having its own entrance (inside or outside) and basic facilities. If the housing unit has people living in it, they constitute a **household.** In 2000, there were 105 million households in the United States, with an average of 2.6 people per household. Except for homeless people, most Americans live in

High light 14.1

Reference Group Image Advertising

At one time, pharmaceutical companies didn't have to worry much about advertising their products to the general public; rather, they concentrated on influencing physicians. But in 1997, the Food and Drug Administration relaxed restraints on television and radio advertising, allowing drug companies to appeal directly to consumers. Since then, a number of these companies have used celebrities to promote their products.

Viagra, a pill created to help men with erectile dysfunction, hit the market in April 1998 to great fanfare. Shortly thereafter Viagra's manufacturer, Pfizer, hired former Republican presidential candidate Bob Dole as a spokesperson for the drug. The decision was somewhat surprising. Many were shocked that a conservative, 70-something World War II veteran like Dole would go on television and talk to millions of viewers about his sexual problems. But that is precisely what he did. Dole never mentioned Viagra by name in the ads, but the implication was obvious. The ads showed close-ups of a serious-looking Dole saying, "When I was diagnosed with prostate cancer, I was primarily concerned with ridding myself of the cancer. But sec-

ondly, I was concerned about postoperative side effects . . . erectile dysfunction . . . E.D." He went on to reassure viewers that "It's a little embarrassing to talk about E.D., but so important to millions of men and their partners . . . and there are many treatments available."

The Dole ad helped sales of Viagra reach $1 billion in 1999. According to one estimate, doctors write 5 million prescriptions for the drug every month. It is logical to assume that the Dole ads hit home with many Viagra users, 80 percent of whom are, like Dole, men over age 50.

Dole is not the only celebrity pharmaceutical companies have enlisted to tout their products. Schering-Plough paid former *Good Morning America* anchor Joan Lunden an estimated $1 million per year to promote its allergy medication Claritin. Merck hired baseball legend Cal Ripken to promote its high blood pressure drug Prinivil. Ripken does not suffer from high blood pressure, but Merck says the ads are designed to compare Ripken's work ethic (he played in a record number of consecutive games) with the hard work Prinivil does in fighting high blood pressure.

Sources: Rita Rubin, "Viagra's Banner Year. First Anniversary Provides Potent Cause to Celebrate," *USA Today,* March 17, 1999, p. 1D; Barbara Lippert, "On the Rise," *Adweek,* March 8, 1999, pp. 29–30; anonymous, "Celebrity Ads Becoming Favored Prescription for Drug Companies Seeking Healthy Profits," *Boston Globe,* February 21, 1999, p. E7.

households involving many different living arrangements, such as houses, townhouses, apartments, college dorm rooms, fraternity houses, military barracks, and nursing homes. Each household has a *householder,* the person who rents or owns the household. Households are categorized into types based on the relationship of the residents to the householder. Marketers are concerned with two main types of households: families and nonfamilies.

Nonfamily households include unrelated people living together, such as college roommates or unmarried couples of the opposite or same sex. In 2000 three of ten American households (32 million) were nonfamilies. In contrast, a **family** has at least two people: the householder and someone who is related to the householder by blood, marriage, or adoption. About 70 percent of American households (72,025,000) are families. The difference between nuclear and extended families is an important distinction. The *nuclear family* includes one or more parents and one or more children living together in a household. The *extended family* is a nuclear family plus other relatives, usually grandparents, living in one household. Extended families are more common in Hispanic and Asian subcultures.

Family Decision Making

Marketers are highly interested in **family decision making**—how family members interact and influence one another when making purchase choices for the household.[13] Research has shown that different people in the family may take on different social roles and perform different behaviors during decision making and consumption.[14] For example, the person who purchases Jif peanut butter for lunchtime sandwiches (the father) may not be the same person who prepares the sandwiches (the mother) or eats them (the children). To fully understand family decision making, marketers need to identify which family members take on which roles. Included among these decision-making roles are the following:

Influencers provide information to other family members about a product or service (a child tells parents about a new brand of breakfast cereal).

Gatekeepers control the flow of information into the family (a mother does not tell her children about a new toy she saw at the store).

Deciders have the power to determine whether to purchase a product or service (a husband decides to buy a new snack chip at the grocery store).

Buyers actually purchase the product or service (a teenager buys milk for the family at the convenience store).

Users consume or use the product or service (the kids eat canned spaghetti bought by the parents).

Northwestern Mutual Life orients its service to the needs of the family unit
Courtesy Northwestern Mutual Life.

Disposers dispose of a product or discontinue use of a service (a father throws out a partially eaten pizza; a mother stops a magazine subscription).

These roles clearly show that different family members may be involved in different aspects of the purchase decision process and in consumption of the product or service that is bought. From the perspective of the Wheel of Consumer Analysis, each family member and his or her roles and behaviors are part of the social environment for the other family members. Thus, studying family decision making requires that marketers study the social interactions among family members and the resulting patterns of reciprocal influence. This can be a difficult research challenge.

Developing successful marketing strategies for products purchased by families requires attention to questions such as these:

1. Is the product likely to be purchased for individual or joint family use?

2. Is the product likely to be purchased with individual or family funds?

3. Is the product so expensive that its purchase involves an important trade-off in purchasing other products for the family?

4. Are family members likely to disagree about the value of the product? If so, what can be done to reduce the conflict?

5. Is the product likely to be used by more than one family member? If so, are product modifications necessary to accommodate different people?

6. Which family members will influence the purchase, and what media and messages should be used to appeal to each?

7. Are particular stores preferred by various family members or by various families in the target market?

Answers to these questions influence the appropriate marketing strategy. For example, if a car is being purchased by a family for a teenager to drive to school, the type of product, method of financing, price, and appropriate promotion message and media should vary from those involved with the family's purchase of a car that the adult head of the household will use to commute to work.

Influences on Family Decision Making   Among the areas explored in research on family decision making are the following: (1) differences in product class and their relationship to family decision making, (2) the structure of husband/wife roles, and (3) the determinants of joint decision making.[15] However, relatively few generalizations for consumer analysis can be offered about family decision making. In fact, several years ago a review of the subject concluded that

1. Husband/wife involvement varies widely by product class.

2. Husband/wife involvement within any product class varies by the specific decision and decision stages.

3. Husband/wife involvement for any consumer decision is likely to vary considerably among families.[16]

Essentially we should expect considerable variance both in the persons involved at each stage of the decision-making process and in the extent to which they are involved.[17] For any given marketing problem, researchers must determine the dynamics of family decision making, which family members are involved, what roles they play, and who has the major influence. This analysis will help them develop effective marketing strategies targeted at the appropriate person.

Children and Family Decision Making   Most research on family decision making has focused on husband/wife roles and influence, whereas children (and other family members in extended families) have received little attention.[18] Yet, as illustrated in the opening example, the children's market is large and important. Children—both younger kids and teenagers—can have major influences on the family's budget allocation decisions and purchase choices. Also, the birth of a child is a major event for a family that creates demand for a wide variety of products most couples never would have considered purchasing previously.

Conflict in Family Decision Making   When more than one person in a family is involved in making a purchase decision, some degree of conflict is likely.[19] **Decision conflict** arises when family members disagree about some aspect of the purchase decision. The means–end chain model provides a useful framework for analyzing decision conflict. Family members may disagree about the desired end goals of a purchase. For instance, in choosing a family vacation, the husband may want to go somewhere for relaxation, the wife may want good shopping and nightlife, and the kids probably want adventure and excitement. Differences in end goals often create major conflict because very different choice alternatives are likely to be related to these incompatible ends. Serious negotiations may be required to resolve the conflict.

In other cases, family members may agree on the desired end goal but disagree about the best means to achieve it. For instance, everyone may want to go out to eat or see a movie, but the kids think a fast-food restaurant or action film is the best choice, whereas the parents prefer a full-service restaurant or a dramatic film. Again, some means of resolving the conflict is necessary. Often a different alternative (a new means to the end) is purchased as a compromise (everyone goes out for pizza or to a comedy film). Finally, when either the ends or the means are in conflict, family members are also likely to disagree about the choice criteria for evaluating the choice alternatives (For a new car, what is the appropriate price range, what options are necessary, what is the best color?).

Clearly there are times when family members disagree about such factors in a purchase situation, and occasionally the conflict may be severe.[20] When this happens, family members can do several things. Some consumers may procrastinate, ignoring the problem and hoping the situation will resolve itself. Others may try to get their way in the purchase decision process by trying to influence other family members. Exhibit 14.3 describes several influence strategies identified in family

---

Exhibit 14.3

Six Common Types of Family Influence Strategies

Expert influence is reflected by a spouse providing specific information concerning the various alternatives. For example, one spouse can try to convince the other that she/he is more knowledgeable concerning the products under consideration by presenting detailed information about various aspects of these products.

Legitimate influence deals with one spouse's attempts to draw upon the other's feelings of shared values concerning their role expectations. Therefore, the spouse's influence is based on the shared belief that she/he should make the decision because she/he is the wife/husband. For example, the husband can argue that since he is the "man of the house," he should make a particular decision.

Bargaining involves attempts by one spouse to turn the joint decision into an autonomous one in return for some favor granted to the other spouse. For example, in return for autonomy in a particular decision, one spouse may agree to give the other autonomy in another decision when she/he had previously refused to do so. "If you do this, I'll do that" may be the common type of bargaining attempt.

Reward/referent influence is based on a combination of the reward and referent power/influence strategies. Reward influence is based on an individual's ability to reward another by doing something that the other would enjoy. Referent influence is the influence based on the identification or feeling of oneness (or desire for such an identity) of one person with another. Referent influence in marriage stems from the desire of spouses to be like their concepts of the "ideal" husband or wife.

Emotional influence attempts involve displaying some emotion-laden reaction. For example, one spouse may get angry at the other. These attempts are often nonverbal techniques. For example, one person may cry or pout, while another may use the "silent treatment."

Impression management encompasses premeditated persuasive attempts to enhance one's influence differential in a dyadic relationship. For example, one spouse may claim that the other's preferred brand was "out of stock" when, in fact, it wasn't. The objective is to convince the spouse to attribute the influence attempt to external pressures beyond the influencer's control.

Source: From Rosann L. Spiro, "Persuasion in Family Decision Making," *Journal of Consumer Research,* March 1983, p. 394. Copyright 1983 Journal of Consumer Research. Reprinted with permission of the publisher, University of Chicago Press.

Exhibit 14.4

Patterns or Styles of Influence Behaviors

> **Noninfluencers.** This group, which characterizes 22 percent of the individuals in the sample, is substantially lowest in reported use of all the influence types. When the people in this group do attempt to influence their spouses, they are most likely to use the expertise type of influence.
>
> **Light Influencers.** This was the largest subgroup in the sample (36 percent). The mean scores on all the influence types are substantially higher than the scores for Noninfluencers but relatively low compared to all the other groups. Their relative use of the various influence strategies is very similar to (although higher than) the Noninfluencers, with the exception of their use of impression management. Light Influencer individuals are more likely to use some impression management as well as "expert" influence.
>
> **Subtle Influencers.** This mix characterizes 18.8 percent of the sample. Relative to their use of other strategies, these people rely heavily on the reward/referent strategy and secondly on the expert strategy. Apparently, they attempt to put their partners in a favorable "mood" (by being very nice, "buttering up") before a decision is made.
>
> **Emotional Influencers.** This category represents one of the two smallest groups (6.6 percent of the sample), yet its profile is quite distinctive. This profile displays the widest variations in the extent to which the different types of influence are used. These people report a high use of emotional influence and almost as high a use of reward/referent influence, a low use of legitimate and impression management, and a moderate use of both expert and bargaining strategies.
>
> **Combination Influences.** This mix (10 percent of the sample) is generally characterized by moderate use of all the influence strategies. In fact, there is less than one-half a scale-point difference between the strategy used least—legitimate—and the strategy used most frequently—expert.
>
> **Heavy Influencers.** The final group (6.6 percent of the sample) uses each of the six types of influence much more than any of the other groups. The people in this group use bargaining, reward/referent influence, and the emotional strategy more than they use expert and legitimate influence and impression management, but all of the mean scale scores are high, indicating their heavy use of all the influence strategies.

Source: From Rosann L. Spiro, "Persuasion in Family Decision Making," *Journal of Consumer Research,* March 1983, p. 397. Copyright 1983 Journal of Consumer Research. Reprinted with permission of the publisher, University of Chicago Press.

research.[21] Depending on the product being considered, the family members involved in the decision, the social class and subculture of the family, and the situational environment, a family member might use any of these strategies to influence other members.

Over time, family members may learn characteristic patterns of influence behaviors that they use repeatedly in conflict situations. In a study of furniture and appliance purchases, Rosann Spiro identified six styles of family influence used by adults.[22] These are described in Exhibit 14.4. Although children's influence behaviors were not considered in this study, strategies that kids use to influence their parents could also be analyzed.

Although serious conflicts can occur in family decision making, many family purchases probably do not involve major conflicts. For one thing, many family purchases are recurring in that several products and brands are bought repeatedly over a long period. So even if conflict was present in the past, it usually will have been resolved. To minimize continuous friction, families may develop choice plans to minimize or avoid potential conflict. For instance, a family with two children might allow one to choose the breakfast cereal or ice cream flavor one week and the other to choose the next week.

Another reason decision conflict among family members concerning purchase and consumption decisions is often not serious is that many purchases in a household are made by individuals to meet their own personal needs or those of other family members. To the degree that such purchases are reasonably consistent with family values and do not place an undue burden on family resources, there is likely to be little conflict. For instance, we would expect that purchases of books, personal care items, and many food products involve little family conflict.

Consumer Socialization

Through socialization processes, families transmit the cultural meanings of society, subcultures, and social class to their children and thereby influence their children's affect, cognitions, and behaviors.[23] **Consumer socialization** refers to how children acquire knowledge about products and services and various consumption-related skills (such as how to search for bargains).[24] Younger children acquire much of their consumer knowledge from their parents, but adolescents also learn from their peers. Both younger and older children learn consumer knowledge and skills from social institutions such as the media (TV, magazines, movies) and advertising.[25]

Socialization can occur directly through intentional instruction or indirectly through observation and modeling. Indirect socialization occurs when parents talk about products and brands or take their children on shopping trips. Sometimes parents intentionally try to teach their children consumer skills such as how to search for products, find the best price, bargain with salespeople, return products to the store for a refund, and dispose of products (recycle, hold a garage sale).[26]

The consumer knowledge formed in childhood can influence people in later years. Some adults still use the same brands of products their parents purchased for them as children. Thus, some long-lived brands may be purchased and used throughout an adult's life (Campbell's soup, Crest or Colgate toothpaste, Heinz ketchup, or Tide laundry detergent, among many others).

Developing early brand awareness and loyalty is an important marketing strategy for many companies. Thus, Chrysler has sponsored events during spring break at Daytona Beach (including building a 250-foot-long sand sculpture on the beach). Even though teens don't buy many cars, they can have a significant influence on their parents' choices, particularly for the second or third car in a household. As GM's basic car division, Chevrolet needs to attract today's teens, so it has advertised on MTV.[27]

The flow of socialization is not restricted to parents influencing their young children. Children can socialize their parents, especially about new products (teens may introduce their parents to new music styles).[28] As another example, adult children can influence the consumption behavior of their aged parents, such as decisions about retirement housing.[29] Finally, consumer socialization can occur throughout life as people continue to learn consumer skills and acquire product knowledge. Consider the socialization that occurs when people marry or begin cohabiting. Both partners learn from each other as they adjust to the other person's preferences and consumption behaviors.

Highlight 14.2

Avon Changes With the Times

Since 1886, the "Avon Lady" has been a part of American culture. For more than a century, Avon thrived by sending its representatives door to door selling cosmetics. However, the changing face of the American family meant trouble for Avon. Increasing numbers of women entering the work force has meant fewer women at home during the day. Moreover, people generally are less willing to open their doors to strangers than they were 20 or 30 years ago.

In 2000, Avon adapted its sales strategy to better reach busy working women. It staffed its website (**www.avon.com**) with live "e-representatives" who could help women make their cosmetics purchases online. In an even more radical move, the company announced plans to sell its products in U.S. stores for the first time in its 115-year history. Avon opened beauty centers and kiosks in malls across the country. Avon has also stepped up its advertising and diversified its product line in an attempt to overhaul its somewhat dowdy image and appeal to a new generation of younger, more active women. Avon's beComing line of beauty products is targeted to women ages 25 to 35 with annual household incomes in excess of $50,000. With its beComing products available in retail locations, Avon hopes to avoid cannibalizing the core Avon brand, which the Avon Ladies will continue to sell directly.

Sources: Emily Nelson and Ann Zimmerman, "Avon Goes Store to Store," *The Wall Street Journal,* September 18, 2000, pp. B1, B4; Mercedes M. Cardona, "Avon Thinks Younger, Wealthier," *Advertising Age,* October 2, 2000, p. 69; **www.avoncompany.com**.

Factors Influencing American Families

Many cultural and social changes have occurred in recent years that have influenced the structure of American families (many of these have happened in other countries, too). We briefly discuss three important changes: in female employment, in marriage and divorce, and in childbirth and child-rearing practices. These changes are highly interrelated.

Changes in Female Employment   At one time in American society (say, 50 years ago) the typical role of women was a homemaker. Today more than half of all women are in the labor force (Highlight 14.2 describes some consequences).[30] Working women are not distributed equally across all age groups, however. More than two-thirds of women in their 20s, 30s, and 40s are employed outside the home, but fewer older women have outside jobs. Of the women who work, 45 percent are employed full-time year round, compared to 65 percent of men who work full-time all year. More than 50 percent of young women with preschool children work, up from 30 percent in 1970.

The disposable income of married-couple households increases dramatically when both spouses work outside the home. The medium household income for dual-earner couples with children was $60,400 in 2001, some $15,000 greater than for one-earner households.[31] The total income of this segment is a staggering $900 billion, creating a vast market for many products.

Changes in Marriage and Divorce   American society has undergone major changes in people's attitudes and behaviors, toward marriage and divorce.[32] Young people have been delaying marriage (in 2001, the median age of first marriage was 25.1 for women and 26.8 for men), and increasing numbers of Americans may never marry.

As the 2000's progress, marriage is likely to become even more of an optional lifestyle.[33] Increasing numbers of single women are remaining unmarried and raising children alone. Although the majority will likely remarry, divorced and widowed people are waiting longer to remarry, and increasing numbers of them will never remarry. In addition, more Americans are living together outside of marriage. Some 2.8 million households contain unmarried, cohabiting couples (17 percent of unmarried people ages 25 to 29 are cohabiting, and nearly half have cohabited at some time). Although some people claim cohabiting is a way to cut the chances of divorce (because people learn more about their future spouses before marriage), divorce rates actually are higher for couples who cohabited before marriage (53 percent of first marriages that begin with cohabitation end in divorce compared to 28 percent of those in which the partners did not live together before marriage).

The net result is that more Americans are spending less of their lives in marriage. These changes will have profound implications for many consumer businesses whose markets have consisted of traditional families. Despite these important trends, however, marketers must remember that most Americans eventually do marry (or remarry), and many of them have children. Current estimates are that 90 percent of American women will marry at some time in their lives. The point is that marketers must consider a greater variety of family types than was necessary previously.

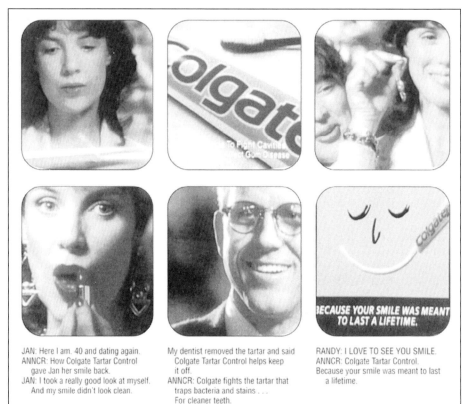

Many companies have recognized segments of the family life cycle such as divorced or widowed middle-aged people *Courtesy Colgate-Palmolive Company.*

JAN: Here I am. 40 and dating again.
ANNCR: How Colgate Tartar Control gave Jan her smile back.
JAN: I took a really good look at myself. And my smile didn't look clean.

My dentist removed the tartar and said Colgate Tartar Control helps keep it off.
ANNCR: Colgate fights the tartar that traps bacteria and stains . . . For cleaner teeth.

RANDY: I LOVE TO SEE YOU SMILE.
ANNCR: Colgate Tartar Control. Because your smile was meant to last a lifetime.

Changes in Childbirth and Child-Rearing Practices   As more baby boomers begin their own families, the number of births has increased to near record levels (3.95 million births in 2002). The number of births is up because there are more potential parents among the baby boomers, not because families are having more children. In fact, the number of children per family has been decreasing steadily since the mid-1960s. Women now bear an average of fewer than two children, down from nearly three in 1965.[34] Despite this trend toward smaller families, there still are some large families in America. Some 8 million families have three or more children (23 percent of families with kids, down from 40 percent in the late 1960s).[35] These larger families constitute very important markets for certain family-oriented products such as breakfast cereal, milk, toothpaste, and toilet paper.

Also, because people are marrying later and having children later than their parents did, changes have occurred in how they raise their kids and relate to them. Finally, parents live many years after the children leave home. All of these changes mean people spend less of their lives in child-oriented households than once was the case.

Demographic Changes in Household Composition

American family and nonfamily households have undergone major demographic changes during the past few decades that have significant implications for marketers. For instance, the number of households grew to 105 million households in 2000. Because the number of households grew faster than the total population (now about 292 million), the average household size dropped to 2.6 people in 2000 from 2.8 in 1980.

American families are highly diverse, and the various types of families constitute distinctive markets for many products. Still the most common family is the *married-couple family*—householders who live with their spouses (53 percent of American households). This category grew about 5 percent over the past 10 years. Most of these households have dual earners; only 21 percent of married-couple households in 1998 contained a male breadwinner and a female homemaker, down from 61 percent in 1960.

The so-called *traditional family* has several definitions, but it usually means a married-couple family with children under 18. This category actually declined slightly during the 1980s and currently stands at 25 percent of all households. Sometimes traditional family means a working husband and a homemaker wife; only 11 percent of households fit this description. Finally, if the traditional family means a working husband, a nonworking wife, and exactly two children, we are talking about only 3 percent of all American households.

So-called *nontraditional families* are also growing in number. Among this type of family, the most common household with children is headed by a woman with no husband present (nearly 10 million American households in 1997).[36] In the late 1990s, the fastest-growing family type was headed by single dads (1.9 million) and growing at 10 percent a year.

Despite this fragmentation into different types of families, the family unit is still America's largest market, accounting for 69 percent of all households. Actually, the 1990s were a family decade, thanks to the large numbers of baby boomers in the midst of their child-rearing years. Three-fourths of all boomer households are families.

Nontraditional families and nonfamily households are growing in number. Among this segment are single-parent families and families headed by gay couples   *(left) Copyright Mary Elenz-Tranter; (right) Suzanne Arms/The Image Works.*

Nonfamily households make up 31 percent of all U.S. households and are growing rapidly. They were up 16 percent during the 1990s, compared to a 7 percent gain for families. For instance, households headed by a single, unmarried person constitute nearly 15 percent of all households. Unrelated people living together constitute a rapidly growing proportion (now about 5 percent) of nonfamily households. Nearly 4 million of these households are made up of unmarried couples of both sexes, sometimes called *cohabiting couples.* Currently one in four nonfamily households consists of a single person living alone. Men living alone make up 11 percent of households and women 15 percent. Two factors are behind this surge. First, unprecedented numbers of consumers are not marrying; second, up to 60 percent of those who do marry will eventually divorce and become single again. These social trends toward living alone have created major opportunities for marketers.

Dealing with the many demographic changes in family composition and structure can be difficult. To organize these complexities, marketers often use the concept of the *family life cycle,* a strategic tool to identify key family segments and develop effective marketing strategies for those households.

Family Life Cycle

Thirty or forty years ago, most Americans followed the same life path and went through about the same stages of life. People got married, had children, stayed married, raised their children and sent them on their way, grew old, retired, and eventually died. The traditional family life cycle identified these typical stages as a linear sequence of family types marked by major life events (marriage, birth of children, aging, departure of children, retirement, death). These major life events create very different social environments (consider the birth of a baby) that influence consumers' affective reactions, cognitions, and consumption behaviors. For instance, the highest purchase rate for home appliances is that of newly married couples.

Exhibit 14.5

A Modern Family Life Cycle

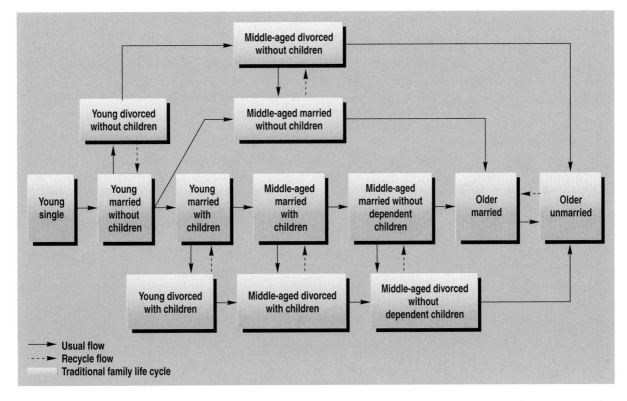

Source: From Patrick E. Murphy and William A. Staples, "A Modernized Family Life Cycle," *Journal of Consumer Research, June* 1979, pp. 12–22. Copyright 1979 Journal of Consumer Research. Reprinted with permission of the publisher, University of Chicago Press.

The recent cultural changes in American society such as delayed marriages, childless marriages, working women, and increased divorce rates have rendered the traditional family life cycle somewhat inadequate. Exhibit 14.5 presents a **modern family life cycle** that incorporates the traditional family life cycle but adds several other family types to account for the more diverse family structures of today.[37] The modern family life cycle captures most types of families in American society, including childless couples, divorced parents, and single parents with children.

Single parents constitute 9 percent of all households. Most are divorced parents, but some mothers who have never married are raising children. Although income is a relatively low $21,400 average, the growing numbers of single parents create a sizable market.

Young singles are people under 45 who live by themselves. Currently they are 9 million households, or 9 percent of all households. The tendency to delay or avoid marriage is increasing in this segment. Their average income level of $25,000 gives this group significant purchasing power, and their lack of responsibilities gives them considerable discretion in spending it. This rapidly increasing market is very important for companies that sell products purchased by households (appliances, kitchen utensils, TVs, basic furniture, and so on).

Older singles are people over 45 who live alone. They are 15 million households, or 16 percent of all households. Although their average income is relatively low ($17,500), their large numbers make them a significant market.

Married couples with children include two important subcategories: (1) dual-earner couples and (2) other married couples (usually a working husband and a homemaker wife). The distinction is important for two reasons: Average household income is $49,600 versus $40,000, and lifestyles differ considerably in these households. Life in the dual-earner households is usually more hectic, and the parents are more pressed for time than in other married-couple households.

Television producers considered some of these stages in the family life cycle in creating television situation comedies, as evidenced by several shows in the late 1990s starring single fathers with children.

Marketing Analysis   In this section, we discuss several considerations for using the family life cycle for marketing analysis. First, it is important to recognize that the modern family life cycle does not include nonfamily households, which currently are nearly 30 percent of all American households. This diverse category includes people who never marry, cohabiting couples, and shared households containing various combinations of unrelated residents. Although these diverse households are difficult to identify and target with marketing strategies, their numbers—28 million—make them very attractive markets for many products.

Also, the family life cycle does not capture every possible change in family status that can occur. For instance, a new life cycle stage has developed called the "boomerang age."[38] This group refers to the increasing number of young adults (mostly in their 20s) who left home for work or college but then returned to live with their parents. Currently there are more of these people than at any time since the Great Depression.

Actually, living with parents past high school and even college is not so unusual. Only one-third of young adults (19 to 24) live independently of their parents (25 percent of men and 38 percent of women). Most young people begin to live independently at ages 22 to 24, but few will live alone (only about 5 percent of young adults live alone). Many will live in a nonfamily household of unrelated adults or cohabit with a potential marriage partner. In addition, as many as 40 percent of young adults return to live in their parents' homes at least once. This "boomerang" segment of the family life cycle may offer some marketing opportunities.

Marketers use the family life cycle to segment the market, analyze market potential, identify target markets, and develop more effective marketing strategies. But the family segments identified by the family life cycle are not entirely homogeneous. In fact, each family type is variable and contains highly diverse types of people. For instance, each family type contains people from every social class and every age, racial, ethnic, and regional subculture in the country. Consider the young single or bachelor stage of the family life cycle. The number of bachelors has increased 21 percent since 1980 to nearly 30 million men.

Much of this growth is due to the "new" bachelors created by divorce. The rate of increase in divorced men (5.6 million) is rising about twice as fast as that of never-married men (21 million). For instance, 18- to 24-year-old men in the swinging years (99 percent have never married, but most will someday) are a prime market for CD players, six-packs, and hot cars. But 35- to 45-year-old unmarried men (51 percent of whom are divorced) are more interested in toys for their kids, living room furniture, and toilet bowl cleaners. Many divorced men (19 percent of all bachelors) are only temporary bachelors; many will remarry within an average of three years. Approximately 7 percent of bachelors are widowers. With an average age of 61, their behavior resembles married men their age more closely than other bachelors. With this type of diversity, developing marketing strategies for the bachelor segment is a challenge for marketers.

Another point to recognize is that some stages in the family life cycle are more important markets than others. For instance, households headed by people ages 35 to 54 spend more on every product category (except health care) than other types of families.[39] Consider food. Middle-aged households spent about $4,700 on food in 1988, 22 percent more than average households. The youngest and oldest households spent considerably less than the average ($2,500 and $2,000, respectively). This segment of middle-aged households became even more important through the 1990s and into the 2000s as all baby boomers entered this life cycle stage. Most of these boomers have children and will spend heavily on them.

Stages of the family life cycle that contain children are quite important to many marketers (toys, clothing, video products). Many companies study the purchasing habits of kids, including quite young children. Highlight 14.3 raises some ethical issues about the approaches used to study the consumer behavior of young teens.

Marketing Implications   The family life cycle can help marketers understand how important cultural trends affect family structures and consumption behavior. For example, consider the estimated 43 million "time-starved" consumers in the United States.[40] Time has become more precious to many people as the pace of family life gets more hectic and as more families have two wage earners (two-thirds of married couples with children are dual-income households) or are headed by single parents. Millions of people are stressed about time, believe they don't have enough time, and are striving to save time. They are prime candidates for convenience products of all types that can save time, which they can then use for more enjoyable or profitable purposes.

For many of these people, shopping is a stressful chore that interferes with their leisure. Fully 63 percent of Americans think most shopping is drudgery. According to one survey, these perceptions are strongest among married-couple families with children, especially if both parents work. Eleven million of these people do not enjoy shopping, and half believe shopping adds to their stress level. Clearly, the thrill of shopping is gone for many (but not all) Americans.

These attitudes are reflected in various consumption-related behaviors. For instance, in 1988, the average consumer spent 90 minutes on a shopping trip to the mall; in 1990, shopping time was down to 68 minutes. Many consumers have developed shopping strategies to save time. For instance, some people shop for clothes only two or three times a year. Some shoppers follow a certain path through the store to eliminate duplication of effort. In one extreme case, a consumer followed a regimented strategy by shopping for groceries each Tuesday from 4:45 to 5:15 PM. As she sprints through the store in a virtual trance, it will be very difficult to catch her attention with a new marketing strategy. One executive bought a car at a dealer located near the airport so he can have the car serviced during business trips.

Relatively few marketers have done much to reduce shopping time and stress, but there are many opportunities for marketers to appeal to the time-stressed shopper. These need not be highly sophisticated strategies; Dayton-Hudson, for example, changed to a central-aisle layout to make it easier for customers to find their way through the store. Following are several ideas for marketing strategies to help reduce shopping time and stress.

Highlight 14.3

Ethical Considerations in Marketing to Kids

Once marketers promoted toys and breakfast cereals to kids. Then it was sneakers and video games. Now kids are sought after as consumers by nearly every company. The main reason is money. The amount of money kids spend or influence is much larger than once thought. Until recently, marketers believed kids spent or influenced about $150 billion annually. Recent evidence suggests that the actual figure is close to $500 billion, roughly the same amount Americans spend annually on all forms of legalized gambling. Thus, U.S. companies spend more than $12 billion a year trying to bring their messages to children.

Kids seem to form brand relationships quite early, perhaps as young as 2 years old. Debbie Solomon, senior researcher at J. Walter Thompson (an advertising agency), suggests that the majority of American adults use the same toothpaste, peanut butter, and canned soup their parents used when they were kids.

Marketers are using various research techniques to learn more about these young consumers.

- To learn what kids do, Levi's supplied kids with throwaway cameras and video cameras and asked them to make photo diaries about how they and their friends spend time.
- BBDO, a New York ad agency, arranged for 30 high school students to spend a chaperoned weekend in a posh New York City hotel to do focus group interviews about new Pepsi ads.

- To learn how young teenage girls think about clothes, a researcher working for Esprit had three girls, age about 14, spend several overnights in her guest room while working as interns for her research firm.
- Sega of America conducts online dialogues with kids (their prime customers) in which they capture about 2,000 names and addresses of potential and future customers each week.
- Sony, IBM, and Columbia Records are among the corporations that use a product called SchoolCards, postcards featuring advertising, social, cultural, and educational messages that are free to students in more than 300 schools in the United Kingdom. Companies learn the pick-up rate of each card and get feedback about students' reactions, thus learning about changes in trends and opinions among kids.
- A research firm called Kid2Kid hires teens as young as 14 to conduct focus groups of kids' reactions to products and ads.
- To learn what products are important to kids, Levi's gave kids from $50 to $100 and asked them to record how they spent every bit of it.

What do you think about the ethics of these marketing practices? Is it OK for business firms to use sophisticated marketing research techniques to understand young consumers? How young should companies go? Should parents be involved in the decision to participate? What other factors would be relevant to your determination of the ethics of each situation?

Sources: Bruce Horovitz, "Retailers in Search of Customers for Life," *USA Today,* December 18, 1997, pp. A1–A2. Copyright 1997. Reprinted with permission; Jo-Anne Flack, "Child Minding," *Marketing Week,* July 8, 1999, pp. 41–44.

Provide Information. Marketers that provide useful information to help consumers make the right choices will save their customers time and reduce shopping stress. For instance, Blockbuster has a computerized database to help customers find films made by a certain director or starring a particular actor. Computer technology could be used to help consumers make the right choices of color, size, styles for clothing, automobiles, and home furnishings. Coordinated displays of related products, such as showing entire ensembles, can serve the same purpose. Amazon.com provides book suggestions based on a consumer's prior purchases.

Assist in Planning. People often try to cope with time stress by carefully planning their shopping excursions. Marketers that help consumers form purchase plans will help them reduce stress. High-quality sales assistance in the clothing store or appliance showroom can help a time-stressed customer develop a decision plan. Marketers might suggest alternatives when a product is unavailable. Blockbuster Video tries to give customers movie alternatives if their first-choice film is unavailable.

Develop Out-of-Store Selling. Although shopping once was a pleasant and desirable experience, today many consumers would rather be relaxing at home. This trend creates problems for retailers but also creates new opportunities for selling in the home or at the workplace. Avon, for example, has begun to sell its products to groups of co-workers at the work site. Many consumers use creative combinations of Internet, catalog, and in-store shopping—even from the same retailer.

Automate Processes. Companies that can automate and thereby speed up transaction processes will appeal to time-stressed consumers. At Wegmen's, a supermarket chain in Rochester, New York, customers can use a computer to enter their deli orders so they don't have to wait in line to be served; they pick up their deli orders as they leave the store. Grocery stores such as A&P and Shop Rite have instituted automated checkout and self-checkout systems to reduce waiting time in the checkout line. Most car rental companies, such as Hertz and Alamo, offer an automated check-in service at major airports. Hand-held computers speed the check-in process so that customers receive the invoice on the spot as they leave the car in the parking lot. Customers can speed to the airport with no waiting.

Improve Delivery. Nothing upsets a time-stressed consumer more than having to wait all day at home for a service person to come to fix an appliance. For years, GE has made precise appointments for its service calls. Sears now offers repair services six days a week and in the evening. In Pasadena, California, Vons grocery offers drive-up service for 1,400 items. How about a service court in a mall where consumers could obtain a variety of services (dry cleaning, shoe repair, small-appliance repairs, mailing) in one stop?

Back To...

Chuck E. Cheese

The opening example illustrates several of the concepts discussed in this chapter. Most obviously, it shows that "kids," even very young children, are a large and growing market. Even though kids don't always spend their own money, children can play a major role in influencing family purchase and consumption decisions. Therefore, restaurants (and other companies) that target young families need to cultivate an image and atmosphere that appeals to both kids and parents. Also, we see how demographic and cultural changes have contributed to Chuck E. Cheese's success. Not only is the number of school-age children growing in the United States, but also parents' increasingly hectic schedules (a cultural factor) have made it more desirable to eat out than cook a meal or host a birthday party at home. Furthermore, in their consumption decisions, parents are influenced by their peers (friendship reference groups) and other relatives in their extended families. Indirectly, parents are also influenced by their children's peers (if your son's friends all go to Chuck E. Cheese, it is likely he will want to go there, too). In sum, marketers can use the concepts of reference group and family to analyze consumers' behaviors, segment the overall market, and develop marketing strategies to influence those segments. ❖

Summary   This chapter described two aspects of the micro social environment: reference groups and family. After defining groups and reference groups, we discussed three types of reference group influence: informational, utilitarian, and value-expressive. Then we discussed how reference groups can influence purchase decisions about products and brands, and looked at ideas for using reference groups in marketing strategies. Next, we distinguished between families and households.

We discussed decision making by families, considering the different decision-making roles taken by family members, including children. We examined conflict in family choices and described several ways family members might try to resolve the decision conflict and influence one another. We also discussed consumer socialization—how consumers obtain knowledge about products and consumer skills. Next, we described several demographic trends that have changed family households. We concluded with a model of the family life cycle and examined how marketers could use the family life cycle to analyze markets and develop marketing strategies.

Key Terms and Concepts

consumer socialization **360**
decision conflict **357**
family **355**
family decision making **356**
group **349**
household **354**
informational reference group
 influence **350**

modern family life cycle **365**
nonfamily households **355**
reference group **349**
utilitarian reference group
 influence **351**
value-expressive reference group
 influence **351**

Review and Discussion Questions

1. Identify two reference groups that influence your consumption behavior. Describe each according to the types listed in the text, and identify the categories of purchases each influences.
2. From a marketing manager's viewpoint, what are some advantages and problems associated with each type of reference group influence?
3. Describe how public visibility and the distinction between luxury and necessity goods affect reference group influence on choice at the product and brand levels.

4. What is the family life cycle? Discuss how it can be used to develop effective marketing strategies.

5. Identify three different family purchases in which you played a role in the decision process. What role did you play? Discuss the interpersonal interactions involved in these decisions.

6. Suggest two ways in which marketing strategies could influence the decision process in your family or household. How are these different from strategies that might be used to influence individual decisions?

7. Offer examples of conflict in family household decision making that you have experienced or observed. What types of marketing strategies could help reduce such conflict?

8. Discuss the differences between households and families. Describe how each is important to marketers.

9. How are family influence strategies similar to or different from other reference group influences? What marketing implications are related to these distinctions?

10. Identify two different household or family compositions. Assume each unit has the same level of income and discuss how the decision processes and conflicts might vary for a product such as an automobile, a vacation, or a stereo system.

Marketing Strategy in Action

The Saturn Family

Consumers are bombarded with advertisements and marketing hype every day. When you log onto the Internet, watch television, listen to the radio, read a newspaper, or open your mail, you are inevitably greeted with a plea to purchase brand X or visit store Y or website Z. In any given day, you are exposed to more information than you can realistically process. In the 1990s, marketers began to look for fresh, innovative ways to make their companies stand out from the media clutter. Few have been as successful as General Motors' subsidiary Saturn, whose 1994 "homecoming" of car owners has been described as "the mother of all marketing programs."

Saturn's mission statement emphasizes the concept of "family." In an industry whose history is replete with labor conflict, Saturn has tried to erase the line between labor and management. In fact, the very words *labor* and *management* are somewhat taboo. Regardless of their positions in the company, all Saturn employees—from vice presidents to the newest workers on the assembly line—are considered "team members." Saturn boasts that no one punches a time clock and that members of labor and management even eat in the same cafeteria! Moreover, the company expects its employees and dealers to make customers feel like a part of the Saturn family.

According to Joe Kennedy, Saturn's corporate vice president of sales, service, and marketing, "Everything at Saturn hinges on our retail operations being enthusiastic about serving their customers." Indeed, salespeople (or, as Saturn prefers to call them, "consultants") have gone far out of their way to make current and potential customers happy. In one legendary story, a woman in Wyoming was interested in purchasing a Saturn only to find that the nearest dealership was hundreds of miles away in Salt Lake City, Utah. Not to worry. A salesperson from Salt Lake City flew to Wyoming, picked the woman up, flew back with her to the dealership in Utah, showed her the car, and made the sale. Saturn instituted a "no-haggle" pricing policy to reduce the traditionally antagonistic relationship between automobile salespeople and customers. Saturn's television ads have featured employees discussing the family feeling at the company and actual customers sharing their own Saturn stories.

The "Saturn family" concept took hold with consumers. Soon delighted customers began calling and writing the company's plant in Spring Hill, Tennessee (near Nashville), to learn how they could tour the facility and maybe meet other Saturn owners from across the country. So management decided to spend $1 million to hold its first "homecoming" of Saturn owners and their cars the weekend of June 24–25, 1994 in Spring Hill. It mailed out 650,000 invitations to Saturn owners and also purchased commercial time on CBS's *Late Show with David Letterman.*

The response was overwhelming. About 30,000 Saturns—and their owners—made the pilgrimage. If you were on the highway that week and saw a Saturn with an orange ball on the radio antenna, that car was probably headed home to Tennessee. Saturn owners came from as far away as Taiwan and filled most of the 24,000 hotel rooms in the Nashville area. In fact, a dealer from Taiwan brought home the first Saturn ever sold in that country. That car was honored with its own tent. Throughout the weekend, car owners met members of the Saturn team, toured the plant, and shared their own Saturn stories. The homecoming had all the trappings of an old-fashioned outdoor revival with music, dancing, testimonials from celebrities (Olympic speed skater Dan Jansen), and food (everything from "southern Chinese egg rolls" to barbecued catfish).

Even though two Herculean thunderstorms blew over some tents, injured a few people, and forced the cancellation of a scheduled concert by country music star Wynonna, it didn't seem to dampen many folks' spirits. Mary Taylor, age 60, was part of a 22-car caravan that trekked 1,800 miles from Nevada to Tennessee to be part of the homecoming. She couldn't stop raving about her dealer. "I couldn't believe how much they cared," Taylor said. "They know us when we walk in. It's such a friendly atmosphere, I look forward to going to the dealership." Another Saturn owner compared the weekend get-together with Woodstock: "This is another gathering in a field, except it's about cars, not music." Ruth Morrissey from South Dakota perhaps summed up the weekend best as she gushed, "We love our Saturns. We are all just a bunch of walking ads." For those who couldn't make it to Spring Hill, Saturn sponsored smaller-scale get-togethers at dealerships around the United States. An estimated 100,000 additional people attended those events.

The homecoming was just a part of Saturn's overall strategy of making customers feel like part of a big Saturn family. Was this approach successful? Apparently it was. Company research in 1994 showed that out of the approximately 650,000 people who owned Saturns, 80 percent planned to buy another Saturn. Furthermore, Saturn reported that during the homecoming ad campaign (which ran from January through June 1994), sales were up 25 percent compared to a year earlier.

Other carmakers took notice and copied the Saturn homecoming model. DaimlerChrysler's Jeep division sponsored an event called Jeep 101 in which Jeep owners—many of whom drive exclusively on paved urban streets—took their vehicles off-road. Mercedes-Benz of North America invited 100,000 current and potential customers to Los Angeles for an unveiling of new models. The opportunity to ogle these pricey new automobiles—plus the lure of good food and wine— apparently was quite compelling. So many people showed up that they had to close down a highway. In another promotion, Mercedes invited 1 million people to "fall in love" with a new Mercedes by attending one of a variety of special customer bonding events at local dealerships.

To be sure, Saturn has had its share of problems since that first homecoming event in 1994. Some critics have sniped at Saturn's boring styling and limited choice of models. Others believe Saturn has slipped compared to other carmakers in terms of performance and reliability. Sales of the L-series mid-size car were very disappointing, which forced production slowdowns and layoffs in 2000. In addition, the harmonious relationship between labor and management hit a snag when Saturn's 7,000 unionized employees began to express dissatisfaction with their special labor agreement with the carmaker. Seeing a problem, General Motors in 2000 pledged to invest $1.5 billion to expand the Spring Hill facility and provide Saturn with an SUV and a redesigned compact car in time for the 2002 model year. (To check out Saturn's current model line and other company information, visit the company's website at **www.saturn.com.**

But make no mistake, Saturn's innovative marketing efforts have accomplished their goal. Even with the recent problems, surveys reveal that most consumers—especially younger people—still believe Saturn is, as its ad campaign declares, "a different kind of car company." In 1999, Saturn held another large, successful homecoming and many industry experts believe that with new models in the offing, Saturn can regain the momentum it had in the mid-1990s.

Discussion Questions

1. Visit the Saturn website and try to determine the market segments the carmaker is targeting. What should Saturn do to better serve those segments? How might Saturn tailor its offerings to address the different stages of the family life cycle?

2. Other vehicles—such as Porsches, Mustangs, and Harley-Davidson motorcycles—also have "cult" followings. But these products also have very strong symbolic meanings associated with them. The Saturn is a solid and reliable, but basically unspectacular, car. Identify and discuss three reasons that you think Saturn has such a devoted following of involved customers.

3. An automobile is a high-involvement purchase. Discuss how the manufacturer of a lower-cost, lower-involvement product could generate greater personal relevance and long-term loyalty. Find and discuss an example of a company that has done so.

4. Saturn is a company that generates sales and loyalty through meaningful one-on-one interactions with customers. What is the role of traditional mass media advertising for firms such as Saturn that use innovative ways to reach consumers?

Sources: Matthew Grimm, "Getting to Know You," *Brandweek,* January 4, 1999, pp. 16–18; Daniel Hill, "Love My Brand," *Brandweek,* January 19, 1998, pp. 26–29; Andy Cohen, "Saturn," *Sales and Marketing Management,* November 1996, p. 58; James Bennett, "Saturn Invites the 'Family' to a Party," *The New York Times,* June 20, 1994 pp. D1, D8; Alan Solomon, "Car Is Big Wheel at Homecoming," *Advertising Age,* July 4, 1994, p. 12; **www.saturn.com.**

five

Consumer Analysis and Marketing Strategy

15

Market Segmentation and Product Positioning

H2—Oh!—Positioning the Hummer H2

In July 2002, General Motors introduced a new SUV: the Hummer H2, a scaled-down version of the Hummer H1 produced by AM General. The H2 stood 6½ feet tall, weighed 6,400 pounds, and was built on a Silverado chassis. It was made of mostly GM parts, although manufactured by AM General at its South Bend, Indiana, plant. The base sticker price was about $50,000, a big number for an SUV. It did not have a gas mileage rating, but GM claimed that it got 10 to 13 miles per gallon (some dealers and owners claimed 8 to 10 mpg), which didn't compare to the mileage of a Ford Expedition (14 to 19 mpg) or a three-quarter-ton Chevy Suburban (13 to 17 mpg), much less a high-mileage passenger car. Environmentalists claimed GM was irresponsible to put a car like the H2 on the road and planned anti-Hummer campaigns denouncing the low mileage, high pollution, and damage it would do to wilderness areas. AM General had sold

only about 700 Hummer H1s per year. Thus, the H2 was big, heavy, expensive, unpopular with environmentalists, and based on a previous unsuccessful product. So it probably wasn't going to sell, right?

Wrong! In the first six months after its introduction, consumers bought nearly 19,000 H2s, and General Motors expected to sell at least 40,000 per year until 2005, when it plans to introduce the H3, a more diminutive and affordable version. It was one of the most successful new-product introductions in GM history. Celebrities like Arnold Schwarzenegger, who already owned five Hummer H1s, bought an H2, as did Arizona Diamondbacks star Luis Gonzalez and Phoenix Suns center Scott Williams. High-school-to-NBA basketball phenomenon Lebron James and rap star Coolio drive H2s. "Anybody who's anybody right now is buying an H2," said Jim Seawards, a general sales director for Legends Cadillac Hummer dealership. "I can't keep enough of them in stock. My sales are predicated on supply. If I get 30 a month, I sell 30 a month. Everything goes." The dealership has an eight-week wait to get an H2, which will sell at full price with no discounts. Many of the H2s are sold with huge chrome wheels, low-profile tires, exotic audio systems, and other accessories, often nearly doubling the list price.

GM markets the vehicle as a "real" SUV that can carry heavy cargo, maneuver easily over rocks, plow through mud, and navigate water 20 inches deep. The website for the Hummer H2 states: "In a world where SUVs have begun to look like their owners, complete with love handles and mushy seats, the H2 proves that there is still one out there that can drop and give you 20. And with a more spacious comfortable interior and a host of standard features, the H2 strikes a perfect balance between interior comfort, on-road capability and off-road capability."

AP/Wide World Photos.

Sources: Bob Golfen, "Buyers Snap Up Hummer H2," azcentral.com, February 10, 2003; "SUV Backlash? Not for Hummer Owners," USATODAY.com, February 3, 2003; Michael McCarthy, "Ad Track: Hummer H2 Makes Impression Despite SUV Backlash," USATODAY.com, January 26, 2002; Melanie Wells, "Muscle Car," *Forbes*, July 22, 2002, p. 181; Alex Taylor III, "Humdinger," *Fortune*, October 28, 2002, p. 225; **www.hummer.com.**

How is the H2 positioned and who buys them? Market segmentation is one of the most important concepts in the consumer behavior and marketing literature. A primary reason for studying consumer behavior is to identify bases for effective segmentation, and a large portion of consumer research concerns segmentation. From a marketing strategy view, selection of the appropriate target market is paramount to developing successful marketing programs.

The logic of market segmentation is quite simple: It is based on the idea that a single product usually will not appeal to *all* consumers. Consumers' purchase goals,

Highlight 15.1

Can Target Marketing Be Unethical?

Dividing markets into segments and then selecting the best ones to serve is one of the cornerstones of sound marketing practice. However, there are situations when target marketing has been criticized as being unethical.

- R. J. Reynolds Tobacco Company (RJR) planned to target African American consumers with a new brand of menthol cigarette, Uptown. This brand was to be advertised with suggestions of glamor, high fashion, and night life. After criticism for targeting a vulnerable population, the company canceled plans for the brand.
- RJR planned to target white, 18- to 24-year-old "virile" females with a new cigarette brand, Dakota. It was criticized for targeting young, poorly educated, blue-collar women and, although it expanded the market to include males, Dakota failed in test markets and was withdrawn.

- Heileman Brewing Company planned to market a new brand of malt liquor called PowerMaster. Malt liquor is disproportionately consumed by blacks and in low-income neighborhoods. Criticism of this strategy led the brand to be withdrawn.

One study suggests that whether targeting a group of consumers is unethical depends on two dimensions. The first is the degree to which the product can harm the consumers; the second is the vulnerability of the group. Thus, to market harmful products to vulnerable target markets is likely to be considered unethical and could result in boycotts, negative word of mouth, and possibly litigation or legislation unfavorable to the industry. Do you think the above examples of target marketing are unethical? For what products and markets do you think target marketing is inappropriate or unethical?

Source: N. Craig Smith and Elizabeth Cooper-Martin, "Ethics and Target Marketing: The Role of Product Harm and Consumer Vulnerability," *Journal of Marketing,* July 1997, pp. 1–20.

product knowledge, involvement, and purchase behavior vary; successful marketers often adapt their marketing strategies to appeal to specific consumer types. Even a simple product such as chewing gum comes in multiple flavors and package sizes, and varies in sugar content, calories, consistency (e.g., liquid centers), and colors to appeal to different consumers. Although a single product will seldom appeal to all consumers, it can almost always serve more than one consumer. Thus, there are usually *groups of consumers* who can be served well by a single item. If a particular group can be served profitably by a firm, it comprises a viable market segment. A marketer should then develop a marketing mix to serve that group, as long as it is ethical (see Highlight 15.1).

In the past, many marketers focused on target markets in a general, nonpersonal way. Although they may have had some idea of the general characteristics of their target market, they could not identify individual consumers who actually purchased and used their products. However, with today's technology, including scanner and other personal data sources, improved methods of marketing research, and efficient computers for handling large databases, marketers can collect detailed, personal information on many members of their target market. For example, one tobacco company is reported to have the names, addresses, and purchasing data for more than 30 million smokers. Marketers can now target a product's best customers and the stores where they are most likely to shop. Also, a variety of companies offer consumer data for use in segmentation. For one example, visit the USA Data website at **www.usadata.com**.

In this chapter, we consider market segmentation. We define **market segmentation** as the process of dividing a market into groups of similar consumers and

Exhibit 15.1

Tasks in Market Segmentation

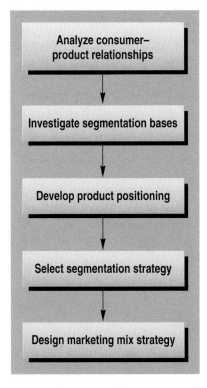

selecting the most appropriate group(s) and individuals for the firm to serve. We can break down the process of market segmentation into five tasks, as shown in Exhibit 15.1. In the remainder of this chapter, we discuss each of the market segmentation tasks shown in the figure. Although we recognize that these tasks are strongly interrelated and their order may vary depending on the firm and the situation, market segmentation analysis can seldom (if ever) be ignored. Even if the final decision is to mass market and not segment at all, this decision should be reached only after a market segmentation analysis has been conducted. Thus, market segmentation analysis is critical for sound marketing strategy development.

Analyze Consumer–Product Relationships   The first task in segmenting markets is to analyze consumer–product relationships. This entails analysis of the affect and cognition, behavior, and environments involved in the purchase/consumption process for the particular product. There are three general approaches to this task. First, marketing managers may brainstorm the product concept and consider what types of consumers are likely to purchase and use the product and how they differ from those less likely to buy. Second, focus groups and other types of primary research can be used for identifying differences in attributes, benefits, and values of various potential markets. Third, secondary research may further investigate differences in potential target markets, determine the relative sizes of those markets, and develop a better understanding of consumers of this or similar products.

For many established product categories, considerable information is available for analyzing various markets. For product categories like automobiles, toothpaste,

The Porsche Boxster is targeted to 35- to 50-year-olds with household incomes of $150,000   *David Young-Wolff/PhotoEdit, Inc.*

and many food products, various target markets are well established. For example, the category of automobile buyers includes luxury, sports, midsize, compact, and subcompact markets.

Within each of these markets, further analysis may offer insights into market opportunities. For example, Porsche sought market growth when it introduced the Boxster. The Porsche 911 is targeted to 45- to 60-year-old men with household incomes of $225,000 or more. Although this is a great market for the car, it is relatively small and limits Porsche's chances for growth. The Boxster is targeted to 35- to 50-year-olds with household incomes of $150,000 and is priced at $40,000, much less than the 911. Also, the Boxster is designed to increase sales to women from 10 to 25 percent. Thus, by further analyzing consumers in the sport-luxury market, Porsche determined that the consumer–product relationships for its products called for a new model to increase growth.[1]

For many products, the initial breakdown in markets is between the prestige and mass markets. The prestige market seeks the highest-quality (and often the highest-priced) product available. Often particular products for consumers in this market have very important meanings, such as expressions of good taste, expertise, and status. Brands such as Rolex watches, Mercedes-Benz automobiles, Hartmann luggage, and Gucci handbags are targeted to these consumers.

For some products, gender can be an important segmentation variable   *(both) The Gillette Company.*

Highlight 15.2

Target Markets for JCPenney's Women's Apparel

	Conservative	Traditional	Update
Size	23% of population	38% of population	16% of population
	16% of total sales	40% of total sales	24% of total sales
Age	35–55 years old	25–49 years old	25–49 years old
Values	Conservative values	Traditional values	Contemporary values
	Satisfied with present status	Active, busy, independent, self-confident	Active, busy, independent, very self-confident
Employment	Has job, not career	Family and job/career oriented	Family and job/career oriented
Income	Limited disposable income	Considerable income	Considerable income
Benefits sought	Price driven, reacts to sales	Quality driven, will pay a little more	Fashion driven, expresses self through apparel
	Wants easy care and comfort	Wants traditional styling, seeks clothes that last	Wants newness in color and style
	Not interested in fashion	Interested in newness Defines value as	Shops often
	Defines value as	Quality	Defines value as
	Price	Fashion	Fashion
	Quality	Price	Quality
	Fashion		Price

Source: Adapted from Michael Levy and Barton A. Weitz, *Retailing Management,* 5th ed. (Boston, MA: McGraw-Hill/Irwin, 2004), p. 134. Reproduced with permission from The McGraw-Hill Companies.

The marketing strategies for these products generally involve selling them in exclusive stores at high prices and promoting them in prestige media. For consumers in this market, affect and cognition (feelings about and meaning of the product), behavior (shopping activities), and environments (information and store contact) differ from those of consumers in the mass market. Thus, the initial analysis of consumer–product relationships has important implications for all of the tasks involved in market segmentation and strategy development. Highlight 15.2 details profiles of the target markets for JCPenney's women's apparel.

Investigate Segmentation Bases

There is no simple way to determine the best bases for segmenting markets. In most cases, however, at least some initial dimensions can be determined from previous purchase trends and managerial judgment. For example, suppose we wish to segment the market for all-terrain vehicles. Several dimensions come to mind for initial consideration: sex (male); age (18 to 35); lifestyle (outdoorsy); and income level (perhaps $25,000 to $40,000). At a minimum, these variables should be included in subsequent segmentation research.

Exhibit 15.2 presents a number of bases for segmenting consumer markets. This is by no means a complete list of possible segmentation bases, but it represents some useful categories. Four specific types of segmentation are discussed next: benefit, psychographic, person/situation, and geodemographic segmentation.

Exhibit 15.2

Useful Segmentation Bases for Consumer Markets

Segmentation Bases	Illustrative Categories
Geographic Segmentation	
Region	Pacific; Mountain; West North Central; West South Central; East North Central; East South Central; South Atlantic; Middle Atlantic; New England
Size of city, county, or standard metropolitan statistical area (SMSA)	Under 5,000; 5,000–19,999; 20,000–49,999; 50,000–99,999; 100,000–249,999; 250,000–499,999; 500,000–999,999; 1,000,000–3,999,999; 4,000,000 or over
Population density	Urban; suburban; rural
Climate	Warm; cold
Demographic Segmentation	
Age	Under 6; 6–12; 13–19; 20–29; 30–39; 40–49; 50–59; 60+
Gender	Male; female
Family size	1–2; 3–4; 5+ persons
Family life cycle	Young, single; young, married, no children; young, married, youngest child under 6; young, married, youngest child 6 or over; older, married with children; older, married, no children under 18; older, single; other
Income	Under $10,000; $10,000–$14,999; $15,000–$24,999; $25,000–$34,999; $35,000–$49,999; $50,000 or over
Occupation	Professional and technical; managers, officials, and proprietors; clerical, sales; craftspeople, foremen; operatives; farmers; retired; students; homemakers; unemployed
Education	Grade school or less; some high school; graduated from high school; some college; graduated from college; some graduate work; graduate degree
Marital status	Single; married; divorced; widowed
Sociocultural Segmentation	
Culture	American, Hispanic, African, Asian, European
Subculture	
Religion	Jewish; Catholic; Muslim; Mormon; Buddhist
Race	European American; Asian American; African American; Hispanic American
Nationality	French; Malaysian; Australian; Canadian; Japanese
Social class	Upper class; middle class; working class; lower class
Affective and Cognitive Segmentation	
Knowledge	Expert; novice
Involvement	High; low
Attitude	Positive; neutral; negative
Benefits sought	Convenience, economy; prestige
Innovativeness	Innovator; early adopter; early majority; late majority; laggard; nonadopter

Exhibit 15.2

Continued

Segmentation Bases	Illustrative Categories
Readiness stage	Unaware; aware; interested; desirous; plan to purchase
Perceived risk	High; moderate; low
Behavioral Segmentation	
Media usage	Newspaper; magazine; TV; Internet
Specific media usage	*Sports Illustrated; Life; Cosmopolitan*
Payment method	Cash; Visa; Mastercard; American Express; check
Loyalty status	None; some; total
Usage rate	Light; medium; heavy
User status	Nonuser; ex-user; current user; potential user
Usage situation	Work; home; vacation; commuting
Combined Approaches	
Psychographics	Achievers; strivers; strugglers
Person/situation	College students for lunch; executives for business dinner
Geodemography	Blue-blood estates; towns and gowns; Hispanic mix

Exhibit 15.3

Toothpaste Market Benefit Segments

	Sensory Segment	Sociable Segment	Worrier Segment	Independent Segment
Principal benefit sought	Flavor, product appearance	Brightness of teeth	Decay prevention	Price
Demographic strengths	Children	Teens, young people	Large families	Men
Special behavioral characteristics	Users of spearmint-flavored toothpaste	Smokers	Heavy users	Heavy users
Brands disproportionately favored	Colgate	Ultra Brite	Crest	Cheapest brand
Lifestyle characteristics	Hedonistic	Active	Conservative	Value-oriented

Source: Adapted from Russell I. Haley, "Benefit Segmentation: A Decision-Oriented Research Tool," *Journal of Marketing,* 32 (July 1969), pp. 30–35. Published by the American Marketing Association. Reprinted by permission.

Benefit Segmentation

The belief underlying the **benefit segmentation** approach is that the *benefits* people seek in consuming a given product are the basic reasons for the existence of true market segments.[2] This approach thus attempts to measure consumer value systems and consumers' perceptions of various brands in a product class. The classic example of a benefit segmentation, provided by Russell Haley, concerned the toothpaste market. Haley identified four basic segments—Sensory, Sociable, Worrier, and Independent—as presented in Exhibit 15.3. Haley argued that this

▶ **High**light 15.3

An Interesting Source of Lifestyle Information

Many consumers use 800 and 900 telephone numbers. Here's how marketers get lifestyle information about consumers who do so. Do you think marketers have a right to this information?

1. *Make a phone call.* You call an 800 or 900 number to buy a product, get information, or express an opinion.

2. *Connect to computer.* In many cases, the call goes to a computer in Omaha, Nebraska, owned by AT&T and American Express. It has 10,000 continuously operating phone lines.

3. *Computer identifies you.* Using your phone number, the computer connects with a marketing service to get your name and address and display it on a salesperson's computer screen. Tens of millions of names can be searched in a second or two.

4. *Do your business.* The salesperson can greet you by name, then take your order, answer questions, or ask you for more information.

5. *Instant check on your credit.* If you order something by credit card, the computer checks an electronic credit authorization bureau to make sure your credit is good.

6. *Your call is recorded.* Your name, address, phone number, and the subject of your call are provided electronically to the sponsoring company or organization, which can then use it for targeted mailing lists or marketing campaigns.

7. *Marketers analyze your lifestyle.* The sponsoring company can match these data with information in other databases—voter lists, magazine subscriptions—to find out even more about your lifestyle.

Source: Robert S. Boyd, "How Big Brother Sees Consumers," *Wisconsin State Journal,* July 8, 1990, p. 4B. Knight Ridder News Service.

segmentation could be very useful for selecting advertising copy, media, commercial length, packaging, and new-product design. For example, colorful packages might be appropriate for the Sensory segment, perhaps aqua packages (to indicate fluoride) for the Worrier group, and gleaming-white packages for the Sociable segment because of their concern with white teeth.[3]

Psychographic Segmentation

Psychographic segmentation divides markets on differences in consumer lifestyles. Generally, psychographic segmentation follows a post hoc model. That is, consumers are first asked a variety of questions about their lifestyles and then are grouped on the basis of the similarity of their responses. Lifestyles are measured by asking consumers about their activities (work, hobbies, vacations), interests (family, job, community) and opinions (about social issues, politics, business). The activity, interest, and opinion (**AIO**) questions in some studies are very general. In others, at least some questions are related to specific products. However, as illustrated in Highlight 15.3, psychographic information can be obtained from sources other than company-sponsored research projects.

Psychographic segmentation studies often include hundreds of questions and provide a tremendous amount of information about consumers. Thus, psychographic segmentation is based on the idea that "the more you know and understand about consumers, the more effectively you can communicate and market to them."[4]

**GET A DENTIST CLEANING TWICE A YEAR.
HAVE A DENTIST-CLEAN FEELING TWICE A DAY.**

Courtesy of the Crest
SpinBrush Pro. It has dual
motions; the head spins
and the soft brushing bristles
move up and down. So you
can have that just-cleaned
feeling you get from the
dentist - every day. And, for
under $7, the price is as
refreshing as the clean.
Satisfaction
guaranteed.

8 out of 10 people who
have tried Crest SpinBrush Pro
said that it was better than any
other brush they've ever
used or tried.

UNDER $7
For guarantee details, call 1800.285.5292

Crest SpinBrush PRO
A BETTER SPIN ON CLEAN.

Crest is targeted to the
Worrier segment concerned
about decay prevention
© *The Procter & Gamble
Company. Used by
Permission.*

To date, no consensus has been reached concerning how many different lifestyle segments exist in the United States or in other countries. Psychographic studies frequently reach different conclusions about the number and nature of lifestyle categories. For this reason, the validity of psychographic segmentation is sometimes questioned.[5]

The best-known psychographic segmentation is called **VALS,**[TM] which stands for "values and lifestyles." It was developed in the 1970s to explain changing U.S. values and lifestyles. It has since been redone to enhance its ability to predict consumer behavior. Segmentation research based on VALS[TM] is a product of SRI Consulting Business Intelligence.

As Exhibit 15.4 shows, the groups are arranged in a rectangle and are based on two dimensions. The vertical dimension segments people based on the degree to which they are innovative and have resources such as income, education, self-confidence, intelligence, leadership skills, and energy. The horizontal dimension represents primary motivations and includes three different types. Consumers driven by knowledge and principles are motivated primarily by *ideals*. These consumers include the Thinkers and Believers groups. Consumers driven by a goal of demonstrating success to their peers are motivated primarily by *achievement*. These consumers include Achievers and Strivers. Consumers driven by a desire for social or physical activity, variety, and risk taking are motivated primarily by *self-expression*. These consumers include both the Experiencers and Makers. At the top of the rectangle are the Innovators, who have such high resources that they could have any of the three primary motivations. At the bottom of the rectangle are the Survivors, who live complacently and within their means without a strong primary motivation of the types listed above. Exhibit 15.4 gives more details about each of the eight groups.

Marketers can purchase research data that show which groups are the primary buyers of specific products and services. This information can be used to better focus elements of the marketing mix, such as promotion, on the best target markets. VALS[TM] types can also be tied to a number of other consumer research databases. In addition, SRI Consulting Business Intelligence offers Geo VALS,[TM] which links VALS[TM] to local marketing initiatives by identifying VALS[TM] consumer groups residing within a specific block group or zip code.[6] Highlight 15.4 shows you how to determine your VALS category.

Person/Situation Segmentation

Markets can often be divided on the basis of the usage situation in conjunction with individual differences among consumers. This approach is known as **person/ situation segmentation.** For example, clothing and footwear markets are divided not only on the basis of the consumer's sex and size but also on usage situation dimensions such as weather conditions, physical activities, and social events.[7]

Exhibit 15.4

VALS™ Framework and Segments

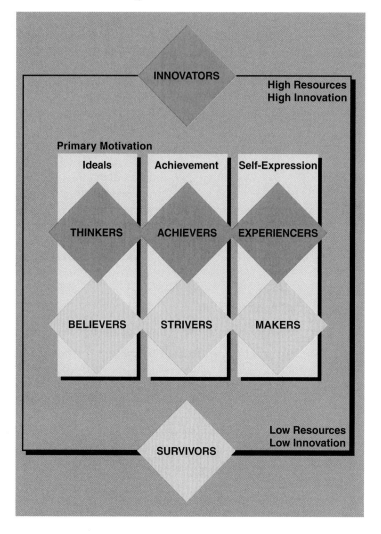

As another example, expensive china is designed for special occasions; Corelle dinnerware is designed for everyday family use. One expert argues, "In practice the product whose unique selling proposition (quality, features, image, packaging, or merchandising) is not targeted for particular people in particular usage situations is probably the exception rather than the rule."[8] Thus, this expert suggests the approach to segmentation outlined in Exhibit 15.5. This approach combines not only the person and the situation but also other important segmentation bases: benefits sought, product and attribute perceptions, and marketplace behavior.

Operationally, this segmentation approach involves the following steps:

Step 1: Use observational studies, focus group discussions, and secondary data to discover whether different usage situations exist and whether they are determinant, in the sense that they appear to affect the importance of various product characteristics.

Exhibit 15.4

Continued

Innovators. These consumers are on the leading edge of change, have the highest incomes, and such high self-esteem and abundant resources that they can indulge in any or all self-orientations. They are located above the rectangle. Image is important to them as an expression of taste, independence, and character. Their consumer choices are directed toward the "finer things in life."

Thinkers. These consumers are the high-resource group of those who are motivated by ideals. They are mature, responsible, well-educated professionals. Their leisure activities center on their homes, but they are well informed about what goes on in the world and are open to new ideas and social change. They have high incomes but are practical consumers and rational decision makers.

Believers. These consumers are the low-resource group of those who are motivated by ideals. They are conservative and predictable consumers who favor American products and established brands. Their lives are centered on family, church, community, and the nation. They have modest incomes.

Achievers. These consumers are the high-resource group of those who are motivated by achievement. They are successful work-oriented people who get their satisfaction from their jobs and families. They are politically conservative and respect authority and the status quo. They favor established products and services that show off their success to their peers.

Strivers. These consumers are the low-resource group of those who are motivated by achievement. They have values very similar to achievers but have fewer economic, social, and psychological resources. Style is extremely important to them as they strive to emulate people they admire.

Experiencers. These consumers are the high-resource group of those who are motivated by self-expression. They are the youngest of all the segments, with a median age of 25. They have a lot of energy, which they pour into physical exercise and social activities. They are avid consumers, spending heavily on clothing, fast foods, music, and other youthful favorites, with particular emphasis on new products and services.

Makers. These consumers are the low-resource group of those who are motivated by self-expression. They are practical people who value self-sufficiency. They are focused on the familiar—family, work, and physical recreation—and have little interest in the broader world. As consumers, they appreciate practical and functional products.

Survivors. These consumers have the lowest incomes. They have too few resources to be included in any consumer self-orientation and are thus located below the rectangle. They are the oldest of all the segments, with a median age of 61. Within their limited means, they tend to be brand-loyal consumers.

Sources: SRI Consulting Business Intelligence, **www.sric-bi.com**, July 27, 2003; Martha Farnsworth Riche, "Psychographics for the1990s," *American Demographics,* July 1989, pp. 24–26ff. Copyright 1989, PRIMEDIA Business Magazines & Media Inc. All rights reserved.

Step 2: If step 1 produces promising results, undertake a benefit, product perception, and reported market behavior segmentation survey of consumers. Measure benefits and perceptions by usage situation as well as by individual difference characteristics. Assess situation usage frequency by recall estimates or usage-situation diaries.

Step 3: Construct a person/situation segmentation matrix. The rows are the major usage situations, and the columns are groups of users identified by a single characteristic or combination of characteristics.

Shoes for different person/situations   *Courtesy Allen-Edmonds.*

Step 4: Rank the cells in the matrix in terms of their submarket sales volume. The person/situation combination that results in the greatest consumption of the generic product would be ranked first.

Step 5: State the major benefits sought, important product dimensions, and unique market behavior for each nonempty cell of the matrix. (Some types of people will never consume the product in certain usage situations.)

Step 6: Position your competitors' offerings within the matrix. The person/situation segments they currently serve can be determined by the product feature they promote and other marketing strategies.

Step 7: Position your offering within the matrix on the same criteria.

Step 8: Assess how well your current offering and marketing strategy meet the needs of the submarket compared to the competition's offering.

Step 9: Identify market opportunities based on submarket size, needs, and competitive advantage.[9]

This approach incorporates all four of the major factors discussed in this text: affect and cognition, behavior, environment, and marketing strategy. It thus offers a more comprehensive analysis than many other approaches.

Geodemographic Segmentation

One problem with many segmentation approaches is that although they identify types or categories of consumers, they do not identify specific individuals or households

Exhibit 15.5

Person/Situation Segmentation

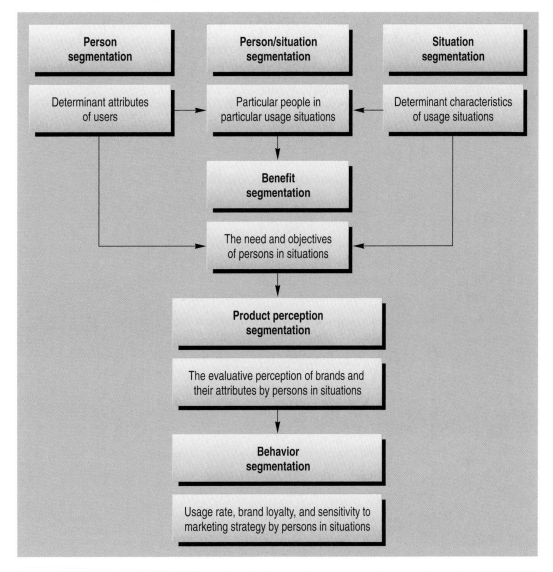

Source: Adapted from Peter R. Dickson, "Person–Situation: Segmentation's Missing Link," *Journal of Marketing,* 46 (Fall 1982), pp. 55–64. Published by the American Marketing Association. Reprinted by permission.

within a market. **Geodemographic segmentation** identifies specific households in a market by focusing on local neighborhood geography (such as zip codes) to create classifications of actual, addressable, mappable neighborhoods where consumers live and shop.[10] One geodemographic system created by Claritas, Inc., is called PRIZM, which stands for Potential Ranking Index by ZIP Markets. This system classifies every U.S. neighborhood into 1 of 62 distinct types or clusters of

Exhibit 15.6

Claritas PRIZM Cluster 01—Blue Blood Estates

The *blue blood estates* cluster contains America's wealthiest suburbs, populated by super-upper established executives, professionals, and heirs to "old money" who are accustomed to privilege and live in luxury, supported by servants. One in ten residents is a multimillionaire, and there is a sharp drop from these heights to the next level of affluence.

Predominant Characteristics

- Households (% U.S.):   729,500 (0.8%)
- Population: 2,181,400
- Demographic caption: Elite super-rich families
- Ethnic diversity: Dominant white, high Asian
- Family type: Married couples w/children
- Predominant age ranges: 35–54
- Education: College graduates
- Employment level: Professional
- Housing type: Owners/single unit
- Density percentile: 66 (1 = sparse, 99 = dense)

More Likely to:

Lifestyle	Products and Services
Belong to a country club	Purchase a car phone
Travel to Japan/Asia	Eat pita bread
Contract home improvement	Drink imported wine
Go sailing	Own a Lexus
Use maid/housekeeper	Spend $250+ on business suit
Lease car for personal use	Buy Montblanc/Waterman pen

Radio/TV	Print
Watch arts and entertainment	Read *National Geographic Travel*
Listen to news/talk radio	Read newspaper business section
	Read *Elle*
Listen to soft contemp radio	Read *Food & Wine*
Watch Masters (Golf)	Read *Fortune*

Source: Adapted from Valarie Walsh and J. Paul Peter, "Claritas Inc.: Using Compass and PRIZM," in *Marketing Management: Knowledge and Skills,* 7th ed., eds. J. Paul Peter and James H. Donnelly, Jr. (Burr Ridge, IL: McGraw-Hill/Irwin, 2004), p. 288. Reproduced with permission from The McGraw-Hill Companies.

consumers. Each PRIZM cluster is based on zip codes, demographic information from the U.S. Census, and information on product usage, media usage, and lifestyle preferences to create profiles of the people who live in specific neighborhoods. Exhibits 15.6 and 15.7 show two sample profiles. The PRIZM system includes maps of different areas that rank neighborhoods on their potential to purchase specific products or services.

The PRIZM system is based on the assumptions that consumers in particular neighborhoods are similar in many respects and that the best prospects are those who actually use a product or other consumers like them. Marketers use PRIZM to better understand consumers in various markets, what they are like, where they live, and how to reach them. These data help marketers with target market

Exhibit 15.7

Claritas PRIZM Cluster 36—Towns and Gowns

The *towns and gowns* cluster describes most of our college towns and university campus neighborhoods. With a typical mix of half locals (towns) and half students (gowns), it is unique, with thousands of penniless 18- to 24-year-old kids, plus highly educated professionals, all with a taste for prestige products beyond their evident means.

Predominant Characteristics

• Households (% U.S.):	1,290,200 (1.4%)
• Population:	3,542,500
• Demographic caption:	College town singles
• Ethnic diversity:	Dominant white, high Asian
• Family type:	Singles
• Predominant age ranges:	Under 24, 25–34
• Education:	College graduates
• Employment level:	White collar/Service
• Housing type:	Renters/Multiunit 10+
• Density percentile:	58 (1 = sparse, 99 = dense)

More Likely to

Lifestyle	**Products and Services**
Go to college football games	Have a personal education loan
Play racquetball	Use an ATM card
Go skiing	Own a Honda
Play billiards/pool	Buy 3+ pairs of jeans annually
Use cigarette rolling paper	Drink Coca-Cola Classic
Use a charter/tour bus	Eat Kraft Macaroni and Cheese

Radio/TV	**Print**
Watch VH1	Read *Self*
Listen to alternative rock music	Read newspaper comics section
Watch *Jeopardy*	Read *Rolling Stone*
Listen to variety radio	Read *GQ*
Watch *The Simpsons*	

Source: Adapted from Valarie Walsh and J. Paul Peter, "Claritas Inc.: Using Compass and PRIZM," in *Marketing Management: Knowledge and Skills,* 7th ed., eds. J. Paul Peter and James H. Donnelly, Jr. (Burr Ridge, IL: McGraw-Hill/Irwin, 2004), p. 289. Reproduced with permission from The McGraw-Hill Companies.

selection, direct marketing campaigns, site selection, media selection, and analyzing sales potential in various areas. You can learn more about geodemography by visiting Claritas's website at **www.claritas.com**.

Develop Product Positioning

By this time, the firm should have a good idea of the basic segments of the market that potentially could be satisfied with its product. The next step involves **product positioning:** positioning the product relative to competing products in the minds of consumers.[11] A classic example of positioning is the 7UP "Uncola" campaign. Before this campaign, Seven-Up had difficulty convincing consumers that the product could be enjoyed as a soft drink and not just as a mixer. Consumers believed colas were soft drinks, but they apparently did not think of 7UP in this way. By promoting

7UP as the Uncola, the company positioned it both as a soft drink that could be consumed in the same situations as colas and as an alternative to colas. This positioning was very successful.[12]

The key objective of positioning strategy is to form a particular brand image in consumers' minds. This is accomplished by developing a coherent strategy that may involve all of the marketing mix elements. There are at least five approaches to positioning strategy: positioning by attribute, by use or application, by product user, by product class, and by competitors.[13] We discuss these approaches next.

Positioning by Attribute

Probably the most frequently used positioning strategy is **positioning by attribute:** associating a product with an attribute, a product feature, or a customer feature. Consider imported automobiles. Hyundai emphasizes low price. Volvo has stressed safety and durability, showing commercials of crash tests and citing statistics on the average long life of its cars. Fiat, in contrast, has made a distinct effort to position itself as a European car with European craftsmanship. BMW has emphasized handling and engineering efficiency, using the tag line "the ultimate driving machine" and showing BMW performance capabilities at a racetrack.

A new product can also be positioned with respect to an attribute that competitors have ignored. Paper towels had emphasized absorbency until Viva stressed durability, using demonstrations supporting the claim that Viva "keeps on working."

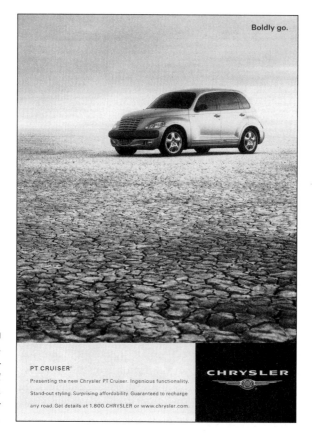

Positioning a product on multiple attributes   *The DaimlerChrysler advertisements are used with permission from DaimlerChrysler Corporation.*

YOU MAY FIND IT
SURPRISING
HOW DIFFERENT
SOUP TASTES
WHEN YOU SERVE
IT ON A PLATE.

Campbell's soup as an ingredient in a main dish—positioning by use   *Courtesy Campbell's Canada.*

Bounty paper towels are positioned as being "microwave safe" with dyes that do not come off in microwave ovens.

Sometimes a product can be positioned in terms of two or more attributes simultaneously. In the toothpaste market, Crest became a dominant brand with positioning as a cavity fighter, a claim supported by a medical group endorsement. Aim, however, achieved its 10 percent market share by positioning in terms of two attributes, good taste and cavity prevention. More recently, Aqua-fresh was introduced by Beecham as a gel/paste that offers both cavity-fighting and breath-freshening benefits.

The price/quality attribute dimension is commonly used for positioning products as well as stores. In many product categories, some brands offer more in terms of service, features, or performance—and a higher price is one signal to the customer of this higher quality. For example, Curtis-Mathes TVs are positioned as high-priced, high-quality products. Conversely, other brands emphasize low price and good quality.

In general-merchandise stores, Neiman Marcus, Bloomingdale's, and Saks Fifth Avenue are near the top of the price/quality scale. Below them are Macy's, Robinson's, Bullock's, Rich's, Filene's, and so on. Stores such as Target and JCPenney are positioned below these but above discount stores such as Kmart or Shopko. Interestingly, JCPenney and Sears have both upgraded their positions to avoid competing directly with successful discount and warehouse stores such as Wal-Mart.

Positioning by Use or Application

Another strategy is **positioning by use** or application. For many years, Campbell's soup was positioned for use at lunchtime and advertised extensively over noontime radio. Now many Campbell's soups are positioned for use in sauces and dips or as ingredients in main dishes. AT&T has positioned long-distance calling by particular uses. For example, the "reach out and touch someone" campaign positioned long-distance calls as a method of communicating with loved ones.

Products can have multiple positioning strategies, although increasing the number involves difficulties and risks. Often a positioning-by-use strategy represents a second or third position designed to expand the market. Thus, Gatorade, introduced as a summer beverage for athletes who need to replace body fluids, attempted to develop a winter positioning strategy as the beverage to drink when one is ill and the doctor recommends drinking plenty of fluids. Similarly, Quaker Oats attempted to position a breakfast food as a natural whole-grain ingredient for recipes. Arm & Hammer has successfully positioned its baking soda as an odor-destroying agent in refrigerators.

Positioning by Product User

Another approach is **positioning by product user** or a class of users. Revlon's Charlie cosmetics line was positioned by associating it with a specific lifestyle profile. Johnson & Johnson increased its market share from 3 to 14 percent when it repositioned its shampoo from a product used for babies to one used by people who wash their hair frequently and therefore need a mild shampoo. A similar strategy was used to get adults to use Johnson's Baby Lotion.

Miller High Life, once the "champagne of bottled beers," was purchased by the upper class and had an image of being a woman's beer. Philip Morris repositioned it as a beer for the "heavily beer-drinking, blue-collar working man." Miller's Lite beer used convincing beer-drinking personalities to position it as a beer for the heavy beer drinker who dislikes that "filled-up feeling." In contrast, earlier efforts to introduce low-calorie beers positioned with respect to the low-calorie attribute were dismal failures. Miller's positioning strategies are in part why it moved up to the number two brewing company in the United States during that period.

Positioning by Product Class

Some critical positioning decisions involve **positioning by product class.** For example, Maxim freeze-dried coffee was positioned with respect to regular and instant coffee. Some margarines are positioned with respect to butter. A maker of dried milk introduced an instant breakfast drink positioned as a breakfast substitute and a virtually identical product positioned as a meal substitute for those on diets. Caress soap, made by Lever Brothers, was positioned as a bath oil product rather than a soap. The 7UP example we discussed earlier is also an example of positioning by product class. Recently dates have been positioned as the "wholesomely sweet alternative to raisins" in television commercials.

Positioning by Competitors

In most positioning strategies, an explicit or implicit frame of reference is the competition (**positioning by competitors**). Often the major purpose of this type of positioning is to convince consumers that a brand is better than the market leader (or another well-accepted brand) on important attributes. Positioning with respect to a competitor is commonly done in advertisements in which a competitor is named and compared. For example, Burger King ads argued that McDonald's burgers had less beef and did not taste as good as Burger King's because McDonald's product was not flame broiled. Both Pepsi and Coke have run comparative ads claiming their brand tastes better than the other one.

A classic example of this type of positioning was the Avis "We're No. 2, so we try harder" campaign. The strategy was to position Avis with Hertz as a major car rental agency and away from National, which at the time was at least as large as Avis. This strategy was quite successful.

Positioning Maps

One way to investigate how to position a product is by using a positioning map. A **positioning map** is a visual depiction of consumers' perceptions of competitive products, brands, or models. It is constructed by surveying consumers about various product attributes and developing dimensions and a graph indicating the relative positions of competitors. Exhibit 15.8 depicts a positioning map for alternative car brands.

Positioning maps can give marketers a sense of how consumers perceives their brands relative to competitors and suggest positioning strategies. In Exhibit 15.8, for example, the Chrysler nameplate is perceived as more luxurious than Buick, but it falls short of its main competitors, Cadillac and Lincoln. Thus, Chrysler may

An ad designed to position a brand relative to sugar rather than other sugar substitutes—positioning by product class   *Courtesy of McNeil Nutritionals.*

reposition itself to be a more luxurious car, such as by adding better upholstery, better wood-grain interior trim, and gadgets and conveniences that meet or exceed its competitors. These might be featured in comparative ads and prices might be increased to try to improve consumers' perceptions about how luxurious Chryslers are. A follow-up study after this strategy change could indicate whether the brand had moved farther above Buick and closer to or above Lincoln and Cadillac.

Exhibit 15.8

Positioning Map for Automobiles

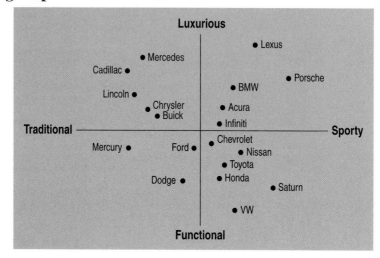

Source: Adapted from Gilbert A. Churchill, Jr. and J. Paul Peter, *Marketing: Creating Value for Customers,* 2nd ed. (Burr Ridge, IL: McGraw-Hill/Irwin, 1998), p. 221. Reproduced with permission from The McGraw-Hill Companies.

Alternatively, an examination of this map might indicate that the company should create a new brand that would be positioned in the luxurious–sporty quadrant, where there are fewer competitors.

Select Segmentation Strategy

After the analysis in the previous stages is completed, the appropriate **segmentation strategy** can be considered. There are four basic alternatives. First, the firm may decide not to enter the market. Analysis to this stage may reveal there is no viable market niche for the product, brand, or model. Second, the firm may decide not to segment but to be a mass marketer. This may be the appropriate strategy in at least three situations:

1. When the market is so small that marketing to a portion of it is not profitable.
2. When heavy users make up such a large proportion of the sales volume that they are the only relevant target.
3. When the brand is dominant in the market and targeting to a few segments would not benefit sales and profits.[14]

Third, the firm may decide to market to only one segment. Fourth, the firm may decide to market to more than one segment and design a separate marketing strategy for each.

In any case, marketers must have some criteria on which to base segmentation strategy decisions. Three important criteria are that a viable segment must be measurable, meaningful, and marketable.

1. *Measurable.* Marketers must be able to measure the segment's size and characteristics. For example, one difficulty with segmenting on the basis of social class is that the concept and its divisions are not clearly defined and measured. Alternatively, income is much easier to measure.

2. *Meaningful.* A meaningful segment is one that is large enough to have sufficient sales and growth potential to offer long-run profits.

3. *Marketable.* A marketable segment is one that can be reached and served profitably.

Segments that meet these criteria are viable markets for the product. The marketer must now give further attention to the marketing mix.

Design Marketing Mix Strategy

The firm is now in a position to complete its marketing strategy by finalizing the marketing mix for each segment. Selecting the target market and designing the marketing mix go hand in hand, and thus many marketing mix decisions should have already been carefully considered. For example, if the target market selected is price sensitive, some consideration has already been given to price levels. Product positioning also has many implications for selecting appropriate promotions and channels. Thus, many marketing mix decisions are made *in conjunction with* (rather than after) target market selection. In the remaining chapters of this section, we discuss consumer behavior and marketing mix strategies in more detail.

Back To...

Positioning the Hummer H2

General Motors stated that 80 percent of H2 buyers are "successful achievers" and the remaining 20 percent can be described as "rugged individualists." The fact that the H2 is derived from the military Humvee helps position it as a "real" SUV on attributes like ruggedness and dependability.

"People from all walks of life are buying it. Everyone from successful Wall Street business executives to style leaders who have to have the new hot thing," says Liz Vanzura, director of advertising and sales promotions for GM's Hummer unit. "The typical buyer is a 41-year-old, college educated 'free spirit,' with an income north of $215,000."

Interestingly, 30 percent of H2 buyers are women like Josefa Salionas, who believes that motoring through the urban wilderness of Los Angeles requires more than your average sport utility vehicle. "I need a car that no matter what happens in this town—earthquake, civil unrest, fire, flood—I can get through it, under it or over it," says Salionas, an entertainment manager and radio host.

GM focused some of its ads on the women's market. One spot showed a woman steering her H2 through city streets with the line "Threaten men in a whole new way." Thus, the H2 positioning to women is by attribute, namely safety. "It has safety written all over it," says Vanzura, who reports that some female buyers believe the H2 gives their kids more protection on the road. "Women say when they drive it, they have a lot of sheet metal around them." In fact, the H2 won the 2003 American Woman Road & Travel Award for the vehicle "Most Likely to Survive Anything."

Thus, GM was able to attract a profitable market of successful, early-middle-aged buyers who wanted an SUV that would be powerful, dependable, rugged, and safe. Some analysts believe the attention H2 buyers receive when driving it is an important reason that they bought it in the first place. Analysts have also suggested that the potential to intimidate other drivers on the road is also considered a plus by many H2 owners. ❖

Summary

This chapter provided an overview of market segmentation analysis. Market segmentation is defined as the process of dividing a market into groups of similar consumers and selecting the most appropriate group(s) for the firm to serve. Market segmentation was analyzed in terms of five interrelated tasks: (1) analyze consumer–product relationships, (2) investigate segmentation bases, (3) develop product positioning, (4) select segmentation strategy, and (5) design marketing mix strategy. Market segmentation is a cornerstone of sound marketing strategy development and is one of the major bridges between the literature on consumer behavior and that dealing with marketing strategy.

Key Terms and Concepts

AIO **384**

benefit segmentation **383**

geodemographic segmentation **389**

market segmentation **378**

person/situation segmentation **385**

positioning by attribute **392**

positioning by competitors **394**

positioning by product class **394**

positioning by product user **393**

positioning by use **393**

positioning map **394**

product positioning **391**

psychographic segmentation **384**

segmentation strategy **396**

VALS™ **385**

Review and Discussion Questions

1. Define *market segmentation* and describe the management tasks involved in applying the concept.
2. Select a product (other than toothpaste) about which you are fairly knowledgeable and develop a preliminary description of possible benefit segments following the structure presented in Exhibit 15.3.
3. Identify potential advantages and problems associated with marketing to benefit segments.
4. Use the VALS™ categories to suggest marketing strategies for psychographic segments of buyers for hotel/motel services.
5. Consider person/situation segmentation as a way to view the snack food market. State the needs and objectives of consumers in situations for at least three segments that you identify.
6. Explain each of the five approaches to product positioning and offer an example (not in the text) for each approach.
7. How does the concept of segmentation relate to positioning strategies?
8. What options are available to the organization after it identifies segments in the market? When would each of these options represent a reasonable choice?
9. How would segmentation and positioning decisions be different for a small-business entrepreneur than for a large corporation?

Marketing Strategy in Action

Hershey Chocolate USA in 2000

Although Hershey Chocolate USA, a division of Hershey Foods Corporation, did not meet its performance expectations in 1999, the company played an important role in increasing U.S. candy sales. Retail confectionery sales grew at a rate of 4 percent in 1999, which was greater than the average growth rate within the general packaged foods industry. The past decade has shown an increase in competition in the candy industry, with companies such as Mars Candy Company introducing a variety of new products, brand extensions, and additional pack types. Similarly, Hershey has diversified its product line and formed alliances with other companies, such as Breyer's.

Record sales in the early 1990s resulted in part from the introduction of a number of new Hershey products, the most significant being Hershey's Kisses with Almonds. This product was introduced in 1990 and became one of the top 20 U.S. candy brands during 1991. By reaching the top 20 in less than one full year of national distribution, Hershey's Kisses with Almonds became the most successful new-product introduction in the corporation's history.

In 1991, Hershey Chocolate also received the Equitrend Outstanding Quality Award. This award was based on a national survey that measured how consumers perceived the quality of 190 nationally recognized brand names. Hershey's milk chocolate bar was the highest-rated confectionary brand.

Part of Hershey's strategy is to target mothers. The company reasons that mothers determine children's early taste in candy. In addition, research shows that adults eat more than 55 percent of all candy sold. Bite-size products are especially popular with adult consumers. When wrapped in seasonal colors, these products have tremendous appeal for adults during Christmas and Easter season. Halloween season, however, is more oriented toward candy bars. In December 1998, Hershey targeted the ever-growing snacking segment of the confectionery industry by transforming some of its most popular bars into "Hershey Bites." Included in this range of products were Hershey's Milk Chocolate with Almonds, Cookies 'n' Creme, Almond Joy, and Reese's Peanut Butter Cups. Unwrapped, bite-size chocolate candy now represents about one-fourth of the packaged chocolate candy category.

Hershey also generates interest and excitement in its product(s) by providing fresh, new looks for standard confections. This strategy has allowed the company to align itself with top-of-mind activities. For instance, in 1997 the company successfully implemented a merchandising strategy with *The Lost World: Jurassic Park*. By using creative selling, marketing, and merchandising techniques, Hershey achieved a retail growth of 5.6 percent in 1998, exceeding the category growth rate and leading to record levels of market share.

In early 2000, Hershey's creative marketing techniques were evident in its "Keep Easter Easy" campaign, which encouraged parents to incorporate nonchocolate treats like jelly beans, lollipops, and gum into their traditional Easter festivities. A brochure full of recipe and game ideas incorporated a variety of Hershey products into activities the whole family could enjoy and could easily be downloaded from Hershey's seasonal website (**www.keepeastereasy.com**). Another incentive for parents to implement nonchocolate sweets into the holiday was a mail-in coupon (located in the brochure) for a limited-edition Jolly Rancher Lollipops Watermelon plush toy that was cross-promoted with the brochure.

In addition, Hershey uses a slightly less conventional approach to increase mind share. Hershey, Pennsylvania, the hometown of the chocolate bar, houses not only the company's headquarters but also a 110-acre amusement park. It may not be the getaway parents dream of, but children seem to enjoy the eight roller coasters, six water rides, more than 20 kiddie rides, monorail, and zoo. At the end of a long day of fun and frolic, families can retire to one of the 235 luxurious rooms in the Hotel Hershey.

The highly competitive nature of the chocolate candy market has individual companies vying for consumers with increasingly inventive

Sherri Zuckerman

advertising campaigns. Cadbury Schweppes has developed several campaigns to specifically target women consumers. One such television ad starred a woman caught in a dilemma: She was unable to choose between her lover and her chocolate bar. More recently the company developed a new line of chocolate bars called Marble (a combination of marbled milk and white chocolate bars with a hazelnut praline center) targeted to women between ages 18 and 24. Hershey has also recently departed from its catchy but childlike jingles in an attempt to draw in a more mature chocolate lover. When introducing its new candy, Bar None, the company aired a TV commercial showing a lion tamer trying to satisfy a "chocolate beast" snarling from behind a door.

Perhaps one of the more popular advertising campaigns Hershey has come up with in the past few years stars the eye-catching Hershey's Syrup animated cows. In mid-1999, the cow commercials were combined with the California Milk Processor Board's popular "Got Milk?" advertisements. The TV spot depicted two cows sitting together on a couch watching the "Got Milk?" commercial on television. One cow turns to the other and says, "That's a silly question."

For more information on Hershey Chocolate USA, see its website at **www.hersheys.com**.

Discussion Questions

1. What are the advantages of targeting candy bars to adults rather than to children?
2. Does targeting to adults require a change in image for candy products?
3. Why do you think bite-size candies are so popular with adults?
4. Describe your most recent purchase of a candy bar in terms of relevant affect and cognition, behavior, and environments.

Sources: Paul Bubny and Winifred Capowski, "The Bunny Hop," *Supermarket Business,* January 15, 2000, pp. 52–53; Hershey Foods Corporation 1999 annual report; Fleming Meeks, "Kids Invited," *Barron's,* October 18, 1999, pp. T10–T12; Justin Dini, "Important Moos for Hershey's," *Adweek,* May 31, 1999, p. 4; anonymous, "A Big Taste in a Little Bite," *Candy Industry,* May 1999, p. 50; anonymous, "Cadbury to Target Women with New Chocolate Countline," *Marketing Week,* April 23, 1998, p. 8; Jennifer Pellet, "Marketing to America's Sweet Tooth," *Discount Merchandiser,* May, 1991, pp. 21–22; Carol Higgins, "Cadbury Unwraps Sinfully Delicious Plea for Self-Indulgence," *Across the Board,* March 4, 1988, p. 36.

16

Consumer Behavior and Product Strategy

Timberland

A howling wind whips the soggy brown leaves as rain pelts the Atlantic seacoast. Timberland chief operating officer Jeffrey Swartz, 33, surveys the miserable weather from the company's headquarters an hour's drive from Boston. "This is a Timberland kind of day," he says.

If the weather were like this every day, Swartz and his father, CEO Sidney Swartz, would be ecstatic. It's nearly perfect for the rugged hiking boots, casual shoes, and outerwear Timberland sells. But no matter the weather, these are sunny times for Timberland.

Boots are in. Heavy work boots, outdoor boots, and even granny boots have appeared everywhere from teenagers' feet to fashion runways. "We have become fashionable when we didn't expect to be fashionable. That certainly hasn't hurt us," says Sidney, 57, clad in blue shirt, tan pants, and, of course, Timberland shoes.

Mike Smith, 38, of Arlington, Virginia, has three or four pairs of Timberland shoes. He was shopping recently for another pair at Nordstrom. "They last, they fit . . . and they're really waterproof." A fashion trend? "Oh yeah, I've heard that. You have to be really young."

At the other end of the fashion spectrum is Jeff Corbin, 23, of Reston, Virginia. When he decided to buy boots, they had to be Timberland. Others offer lookalikes, but they don't have the Timberland tree stamped into the leather. "That emblem is like a Ralph Lauren logo," Corbin says. Adds Scott Davis, marketing analyst, "Timberland is No. 1 in this market. Everyone else is playing catch-up."

One of the most important things the company did to improve its products was in manufacturing. Timberland switched from an assembly line to a team approach where marketing, finance, manufacturing, and product development work together.

This helped eliminate waste, cut product development time from 18 months to 6, and reduced the time it takes to deliver goods. According to its website, Timberland has earned a reputation for crafting the best boots in the world.

Timberland outerwear products   *Robert Holmes/CORBIS.*

Sources: M. Tedeschi, "Rugged Shoe Makers Prolong the Adventure," *Sporting Goods Business,* February 24, 1999, p. 36; M. Tedeschi, "Timberland Bones Up with Endoskeleton," *Sporting Goods Business,* August 6, 1999, p. 18; Donna Rosato and Judith Schroer, "Timberland Steps into Fashion," *USA Today,* December 14, 1993, pp. 1B, 2B. Copyright 1993, *USA Today.* Reprinted with permission; **www.timberland.com**.

Why do you think Timberland has been so successful? Many experts consider the product area the most important element of the marketing mix. Booz, Allen & Hamilton, a business consulting company, noted a number of years ago, "If it is accepted that products are the medium of business conduct, then business strategy is fundamentally product planning."

Of course, a key element in product planning is the matching of products with consumer markets. Although products may be the medium of business conduct from the producer's viewpoint, the exchange of consumer assets for products is the acid test that determines whether products will succeed or fail.

In this chapter, we focus on product strategy and some consumers' product-related affect and cognition, behavior, and environmental factors. Exhibit 16.1 provides the framework for this chapter and lists the topics to be discussed. Although many of the topics previously discussed in the text concern consumer–product relationships, the topics in this chapter have special relevance for product strategy. We begin by investigating product affect and cognition, behavior, and environmental elements, and then discuss product strategy in terms of a number of characteristics that influence product success.

Product Affect and Cognition

Much of our discussion of affect and cognition in Section Two of the text focused on products and how consumers feel about, interpret, and integrate information about them. One area of research that deserves special consideration in product strategy is *satisfaction/dissatisfaction.*

Exhibit 16.1

The Wheel of Consumer Analysis: Product Strategy Is

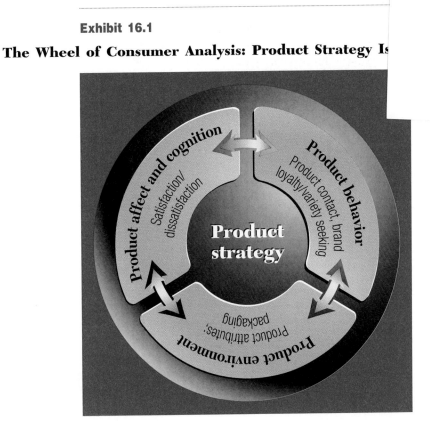

Satisfaction/Dissatisfaction

Consumer satisfaction is a critical concept in marketing thought and consumer research. It is generally argued that if consumers are satisfied with a product, service, or brand, they will be more likely to continue to purchase it and tell others about their favorable experiences with it. If they are dissatisfied, they will more likely switch products or brands and complain to manufacturers, retailers, and other consumers.

Given its importance to marketing strategy, satisfaction has been the subject of considerable academic and practitioner consumer research. Although there are a variety of theories and approaches to studying satisfaction, the *expectancy disconfirmation with performance approach* is the most current formulation.[1] Basically this approach views consumer satisfaction as the degree to which a product or service provides a pleasurable level of consumption-related fulfillment.[2] In other words, it is the degree to which a product's performance exceeds the consumer's expectations for it. Exhibit 16.2 shows a more complete view of this approach. **Prepurchase expectations** are the consumer's beliefs about anticipated performance of the product. **Postpurchase perceptions** are the consumer's thoughts about how well the product performed. **Disconfirmation** refers to the difference between the two.

There are three types of disconfirmation. First, *positive disconfirmation* occurs when product performance is better than expected. This situation is thought to lead to satisfaction or a pleasurable level of fulfillment. For example, suppose a consumer expected a Gateway computer to be pretty good but not as good as an IBM.

A&W
All American Food

Jerry's Subs and Pizza

Thank you for dining with us today.   Our goal is to provide our customers with the very best products and service possible.   Your opinions are very important to us. In order to better serve you, would you please take a moment to complete this comment card and drop it in our suggestion box. **Thank You!**

1. Was today your first visit to our restaurant?   YES ____   NO ____
2. Time: _____   Date: _____   Food - A&W _____   Food - Jerry's Subs & Pizza _____
3. How would you rate your experience today? (Please check)

QUALITY (taste, temperature)	Excellent ____	Good ____	Fair ____	Poor ____
SERVICE (prompt, courteous, friendly)	Excellent ____	Good ____	Fair ____	Poor ____
VALUE FOR MONEY SPENT	Excellent ____	Good ____	Fair ____	Poor ____
CLEANLINESS (restaurant, bathrooms)	Excellent ____	Good ____	Fair ____	Poor ____

(If fair or poor, please comment below)

4. Would you return based on your experience here today? Yes ____   No ____
5. If a problem occurred, was it resolved to your satisfaction? Yes ____   No ____
6. Age Group: Under 15 ____   15-20 ____   21-30 ____   31-40 ____   Above 40 ____
7. Number in party: ____   **COMMENTS - SUGGESTIONS:** _____

As a special Thank You for completing this form . . .

NAME: _____
ADDRESS: _____
_____
TELEPHONE (optional)   _____

We would like to mail you a coupon for a FREE A&W ROOT BEER

We appreciate and value your comments and patronage!

A survey designed to measure consumer satisfaction with a restaurant Courtesy Jerry's Subs and Pizzas.

Exhibit 16.2

An Expectancy Disconfirmation Approach to Satisfaction

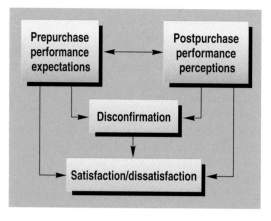

Source: Based on Richard L. Oliver, *Satisfaction: A Behavioral Perspective on the Consumer* (New York: McGraw-Hill, 1997), chap. 4. Reprinted with permission.

After buying and using one, the consumer perceived it to be even better than an IBM. In this case, the consumer's expectations would be positively disconfirmed and the theory would suggest that she or he would be satisfied. Second, *negative disconfirmation* occurs when product performance is lower than expected. This situation is thought to lead to **dissatisfaction.** For example, if the consumer perceived the Gateway computer to be far inferior to an IBM after using it, she or he would be negatively disconfirmed and, according to the theory, would be dissatisfied. Finally, *neutral disconfirmation* occurs when performance perceptions just meet expectations. Whether the consumer is satisfied or not in this case depends on other variables, such as the levels of expectation and performance.

Consumer research has generally supported this approach, and it has been used to investigate consumer dissatisfaction and complaint behavior. Several generalizations about these have been offered:

1. Those who complain when dissatisfied tend to be members of more upscale socioeconomic groups than those who do not complain.

2. Personality characteristics, including dogmatism, locus of control, and self-confidence, are only weakly related to complaint behavior, if at all.

3. The severity of dissatisfaction or problems caused by the dissatisfaction are positively related to complaint behavior.

4. The greater the blame for the dissatisfaction placed on someone other than the dissatisfied party, the greater the likelihood of a complaint.

5. The more positive the perception of retailer responsiveness to consumer complaints, the greater the likelihood of a complaint.[3]

Not all consumer researchers agree with the disconfirmation paradigm, however. One alternative is the *balancing paradigm* suggested by Susan Fournier and David Mick.[4] This approach argues that satisfaction should be studied more broadly than at the level of a single transaction. From this perspective, satisfaction is a more active and dynamic phenomenon that changes across time with usage and other situational factors. Satisfaction with products can also be strongly influenced by the satisfaction of other household members. Meaning and emotions are viewed as critical components of satisfaction with products across time.

Product Behavior

From a strategic viewpoint, a major objective of marketing is to increase the probability and frequency of consumers coming into contact with products, purchasing and using them, and repurchasing them. We will discuss this objective in terms of two classes of consumer behavior: product contact and brand loyalty.

Product Contact

When we introduced the idea of *product contact* in this text, we discussed it in terms of a common retail purchase sequence. We argued that in the context of a retail store purchase, product contact involves behaviors such as locating the product in the store, examining it, and taking it to the checkout counter. In addition, we examined a number of marketing tactics designed to increase product contact.

Product contact can occur in other ways besides visits to retail stores. For example, many students may become familiar with personal computers from courses taken in school. When the time comes to purchase a personal computer, the product contact at school may strongly influence the brand purchased. Computer firms seem aware of this possibility, since they frequently donate their products to universities or offer them at reduced costs.

Consumers may come in contact with products and experience them in a variety of other ways. A consumer may receive a free sample in the mail or on the doorstep or be given a sample in a store, borrow a product from a friend and use it, receive a product as a gift, or simply see someone else using the product and experience it vicariously.

Brand Loyalty/Variety Seeking

From a marketing strategy viewpoint, understanding the pattern of consumers' brand purchases is critical. In today's hypercompetitive marketplace, retaining customers is crucial for survival and far more profitable than constantly fighting to attract new customers. However, because of factors such as the abundance of choices available in most product categories, the availability of information about them, the similarity of many offerings, the demand for value, and the lack of time to always find a particular brand, there is evidence that loyalty to particular brands is decreasing in many product categories.[5]

Exhibit 16.3 presents four categories of consumer purchasing patterns based on the degree of cognitive commitment and number of brands purchased in a particular period. For consumers to be brand loyal, they must not only purchase the same brand repeatedly but also have a cognitive commitment to do so. The brand must have sufficient meaning for them that they purchase it not because of convenience or deals but because the brand represents important benefits or values to them. **Brand loyalty** is an intrinsic commitment to repeatedly purchase a particular brand. It is differentiated from *repeat purchase behavior* because the latter focuses only on the behavioral action without concern for the reasons for the habitual response.

Exhibit 16.3

Categories of Brand Commitment and Purchasing Patterns

Source: Based on Hans C. M. Van Trijp, Wayne D. Hoyer, and J. Jeffrey Inman, "Why Switch? Product Category—Level of Explanations for True Variety-Seeking Behavior," *Journal of Marketing Research,* August 1996, pp. 281–292; conversations with Jeffrey Inman.

Variety seeking is a cognitive commitment to purchase different brands because of factors such as the stimulation involved in trying different brands, curiosity, novelty, or overcoming boredom with the same old thing.[6] It is the antithesis of brand loyalty in that consumers' purchase behavior differs and the cognitive commitment to purchase is opposite that of brand-loyalty purchases. Variety seeking has also been differentiated from *derived varied behavior* in that the latter does not involve intrinsically motivated behavior. Derived varied behavior results from external cues in the environment; for example, a store is out of stock of a particular brand or a deal is available for a different brand.

The degree to which consumers are brand loyal or seek variety can be viewed as a continuum. For example, consumers might be completely brand loyal, loyal but switch occasionally, change loyalty from one brand to another, variety seek among a limited set of brands and options, or variety seek among all brands and options during a particular consumption period. Multiple brand strategies are designed not only to appeal to different target markets but also to capitalize on consumers who seek variety. Brand extensions are designed in part to appeal to brand-loyal customers who also seek variety within a branded group and increase sales to them. Highlight 16.1 discusses the value of brand names.

Although marketers seek to develop brand-loyal customers, they also need to be concerned with the *usage rate* of particular products by various target markets and consumers. For example, the 18- to 24-year-old group uses almost twice as much shampoo as the average user, and families of three or more people make up 78 percent of heavy users of shampoo. Clearly, obtaining brand loyalty among these consumers is preferable to attracting consumers who purchase and use shampoo less frequently, other things being equal.

Exhibit 16.4 shows the relationship between brand loyalty and usage rate. For simplicity, we have divided the dimensions into four categories of consumers rather than consider each dimension as a continuum.

Exhibit 16.4 shows that attracting brand-loyal consumers is most valuable when the consumers are also heavy users. This figure could be used as a strategic tool to plot consumers of both the firm's brands and competitive brands on the basis of brand loyalty and usage rates. Depending on the location of consumers and whether they are loyal to the firm's brand or a competitive one, several strategies might be useful:

1. If the only profitable segment is the brand-loyal heavy user, focus on switching consumer loyalty to the firm's brands. For example, comparative advertising such as that used by Avis in the car rental industry or by Burger King in the fast-food industry may have been an appropriate strategy for switching heavy users.

2. If there is a sufficient number of brand-loyal light users, focus on increasing their usage of the firm's brand. For example, the baking soda market might have been characterized as being composed of brand-loyal light users of Arm & Hammer baking soda. This brand then demonstrated new uses of the product, such as for freshening refrigerators. It is reported that half the refrigerators in America now contain a box of baking soda.

3. If there is a sufficient number of variety-seeking heavy users, attempt to make the firm's brand name a salient attribute and/or develop a new relative advantage. For example, no firm in the hot dog market has more than a 12 percent market share. Firms such as Oscar Mayer stress the brand name in advertising in an attempt to increase the importance of brand name to the consumer. In

Highlight 16.1

Valuing Manufacturer and Store Brands

Some portion of a product's sales can be attributed to the brand name it carries. Consumers often prefer branded products because the brand names represent higher-order values and meanings. For example, Levi's core meanings of democracy, freedom, and independence help make its products big sellers in Asia. It is useful for marketers to know just how much their brands are worth so they can assess how successful their marketing strategies have been at creating positive affect and future purchases by consumers.

Interbrand Corporation evaluates brands on the basis of how much they are likely to earn in the future and discounts the projected profits to their present value based on how risky the projected earnings are. Below are the world's 10 most valuable brands in 2003:

Rank	Brand	Value ($ in billions)
1	Coca-Cola	$70.45
2	Microsoft	65.17
3	IBM	51.77
4	GE	42.34
5	Intel	31.11
6	Nokia	29.44
7	Disney	28.04
8	McDonald's	24.70
9	Marlboro	22.18
10	Mercedes	21.37

Interestingly, 8 of these 10 brands are American companies, as are 62 of the top 100, in spite of the fact that many global consumers are anti-American. For example, Ahmad Tarouat, a 23-year-old Parisian, insists he will never eat a Big Mac because McDonald's stands for American imperialism. However, he seems oblivious to the fact that the Nike sneakers on his feet or the pack of Marlboro Lights in his pocket are also American products.

Marketers are rightly concerned with the value of their brands and the future earnings they will produce both domestically and globally. One trend that may affect the future value of manufacturer brands is the increase in purchases of private-label or store-brand merchandise. One in five items sold in U.S. stores is a store-branded product that can reduce the value of manufacturer brand names. For example, Wal-Mart's Ol' Roy dog food has surpassed Nestlé's Purina as the world's top-selling dog chow. Grocery giant Kroger now has 4,300 of its own food and drink items that are manufactured in 41 factories that it owns and operates. One out of two ceiling fans sold in the United States is from Home Depot, and most of these are its Hampton Bay brand. Other retailers, such as Target, Costco, and Albertson's, also enjoy the higher margins, lower marketing costs, and low overhead of private-label products. The improved quality of private-label products in recent years and their lower prices are reasons many consumers are increasing their purchases of them. Could a store brand ever make the top 10 list of most valuable brands?

Sources: Matthew Boyle, "Brand Killers," *Fortune,* August 11, 2003, pp. 88–100. Copyright 2003 Time Inc. All rights reserved. Reprinted by permission; Reprinted with permission from Gerry Khermouch, Diane Brady, Stanley Holmes, Moon Ihlwan, Manjeet Kripalani, and Jennifer Picard, "Brands in an Age of Anti-Americanism," *Business Week,* August 4, 2003, pp. 69–78. Copyright 2003 by the McGraw-Hill Companies, Inc.

addition, Oscar Mayer successfully developed the market for hot dogs containing cheese to increase sales.

4. If there is a sufficient number of variety-seeking light users, attempt to make the firm's brand name a salient attribute and increase usage of the brand among consumers, perhaps by finding a sustainable relative advantage. For example, a portion of the market that shops at Wal-Mart consists of variety-seeking consumers attracted by lower prices.

Exhibit 16.4

Brand Loyalty and Usage Rate

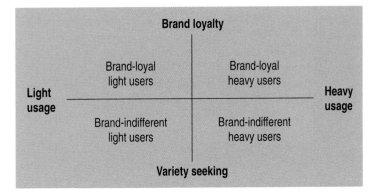

As we noted, it is also important to plot consumers of competitive brands to develop appropriate strategies. For example, if a single competitor dominates the brand-loyal heavy-user market and has too much market power to be overcome, strategies may have to focus on other markets. For example, because Nike dominates the men's athletic shoe market, companies like Avia and Ryka are focusing on women's casual and athletic shoes.

The Product Environment

The *product environment* refers to product-related stimuli that consumers attend and comprehend. In general, the majority of these stimuli are received through the sense of sight, although there are many exceptions. For example, the way a stereo sounds or how a silk shirt feels also influences consumer affect, cognition, and behavior. In this section, we focus on two types of environmental stimuli: product attributes and packaging.

Product Attributes

Products and product attributes are major stimuli that influence consumer affect, cognition, and behavior. Consumers may evaluate these attributes in terms of their own values, beliefs, and past experiences. Marketing and other information also influences whether purchase and use of the product is likely to be rewarding. For example, the product attributes of a new shirt might include color, material, sleeve length, type and number of buttons, and type of collar. By investigating these attributes and trying the shirt on, a consumer might conclude, "This shirt is well made but just isn't for me."

It is unlikely that many consumers would purchase a shirt based on these product attributes alone, however. The price of the shirt would likely be important; the store selling the shirt (and the store's image) might be considered. In addition, the packaging, brand name, and brand identification would likely be factors. In fact, for many purchases, the image of the brand created through the nonproduct variables of price, promotion, and channels of distribution may be the most critical determinant of purchase.

Packaging

Packaging is an element of the product environment on which marketers spend billions of dollars annually. Traditionally, four packaging objectives are considered. First, packaging should *protect* the product as it moves through the channel to the consumer. Second, packaging should be *economical* and not add undue cost to the product. Third, packaging should allow *convenient* storage and use of the product by the consumer. Fourth, packaging can be used effectively to *promote* the product to the consumer.

In some cases, packaging can obtain a relative advantage for a product. For example, Oscar Mayer's use of zip-lock packages for its hot dogs, bacon, and lunch meats made these products easier for consumers to keep fresh after opening. Procter & Gamble introduced the Crest Neat Squeeze dispenser, which draws unused toothpaste back into the container to make it neater and more economical. Duracell uses a package with a built-in tester to allow consumers to ensure the batteries they buy are fresh. Glad's zip-lock bags use blue and yellow channels that turn green when they are sealed, ensuring that the bags are sealed properly. In these examples, mature products were differentiated on the basis of packaging alone. Highlight 16.2 discusses other examples and lists some findings from a packaging study.

Package Sizes

Package sizes can influence not only which brands consumers choose but also how much of a product they use on particular occasions.[7] In general, consumers believe that larger package sizes offer lower unit costs and, as such, may be willing to use their contents more freely than from smaller packages. Consumers may also use the contents of smaller packages more sparingly to avoid the hassle of a trip to the store or pantry in order to get more of the product in the short term. Larger packages and larger home inventories of products may also increase the frequency of a product's usage. For example, if a consumer has a large box of Wheaties or 10 cans of Campbell's tomato soup in the pantry, more occasions for use may be found because the products are readily available and convenient.

An interesting issue is whether the size of a pour spout or the diameter of a package's opening influences how much of a product is used on a particular occasion. Although there is evidence that it does not,[8] many consumers seem to use more toothpaste and shampoo when the product is dispensed from a container with a larger opening. Also, many believe the beer drunk from "big mouth" cans is consumed more rapidly than from conventional openings.

Package Colors

In addition to the nature of the package itself, package colors are thought to have an important impact on consumers' affect, cognition, and behavior. This impact is more than just attracting attention by using eye-catching colors (like Tide's orange). Rather, it has been argued that package colors connote meanings to consumers and can be used strategically.[9]

For instance, the color of the Ritz cracker box was changed to a deeper red trimmed with a thin gold band. This change was made to appeal to young, affluent consumers. Microsoft Corporation changed its software packages from green to red and royal blue because consultants argued that green was not eye-catching and connoted frozen vegetables and gum to consumers rather than high-tech software.

Highlight 16.2

Can Packaging Enhance Trial of Both Old and New Products?

Everyone is familiar with the old maxim about judging a book by its cover. But consumers judge products constantly by their boxes, bags, and shrink-wrapping. Effective packaging is often what gets a potential consumer to pick up a product, examine it, and perhaps give it a try. In fact, some analysts argue that consumers go through a two-step process for many products. First, they decide whether to examine the product more closely. Second, they decide whether to buy it. For example, when AriZona Beverages decided to spice up its offering, it didn't tamper with its formula of water, sugar, tea, and flavorings. Rather, it came up with a snazzier container, a squeezable sports bottle with a nozzle just like the ones athletes use to guzzle on the run. Although consumers will pay 28 cents for this container, four times the cost of an aluminum can,

Modern beverage packaging   *Tom McCarthy/PhotoEdit, Inc.*

the package could entice them to both look it over and buy it. When Coke came up with a contoured plastic bottle, consumers increased purchases by 50 percent in some markets and sales growth averaged 20 percent since then. Pepsi's 20-ounce "Big Slam" bottles earned it an extra $400 million in high-margin sales its first year-and-a-half on the market.

One packaging study offered the following generalizations:

- Consumers appreciate packaging with utility that goes beyond the original purchase. Tins that once contained lozenges and mints, for example, can be used again to store other small items.
- A package should be consistent with the product it holds. Graphics and information that clash with the product's purpose create confusion in consumers' minds.
- Good packaging both attracts the consumer to the product and encourages selection, as these are two separate decisions.
- Consumers want a good deal, but they can be lazy about clipping coupons or looking for the cheapest price. Packaging that communicates a price break helps differentiate the product at the point of the decision. Good packaging can convey a solid or upscale image, whereas poor packaging detracts from the product's image.

Although packaging is critical for new-product launches, its effects on trial can be extended to any phase of the product life cycle. Any undiscovered product is a new product to consumers. Even old brands can benefit from a new package designed to enhance trial.

Sources: Catherine Arnold, "Way Outside the Box," *Marketing News,* June 23, 2003, pp. 13–15; Ian P. Murphy, "Study: Packaging Important in Trial Purchase," *Marketing News,* February 3, 1997, p. 14. Reprinted by permission of the American Marketing Association; Reprinted with permission from Stephen Baker and Nicole Harris, "What's Foiling the Aluminum Can," *Business Week,* October 6, 1997, pp. 106–108. Copyright 1997 by The McGraw-Hill Companies.

Swanson dropped the turquoise triangle from its frozen dinners because that color was thought to give the product a dated 1950s look. Canada Dry changed the color of its cans and bottles of sugar-free ginger ale from red to green and white when consultants claimed that red sent a misleading "cola" message to consumers. Canada Dry sales were reported to increase 25 percent after this color change.

Packaging can give a
product a competitive
advantage   *Courtesy Lever
Brothers Company.*

Label information can
influence purchase behavior
Alan Becker/Getty Images.

It has also been reported that consumer perceptions of products may change with a change in package color. For example, when designers at Berni Corporation changed the background hue on Barrelhead sugar-free root beer cans from blue to beige, consumers reported that the product tasted more like old-fashioned root beer, even though the beverage remained the same. Similarly, consumers ascribed a sweeter taste to orange drinks when a darker shade of orange was used on the can or bottle.

Brand Identification and Label Information   The brand identification and label information on the package (as well as on the product) provide additional stimuli for consideration by the consumer. In many cases, brand identification simplifies purchase for the consumer and makes the loyalty development process possible. As we noted previously, brand names such as Tide, Crest, and Rolex may well be discriminative stimuli for consumers.

Label information includes use instructions, contents, lists of ingredients or raw materials, warnings for use and care of the product, and the like. For some products, this information can strongly influence purchase. For example, consumers often carefully examine label information on over-the-counter drugs such as cough medicines. Health-conscious consumers often consult package information to determine the nutritional value, sugar content, and calories in a serving of products such as cereal.

Product Strategy   Product strategies are designed to influence consumers in ...
run. In the short run, new-product strategies aim to influe...
product; in the long run, product strategies are designed ...
and obtain large market shares.

A critical aspect of designing product strategies invol...
product relationships. This means consumers' product–...
behavior, and environments should be carefully considered ... ... ,
ductions and should be monitored throughout a product's life cycle. In this section,
we first examine some personal characteristics of consumers that influence product
adoptions. Then we look at some characteristics of products that influence the adoption process.

Characteristics of Consumers

In analyzing consumer–product relationships, it is important to recognize that consumers vary in their willingness to try new products. Different types of consumers
may adopt a new product at different times in the product's life cycle. Exhibit 16.5
presents the classic **adoption curve** and five categories of adopters. The adoption
curve represents the cumulative percentage of purchasers of a product across time.

Traditionally, the five adopter groups are characterized as follows: **Innovators**
are venturesome and willing to take risks; **early adopters** are respectable and often
influence the early majority; the **early majority** avoid risks and are deliberate in
their purchases; the **late majority** are skeptical and cautious about new ideas;
laggards are very traditional and set in their ways.

Designers of product strategies find innovators particularly important because
they may influence early adopters, who in turn may influence the early majority to
purchase. Thus, a new product's chances of success increase once innovators

---

Exhibit 16.5

The Adoption Curve

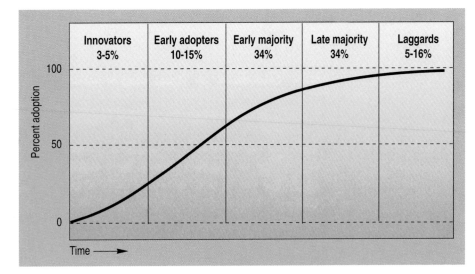

purchase the product and tell others about it. Also, early adopters and others can learn about the product vicariously by seeing innovators use it.

A major focus of consumer research has been to identify the characteristics of innovators and their differences from other consumers. A review of this research found that innovators tend to be more highly educated and younger and to have greater social mobility, more favorable attitudes toward risk (more venturesome), greater social participation, and higher opinion leadership than other consumers.[10]

Innovators also tend to be heavy users of other products within a product class. For example, Mary Dickerson and James Gentry found that adopters of home computers had greater experience with other technical products, such as programmable pocket calculators and video television games, than did nonadopters.[11] Innovators may have better-developed knowledge structures for particular product categories. This may enable them to understand and evaluate new products more rapidly and thus adopt earlier than other consumers.[12]

Finally, note that the five adopter categories and the percentages in Exhibit 16.5 are somewhat arbitrary. These categories were developed in research in rural sociology that dealt with major farming innovations. Their validity has not been fully supported in consumer research, particularly for low-involvement products.[13]

However, the idea that different types of consumers purchase products in different stages of the products' life cycles does have important implications for product strategy: Namely, product strategy (and other elements of marketing strategy) must change across time to appeal to different types of consumers.

Characteristics of Products

In analyzing consumer–product relationships, it is also important to consider the product characteristics listed in Exhibit 16.6. A number of these characteristics have been found to influence the success of new products and brands.[14] There is no absolute demarcation, but some of the dimensions are more directly involved with facilitating trial, whereas others both facilitate trial and encourage brand loyalty. We will discuss each of these characteristics next.

Exhibit 16.6

Some Important Questions in Analyzing Consumer–Product Relationships

Compatibility: How well does this product fit consumers' current affect, cognitions, and behaviors?

Trialability: Can consumers try the product on a limited basis with little risk?

Observability: Do consumers frequently see or otherwise sense this product?

Speed: How soon do consumers experience the benefits of the product?

Simplicity: How easy is it for consumers to understand and use the product?

Competitive advantage: What makes this product better than competitive offerings?

Product symbolism: What does this product mean to consumers?

Marketing strategy: What is the role of other marketing mix elements in creating a functional or image-related relative advantage?

A marketing strategy to increase trialability
Courtesy Oreck Corporation.

Compatibility **Compatibility** refers to the degree to which a product is consistent with consumers' current affect, cognition, and behavior. Other things being equal, a product that does not require an important change in consumer values and beliefs or purchase and use behaviors is more likely to be tried by consumers. For example, Chewels chewing gum—the gum with a liquid center—required little change on the part of consumers to try the product.

Trialability **Trialability** refers to the degree to which a product can be tried on a limited basis or divided into small quantities for an inexpensive trial. Other things being equal, a product that facilitates a nonpurchase trial or a limited-purchase trial is more likely to influence consumers to try the product. Test-driving a car, trying on a sweater, tasting bite-size pieces of a new frozen pizza, accepting a free trial of a new software package, or buying a sample-size bottle of a new shampoo are ways consumers can try products on a limited basis and reduce risk.

Observability **Observability** is the degree to which products or their effects can be sensed by other consumers. New products that are public and frequently discussed are more likely to be adopted rapidly. For example, many clothing styles become popular after consumers see movie and recording stars wearing them. Satellite dishes are highly observable, and this feature likely influences their purchase.

Speed **Speed** refers to how rapidly consumers experience the benefits of the product. Because many consumers are oriented toward immediate rather than delayed gratification, products that can deliver benefits sooner rather than later have a higher probability of at least being tried. For example, weight-loss programs that promise results within the first week are more likely to attract consumers than those that promise results in six months.

Simplicity **Simplicity** refers to the degree to which a product is easy for a consumer to understand and use. Other things being equal, a product that does not require complicated assembly and extensive consumer training has a higher chance of trial. For example, many computer products, are promoted as being user-friendly to encourage purchase.

Competitive Advantage **Competitive advantage** is the degree to which an item has a *sustainable competitive advantage* over other product classes, product forms, and brands. There is no question that relative advantage is a most important product characteristic not only for obtaining trial but also for encouraging continued purchase and development of brand loyalty.

In some cases, a relative advantage may be obtained through technological developments. For example, at the product class level, RCA introduced the videodisk player, which showed movies on any TV set. The disk player cost half as much as a cassette machine, and the disks were cheaper than videocassettes. However, videocassette players had a relative advantage over disk players: They could record programs, and the disk players could not. RCA thought recording ability was not an important factor to consumers—and lost more than $500 million finding out otherwise.

At the brand level, however, it is often difficult to maintain a technological relative advantage. This is because new or improved technology is often quickly copied by competitors. In addition, many brands within product groups are relatively homogeneous in terms of their functional benefits for consumers. For these reasons, we believe one of the most important sources of a sustainable competitive advantage comes from product symbolism rather than technological changes or functional differences in products.

Product Symbolism   **Product symbolism** refers to what the product or brand means to the consumer and what the consumer experiences in purchasing and using it. Consumer researchers recognize that some products possess symbolic features and that consumption of them may depend more on their social and psychological meaning than on their functional utility.[15] For example, the blue jean market has many successful brands, and it is difficult to determine clear differences among them except in pocket design and brand labeling. If these brand names meant nothing to consumers and were purchased only on the basis of product attributes such as materials and styles, it would be difficult to explain differences in market shares, given the similarity among brands. Similarly, it would be difficult to describe how a brand such as Guess? jeans took in $200 million in sales in its first three years.

It seems clear that jeans brand names have meanings and symbolize different values for consumers. For example, teenagers make up a large portion of the market for Guess? jeans. These consumers may be seeking to convey an identity different from that of wearers of traditional brands, such as their parents.

Sexy, trendy product symbolism for Guess? jeans
Courtesy Guess, Inc.

Marketing Strategy   To this point, we have suggested that a variety of product characteristics partially account for the success or failure of products and brands. Though not strictly a product characteristic, the quality of the *marketing strategy* employed also has an important bearing on whether a product is successful and profitable.

We have also argued that at the brand level, the image or symbolism a brand carries is often the only competitive advantage a firm has to offer. This frequently

Highlight 16.3

Tips for Global Consumer Products' Marketing Strategies

Many consumer goods companies have sought growth by expanding into global markets. For U.S. companies, this is sound strategy since 95 percent of the world's population and two-thirds of its purchasing power are located outside their country. The potential for success in global markets is enhanced when companies carefully research and analyze consumers in foreign countries, just as it is in domestic markets. Below are some suggestions for companies seeking to successfully market to global consumers.

- Research the cultural nuances and customs of the market. Be sure that the company and brand name translate favorably in the language of the target country and, if not, consider using an abbreviation or entirely different brand name for the market. Consider using marketing research firms or ad agencies that have detailed knowledge of the culture.

An example of Ford's global advertising   *Courtesy Ford Motor Company.*

- Determine whether the product can be exported to the foreign country as is or whether it has to be modified to be useful and appealing to targeted consumers. Also, determine what changes need to be made to packaging and labeling to make the product appealing to the market.
- Research the prices of similar products in the target country or region. Determine the necessary retail price to make marketing it profitable in the country and research whether a sufficient number of consumers would be willing to pay that price. Also, determine what the product has to offer that should make consumers willing to pay a higher price.
- Based on research, decide whether the targeted country or region will require a unique marketing strategy or whether the same general strategy can be used in all geographic areas.
- Research the ways consumers purchase similar products in the targeted country or region and whether the company's product can be sold effectively using this method of distribution. Also, determine if a method of distribution not currently being used in the country could create a competitive advantage for the product.
- Pretest integrated marketing communication efforts in the targeted country to ensure not only that messages are translated accurately, but also that subtle differences in meaning are not problematic. Also, research the effectiveness of planned communication efforts.

Marketing consumer goods successfully in global markets requires a long-term commitment as it may take time to establish an identity in new markets. However, with improving technology and the evolution of a global economy, both large and small companies have found global marketing both feasible and profitable.

Source: Based on Dom Del Prete, "Winning Strategies Lead to Global Marketing Success," *Marketing News,* August 18, 1997, pp. 1, 2. Reprinted by permission of the American Marketing Association.

happens because in many product classes, the brands offered are relatively homogeneous in their functional utility to the consumer.

In many cases, a favorable image is created through the other elements of the marketing mix. *Promotion* in the form of advertising is commonly used to create a favorable image for the brand by pairing it with positively evaluated stimuli, such as attractive models. In addition, promotion tells consumers what attributes they should look for in the product class and emphasizes the superiority of the brand in terms of those attributes. Few consumers can tell the difference in the taste of various brands of beer—and, in fact, many consumers initially do not like the taste of beer. Thus, many commercials try to teach consumers that a particular brand tastes great, or a least as good as more expensive beers. We suspect brand image is a key determinant of beer brand choice, although many consumers would likely disavow image and insist that taste is the most important consideration.

Price can also create brand images as well as provide a functional competitive advantage. In terms of brand images, high prices can connote high quality for some products; and it is often stated that consumers perceive a relationship between price and quality. Price can also be used to position a brand as a good value for the money; for example, Suave hair care products are reportedly as good as the expensive brands, but much cheaper. As a functional competitive advantage, through vast economies of scale and large market shares, a firm can sometimes sustain a price advantage that no competitor can meet. Campbell's soups have long enjoyed such an advantage.

Finally, a variety of *distribution* tactics can be used to gain a relative advantage. Good site locations and a large number of outlets are important advantages in the fast-food market and in the markets for other products and services. Also, a variety of in-store stimuli, such as displays, can offer products at least a temporary competitive advantage. Highlight 16.3 discusses some ideas for developing successful global marketing strategies.

Back To...

Timberland

Timberland's success can be traced to several of the factors mentioned in this chapter. First, there is no question that the product is of high quality and functionally keeps feet dry. It has a number of favorable product characteristics such as compatibility, trialability, observability, speed, and simplicity.

Second, Timberland shoes and boots have a distinctive tree brand mark that differentiates the product from other brands. This emblem may be a discriminative stimulus for buyers and serves the role of imparting meaning to the products. Thus, product symbolism may be a key to the company's success. As such, the emblem also may serve to give Timberland boots a competitive advantage.

Third, Timberland changed a number of components of its marketing strategy. It cut prices on its Weatherbuck casual shoes from $130 to $95 a pair. Sales increased 300 percent, leading Timberland to consider price cuts on other models. It redesigned products, adding colors and improving styling of its shoes and clothing. It increased advertising to $25 million and targeted 25- to 44-year-olds. It expanded U.S. distribution beyond the Northeast. In a recent quarter, the Midwest and South were Timberland's fastest-growing regions. Finally, Timberland continued to expand overseas. In one recent year, 40 percent of its revenues came from overseas.

Analysts believe that the boots-as-fashion trend will last only a couple of years and then cool down. However, Timberland will remain strong because it is sticking with its core business. Jeff Swartz says, "We transcend language and geography. We represent something that's more than a product. It's also a point of view. Whether it's the '60s or '70s, whether it's grunge or hip-hop or bebop, it still snows and it still rains, and you're going to get dressed for the snow and the rain."

In addition, the expanding worldwide adventure travel market (African Safari, not Walt Disney's Frontier Land), which is among the fastest-growing segments of the outdoor industry, has meant only good news for Timberland. According to Timberland, the travel industry will grow 55 percent to $7.2 trillion in a few years, with adventure travel leading the pack. The category is made up primarily of aging baby boomers, and 50 percent of the segment are women. To meet the needs of this expanding market, Timberland is developing new shoe technologies and expanding its mountain athletic line. With the demand for quality outdoor apparel and gear increasing at such a rapid rate, Timberland is in a strong position indeed. ❖

Summary   In this chapter we investigated some product-related affect, cognition, behavior, and environmental factors, as well as several aspects of product strategy. Initially we discussed product affect and cognition in terms of consumer satisfaction and dissatisfaction. Developing satisfied consumers is clearly a key to successful marketing. Our analysis of behavior looked at product contact and brand loyalty, and emphasized several strategies based on the relationships between brand loyalty and usage rates. Product attributes and packaging were among the environmental factors examined. Finally, we discussed product strategy, focusing on a number of characteristics of consumers and products that influence whether products are adopted and become successful.

Key Terms and Concepts

adoption curve **413**
brand loyalty **406**
compatibility **415**
competitive advantage **415**
consumer satisfaction **403**
disconfirmation **403**
dissatisfaction **405**
early adopters **413**
early majority **413**
innovators **413**

laggards **413**
late majority **413**
observability **415**
prepurchase expectations **403**
postpurchase perceptions **403**
product symbolism **416**
simplicity **415**
speed **415**
trialability **415**
variety seeking **406**

Review and Discussion Questions

1. Describe the process by which the consumer comes to experience satisfaction or dissatisfaction. Illustrate each result with an experience of your own.
2. Gather several consumer complaints from friends or classmates and make recommendations for marketing strategies to prevent similar problems.
3. Explain each of the four categories in Exhibit 16.3. Offer an example of a product for which your purchasing patterns fit each category.
4. Recommend a marketing strategy for a brand that competes with one for which you are a brand-loyal heavy user. How successful do you believe the strategy would be, and why?
5. Identify the key stimuli in the product environment that influence your purchasing behavior for (*a*) soft drinks, (*b*) frozen pizza, (*c*) shampoo, and (*d*) jeans.
6. To which adopter category do you belong in general? Explain.
7. Describe characteristics of new products that would be useful for predicting success and for prescribing effective marketing strategies.
8. Discuss the problems and advantages that could be associated with appealing to innovators when marketing a new consumer packaged good.
9. Analyze the consumer–product relationships for a new presweetened cereal product. Include both product and consumer characteristics.

Marketing Strategy in Action

Harley-Davidson, Inc.

Harley-Davidson, Inc., founded in 1903, is the only remaining American motorcycle manufacturer, although there are some new upstart companies. During the 1950s and 1960s, Harley-Davidson had a virtual monopoly on the heavyweight motorcycle market. Japanese manufacturers entered the market in the 1960s with lightweight motorcycles backed by huge marketing programs that increased demand for motorcycles. These manufacturers, which included Honda, Kawasaki, Suzuki, and Yamaha, eventually began building larger bikes that competed directly with Harley-Davidson.

Recognizing the potential for profitability in the motorcycle market, American Machine and Foundry (AMF, Inc.) purchased Harley-Davidson in 1969. AMF almost tripled production to 75,000 units annually over a four-year period to meet increased demand. Unfortunately, product quality deteriorated significantly.

More than half the cycles came off the assembly line missing parts, and dealers had to fix them to make sales. Little money was invested in improving design or engineering. The motorcycles leaked oil, vibrated badly, and could not match the excellent performance of the Japanese products. Although hard-core motorcycle enthusiasts were willing to fix their Harleys and modify them for better performance, new motorcycle buyers had neither the devotion nor the skill to do so.

In late 1975, AMF put Vaughn Beals in charge of Harley-Davidson. Beals set up a quality control and inspection program that began to eliminate the worst of the production problems. However, Beals and the other senior managers recognized that it would take years to upgrade the quality and performance of their products to compete with the faster, high-performance Japanese bikes.

To stay in business while the necessary changes in design and product were being accomplished, the executives turned to William G. Davidson, Harley's styling vice president. Known as "Willie G." and a grandson of one of the company founders, he frequently mingled with bikers and, with his beard, black leather, and jeans, was accepted by them. Willie G. understood Harley customers and noted:

> They really know what they want on their bikes: the kind of instrumentation, the style of bars,, the cosmetics of the engine, the look of the exhaust pipes, and so on. Every little piece on a Harley is exposed, and it has to look just right. A tube curve or the shape of a timing case can generate enthusiasm or be a total turnoff. It's almost like being in the fashion business.

Willie G. designed a number of new models by combining components from existing models. These included the Super Glide, the Electra Glide, the Wide Glide, and the Low Rider. Although these were successful, Harley-Davidson was still losing market share to

An example of Harley's eye-catching styling   *AP/Wide World Photos.*

Japanese competitors that continued to pour new bikes into the heavyweight market.

By 1980, AMF was losing interest in investing in the recreational market and sold the company to 13 senior Harley executives in a leveraged buyout on June 16, 1981. Although the company was starting to make money in the early 1980s, its creditors wanted payment, and Harley-Davidson nearly had to file for bankruptcy at the end of 1985. However, through some intense negotiations, it stayed in business and rebounded to become a highly profitable company.

By 1996, Harley-Davidson controlled more than 47 percent of the heavyweight (651cc and larger) motorcycle market, far more than its all-time low of 23 percent. Its products are considered to have "bulletproof reliability" because of manufacturing and management changes that resulted in products of excellent quality.

Owners of Harleys are highly brand loyal, and more than 94 percent of them state they would buy another Harley. The company sponsors the Harley Owner Group (HOG), which has more than 1,200 chapters and 750,000 members worldwide. Executives of the company frequently meet with chapters to obtain suggestions for product improvements.

In 2002, Harley sold 215,454 motorcycles domestically and 48,199 in the global market. It also sold 10,943 Buell motorcycles in that year. Its net revenue for 2002 was over $4 trillion, about double its 1998 net revenue. Its net income for 2002 was $580 million compared to $213 million 5 years earlier. In 2003, its 100th anniversary product line included 7 Softtail models, 7 Sportster models, 5 Dynaglide models, and 7 Touring models. In addition, its VRSCA V-Rod, a new-style, $17,000 Harley was selling quickly even though it was a departure from the retro look of traditional Harleys.

Harley-Davidson motorcycles are distributed worldwide by a network of over 1,300 dealers. These dealers typically have upgraded facilities that merchandise not only motorcycles and service but also a variety of parts, clothing, and accessories. Clothing and accessories are highly profitable items that enhance the motorcycle-owning and riding experience. For more information, visit the company's website at **www.Harley-Davidson.com**.

Discussion Questions

1. What kind of consumer owns a Harley?
2. What accounts for Harley owners' satisfaction and brand loyalty?
3. What role do you think the Harley Owner Group plays in the success of the company?
4. What threats do you think Harley-Davidson faces in the next few years?

Sources: John Helyar, "Will Harley-Davidson Hit the Wall?" *Fortune,* August 12, 2002, pp. 120–124; Leslie Norton, "Potholes Ahead," *Barron's,* February 1, 1999, pp. 16–17; 1998 Annual Report, Harley-Davidson, Inc.; Richard A. Melcher, "Tune-Up Time for Harley," *Business Week,* April 8, 1996, pp. 90, 94; Kevin Kelly and Karen Lowry Miller, "The Rumble Heard Round the World: Harley," *Business Week,* May 24, 1993, pp. 58–60; John Kekis, "Business Rev Charges Harley after Long Slump," *Wisconsin State Journal,* June 17, 1991, p. 6B; Bob Wiedrich, "Harley Zooms Crest of Cycle Comeback," *Wisconsin State Journal,* January 7, 1990, p. 1F; Thomas Gelb, "Overhauling Corporate Engine Drives Winning Strategy," *Journal of Business Strategy,* November–December 1989, pp. 8–12; "How Harley Beat Back the Japanese," *Fortune,* September 25, 1989, pp. 155–164.

Consumer Behavior and Promotion Strategy

Winning Promotions

Each year the Promotion Marketing Association of America (PMA) honors the most effective promotions in the country with Reggie Awards, in the form of small gold, silver, and bronze cash registers. In 2000, American Express won the top prize, the Super Reggie, for its "Central Park in Blue" promotion. Although American Express generally is considered a card for older, wealthier, more conservative consumers, the company's new Blue card was designed to appeal to a younger demographic, people ages 25 to 40. To reach that market, American Express sponsored a rock concert in New York's Central Park featuring Sheryl Crow, Eric Clapton, Keith Richards, and Stevie Nicks, among others. In the weeks leading up to the concert, teams of "Blue Crews" hit the streets on scooters and skateboards to give out instant win game pieces, one in four of which were good for concert tickets.

The Blue Crews alone were directly responsible for 3,000 card applications. At the concert, photographers took digital photos of fans and then directed those folks to a website

where they could see their photos online and apply for a card. In addition to the crowd of 25,000 in Central Park, 13 million people enjoyed the music on Fox television, a network of radio stations, and the Internet. A survey of TV viewers revealed that two-thirds of them could successfully recall American Express Blue as the sponsor. By the end of 1999, the number of Blue cards in circulation was 71 percent above the company's goal, while Internet applications beat estimates by 150 percent. In fact, American Express is still getting mileage from its concert promotion: CDs, home videos, and DVDs of the "Central Park in Blue" performance all include Blue card applications.

Oscar Mayer snagged a Reggie for its "Share the Smiles" campaign, an effort to fight hunger and build brand image for Oscar Mayer hot dogs. The company put its fleet of six 26-foot-long, hot-dog-shaped Weinermobiles on the road to visit 200 cities across the

United States. In exchange for a contribution to their local Second Harvest food bank, people could have their picture taken in the Weinermobile. They would also receive a commemorative photo holder and coupons for Oscar Mayer products. A program for retailers provided Weinermobile pedal cars and bean-bag toys in exchange for promotional displays. About 6,500 stores bought in. According to Lori Farley, manager of the Oscar Mayer in-house promotions team, "We built goodwill with retailers. On those days when the Weinermobile was parked out front, they had problems keeping any product on the shelf. That's a good problem to have." The promotion earned $500,000 for Second Harvest, which meant 18 million meals delivered to families in need. It also allowed Oscar Mayer to reach more than 700,000 potential consumers.

In 2003, DVC Worldwide received the Super Reggie Award for the overall marketing promotion of the year. The campaign, "Do you know a Brawny man?", was created for Georgia-Pacific Company to promote its brand, Brawny paper towels. The promotion encouraged female consumers to nominate a real-life rugged guy who exemplified the characteristics of strength, toughness, and dependability of the fictitious Brawny man shown on the package and in TV commercials. DVC designed a multipronged plan that included national TV and online advertising, in-store displays, a website to make nominations, and an interactive game in which consumers could create a virtual Brawny man. After receiving 4,131 photo-and-essay entries and 40,000 votes, 12 finalists were selected, and their pictures appeared on a calendar that was sold in stores (self-liquidating). The winner, firefighter Mario Cantacessi, received a Dodge Durango truck, and his picture appeared on Brawny packages for a time. PMA pointed out that this promotion also showed how a fully integrated promotion campaign can build brand recognition and drive sales, even in usually low-interest product categories, by involving consumers with the product in an emotional way. The results? Brawny's household penetration grew by 10 percent and sales volume increased by 12 percent.

Sources: For a description of 2003 Reggie Award winners, visit the *PROMO* magazine website (**http://promomagazine.com**), click on "PROMO Archive," then click on 2003 Features; Terry Lefton, "Ablue's Crew Mastermind," *Brandweek,* April 3, 2000, pp. R4–R5; T. L. Stanley, "Unfurling a Tall Order," *Brandweek,* April 3, 2000, pp. R8–R9; Sonia Reyes, "Hotdoggin' Cross-Country," *Brandweek,* April 3, 2000, pp. R16, R25; anonymous, "Brand Names" *PROMO,* January 1, 2003, pp. 28–39.

This example describes three highly successful sales promotion strategies. Marketers develop **promotions** to communicate information about their products and to persuade consumers to buy them. There are four major types of promotions: *advertising, sales promotions, personal selling,* and *publicity*. Like all marketing strategies, promotions are experienced by consumers as social and physical aspects of the environment that may influence consumers' affective and cognitive responses as well as their overt behaviors. From the view of marketing management, the importance of promotion cannot be overstated. Most successful products and brands require promotions such as those described in the opening example to create and maintain a *differential advantage* over their competitors.

Because they are so highly visible, promotion strategies are often the target of marketing critics. Some critics claim promotions are expenses that add nothing to the value of products but increase their cost to the consumer. Supporters counter that marketing promotions inform consumers about product attributes and consequences, as well as prices and places where products are available. This information saves consumers both time and money by reducing the costs of search. Moreover, advocates of promotion point out that some promotion strategies save consumers money directly. According to NCH Promotional Services, a division of Dun & Bradstreet, coupons, the most popular type of sales promotion, saved American consumers an estimated $115 million in 1999, up from $104 million in 1997 and $93 million in 1995.[1]

In this chapter we discuss how promotion strategies affect consumers' affective and cognitive responses and their overt behaviors. We begin by briefly describing the four types of promotion strategies. Then we discuss the communication process. Next, we examine selected aspects of the promotion environment, consumers' affective and cognitive responses to promotions, and promotion-related behaviors. These topics are shown in the Wheel of Consumer Analysis in Exhibit 17.1. We conclude by detailing how marketing managers can use their understanding of consumers to manage promotion strategies.

Exhibit 17.1

Types of Affective Response

Types of Promotion

The four types of promotion—advertising, sales promotions, personal selling, and publicity—together constitute a promotion mix that marketers try to manage strategically to achieve organizational objectives. The most obvious type of promotion is advertising.

Advertising

Advertising is any paid, nonpersonal presentation of information about a product, brand, company, or store. It usually has an identified sponsor. Advertising is intended to influence consumers' affect and cognitions—their evaluations, feelings, knowledge, meanings, beliefs, attitudes, and images concerning products and brands. In fact, advertising has been characterized as *image management:* creating and maintaining images and meanings in consumers' minds.[2] Even though ads first influence affect and cognition, the ultimate goal is to influence consumers' purchase behavior.

Advertisements may be conveyed via a variety of media—the Internet, TV, radio, print (magazines, newspapers), billboards, signs, and miscellaneous media such as hot-air balloons or T-shirt decals. Although the typical consumer is exposed to hundreds of ads daily, the vast majority of these messages receive low levels of attention and comprehension. Thus, it is a major challenge for marketers to develop ad messages and select media that expose consumers, capture their attention, and generate appropriate comprehension.

For many years, Nike Corporation used print ads and billboards featuring strong visual images of athletes—Carl Lewis long jumping, Michael Jordan leaping for the basket, or unknown ordinary people jogging—and little else. Some outdoor ads contained only the Nike "swoosh" logo in the corner and the athletes wearing Nike shoes and clothes. At first, consumers probably had to look twice to comprehend what product was being advertised. But once the association was made, Nike-related meanings were easily activated when consumers encountered other ads in the series. In markets where the ads were run, Nike sales increased an average of 30 percent.[3]

Sales Promotions

Sales promotions are direct inducements to the consumer to make a purchase.[4] TV advertising may be more glamorous, but more money is spent on sales promotions in the United States.

The many types of sales promotions—including temporary price reductions through coupons, rebates, and multipack sales; contests and sweepstakes; trading stamps; trade shows and exhibitions; point-of-purchase displays; free samples; and premiums and gifts—make defining them difficult. According to Parker Lindberg, president of the Promotion Marketing Association of America, the key aspect of sales promotions is to "move the product today, not tomorrow. A sales promotion gets people to pick the product up at retail and try it by offering something concrete—a premium, cents off, or whatever."[5] In sum, most sales promotions are oriented at changing consumers' immediate purchase behaviors.

Consider a promotion by ITT Sheraton, owners of Sheraton hotels, to increase bookings by travel agents. Research indicated that most travel agents knew little about the $1 billion in improvements Sheraton had made to many of its 430 properties nationwide. Also, many agents did not know the differences among Sheraton hotels, resorts, suites, and inns. The campaign, called "Wish You Were Here," featured two fictitious travel agents, Ellen and Carol, who sent funny postcards to real-life travel agents describing their "cross-country trip." In the cards, Ellen and Carol described the Sheraton properties where they stayed, explained the different Sheraton properties, and talked up the renovations and upgrades. Agents who answered five questions on a postcard could enter a sweepstakes contest with prizes such as a free weekend at the Sheraton New York, magazine subscriptions, and cosmetics. The three-month promotion increased awareness of the renovations to 90 percent of travel agents and increased bookings at Sheraton properties by 35 percent.[6]

Coupons directed at consumers remain the most popular form of sales promotion, with cents-off promotions in second place. Other forms of sales promotions, particularly coupons distributed in the store (electronically at the checkout or via dispensers on the shelf), have increased in popularity, as has the old standby, sampling (giving away free or trial samples of new products). An interesting sales promotion called "Win Your Own Pub in Ireland" was devised by Guinness Import Company in 1994. The prize was Connie Doolan's pub in the sea town of Cobh. To win, consumers had to write a 50-word essay describing the "perfect pint of Guinness," and 10 finalists competed in dart throwing and beer pouring. Besides generating worldwide publicity, Guinness received more than 30,000 entries and a 29 percent increase in draft sales.[7] The promotion was so successful that Guinness ran another promotion in 1995 offering the Kilgoban Pub in Bantry as the prize.

Personal Selling

Personal selling involves direct personal interactions between a potential buyer and a salesperson. Personal selling can be a powerful promotion method for at least two reasons. First, the personal communication with the salesperson may increase consumers' involvement with the product and/or the decision process. Thus, consumers may be more motivated to attend to and comprehend the information the salesperson presents about the product. Second, the interactive communication situation allows salespeople to adapt their sales presentations to fit the informational needs of each potential buyer.

Certain consumer products, such as life insurance, automobiles, and houses are traditionally promoted through personal selling (see Highlight 17.1). In retailing, personal selling has decreased over the past 20 years as self-service has become more popular. However, some retailers, like Nordstrom, have established a differential advantage by emphasizing personal selling and customer service. Besides lots of personal attention from a courteous sales staff, customers are coddled by pianos softly playing in the store and champagne at fashion shows.

For other businesses, personal selling by telephone, or *telemarketing*, has become popular as the total costs of a direct sales call keep increasing (from $295 in 1993 to $330 in 2001).[8] Telemarketing selling differs considerably from face-to-face selling. The telemarketer usually follows a prepared script, never travels, makes 20 to 50 calls per day that last from one to two minutes, works about four to six hours per day, and is closely supervised. In contrast, a conventional salesperson often travels, usually must improvise the sales presentation to fit the buyers' needs, makes only 2 to 10 sales calls per day that last about 1 hour each, works about 8 to 12 hours per day, and is loosely supervised.[9]

Both Avon and Mary Kay Cosmetics, among the largest U.S. marketers of skin care products, were built on personal selling. In their earlier days, neither company spent much on advertising or customer sales promotions. In 2002, Mary Kay did

➤ **High**light 17.1

Youwannadeal?

The stuff of American dreams is on sale at Landmark Chevrolet in Huntsville, Alabama, for $10,987 (plus tax, freight, a document fee, a $395 fabric protection package, and a $1,500 down payment). That's the price of the 1991 Camaro convertible that 21-year-old Jacoby Rice is eyeing. "Bubba" Phelps, a top salesman at Landmark, looks straight into Rice's nervous eyes, smiles broadly, and says, "If you had all the money in the world, you'd buy this car today, wouldn't you? You wouldn't worry about the price."

This sort of hard sell approach to personal selling is alive and well at many car dealerships in America. However, many car manufacturers have concluded the hard sell approach is bad business and have instituted training programs for salespeople as well as dealer incentives to reduce the predatory sales practices once common in the industry. Ford and Chrysler, for example, have elaborate programs in place to induce dealers to give customers better and more respectful treatment both before and after the purchase.

But not all dealerships have embraced the new look in personal selling. Many so-called blow and glow dealerships continue to sell cars the old-fashioned way—with urgency, excitement, dickering, low-price teasers, and lots of eye contact and earnest discussions. To create excitement (and a reason to visit the lot), Landmark holds tent sales, provides giveaways (free diamond [chip] necklaces), hosts free breakfasts, arranges helicopter visits from Santa Claus, and conducts stunts like burying a disk jockey alive.

These promotions, although seemingly hokey and contrived, move metal off the lot. For example, Landmark held a five-day sale over the Fourth of July weekend. Promoted with newspaper ads and live radio broadcasts, Landmark gave away free Cokes, hot dogs, and apple pie. Hundreds of people visited the dealership, where they were offered temporary sales incentives such as doubling the manufacturer's rebate. Landmark sold 253 new and used cars during the weekend, in contrast to the 21 cars sold during the same period at the low-pressure Saturn dealership down the road, where there is no dickering over price.

These promotional events influence people to show up at the dealership, but once they are there the sales staff takes over. At Landmark personal selling is taken seriously. Landmark salesmen (only one is a woman) joke about Saturn "sales consultants" who "don't understand the excitement of buying a car" or "how to build relationships with customers." At Landmark the salesperson is expected to "control" the customer, "work the deal" for maximum profit and "sell what you see" (sell the cars on the lot, not necessarily what the customer wants to buy). Salespeople at Landmark follow the age-old ritual of taking every purchase offer to the sales manager, presumably to plead for a better deal on behalf of the customer. These price negotiations can be drawn out and intense.

Not all customers like this hard sell bargaining style, of course, but many customers know what to expect and see the negotiation process as "fun" and "a challenge." Says one, "They are full of tricks, but I expect all this. I love the wheeling and dealing. I know from experience, Bubba will try to lowball you on the trade-in and stick on all kinds of fees."

Salespeople at Landmark believe the consumer "wants to be sold." Consider how Bubba sold a Caprice sedan to an elderly couple. After he determined they had been married about 45 years, he asked the husband to close his eyes and think back 45 years to the day they were married. "Do you remember how much you loved your wife that day? Do you still love her as much today as you did 45 years ago? If you could have afforded to buy this car for her then, would you have done it?" The husband responded with a hint of anger in his voice, "Boy, you really got me there." To make him feel better, Bubba knocked off another $50 and closed the sale.

In this age of self-service retailing, personal selling can be very effective, especially at car dealerships such as Landmark.

$1.6 billion in wholesale business with little advertising. Most of the Mary Kay promotion budget is spent on sales incentives intended to motivate sales consultants. In addition to symbolic prizes such as medals, ribbons, and commemorative certificates, Mary Kay gives jewelry, calculators, briefcases, and furs as rewards to salespeople. Top sellers receive the use of pink Cadillacs or Buicks. Mary Kay also spends heavily on motivational and training programs for its 1 million female sales consultants worldwide (Mary Kay has very few male salespeople).[10]

Publicity

Publicity is any unpaid form of communication about the marketer's company, products, or brands. For instance, an article in *PC World* comparing various brands of word processing software provides useful product information to consumers at no cost to the marketers of the software. Similarly, descriptions of new products or brands; brand comparisons in trade journals, newspapers, or news magazines; or discussions on radio and TV talk shows provide product information to consumers.

Publicity can be either positive or negative. Nike received a bonanza of free publicity in the form of favorable news stories about its billboard campaign. One TV news segment in Los Angeles concluded with the reporter urging viewers to "give a honk for Nike, which has raised the billboard from visual blight to at least camp art."[11] Exxon, on the other hand, received considerable unfavorable publicity when a tanker spilled oil in a pristine bay in Alaska.

Sometimes publicity can be more effective than advertising because consumers may not screen out the messages so readily. In addition, publicity communications may be considered more credible because they are not presented by the marketing organization. Publicity is difficult to manage, however. Marketers sometimes stage "media events" in the hope of garnering free publicity. For instance, in 1997 IBM spent about $5 million to set up a rematch between world champion chess player Gary Kaparov and its supercomputer named Deep Blue. The match attracted the interest of the media and many people, even non–chess players. Countless stories appeared around the world, including "The Brain's Last Stand," a cover story in *Newsweek*. The IBM Internet site covered the competition live and, during one game, had an astounding I million viewers, at the time perhaps the most traffic for an event on the World Wide Web. IBM claimed to have reaped the equivalent of more than $100 million in free publicity, nearly all of it favorable.[12]

The Promotion Mix

Ideally, marketing managers should develop a coherent overall promotion strategy that integrates the four types of promotions into an effective promotion mix. Major environmental forces in the United States over the past three decades have changed the balance of marketing effort devoted to the various types of promotions. The share of total promotion dollars going to media advertising has been decreasing since 1980, while spending on promotions has increased. In 2002, promotion spending was $234 billion, while ad expenditures were $212 billion.[13]

A controversy continues in marketing about the relative importance of advertising versus sales promotions. As you might expect, most advertising agencies argue that advertising is the best (only?) way to create a strong consumer–brand relationship.[14] Other marketers believe sales promotion can also enhance the consumer–brand relationship and has more powerful effects on immediate buying behaviors and

Highlight 17.2

Promotion through Sponsorships

In these times when a 30-second ad during the Super Bowl costs in excess of $2 million, more companies have been seeking alternatives to advertising to promote their brands. One increasingly popular option is the sponsoring of various events, such as rock concerts and tours, football games, and tennis tournaments.

One of the first companies to sponsor a college football bowl game was John Hancock Financial Services, which plunked down $1.6 million in 1990 to rename the Sun Bowl the John Hancock Bowl. For that $1.6 million expenditure, the company garnered about $5.1 million in equivalent advertising value. That total included the 7,800 newspaper and magazine articles mentioning the John Hancock Bowl, references to the company during the game broadcast, drawing the mid-field logo, and the patches on the players' uniforms. Following the game, the number of people who claimed they would consider buying from Hancock rose from 41 to 54 percent, while awareness of the Hancock advertising campaign rose from 90 to 96 percent. Today all college bowl games carry some form of title sponsorship.

Some companies go even further, sponsoring not only an event but also athletes. Olympic sponsor UPS operates an Athletes' Training Assistance program. Interested athletes apply for UPS jobs just as anyone else would. After 90 days on the payroll, they can apply for ATAP. If they are among the top 40 in their sport, they are eligible for full-time pay for half-time work. UPS also covers some of the athletes' other expenses. Prior to the 2000 Olympics in Sidney, Australia, UPS circulated 65 million envelopes worldwide with images of its employee-athletes. The athletes also participated in a welcome dinner in Sidney for customers from around the globe, discussing their training and their sports, answering questions, and signing autographs.

Increasingly, companies are creating their own events, which gives them more control and may also save money. In 1996, H. J. Heinz could not find an event to sponsor that related to the key meanings of its Kibbles and Bits dog food: superior taste and the great lengths to which dogs would go to get it. So Heinz created an event called "Do Your Bit for Kibbles and Bits." The premise was to select a dog for a TV commercial based on the trick the dog would perform to get Kibbles and Bits. Consumers entered more than 2,500 dogs and submitted 1,600 additional entries on videotape. At the events, Heinz gave away coupons, sold plush toys, and donated profits to local animal shelters. Sales of Kibbles and Bits increased from one to four share points in the key retail markets where the promotion ran.

Sources: Anonymous, "Companies Hire Athletes, Aid Olympic Hopefuls in Exchange for PR Gold," *PR News,* September 25, 2000. p.1; Wayne D'Orio, "The Main Event," *PROMO,* March 1997, pp. 19–32; Michael J. McCarthy, "Keeping Careful Score on Sports Tie-Ins," *The Wall Street Journal,* April 24, 1991, pp. B1, B5.

eventual brand success.[15] A long-range trend may be occurring in which TV and print advertising are no longer the centerpieces of a company's promotion mix.[16] There is evidence that advertising is having a decreasing influence on consumers' behaviors, partly owing to people's increasingly hectic lifestyles and the resulting pressures on their time.

The promotion mix of the future is likely to be more eclectic with many more options, including event sponsoring (see Highlight 17.2), sports marketing (e.g., Volvo sponsors tennis matches), direct marketing (sending coupons to purchasers of a competitor's brand), and public relations. These promotion types are being developed partly because of the high costs of advertising and partly because of the need to target customers more precisely. For instance, Nintendo of America created a 13-minute MTV-style documentary video to promote its new game, Donkey

Kong Country. The company sent more than 2 million copies of the video to a highly targeted group of potential buyers—subscribers of Nintendo Power and recent buyers of the Super Nintendo Entertainment system. (Video promotions have become cost effective; a 10-minute video can be produced and mailed in a four-color box for about $1.50 per unit, compared to perhaps $8.00 for a fancy brochure.) Partly because of this unusual promotion, Nintendo sold 6.1 million units of the game in the pre-Christmas season of 1994, making Donkey Kong Country the fastest-selling game in the history of the videogame industry.[17]

Another factor in advertising's decline is the documented decrease in consumers' ability to remember ads they have seen. In 1986, 64 percent could remember, unaided, an ad campaign seen in the previous month. This figure plunged to 48 percent in 1990.[18] Attention to individual ads has decreased even further because of remote controls, the clutter of 30- and 15-second ads during commercial breaks, and consumers' dropping loyalty to favorite brands. Simultaneously, price has become more important as a choice criterion, further increasing the effectiveness of sales promotions, which are often based on price reduction.

A Communication Perspective

Consumers experience all promotions as information in the environment. Thus, the cognitive processing model of decision making (see Exhibit 3.5 on page 52) is relevant to an understanding of the effects of promotions on consumers. First, consumers must be exposed to the promotion information. Then they must attend to the promotion communication and comprehend its meaning. Finally, the resulting knowledge, meanings, and beliefs about the promotion must be integrated with other knowledge to create brand attitudes and make purchase decisions (form purchase intentions).

The Communication Process

A cognitive processing perspective suggests that developing successful promotion strategies is largely a communication problem.[19] Exhibit 17.2 presents a simple model that identifies the key factors in the **communication process.** The process begins when the *source* of the promotion communication determines what information is to be communicated and *encodes* the message in the form of appropriate symbols (using words, pictures, and actions). Then the message is *transmitted* to a receiver over some medium such as a television show, direct mail, signs, or a magazine. The *receiver* or consumer, if exposed to the promotion, must *decode* it or interpret its meaning. Then the consumer might take *action*, which could include going to a store or making a purchase. Marketing managers are usually the sources of promotion communications, and managing the promotion mix is their responsibility. As the target of promotion communications, consumers may be influenced by them.

Two stages of the communication model are particularly important to the success of promotion strategies. The first occurs when the marketer creates the promotion communication to encode a particular meaning. As you learned in Chapter 12, the marketer selects cultural meanings from the environment to create a message that will convey the intended meaning about the brand to the consumer.[20] The other critical stage is decoding, when consumers attend to and comprehend the information in the promotion communication and construct their personal interpretations of its meaning. Consumers' interpretations, of course, may not have the same meaning as that intended by the marketer.

Exhibit 17.2

A General Model of the Communication Process for Promotions

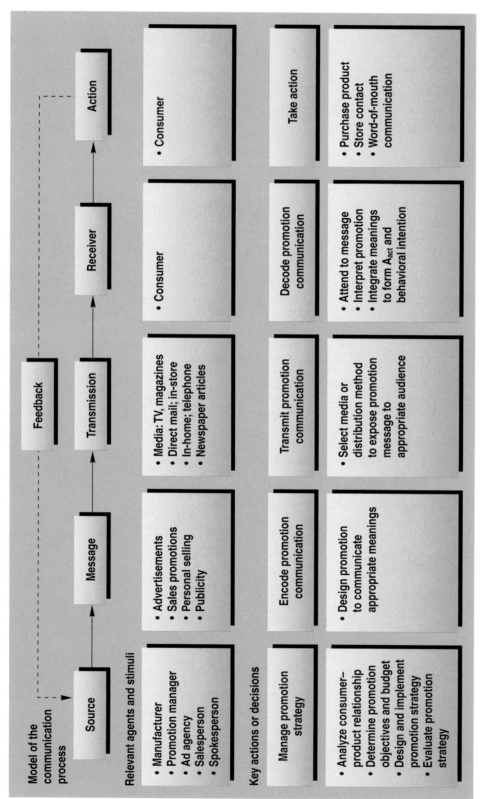

Source: Adapted from Figure 8.1 in Henry Assael, *Consumer Behavior and Marketing Action*, 3rd ed. (Boston: PSW-KENT Publishing Company, 1987), p. 210 © by Wadsworth, Inc. More recently found in Henry Assael, *Consumer Behavior: A Strategic Approach* (Houghton Mifflin, 2004), p. 504. Used with permission.

Companies that sponsor race cars gain publicity if photos are shown in news media.
Darrell Ingham/Getty Images.

Goals of Promotion Communications

Researchers have identified five types of communication effects that promotion information can have on consumers.[21] These effects can be ordered in a hierarchical sequence of events or actions that are necessary before consumers can or will purchase a brand. From the marketing manager's perspective, these effects can be treated as a sequence of goals or objectives for promotion communications.

- Consumers must have a *recognized need* for the product category or product form.
- Consumers must be *aware* of the brand.
- Consumers must have a *favorable brand attitude*.
- Consumers must have an *intention to purchase* the brand.
- Consumers must *perform various behaviors* to purchase the brand (such as travel to the store, find the brand in the store, talk to salespeople).

In this section we discuss each communication goal, identify the types of promotion strategies best suited for each goal, and briefly describe how these communication effects can be created. Several concepts discussed earlier in the text will be relevant for our analysis.

Stimulate Category Need   Before they make any brand purchase, consumers must recognize (feel) a need for the product category or the product form. Only consumers who have recognized the self-relevance of the product and have formed a general intention to purchase it are "in the market" for the product. As you learned in Chapters 6 and 7, consumers' intentions to buy a brand are based on their attitudes toward buying and their social beliefs about what others want them to buy. A_{act} in turn is based on consumers' beliefs about the consequences of buying the brand. Thus, to stimulate a category need, marketers need to create beliefs about the positive consequences of buying and using the product category or form.

When consumers in the target market already recognize a category need, marketers can concentrate promotion strategies on other goals. However, at any given time, relatively few consumers are likely to have a general intention to buy a product. For instance, perhaps 20 percent of consumers might intend to buy laundry detergent at any time, compared to 1 percent who intend to buy a new car. Moreover, it can be difficult to distinguish the consumers who have formed such intentions from those not fully in the market.

Marketers usually use advertising to stimulate a category need among additional consumers, although publicity and personal selling also can influence category need to some extent. These strategies should be designed to convince consumers that the product category or form is associated with important end goals and values. Essentially, stimulating product need involves creating positive means–end chains at the level of the product category or product form.

Brand Awareness   Because consumers cannot buy a brand unless they are aware of it, brand awareness is a general communication goal for all promotion strategies. By creating brand awareness, the marketer hopes that whenever the category need arises, the brand will be activated from memory for inclusion in the consideration set of choice alternatives for the decision (see Exhibit 7.3). Advertising probably has the greatest influence on brand awareness,[22] although publicity, personal selling, and sales promotion also can increase awareness.

In the store, sales personnel can generate brand awareness by bringing certain brands to consumers' attention. Various sales promotion strategies, such as colorful price discount signs and end-of-aisle displays (a large stack of brand packages at the end of the supermarket aisle), draw consumers' attention to brands. Also, shelf position and brand placement within the store can influence brand awareness. Finally, prominent brand-name signs (buses and billboards) also remind consumers of the brand name and maintain brand awareness.

The level of consumers' brand awareness necessary to induce purchase varies depending on how and where they make their purchase decisions for that product category or form. Many brand choice decisions about grocery and personal care products, clothing items, appliances, and electronic products are made in the store. Consumers do not need to recall a brand name; they need only to be able to quickly recognize familiar brands (often based on package cues), which then activates their relevant brand knowledge in memory. Thus, an implication is to show the brand package in the advertising so consumers can more easily recognize the brand in the store.[23]

In other decision situations, a higher level of brand awareness is necessary to influence brand choice. If the purchase decision is made at home or in another environment where few brand-related cues are available, the brand must be recalled from memory to enter the consideration set. Restaurant choices are an example. In such cases, knowledge in memory may be more important than environmental factors. Unless consumers are able to recall the brand name (activate it from memory), the brand is not likely to be considered or purchased.

Marketers can measure the level of consumers' brand awareness by asking them to state the brand names they can remember (with no hints—unaided recall) or by observing which brands consumers recognize as familiar. Whether brand recall or recognition is suitable depends on where and when the purchase decision is made.[24]

A company's brand awareness strategy depends on how well known the brand is. Sometimes the marketing goal is to maintain already high levels of brand awareness.

Much of the advertising for well-known brands such as Coca-Cola, IBM, and Tylenol serves a reminder function that keeps the brand name at a high level of awareness.[25] This makes brand activation more likely in a decision situation. Publicity and sales promotions also can have reminder effects. Managers of less familiar brands have a more difficult task and may have to spend heavily to create brand awareness.

Brand Attitude   As you learned in Chapter 6, consumers are likely to have an attitude toward every brand they purchase. Each promotion strategy can influence consumers' brand attitudes, but the specific communication objective depends on consumers' current attitudes toward the brand. More specifically, for a new or unfamiliar brand, the goal might be to *create* a brand attitude. For an already popular brand, marketers may be content to *maintain* existing favorable brand attitudes. For brands with neutral or slightly unfavorable attitudes, marketers may wish to *increase* the existing attitude. In each case, the general promotion strategy will be to create more beliefs about the favorable consequences of salient brand attributes.[26]

Marketers make a big mistake if they analyze consumers' brand attitudes in an absolute or very general sense without specifying the situational context. Usually the salient beliefs about important attributes, consequences, and end goals will vary across situations and contexts. Therefore, brand attitudes are likely to vary from one decision context to another. As you learned in Chapter 4, the meanings of beliefs about brand consequences depend on the ends to which they are related. For instance, in different circumstances, consumers may believe that a functional consequence for toothpaste such as "makes my mouth feel fresh" leads to different ends, including "sensory enjoyment, eliminate bad breath and avoid offending others, or feel more alive." In general, the overall communication goal is to create means–end knowledge structures that link the brand to important consequences and values.

Brand Purchase Intention   Marketers intend most promotion strategies to increase (or maintain) the probability that consumers will buy the brand (increase *BI*). As you learned in Chapters 6 and 7, all voluntary behaviors are based on intentions to behave (I will buy Pert shampoo this afternoon). Behavioral intentions (*BI*) may be activated from memory as stored decision plans (When I run low on mouthwash, I will buy more Scope). Alternatively, *BI* can be constructed through integration processes at the time of the decision choice, usually in the store (I'll buy this red Hanes T-shirt). An intention to buy a brand is based on a consumer's attitude toward buying the brand (A_{act}) as well as the influence of social norms (*SN*) about what other people expect. A_{act} is based on means–end chains of beliefs about the consequences and values associated with the acts of buying or using the brand.

To develop effective promotion strategies directed at brand purchase intentions, marketers must know when *BI* are formed by most of the target consumers. Consumers do not necessarily form an intention to buy immediately on exposure to advertising information about the brand. Only consumers who recognize the category need and are actively in the market for the product (they have a general intention to buy the product) are likely to form a brand purchase intention at the time of exposure to an ad.[27]

More typically, formation of a brand *BI* is delayed until well after exposure to advertising, when the consumer is in a purchase context such as a store. This situation is more likely for brands that are not high in intrinsic self-relevance (candy bars), which are more likely to be purchased on impulse (that is, environmental factors tend to trigger purchase). An estimated 85 percent of candy purchases, 83 percent of snack purchases, and 45 percent of soft-drink purchases are based on impulse where the *BI* to purchase is formed in the store.[28]

In contrast, personal selling and sales promotions usually are designed to influence purchase intentions at the time of exposure to the promotion information.[29] The goal is for consumers to immediately form a connection between the brand and important consequences and values. For example, a lower price due to a 25-percent-off price promotion might be seen as leading to "saving money" and "having more money to use for other things," which in turn is linked to the values of "being a careful consumer" and "self-esteem." Thus, consumers might form a positive A_{act} and *BI* on the spot.

Facilitate Other Behaviors   Finally, some promotion strategies are designed to facilitate behaviors other than purchase. As you learned in Chapter 10, consumers often must perform several other behaviors prior to making a brand purchase. For instance, buying certain brands of clothing requires consumers to enter the stores that carry such brands and then find the brand. Sales promotions and publicity are likely to have little influence on these other behaviors, but advertising and personal selling strategies may increase their probability. For instance, an ad might be directed at encouraging consumers to come to the dealership to test-drive a new car. Salespeople might encourage consumers to operate the controls of an appliance or a digital camera, which increases the probability of making a purchase. Other advertising strategies might encourage consumers to engage in positive word-of-mouth communication by telling other people about the brand.

The Promotion Environment

The *promotion environment* includes all the stimuli associated with the physical and social environment in which consumers experience promotion strategies. Many of these factors can affect the success of a promotion. In this section we discuss two environmental factors that can influence advertising and sales promotion strategies—promotion clutter and level of competition.

Promotion Clutter

A key promotion objective is to increase the probability that consumers will come into contact with, attend to, and comprehend the promotion message. In recent years, however, the amount of marketing promotion has so increased that the effectiveness of any given promotion strategy may be impaired by *promotion clutter,* the growing number of competitive strategies in the environment.[30]

Advertisers have long worried that the clutter created by multiple ads during commercial breaks and between TV programs will reduce the communication effectiveness of each ad. There is good reason for alarm: Fewer consumers can remember ads they have seen. A 1994 survey of 20,000 consumers found that a surprising 40 percent could not identify a single "outstanding" commercial. These consumers could not remember enough details of any ad to establish that they actually recalled it.[31]

Clutter also affects other types of promotion strategies, especially sales promotions. Over the past decade, marketers have dramatically increased their spending on sales promotions. Traditionally, *couponing* has been the most popular form of sales promotion, and its use grew steadily until the mid-1990s. Nearly every major U.S. consumer goods company used coupon promotions in 1995. These firms

Comparative ads make direct comparisons with key competitors *Courtesy of GlaxoSmithKline.*

distributed a staggering 310 billion coupons, about 3,000 per household. Yet redemption rates by consumers were quite low—only about 4.4 percent of all types of coupons were redeemed. By 2002, marketers had distributed 336 billion (3100 per household per year), and saw overall redemption rates of about 1.2 percent. Consumers do not respond to all coupons in the same way, of course. For instance, the so-called FSI (freestanding insert coupons distributed in supplements to Sunday newspapers) are the most popular form of coupon, accounting for more than 80 percent of coupons. But they have the lowest usage rate; only about 1.0 percent were redeemed in 2002.[32]

Level of Competition

The *level of competition* for a product category is a key aspect of the promotion environment. As competition heats up, marketers' use of promotions usually increases. We saw this in the large number of promotions tried by the airlines and telephone companies when deregulation created a more competitive environment. Moreover, the types of promotion strategies change as competitive pressures increase.

Comparative advertising, featuring direct comparisons with competitive brands, has become more common.[33] Sometimes miniature "wars" are fought through TV commercials. In one notable example, Pepsi "challenge" ads claimed taste preference superiority over Coke, and Coca-Cola retaliated with taste tests that showed consumers preferring Coke. New battles erupted in the 1990s when Coke claimed Pepsi drinkers were switching to Diet Coke, and Pepsi showed archaeologists of the future puzzled by their discovery of an "old" can of Coke.

In fiercely competitive environments, promotion often becomes the key element in the marketers' competitive arsenal. Marketers of breakfast cereals, for instance, have developed complex promotion mixes that include couponing, in-pack prizes, premiums, advertisements, price reductions, contests, games, and publicity. Rental car companies such as Hertz, Avis, and Budget promote continuously, mostly on price, by offering various deals and discounts, but they also mount extensive advertising campaigns and offer frequent-traveler programs along with occasional contests and prizes.

Promotion Affect and Cognition

Promotion affect and cognition include all of the affective and cognitive responses we discussed in Section Two. Interpretation of promotion communications (attention and comprehension) and integration processes (forming attitudes and intentions) are extremely important. But some researchers claim ad information can influence consumers without any affective or cognitive responses (see Highlight 17.3).

As we discussed in Chapter 5, consumers' comprehension processes vary in depth and elaboration, depending on their levels of knowledge and involvement.[34] Thus, exposure to a promotion communication—whether an ad, a coupon, or a sales presentation—may produce meanings that vary in number (elaboration), level (deep

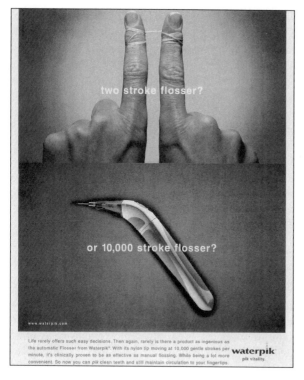

Advertising can be quite effective in influencing consumers' affect and cognition about a product. *Reprinted with permission of Water Pik, Inc.*

versus shallow), and interconnectedness. Consumers also may form inferences about product attributes or consequences or the marketer's motivation.[35] In this section, we examine two other concepts relevant to understanding the effects of advertising: consumers' attitudes toward ads and persuasion processes.

Attitude toward the Ad

Advertisers have long been interested in measuring consumers' evaluations of advertisements.[36] Researchers have established that consumers' **attitude toward the ad**—their affective evaluations of the ad itself—can influence their attitudes toward the advertised product or brand.[37] That is, ads that consumers like seem to create more positive brand attitudes and purchase intentions than ads they don't like. Exactly how liking an ad influences brand attitude is not known. It may be that ad liking influences attention (people pay more attention to ads they like)[38] and comprehension (consumers devote more effort to elaborating the information in likable ads).

Currently a number of other issues remain to be resolved, including what aspects of the ads (perhaps the visual material in print ads) have the greatest influence on ad attitudes and whether consumers' evaluative reactions to the ads make purchase more likely.[39] Apparently a positive attitude toward an ad may not always lead to increased purchase of the brand. At one time in the mid-1990s, the Energizer Bunny campaign was the 13th most popular ad on TV, but sales of Energizer batteries were up just 3.8 percent compared to a 5 percent increase for batteries in general. As another example, Nestlé developed a very popular, long-running campaign featuring a flirtatious relationship between Tony and Sharon, two 30-somethings with a common attraction to Taster's Choice coffee. When Tony and Sharon finally shared their first kiss, sales of Taster's Choice had decreased 2.7 percent, while sales in the instant-coffee category decreased even more (down 5.8 percent).[40]

The Persuasion Process

Persuasion refers to changes in beliefs, attitudes, and behavioral intentions caused by a promotion communication. For the most part, marketing researchers have studied the persuasive effects of advertising communication, but sales promotions, personal selling, and publicity can also persuade consumers.

The Elaboration Likelihood Model The **Elaboration Likelihood Model (ELM)** identifies two cognitive processes by which promotion communication such as advertising can persuade consumers: the central and peripheral routes to persuasion.[41] Exhibit 17.3 shows how these two processes work. Which persuasion process occurs is determined by consumers' level of involvement with the product message.[42] The central route to persuasion is more likely when consumers' involvement is higher; the peripheral route to persuasion is more likely when involvement is lower.

Highlight 17.3

Subliminal Advertising

Although most advertisers pay little or no attention to it, the topic of *subliminal persuasion* in advertising won't go away. In 1957, an advertising executive named James Vicary claimed that sales of popcorn and Coke in movie theaters increased dramatically when messages stating "Eat Popcorn" and "Drink Coke" were quickly flashed on-screen throughout a movie. Six years later, Vicary backed away from his assertion, claiming he had used "a small amount of data—too small to be meaningful." But by then many others had eagerly latched onto his original claim. Writers like Wilson Key keep turning out widely read books that claim subliminal advertising is all around us. Key claims marketers intentionally embed subliminal stimuli—usually sexual objects, symbols, or words—in advertisements. Moreover, he claims these hidden, subliminal stimuli affect us in powerful ways of which we are unaware.

What do we know about the effects of subliminal stimulation? First, it is clear that stimulation below the level of a person's conscious awareness *can* be shown to have measurable effects on some aspects of that person's behavior. That is, people do respond to stimuli without being consciously aware of the stimuli. But these stimuli are not necessarily subliminal; that is, they are not presented at intensities below a person's perceptual threshold. They simply are not consciously noticed as consumers go about their business. As we have seen throughout this text, a great deal of cognitive activity occurs automatically, without awareness. Often consumers are unable to report the existence of a stimulus or an awareness that some cognitive process occurred.

With regard to Key's claims about sexual embedding, two issues are in question. First, are advertisers doing subliminal embedding in advertisements as a matter of course, as Key claims? Virtually no evidence exists that this is so. Certainly overt sexual stimuli are found in a great many advertisements, but these are not subliminally embedded. Second, can subliminal stimuli affect goal-directed behaviors like purchase choices?

Most stimuli have little or no influence on our cognitions or behaviors when presented at a recognizable level. Why, then, should they suddenly have a strong impact when presented subliminally? Key claims that humans have two processing systems, one of which operates on a completely unconscious level and immediately picks up on the alleged subliminally embedded information. However, no psychological theories or data support such a system of recognition.

A key finding in cognitive psychology that we have emphasized throughout this text is that the meaning of a stimulus is not inherent in the stimulus itself. Rather, consumers construct meanings in active and sometimes complex ways as they come into contact with the stimulus.

In sum, it seems that ads may be able to influence consumers' meanings at a subconscious level, but the stimuli don't have to be a subliminal in order for that to occur.

Sources: Raja Mishra, "TV Spot Gaffe Revives Decades-Old Suspicion," *Boston Globe,* September 13, 2000, p. A26; Jack Haberstroh, "Can't Ignore Subliminal Ad Charges," *Advertising Age,* September 17, 1984, pp. 3, 42; Timothy E. Moore, "Subliminal Advertising: What You See Is What You Get," *Journal of Marketing,* Spring 1982, pp. 38–47; check out the website **www.poleshift.org/sublim**.

The ELM also distinguishes between two types of information in the promotion communication. Specific claims about product attributes or demonstrations of functional and psychosocial consequences, along with supporting evidence, are central information; information about anything other than the product is peripheral.

In the *central route to persuasion,* consumers who experience higher levels of involvement with the product or promotion message are motivated to pay greater attention to the central, product-related information and comprehend it at deeper and more elaborate levels.[43] Consumers' comprehension of the product-related information is indicated by the types of cognitive responses (thoughts) they have to

Exhibit 17.3

Two Routes to Persuasion in the ELM

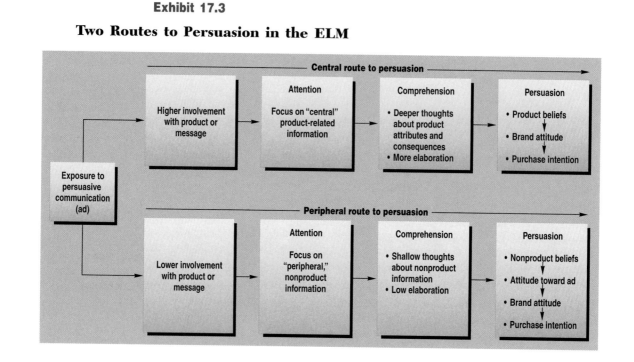

the promotion message.[44] *Support arguments* are positive thoughts about product attributes and the self-relevant consequences of product use (Head and Shoulders does seem like an effective dandruff shampoo). Support arguments enhance persuasion by leading to favorable product beliefs, positive brand attitudes, and stronger intentions to buy the product. During comprehension, consumers may produce unfavorable thoughts about the product called *counterarguments* (I don't think that taking this vitamin every day will make a difference in my health). Counterarguing reduces persuasion by leading to unfavorable product beliefs, negative brand attitudes, and weaker intentions or no intention to buy the product.

The *peripheral route to persuasion* is quite different. Consumers who have low involvement with the product message (perhaps they are not in the market for the product) have little motivation to attend to and comprehend the central product information in the ad. Therefore, direct persuasion is low because these consumers form few brand beliefs and are unlikely to form brand attitudes or purchase intentions. However, these consumers might pay attention to the peripheral (nonproduct) aspects of the promotion communication, such as the pictures in a print ad or the scenery or actors in a TV commercial, perhaps for their entertainment value. For instance, ads for Pepsi featuring entertainers such as Faith Hill and Beyoncé Knowles are intended to attract such attention. Consumers' affective and cognitive responses to these peripheral features may be integrated to form an attitude toward the ad (This is a fun or a creative ad). Later, if consumers need to evaluate a brand during decision making, these ad-related meanings could be activated and used to form a brand attitude or a purchase intention.[45] In this way, the peripheral route to persuasion can also persuade consumers to buy, but in an indirect manner.

Because relatively few consumers are in the market for a particular product, much of the advertising they are exposed to each day is not particularly relevant to their end goals and values. These typically low levels of involvement suggest that most mass media advertising receives peripheral processing. Certainly the low levels of day-after recall for most ads (about 20 percent on average) suggest this is the case. In some cases, however, marketers may want consumers to engage in peripheral route processing. If a brand is similar to competing brands (soft drinks, beer, and cigarettes are examples), marketers may not be able to make credible claims about unique product attributes or consequences. Promotion strategies will therefore tend to focus on image advertising for which peripheral processing is appropriate.

In situations where a brand has a distinctive advantage, marketers may want to encourage consumers to engage in central route processing by increasing their involvement with the ad message and the product or brand.[46] For instance, comparative advertisements make explicit comparisons with other brands, which tend to make the ad messages more interesting and involving. Sending promotion messages directly to consumers who are in the market for the product category or product form ensures some level of motivation in the brand information.

Promotion Behaviors

Ultimately promotion strategies must affect not only consumers' cognitions but also their behaviors. A firm's sales, profits, and market share objectives can be accomplished only if consumers perform a number of behaviors, including purchase of its product. Different types of promotions can be used to influence the various behaviors in the purchase–consumption sequence. Because we have already discussed purchase behavior in this chapter and throughout the book, we focus here on two other behaviors that are critical to the success of promotion strategies: information contact and word-of-mouth communication with other consumers.

Information Contact

For promotion information to be successful, consumers must come in contact with it. *Information contact* with promotions can be *intentional* (the consumer searches the newspapers for food coupons) but probably is most often *incidental* (the consumer just happens to come into contact with a promotion when engaging in some other behavior). Sometimes promotion contact can even trigger the purchase decision process, as might occur when the consumer accidentally comes across a sale or other incentive promotion. As a practical matter, the marketer must place the promotion message in the target consumers' physical environment to maximize chances for exposure and must design the promotion so it will be noticed (attended to). For advertising promotions, this requires knowledge of the media habits of the target market— what TV shows do they watch, what radio shows do they listen to, what magazines do they read?

Placing information in consumers' environments can be easy when target consumers can be identified accurately. For example, catalog marketers can buy lists of consumers who have made mail-order purchases in the past year. Then they can send promotion materials directly to these target consumers. Of course, sending coupons or a sweepstakes promotion through the mail does not guarantee consumers

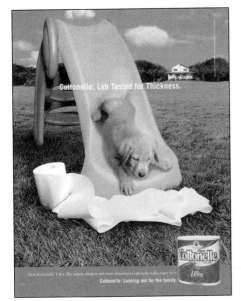

Consumers who are involved with their dogs may attend to this ad and engage in more elaborate comprehension processes— the central route to persuasion © 2003 KCWW. Reprinted with permission.

Highlight 17.4

Quirky Quisp Takes to the Internet

Quaker Oats used the Internet to bring a spark of life to a moribund breakfast cereal brand. In the late 1960s, Quisp's popularity skyrocketed thanks to funny TV advertising and a lovable pink, propeller-headed alien mascot (created by the same two men who brought the world Rocky and Bullwinkle). But sales plummeted in the 1970s and 1980s, and by the 1990s Quisp was available in only six U.S. cities. In 1999, Quaker sold a mere 92,000 boxes of Quisp. By contrast, consumers that year gobbled up 122 million boxes of market-leader Cheerios.

Despite anemic sales, Quaker executives couldn't bring themselves to kill off Quisp. According to Quisp marketing manager Pat Culligan, "It's the cereal I ate when I was a kid, and people around here want to keep it going." Apparently many consumers also retained a soft spot in their hearts for Quisp. Quaker's Quisp website (**www.quisp.com**) generated much more traffic than the sites of Quaker's bigger brands like Life and Cap'n Crunch. Furthermore, Quisp and Quisp-related products were commanding premium prices on Internet auction sites. For example, bidders were willing to shell out up to $10 for a box of the cereal, while an old Quisp decoder ring went for more than $600.

So Quaker decided to capitalize on Quisp's cult following in October 1999 by creating a link between the Quisp website and **www.netgrocer.com**, a nationwide online grocery retailer. Before long, Quisp had become NetGrocer's top-selling cereal, easily outpacing better-known names like Cheerios and Frosted Flakes. The ensuing buzz carried over to in-store sales as well. All told, Quaker moved seven times more boxes of Quisp than projected during the first four months of 2000.

Quaker began to use the Quisp website (which was receiving about 30,000 hits per week) to sell watches and T-shirts featuring the goofy little Quisp alien. But this Quisp revival notwithstanding, Quaker has no plans to expand the cereal's in-store distribution. There is only so much shelf space available, and the company fears Quisp would get lost in the clutter. Quaker would rather use in-store space to sell its more mainstream cereal brands. So consumers in most of the country will have to rely on the Internet for their Quisp fix. But Quaker executives hope this experiment will provide them with a stronger understanding of online grocery shopping, a market that is expected to become more lucrative in the coming years.

Sources: Wall Street Journal. Central Edition [Staff Produced Copy Only]. Jonathan Eig, "How the Web Rescued Quisp From a Cereal Killing," *The Wall Street Journal,* April 24, 2000, pp. B1, B10. Copyright 2000 by Dow Jones & Co. Inc. Reproduced with permission of Dow Jones and Co. Inc. in the format Textbook via Copyright Clearance Center; www.quisp.com.

will open the envelope and read its contents. Highlight 17.4 describes information contact through the Internet.

Contact for personal selling promotions can be achieved through "cold calls" on consumers. But referrals and leads (or consumers who initiate contact with salespeople during the search process) are likely to be more successful. Marketers sometimes encourage referrals by offering gifts in return for the names of potential customers.

Telemarketing is a popular and increasingly controversial method of information contact. State Farm Insurance, for example, used a telemarketing approach in which consumers were called and asked what time of the year they pay their homeowners' and automobile insurance premiums. Then, just before that time, rate information was sent to these consumers to encourage a switch to State Farm's insurance products.

Exposure to promotion messages is not enough, however. Consumers must also attend to the promotion messages. Big promotions (large discounts, expensive prizes) tend to be situational sources of involvement and thus are more likely to be noticed and receive higher levels of attention. How well the promotion interacts with such consumer characteristics as intrinsic self-relevance and existing knowledge also affects the level of attention. For instance, the effectiveness of price reduction promotions depends largely on consumers' price sensitivity.

Word-of-Mouth Communication

Marketers sometimes encourage consumers' **word-of-mouth communication** about a promotion. This helps to spread awareness beyond those consumers who come into direct contact with the promotion.[47] Consumers may share information with friends about good deals on particular products, a valuable coupon in the newspaper, or a sale at a retail store. For example, a consumer may phone a friend who is looking for tires to say Sears is having a great sale. Consumers sometimes recommend that their friends see a particular salesperson who is especially pleasant or well informed or who offers good deals on merchandise. Consumers often pass on impressions of new restaurants, retail stores, or movies to their friends.

As these examples illustrate, simply by placing promotion information in consumers' environments, marketers can increase the probability that the information will be communicated to other consumers. And because personal communication from friends and relevant others is a powerful form of communication, marketers may try to design promotions that encourage word-of-mouth communication (convince a friend to join the health club and you will get two months' membership free).

Managing Promotion Strategies

Developing and implementing effective promotion strategies is a complex, difficult task. There are four key activities in managing promotion strategies: (1) analyze consumer–product relationships, (2) determine the promotion objectives and budget, (3) design and implement a promotion strategy, and (4) evaluate the effects of the promotion strategy.

Analyze Consumer–Product Relationships

Developing effective promotion strategies begins with an analysis of the relationships between consumers and the products or brands of interest. This requires identifying the appropriate target markets for the product. Then marketers must identify consumers' needs, goals, and values, their levels of product and brand knowledge and involvement, and their current attitudes and behavior patterns. Ideally, marketers should also understand the deeper symbolic meaning of their brand. In short, marketers must strive to understand the relationship between their target consumers and the product or brand of interest.

When dealing with a new product or brand, marketers may have to conduct considerable marketing research to learn about the consumer–product relationship. This research could include interviews to identify the dominant means–end chains that reveal how consumers perceive the relationships between the product or brand and their own self-concepts.[48] Other methods might include focus group interviews, concept tests, attitude and use surveys, and even test marketing. For existing products and brands, marketers may already know a great deal about consumer–product relationships. Perhaps only follow-up research may be necessary.

Exhibit 17.4

The Foote, Cone & Belding Grid for Analyzing Consumer–Product Relationships

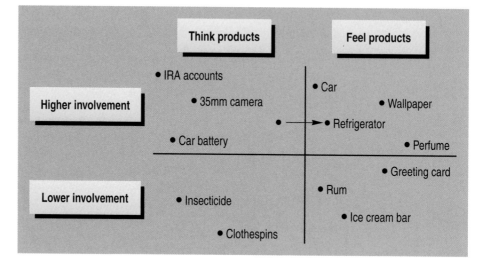

Source: David Berger, "Theory into Practice: The FCB Grid," *European Research,* January 1986, p. 35.

The FCB Grid   Exhibit 17.4 presents a simple grid model used by Foote, Cone & Belding, a major advertising agency, to analyze consumer–product relationships.[49] The figure also shows the typical locations of several different products based on extensive consumer research conducted around the world. The **Foote, Cone & Belding (FCB) grid** is based on two concepts you studied in earlier chapters: consumers' involvement and their salient knowledge, meanings, and beliefs about the product.

Consumers have varying degrees of involvement with a product or brand because of intrinsic and situational sources of self-relevance. Moreover, various types of knowledge, meanings, and beliefs may be activated when consumers evaluate and choose among alternative products or brands. Some products are considered primarily in terms of rational meanings, such as the functional consequences of using the product.[50] These are termed *think products* in the grid model. Included in this category are such products as investments, cameras, and car batteries—all products purchased primarily for their functional consequences.

In contrast, *feel products* are considered by consumers primarily in terms of nonverbal images (visual or other types of sensory images) and emotional factors, such as psychosocial consequences and values.[51] For instance, products purchased primarily for their sensory qualities—ice cream, soft drinks, cologne—as well as products for which emotional consequences are dominant—flowers or jewelry—are feel products in the FCB grid.

Because the consumer–product relationships are quite different in the four quadrants of the grid, the FCB grid also has implications for developing creative advertising strategies, measuring advertising effects, and selecting media in which to place ads.

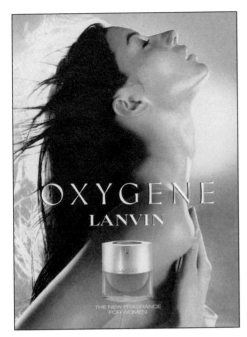

Ads for feel products such as cologne tend to use strong visual images that connote sensory and emotional meanings
Photographer: Steven Meisel; Model: Gisele Bündchen; Agency: A/R Media.

The appropriate promotion strategy depends on the product's position in the grid. Sometimes a product can be moved within the grid, like the refrigerator in Exhibit 17.4, which was shifted from a think to a feel product by the following strategy. A South American client of FCB once had a problem: 5,000 ugly green refrigerators in inventory were not selling, while competing brands offered desirable product features such as ice makers. High-involvement products such as refrigerator tend to be sold in terms of functional consequences, but in this case there was no rational benefit to promote. So FCB designed a promotion strategy to move refrigerators from the think quadrant to the feel quadrant. The agency created ads that featured Venezuelan international beauty queens and termed the refrigerators "another Venezuelan beauty." The 5,000 refrigerators sold out in 90 days. In general, FCB has found that traditional *think* products often can be marketed successfully using *feel* advertising promotion strategies. In sum, the FCB grid model helps marketers analyze consumer–product relationships to develop more effective promotions.

Determine Promotion Objectives and Budget

Promotions can affect consumers' affect, cognitions, and behaviors.[52] Thus, promotion strategies may be designed to meet one or more of the following objectives:

- *To influence behaviors.* Change or maintain consumers' specific behaviors concerning the product or brand—usually purchase behaviors.
- *To inform.* Create new knowledge, meanings, or beliefs about the product or brand in consumers' memories.
- *To transform affective responses.* Modify the images, feelings, and emotions that are activated when consumers consider the product or brand.
- *To remind.* Increase the activation potential of the brand name or some other product meaning in consumers' memories.

Before designing a promotion strategy, marketers should determine their specific promotion objectives and the budget available to support them. The long-run objective of most promotion strategies is to influence consumer behaviors, especially store patronage and brand purchase. Shopping malls sponsor auto, boat, or home-builder shows to build consumer traffic. Many sales promotions are designed to directly and quickly affect consumer purchases of a particular brand. The rebate programs and low-interest financing offered by automakers are intended to stimulate short-run sales of certain brands and models.

Finally, some promotions have multiple objectives. Frito-Lay has used a sales promotion strategy of placing coupons on the package. This promotion is designed to do two things—stimulate immediate sales and encourage repeat sales—with the long-run goal of creating more brand-loyal consumers.

Some promotions are designed to first influence consumers' cognitions in anticipation of a later influence on their overt behaviors. When a new product or brand is introduced, a primary objective for advertising promotions may be to create awareness of the product and some simple beliefs about it. Marketers also try to generate publicity for new products for these reasons, as well as to create a favorable brand attitude. These cognitions are intended to influence purchase intentions and sales behaviors later.

Design and Implement a Promotion Strategy

Designing alternative promotion strategies and selecting one to meet the promotion objectives are based largely on the consumer–product relationships identified through marketing research. Implementing the promotion strategy may include creating ads and placing them in various media, designing and distributing coupons, putting salespeople to work, and developing publicity events. Many of these tasks may be done with the aid of an advertising agency or a promotion consultant.

Designing Promotion Strategies The design of effective promotion strategies must be sensitive to the consumer–product relationships represented in different market segments. Consider the various consumer segments portrayed in Exhibit 17.5. These groups are defined by consumers' past purchase behavior and current attitudes toward a brand. Consumers who dislike the brand and never buy it are not likely to be influenced by any promotions and can be ignored. But consumers who never buy the brand but have a favorable (or at least neutral) attitude toward it are vulnerable to the company's promotions. Free samples, premiums, contests, or coupons may create an intention to try the brand and move consumers to an occasional-user segment.

Occasional purchasers of the brand are vulnerable to the promotion strategies for competing brands. In that situation, marketers may have a promotion objective

Exhibit 17.5

An Analysis of Consumer Vulnerability

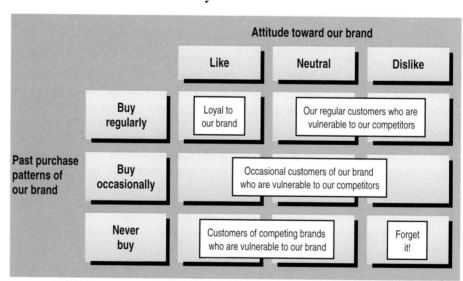

Source: Adapted from Yoram Wind, "Brand Loyalty and Vulnerability," in *Consumer and Industrial Buying Behavior*, eds. A. G. Woodside, J. N. Sheth, and P. D. Bennett (New York: North Holland Publishing, 1977), pp. 313–320.

to encourage repeat purchases of the brand. A purchase plan such as offering a free doughnut after the consumer has bought 12 or a premium for saving proofs of purchase may be effective strategies. Or a firm might try to demonstrate the superiority of its brand over competing brands. For example, Burger King and Pepsi-Cola have used comparative advertising to try to "prove" their brand is better than McDonald's and Coca-Cola, respectively.[53]

Finally, brand-loyal consumers who like a company's brand and purchase it consistently can be influenced by promotions designed to keep them happy customers. The airlines have used a phenomenally successful promotion, frequent-flier programs, to reinforce the attitudes and purchase behavior of their frequent customers. Consumers rack up mileage on flights taken with the airline and receive free trips when they have accumulated sufficient mileage. The programs are supposed to be limited to frequent fliers, originally defined as those taking 12 or more plane trips per year. However, by 1984 an estimated 7 million Americans had enrolled in frequent-flier programs, many more than the estimated 1 million frequent fliers. Currently more than a third of air travelers are enrolled in four such programs— not exactly what the airlines had in mind when the promotion began.[54] In any case, these incentive programs have seemed so successful that they are being copied by hotels, car rental firms, restaurants, and other types of companies.

Phone calls by salespeople to "check on how things are going" may reinforce past customers' attitudes and intentions to rebuy when the need arises. When Joe Girard was the top car salesperson in the United States for 11 years in a row, he sent out more than 13,000 cards to his customers each month, wishing them Happy New Year from Joe Girard, Happy St. Patrick's Day, and so on.[55] Finally, promotions can inform current consumers of new uses for existing products. Advertising campaigns promoted Saran Wrap for use in microwave cooking and Static Guard to eliminate static electricity from carpets around computers.

These brief examples illustrate three important points. First, appropriate promotions depend on the type of relationship consumers have with the product or brand, especially their intrinsic self-relevance.[56] Second, promotion methods vary in their effectiveness for achieving certain objectives. Personal selling, for example, is usually more effective for closing sales, whereas advertising is more effective for increasing brand awareness among large groups of consumers. Third, promotion objectives will change over a product's life cycle as changes occur in consumers' relationships with the product and the competitive environment.[57] The promotion strategy that worked well when the product was introduced is not likely to be effective at the growth, maturity, or decline stage.

Developing Advertising Strategy   Marketers should specify advertising strategy in terms of the type of relationship the consumer will have with the product or brand. Then ads should be created to communicate the appropriate means–end connections between the product attributes and consumers' goals and values.[58] The **MECCAS model** shown in Exhibit 17.6 can help marketers understand the key aspects of ad strategy and make better strategic decisions.[59] MECCAS defines four elements of *advertising strategy*—the driving force, the leverage point, consumer benefits, and message elements—based on analyses of consumers' means–end chains (MECCAS stands for *means–end chain conceptualization of advertising strategy*). The fifth component of the MECCAS model, the executional framework, is part of the *creative strategy* that must develop the details of the actual advertisement that will communicate the ad strategy.

Exhibit 17.6

The MECCAS Model

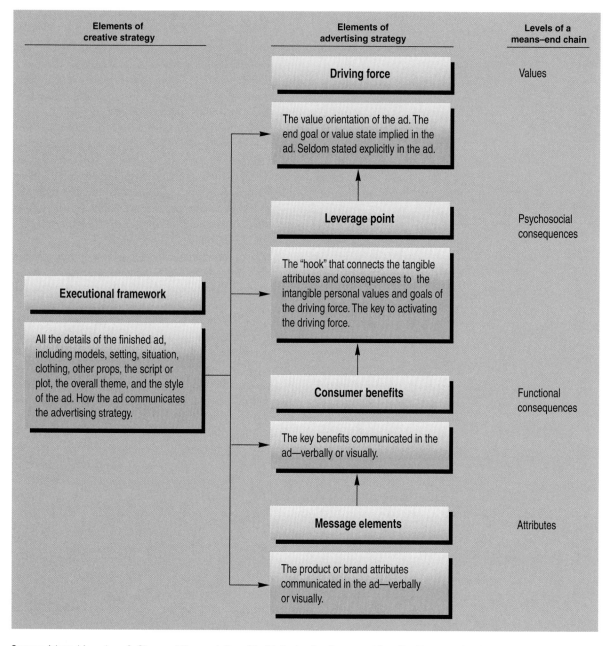

Source: Adapted from Jerry C. Olson and Thomas J. Reynolds, "Understanding Consumers' Cognitive Structures: Implications for Advertising Strategies," in *Advertising and Consumer Psychology,* eds. Larry Percy and Arch Woodside (Lexington, MA: Lexington Books, 1983), pp. 77–90. Copyright © 1983 The New Lexington, an imprint of the Rowman & Littlefield Publishing Group, Lanham, MD.

The first step in creating an advertising strategy is to *understand the consumer–product relationship* by measuring consumers' means–end chains for the product category or product form. Then the marketer should select one means–end chain to convert into an advertising strategy. The most important means–end chain in the decision-making process is a likely candidate (unless a competitor already "owns" that chain). Knowing which product attributes are most important for consumers helps marketers decide which information to include as *message elements* in the ad strategy. (Should the ads for Ruffles potato chips emphasize their flavor, their crunchiness, or their ridges?) Knowing what functional consequences are linked to these salient attributes helps marketers identify the key *consumer benefits* to be emphasized. (If Ruffles chips are for dipping, focus on the ridges. If Ruffles are an accompaniment for sandwiches, emphasize flavor and crunchiness.)

The *driving force* is the basic value or end goal to be communicated by the ad. The driving force usually is communicated indirectly and in a subtle fashion; values are seldom mentioned explicitly in ads. That would be perceived as heavy-handed by most consumers, who may react negatively to being told what value they should be thinking of. Values and end goals are part of the consumer, not the product, and should be aroused or activated "in" the consumer. Explicitly stating a value in an ad does not ensure that it will be activated and felt by consumers. Once activated, the emotional and motivational power of the end goals or values provides the driving force for action, including purchase of the brand.

The final component of an ad strategy is the important *leverage point* by which the relatively concrete, tangible message elements and benefits (attributes and functional consequences of the product) are linked to the abstract driving force (values of the consumer). The leverage point can be thought of as a "hook" that "reaches into" the consumer and attaches the product to the activated value that is the driving force of the ad strategy. In advertising, the leverage point is often portrayed as a psychosocial consequence of using the brand. Because consumers automatically perceive the values associated with most psychosocial consequences, the leverage point should activate the driving force and form a connection to it. Thus, the ad does not have to explicitly mention the value in order to communicate the ad strategy.

In sum, an advertising strategy should specify how a brand will be connected to the important ends the consumer wants. The advertising team must then create an ad that will persuasively communicate these meanings and the linkages among them. The *executional framework* refers to the various details of the creative strategy (the type of models, how they are dressed, the setting, what people are saying) that are designed to communicate the ad strategy. In general, an effective advertisement should communicate each of the four means–end levels of meaning in the ad strategy (from message elements to driving force) and the links or connections among the levels.

The MECCAS model is not a foolproof tool for creating successful ads; rather, it is a guide to developing advertising strategies and creating effective ads.[60] Marketers still must carefully analyze consumers and use their creative imaginations. Marketers can use the MECCAS model to translate several means–end chains into possible ad strategies, which can then be evaluated for their competitive advantages. Although any means–end chain can be translated into an advertising strategy using the MECCAS model, not every means–end chain is a viable strategy. Some strategies, for instance, may already be taken by one's competitors. Some means–end chains may lack sufficient motivational "power." Marketers also can use the MECCAS model as a framework for analyzing the meanings communicated in their current advertising and for considering how these ads could be made more persuasive.[61]

Developing Personal Selling Strategies   The process of developing a personal selling promotion strategy is illustrated in Exhibit 17.7.[62] This is the **ISTEA model,** which stands for *impression, strategy, transmission, evaluation,* and *adjustment.* This model suggests salespeople's influence depends on their skills at performing five basic activities: (1) developing useful *impressions* of the customer, (2) formulating selling *strategies* based on these impressions, (3) *transmitting* appropriate messages, (4) *evaluating* customer reactions to the messages, and (5) making appropriate *adjustments* in presentation should the initial approach fail.

According to this model, the personal selling process works as follows:

> In the first activity, the salesperson combines information gained through past experience with information relevant to the specific interaction to develop an impression of the customer. Salespersons can derive information about their target customers by examining past experiences with this and other customers, by observing the target customer during an interaction, and by projecting themselves into the target customer's decision-making situation.
>
> In the second activity, the salesperson analyzes his/her impression of the customer and develops a communication strategy which includes an objective for the strategy, a method for implementing the strategy, and specific message formats.
>
> Having formulated the strategy, the salesperson transmits the messages to the customer. As the salesperson delivers the messages, she/he evaluates their effects by observing the customer's reactions and soliciting opinions. On the basis of these evaluations, the salesperson can make adjustments by either reformulating the impression of the customer, selecting a new strategic objective, or changing the method for achieving the strategic objective, or the salesperson can continue to implement the same strategy.[63]

Although the ISTEA model was developed for industrial (business-to-business) marketing situations, it is consistent with the communication approach to consumer promotion discussed here. The model emphasizes analysis of the customer as the starting point for strategy development. Research confirms that impression formation (consumer analysis) and strategy formulation by salespeople improve their sales performance. Similarly, research on sales transactions in retail sporting goods stores suggests that successful salespeople adapt their communication style to interact appropriately with customers.[64]

Evaluate Effects of the Promotion Strategy

Evaluating the effects of a promotion strategy involves comparing its results with the objectives. Although this may seem simple, determining promotion effects can be difficult. For example, even clearly stated cognitive objectives, such as "increase brand awareness by 25 percent," are not easily evaluated because different methods of measuring awareness may give different results. Moreover, it is often difficult to determine whether a change in brand awareness resulted from the promotion strategy or from something else, such as word-of-mouth communication.

Similarly, promotion objectives stated in behavior terms—"increase sales by 10 percent"—can be hard to evaluate. It is often difficult to determine what factors

Exhibit 17.7

A Model of the Personal Selling Process

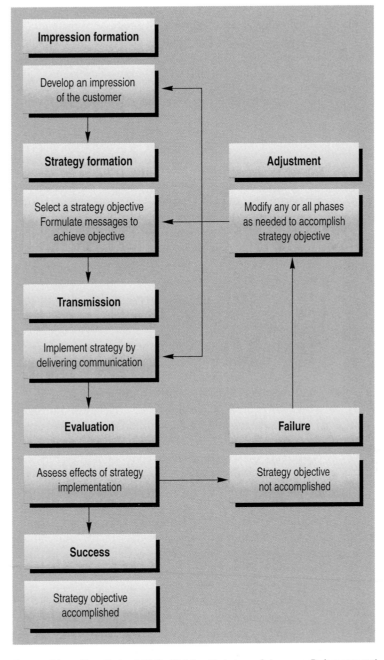

Source: Adapted from Barton A. Weitz, "Relationship between Salesperson Performance and Understanding Customer Decision Making," *Journal of Marketing Research* 15, November 1978, p. 502. Published by the American Marketing Association. Reprinted with permission.

caused a sales increase. Increases in competitors' prices, opening new territories and outlets, changes in consumers' attitudes, and various other factors may be responsible for the increase in sales. Likewise, if sales decrease or remain the same during the promotion period, it is difficult to determine whether the promotion strategy was ineffective or whether other factors were responsible.[65]

In other cases, however, evaluation of promotion effects can be relatively straightforward. Sales promotion tools such as coupons are used to stimulate short-term sales, and coupon redemption rates can give a good idea of effectiveness.[66] The dollar amounts sold by different salespeople can also be compared to determine their relative effectiveness. In sum, although measuring the effectiveness of promotion strategies may be difficult, marketers do have methods for estimating these effects.

Measuring Advertising Effects   Because the main immediate impact of advertising is on consumers' affective responses and cognitions, measuring the effects of advertising is difficult. However, because the costs of advertising are very high (an estimated $201 billion was spent in the United States in 1998), marketers are very interested in determining the communication effectiveness of their ads so they can improve them. A wide variety of approaches have been taken to measuring advertising effects, including *pretesting* (testing the effects of ads that are in rough, unfinished form before the ad is run in the natural environment) and *copy testing* (determining the meanings consumers derive from ads.)[67]

Three broad criteria have been used as indicators of advertising effectiveness: sales, recall, and persuasion. Many researchers have tried to relate advertising to *sales* by measuring the aggregate purchase behavior of large groups of consumers who supposedly were exposed to the ads. Linking sales to advertising has proven quite difficult because of the number of factors, in addition to advertising, that influence purchase behavior. However, current technology is moving marketers closer to the day when they will be able to relate advertising exposure to purchase of the product.

Another common measure of ad effectiveness is consumers' *recall* of the ad or some aspect of the ad. For example, in day-after recall studies, researchers telephone consumers the day after a TV commercial has run and ask them if they watched the TV program the previous evening. If so, consumers are asked if they remember any ads, and what they specifically recall about the ad in question. Only viewers who can remember a visual element or a sales message are counted as having recalled the ad. In 2000 the average ad received a recall rating of about 13 percent, down from about 24 percent in the late 1970s.[68] Of course, many ads score both lower and higher than that. Recall has been criticized for not really measuring the most important impacts of ads (such as creating product meanings or affective responses), but it can be an important objective in certain cases.[69] For ads that are intended primarily to enhance consumers' awareness of the brand, recall may be an appropriate measure of effectiveness.

The third major criterion for advertising effectiveness is *persuasion*.[70] Most studies of persuasion measure whether consumers' comprehension of the ad produced changes (positive ones, preferably) in beliefs about the attributes or consequences of the product, brand attitudes (A_o), attitudes toward buying the brand (A_{act}), or purchase intentions (BI).[71] Another useful approach is to see if the ad created the desired means–end chains of product knowledge—that is, find out whether consumers formed an appropriate association between the brand and self-relevant ends.[72]

Back To…

Winning Promotions

The opening example described three successful promotion strategies to change customers' short-term behaviors. The American Express campaign is an example of publicity at work. The Brawny promotion is a combination of publicity, advertising, and sales promotion. Although not mentioned in this example, these companies utilize other types of promotion strategies besides publicity and sales promotions, including advertising and personal selling. All of these promotions create information in consumers' environments that may influence their behaviors (brand purchases or television viewing selections, for example) and affective and cognitive responses. Each type of promotion has unique advantages and disadvantages that must be considered in developing an overall mix of promotion strategies. In designing effective promotion strategies, marketers must use all the concepts discussed in the first four sections of this book. ❖

Summary   This chapter discussed how marketers can use knowledge about consumers' affect and cognitions, behaviors, and environments in developing more effective promotion strategies. We began by describing four types of promotions: advertising, sales promotions, personal selling, and publicity. Then we detailed how the basic communication model can be used to create promotions as forms of marketing communications. Next, we discussed some important aspects of the promotion environment (clutter and level of competition), affective and cognitive responses to promotions (attitudes toward the ad and persuasion processes), and promotion-related behaviors (information contact and word-of-mouth communication). Finally, we examined a managerial model for designing and executing promotion strategies. We described the various goals and objectives marketers may have for promotion strategies and looked at two models for developing advertising strategies and personal selling strategies. We concluded with a discussion of how to evaluate the effectiveness of promotion strategies.

Key Terms and Concepts

advertising   **426**
attitude toward the ad   **438**
communication process   **431**
Elaboration Likelihood Model
    (ELM)   **438**
Foote, Cone & Belding (FCB) grid   **444**
ISTEA model   **450**

MECCAS model   **447**
personal selling   **427**
persuasion   **438**
promotions   **424**
publicity   **428**
sales promotions   **426**
word-of-mouth communication   **443**

Review and Discussion Questions

1. As a consumer of fast-food products, discuss the effects of promotion strategies on your decision processes.
2. Using the soft-drink industry as an example, define and illustrate each of the four major types of promotion strategies.
3. Are the major promotion methods equally effective in influencing high- and low-involvement decisions? Explain.
4. Select a specific advertisement or sales promotion strategy and evaluate it in terms of the elements of the communication model.
5. Describe how the two routes to persuasion differ, and discuss their implications for developing effective advertising strategies.
6. Use the FCB grid model to illustrate consumer–product relationships for four products you have purchased in the last six months. How would this information be helpful to the promotion managers for these products?
7. Describe the MECCAS model for developing an effective advertising strategy. Illustrate the use of the model by suggesting a strategy for an athletic shoe promotion.
8. Do you agree with the suggestion that personal selling tends to create higher levels of involvement than other promotion strategies? How would your conclusion affect your use of the ISTEA model of personal selling (Exhibit 17.7)?
9. Identify a specific promotional strategy. Use the Wheel of Consumer Analysis model to analyze its effects on target consumers. Then suggest specific criteria that could be used to measure the effects of the promotion.
10. Suggest reasons for the increasing emphasis on sales promotion and publicity in the promotion mix of many marketing organizations.

Marketing Strategy in Action

The Cereal Wars

What's for breakfast? For more and more Americans, the answer to that question is "nothing."

For decades, the breakfast cereal market was marked by steady growth—which seemed logical. An expanding population meant more mouths to feed and thus more people eating breakfast. But in the mid-1990s, lifestyles began to change. As Americans watched their lives become more hectic, many opted to eat breakfast on the run or skip it entirely. They didn't have time to take the cereal from the cupboard and the milk from the fridge and sit down to a leisurely breakfast. According to one expert, "People wish they could just get breakfast injected into them on the run." From 1995 to 2000, the size of the breakfast cereal market slipped nearly $1 billion, down to $7.7 million. But in the midst of all this was a success story: General Mills. While the industry as a whole was taking a beating, General Mills saw its cereal sales grow an average of almost 6 percent per year between 1996 and 1999. At the end of 1999, General Mills became the nation's number one cereal seller for the first time ever, supplanting Kellogg. How could a company thrive in such a seemingly bleak market? Why had General Mills flourished while Kellogg tumbled? A primary reason is General Mills' increasingly aggressive marketing strategies.

The cereal market is highly competitive, with the top four companies—General Mills, Kellogg, Quaker Oats, and General Foods (Post Cereals)—controlling more than 80 percent of the market in 1999. In the early 1980s, Kellogg turned up the competitive heat by increasing promotion expenditures, especially for advertising. Kellogg saw its market share bounce 4.5 percent, from 36.7 percent in 1983 to 41.2 percent in 1988. Over this same span, General Mills' market share was basically flat, moving up from 20 to 21 percent over the five years, while Post's market share fell nearly 3 percent. These changes were significant. In 2000 ready-to-eat cereal was a $7.7 billion market in the United States, making each share point worth about $75 million in sales.

Kellogg did not introduce any highly successful new products during these years. In fact, it did not roll out one successful new product from 1964 through 1991. What it did do was promote its existing cereals extremely well, targeting especially the pool of 80 million baby boomers. For instance, Kellogg positioned Frosted Flakes (and its famed Tony the Tiger) as cereal appropriate for adults, with ads that claimed, "Frosted Flakes have the taste adults have grown to love." The extensive promotion catapulted Frosted Flakes ahead of General Mills' Cheerios to become the nation's number one breakfast cereal brand by 1988. Kellogg supported its products with a promotion mix of extensive TV and print advertising combined with various types of sales promotions. For years, more coupons were distributed for breakfast cereal than for any other category. A 1992 study of cereal ads containing coupons found that 55 percent were from Kellogg, 22 percent from General Foods, and 15 percent from General Mills. Kellogg's most frequently used promotion technique was to offer two boxes of cereal for the price of one, sometimes three for the price of two (31 percent of their ads made this offer). By the mid-90s, Kellogg still had a comfortable grip on market leadership.

But then the cereal market began to change, and General Mills' marketing department was up to the task. More than most products, breakfast cereal is "marketing sensitive." That is, dollars spent on mediocre promotions simply fall into the void; they have no noticeable effect on consumers. But the same amount of money spent on a well-designed promotion strategy can dramatically increase sales and produce significant shifts in market shares. For example, in 1996 General Mills ran a very successful promotion tied into its sponsorship of the Olympics. Customers who sent in eight proofs of purchase from General Mills products received a coffee table book entitled *The Olympic Spirit*. It was an immediate hit. "Within one week, General Mills went through 20,000 books and generated sales of more than 200,000 boxes of cereal," according to one expert. "It was the most successful in-store promotion they've ever run."

General Mills has also successfully (and creatively) targeted the kids' market over the past few years. In 1999, the company put the 59-year-old Cheerios brand in front of a new generation of consumers by publishing a pair of children's books with the Cheerios logo on the cover. Normally such books would sell about 25,000 copies a year. The two Cheerios books sold more than 1 million. General Mills followed up in 2000 with the introduction of Cheerios puzzles, toys, and clothing. Among the new products was a toy cell phone that dispensed Cheerios and pajamas adorned with the smiling face of the Honey Nut Cheerios bee. Leigh Ann Schwarzkopf, General Mills' manager of trademark licensing, says, "Since 1998 we've gone from zero to about $100 million at retail." General Mills has also tied in several of its cereal brands with popular children's movies and products. In 1998 it capitalized on Saban Entertainment's direct-to-video release of *Casper Meets Wendy*, a movie featuring the lovable Casper the Friendly Ghost. General Mills' Count Chocula, Frankenberry, and Boo Berry cereals all contained marshmallows shaped like characters from the movie. Parents appreciated the corresponding mail-in offer: $15 in coupons in exchange for the purchase of two General Mills cereals and three Hershey products. In 1999, a similar tie-in with Time Warner put Scooby Doo on (and in) 4 million boxes of Count Chocula. When the company decided to place figurines from the movie *Toy Story2* inside cereal boxes, it created a new kind of packaging that allowed kids to see the toy before they even opened the box. Also in 1999, General Mills reached out to teenagers, printing $5 coupons for Sony PlayStation video games on boxes of Lucky Charms, Trix, Cocoa Puffs, and several other popular kids' cereals. The General Mills website (**www.generalmills.com**) has a "You

455

Rule School" section, which includes games, educational information, and an opportunity for kids to e-mail their favorite cereal characters.

Nor did General Mills forget the adult consumer. In 2000 it launched Harmony, an oatmeal-fortified cereal geared toward health-conscious women. It promoted the new brand with a multimillion-dollar TV and print advertising campaign. The company also persuaded the American Heart Association to endorse the health benefits of Cheerios and added calcium to Lucky Charms. Moreover, in response to Americans' yearning for breakfast-on-the-go, General Mills launched a line of Milk 'n Cereal bars made from its Honey Nut Cheerios, Cinnamon Toast Crunch, and Chex brands. It also supported these new products with an extensive advertising campaign. Consumers also like General Mills' annual Salute to Savings coupon book, which offers discounts of up to $60 on future purchases.

While General Mills was using these promotions to build market share, Kellogg seemingly could do nothing right. For one, its brands were familiar, but not particularly strong. Analyst William Leach of Donaldson, Lufkin, & Jenrette explains, "At General Mills, Wheaties is a brand. But Kellogg's Corn Flakes? That just describes what's in the box." The lack of strong brand identification has made Kellogg cereals especially vulnerable to private-label imitators. Furthermore, Kellogg blundered in adapting to the healthier, faster-paced American lifestyle. Whereas General Mills rolled out healthier cereals, Kellogg was more tentative, creating a campaign called "K-Sentials," which emphasized the nutritional value of its existing cereals. It flopped. As a writer for *Fortune* illustrates, "Who thinks 'This is good for me!' while munching on Froot Loops?" Kellogg's early foray into quickie breakfasts was also a disaster. Breakfast Mates crammed cereal, milk, a bowl, and a spoon all into one package. Unfortunately, it was all but impossible to eat while driving. Sales were weak and the company killed the product in 1999. In addition, as the market for traditional breakfast cereals declined, Kellogg was reluctant to reduce prices. Then, after finally deciding to offer dollar-off coupons, it tried to preserve earnings by cutting back on advertising. That strategy played right into General Mills' hands. In 1999, General Mills outspent Kellogg in advertising by nearly 2 to 1.

Kellogg, however, is now fighting back by boosting advertising expenditures. It is also making a concerted effort to win back children by, among other things, offering various gift items inside boxes of selected cereals and developing new, more mobile breakfast products. Its website (**www.kelloggs.com**) discusses other promotional efforts that are under way.

An important battleground in the future could be the international arena, where Kellogg has traditionally been very successful. Kellogg has been a leader in promoting cereal and milk to start the day in countries where such a breakfast has not been the norm. For example, in the early 1990s, Kellogg forayed into India with the launch of a product made from basmati rice, a premium, aromatic rice. To help entice consumers to switch from fried breakfasts high in fat, its advertising communicated a theme commonly used in the Asia/Pacific Rim area: eating too many fatty products such as butter and fried foods is bad for you, and so is skipping breakfast altogether (which about 20 percent of Indians did). Kellogg also sponsored TV and radio shows featuring dieticians and nutritionists, and set up billboards with nutritional messages along busy highways near big cities like Bombay. Kellogg also managed, after many years, to crack the Mexican and European markets.

General Mills has begun making strides internationally as well, thanks to partnerships with Pepsi and Nestlé. In addition, it has launched a line of cereals (*Para su Familia*) with bilingual packaging to appeal to the growing Hispanic population in the United States.

For General Mills and Kellogg, product diversity and creative marketing strategies appear to be the keys to future success both in the United States and around the world as the cereal wars continue.

Discussion Questions

1. Use the means–end model to describe (based on your intuition) the consumer–product relationship for three segments of the breakfast cereal market: kids (ages 6 to 12), teens/young adults (ages 16 to 22), and baby boomers (ages 35 to 50). What implications do your ideas suggest for promotion strategies targeted toward these three groups?

2. Find a current print ad for either Kellogg's or General Mills' cereal. Describe the ad strategy using the MECCAS model described in the text (identify the driving force, message elements, leverage point, and so on). Use the means–end approach to critique the ad strategy and make suggestions for improving the ad.

3. Both companies discussed in this case use a mix of promotions to market their cereals. Discuss how consumer reactions to brand-oriented advertising and sales promotions (coupons versus prizes and premiums) are likely to differ. Discuss the likely effects on consumers' behavior, affect, and cognition for a 75-cent coupon for cereal versus a price reduction deal such as "buy three for the price of two."

4. Discuss the likely effect on consumers' behavior, affect, and cognition of the various forms of promotion General Mills has used to target children. What do you think are the effects on both parents and kids?

5. Discuss the cultural issues faced by Kellogg and General Mills in trying to induce consumers in other cultures to adopt ready-to-eat cereal as a food for breakfast. What types of changes in consumers' meanings and behaviors must occur before these consumers will accept ready-to-eat breakfast cereal? In addition to what is described in the case, what other promotional strategies could these companies use?

6. Why do you think the breakfast cereal market is so "marketing sensitive"? Why do consumers respond to good marketing promotions but not at all to weak ones?

Sources: Amy Kover, "Why the Cereal Business Is Soggy," *Fortune,* March 6, 2000, p. 74; Linda Formichelli, "Scoring Points with Sports Incentives," *Incentive,* September 1999, pp. 94–99; Keith Naughton, "Crunch Time at Kellogg," *Newsweek,* February 14, 2000, pp. 52–53; Melinda Fulmer, "Food Makers Cashing in by Turning Brands into Books, Toys," *Los Angeles Times,* March 26, 2000, p. C4; www.kelloggs.com.

Consumer Behavior and Pricing Strategy

Vinnie Bombatz

Vinnie Bombatz is a construction worker who makes $12 per hour. Although he could work overtime on Saturday at $18 per hour, he takes off two consecutive Saturdays to go fishing.

Vinnie is a heavy drinker of Diet Pepsi. On the morning of his first Saturday off, he walks two blocks to a convenience food store to purchase a 12-pack for his fishing trip. The price is $5 plus 5 percent sales tax. Vinnie complains about the high price and is told by the clerk, "I don't set the prices. Take it or leave it!" Vinnie is more than a little upset, but he pays the money because he's in a rush to get to the lake. He vows to himself never to get ripped off like this again. He walks home. The whole trip has taken 10 minutes.

On the next Saturday, Vinnie again needs a 12-pack of Diet Pepsi for his fishing trip. Remembering his previous experience at the convenience store, he decides to get in his car and drive 6 miles each way to the discount supermarket. He is pleasantly surprised that Diet Pepsi is on sale for $2.99 a dozen plus tax. Although the store is a bit crowded and it takes him a while to get through the checkout, he drives home feeling good about the purchase and the money he saved. This shopping trip has taken 45 minutes.

O n which Saturday did Vinnie get a better price? In several ways, *price* is the most unusual element of the marketing mix. For one thing, it is the only one that involves revenues; all the other elements, as well as marketing research, involve expenditures of funds by organizations. Another difference is that although price may seem tangible and concrete, it is perhaps more intangible and abstract than other elements of the marketing mix.

For example, in the product area, consumers often have a tangible product to examine or at least information about a service to evaluate. In the promotion area, consumers have magazine and newspaper ads and information from salespeople to look at, listen to, and evaluate. In the distribution area, consumers have malls, stores, catalogs, and websites to experience. However, the price variable is a rather abstract concept that, while represented as a sign or tag, has relatively little direct sensory experience connected with it. Perhaps because of this, basic research on pricing issues in marketing has been relatively modest compared to work done on the other marketing mix elements.

These differences should not lead you to underestimate the importance of price to marketing and consumer behavior, however. For example, Vithala Rao states:

> The effects of price changes are more immediate and direct, and appeals based on price are the easiest to communicate to prospective buyers. However, competitors can react more easily to appeals based on price than to those based on product benefits and imagery. It can be argued that the price decision is perhaps the most significant among the decisions of the marketing mix (strategy) for a branded product.[1]

In this chapter, we focus on some important relationships among consumer affect, cognition, behavior, and the environment as they relate to the price variable of the marketing mix. These variables and relationships are shown in Exhibit 18.1, which provides an overview of the topics to be discussed. We begin our discussion by examining a conceptual view of the role of price in marketing exchanges. We then discuss price affect and cognition, behavior, the environment, and, finally, pricing strategy.

Conceptual Issues in Pricing

From a consumer's point of view, *price* is usually defined as what the consumer must give up to purchase a product or service. Research typically views price only in terms of dollar amount asked or paid for an item or a service. Because we believe price is a pivotal element in the exchange process, we offer a conceptual view of price that encompasses more than the dollar amount or financial cost to the consumer. Our discussion is intended to help you better understand the role of price in marketing strategy development.

Exhibit 18.2 offers a general model of the nature of marketing exchanges and highlights the role of price in this process. Although we will focus on for-profit organizations, the model could be developed and discussed in terms of nonprofit marketing. The major differences in nonprofit exchanges are that (1) although nonprofit organizations may seek money from consumers, they (at least in theory) do not seek surplus funds beyond costs, and (2) the value derived by consumers in nonprofit exchanges is often less tangible.

Exhibit 18.2 identifies four basic types of consumer costs: money, time, cognitive activity, and behavior effort. When paired with whatever value or utility the product offers, these costs are a convenient way to consider the meaning of price to the consumer. Although we do not argue that the consumer painstakingly

Exhibit 18.1

The Wheel of Consumer Analysis: Pricing Strategy Issues

Exhibit 18.2

The Pivotal Role of Price in Marketing Exchanges

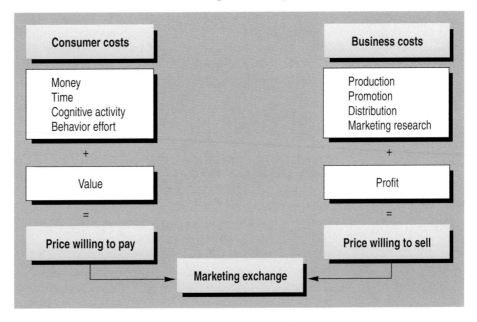

A marketing strategy designed to reduce consumer money cost   *Ad reproduced courtesy of GRW Advertising. Creative Director: Glen Wielgus; Account Director: Ed Ronk.*

calculates each of these costs for every purchase, we do believe they are frequently considered in the purchase of some products.

Exhibit 18.2 also divides marketing costs into the four categories of production, promotion, distribution, and marketing research. Most business costs and investments could be attributed to one or another of these categories. When paired with the level of profit a firm seeks, these costs offer a convenient way to consider the marketing side of the exchange equation. Basically, the model implies that products usually must cover at least variable costs and make some contribution to overhead or profits for the offering to be made to the marketplace.

For marketing exchanges to occur, the price consumers are willing to pay must be greater than or equal to the price at which marketers are willing to sell. However, although this view seems simple enough, a number of complex relationships need to be considered when examining pricing from this perspective. Of major importance is the nature of consumer costs and the relationships among them. It should become clear that the dollar price of an item often is only a part of the total price of an exchange for the consumer.

Money

As we have noted, most pricing research has focused only on *money:* the dollar amount a consumer must spend to purchase a product or service. This research has recognized that the same dollar amount may be perceived differently by different individuals and market segments, depending on income levels and other variables. However, several important aspects of the dollar cost of offerings are not always considered. One of these concerns the *source* of funds for a particular purchase. We suspect that money received as a tax rebate, gift, interest, or gambling winnings has a different value to many consumers than money earned through work. Consequently, the dollar price of a particular item may be perceived differently by the same individual, depending on what sources of funds are used to pay for it.

Similarly, the actual price of a credit card purchase that will be financed at 16 percent for an extended period is much different from the price if cash is used. To consumers who are accustomed to carrying large credit card balances, this difference may be irrelevant; to others, the difference may forestall or eliminate a purchase. In addition, the type of work consumers do may affect how valuable a particular amount of money is to them, as well as affect their willingness to spend that money on particular products and services. Shipping costs and return shipping costs for Internet purchases increase dollar costs for consumers.

A number of methods can reduce the dollar amount spent for a particular item, although they often involve increasing other costs. For example, time, cognitive activity, and behavior effort are required to clip and use coupons, mail in for rebates, or download coupons from Internet sites. Shopping at different stores seeking the lowest price not only involves time, cognitive activity, and behavior effort but also increases other dollar costs, such as transportation or parking. Highlight 18.1 discusses some sources of coupons on the Web.

Time

The *time* necessary to learn about a product or service and to travel to purchase it, as well as the time spent in a store, can be important costs to the consumer.[2] Most consumers are well aware that convenience food stores usually charge higher prices than supermarkets. Many convenience food stores are very profitable, for most consumers purchase from them at least occasionally. Clearly these consumers often make a trade-off of paying more money to save time, particularly if only a few items are to be purchased. Time savings may result because the convenience outlets are located closer to home and thus require less travel time or because less time is required in the store to locate the product and wait in line to pay for it. Given the high cost of operating an automobile, it may even be cheaper in dollar terms to shop at stores that are closer to home, even if they have higher prices! Thus, bargain hunters who travel all over town to save 25 cents here and 50 cents there may be fooling themselves if they think they are saving money. Internet purchasing may save time for some consumers, but they must wait at least a few days for delivery of most products.

However, we should not treat time only as a cost of purchasing. In some situations, the process of seeking product information and purchasing products is a very enjoyable experience—rather than a cost—for consumers. For instance, many consumers enjoy Christmas shopping and spend hours at it. Some consumers enjoy window shopping and purchasing on occasion, particularly if the opportunity cost of their time is low. In areas that offer shopping on Sunday, some consumers prefer going to the mall rather than sitting at home watching football games. Similarly, some consumers enjoy spending hours looking through catalogs or surfing the Web for their favorite merchandise. Thus, although in an absolute sense consumers must spend time to shop and make purchases, in some cases this may be perceived as a benefit rather than a cost.

Cognitive Activity

One frequently overlooked cost of making purchases is the *cognitive activity* involved. Thinking and deciding what to buy can be very hard work. For example, when all of the styles, sizes, colors, and component options are considered, one Japanese manufacturer offers more than 11 million variations of custom-made bicycles.

Highlight 18.1

Saving Money with Coupons: An Evaluation of Six Coupon Websites

Consumers can reduce how much money they spend on purchases by using coupons clipped from the newspaper or magazines. They can also get coupons from a number of websites. Below is an evaluation of several websites that offer coupons to consumers.

	Features	Navigation
www.coolsavings.com	Excellent. A cool pig in shades digs up hundreds of online and offline deals, plus daily specials. Register for free to download coupons for local stores.	Great. Browse 20 coupon categories or use Quick Search to see deals offered by specific merchants. Downside: no keyword search for a specific product; Macs with Internet Explorer can't download coupons.
www.deal-finder.com	Great. No need to sign up to access these online coupons, which are updated daily. However, you must register if you want to receive savings news from Deal-Finder.com's free e-newsletter.	Excellent. Homepage features the newest deals. Or, search by category or keyword. Click on a coupon description, and Deal-Finder.com opens the vendor's homepage with the coupon information at the top.
www.couponsurfer.com	Good. If you join the site, you can get more than 100 deals at online merchants. Members receive e-mails about offers in categories they choose.	Excellent. Click on All Coupons to scan every offer, or choose from nearly 20 categories, including As Seen on TV and Small Business. You also can browse by merchant or try a keyword search.
www.mycoupons.com	Great. Some online coupons are accompanied by merchant ratings and customers' comments. However, the Local Coupons and Grocery Coupons sections are skimpy.	Good. Pick a category in the Online Coupons section to view the deals; loading all of the coupons takes too long. Jot down the offer code, and click on its description to go to the site and start shopping.
www.thatscheap.com	Good. This thrifty site lists the latest coupons for major Internet vendors plus potential shipping fees, making it easier to find the best deals.	Fair. Click on All Internet Coupons and scan an alphabetical list of merchants; they aren't organized by category. Grab the deal you want, but don't forget to write down the coupon code before going to the vendor's site.
www.valupage.com	Good. Instead of coupons, this site awards Web Bucks when shoppers buy certain items at participating grocery stores. The catch: The money you save isn't deducted from your bill until your next visit to the store.	Good. Easy to use: Just type in your ZIP code for a list of ValuPage grocery chains near you, then print out weekly deals. Purchase listed items, and the cashier will give you a receipt to get a credit on your next shopping trip.

Bottom line: At our faves CoolSavings and Deal-Finder.com, it's a cinch to click the latest coupons for online vendors.— *Lauren Wiley*

Sources: Lauren Wiley, "Coupons," *Access,* July 30, 2000, p. 17. Reprinted with permission; also see "Buying without Spending: The New Coupon-Clipping," *Fortune,* March 6, 2000, pp. 386–388.

Consumers would never evaluate all 11 million options, but consider the cognitive activity required to evaluate even a small fraction of them. Clearly, it would not only take a lot of time but also involve very taxing cognitive work.[3] If even a few comparisons are made, some cognitive effort must be expended; excessive cognitive effort can cause negative affect.[4]

In addition to all the cognitive work involved in comparing purchase alternatives, the process can be stressful. Some consumers find it very difficult and dislike making purchase (or other types of) decisions. To some, finding a parking space, shopping in crowded malls and stores, waiting in long checkout lines, and viewing anxiety-producing ads can be very unpleasant emotional experiences. Consumers who lack the skills to surf the Net efficiently can find shopping online stressful. Also, the perceived risks of shopping online, such as sending credit card numbers or uncertainty about product quality, can be distressing. Thus, the cognitive activity involved in purchasing can be a very important cost.

The cost involved in decision making is often the easiest one for consumers to reduce or eliminate. Simple decision rules or heuristics can reduce this cost considerably. By repeatedly purchasing the same brand, for example, consumers can practically eliminate any decision making within a product class. Other heuristics might entail purchasing the most expensive brand, the brand on sale or display, the brand Mom or Dad used to buy, the brand a knowledgeable friend recommends, or the brand a selected dealer carries.

On the other hand, in some situations consumers actively seek some form of cognitive involvement. Fishing enthusiasts frequently enjoy comparing the attributes of various types of equipment, judging their relative merits, and assessing the ability of different equipment to catch fish. We suspect that although consumers may enjoy periods in which they are not challenged to use much cognitive energy or ability, they may also seek purchasing problems to solve as a form of entertainment.

Behavior Effort

Anyone who has spent several hours walking around in malls can attest to the fact that purchasing involves *behavior effort*. When large shopping malls were first developed, one of the problems they faced was that consumers had long walks from the parking lot and considerable distance to cover within the mall itself. Many consumers were not physically comfortable with this much effort, and some avoided malls or shopped in only a small number of the stores available. Primarily to overcome this problem, benches and chairs were placed in malls to give consumers places to rest while shopping. Shopping online is a welcome alternative for disabled people and others who have trouble walking long distances in stores and malls. However, returning unwanted or damaged merchandise ordered online is considered wasted time by most consumers.

Like time and cognitive activity, behavior effort can be a benefit rather than a cost. For example, walking in malls and stores is good exercise and is sometimes done as a source of relaxation. Some malls provide early-morning mall-walking programs for senior citizens. These programs aim to create a positive image for malls and bring in potential buyers.

Perhaps the most interesting aspect of behavior effort is the willingness of consumers to take on some marketing costs to reduce the dollar amount they spend and to make trade-offs among various types of costs. In some cases, consumers will perform part of the production process to get a lower dollar price. For example, consumers may forgo the cost of product assembly for bicycles and toys and do it themselves to save money.

There are also cases in which consumers will take on at least part of the cost of distribution to lower the dollar price. At one time, for example, milk was commonly delivered to the home; now most consumers purchase it at stores. Consumers with access to a pickup truck frequently bring home their own furniture and appliances rather than pay a store for delivery. Catalog purchases require the consumer to pay the cost of shipping directly, yet may be less expensive than store purchases. If they are not, the consumer at least saves shopping time and effort to have the product delivered to the home. As we noted earlier in the text, consumers will also perform promotion and marketing research for firms to receive lower prices or other merchandise "free."

A final trade-off of interest in terms of pricing concerns the degree to which consumers participate in purchase/ownership. Consumers have several options with regard to purchase: (1) They can buy the product and enjoy its benefits as well as incur other costs, such as inventory and maintenance; (2) they can rent or lease the product and enjoy its benefits but forgo ownership and often reduce some of the other costs, such as maintenance; (3) they can hire someone else to perform whatever service the product is designed to perform and forgo ownership and other postpurchase costs; or (4) they can purchase the product and hire someone else to use and maintain it for them. For many durable goods, such as automobiles, appliances, power tools, furniture, and lawn mowers, at least several of these options are available. Clearly, as we stated at the beginning of the chapter, price is a lot more than just dollars and cents!

Value

We have discussed four aspects of price from the consumer's point of view. We have suggested that consumers can sometimes reduce one or more of these costs, but this usually requires an increase in at least one of the other costs. Purchases can be viewed in terms of which of the elements is considered a cost or a benefit and which is considered most critical for particular purchases. However, regardless of what cost trade-offs are made, it seems that whatever is being purchased must be perceived to be of greater *value* to the consumer than merely the sum of the costs. In other words, the consumer perceives that the purchase offers benefits greater than the costs and is willing to exchange to receive these benefits.

Although this view of price is useful, we want to restate that consumers seldom (if ever) thoroughly calculate each of these costs and benefits in making brand-level decisions. Rather, for many types and brands of consumer packaged goods, the amounts of money, time, cognitive activity, and behavior effort required for a purchase are very similar. For these goods, choices among brands may be made on the basis of particular benefits or imagery, although price deals are often important.

For some purchases, consumers may consider all the costs and trade-offs. But the major importance of our view of price is not the degree to which consumers actively analyze and compare each cost of a particular exchange. Instead, this view is important because it has direct implications for the design of marketing strategy, as discussed later in the chapter.

Price Affect and Cognition

As we noted, little sensory experience typically is connected with the price variable. Yet information about prices is often attended to and comprehended, and the resulting meanings may influence consumer behavior. For some purchases, consumers

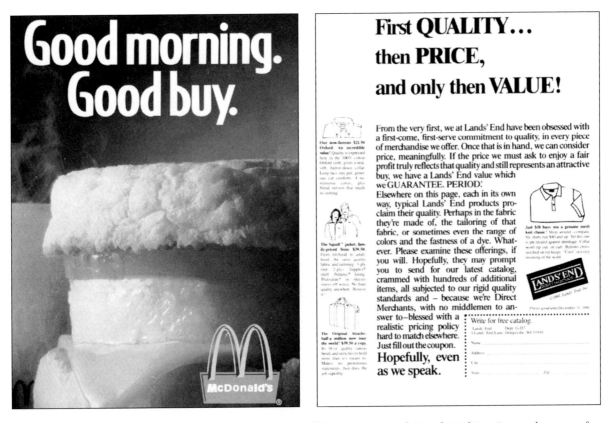

Creating perceptions of value   *(left) Used with permission of McDonald's Corporation; (right) Lands' End, Inc. Reprinted courtesy of Lands' End, Inc.*

may make a variety of price comparisons among brands and evaluate trade-offs among the various types of consumer costs and values.

Several attempts have been made to summarize the research on the effects of price on consumer affect, cognition, and behavior, but these reviews have found few generalizations.[5] For example, it has long been believed that consumers perceive a strong relationship between price and the quality of products and services. Experiments typically find this relationship when consumers are given no other information about the product except dollar price. However, when consumers are given additional information about products (which is more consistent with marketplace situations), the price–quality relationship diminishes.

In general, all of these reviews conclude that research on the behavioral effects of pricing has not been based on sound theory and that most of the studies are seriously flawed methodologically. Thus, it should not be surprising that there is little consensus on basic issues regarding how price influences consumer choice processes and behavior.

Price Perceptions and Attitudes

Price perceptions concern how price information is comprehended by consumers and made meaningful to them. One approach to understanding price perceptions is information processing, which has been advocated by Jacob Jacoby and Jerry Olson.[6] Exhibit 18.3 outlines an adaptation of this approach.

Exhibit 18.3

Conceptual Model of Cognitive Processing of Price Information

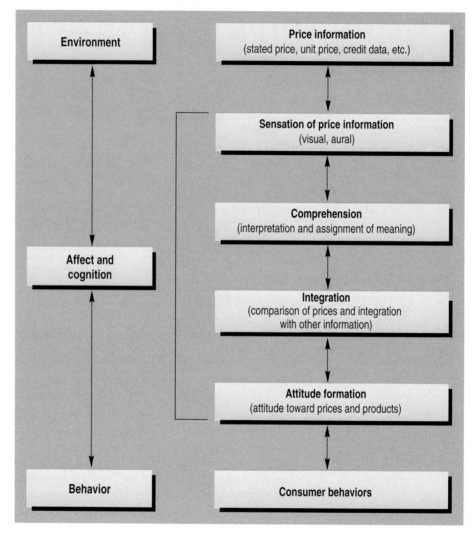

This model illustrates an approach to describing price effects for a high-involvement product or purchase situation. Basically it suggests that price information is received through the senses of sight and hearing. The information is then comprehended, which means it is interpreted and made meaningful (i.e., consumers understand the meanings of price symbols through previous learning and experience).

In the cognitive processing of price information, consumers may make comparisons between the stated price and a price or price range they have in mind for the product. The price they have in mind for making these comparisons is called the **internal reference price.** The internal reference price may be what consumers think is a fair price, what the price has been historically, or what consumers think is a low or a high market price. Basically an internal reference price serves as a

These prices may influence purchase because they are below consumers' reference prices. *Courtesy of the Procter & Gamble Company. Used by permission.*

Would this price lead you to a purchase? *Mary Kate Denny/PhotoEdit, Inc.*

guide for evaluating whether the stated price is acceptable to the consumer.[7] For example, a consumer may think 50 cents is about the right price to pay for a candy bar. When a vending machine offers candy bars for 75 cents, the internal reference price may inhibit purchase because the asking price is too high.

The stated price for a particular brand may be considered a product attribute. This knowledge may then be compared with the dollar prices of other brands in a product class, other attributes of the brand and other brands, and other consumer costs. An attitude is formed toward the various brand alternatives that may lead to purchase behavior.

For a low-involvement product or purchase situation, dollar price may have little or no impact on consumer affect and cognition or behavior. For many products, consumers may have an implicit price range, and as long as prices fall within it, price is not even evaluated as a purchase criterion. Similarly, some products are simply purchased without ever inquiring as to the price but simply paying whatever is asked for at the point of purchase. Impulse items located in the checkout area of supermarkets and drugstores are frequently purchased this way, as are other products for which the consumer is highly brand loyal. In the latter cases, consumers may make purchases on the single attribute of brand name without comparing dollar price, other consumer costs, or other factors.

In other cases, price information may not be carefully analyzed because consumers have a particular price image for the store they are shopping in. Discount stores such as Wal-Mart or Shopko may be generally considered low-priced outlets, and consumers may forgo comparing prices at these outlets with those at other stores.

Consumers often do not carefully store detailed price information in memory, even for products they purchase. For example, in a study of grocery shoppers, the researchers concluded:

What is surprising is just how imperfect [price] information attention and retention are at the very point of purchase. The fact is that less than half of the shoppers could recall the price of the item they had just placed in their shopping basket, and less than half were aware they had selected an item that was selling at a reduced price. Only a small minority of those who bought a special knew both its price and the amount of the price reduction.[8]

There are good reasons many consumers do not methodically store in memory the prices of individual products. Consumers probably do not want to exert the considerable effort necessary to obtain, store, and revise prices for the many products they buy. For many purchases, other than using coupons or haggling, consumers must pay the stated price or forgo purchase. Thus, if they choose to purchase, the price is uncontrollable by them and it likely makes little sense to carefully store price information when it has little impact on saving money. In sum, the cognitive activity costs, behavior effort costs, and time costs involved in storing price information and shopping carefully are often not worth expending to save a few dollars.

Price Behavior

Depending on the consumer, the product, and its availability in various stores and other channels, and other elements of the situation, price can affect a variety of consumer behaviors. Two types of behaviors are particularly relevant to the price variable: funds access and transactions.

Funds Access

One source of embarrassment for most of us as consumers is to arrive at the point in the purchase process where we have to produce funds for an exchange and realize we do not have sufficient funds. Not having enough money at the grocery checkout and having to replace several items can be embarrassing, particularly when the total amount of money needed is quite small. Similarly, it is embarrassing to bounce a check, to have a credit card purchase refused because we have exceeded our limit, or to be refused a purchase because of a poor credit rating. For these reasons, most of us are likely to plan for funds access to ensure sufficient funds are available when we go shopping.

As noted previously, there are several ways consumers can access funds. First, many consumers carry a certain amount of cash to pay for small purchases. This cash supply may be replenished as needed for day-to-day activities. Second, many consumers also carry checkbooks (or at least a few blank checks) in case a need arises for a larger amount of money. Third, millions of Americans carry credit cards to handle purchases. Although the interest rates on credit cards are often high, this method of accessing funds is very popular.

Credit card purchases and payments not only are convenient for the consumer but may also make the purchase seem less expensive. This is because consumers do not see any cash flowing from their pockets or a reduction in their check-book balances; they merely need to sign their names and not even think about payment until the end of the month. In one sense, if no balance is carried over on the credit card, the purchase is "free" for the time between the exchange and the payment. We suspect that although many consumers keep tabs on their checkbook balances, they may be less concerned about their credit card balances throughout the month, unless they are close to their credit limits.

Credit cards also facilitate purchasing because little effort is required to access funds. Even going to a bank to cash a check before shopping requires more effort than using a credit card. Thus, overall, the use of credit cards may reduce consumers' time, cognitive activity, and behavior effort costs. Highlight 18.2 discusses credit card purchases from priceline.com.

Transactions

The exchange of funds for products and services is typically a relatively simple transaction. It usually involves handing over cash, filling out a check, signing a credit slip, sending a credit card number to a website, or signing a credit contract and following up by making regular payments.

Highlight 18.2

priceline.com: Bust a Move, Dog

In a popular commercial, William Shatner, formerly Captain Kirk on *Star Trek,* asks the TV audience if it wants some "Dope airfares, hip hotel rooms, and fly rental cars" and, if so, to "Bust a move, dog" and get them from priceline.com. This company offers consumers another way to save money on such things as airfares, long-distance phone rates, hotel rooms, rental cars, and home equity loans. Consumers specify how much they are willing to pay for these products and services, and priceline.com communicates the offers to participating sellers or their databases. Consumers guarantee their offers with a credit card and agree to hold their offers open for a specified period of time to enable priceline.com to fulfill their offers from inventory provided by sellers. Once fulfilled, offers generally cannot be canceled. By requiring consumers to be flexible about brands, sellers, and/or

product features, sellers can generate incremental revenue without disrupting their existing distribution channels or retail pricing structures, according to priceline.com's website.

To get the best deals, consumers should know the lowest price for which they can get the product or service elsewhere and then discount it and hope that priceline.com can get a company to sell it to them for that price. Consumers also have to be willing to pay the price they offer and be flexible with respect to brands, sellers, and/or product features. This increases consumer risk and the possibility of receiving products and services that don't meet their needs. However, for such things as airline tickets, consumers apparently feel that one airline is as good as another. In its first six weeks, priceline.com reported that it sold more than 10,000 airline tickets.

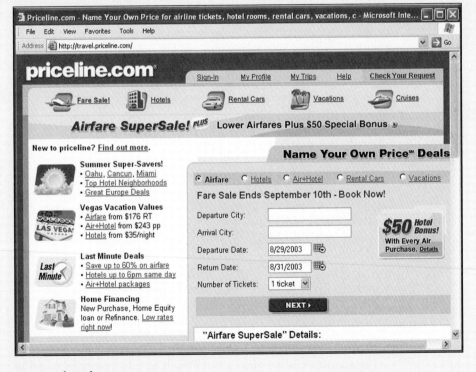

Courtesy of priceline.com.

However, as we have emphasized throughout this chapter, consumers exchange much more than simply money for goods and services. They also exchange their time, cognitive activity, and behavior effort—not only to earn money but also to shop and make purchases. Thus, analysis of these elements, and of the value consumers receive in purchase and consumption, may provide better insights into the effects of price on consumer behavior.

Price Environment

As we stated at the beginning of the chapter, price is perhaps the most intangible element of the marketing mix. From an environmental perspective, this means the price variable typically offers very little for the consumer to experience at the sensory level, although it may generate considerable cognitive activity and behavior effort. In the environment, price is usually a sign, a tag, a few symbols on a package, or a few words spoken on TV, on radio, or by a salesperson in a store or on the phone. The price variable also includes purchase contracts and credit term information.

The price variable may also include an external reference price. An **external reference price** is an explicit comparison of the stated price with another price in advertising, catalog listings, price guides, shopping tags and store displays, or sales presentations. For example, the stated price may be compared with the seller's former price ("$11.95, marked down from $15.00"), with the manufacturer's suggested retail price ("Manufacturer's suggested retail price—$50, on sale today for $39.95"), or with prices at competing stores ("$54.95, lowest price in town"). External reference prices are used to enhance the attractiveness of the stated price.[9]

How price information is communicated also has an effect. For example, the advent of scanner checkout systems has reduced price information in the environment for many grocery products because prices are no longer stamped on each package or can. A study by Valerie Zeithaml found that having each item marked increased consumers' certainty of price recall and decreased errors in both exact price and unit price recall.[10] The study also found some differences in the impacts of shelf price tags, supporting the idea that not only the price itself but also the method by which price information is communicated influences consumer affect, cognition, and behavior.

Pricing Strategy

Pricing strategy is of concern in three general situations: (1) when a price is being set for a new product, (2) when a long-term change is being considered for an established product, and (3) when a short-term price change is being considered. Marketers may change prices for a variety of reasons, such as an increase in costs, a change in the price of competitive products, or a change in distribution channels.

Many models have been offered to guide marketers in designing pricing strategies.[11] Most of these models contain very similar recommendations and differ primarily in terms of how detailed the assumptions are, how many steps the pricing process is divided into, and in what sequence pricing tasks are recommended. For our purposes, we have developed a six-stage model, shown in Exhibit 18.4. Our model differs from traditional approaches primarily in that it places greater emphasis on consumer analysis and gives greater attention to the four types of consumer costs in developing pricing and marketing strategies.

The six stages in our strategic approach to pricing are discussed next. Although consumer analysis is not the major focus in all the steps, our discussion is intended to clarify the role of consumer analysis in pricing and to offer a useful overview of the pricing process.

Exhibit 18.4

A Strategic Approach to Pricing

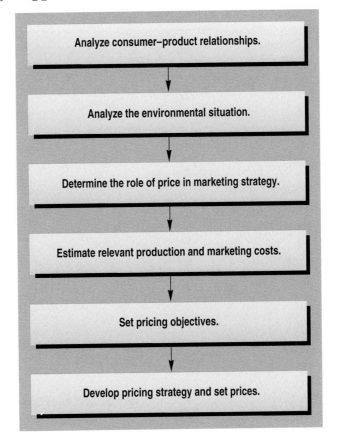

Analyze consumer–product relationships.

↓

Analyze the environmental situation.

↓

Determine the role of price in marketing strategy.

↓

Estimate relevant production and marketing costs.

↓

Set pricing objectives.

↓

Develop pricing strategy and set prices.

Analyze Consumer–Product Relationships

Pricing strategy for a new product generally starts with at least one given: The firm has a product concept or several variations of a product concept in mind. When a price change for an existing product is being considered, much more information is typically available, including sales and cost data.

Whether the pricing strategy is being developed for a new or existing product, a useful first stage in the process is to analyze the consumer–product relationships. Answers must be found for questions such as: How does the product benefit consumers? What does it mean to them? In what situations do they use it? Does it have any special psychological or social significance to them? Of course, the answers to these questions depend on which current or potential target markets are under consideration.

A key question is whether the product itself has a clear competitive advantage that consumers would be willing to pay for or whether a competitive advantage must be created on the basis of other marketing mix variables. This question has important implications for determining which of the four areas of consumer costs (time, money, cognitive activity, or behavior effort) can be appealed to most effectively.

Exhibit 18.5

Analyzing Consumer–Product Relationships: Comparing Consumer Costs for In-store versus Online Purchases

Type of Cost	In-store	Online
Money Costs		
Travel costs	More	Less
Price of product	More	Less
Shipping charges	Less	More
Time Costs		
Shopping time	More	Less
Travel time	More	Less
Delivery time	Less	More
Cognitive Costs		
Shopping skill	Less	More
Decision-making effort	Less	More
Perceived risk	Less	More
Behavioral Costs		
Energy spent traveling	More	Less
Energy spent shopping	More	Less
Effort to return products	Less	More

Suppose a firm is deciding whether to sell its products in traditional stores or on the Internet. After delineating its target market, one thing the firm should do is evaluate consumer costs for shopping and purchasing from these two alternatives. Surely, for most convenience goods, selling in-store is the likely alternative. However, for some shopping and specialty goods, e-tailing to consumers makes sense.

Exhibit 18.5 compares consumer costs for in-store versus online purchases. In terms of money, it is likely a company would sell its products at a lower price on the Web. Most companies have tried to attract consumers to make Internet purchases by offering lower prices. Web purchases also save consumers travel costs, such as the costs of gasoline to drive to stores and to park their cars. However, consumers usually pay shipping charges for products bought on the Internet. Even so, money costs are likely to be lower for most products when bought online. The firm would have to decide whether it should compete on the basis of money costs or on other costs or benefits to consumers.

There is no question that skillful consumers can save time shopping on the Internet. The ability to shop at a number of sites while sitting at home or in one's office is a convenience compared to traveling all over town looking at a variety of stores and merchandise. However, many consumers prefer to get merchandise immediately rather than wait a few days or weeks for delivery. The firm should determine whether consumers in their target market want the product immediately or don't mind waiting for delivery.

Effective online shopping likely takes more skill than simply going to a store or two and picking out a product. The consumer needs skills to navigate websites efficiently and must be willing to put up with websites that are not user-friendly. In addition, decision-making effort is likely greater online, since many more sites and alternative products are readily available for consideration. This, coupled with risks associated with unknown Web companies, credit card security, and uncertainty about product quality prior to purchase, may increase the stress of online purchasing. In addition, some commercial websites cannot handle a large number of orders during peak demand periods, such as the Christmas season, increasing stress and disappointment if the product is not delivered in a timely fashion. The firm should determine the computer sophistication of its target market and consumers' willingness to shop for that type of product online before selecting this channel.

As noted previously, the energy spent traveling and shopping in stores and malls can be a significant barrier for some consumers. This makes online shopping more convenient for many consumers. However, repackaging and returning merchandise that does not meet the consumer's needs usually requires greater effort than simply returning a product to a store. For products that vary greatly in terms of style and quality, this is an important consideration.

This discussion suggests several generalizations about analyzing consumer–product relationships in terms of consumer costs. First, one important outcome of analyzing consumer–product relationships is an estimate of how sensitive the target market is to money costs. In economics, one measure of this sensitivity is **price elasticity,** the relative change in demand for a product for a given change in dollar price. If consumers are highly price sensitive, this suggests that competing on price may be the only alternative. Amazon.com has become one of the best-known e-marketers primarily by competing on low price, although some analysts argue that this company loses money on every product it sells. The strategy of trying to build an online market primarily by focusing consumers only on low prices has led many online marketers to bankruptcy.

Second, competing on marketing mix variables other than money costs is often a more defensible and more profitable strategy. The ability to save consumers time, cognitive activity, or behavioral effort can give a company a competitive advantage and be more profitable than competing on money costs alone. Offering superior product quality through research and development, creating superior brand equity through advertising, or offering superior customer service or outstanding product assortments often is a better strategy than competing on money costs alone.

Finally, there is the question of what value consumers receive from purchasing a product in-store versus online. In-store purchases can provide value in that they lower purchasing risks and can be enjoyable experiences. Online purchases can provide value by saving time and effort and offering lower money costs and larger product assortments.

Analyze the Environmental Situation

There is no question that a firm must consider elements of the environment—economic trends, political views, social changes, and legal constraints—when developing pricing strategies. These elements should be considered early in the process of formulating any part of marketing strategy and should be monitored continually. By the time a firm is making pricing decisions, many of these issues have already been considered. Although this may also be true for competitive analysis, consideration of competition at this point is critical in developing pricing strategies.

In setting or changing prices, the firm must address its competition and how that competition will react to the product's price. Initially consideration should be given to such factors as

- Number of competitors.
- Market share of competitors.
- Location of competitors.
- Conditions of entry into the industry.
- Degree of vertical integration of competitors.
- Financial strength of competitors.
- Number of products and brands sold by each competitor.
- Cost structure of competitors.
- Historical reaction of competitors to price changes.

Analysis of these factors helps determine whether the dollar price should be at, below, or above competitors' prices. However, this analysis should also consider other consumer costs relative to competitive offerings. Consumers often pay higher dollar prices to save time and effort.

Determine the Role of Price in Marketing Strategy

This step involves determining whether the dollar price is to be a key aspect of positioning the product or whether it is to play a different role. If a firm is attempting to position a brand as a bargain product, setting a lower dollar price is clearly an important part of this strategy. Barbasol shaving cream positions itself as just as good as but half the price of other brands, for example. Similarly, if a firm is attempting to position a brand as a prestige, top-of-the-line item, a

A pricing strategy for a prestige product *Courtesy BMW of North America, LLC.*

higher dollar price is a common cue to indicate this position. For example, BMW has long used this approach for its automobiles. The success of these types of strategies also depends on analyzing the trade-offs with other elements of consumer costs.

In many situations, dollar price may not play a particularly important positioning role other than in terms of pricing competitively. If consumers enjoy greater convenience in purchasing (e.g., free delivery), or if the product has a clear competitive advantage, the price may be set at or above those of the competition but not highlighted in the positioning strategy. In other cases, when the price of a product is higher than that of the competition but there is no clear competitive advantage, the price may not be explicitly used in positioning. For example, premium-priced beers do not highlight price as part of the appeal.

Estimate Relevant Production and Marketing Costs

The costs of producing and marketing a product provide a useful benchmark for making pricing decisions. The variable costs of production and marketing usually determine the lowest dollar price a firm must charge to make an offering in the market. However, there are some exceptions to this rule. These exceptions typically involve interrelationships among products. For example, a firm may sell an item below cost (i.e., a loss leader) to build traffic and increase sales of other items.

Set Pricing Objectives

Pricing objectives should be derived from overall marketing objectives, which in turn should be derived from corporate objectives. In practice, the most common objective is to achieve a target return on investment. This objective has the advantage of being quantifiable, and also offers a useful basis for making not only pricing decisions but also decisions on whether to enter or remain in specific markets. For example, if a firm demands a 20 percent return on investment, and the best estimates of sales at various prices indicate a product would have to be priced too high to generate demand, the decision may be to forgo market entry. However, marketers should be aware of the sensitivity of profits to small differences in the prices they receive for their products and services, as discussed in Highlight 18.3.

Develop Pricing Strategy and Set Prices

A thorough analysis in the preceding stages should provide the information necessary to develop pricing strategies and set prices. Basically, the meaning of the product to the consumer and consumer costs have been analyzed. The environment has been analyzed, particularly competition. The role of pricing marketing strategy has been determined. Production and marketing costs have been estimated. Pricing objectives have been set. The pricing task now is to determine a pricing strategy and specific prices that are (1) sufficiently above costs to generate the desired level of profit and achieve stated objectives, (2) related to competitive prices in a manner consistent with the overall marketing and positioning strategy, and (3) designed to generate consumer demand based on consumer cost trade-offs and values.

Highlight 18.3

Effects on Profitability of Small Changes in Price

Small changes in the price marketers receive can lead to large differences in net income. For example, at Coca-Cola a 1 percent increase in the price received for its products would result in a net income boost of 6.4 percent; at Fuji Photo, 16.7 percent; at Nestlé, 17.5 percent; at Ford, 26 percent; and at Philips, 28.7 percent. In some companies, a 1 percent increase in the price received would be the difference between a profit and a significant loss. Given the cost structure of large corporations, a 1 percent boost in realized price yields an average net income gain of 12 percent. In short, when setting pricing objectives and developing pricing strategies, it's worth the effort to do pricing research to see what prices consumers are willing to pay and still believe they are receiving good value.

Sources: Based on Robert J. Dolan and Hermann Simon, *Power Pricing: How Managing Price Transforms the Bottom Line* (New York: The Free Press, 1997), p. 4; also see Kent Monroe, *Pricing: Making Profitable Decisions* (Burr Ridge, IL: McGraw-Hill/Irwin, 2003).

In some cases, prices are developed with a long-run strategy in mind. For example, **penetration pricing** may include a long-run plan to sequentially raise prices after introduction at a relatively low price. **Skimming pricing** may include a long-run plan to systematically lower prices after a high-price introduction.

However, most price changes occur as a result of changes in consumer behavior, the environment, competition, costs, strategies, and objectives. A dramatic example of the relationships among these variables is the pricing of air fares.

Before deregulation, prices were set by the Civil Aeronautics Board. Price increases were the result of petitions to this agency based on evidence of increased costs of operation. Thus, price was not a very important competitive weapon, as all carriers charged the same fare for the same route. Shortly after deregulation, however, price became a critical competitive tool; in fact, in some periods up to 5,000 price changes were made in a single day! Major carriers attempted to compete with low-price, "no-frills" airlines by lowering the prices on competitive routes and raising the prices on routes the low-price airlines did not serve. In addition, the major carriers engaged in cost cutting in an effort to be more competitive with the no-frills airlines. Consumers had a basic choice between attempting to minimize dollar cost by spending more time shopping for low prices, forgoing some flexibility in departure times and dates, and giving up some additional services versus paying full fare and receiving these benefits. Business travelers often paid the higher full-fare price, whereas leisure travelers spent the time and effort necessary to get cheaper fares.

A pricing strategy offering more items for the same price *Courtesy Tyco.*

Highlight 18.4

Who Gets What When You Use Plastic?

Consumers have two options when using plastic to pay for their purchases: They can use a credit card and charge their purchases for later payment, or they can use a debit card and have the payment taken directly from their checking accounts. While credit cards are handy, the interest expenses on them can be considerable if the balance isn't paid off each month. However, since a debit card requires consumers to have money in their checking accounts in order to use it, they are less likely to run up huge debts overall. So both options have advantages and disadvantages for consumers.

Whether a credit or debit card is used, someone has to pay for the service. However, different organizations receive varying amounts depending on which type of card is used. For a credit card or signature debit card (where the receipt is signed just like a credit card) transaction, more money goes to banks and card issuers. For a PIN debit card transaction (where the consumer punches in a personal identification number, or PIN), more money goes to the retailer. For example, for a $100 consumer purchase, the organizations involved receive the following amounts:

	Credit Card	Debit Card
Retailer	$98.20	$99.80
Processing agent	.05	.05
Retailer's bank	.23	.00
Issuing bank	1.48	.13
Visa or Mastercard	.04	.00
PIN debit card network	.00	.02

Retailers make more money with debit cards, so they prefer them for some purchases. However, since consumers tend to make bigger-ticket purchases with credit cards rather than with debit cards, checks, or cash, retailers also greatly value credit cards.

Ultimately consumers end up paying these costs since merchants raise retail prices to cover them. So how much money are we really talking about? In one recent year, total consumer spending in the United States amounted to $5.5 trillion, and $1.2 trillion of this was paid by check. If this $1.2 trillion had been paid by credit cards instead of by check, it would have generated about $8 billion in fees for the credit industry.

Sources: Roger Parloff, "The $50 Billion Card Game," *Fortune,* May 12, 2003, pp. 109–119; Danie Lyons, "Visa's Vision," *Forbes,* September 16, 2002, pp. 78–86.

This example illustrates how a change in the environment (deregulation) led to a change in competitors (entrance of no-frills airlines), which led to a change in pricing strategies (price cuts for some seats but overall attempts to maximize revenues per flight) and cost-cutting efforts. Many consumers also changed their behavior as they became more involved in the purchase of airline tickets and perhaps even traveled more by plane as dollar prices fell, at least in the short run. Highlight 18.4 discusses another factor that influences consumer prices: the use of credit and debit cards.

Back To...

Vinnie Bombatz

When considering only the money cost of the Diet Pepsi, at first glance it may appear that the discount supermarket price is better: $2.99 plus $.15 tax, which equals $3.14, versus the convenience store price of $5 plus $.25 tax, which equals $5.25.

Now let's consider the cost of operating Vinnie's car. Assume it cost $.20 per mile; driving twelve miles equals $2.40. The supermarket purchase now cost Vinnie $3.14 plus $2.40, which equals $5.54—more than the convenience store price of $5.25.

Next, it seems reasonable to estimate the cost of Vinnie's time. Several rates could be considered. Although his market value for this time is $18 per hour, because of taxes and other deductions Vinnie does not take home the full amount. Let's assume he takes home $9 per hour and agree this is the value of the time to Vinnie.

The convenience store trip had a time cost of 10 minutes at $9 per hour, which equals $1.50, for a total of $5.25 plus $1.50, which equals $6.75. The supermarket trip had a time cost of 45 minutes at $9 per hour, which equals $6.75, for a total of $5.54 plus $6.75, which equals $12.29. The convenience store trip now appears to be a real bargain: $6.75 versus $12.29!

Finally, let's consider how Vinnie felt about the two trips and what he experienced. In terms of cognitive activity, the convenience store trip was clearly stressful and unpleasant, and likely required more behavior effort than the trip to the supermarket. However, the two-block walk provided beneficial exercise. On the other hand, the supermarket trip was pleasant, and Vinnie felt very good about the purchase.

So which was the better trip? To Vinnie it was the supermarket, since he ignored costs other than the price paid. However, if we accept the economic assumptions involved in valuing Vinnie's automobile operating costs and time, we might conclude that the convenience store price was a better buy. Depending on how the cognitive activity and behavior effort are evaluated, either of the two may be considered the better purchase.

Finally, consider the fact that Diet Pepsi was on sale at the convenience store for $2.79 plus tax on the same day that Vinnie went to the supermarket and paid $2.99 plus tax. Had he known this, Vinnie could have walked to the convenience store and saved both money and time.

Which was the better price? It depends on whether we consider the question from Vinnie's point of view or from that of an outside observer with perfect information. In addition, it depends on whether we analyze only the dollar price of the item or also consider the other dollar costs, time, cognitive activity, and behavior effort involved. ❖

Summary   This chapter presented an overview of pricing decisions and consumer behavior. Initially we focused on developing a conceptual framework for considering pricing decisions that includes four types of consumer costs: money, time, cognitive activity, and behavior effort. These elements, when coupled with value, provide a framework for examining price from the consumer's point of view. Next, we discussed affect and cognitions, behaviors, and environmental factors relative to price. The cognitive factors examined included price perceptions and attitudes; the behaviors described included funds access and transactions. The discussion of the environment focused on price information. Finally, we developed a pricing strategy model for use in pricing new products or for making price change decisions.

Key Terms and Concepts

external reference price   **470**
internal reference price   **466**
penetration pricing   **476**

price elasticity   **473**
price perceptions   **465**
skimming pricing   **476**

Review and Discussion Questions

1. Define *price* and explain the differences between price strategy and other elements of the marketing mix.
2. In what situations are consumers willing to pay a higher dollar cost to save time, cognitive activity, and behavior effort?
3. Use the Wheel of Consumer Analysis to identify the interactions associated with consumer response to a credit card pricing strategy. You might consider Discover Card or select your own example.
4. How can price be used to position a product like basketball shoes or luggage?
5. Explain how consumers determine that a particular price is too high. Use the conceptual model of cognitive processing (Exhibit 18.3) to structure your answer.
6. Offer alternative behavioral views of consumer response that could explain the response to price in question 5.
7. Could a marketing manager change price perceptions with strategies aimed at funds access and transaction behaviors? Explain and give examples.
8. The text suggests little research has examined the price environment. Use your experiences to suggest some areas for research on the price environment.
9. Analyze consumer costs associated with the purchase of automobile insurance or airline tickets. What are some strategy implications suggested by your analysis?
10. How would changing environmental factors influence price setting or price changes for fast-food hamburgers in your community?

Marketing Strategy in Action

Pleasant Company

"Samantha Parkington fights for women's suffrage. Addy Walker escapes from slavery. Kirsten Larson builds a life on the frontier. Characters from a feminist novel? No, these plucky heroines are part of The American Girls Collection, a line of historical dolls that are the darlings of 7- to 12-year-olds. Christmas orders piled up so fast at Pleasant Co.—the privately held dollmaker—that company vice presidents had to pack boxes in the warehouse.

Former president, Pleasant Rowland, who began the company with royalties she received from writing primary school reading books knew her vision had to be broad. Simply launching a me-too doll would have meant failure.

Before Rowland got her idea she went shopping for dolls for her two nieces. All she found were Barbies that wore spiked heels, drove pink Corvettes, and looked as if they belonged in strip joints. Though industry sources told her she couldn't sell a mass market doll for over $40—some Barbies cost less than $10—Rowland gambled that boomer parents would pay more for one that was fun and educational.

Each of Pleasant Co.'s five dolls represents an era of American history. Addy is from the Civil War, and Samantha is described as a

A Pleasant Company catalog   *Courtesy Pleasant Company.*

"bright Victorian beauty." Parents can also buy historically accurate replicas of clothes, furniture, and memorabilia, such as the June 6, 1944, Chicago *Daily Tribune* headlined "Allies Invade France," made for Molly McIntire, the 1940s doll. The 18-inch dolls cost $84; add in all the accessories, including $80 dresses for the doll's owner, and the price exceeds $1,000. Every doll also stars in its own series of novels, with titles like *Kirsten Learns a Lesson* and *Samantha Saves the Day.* The heroines go on adventures and cope with moral dilemmas; for example, Felicity Merriman, a colonial girl, has to decide whether to continue her tea parties while her father fights King George III's tea tax. Says Rowland: "We try to give girls chocolate cake with vitamins."

Pleasant Co. decided early on not to compete doll to doll on toy store shelves. Defying industry wisdom, Rowland began selling only through her own catalog. She counted on her dolls' being so different that word of mouth would take care of sales. She also coddled her customers. Pleasant Co. opened a "hospital" for broken dolls, so when brother sticks a pair of scissors through Molly's head, Mom can return her to Pleasant Co. for repairs. For $35 the company does the surgery then mails Molly—now wearing a hospital gown and carrying a certificate of health from the house doctor—home to recuperate.

Will Pleasant Co.'s dolls have legs? Rowland says movies, CD-ROMs, and theme parks aren't out of the question. But she'll expand only as long as she can keep the business special. She refuses to license her products on T-shirts and lunch boxes, fearing that too much exposure would cheapen the dolls' image. Says Rowland: 'It never hurts to play hard to get.'"

In 1998, Mattel, Inc., purchased Pleasant Co., which continues to operate as an independent subsidiary. During the same year, American Girl Place, the company's first retail and entertainment site, opened in downtown Chicago, and a second store opened in New York in 2003. The stores are a little girl's delight. Visitors can purchase dolls, books, and clothing; view a musical revue; and have tea, lunch, or dinner at the Café at American Girl Place. The Chicago store sold $35 million worth of products in 2003.

Discussion Questions

1. Why do consumers pay $84 for a Pleasant Company doll when they can buy other dolls much more cheaply at retail stores?
2. Considering money, time, cognitive activity, and behavioral effort costs, are Pleasant Company dolls more or less costly than dolls that can be purchased at retail stores?
3. What recommendations do you have for Pleasant Company to increase sales and profits?

Sources: Brian Dumaine, "How to Compete with a Champ," *Fortune,* January 10, 1994, p. 106. © 1994 Time Inc. All rights reserved. All material in quotes is from *Fortune;* Leah Eskin, "American Girl Place: A Female Theme Park," *Wisconsin State Journal,* August 17, 2003, p. A1, A10; http://www.americangirl.com.

Consumer Behavior, Electronic Commerce, and Channel Strategy

IBM

A bear when it sells big computers to corporations, IBM was a Bambi of a storefront retailer. In the early 1980s, the company began opening grandly decorated computer stores called IBM Product Centers in high-rent business districts all over America. Although the first 81 stores had sales estimated at $100 million in 1983, IBM shelved plans to expand the chain to 100 stores. The centers sold IBM's personal computers (PCs) and typewriters along with add-on gear and software made by IBM and others. Burdened with start-up costs and high overhead, the stores made far less than the 20 percent per year IBM is accustomed to earning on invested capital.

Glimpsing the chance to sell typewriters to small businesses and branch offices of big companies without costly door-to-door calls, IBM had opened three Product Centers by mid-1981. Then, when the PC burst on the scene, the company decided to plunk stores down in every metropolitan area. However, most of the 1,600-odd independent stores that carried the firm's PC and competing makes

had done a better job of selling to the target clientele. The rival stores belonged mostly to big chains such as ComputerLand, Entré Computer Centers, and Sears Business Systems Centers.

IBM made mistakes right off the bat. Although it was a major producer of sophisticated point-of-sale computer systems to centralize billing, inventory, and sales audits, the company forced its own salespeople to record transactions on Stone Age carbon paper invoices. At the end of each day, clerks typed the information into a computer in the back room. Result: mistakes galore in recordkeeping and billing.

In choosing the Product Centers' decor, IBM revealed retailing naiveté. Anxious not to appear cold and remote, it abandoned its traditional icy blue and decorated the centers in bright red. "Red doesn't just irritate bulls," remarked Warren Winger, chairman of CompuShop, a Dallas-based chain, "it makes salesmen hostile and alarms customers." To keep its stores classy, IBM eschewed the usual tacky trapping of computer retailing—flashy in-store displays, brochures, and racks of impulse items near the cash registers. "The in-store merchandising—we never realized how important it was," confessed Jim Turner, the IBM vice president in charge of the centers. IBM also staffed the stores entirely with its own career salespeople, few of whom had retailing experience. Consumer research by a large New York ad agency showed the staff intimidated first-time customers. In interviews the customers revealed they expected more of IBM Product Centers than of other computer stores, but they came away disillusioned.

Source: Excerpted from Peter Petre, "IBM's Misadventures in the Retail Jungle," *Fortune,* July 23, 1984, p. 80. Copyright 1984 Time Inc. All rights reserved. Reprinted by permission.

What mistakes did IBM make in operating its own retail stores? From an economic perspective, channels of distribution are thought of as providing form, time, place, and possession utilities for consumers. **Form utility** means channels convert raw materials into finished goods and services in forms the consumer seeks to purchase. **Time utility** means channels make goods and services available *when* the consumer wants to purchase them.

7-Eleven provides time and place utility, while Mont Blanc provides form utility.   *(left) Tony Freeman/PhotoEdit, Inc.; (right) Courtesy Mont Blanc North America.*

Exhibit 19.1

The Wheel of Consumer Analysis: Channel Strategy Issues

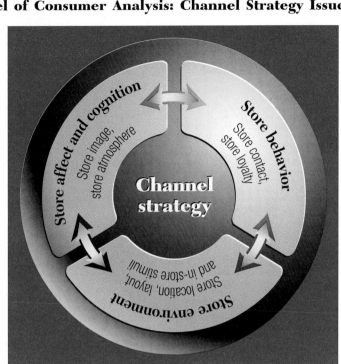

Place utility means goods and services are made available *where* the consumer wants to purchase them. **Possession utility** means channels facilitate the transfer of ownership of goods to the consumer.

Although this view of channels is useful, it perhaps understates their role in our society. Channels of distribution have a very important impact on consumer affect, cognition, and behavior. The locations of malls, shopping centers, and stores, as well as specific products and other stimuli within these environments, strongly influence what consumers think and feel and what behaviors they perform, such as store contacts, product contacts, and transactions. In return, consumer actions at the retail level determine the success or failure of marketing strategies and have an important impact on the selection of future strategies.

In this chapter, we focus on the relationships among consumer affect, cognition, behavior, and environments at the retail store level. Initially we focus on these interactions for store retailing rather than for nonstore retailing because some form of store is involved in more than 90 percent of product sales to the consumer and in the majority of service sales. We then turn to nonstore retailing and electronic commerce.

Exhibit 19.1 provides a model of the store issues addressed in this chapter. We begin by discussing store-related affect and cognition, behavior, and environmental factors and then turn to issues in channel strategy development.

Store-Related Affect and Cognition

A variety of affective and cognitive processes could be discussed in relation to retail stores. However, we will focus on two major variables of managerial concern at the retail level: *store image* and *store atmosphere*. Although the marketing literature is

Dressing salespeople as referees helps create a sports image for this store
Rob Crandall/Stock, Boston, LLC.

not clear on the exact differences between these two variables, it is evident that both deal with the influence of store attributes on consumers' affect and cognition rather than on how marketing managers perceive the stores.

Store Image

For our purposes, we will treat **store image** as what consumers *think* about a particular store. This includes perceptions and attitudes based on sensations of store-related stimuli received through the five senses. Operationally, store image is commonly assessed by asking consumers how good or how important various aspects of a retail store's operation are. Commonly studied dimensions of store image include merchandise, service, clientele, physical facilities, promotion, and convenience. Store atmosphere is also often included as part of store image.

Store image research involves polling consumers concerning their perceptions of and attitudes about particular store dimensions. Typically these dimensions are broken into a number of store attributes. For example, the merchandise might be studied in terms of quality, assortment, fashion, guarantees, and pricing. The service dimension might be studied in terms of general service, salesclerk service, degree of self-service, ease of merchandise return, and delivery and credit services.

Often the same attributes are studied for competitive stores to compare the strengths and weaknesses of a particular store's image with that of its closest competitors. Based on this research, store management may then change certain attributes of the store to develop a more favorable image.

Developing a consistent store image is a common goal of retailers. This involves coordinating the various aspects of store image to appeal to specific market segments. However, store images sometimes have to be changed to adapt to changes in consumers' shopping habits and in competitive position.

For example, in the early 1980s JCPenney was a traditional general merchandiser. As discount chains began to dominate the general-merchandise market, Penneys began repositioning its stores to create the image of a moderately priced fashion specialist. The company stopped selling hard goods, such as sporting goods and photography products, and focused its efforts on clothing and home leisure products. More recently it changed its apparel strategy from selling designer names such as Halston and Mary McFadden to improving its private-label fashions and adding more national brands such as Levi's and Bugle Boy. Nearly half of its sales today are women's wear, and its gross margins have improved dramatically. It has one of the most successful sites on the Web. Apparently the company successfully changed its store image in the minds of consumers.

Store Atmosphere

Robert Donovan and John Rossiter argue that **store atmosphere** involves primarily affect in the form of in-store *emotional states* that consumers may not be fully conscious of when shopping.[1] Thus, many controlled studies have failed to find that store atmosphere has significant effects on behavior because these emotional states are difficult for consumers to verbalize, are rather transient, and influence in-store behavior in ways of which consumers may not be aware.

The basic model underlying the Donovan and Rossiter research, shown in Exhibit 19.2, is taken from the environmental psychology literature. Basically the model posits that environmental stimuli affect consumers' emotional states, which in turn affect approach or avoidance behaviors. *Approach behaviors* refer to moving toward and *avoidance behaviors* refer to moving away from various environments and stimuli, Four types of approach or avoidance behaviors are related to retail stores:

1. *Physical* approach and avoidance, which can be related to store patronage intentions at a basic level.

2. *Exploratory* approach and avoidance, which can be related to in-store search and exposure to a broad or narrow range of offerings.

3. *Communication* approach and avoidance, which can be related to interactions with sales personnel and floor staff.

4. *Performance and satisfaction* approach and avoidance, which can be related to frequency of repeat shopping as well as reinforcement of time and money expenditures in the store.

These authors investigated the relationships among the three types of emotional states shown in Exhibit 19.2 (pleasure, arousal, and dominance) and stated intentions to perform certain store-related behaviors. *Pleasure* refers to the degree to which the consumer feels good, joyful, happy, or satisfied in the store; *arousal* refers to the degree to which the consumer feels excited, stimulated, alert, or active in the store; and *dominance* refers to the extent to which the consumer feels in control of or free to act in the store. The study was conducted in 11 different types of retail outlets, including department, clothing, shoe, hardware, and sporting goods stores.

The Donovan and Rossiter research found that simple *affect,* or store-induced pleasure, is a very powerful determinant of approach–avoidance behaviors within the store, including spending behavior. Further, their research suggests *arousal,*

Exhibit 19.2

A Model of Store Atmosphere Effects

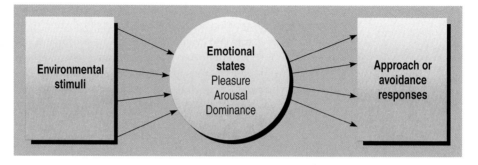

Sources: Robert J. Donovan and John R. Rossiter, "Store Atmosphere: An Environmental Psychology Approach," *Journal of Retailing,* Spring 1982, p. 42. Copyright, New York University, Stern School of Business; also see Charles S. Areni, John R. Sparks, and Patrick Dunne, "Assessing Consumers' Affective Responses to Retail Environments: A Tale of Two Simulation Techniques," in *Advances in Consumer Research,* vol XXIII, eds. Kim P. Corfman and John G. Lynch, Jr. (Provo, UT: Association for Consumer Research, 1996), pp. 504–509.

or store-induced feelings of alertness or excitement, can increase time spent in the store as well as willingness to interact with sales personnel. They suggest that in-store stimuli that induce arousal include bright lighting and upbeat music. However, the inducement of arousal works positively only in store environments that are already pleasant; arousal may have no influence, or may even have a negative influence, in unpleasant store environments.

Overall, then, pleasure and arousal were found to influence consumers' stated (1) enjoyment of shopping in the store, (2) time spent browsing and exploring the store's offerings, (3) willingness to talk to sales personnel, (4) tendency to spend more money than originally planned, and (5) likelihood of returning to the store. The third emotional dimension, *dominance,* or the extent to which consumers feel in control of or free to act in the store, was found to have little effect on consumer behaviors in the retail environment.

Store-Related Behavior

Marketing managers aim to encourage many behaviors in the retail store environment. Two basic types of behavior are discussed here: store contact and store loyalty. Highlight 19.1 discusses the most successful retailer in history at influencing consumer behavior.

Store Contact

As we mentioned in Chapter 8, *store contact* involves the consumer locating, traveling to, and entering a store. We also noted that putting carnivals in parking lots, having style shows in department stores, and printing maps and location instructions in the Yellow Pages are common tactics to increase these behaviors. Other commonly used tactics include store coupons, rebates, and local advertising.

A number of the variables discussed in this chapter also concern obtaining store contacts. For example, store location decisions are strongly influenced by heavy traffic and pedestrian patterns, which facilitate store contact.

Highlight 19.1

Wal-Mart: Premier Consumer Marketer

In 2003, Wal-Mart became the first company to be not only the largest company in the world but also the most admired in *Fortune*'s annual poll of 10,000 executives. Wal-Mart has been so successful in marketing to consumers that it had sales of over $244 billion in 2002, accounting for an estimated 2.3 percent of the total U.S. GNP. It has redefined what it means to be a big marketer! Some other startling facts about Wal-Mart's success include the following:

- It employs 1.3 million people.
- It is the biggest employer in 21 states, with more people in uniform than the U.S. Army.
- Some 70 million consumers shop in Wal-Mart stores each week.
- Wal-Mart's sales on a single day in Fall 2002, $1.42 billion, were larger than the GDPs of 36 countries.

- Its losses to theft each year, estimated at $2 billion, are equivalent to the size of the revenues of the 694th company on the Fortune 1000.
- It accounts for 39 percent of sales of Tandy Brands, 23 percent of Clorox, 20 percent of Revlon, 20 percent of RJR Tobacco, and 17 percent of Procter & Gamble.
- Its U.S. market share is 36 percent for dog food, 32 percent for disposable diapers, 30 percent for photographic film, 26 percent for toothpaste, and 21 percent for pain remedies.

Wal-Mart is so influential in the economy that its low prices are considered a key reason inflation has stayed low in recent years. Apparently Wal-Mart understands consumers well and delivers value to them.

Sources: Jerry Useem, "One Nation under Wal-Mart," *Fortune,* March 3, 2003, pp. 64–78; Nicholas Stein, "America's Most Admired Companies," *Fortune,* March 3, 2003, pp. 81–85; **www.walmart.com.**

The visibility of the store and its distance from consumers are other variables used to select locations that can increase store contact. For many small retail chains and stores, selecting locations in the vicinity of major retail stores such as Sears, JCPenney, Wal-Mart, or a major grocery store may greatly increase the probability that consumers will come into contact with them. In fact, one major advantage of locating in a successful shopping center or mall is the store contact available from pedestrians passing by on their way to another store. From the consumer's viewpoint, such locations can reduce shopping time and effort by allowing a form of one-stop shopping.

Store Loyalty

Most retailers do not want consumers to come to their stores once and never return; rather, they seek repeat patronage. **Store loyalty**—repeat patronage intentions and behavior—can be strongly influenced by the arrangement of the environment, particularly the reinforcing properties of the retail store. For example, the in-store stimuli and the attributes discussed in this chapter in terms of store image are the primary variables used to influence store loyalty.

Consider one further example of a tactic that may be used to develop store loyalty: in-store unadvertised specials. These specials are often marked with an attention-getting orange sign. Typically, consumers go to a store shopping for a particular product or just to go shopping. While going through the store, a favorite brand or long-sought-after product the consumer could not afford is found to be an unadvertised special. This can be quite reinforcing and strongly influence the

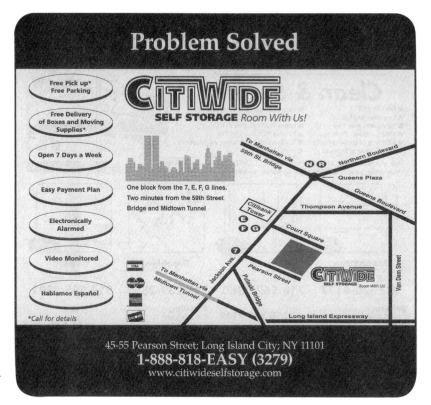

probability that the consumer will return to the same store, perhaps seeking other unadvertised specials. Quite likely, the consumer would not have to find a suitable unadvertised special on every trip to the store; a variable ratio schedule might well be powerful enough to generate a high degree of store loyalty.

These additional trips to the store allow the consumer to experience other reinforcing properties, such as fast checkout, a pleasant and arousing store atmosphere, or high-quality merchandise at competitive prices. In sum, reinforcing tactics and positive attributes of the store are used to develop store loyalty.

Store loyalty is a major objective of retail channel strategy, and it has an important financial impact. For example, it has been estimated that the loss of a single customer to a supermarket can cost the store about $3,100 per year in sales. Thus, analysis of the store environment and of consumers' store-related affect, cognition, and behavior is critical for successful marketing.

Store Environment

As we noted previously, retail stores are relatively closed environments that can exert a significant impact on consumer affect, cognition, and behavior. In this section, we consider three major decision areas in designing effective store environments: store location, store layout, and in-store stimuli.

Store Location

Although not part of the internal environment of a store, **store location** is a critical aspect of channel strategy. Good locations allow ready access, can attract large numbers of consumers, and can significantly alter consumer shopping and purchasing patterns. As retail outlets with very similar product offerings proliferate, even slight differences in location can have a significant impact on market share and profitability. In addition, store location decisions represent long-term financial commitments, and changing poor locations can be difficult and costly.

Research on retail location has been dominated by a regional urban economics approach rather than a behavioral approach. Thus, many of the assumptions on which the models are based offer poor descriptions of consumer behavior. For example, these approaches generally assume consumers make single-purpose shopping trips from a fixed origin. Considerable behavioral research suggests, however, that 50 to 60 percent of all shopping trips are multipurpose. The regional models also assume consumers have equal levels of knowledge about different stores, and they often ignore the impact of store advertising and promotion on consumers.

Although recent work has begun to integrate behavioral variables such as store image into location models, the models still place primary emphasis on economic variables and assumptions and on *predicting* rather than *describing* consumer behavior. Consumers are considered primarily in terms of demographic and socioeconomic variables and of traffic patterns and distances to various locations.

Despite these criticisms, many retail location models are quite sophisticated and can deal with a variety of criteria. Although we do not review all the approaches available for selecting trading areas, business districts, shopping centers, and optimal store sites,[2] we briefly discuss four general approaches to store location. These include the checklist method, the analog approach, regression models, and location allocation models.[3]

Checklist Method   The *checklist method* attempts to systematically evaluate the relative value of a site compared to other potential sites in the area. Essentially it involves an evaluation of various factors likely to affect sales and costs at a site. Marketing managers then make decisions about the desirability of the site based on these comparisons. Checklists commonly include information about socioeconomic and demographic composition of consumers in the area, level of consumption, and consumer expenditure patterns. Site-specific factors such as traffic count, parking facilities, ease of entry and exit, and visibility are often considered.

Analog Approach   The *analog approach* first identifies an existing store or stores similar to the one to be located. Surveys are used to observe the power of these analog stores to draw consumers from different distance zones. The ability of the analog stores to attract consumers is then used to estimate the trading area and the expected sales at alternative sites. The site with the best expected performance is chosen for the new store.

Regression Models   *Regression models* are commonly used to investigate the factors that affect the profitability of retail outlets at particular sites. Retail performance has frequently been studied in regression models as a function of store location, store attributes, market attributes, price, and competition. In most of the studies, performance has been found to be affected by population size and socioeconomic characteristics of consumers in the store's market area, as well as by service factors such as local promotion and advertising.

Location Allocation Models   Although the previous approaches are most commonly used to evaluate store location sites, *location allocation models* typically have been used to assess an entire market or trading area. Location allocation models generally involve the simultaneous selection of several locations and the estimation of demand at those locations to optimize some specified criteria. These models allow the investigation of the effects on profitability of one store in a chain if another store is added in the same trading area, and they can be used to systematically consider the impacts of possible changes in the future marketing environment, such as competitive reactions.

Store Layout

Store layout can have important effects on consumers. At a basic level, the layout influences such factors as how long the consumer stays in the store, how many products the consumer comes into visual contact with, and what routes the consumer travels within the store. Such factors may affect what and how many purchases are made. There are many types and variations of store layouts; two basic types are grid and free form.

Grid Layout   Exhibit 19.3 presents an example of a **grid layout** common in many grocery stores. In a grid, all counters and fixtures are at right angles to each other and resemble a maze, with merchandise counters acting as barriers to traffic flow. The grid layout in a supermarket forces customers to the sides and back of the store, where items such as produce, meat, and diary products are located. In fact, 80 to 90 percent of all consumers shopping in supermarkets pass these three counters.

In a supermarket, such a layout is designed to increase the number of products a consumer comes into visual contact with, thus increasing the probability of purchase. In addition, because produce, meat, and dairy products are typically high-margin items, the grid design can help channel consumers toward these more profitable products. Similarly, the location of frequently purchased items toward the back of the store requires consumers who are shopping only for these items to pass many other items. Because the probability of purchasing other items increases once the consumer is in visual contact with them, the grid layout can be very effective in increasing the number of items purchased.

The grid layout is more likely to be used in department and specialty stores to direct customer traffic down the main aisles. Typically these retailers put highly sought merchandise along the walls to pull customers past other slow-moving merchandise areas. For example, sale merchandise may be placed along the walls not only to draw consumers to these areas but also to reward consumers for spending more time in the store and shopping carefully. This may increase the probability that consumers will return to the store and follow similar traffic patterns on repeat visits. Expensive items can be placed along the main aisles to facilitate purchases by less price-sensitive consumers. The grid layout is commonly found on the main floors of multilevel department and specialty stores and at mass merchandisers.

Exhibit 19.3

Examples of Grid and Free-Form Store Layouts

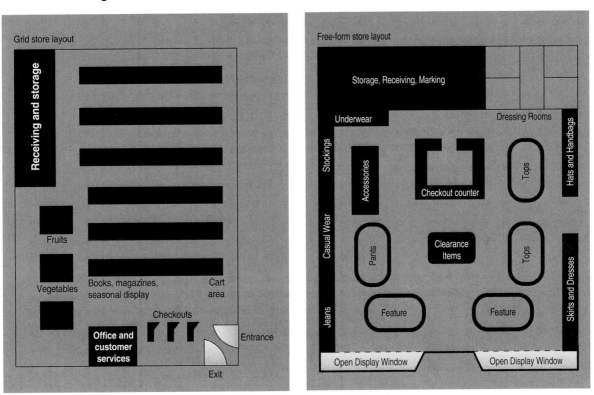

Source: Adapted from Michael Levy and Barton A. Weitz, *Retailing Management,* 5th ed. (Burr Ridge, IL: McGraw-Hill/Irwin, 2004), pp. 592, 595. Reproduced with permission from The McGraw-Hill Companies.

Free-Form Layout   Exhibit 19.3 also presents an example of a **free-form layout.** The merchandise and fixtures are grouped into patterns that allow unstructured flow of customer traffic. Merchandise is divided on the basis of fixtures and signs, and customers can come into visual contact with all departments from any point in the store. A free-form arrangement is often used in specialty stores, boutiques, and apparel stores. This arrangement is particularly useful for encouraging relaxed shopping and impulse purchases. It may also help store salespeople move consumers to several different types of merchandise. For example, it may aid in selling a collection of different items, such as a suit, shirt, tie, and shoes in a clothing store, thus increasing the total sale.

Exhibit 19.4 summarizes the major advantages and disadvantages of the grid and free-form layouts.

In-Store Stimuli

In most environments, an endless number of stimuli can influence affect, cognitions, and behavior. A retail store is no exception. Stores have many stimuli that

Exhibit 19.4

Advantages and Disadvantages of Grid and Free-Form Layouts

Advantages	Disadvantages
Grid	
Low cost	Plain and uninteresting
Customer familiarity	Limited browsing
Merchandise exposure	Stimulator of rushed shopping behavior
Ease of cleaning	Limited creativity in décor
Simplified security	
Possibility of self-service	
Free-Form	
Allowance for browsing and wandering freely	Loitering encouraged
Increased impulse purchases	Possible confusion
Visual appeal	Waste of floor space
Flexibility	Cost
	Difficulty of cleaning

Source: From Robert F. Lusch, *Management of Retail Enterprises* (Boston: Kent Publishing Company, 1982), p. 471. © by Wadsworth Inc. Reprinted by permission of the author.

influence consumers: the characteristics of other shoppers and salespeople, lighting, noises, smells, temperature, shelf space and displays, signs, colors, and merchandise. Highlight 19.2 discusses the importance of store design.

Although the effects of some in-store stimuli have been studied extensively, much of this research is proprietary. (It is not available in the marketing or consumer research literature because it has been conducted by firms seeking a differential advantage over competitors.) Much of the research available in the literature is dated and of questionable validity in today's marketplace. In addition, in the research that is available, the results are seldom consistent; some studies find large effects of in-store stimuli, some find small effects, and some find no effects. Differences in findings are often attributable to methodological issues, but we believe effects are highly situation specific and no single in-store tactic should be expected to succeed in all cases.

With these caveats, we turn to some of the research findings concerning the effects of in-store stimuli on consumer affect, cognition, and behavior. Five areas are discussed: the effects of signs and price information, color, shelf space and displays, music, and scent.

Signs and Price Information   In-store signs are useful for directing consumers to particular merchandise and for offering product benefit and price information. Gary McKinnon et al. conducted an experiment that investigated the use of signs, the type of message included on the sign (price-only or product benefit statements), and the effects of including a regular versus a sale price on the sign.[4] The six products studied were bath towels, pantyhose,

Highlight 19.2

Can Store Design Influence Consumer Behavior?

"Retailers can have absolute control over the response of their customers," maintains Joseph Weishar, author of *Design for Effective Selling Space.* Shoppers move in predictable patterns, he says. They respond predictably to light and color stimuli. The right store design can turn a browser into a buyer. "If you can get the customers to see what you want them to see, they will probably buy what you want to sell them."

More and more retailers are buying his theory. Renovation, remodeling, and attention to store design are on the rise. A survey of retailers by the International Mass Retail Association found that 60 percent were boosting plans for renovating stores and building stores based on new designs. Among full-price specialty stores, 80 percent had hired store-design consultants.

Sears is spending $4 billion to upgrade its stores, and Kmart is spending $2.3 billion for store improvement. J.C. Penney has been spending more than $500 million a year on redesigning its stores. Benetton is redoing its 200 U.S. locations, spending up to $400,000 per store.

Cosmetic changes? Not at all. According to Weishar, there is a science to store design. For example, did you know, as store designers do, that customers walk into a store and turn right 80 percent of the time? Whatever you encounter to the right of the entrance is what the retailer most wants you to buy that day. Did you know that wide aisles will persuade you to pay higher prices and that fluorescent lights flash the words "good value" through your brain?

Weishar cites luxury retailer Bergdorf Goodman as an example of his wide-aisles-equal-high-prices theory. "Bergdorf Goodman has less merchandise per cubic foot than any large specialty store in New York, yet it reports one of the highest sales per square foot in the country—as high as $2,000 per square foot," he says. The spacious look ignites thoughts of exclusivity and helps persuade customers to buy the high-priced goods, he says.

Other high-profile success stories include The Gap and Disney stores. "The Gap has designed a perfect store for its merchandise," he says. The table at the front of the store is angled so that it appears as a diamond shape. That is intentional. The angle guides the customer to the right, straight into a collection of newly arrived, full-priced clothing.

Disney stores are designed to communicate the fun and excitement of the theme parks and famous characters, creators say. They also have another purpose: to get customers to walk to the back wall. That's the goal of every boutique and department, says Weishar. Chances are good that when you get to the wall, you won't walk back out along the route you came in on. And if you go back by another route you'll pass by more merchandise. Disney stores run a huge video screen at the back of every store. The full-screen animation with familiar songs lures customers back—often dragged by their kids. By the time you walk all the way in and all the way out, your chances of avoiding a purchase are slim. A Disney store does three times the business of its average mall competition.

Sources: Based on Ellen Neuborne, "Stores Say Remodeling Boosts Sales," *USA Today,* April 19, 1993, pp. 1B, 2B. Copyright 1993. Reprinted with permission. Also see Julie Baker, A. Parasuraman, Dhruv Grewal, and Glenn B. Voss, "The Influence of Multiple Store Environment Cues on Perceived Merchandise Value and Patronage Intentions," *Journal of Marketing,* April 2002, pp. 120–141.

women's slacks, men's dress slacks, men's jeans, and men's shirts. All six products were studied in varying conditions over a three-week period in three department stores. Based on statistical analysis of sales differences, the following conclusions were drawn:

1. Price influences sales more than sign type does.

2. At regular prices, the addition of a price sign will not increase sales, but when the item is on sale, a price sign will increase sales.

3. Benefit signs increase sales at both regular and sale prices, but at a greater rate when the item is on sale.

4. A benefit sign is more effective than a price-only sign at both a regular and a sale price.

Overall, these results suggest that at regular prices, a benefit sign should be the only type of sign used, whereas at a sale price, both a price-only and a benefit sign will increase sales over a no-sign condition, with a benefit sign being the most effective. Thus, these results support the idea that signs affect consumer cognition (consumers apparently processed different sign information) and consumer behavior (sales increased with the use of certain types of signs).

Color   Color has been shown to have a variety of physical and psychological effects on both humans and animals. Joseph Bellizzi et al. examined the effects of color on consumer perceptions of retail store environments in a laboratory experiment.[5] While noting the limitations of their study, the authors concluded that color can have customer drawing power as well as image-creating potential. An interesting finding was that consumers were drawn to warm colors (red and yellow) but felt that warm-color environments were generally unpleasant; cool colors (blue and green) did not draw consumers but were rated as pleasant. The authors offered the following summary of the implication of their work for store design:

> Warm-color environments are appropriate for store windows and entrances, as well as for buying situations associated with unplanned impulse purchases. Cool colors may be appropriate where customer deliberations over the purchase decision are necessary. Warm, tense colors in situations where deliberations are common may make shopping unpleasant for consumers and may result in premature termination of the shopping trip. On the other hand, warm colors may produce a quick decision to purchase in cases where lengthy deliberations are not necessary and impulse purchases are common.[6]

Plentiful shelf space and in-store displays can increase sales   *Steve Niedorf.*

Shelf Space and Displays   Research generally supports the idea that more shelf space and in-store displays increase sales. In a portion of a larger study, J. B. Wilkinson et al. examined the impact of these two variables on sales of four grocery products in an in-store experiment.[7] Comparisons were made between normal display (regular shelf space), expanded display (double the regular shelf space allocation), and special display (regular shelf space plus special end-of-aisle or within-aisle product arrangement).

Although the percentage increases varied by product, as would be expected, both expanded and special displays consistently increased sales for all of the products. Further, special displays consistently outperformed expanded shelf spaces. These results support the idea that the presentation of merchandise in the store has an important impact on consumer behavior.

The study also found that in-store price reductions influenced sales, but newspaper advertising was not a strong short-term strategy variable for three of the four products. This supports the idea that in-store stimuli have very important effects on consumer behavior—and, in this case, are more important than out-of-store advertising.

Music   Considerable research supports the idea that music played in the background while other activities are being performed influences attitudes and behavior. Music is played in many retail stores, but relatively little basic research has been conducted on its effects on consumer behavior. Ronald Milliman examined the effects of one aspect of music—tempo—on the behavior of supermarket shoppers.[8] Three treatments were used: no music, slow music, and fast music. The basic hypotheses investigated were that these treatments would differentially affect (1) the pace of in-store traffic flow of supermarket shoppers, (2) the daily gross volume of customer purchases, and (3) the number of shoppers expressing an awareness of the background music after they left the store.

The findings supported the idea that the tempo of background music influences consumer behavior. The pace of in-store traffic flow was slowest under the slow-tempo treatment and fastest under the fast-tempo treatment. Further, the slow-tempo musical selections led to higher sales volumes, because consumers spent more time and money under this condition. On average, sales were 38.2 percent greater under the slow-tempo condition than under the fast-tempo condition. Interestingly, when questioned after shopping, consumers showed little awareness of the music that had been playing in the supermarket. Thus, it seems likely that music influenced behavior without consumers being totally conscious of it. In terms of marketing strategy, the author suggests:

> It is possible to influence behavior with music, but this influence can either contribute to the process of achieving business objectives or interfere with it. . . . Certainly, in some retailing situations, the objective may be to slow customer movement, keeping people in the store for as long as possible in an attempt to encourage them to purchase more. However, in other situations, the objective may be the opposite, that is, to move customers along as a way of increasing sales volume. A restaurant, for instance, will most likely want to speed people up, especially during lunch, when the objective is to maximize the "number of seats turned" in a very short period of time, normally about two hours or less. Playing slow-tempo music in a restaurant might result in fewer seats turned and lower profit, although it could encourage return visits if customers preferred a relaxed luncheon atmosphere. Again, the point is that the music chosen must match the objectives of the business and the specific market situation.[9]

Scent   Scents in stores can influence consumer affect, cognition, and behavior. For example, the smell of particular products, such as leather goods, perfume, chocolate, coffee, or flowers, can attract consumers to come into contact with and purchase these products. In addition, *ambient scent*—scent that is not emanating from a particular product but is present in the store environment—can influence store and product evaluations and shopping behavior.[10] Ambient scent can influence feelings about stores and their products, including products that are difficult to scent such as office supplies and furniture. Scents vary in terms of how pleasant they are perceived to be, how likely they are to evoke physiological responses, and how strong they are. Neutral and pleasant scent categories, such as florals, spices, woods, citrus, and mints, can be diffused in a store to influence consumers.

A study by Eric Spangenberg et al. found that in a simulated store environment, lavender, ginger, spearmint, and orange scents had greater influence on the evaluations of both the store and its products and on shopping behaviors than a no-scent environment. The differences were observed even though no other changes occurred in the environment and none of the participants mentioned the presence of a scent. The authors recommend that marketers use distinctive scents in their stores to differentiate them from competitors. In addition, stores should be scented so that the odor is not specific to any single product category. Finally, the authors point out that because many commercially available scenting oils are prohibitively expensive, marketers could use less costly scents that can be spread by a diffuser or through the heating and ventilation system.

Nonstore Consumer Behavior

As noted, more than 90 percent of all consumer purchases are from retail stores. However, consumers shop for and purchase products in a variety of other ways. These include catalogs and direct mail, vending machines, direct sales purchases, TV home shopping, and electronic exchanges, such as purchasing on the Internet.[11] Exhibit 19.5 illustrates the relative sales from each of these venues. Although catalogs and vending machines dominate consumer purchases, other methods, such as electronic exchanges, are expected to grow dramatically in the near future. We refer to the method a consumer uses to shop and purchase from store or nonstore alternatives as the **consumer purchase mode.**

Choices made among the various consumer purchase modes are influenced by many factors. Each may involve different environmental influences and different amounts and types of cognition, affect, and behavior. Brick-and-mortar stores have dominated consumer purchases because they allow consumers to shop efficiently, compare product offerings, and experience them directly. They also create in-store affect and often have lower prices. However, each of the other purchase mode alternatives has advantages in some situations. We will briefly discuss each nonstore purchase mode and compare them with store consumer behavior.

Catalog and Direct Mail Purchases

Most consumers are familiar with catalogs and other direct mail letters and brochures sent to their homes to present merchandise and solicit orders. With the increase in dual-income families and consumers' general need to save time, catalogs and direct mail have grown dramatically. In addition to enjoying convenient

Exhibit 19.5

Annual Purchases from Nonstore Modes

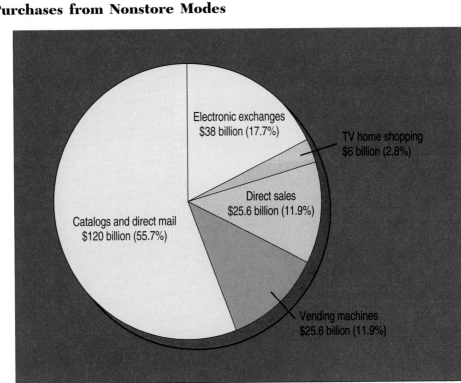

Electronic exchanges
$38 billion (17.7%)

TV home shopping
$6 billion (2.8%)

Direct sales
$25.6 billion (11.9%)

Catalogs and direct mail
$120 billion (55.7%)

Vending machines
$25.6 billion (11.9%)

Source: Adapted from Michael Levy and Barton A. Weitz, *Retailing Management,* 5th ed. (Burr Ridge, IL: McGraw-Hill/Irwin. 2004), pp. 57–62. Reproduced with permission from The McGraw-Hill Companies.

Online purchasing continues to grow
David Young-Wolff/PhotoEdit, Inc.

in-home shopping, many consumers like browsing through catalogs searching for unique items. For example, the Willis & Geiger catalog offered a Resistance Movement Portable Landing Strip complete with obstacle lights, combat heads, mast adapters, buy clamps, strapping, lamps, stakes, tools, and bulletins and manuals, which is identical to the kits used in World War II. Catalogs can also offer more complete product assortments. For example, Bass Pro Shop catalogs have perhaps the best selection of fishing equipment in the world.

Catalogs, however, have some disadvantages for consumers. First, catalog prices are often higher than prices for comparable products in stores and consumers have to pay shipping charges, which increase the dollar price. Second, although catalogs can describe and provide pictures of merchandise, this does not allow consumers to experience the feel, fit, or other sensory stimuli directly. Third, although consumers save shopping time using catalogs, they must wait for

Vending machines provide convenience for consumers
Owen Franken/Stock, Boston, LLC.

merchandise until it is shipped and received. When purchasing in stores, consumers can usually receive products and use them immediately. Finally, if a catalog purchase is made and found to be unsatisfactory, consumers usually must repackage the product and ship it back, often at their own expense. However, some catalog companies have tried to minimize this problem by having representatives pick up return merchandise from consumers' homes. Levenger, which sells pens, desks, and other "tools for serious readers," sends consumers a postage-paid label to return unwanted merchandise to reduce the risk of purchasing from the catalog.

Vending Machine Purchases

Most vending machine purchases made by consumers are for hot and cold beverages, food, and candy. Vending machine sales have experienced little growth in recent years, and merchandise selling for more than $1 has not sold well from them. Not all vending machines take dollar bills, or accept credit cards. The primary advantage of vending machines is that they provide merchandise in convenient locations and are often available for purchases 24 hours a day. However, products in vending machines typically are priced higher than the same merchandise in a store. Also, when vending machines fail to deliver the merchandise, consumers often cannot recover their money. Thus, consumers typically use vending machines rather than stores for occasional purchases of convenience goods.

Television Home Shopping

Television home shopping includes cable channels dedicated to shopping, infomercials, and direct-response advertising shown on cable and broadcast networks. Although 60 million Americans have access to a television shopping channel network, only about 20 percent watch it. The Home Shopping Network and QVC are the leaders in this market. Consumers who purchase using this mode buy primarily inexpensive jewelry, apparel, cosmetics, and exercise equipment. This purchase mode allows consumers to purchase conveniently from their homes by telephone and can offer and demonstrate products. It also allows better visual display than catalogs. However, it has several weaknesses for consumers. First, consumers must be watching the channel when the merchandise is offered; if they are not, they have no way to know or find what was offered. Second, consumers must pay shipping charges and thus have the same problem as with catalog purchases if the merchandise is unsatisfactory. Third, although the visual display may be better than a still picture, it is less informative than experiencing products directly in stores. It is not surprising that attempts to sell upscale merchandise using this approach have not been successful.

Jewelry is a good seller on TV home-shopping networks
David Young-Wolff/PhotoEdit, Inc.

Direct Sales Purchases

Consumers make direct sales purchases in their homes or at work from salespeople in a face-to-face or telephone transaction. The most common products purchased this way are cosmetics, fragrances, decorative accessories, vacuum cleaners, home appliances, cooking utensils and kitchenware, jewelry, food and nutritional products, and encyclopedias and educational materials. Consumers can benefit from direct sales purchases because salespeople can provide in-depth product usage information. For example, Avon salespeople can demonstrate the various uses and shades of cosmetics and match them to the consumer's complexion and facial features. Tupperware salespeople can show how to use various storage containers and kitchen gadgets. Thus, direct sales purchases benefit consumers when buying products that need demonstration. However, direct sales merchandise is often higher priced than similar merchandise in stores. Also, consumers often must spend a good deal of time watching the demonstration and discussing products. Finally, consumers sometimes feel pressured by overzealous salespeople to purchase products they don't really need.

Electronic Exchanges

Electronic exchanges involve consumers in collecting information, shopping, and purchasing from websites on the Internet. It is the fastest-growing purchase mode. Many companies are unsure of when electronic commerce will blossom but want to be on the Internet with an effective website when it does. More will be said about electronic exchanges later in this chapter. Highlight 19.3 offers recommendations for developing effective commercial websites.

A Comparison of Consumer Purchase Modes

Exhibit 19.6 presents a comparison of six consumer purchase modes that can partially account for the relative use of each. Stores dominate consumer purchases because they offer the deepest and widest product assortment. In addition, they offer the greatest potential for fun and status. For example, many consumers enjoy shopping in stores on some occasions, and purchasing from stores like Nordstrom or even The Gap offers additional psychological and social benefits. Stores also have the broadest range of prices for most types of merchandise, offering this purchase mode a selection advantage over nonstore modes. Thus, even though purchasing from stores may take more shopping effort and time in some cases, it continues to dominate consumer retail purchasing.

Catalogs offer consumers the convenience of shopping from home or work and offer some products and brands not available in stores. Also, some catalogs, such as Orvis, L. L. Bean, and Lands' End, have established strong reputations with consumers for providing quality merchandise. However, many products are not available in catalogs.

Vending machines are highly limited in the products offered but provide consumers with time and place utility for convenience goods. Direct sales offer consumers only a limited number of products, although some are highly respected, such as Tupperware storage containers and Avon cosmetics. However, such purchases often require a good deal of consumers' time, and goods of similar quality are available at lower prices from stores.

Highlight 19.3

Recommendations for Developing Successful Commercial Websites

Because electronic commerce is expected to grow dramatically, many companies are spending heavily to develop effective websites. In one study, 32 percent of the companies polled were spending from $500,000 to more than $5 million to create a commerce-based website. Like most marketing strategies, designing successful websites requires careful analysis of consumers. Below are five recommendations for designing websites that consumers will be able to use efficiently and effectively:

"1. Make sure your site has contact information that is accurate and complete. Many websites lack basics such as postal address, phone and fax numbers, and e-mail addresses. Don't hide this stuff five levels deep in a back corner; make it easy to find.

2. Don't make factual information, such as product updates and prices, hard to come by. Make someone who isn't the Webmaster responsible for keeping track of this information and keeping it up to date.

3. Make sure users can find you with straightforward keywords. Make it simple to find your site via the various search engines. Next, improve searching on the site itself. Make sure you think about these issues: How good is the search function, and how many screens does it take to get to it? Are there any instructions on how to enter multiple keywords near the big search button? Can particular areas of the site be restricted, such as the press area or by the date of a document?

4. Make it just as easy for users to exit your site as it is for them to find it and use it. Can someone get back out of the site the way he or she came in—using the browser navigation features (history of back buttons)? Can the user move from one section of a site to another without having to go back to the home page? The layout and design of your site should be fairly obvious to viewers, no matter where they land inside.

5. Create a good table of contents and index. Website designers need to realize that not everyone is going to start at the front door and proceed in an orderly fashion through the site. Most users want to get in, grab a few pages (probably print them out), and then get out. That means you should keep the number of screens and subscreens for contents and site organization down to the bare minimum. And put links both to the table of contents and to an index on your front page, so that visitors can find them quickly.

A good place to read more about usability is the Alertbox, written by Jakob Nielsen of SunSoff (**www.useit.com/alertbox**), or *Understanding Electronic Commerce* by David Kosiur, available through **www.Amazon.com**."

Sources: Adapted from Mark Halper, "So Does Your Web Site Pay?" *Forbes ASAP*, August 25, 1997, pp. 117–118; All text in quotation marks from Davi Strom, "Five Steps for Site Success," *Forbes ASAP*, August 25, 1997, p. 118. Reprinted by permission of FORBES ASAP Magazine © 2003 Forbes Inc.

The growth potential for sales from TV home shopping and electronic exchanges will likely increase as these modes become more interactive. In fact, several experts have argued for interactive home shopping systems that have the following characteristics:

1. Faithful reproduction of descriptive and experiential product information.

2. A greatly expanded universe of offerings relative to what can be accessed now through local or catalog shopping.

3. An efficient means of screening the offerings to find the most appealing options for more detailed consideration.

Exhibit 19.6

A Comparison of Six Consumer Purchase Modes

Criteria	Stores	Catalogs/ Direct Mail	Vending Mechines	Direct Sales	TV Home Shopping	Electronic Exchange
Types of products available	All types	Shopping Specialty	Convenience	Shopping Specialty	Shopping Specialty	All types
Number of products and brands available	Almost all	Some	Few	Few	Few	Many
Potential for status for purchasing from this mode	High	High	None	Moderate	Low	Moderate
Potential for fun	High	Some	Low	Moderate	Low	Moderate
Price level	Mixed	Mixed	High	High	High	Low/mixed
Additional shipping/delivery charges	Seldom	Usually	No	Often	Usually	Usually
Return effort	Little	Some	NA	Some	Some	Some
Purchase time required	Moderate	Low	Low	High	Low	Low
Shopping effort	High	Low	Low	Moderate	Low	Low
Wait for delivery	Seldom	Yes	No	Usually	Yes	Yes

4. Unimpeded search across stores and brands.

5. Memory for past selections that simplifies information search and purchase decisions.[12]

Although such systems are not currently available, they clearly could offer consumers greater convenience and selection than many other purchase modes.

A new purchase mode for tickets *David Young-Wolff/PhotoEdit, Inc.*

Catalogs offer consumers a number of benefits. This is why they are the second largest consumer purchase mode   *Rhoda Sidney/Stock, Boston, LLC.*

Electronic Commerce

Electronic commerce, or e-commerce, is the process by which buyers and sellers conduct exchanges of information, money, and merchandise by electronic means, primarily on the Internet. Electronic commerce has many advantages for marketers, since large amounts of product information and large assortments of products can be transmitted efficiently to people throughout the world. However, unlike with traditional marketing, where marketers can put information and products into consumer environments, electronic commerce often requires consumers to seek out marketers by going to particular websites. While e-marketers can advertise in traditional media as well as on the Internet, many do not and count on consumers to find them. This is unlike traditional marketers that regularly put stores and advertising in consumers' environments to influence their behavior. Even if consumers go to a marketer's website, they commonly collect information but do not actually buy anything.

Consumer Strategies for Electronic and Store Exchanges

For most products, consumers can use both electronic exchanges and traditional stores for shopping and purchasing. As Exhibit 19.7 shows, there are four strategies consumers can use to make exchanges involving these two purchase modes. First, consumers can both shop and purchase electronically, making a pure electronic exchange. For example, suppose a consumer is looking for books to read on the beach and decides simply to go online and order a novel. She starts with amazon.com and checks through the bestsellers and recommendations, and then goes to barnesandnoble.com and does the same. She notes that *The Da Vinci Code* by Dan Brown is on its bestseller list. She then checks booksamillion.com, powells.com, and 1bookstreet.com. She finds that amazon.com has the lowest price on Brown's book, orders it and several others, and uses the one-click shopping option to pay for them and the $3.00 plus $.99-per-book shipping charge

Exhibit 19.7

Point-and-Click and Brick-and-Mortar Consumer Strategies

		Shopping	
		Online	In-store
Purchasing	Online	Electronic Exchange	Store-aided Electronic Exchange
	In-store	Web-aided Store Exchange	Traditional Exchange

with her Mastercard. In this case, the entire shopping and purchasing sequence is done electronically. For some products, such as books, CDs, and computers, electronic exchanges such as this are common among computer-savvy consumers.

A second strategy consumers can use is the store-aided electronic exchange. In this case, consumers shop at stores first to examine and experience products. After deciding which product they want to buy, they go home to their computers and purchase the product online. For example, suppose a consumer is going on a camping trip and wants to buy a knife for cutting kindling, vegetables, and other camp chores. He stops by a local sporting goods store and examines a number of different options, discussing their attributes with a knowledgeable salesperson. He decides that the Gil Hibbon Kempo II is the ideal knife for his needs. However, he doesn't like the $119 price and leaves the store. At home, he goes online and checks out a number of knife outlets such as 4bestblades.com, discountknivesonline.com, and knifecastle.com. He finds the knife is cheapest at onestopknifeshop.com at $79.95 and orders one. For some specialty items for which consumers have limited information and want to examine products before seeking the best deal, this strategy is effective. However, critics argue that collecting information from the store is a form of freeloading since the store gets nothing for providing information to consumers who buy the product elsewhere.

A third strategy consumers can use involves collecting information online and then going to a brick-and-mortar store or dealer to make a purchase. Consumers can collect information about products on the Web from manufacturers, dealers, and rating services. They can do comparison shopping at sites like consumerreports.org, dealtime.com, deja.com, and productopia.com. Consumers can research automobiles on the Web, including dealer cost and price data, and then go to the dealership and bargain for a low price. A consumer can get such information from Edmunds.com or Autobytel.com. This is a major use of the Internet by consumers and has lowered the average markup for car dealers.

Finally, consumers can shop and purchase in stores without using the Internet at all. This is the most common strategy for most purchases. While electronic exchanges are increasing, they likely will not soon become the leading purchase mode for most products. To understand why, let's evaluate electronic exchanges from the consumer's viewpoint.

Exhibit 19.8

Evaluation of Electronic Commerce from Consumers' Point of View

Product Advantages

- Increased product and brand selection

- Increased product and brand availability

Promotion Advantages

- Increased information about products and brands from manufacturers and dealers
- Increased information about products and brands from independent agencies

Price Advantages

- Increased opportunity to get lower prices for many products and brands
- Increased cost and price information for many products and brands

Channel Advantages

- Increased dealer selection
- Convenience of shopping from home or office

Product Disadvantages

- Uncertainty about quality of some products and brands
- Inability to experience product before purchase

Promotion Disadvantages

- Information overload from too much readily available data or unwanted online ads
- Time and effort costs to access information

Price Disadvantages

- Shipping costs and costs of returning unacceptable merchandise may increase price
- Credit card and other personal information perceived to be at risk

Channel Disadvantages

- Time cost in waiting for delivery
- Hassles' in returning unacceptable merchandise

Electronic Exchanges from the Consumer Side

Exhibit 19.8 compares some of the advantages and disadvantges of electronic exchanges from the consumer's point of view. Certainly the consumer realizes some advantages when shopping and purchasing on the Internet rather than in brick-and-mortar stores. Compared to local brick-and-mortar stores, the many virtual stores offer a greater variety of products, brands, and dealers from which to choose and abundant information that can be accessed from home or office. Products that are out of stock in stores or at some websites are likely to be available at other websites. Electronic exchanges offer many consumers, such as elderly or disabled people, the ability to shop and purchase if they are unable to do so by traditional means. Comparing products on the Internet is usually easier than going to a variety of stores to do so.

Many analysts predicted that electronic exchanges would rapidly take a large share of consumer spending. However, while electronic exchanges have been growing, they still remain a relatively small part of consumer purchasing. Many dot-com businesses have failed, for several likely reasons. Problems with electronic exchanges for consumers include uncertainty about product quality and the inability to experience products prior to purchasing and receiving them. Of course, for companies selling well-known and well-trusted brands, these problems can be overcome since many consumers already have strong beliefs about the brand's quality and considerable brand knowledge. A second problem is the amount of information available on the Internet and the time and effort necessary to access it. Surely, for skilled computer users, this is not the barrier that it is for most consumers. However, the time and effort it takes to find and work through a variety of websites collecting and comparing information and making purchases can be considerable for the average consumer, particularly if the computer used is slow or the websites are difficult to navigate.

It is also not clear whether consumers get the lowest prices by shopping on the Web when shipping costs and return costs are considered. Many traditional brick-and-mortar stores have prices competitive with electronic retailers when these other costs are included. While sites that encrypt consumer credit card numbers and other consumer information are mostly safe, many consumers still fear identity theft by hackers in cyberspace. Finally, many consumers enjoy obtaining products immediately upon purchase and do not want to wait for delivery. This makes Web-based purchases less attractive for this group.

The Future of Consumer Electronic Exchanges

Electronic exchanges by consumers will continue to grow rapidly. However, several factors may limit consumer electronic purchases from equaling or overtaking traditional brick-and-mortar stores in the near future.

1. *Many consumers do not have access to computers or are not savvy enough to perform electronic exchanges effectively.* While a large percent of U.S. households have personal computers,[13] not all can use them efficiently for electronic exchanges. However, as younger consumers with high levels of computer-surfing skills become older and more affluent, electronic exchanges are likely to grow. Globally, while a few countries have higher personal computer market penetration than the United States, most do not. Thus, many global consumers do not have access to electronic exchanges, limiting the growth of this purchase mode.

2. Since lower prices are a major attraction of electronic exchanges, many *e-marketers do not make enough profit to reinvest in growing consumer markets*. Comparing the cost structure of a brick-and-mortar superstore with an online store, for an average sale of $100, the superstore has an operating profit of $12.50 and the online store has an operating loss of $1.24.[14] In addition, price is not the only variable consumers consider when making purchases and, for many, electronic exchanges are less convenient and offer less value than traditional purchases.

3. *Making electronic exchanges requires consumers to change long-standing ways of buying.* Most consumers grew up buying the majority of their products and services from stores, vending machines, and occasionally catalogs. They have well-established methods of meeting their consumption needs and may have considerable resistance to change. In addition, for many purchases, consumers enjoy shopping in stores and malls.

4. *Many consumer products do not fit an electronic exchange format.* Perishable products, products that are wanted immediately, and low-cost convenience goods are not likely to be sold effectively on the Web given current technology. While companies like Peapod can bundle assortments of convenience goods and sell to households too busy to shop in stores, many such companies have yet to find a way to do so profitably. While consumers can purchase cars and trucks on the

Internet, most still go to local dealers for test drives and purchase there in most cases. Auto manufacturers are not likely to sell directly to consumers at lower prices, since they have long-standing contractual relationships with their dealers and need the dealers for sales help and service.

5. *Many consumers trust brick-and-mortar stores where they have shopped and purchased for many years more than Web-based companies that haven't been around as long.* Consumers who have purchased in particular stores and chains and have been satisfied with the exchanges may find little reason to change their purchase mode. In addition, long-established brick-and-mortar stores likely have an advantage when they go online over newer, electronic-commerce-only companies. For example, stores with websites such as Wal-Mart, JCPenney, and Cabela's may have store equity that transfers when consumers decide to purchase online.

In sum, while electronic commerce has not met the growth expectations of many marketers, it is an established alternative to traditional stores for some products and services. In addition, the vast information available on the Web offers consumers the opportunity to be the best informed in history.

Channel Strategy

Marketing managers have many decisions to make when designing effective channels to serve consumers. For example, decisions must be made whether to market directly to the consumer through company-owned or franchised stores or indirectly through combinations of intermediaries such as independent retailers, wholesalers, and agents. Decisions must be made whether to use store retailing, nonstore retailing, or some combination of the two. Decisions must be made about plant and warehouse locations, how products will be delivered to consumers, and who will perform what marketing functions within the channel.

In some cases, manufacturers market products in their own stores. For example, Sherwin-Williams, a paint company, owns and operates its own retail outlets, and Hart, Shaffner & Marx, a clothing manufacturer, operates its own specialty clothing stores. However, most manufacturers sell through independent retailers and retail chains.

Selling through independent retailers can lead to a conflict in objectives for the two types of marketing institutions. That is, although *manufacturers* are concerned with developing consumer brand loyalty (commitment to and repeated purchase of their brands), *retailers* are concerned with developing consumer store loyalty (commitment to and repeated patronage of their stores). For instance, retailers may not be highly concerned with which brand of coffee the consumer buys, as long as it is purchased in their particular stores. This situation has led many manufacturers to put a large portion of their marketing budgets into trade promotions directed at retailers (e.g., 1 case free for every 10 purchased by the retailer). Trade promotions may influence retailers to put up special displays, give more shelf space to a brand, offer lower prices to consumers, and sponsor local advertising of the brand for the manufacturer.

Our discussion highlights the fact that different members of a distribution channel may be concerned primarily with influencing different consumer behaviors. This is an important point; the role of retail management is often overlooked in discussions of marketing and consumer behavior. Retailers affect consumers most directly, and perhaps most influentially, for many types of products and most services. As a result, in this part of the chapter we view channel strategy from the manufacturer's

Exhibit 19.9

Channel Design Criteria

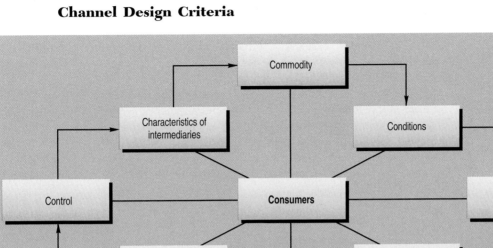

perspective and consider criteria for selecting channel members, particularly retailers.

As with the other elements of the marketing mix, the starting point for designing effective channels is an analysis of consumer–product relationships. At least six basic questions must be considered:

1. What is the potential annual market demand? That is, given a particular marketing strategy, how many consumers are likely to purchase the product, and how often?
2. What is the long-run growth potential of the market?
3. What is the geographic dispersion of the market?
4. What are the most promising geographic markets to enter?
5. Where and how do consumers purchase this and similar types of products?
6. What is the likely impact of a particular channel system on consumers? That is, will the system influence consumer affect, cognition, and behavior sufficiently to achieve marketing objectives?

Although these questions emphasize that consumers are the focal point in channel design, the answers require an analysis of a variety of other factors. As suggested in Exhibit 19.9, these factors must be analyzed both in terms of their relationships with and impact on the consumer and in terms of their relationships with the other variables. We briefly discuss each of these factors, starting with commodity.

Commodity

By *commodity* we mean the nature of the product or service offered to the consumer. Different products and services vary in their tangibility, perishability, bulkiness, degree of standardization, amount of service required, and unit value. These factors influence whether it is effective to market the commodity directly to consumers (as with hairstyling services) or indirectly through a number of intermediaries (as with designer jeans).

Key consumer-related questions in considering the nature of the product or service are (1) what consequences or values the product or service provides the target market, (2) how much time and effort target-market consumers are willing to expend to shop for, locate, and purchase the product, and (3) how often target-market consumers purchase the product. Thus, it is the *relationships* among consumers, the commodity, and the channel that are critical rather than analysis of these factors in isolation.

Conditions

Conditions refer to the current state of and expected changes in the economic, social, political, and legal environments in which the firm operates. This information is critical in channel design because channels typically involve long-term commitments by the firm that may be difficult to change. For example, one major problem that led to the dramatic loss of market share and consolidation of A&P supermarkets was that A&P had long-term leases for many small stores in inner cities. Consumers were moving to the suburbs and purchasing in the larger, well-stocked, conveniently located suburban stores of competitors. Thus, situational analysis of the macroenvironment is critical in channel design to allow response to potential problems and to exploit opportunities.

Competition

The size, financial and marketing strengths, and market share of a firm's competitors are major concerns in designing effective marketing strategies. For channel decisions, a key issue is how major competitors distribute products and how their distribution system influences consumers. In some cases, emulating the channels of major competitors in the industry is the only feasible alternative. For example, many convenience goods require intensive distribution to all available retailers.

In other cases, a competitive advantage can be obtained by selecting nontraditional channels. For example, one reason for the success of companies such as Mary Kay Cosmetics and Tupperware is that they sell their products in homes rather than in traditional retail outlets.

Costs

Although channel strategies seek to provide form, time, place, and possession utilities to influence consumer affect, cognition, and behavior, these strategies are constrained by the cost of distribution. In general, a basic goal is to design a distribution system that facilitates exchanges between the firm and consumers, but does so in a cost-efficient manner. Distribution costs include transportation, order processing, cost of lost business, inventory carrying costs, and materials handling. Thus, costs can be viewed as a constraint on the firm's ability to distribute products and services and to serve and influence consumers. In general, firms seek distribution systems that minimize total distribution costs at a particular level of customer service.

Coverage

The term *coverage* has two separate meanings in channel strategy. First is the idea that seldom can every member of a selected target market receive sufficient marketing coverage to bring about an exchange. Because of cost considerations, even major consumer goods companies often cannot afford to distribute their products in outlets that do not serve a relatively large population.

Second, coverage refers to the number of outlets in a particular geographic area in which the product or service will be sold. Distribution coverage can be viewed along a continuum ranging from intensive through selective to exclusive distribution. Intensive distribution involves marketing the product in as many outlets as available, selective distribution entails a more limited number, and exclusive distribution involves only one outlet in an area.

Competence

A frequently overlooked criterion in designing channels is the firm's *competence* to administer the channels and to perform channel tasks at all levels to ensure effective distribution to the consumer. Both financial strength and marketing skills are crucial, but many production-oriented firms seriously underestimate the importance of marketing and overestimate their marketing abilities. Further, many manufacturers do not have a sufficiently large product line to develop their own retail stores. These firms opt for intermediaries such as Sears. Finally, marketing skills effective for one market are not always transferable to other markets. For example, many global marketing efforts have failed because firms did not adapt their products and marketing strategies to foreign markets.

Critics of marketing frequently point out that marketing intermediaries increase the cost of products because the profits these wholesalers and retailers make add to the cost of the product to the consumer. These critics generally do not understand that intermediaries are used because they can perform some marketing functions more efficiently and cheaply than the manufacturer can.

Control

An important managerial criterion in designing channels is the *degree of control* desired for effective marketing of the product to the consumer. In general, there is greater control in direct channels because no intermediaries are involved. Franchised channels also involve greater control than indirect channels because the franchiser typically places strong contractual constraints on the franchisee's operations. This control is quite important in delivering the major benefit of franchises to the consumer (i.e., standardized products and services).

Characteristics of Intermediaries

A final but extremely important consideration in designing channels concerns the characteristics of the intermediaries that are available and willing to handle the manufacturer's product. If no acceptable intermediaries are available, the firm must either market directly, encourage the development of intermediaries, or forgo entering a particular market.

In addition to such factors as the size, financial strength, and marketing skills of intermediaries, *consumer perceptions* of intermediaries can be crucial in channel strategy. For example, many consumers view discount stores as places to purchase good-quality merchandise but not necessarily prestige items. Manufacturers of prestige products (such as Polo shirts by Ralph Lauren) may lower the image of their products by selling them in discount stores. Thus, manufacturers (and retailers) must consider the consumer–store relationships: the relationships among the store environment, consumer affect and cognition, and consumer behavior.

Back To...

IBM

This classic case demonstrates a number of points raised in this chapter and provides evidence for some of them. First, IBM is an effective producer and marketer of computers when selling door to door in the industrial market as well as when selling through independent retailers. However, these marketing skills clearly did not transfer when the firm began selling in its own retail stores. Consider IBM's store image. Consumers initially had a very positive image, but this image changed—in the wrong direction for IBM. Also, consider IBM's mistakes in the selection of a red decor, in-store merchandising, and salespeople inexperienced in retail sales.

This case is also a good example of management changing an environment based on consumer affect, cognition, and behavior. Because the original strategy resulted in a poor store image and store atmosphere, and with store contact, product contact, and transactions at unsatisfactory levels, IBM changed the store environment.

For one thing, salespeople started to receive formal training to deal more effectively with customers. A point-of-sales computer system was installed, and a less forbidding store design with cozier colors, point-of-sale promotions, and the look of a place where you can "get a deal" were implemented.

However, the stores still avoided price cutting and "bundling"—mixing and matching computer components to make up specially priced packages. IBM's emphasis on service rather than on price and bundling led one retail competitor to remark that the Product Centers were "a delight to compete with."

Although IBM no longer sells directly to consumers, it is still a major player in the market. To learn more about it, visit the IBM website at **www.ibm.com**. ❖

Summary   This chapter presented an overview of consumer behavior and channel strategy. Initially we focused on consumer store-related affect and cognition, behavior, and environmental factors. The two most critical store-related affect and cognitions for channel strategy are store image and store atmosphere. The store-related behaviors discussed in this chapter included store contact and store loyalty, both of which are primary objectives of retail channel strategy. Our examination of store environment emphasized store location, store layout, and in-store stimuli. Then we discussed a variety of consumer purchase modes, with emphasis on nonstore modes. Electronic commerce was evaluated from a consumer point of view. While it has many advantages for consumers, its major use has been to collect information about products rather than make purchases. Finally, we delineated several criteria relevant for designing effective channels, emphasizing that it is the consumer and the relationships the consumer has with the other criteria that determine appropriate channel strategy.

Key Terms and Concepts

consumer purchase mode   **496**
form utility   **482**
free-form layout   **491**
grid layout   **490**
place utility   **483**
possession utility   **483**

store atmosphere   **485**
store image   **484**
store layout   **487**
store location   **488**
store loyalty   **490**
time utility   **482**

Review and Discussion Questions

1. Offer examples of situations in which you have experienced each of the four types of approach or avoidance responses to retail store environments.
2. Relate the concept of shaping to the store contact and store loyalty concerns in this chapter. Make a series of strategy recommendations to achieve the desired ends.
3. Why do many retailers put impulse goods near the front of the store?
4. Research suggests many consumers make more than 80 percent of their grocery purchase decisions while in the store. What do you think are the most important in-store influences on these purchases? (Examples such as cookies, chips, apples, or frozen entrees could be used to focus your answer.)
5. What specific environmental factors account for the difference in atmosphere between eating at McDonald's and eating at a fine-dining restaurant?
6. What are the advantages and disadvantages to the consumer in purchasing from a mail-order catalog rather than from a retail store?
7. From a retailer's point of view, what would be the advantages and disadvantages of mail-order selling?
8. If you were recommending a store location site for a clothing specialty store, which methods or models of store location would you use, and why?
9. Identify some circumstances in which the desired consumer response guiding channel strategy development would be different for the retailer than for the manufacturer.

Marketing Strategy in Action

Amazon.com

In 1994 Jeff Bezos, a young senior vice president at a Wall Street investment firm, decided to become a part of the Internet revolution. He decided to try to sell books via the World Wide Web. Why books? Because about 1.3 million books were in print at the time. Also, Bezos thought he would be able to provide the customer with discounted prices, the opportunity to get any book wanted, and convenience. Bezos initially came up with a list of possible items to sell online, including books, music, PC hardware and software, and magazines. After eliminating all but books and music, he realized that only 250,000 music CDs were available at any one time compared to 1.5 million English book titles (3 million titles if all languages were considered). So Bezos decided to go with books and drew up a business plan as he and his wife drove westward in search of their new home. He subsequently decided to start his new business in Seattle and sold his first book in July 1995. And with that, Amazon.com began its rapid ascent toward becoming one of the most recognized businesses in the world.

While it still hasn't turned a profit, Amazon.com has succeeded where so many other fledgling Internet companies have failed. Bezos, who was recently named *Time* magazine's "Person of the Year" and *Advertising Age*'s 1999 "Marketer of the Year," is the first to admit that first-mover advantage was instrumental in the growth of his company. He also credits the company's success to the comprehensive selection of books available. "There's no way to have a physical bookstore with 1.1 million titles," he says. "Our catalog, if you were to print it, would be the size of seven New York City phone books." In addition, Amazon.com is known for its ability to fulfill and deliver, thanks to large investments in nationwide warehouse distribution centers.

If you are worried that your local Barnes & Noble bookstore might be forced out of business any time soon, however, don't be. Amazon.com cannot compete when customers want the physical presence of a bookstore. The online book behemoth cannot provide soft, comfortable couches, music, and gourmet coffee. Nor does it allow consumers the opportunity to page through a book before purchasing it, savoring the crisp new pages and the creaking of the binding when first opened. The company does, however, offer several advantages in the way of customer-to-customer and customer-to-author interaction. Customers can log on to the site, post a review on any book they have read, and have it permanently associated with that book's entry in the online catalog. Also, authors are able to answer a variety of stock interview questions, which are then posted on the site associated with all of their books. Authors can also leave their e-mail addresses so readers may e-mail their own opinions or comments.

Bezos believes that his is the world's most "customer-centric" company.

Another unique feature the company offers readers who have their own websites is the opportunity to set up their own specialized bookstores. For example, an expert on investing can list several investment strategy books on his or her website and then link them from the site directly into the Amazon.com catalog. The company is able to track books that are purchased in this manner and gives the individual a commission on all sales.

What else can customers expect when purchasing a book from Amazon.com? Discounts. Roughly 30 percent of the book titles are discounted by 10 to 30 percent. The others are sold at list price.

The company's strategy of providing customers with a sense of community within its website seems to be working. While many e-tailers went out of business and many others were barely surviving, Amazon.com's revenues were growing at 20 percent per year and reached $4 billion in 2003. Its operating profit margin at 5 percent beat most retailers' and approached Wall-Mart's 6 percent. One analyst projected the company's net income to be $800 million on $8 billion in revenues by 2007.

Recently the mammoth bookseller has branched into other areas. You can now purchase CDs, toys, home improvement products, software, videos and DVDs, and small appliances at Amazon.com. With this push into selling other products, the company faces increasing competition from traditional retailers and e-commerce startups. Some believe the company risks diluting its brand name by expanding its business to too many lines, too quickly. But Bezos begs to differ. He says, "I get asked a lot, 'Are you trying to be the Wal-Mart of the Web?' The truth is, we're not trying to be the Anything of the Web. We're genetically pioneers." The company's former UK managing director, Simon Murdoch, adds, "It's a great name. 'Amazon' is not tied to any product category. The brand is extendible; it stands for delivery."

Time will tell if the company will continue to deliver. For now, Amazon.com is one of the few Internet brands recognized around the world. It is the most frequented website in America and one of the top few in France, Britain, Germany, and Japan. Jeff Bezos's vision has certainly become one of the great entrepreneurial success stories.

Discussion Questions

1. Why have books and CDs sold successfully online while many other products haven't sold well?
2. Do you think consumers who buy from Amazon.com also shop at other websites for books and CDs and buy from the site that offers the lowest price?

3. What aspects of customer service have contributed to Amazon.com's success?

4. Why do you think Amazon.com isn't profitable even though it generates high sales dollars?

5. What are the differences in the purchasing experience between buying a book at Amazon.com and at a Barnes & Noble brick-and-mortar store?

6. What problems may arise as Amazon.com expands its offerings to products other than books?

Sources: Fred Vogelstein, "Mighty Amazon," *Fortune,* May 26, 2003, pp. 60–74; K.J. Bannan, "Book Battle," *Adweek,* February 28, 2000, pp. 90–94; anonymous, "Survey: E-Commerce: Amazon's Amazing Ambition," *The Economist,* February 26, 2000, p. S24; B. Rosier, "Amazon Leads Race to Expand Web Services," *Marketing,* February 24, 2000, pp. 19–20; D. A. Williamson, "Marketer of the Year: Amazon.com—Dot-Commerce: World's Biggest E-tail Brand Writes Book on Marketing Savvy," *Advertising Age,* December 13, 1999, pp. 1, 36–40; K. Brooker, "Amazon vs. Everybody," *Fortune,* November 8, 1999, pp. 120–128; M. H. Martin, "The Next Big Thing: A Bookstore?" *Fortune,* December 9, 1996, pp. 168–170; K. Southwick, "An Interview: Jeff Bezos, Amazon.com," *Upside,* October 1996, pp. 29–33.

Notes

CHAPTER 1

1. Peter D. Bennett, ed., *Dictionary of Marketing Terms,* 2nd ed. (Chicago: American Marketing Association, 1995), p. 59.
2. Andy Pargh, "Competition Boots Up in the Home Computer Market," *USA Today,* June 17, 1997, p. 4E.
3. David Leonhardt, "Two-Tier Marketing," *Business Week,* March 17, 1997, pp. 82–90.

CHAPTER 2

1. The idea of viewing human processes as a reciprocal system is taken from Albert Bandura, "The Self System in Reciprocal Determinism," *American Psychologist,* April 1978, p. 346, and Albert Bandura, *Social Foundations of Thought and Action: A Social Cognitive Theory* (Englewood Cliffs, NJ: Prentice-Hall, 1986).
2. For a review of these topics, see Gilbert A. Churchill, Jr., and J. Paul Peter, *Marketing: Creating Value for Customers,* 2d ed. (Burr Ridge, IL: McGraw-Hill/Irwin, 1998).
3. See Keith H. Hammonds, "The 'Blacktop' Is Paving Reebok's Road to Recovery," *Business Week,* August 12, 1991, p. 27.
4. For additional information, see Resa King, "What Do Women Want? Guns, Actually," *Business Week,* June 2, 1997, p. 91.

CHAPTER 3

1. C. E. Izard, "Emotion–Cognition Relationships and Human Development," in *Emotions, Cognition and Behavior,* ed. C. E. Izard, J. Kagan, and R. B. Zajonc (New York: Cambridge University Press, 1984), pp. 17–37; Rom Harre, David Clarke, and Nicola De Carlo, *Motives and Mechanisms: An Introduction to the Psychology of Action* (London: Methuen, 1985), chap. 2, pp. 20–39; Jaak Panksepp, "Toward a General Psychobiological Theory of Emotions. With Commentaries," *The Behavioral and Brain Sciences* 5 (1982), pp. 407–67; Robert Plutchik, *Emotion: A Psychoevolutionary Synthesis* (New York: Harper & Row, 1980).
2. Rik G. M. Pieters and W. Fred Van Raaij, "Functions and Management of Affect: Applications to Economic Behavior," *Journal of Economic Psychology* 9 (1988), pp. 251–82.
3. Werner Kroeber-Riel, "Activation Research: Psychobiological Approaches in Consumer Research," *Journal of Consumer Research,* March 1979, pp. 240–50.
4. Meryl Paula Gardner, "Mood States and Consumer Behavior: A Critical Review," *Journal of Consumer Research,* December 1985, pp. 281–300.
5. See Harre et al., *Motives and Mechanisms: An Introduction to the Psychology of Action:* Robert B. Zajonc and Hazel Markus, "Affective and Cognitive Factors in Preferences," *Journal of Consumer Research* 9 (1982), pp. 123–31; Hoffman, "Affect, Cognition, and Motivation," pp. 244–80; Robert B. Zajonc, "On the Primacy of Affect," *American Psychologist* 39 (1984), pp. 117–23; Richard S, Lazarus, "On the Primacy of Cognition," *American Psychologist* 39 (1984), pp. 124–29.
6. Michael K. Hui and John E. G. Bateson, "Perceived Control and the Effects of Crowding and Consumer Choice on the Service Experience," *Journal of Consumer Research,* September 1991, pp. 174–84.
7. John R. Anderson, *Cognitive Psychology and Its Implications* (San Francisco: W. H. Freeman, 1985).
8. For example, see the exchange between Yehoshua Tsal, "On the Relationship between Cognitive and Affective Processes: A Critique of Zajonc and Markus," *Journal of Consumer Research* 12 (1985), pp. 358–64; Zajonc and Markus, "Affective and Cognitive Factors in Preferences"; Robert B. Zajonc and Hazel Markus, "Must All Affect Be Mediated by Cognition?" *Journal of Consumer Research* 12 (1985) pp. 363–64.
9. S. S. Tomkins, "Affect Theory," in *Emotion in the Human Face,* ed. P. Ekman (Cambridge, UK: Cambridge University Press, 1983); Robert B. Zajonc, "On the Primacy of Affect,"

American Psychologist 39 (1984), pp. 117–23; and Richard S. Lazarus, "On the Primacy of Cognition," *American Psychologist* 39 (1984), pp. 124–29.

10. Lazarus, "On the Primacy of Cognition," pp. 124–29; Pieters and Van Raaij, "Functions and Management of Affect: Applications to Economic Behavior," pp. 251–82; Richard S. Lazarus, "Cognition and Motivation in Emotion," *American Psychologist*, April 1991, pp. 352–67.

11. For example, see Julie A. Edell and Marian Chapman Burke, "The Power of Feelings in Understanding Advertising Effects," *Journal of Consumer Research*, December 1987, pp. 421–33; William J. Havlena and Morris B. Holbrook, "The Varieties of Consumption Experience: Comparing Two Typologies of Emotion in Consumer Behavior," *Journal of Consumer Research*, December 1986, pp. 394–404; Morris B. Holbrook and Rajeev Batra, "Assessing the Role of Emotions as Mediators of Consumer Responses to Advertising," *Journal of Consumer Research*, December 1987, pp. 404–20; Rajeev Batra and Douglas M. Stayman, "The Role of Mood in Advertising Effectiveness," *Journal of Consumer Research*, September 1990, pp. 203–14.

12. For example, see Hoffman, "Affect, Cognition, and Motivation," pp. 244–80.

13. Richard Oliver, *Satisfaction: A Behavioral Perspective on the Consumer* (New York: McGraw-Hill, 1997).

14. Dawn Dobni and George M. Zinkhan, "In Search of Brand Image: A Foundation Analysis," in *Advances in Consumer Research*, vol. 17 (Provo, UT: Association for Consumer Research, 1990), pp. 110–19; Ernest Dichter, "What's in an Image?" *Journal of Consumer Marketing*. Winter 1985, pp. 75–81.

15. John R. Rossiter, Larry Percy, and Robert J. Donovan, "A Better Advertising Planning Grid," *Journal of Advertising Research*, October–November 1991, pp. 11–21; Brian Ratchford, "New Insights about the FCB Grid," *Journal of Advertising Research*, August–September 1987, pp. 24–38.

16. Mark Maremont, "They're All Screaming for Haagen-Dazs," *Business Week*, October 14, 1991, p. 121.

17. George Lakoff and Mark Johnson, *Metaphors We Live By* (Chicago and London: University of Chicago Press, 1980); George Lakoff and Mark Johnson, *Philosophy in the Flesh: The Embodied Mind and Its Challenge to Western Thought* (New York: Basic Books, 1999).

18. George Lakoff, "The Contemporary Theory of Metaphor," in Andrew Ortony, ed., *Metaphor and Thought,* 2nd ed (Cambridge, UK: Cambridge University Press, 1993),

pp. 202–251; Gerald Zaltman and Robin Higie Coulter, "Seeing the Voice of the Customer: Metaphor-Based Advertising Research," *Journal of Advertising Research,* July–August 1995, pp. 35–51.

19. A complex information-processing model of consumer decision making was developed by John Howard and Jagdish Sheth, *The Theory of Buyer Behavior* (New York: Wiley, 1969). More recently Bettman introduced another complex information-processing model; see James R. Bettman, *An Informaton Processing Model of Consumer Choice* (Reading, MA: Addison-Wesley, 1979). Also see Robert Chestnut and Jacob Jacoby, "Consumer Information Processing: Emerging Theory and Findings," in *Consumer and Industrial Buying Behavior,* ed. A. Woodside, J. N. Sheth, and P. D. Bennett (New York: Elsevier-North Holland, 1977), pp. 119–33; Roy Lachman, Janet Lachman, and Earl Butterfield, *Cognitive Psychology and Information Processing: An Introduction* (Hillsdale, NJ: Lawrence Erlbaum, 1979).

20. For example, see William J. McGuire, "The Internal Psychological Factors Influencing Consumer Choice," *Journal of Consumer Research*, March 1976, pp. 302–19; and Ivan L. Preston, "The Association Model of the Advertising Communication Process," *Journal of Advertising* 2 (1982), pp. 3–15.

21. F. C. Bartlett, *Remembering: A Study in Experimental and Social Psychology* (Cambridge, UK: Cambridge University Press, 1932); Jerry C. Olson, "Theories of Information Encoding and Storage: Implications for Consumer Research," in *The Effect of Information on Consumer and Market Behavior,* ed. A. A. Mitchell (Chicago: American Marketing Association, 1978), pp. 49–60.

22. Alan M. Collins and Elizabeth F. Loftus, "A Spreading Activation Theory of Semantic Memory," *Psychological Review* 82 (1975), pp. 407–28.

23. John R. Anderson, "A Spreading Activation Theory of Memory," *Journal of Verbal Learning and Verbal Behavior* 22 (1983), pp. 261–75.

24. Collins and Loftus, "A Spreading Activation Theory of Semantic Memory," pp. 407–28.

25. Allan Newell and Herbert A. Simon, *Human Problem Solving* (Englewood Cliffs, NJ: Prentice-Hall, 1972).

26. John A. Bargh, "Automatic and Conscious Processing of Social Information," in *Handbook of Social Cognition,* vol. 3, ed. R. S. Wyer and T. K. Srull (Hillsdale, NJ: Lawrence Erlbaum, 1984), pp. 1–43; Richard M. Schiffrin and Susan T. Dumais, "The Development of Automatism," in *Cognitive Skills and Their*

Development, ed. John R. Anderson (Hillsdale, NJ: Lawrence Erlbaum, 1981), pp. 111–40.

27. Jeffrey F. Durgee and Robert W. Stuart, "Advertising Symbols and Brand Names That Best Represent Key Product Meanings," *Journal of Advertising,* Summer 1987, pp. 15–24.

28. Wayne A. Wickelgren, "Human Learning and Memory," in *Annual Review of Psychology,* ed. M. R. Rosenzweig and L. W. Porter (Palo Alto, CA: Annual Reviews, 1981), pp. 21–52.

29. John R. Anderson, *The Architecture of Cognition* (Cambridge, MA: Harvard University Press, 1983); Terence R. Smith, Andrew A. Mitchell, and Robert Meyer, "A Computational Process Model of Evaluation Based on the Cognitive Structuring of Episodic Knowledge," in *Advances in Consumer Research,* vol. 9, ed. Andrew A. Mitchell (Ann Arbor, MI: Association for Consumer Research, 1982), pp. 136–43.

30. Endel Tulving, "Episodic and Semantic Memory," in *Organization of Memory,* ed. Endel Tulving (New York: Academic Press, 1972), pp. 382–404.

31. Merrie Brucks and Andrew Mitchell, "Knowledge Structures, Production Systems, and Decision Strategies," in *Advances in Consumer Research,* vol. 8, ed. Kent B. Monroe (Ann Arbor, MI: Association for Consumer Research, 1982).

32. Donald A. Norman, *The Psychology of Everyday Things* (New York: Basic Books, 1988).

33. Bruce Nussbaum and Robert Neff, "I Can't Work This Thing!" *Business Week,* April 29, 1991, pp. 58–66.

34. Although many types of memory structures have been proposed, most can be reduced to the more general associative network model. See James R. Bettman, "Memory Factors in Consumer Choice: A Review," *Journal of Marketing,* Spring 1979, pp. 37–53: Andrew A. Mitchell, "Models of Memory: Implications for Measuring Knowledge Structures," in *Advances in Consumer Research,* vol. 9, ed. Andrew A. Mitchell (Ann Arbor, MI: Association for Consumer Research, 1982), pp. 45–51; Edward Smith, "Theories of Semantic Memory," in *Handbook of Learning and Cognitive Processes,* vol. 6, ed. W. K. Estes (Hillsdale, NJ: Lawrence Erlbaum, 1978), pp. 1–56.

35. Joseph W. Alba and Lynn Hasher, "Is Memory Schematic?" *Psychological Bulletin,* March 1983, pp. 203–31; Donald E. Rumelhart and Anthony Ortony, "The Representation of Knowledge in Memory," in *Schooling and the Acquisition of Knowledge,* ed. R. C. Anderson, R. J. Spiro, and W. E. Montague (Hillsdale, NJ: Lawrence Erlbaum, 1977), pp. 99–136.

36. Thomas W. Leigh and Arno J. Rethans, "Experiences with Script Elicitation within Consumer Decision-Making Contexts," in *Advances in Consumer Research,* vol. 10, ed. R. P. Bagozzi and A. M. Tybout (Ann Arbor, MI: Association for Consumer Research, 1983), pp. 667–72; Roger C. Schank and Robert P. Abelson, *Scripts, Plans, Goals, and Understanding: An Inquiry into Human Knowledge Structure* (Hillsdale, NJ: Lawrence Erlbaum, 1977).

37. David E. Rumelhart and Donald A. Norman, "Accretion, Timing, and Restructuring: Three Modes of Learning," in *Semantic Factors in Cognition,* ed. J. R. Cotton and R. L. Klatsky (Hillsdale, NJ: Lawrence Erlbaum, 1978), pp. 37–53.

CHAPTER 4

1. For example, see Roy Lachman, Janet L. Lachman, and Earl C. Butterfield, *Cognitive Psychology and Information Processing* (Hillsdale, NJ: Lawrence Erlbaum, 1979).

2. Eleanor Rosch, Carolyn B. Mervis, Wayne D. Gray, David M. Johnson, and Penny Boyes-Braem, "Basic Objects in Natural Categories," *Cognitive Psychology,* July 1976, pp. 382–439.

3. For examples, see Joseph W. Alba and Amitava Chattopadhyay, "The Effects of Context and Part-Category Cues on the Recall of Competing Brands," *Journal of Marketing Research,* August 1985, pp. 340–9; Mita Sujan and Christine Dekleva, "Product Categorization and Interference Making: Some Implications for Comparative Advertising," *Journal of Consumer Research,* September 1987, pp. 14–54; Mita Sujan and James R. Bettman, "The Effects of Brand Positioning Strategies on Consumers' Brand and Category Perceptions: Some Insights from Schema Research," *Journal of Marketing Research,* November 1989, pp. 454–67.

4. Mita Sujan, "Consumer Knowledge: Effects on Evaluation Strategies Mediating Consumer Judgments," *Journal of Consumer Research,* June 1985, pp. 31–46; Joel Cohen and Kunal Basu, "Alternative Models of Categorization: Toward a Contingent Processing Framework," *Journal of Consumer Research,* March 1987, pp. 455–72; Carolyn B. Mervis, "Category Structure and the Development of Categorization," in *Theoretical Issues in Reading Comprehension,* ed. Rand Spiro et al. (Hillsdale, NJ: Lawrence Erlbaum, 1980), pp. 279–307.

5. Michael D. Johnson, "The Differential Processing of Product Category and Noncomparable Choice Alternatives," *Journal of Consumer Research,* December 1989, pp. 300–9.

6. Zachary Schiller and Mark N. Varmos, "Liquid Tide Looks Like Solid Gold," *Business Week,* December 24, 1984, p. 32.

7. For example, see Elizabeth C. Hirschman, "Attributes of Attributes and Layers of Meaning," in *Advances in Consumer Research*, vol. 7, ed. Jerry C. Olson (Ann Arbor, MI: Association for Consumer Research, 1980), pp. 7–12.

8. Lyle V. Geistfeld, George B. Sproles, and Susan B. Badenhop, "The Concept and Measurement of a Hierarchy of Product Characteristics," in *Advance in Consumer Research*, vol. 4. ed. H. Keith Hunt (Ann Arbor, MI: Association for Consumer Research, 1977), pp. 302–7.

9. Theodore Levitt, "Marketing Myopia," *Harvard Business Review*, July–August 1960, pp. 45–56.

10. Paul E. Green, Yoram Wind, and Arun K. Jain, "Benefit Bundle Analysis," *Journal of Advertising Research*, April 1972, pp. 32–36.

11. Russell I. Haley, "Benefit Segmentation: A Decision-Oriented Research Tool," *Journal of Marketing*, July 1972, pp. 30, 35.

12. Lynn Coleman, "Advertisers Put Fear into the Hearts of Their Prospects," *Marketing News*, August 15, 1988, pp. 1–2.

13. For instance, see Jonathan Gutman and Donald E. Vinson, "Values Structures and Consumer Behavior," in *Advances in Consumer Research*, vol. 6, ed. William L. Wilkie (Ann Arbor, MI: Association for Consumer Research, 1979), pp. 335–39: Janice G. Hanna, "A Typology of Consumer Needs," in *Research in Marketing*, vol. 3. ed. Jagdish N. Sheth (Greenwich, CT: JAI Press, 1980), pp. 83–104; Lynn Kahle, "The Values of Americans: Implications for Consumer Adaptation," in *Personal Values and Consumer Psychology*, ed. Robert E. Pitts, Jr., and Arch G. Woodside (Lexington, MA: Lexington Books, 1984), pp. 77–86.

14. Milton J. Rokeach, *The Nature of Human Values* (New York: Free Press, 1973).

15. Anthony G. Greenwald and Anthony R. Pratkanis, "The Self," in *The Handbook of Social Cognition*, ed. Robert S. Wyer and Thomas K. Srull (Hillsdale, NJ: Lawrence Erlbaum, 1984), pp. 129–78; Hazel Markus and Paula Nurius, "Possible Selves," *American Psychologist*, September 1986, pp. 954–69.

16. John F. Kihlstrom and Nancy Cantor, "Mental Representations of the Self," in *Advances in Experimental Social Psychology* 17 (1984), pp. 1–47; Hazel Markus, "Self-Schemata and Processing Information about the Self," *Journal of Personality and Social Psychology* 35 (1977), pp. 63–78; Hazel Markus and Keith Sentis, "The Self in Social Information Processing," in *Psychological Perspective on the Self*, ed. J. Suls (Hillsdale, NJ: Lawrence Erlbaum, 1982), pp. 41–70.

17. The basic idea of means–end chains can be traced back at least to Edward C. Tolman, *Purposive Behavior in Animals and Men* (New York: Century, 1932). Among the first to suggest its use in marketing was John A. Howard. *Consumer Behavior Application and Theory* (New York: McGraw-Hill, 1977). More recently Jon Gutman, Tom Reynolds, and Jerry Olson have been active proponents of means–end chain models. For example, see Jonathan Gutman and Thomas J. Reynolds, "An Investigation of the Levels of Cognitive Abstraction Utilized by Consumers in Product Differentiation," in *Attitude Research under the Sun*, ed. John Eighmey (Chicago: American Marketing Association, 1979), pp. 125–50; Jonathan Gutman, "A Means–End Chain Model Based on Consumer Categorization Processes," *Journal of Marketing*, Spring 1982, pp. 60–72; Jerry C. Olson and Thomas J. Reynolds, "Understanding Consumers' Cognitive Structures: Implications for Marketing Strategy," in *Advertising and Consumer Psychology*, vol. 1, ed. Larry Percy and Arch Woodside (Lexington, MA: Lexington Books, 1983), pp. 77–90.

18. Shirley Young and Barbara Feigen, "Using the Benefit Chain for Improved Strategy Formulation," *Journal of Marketing*, July 1975, pp. 72–74; James H. Myers and Alan D. Schocker, "The Nature of Product-Related Attributes," in *Research in Marketing*, ed. J. N. Sheth (Greenwich, CT: JAI Press, 1981), pp. 211–36; Gutman and Reynolds, "An Investigation of the Levels of Cognitive Abstraction Utilized by Consumers in Product Differentiation," pp. 128–50; Joel B. Cohen, "The Structure of Product Attributes: Defining Attribute Dimensions for Planning and Evaluation," in *Analytic Approaches to Product and Marketing Planning*, ed. A. D. Shocker (Cambridge, MA: Marketing Science Institute, 1979), pp. 54–86.

19. Olson and Reynolds, "Understanding Consumers' Cognitive Structures," pp. 77–90.

20. For a good example, see Sunil Mehrotra and John Palmer, "Relating Product Features to Perceptions of Quality: Appliances," in *Perceived Quality*, ed. Jacob Jacoby and Jerry Olson (Lexington, MA: Lexington Books, 1985), pp. 81–96.

21. Thomas J. Reynolds and Jonathan Gutman, "Laddering Theory, Method, Analysis, and Interpretation," *Journal of Advertising Research*, February–March 1988, pp. 11–31; Jonathan Gutman, "Exploring the Nature of Linkages between Consequences and Values," *Journal of Business Research* 22 (1991), pp. 143–148.

22. For a good example, see Jonathan Gutman and Scott D. Alden, "Adolescents' Cognitive Structures of Retail Stores and Fashion Consumption: A Means–End Chain Analysis of

Quality," in *Perceived Quality*, ed. Jacob Jacoby and Jerry Olson (Lexington, MA: Lexington Books, 1985), pp. 99–114.

23. Glenn L. Christensen and Jerry C. Olson, "Mapping Consumers' Mental Models with ZMET," *Psychology and Marketing*, June 2002, pp. 477–502.

24. Gerald Zaltman, "Rethinking Market Research: Putting People Back In," *Journal of Marketing Research*, 34 (November), pp. 424–37.

25. For more information about the steps in the ZMET process, see Gerald Zaltman and Robin Higie Coulter, "Seeing the Voice of the Customer: Metaphor-Based Advertising Research," *Journal of Advertising Research*, July–August 1995, pp. 35–51.

26. Zaltman, "Rethinking Market Research: Putting People Back In," pp. 424–37.

27. One of the first and most influential writers about involvement was Herbert E. Krugman. See Herbert E. Krugman, "The Impact of Television Advertising: Learning without Involvement," *Public Opinion Quarterly* 29 (1965), pp. 349–56; Herbert E. Krugman, "The Measurement of Advertising Involvement," *Public Opinion Quarterly* 30 (1967), pp. 583–96.

28. For instance, see John H. Antil, "Conceptualization and Operationalization of Involvement," in *Advances in Consumer Research*, vol. 11, ed. Thomas C. Kinnear (Ann Arbor, MI: Association for Consumer Research, 1984), pp. 203–9; Andrew A. Mitchell, "Involvement: A Potentially Important Mediator of Consumer Behavior," in *Advances in Consumer Research*, vol. 6, ed. William Wilkie (Ann Arbor, MI: Association for Consumer Research, 1979), pp. 191–96; Robert N. Stone, "The Marketing Characteristics of Involvement," in *Advances in Consumer Research*, vol. 11, ed. Thomas C. Kinnear (Ann Arbor, MI: Association for Consumer Research, 1984), pp. 210–15. Also see Peter N. Bloch, "An Exploration into the Scaling of Consumers' Involvement with a Product Class," in *Advances in Consumer Research*, vol. 8, ed. Kent B. Monroe (Ann Arbor, MI: Association for Consumer Research, 1981), pp. 61–65; Judith Lynne Zaichkowsky, "Measuring the Involvement Construct," *Journal of Consumer Research*, December 1985, pp. 341–52.

29. Joel B. Cohen, "Involvement and You: 100 Great Ideas," in *Advances in Consumer Research*, vol. 9, ed. Andrew A. Mitchell (Ann Arbor, MI: Association for Consumer Research, 1982), pp. 324–27.

30. Richard L. Celsi and Jerry C. Olson, "The Role of Involvement in Attention and Comprehension Processes," *Journal of Consumer Research*, September 1988, pp. 210–24; Andrew A. Mitchell, "The Dimensions of Advertising Involvement," in *Advances in Consumer Research*, vol. 8, ed. Kent B. Monroe (Ann Arbor, MI: Association for Consumer Research, 1981), pp. 25–30; William L. Moore and Donald R. Lehmann, "Individual Differences in Search Behavior for a Nondurable," *Journal of Consumer Research*, December 1980, pp. 296–307.

31. Beth A. Walker and Jerry C. Olson, "Means–End Chains: Connecting Products with Self," *Journal of Business Research*, no. 2 (1991), pp. 111–18.

32. Celsi and Olson, "The Role of Involvement in Attention and Comprehension Processes," pp. 210–24.

33. Harold H. Kassarjian, "Low Involvement—A Second Look," in *Advances in Consumer Research*, vol. 8, ed. Kent B. Monroe (Ann Arbor, MI: Association for Consumer Research, 1981), pp. 31–34.

34. Celsi and Olson, "The Role of Involvement in Attention and Comprehension Processes," pp. 210–24.

35. See Celsi and Olson, "The Role of Involvement in Attention and Comprehension Processes," pp. 210–24. A similar perspective is provided by Peter H. Bloch and Marsha L. Richins, "A Theoretical Model of the Study of Product Importance Perceptions," *Journal of Marketing*, Summer 1983, pp. 69–81. Some researchers treat these two factors as two forms of involvement: enduring and situational involvement, respectively. For instance, see Michael J. Houston and Michael L. Rothschild, "Conceptual and Methodological Perspectives on Involvement," in *1978 Educators' Proceedings*, ed. S. C. Jain (Chicago: American Marketing Association, 1978), pp. 184–87. We believe it is clearer to treat these factors as sources of involvement.

36. For a similar proposal, see Peter H. Bloch, "Involvement beyond the Purchase Process: Conceptual Issues and Empirical Investigation," in *Advances in Consumer Research*, vol. 9, ed. Andrew A. Mitchell (Ann Arbor, MI: Association for Consumer Research, 1982), pp. 413–17. Some researchers have called this "enduring involvement"; see, for example, Houston and Rothschild, "Conceptual and Methodological Perspectives on Involvement," pp. 184–87.

37. John Harris, "I Don't Want Good, I Want Fast," *Forbes*, October 1, 1990, p. 186; Nancy J. Perry, "Hit 'Em Where They Used to Be," *Fortune*, October 19, 1992, pp. 112–13.

38. Russell W. Belk, "Worldly Possessions: Issues and Criticisms," in *Advances in Consumer*

Research, vol. 10, eds. Richard P. Bagozzi and Alice M. Tybout (Ann Arbor, MI: Association for Consumer Research, 1983), pp. 514–19; Terence A. Shimp and Thomas J. Madden, "Consumer–Object Relations: A Conceptual Framework Based Analogously on Sternberg's Triangular Theory of Love," in *Advances in Consumer Research,* vol. 15, ed. Michael J. Houston (Ann Arbor, MI: Association for Consumer Research, 1988), pp. 163–68.

39. For a similar idea in an advertising context, see Thomas J. Reynolds and Jonathan Gutman, "Advertising Is Image Management," *Journal of Advertising Research,* February–March 1984, pp. 27–37.

40. Bill Brubaker, "Athletic Shoes: Beyond Big Business," *Washington Post,* March 10, 1991, pp. A1, A18.

41. For a detailed description of the perceived personal relevance (felt involvement) of some consumer researchers, see Donald R. Lehmann, "Pumping Iron III: An Examination of Compulsive Lifting," in *Advances in Consumer Research,* vol. 14, ed. Melanie Wallendorf and Paul Anderson (Ann Arbor, MI: Association for Consumer Research, 1987), pp. 129–31; Debra Scammon, "Breeding, Training, and Riding: The Serious Side of Horsing Around," in *Advances in Consumer Research,* vol. 14, ed. Melanie Wallendorf and Paul Anderson (Ann Arbor, MI: Association for Consumer Research, 1987), pp. 125–28.

42. Peter Cushing and Melody Douglas-Tate, "The Effect of People/Product Relationships on Advertising Processing," in *Psychological Processes and Advertising Effects,* ed. Linda Alwitt and Andrew A. Mitchell (Hillsdale, NJ: Lawrence Erlbaum; 1985), pp. 241–59.

43. Sunil Mehrotra and John Palmer, "Relating Product Features to Perceptions of Quality: Appliances," in *Perceived Quality,* ed. Jacob Jacoby and Jerry C. Olson (Lexington, MA: Lexington Books, 1985), pp. 81–96.

44. Grant McCracken, "Advertising: Meaning or Information," in *Advances in Consumer Research,* vol. 14, ed. Melanie Wallendorf and Paul Anderson (Ann Arbor, MI: Association for Consumer Research, 1987), pp. 121–24.

45. Joshua Levine, "I Gave at the Supermarket," *Forbes,* December 25, 1989, pp. 138–40.

CHAPTER 5

1. See Anthony A. Greenwald and Clark Leavitt, "Audience Involvement in Advertising: Four Levels," *Journal of Consumer Research,* June 1984, pp. 581–92.

2. For example, see William Schneider and Richard M. Shiffrin, "Controlled and Automatic Human Information Processing: I. Detection, Search, and Attention," *Psychological Review,* January 1977, pp. 1–66; Richard M. Shiffrin and William Schneider, "Controlled and Automatic Human Information Processing: II. Perceptual Learning, Automatic Attending, and a General Theory," *Psychological Review,* March 1977, pp. 127–90.

3. Daniel Kahneman and Anne Treisman, "Changing Views of Attention and Automaticity," in *Varieties of Attention,* ed. R. Parasuraman and D. R. Davies (New York: Academic Press, 1984), pp. 29–61; John G. Lynch, Jr., and Thomas K. Snull, "Memory and Attention Factors in Consumer Choice: Concepts and Research Methods," *Journal of Consumer Research,* September 1982, pp. 18–37.

4. Sharon E. Beatty and Scott M. Smith, "External Search Effort: An Investigation across Several Product Categories," *Journal of Consumer Research,* June 1987, pp. 83–95; Peter H. Bloch, Daniel Sherrell, and Nancy M. Ridgway, "Consumer Search: An Extended Framework," *Journal of Consumer Research,* June 1986, pp. 119–26; Joseph W. Newman, "Consumer External Search: Amount and Determinants," in *Consumer and Industrial Buying Behavior,* ed. A. G. Woodside, J. N. Sheth, and P. D. Bennett (New York: Elsevier-North Holland, 1977), pp. 79–94; Richard R. Olshavsky and Donald H. Granbois, "Consumer Decision Making—Fact or Fiction?" *Journal of Consumer Research,* June 1979, pp. 63–70.

5. Leo Bogart, "Executives Fear Ad Overload Will Lower Effectiveness," *Marketing News,* May 25, 1984, pp. 4–5.

6. Peter H. Bloch and Marsha L. Ritchins, "Shopping without Purchase: An Investigation of Consumer Browsing Behavior," in *Advances in Consumer Research,* vol. 10, ed. R. P. Baggozi and A. M. Tybout (Ann Arbor, MI: Association for Consumer Research, 1983), pp. 389–93.

7. Joanne Lipman, "CNN Ads Get Extra Mileage during the War," *The Wall Street Journal,* February 27, 1991, pp. B1, B4.

8. Avery Abernethy and Herbert Rotfield, "Zipping through TV Ads Is Old Tradition—But Viewers Are Getting Better at It," *Marketing News,* January 7, 1991, pp. 6, 14.

9. Suzanne Alexander, "Saturating Cities with Stores Can Pay," *The Wall Street Journal,* September 11, 1990, p. B1.

10. Betsy Morris, "The Brand's the Thing," *Fortune,* March 4, 1996, pp. 72–86.

11. This section is adapted from David W. Schumann, Jennifer Gayson, Johanna Ault, Kerri Hargrove, Lois Hollingsworth, Russell Ruelle, and Sharon Seguin, "The Effectiveness of Shopping Cart Signage: Perceptual Measures Tell a Different Story," *Journal of Advertising Research,* February–March 1991, pp. 17–22.

12. Joanne Lipman, "Brand-Name Products Are Popping Up in TV Shows," *The Wall Street Journal,* February 19, 1991, pp. B1, B3.

13. Sana Siwolop, "You Can't (Hum) Ignore (Hum) That Ad," *Business Week,* September 21, 1987, p. 56.

14. Bill Saporito, "IKEA's Got 'Em Lining Up," *Fortune,* March 11, 1991, p. 72.

15. Roy Lachman, Janet L. Lachman, and Earl C. Butterfield, *Cognitive Psychology and Information Processing: An Introduction* (Hillsdale, NJ: Lawrence Erlbaum, 1979).

16. Daniel Kahneman, *Attention and Effort* (Englewood Cliffs, NJ: Prentice-Hall, 1973).

17. Anthony A. Greenwald and Clark Leavitt, "Audience Involvement in Advertising: Four Levels," *Journal of Consumer Research,* June 1984, pp. 58–92; Chris Janiszewski, "The Influence of Nonattended Material on the Processing of Advertising Claims," *Journal of Marketing Research,* August 1990, pp. 263–78.

18. Schumann et. al., "The Effectiveness of Shopping Cart Signage."

19. David M. Sanbonmatsu and Frank R. Kardes, "The Effects of Physiological Arousal on Information Processing and Persuasion," *Journal of Consumer Research,* December 1988, pp. 379–85.

20. Meryl Paula Gardner, "Mood States and Consumer Behavior," *Journal of Consumer Research,* December 1985, pp. 281–300; Noel Murray, Harish Sujan, Edward R. Hirt, and Mita Sujan, "The Effects of Mood on Categorization: A Cognitive Flexibility Hypothesis," *Journal of Personality and Social Psychology,* September 1990, pp. 411–25.

21. Marvin E. Goldberg and Gerald J. Gorn, "Happy and Sad TV Programs: How They Affect Reactions to Commercials," *Journal of Consumer Research,* December 1987, pp. 387–403.

22. See Richard L. Celsi and Jerry C. Olson, "The Role of Involvement in Attention and Comprehension Processes," *Journal of Consumer Research,* September 1988, pp. 210–24.

23. Adapted from an advertisement in *Advertising Age,* November 4, 1985, p. 69.

24. Both examples were taken from "Intuition, Microstudies, Humanized Research Can Identify Emotions That Motivate Consumers," *Marketing News,* March 19, 1982, p. 11.

25. Celsi and Olson, "The Role of Involvement in Attention and Comprehension Processes."

26. Ann L. McGill and Punam Anand, "The Effect of Vivid Attributes on the Evaluation of Alternatives: The Role of Differential Attention and Cognitive Elaboration," *Journal of Consumer Research,* September 1989, pp. 188–96.

27. "Four More Years: The Marketing Implications," *Marketing News,* January 4, 1985, pp. 1, 50, 52.

28. Brian Davis, "FCO's Run of Bad Luck," *Advertising Age,* June 10, 1985, p. 58.

29. Patricia Winters, "Topsy-Turvy Look Puts a New Spin on Ad Placements," *Advertising Age,* September 12, 1988, p. 4.

30. Cathryn Donohoe, "Whittle Zeroes in on His Target," *Insight,* August 14, 1989, pp. 50–52.

31. Fergus I. M. Craik and Robert S. Lockhart, "Levels of Processing: A Framework for Memory Research," *Journal of Verbal Learning and Verbal Behavior,* 1972, pp. 671–89; Jerry C. Olson, "Encoding Processes: Levels of Processing and Existing Knowledge Structures," in *Advances in Consumer Research,* vol. 7, ed. J. C. Olson (Ann Arbor, MI: Association for Consumer Research, 1980), pp. 154–59.

32. The term *depth* is being used as a metaphor, of course. Depth does not connote any physical dimension of brain storage.

33. John R. Anderson and Lynne M. Reder, "An Elaboration Processing Explanation of Depth of Processing," in *Levels of Processing in Human Memory,* ed. Larry S. Cermak and Fergus I. M. Craik (Hillsdale, NJ: Lawrence Erlbaum, 1979), pp. 385–404; Richard E. Petty and John T. Cacioppo, "The Elaboration Likelihood Model of Persuasion," in *Advances in Experimental Social Psychology,* vol. 19, ed. Leonard Berkowitz (New York: Academic Press, 1986), pp. 123–205.

34. Anderson and Reder, "An Elaboration Processing Explanation of Depth in Processing," pp. 385–404.

35. Alain d'Astous and Marc Dubuc, "Retrieval Processes in Consumer Evaluative Judgment Making: The Role of Elaborative Processing," in *Advances in Consumer Research,* vol. 13, ed. Richard J. Lutz (Provo, UT: Association for Consumer Research, 1986), pp. 132–37; Jerry C. Olson, "Encoding Processes: Levels of Processing and Existing Knowledge Structures," in *Advances in Consumer Research,* vol. 7, ed. J. C. Olson (Ann Arbor, MI: Association for Consumer Research, 1980), pp. 154–59; Douglas M. Stayman and Rajeev Batra, "Encoding and Retrieval of Ad Affect in Memory," *Journal of Consumer Research,* May 1991, pp. 232–39.

36. Kevin Lane Keller, "Memory Factors in Advertising: The Effect of Advertising Retrieval Cues on Brand Evaluations," *Journal of Consumer Research,* December 1987, pp. 316–33; Joan Myers-Levy, "Priming Effects on Product Judgments: A Hemispheric Interpretation," *Journal of Consumer Research,* June 1989, pp. 76–86.

37. Gary T. Ford and Ruth Ann Smith, "Inferential Beliefs in Consumer Evaluations: An

Assessment of Alternative Processing Strategies," *Journal of Consumer Research,* December 1987, pp. 363–71; Richard J. Harris, "Interference in Information Processing," in *The Psychology of Learning and Motivation,* vol. 15, ed. Gordon A. Bower (New York: Academic Press, 1981), pp. 81–128; Mita Sujan and Christine Dekleva, "Product Categorization and Interference Making: Some Implications for Comparative Advertising," *Journal of Consumer Research,* December 1987, pp. 372–78.

38. Amna Kirmani, "The Effect of Perceived Advertising Costs on Brand Perceptions," *Journal of Consumer Research,* September 1990, pp. 160–71; Amna Kirmani and Peter Wright, "Money Talks: Perceived Advertising Expense and Expected Product Quality," *Journal of Consumer Research,* December 1989, pp. 344–53.

39. For examples of inferring means–end chains, see Valarie A. Zeithaml, "Consumer Perceptions of Price, Quality, and Value," *Journal of Marketing,* July 1988, pp. 2–22; Sunil Mehrotra and John Palmer, "Relating Product Features to Perceptions of Quality: Appliances," in *Perceived Quality,* ed. Jacob Jacoby and Jerry C. Olson (Lexington, MA: Lexington Books, 1985), pp. 81–96.

40. See Joseph W. Alba and J. Wesley Hutchinson, "Dimensions of Consumer Expertise," *Journal of Consumer Research,* March 1987, pp. 411–54; Jerry C. Olson, "Inferential Belief Formation in the Cue Utilization Process," in *Advances in Consumer Research,* vol. 5, ed. H. Keith Hunt (Ann Arbor, MI: Association for Consumer Research, 1978), pp. 706–13.

41. Carl Obermiller, "When Do Consumers Infer Quality from Price?" in *Advances in Consumer Research,* vol. 15, ed. Michael J. Houston (Provo, UT: Association for Consumer Research, 1988), pp. 304–10; Jerry C. Olson, "Price as an Informational Cue: Effects on Product Evaluations," in *Consumer and Industrial Buying Behavior,* ed. Arch G. Woodside, Jagdish N. Sheth, and Peter D. Bennett (New York: North Holland, 1977), pp. 267–86; Zeithaml, "Consumer Perceptions of Price, Quality, and Value," pp. 2–22.

42. Frank R. Kardes, "Spontaneous Interference Processes in Advertising: The Effects of Conclusion Omission and Involvement on Persuasion," *Journal of Consumer Research,* September 1988, pp. 225–33; Richard D. Johnson and Irwin P. Levin, "More Than Meets the Eye: The Effect of Missing Information on Purchase Evaluations," *Journal of Consumer Research,* June 1985, pp. 169–77; Carolyn J. Simmons and John G. Lynch, Jr., "Inference Effects with Inference Making? Effects of Missing Information on Discounting and Use

of Presented Information," *Journal of Consumer Research,* March 1991, pp. 477–91.

43. Durairaj Maheswaran and Brian Sternthal, "The Effects of Knowledge, Motivation, and Type of Message on Ad Processing and Product Judgments," *Journal of Consumer Research,* June 1990, pp. 66–73.

44. James R. Bettman and Mita Sujan, "Effects of Framing on Evaluation of Comparable and Noncomparable Alternatives by Expert and Novice Consumers," *Journal of Consumer Research,* September 1987, pp. 141–54; Joseph W. Alba and J. Wesley Hutchinson, "Dimensions of Consumer Expertise," *Journal of Consumer Research,* March 1987, pp. 411–54; Eric J. Johnson and J. Edward Russo, "Product Familiarity and Learning New Information," *Journal of Consumer Research,* June 1984, pp. 542–50; Larry J. Marks and Jerry C. Olson, "Toward a Cognitive Structure Conceptualization of Product Familiarity," in *Advances in Consumer Research,* vol. 8, ed. Kent B. Monroe (Ann Arbor, MI: Association for Consumer Research, 1981), pp. 145–50.

45. Mita Sujan, "Consumer Knowledge: Effects on Evaluation Processes Mediating Consumer Judgments," *Journal of Consumer Research,* June 1985, pp. 31–46.

46. Michael Oneal, "Attack of the Bug Killers," *Business Week,* May 16, 1988, p. 81.

47. Richard E. Petty, John T. Cacioppo, and David Schumann, "Central and Peripheral Routes to Advertising Effectiveness: The Moderating Role of Involvement," *Journal of Consumer Research,* September 1983, pp. 135–44.

48. Peter L. Wright and Barton Weitz, "Time Horizon Effects on Product Evaluation Strategies," *Journal of Marketing Research,* November 1977, pp. 429–43.

49. Christine Moorman, "The Effects of Stimulus and Consumer Characteristics on the Utilization of Nutrition Information," *Journal of Consumer Research,* December 1990, pp. 362–74.

50. Deborah J. MacInnis and Linda L. Price, "The Role of Imagery in Information Processing: Review and Extensions," *Journal of Consumer Research,* March 1987, pp. 473–91.

51. Elizabeth C. Hirschman, "Point of View: Sacred, Secular, and Mediating Consumption Imagery in Television Commercials," *Journal of Marketing Research,* December–January 1991, pp. 38–43.

52. Ronald Alsop, "Marketing: The Slogan's Familiar, But What's the Brand?" *The Wall Street Journal,* January 8, 1988, p. B1.

53. Jacob Jacoby and Wayne D. Hoyer, "Viewer Miscomprehension of Televised Communications: Selected Findings," *Journal of Marketing,* Fall 1982, pp. 12–26; Jacob Jacoby and

Wayne D. Hoyer, "The Comprehension/ Miscomprehension of Print Communication: Selected Findings," *Journal of Consumer Research,* March 1989, pp. 434–43.

54. Some researchers believe these estimates are too high because of problems in measuring miscomprehension. See Gary T. Ford and Richard Yalch, "Viewer Miscomprehension of Televised Communication—A Comment," *Journal of Marketing,* Fall 1982, pp. 27–31; Richard W. Mzerski, "Viewer Miscomprehension Findings Are Measurement Bound," *Journal of Marketing,* Fall 1982, pp. 32–34.

55. Gary T. Ford and John E. Calfee, "Recent Developments in FTC Policy on Deceptions," *Journal of Marketing,* July 1986, pp. 82–103; Ivan L. Preston and Jef I. Richards, "The Relationship of Miscomprehension to Deceptiveness in FTC Cases," in *Advances in Consumer Research,* vol. 13, ed. Richard J. Lutz (Provo, UT: Association for Consumer Research, 1986), pp. 138–42.

56. Bruce Ingersoll, "FDA Takes on 'No Cholesterol' Claims," *The Wall Street Journal,* May 15, 1991, pp. B1, B10.

57. Chris Janiszewski, "The Influence of Print Advertisement Organization on Affect toward a Brand Name," *Journal of Consumer Research,* June 1990, pp. 53–65; James M. Munch and Jack L. Swasy, "Rhetorical Question, Summarization Frequency, and Argument Strength Effects on Recall," *Journal of Consumer Research,* June 1988, pp. 69–76; Thomas J. Olney, Morris B. Holbrook, and Rajeev Batra, "Consumer Responses to Advertising: The Effects of Ad Content, Emotions, and Attitude toward the Ad on Viewing Time," *Journal of Consumer Research,* March 1991, pp. 440–53.

58. Jacob Jacoby, Robert W. Chestnut, and William Silberman, "Consumer Use and Comprehension of Nutrition Information," *Journal of Consumer Research,* September 1977, pp. 119–28; Joyce A. Vermeersch and Helene Swenerton, "Interpretations of Nutrition Claims in Food Advertisements by Low-Income Consumers," *Journal of Nutrition Education,* January–March, 1980, pp. 19–25; and Moorman, "The Effects of Stimulus and Consumer Characteristics."

CHAPTER 6

1. Martin Fishbein and Icek Ajzen, *Belief, Attitude, Intention, and Behavior: An Introduction to Theory and Research* (Reading, MA: Addison-Wesley, 1975), p. 2.

2. Martin Fishbein, "Attitude, Attitude Change, and Behavior: A Theoretical Overview," in *Attitude Research Bridges the Atlantic,* ed. Phillip Levine (Chicago: American Marketing Association, 1975), pp. 3–16.

3. Many authors have defined attitudes in this way, including Russell H. Fazio, "How Do Attitudes Guide Behavior?" in *Handbook of Motivation and Cognition: Foundations of Social Behavior,* ed. R. M. Sorrentino and E. T. Higgins (New York: Guiford Press, 1986), pp. 204–43.

4. Fishbein and Ajzen, *Belief, Attitude, Intention, and Behavior;* Andrew A. Mitchell and Jerry C. Olson, "Are Product Attributes the Only Mediators of Advertising Effects on Brand Attitude?" *Journal of Marketing Research,* August 1981, pp. 318–32; Richard E. Petty and John T. Cacioppo, "Central and Peripheral Routes to Advertising Effectiveness: The Moderating Role of Involvement," *Journal of Consumer Research,* September 1983, pp. 135–46; Danny L. Moore and J. Wesley Hutchinson, "The Influence of Affective Reactions to Advertising: Direct and Indirect Mechanisms of Attitude Change," in *Psychological Processes and Advertising Effects: Theory, Research, and Application,* ed. L. F. Alwitt and A. A. Mitchell (Hillsdale, NJ: Lawrence Erlbaum, 1985), pp. 65–87.

5. For an excellent overview, see Elenora W. Stuart, Terence A. Shimp, and Randall W. Engle, "Classical Conditioning of Consumer Attitudes: Four Experiments in an Advertising Context," *Journal of Consumer Research,* December 1987, pp. 334–49. Also see Chris T. Allen and Thomas J. Madden, "A Closer Look at Classical Conditioning," *Journal of Consumer Research,* December 1985, pp. 301–15; Terence A. Shimp, Elenora W. Stuart, and Randall W. Engle, "A Program of Classical Conditioning Experiments Testing Variations in the Conditioned Stimulus and Context," *Journal of Consumer Research,* June 1991, pp. 1–12.

6. Alain d'Astous and Marc Dubuc, "Retrieval Processes in Consumer Evaluative Judgment Making: The Role of Elaborative Processing," in *Advances in Consumer Research,* vol. 13, ed. Richard J. Lutz (Provo, UT: Association for Consumer Research, 1986), pp. 132–37; Paul W. Miniard, Thomas J. Page, April Atwood, and Randall L. Ross, "Representing Attitude Structure Issues and Evidence," in *Advances in Consumer Research,* vol. 13, ed. Richard J. Lutz (Provo, UT: Association for Consumer Research, 1986), pp. 72–76.

7. Russell H. Fazio, Martha C. Powell, and Carol J. Williams, "The Role of Attitude Accessibility in the Attitude-to-Behavior Process," *Journal of Consumer Research,* December 1989, pp. 280–88; Ida E. Berger and Andrew A. Mitchell, "The Effect of Advertising on Attitude Accessibility, Attitude Confidence, and the Attitude–Behavior Relationship," *Journal of Consumer Research,* December 1989, pp. 269–79.

8. Peter H. Farquhar, "Managing Brand Equity," *Marketing Research,* September 1989, pp. 24–33.

9. For instance, see Joan Myers-Levy, "Priming Effects on Product Judgments: A Hemispheric Interpretation," *Journal of Consumer Research,* June 1989, pp. 76–86.

10. Kenneth E. Miller and James L. Ginter, "An Investigation of Situational Variation in Brand Choice Behavior and Attitude," *Journal of Marketing Research,* February 1979, pp. 111–23.

11. Farquhar, "Managing Brand Equity."

12. Norman C. Berry, "Revitalizing Brands," *Journal of Consumer Marketing,* Summer 1988, pp. 15–20.

13. Farquhar, "Managing Brand Equity."

14. Ibid.

15. David M. Boush and Barbara Loken, "A Process-Tracing Study of Brand Extension Evaluation," *Journal of Marketing Research,* February 1991, pp. 16–28.

16. C. Whan Park, Sandra Milberg, and Robert Lawson, "Evaluation of Brand Extensions: The Role of Product Feature Similarity and Brand Concept Consistency," *Journal of Consumer Research,* September 1991, pp. 185–93.

17. This example is adapted from John Merwin, "The Sad Case of the Dwindling Orange Roofs," *Forbes,* December 30, 1985, pp. 75–79.

18. Fishbein and Ajzen, *Belief, Attitude, Intention, and Behavior;* Mitchell and Olson, "Are Product Attributes the Only Mediators of Advertising Effects on Brand Attitude?"

19. Susan B. Hester and Mary Yuen, "The Influences of Country of Origin on Consumer Attitudes and Buying Behavior in the United States and Canada," in *Advances in Consumer Research,* vol. 14, ed. Melanie Wallendorf and Paul Anderson (Provo, UT: Association for Consumer Research, 1987), pp. 538–42; Sung-Tai Hong and Robert S. Wyer, "Determinants of Product Evaluation: Effects of the Time Interval between Knowledge of a Product's Country of Origin and Information about Its Specific Attributes," *Journal of Consumer Research,* December 1990, pp. 277–88.

20. William B. Dodds, Kent B. Monroe, and Dhruv Grewal, "Effects of Price, Brand, and Store Information on Buyer's Product Evaluations," *Journal of Marketing Research,* August 1991, pp. 307–19; Meryl P. Gardner, "Advertising Effects on Attributes Recalled and Criteria Used for Brand Evaluations," *Journal of Consumer Research,* December 1983, pp. 310–18; Richard Paul Hinkle, "Medals from Wine Competitions Win Sales," *Advertising Age,* January 31, 1985, p. 31.

21. Kenneth E. Miller and James L. Ginter, "An Investigation of Situational Variation in Brand Choice Behavior and Attitude," *Journal of Marketing Research,* February 1979, pp. 111–23.

22. See William L. Wilkie and Edgar A. Pessemier, "Issues in Marketing's Use of Multiattribute Attitude Models," *Journal of Marketing Research,* November 1973, pp. 428–41. However, relatively little work has investigated the integration process itself; see Joel B. Cohen, Paul W. Miniard, and Peter R. Dickson, "Information Integration: An Information Processing Perspective," in *Advances in Consumer Research,* vol. 11, ed. Thomas C. Kinnear (Ann Arbor, MI: Association for Consumer Research, 1980), pp. 161–70. Another influential model, particularly in the early days of marketing research on attitudes, was developed by Milton J. Rosenberg, "Cognitive Structure and Attitudinal Affect," *Journal of Abnormal and Social Psychology,* November 1956, pp. 367–72. Although different terminology is used, the structure of Rosenberg's model is quite similar to Fishbein's.

23. Fishbein and Ajzen, *Belief, Attitude, Intention, and Behavior.*

24. See Phillip A. Dover and Jerry C. Olson, "Dynamic Changes in an Expectancy–Value Attitude Model as a Function of Multiple Exposures to Product Information," in *Contemporary Marketing Thought,* ed. B. A. Greenberg and D. N. Dellenger (Chicago: American Marketing Association, 1977), pp. 455–59; Robert E. Smith and William R. Swinyard, "Information Response Models: An Integrated Approach," *Journal of Marketing,* Winter 1982, pp. 81–93; Russell H. Fazio and Mark P. Zanna, "Attitudinal Qualities Relating to the Strength of the Attitude–Behavior Relationship," *Journal of Experimental Social Psychology* 14 (1987), pp. 398–408.

25. Fishbein and Ajzen, *Belief, Attitude, Intention, and Behavior.*

26. Richard J. Lutz, "The Role of Attitude Theory in Marketing," in *Perspectives in Consumer Behavior,* ed. H. H. Kassarjian and T. S. Robertson (Glenview, IL: Scott, Foresman, 1981), pp. 233–50. An early discussion of this idea was provided by James M. Carmen, "Values and Consumption Patterns: A Closed Loop," in *Advances in Consumer Research,* vol. 5, ed. H. Keith Hunt (Ann Arbor, MI: Association for Consumer Research, 1978), pp. 403–7; Jonathan Gutman, "Exploring the Nature of Linkages between Consequences and Values," *Journal of Business Research,* 1991, pp. 143–48.

27. Jerry C. Olson and Phillip A. Dover, "Attitude Maturation: Changes in Related Belief Structures over Time," in *Advances in Consumer Research,* vol. 5, ed. H. Keith Hunt (Ann Arbor, MI: Association for Consumer Research, 1978), pp. 333–42.

28. Richard J. Lutz and James R. Bettman, "Multiattribute Models in Marketing: A Bicentennial Review," in *Consumer and Industrial Buying Behavior,* ed. A. G. Woodside, J. N. Sheth, and P. D. Bennett (New York: Elsevier-North Holland Publishing, 1977), pp. 137–50.

29. Monci Jo Williams, "Why Is Airline Food So Terrible?" *Fortune,* December 19, 1988, pp. 169–72.

30. Christopher Power, Walecia Konrad, Alice Z. Cuneo, and James B. Treece, "Value Marketing: Quality, Service, and Fair Pricing Are the Keys to Selling in the '90s," *Business Week,* November 11, 1991, pp. 132–40.

31. John B. Palmer and Russ H. Crupnick, "New Dimensions Added to Conjoint Analysis," *Marketing News,* January 3, 1986, p. 62.

32. Richard J. Lutz, "Changing Brand Attitudes through Modification of Cognitive Structure," *Journal of Consumer Research,* March 1975, pp. 49–59; Andrew A. Mitchell, "The Effect of Verbal and Visual Components of Advertisements on Brand Attitudes and Attitude toward the Advertisement," *Journal of Consumer Research,* June 1986, pp. 12–24.

33. Michael J. McCarthy, "Chew on This: Crunch Is Latest Food Fad," *The Wall Street Journal,* April 2, 1997, p. B1.

34. Sanford Grossbart, Jim Gill, and Russ Laczniak, "Influence of Brand Commitment and Claim Strategy on Consumer Attitudes," in *Advances in Consumer Research,* vol. 14, ed. Melanie Wallendorf and Paul Anderson (Provo, UT: Association for Consumer Research, 1987), pp. 510–13.

35. Richard Gibson, "Popular Pizza Chain's Gimmick Is Taste," *The Wall Street Journal,* April 28, 1997, pp. B1, B9.

36. Frank Rose, "If It Feels Good, It Must Be Bad," *Fortune,* October 21, 1991, pp. 91–108.

37. Kathleen Deveny, "Seeking Sunnier Sales, Lotion Makers Play on Fears, Target Teens and Men," *The Wall Street Journal,* May 24, 1991, pp. B1, B3.

38. See, for example, James Jaccard and Grant Wood, "An Idiothetic Analysis of Attitude–Behavior Models," in *Advances in Consumer Research,* vol. 13, ed. Richard J. Lutz (Provo, UT: Association for Consumer Research, 1996), pp. 600–5.

39. Martin Fishbein, "An Overview of the Attitude Construct," in *A Look Back, A Look Ahead,* ed. G. B. Hafer (Chicago: American Marketing Association, 1980), p. 3.

40. See, for example, Icek Ajzen and Martin Fishbein, "Attitude–Behavior Relations: A Theoretical Analysis and Review of Empirical Research," *Psychological Bulletin,* September 1977, pp. 888–918; Alan W. Wicker, "Attitudes versus Action: The Relationship of Verbal and Overt Behavioral Responses to Attitude Objects," *Journal of Social Issues* 25 (1969), pp. 41–78.

41. See Fishbein, "An Overview of the Attitude Construct," pp. 1–19; Fishbein and Ajzen, *Belief, Attitude, Intention, and Behavior.*

42. Icek Ajzen and Martin Fishbein, *Understanding Attitudes and Predicting Social Behavior* (Englewood Cliffs, NJ: Prentice-Hall, 1980); Fishbein and Ajzen, *Belief, Attitude, Intention, and Behavior.* Note that this notion is consistent with our means–end chain conceptualization of consumers' product knowledge.

43. For a detailed exposition, see Terence A. Shimp and Alican Kavas, "The Theory of Reasoned Action Applied to Coupon Usage," *Journal of Consumer Research,* December 1984, pp. 795–809.

44. Ajzen and Fishbein, "Attitude–Behavior Relations: A Theoretical Analysis and Review of Empirical Research," pp. 888–918.

45. Richard P. Bagozzi and Paul R. Warshaw, "Trying to Consume," *Journal of Consumer Research,* September 1990, pp. 127–40.

46. Barbara Loken, "Effects of Uniquely Purchased Information on Attitudes toward Objects and Attitudes toward Behaviors," in *Advances in Consumer Research,* vol. 10, ed. R. P. Bagozzi and A. M. Tybout (Ann Arbor, MI: Association for Consumer Research, 1983), pp. 88–93.

47. Some researchers have argued that the strong distinction between A_{act} and SN may not be justified. See Paul W. Miniard and Joel B. Cohen, "Isolating Attitudinal and Normative Influences in Behavioral Intentions Models," *Journal of Marketing Research,* February 1979, pp. 102–10; Paul W. Miniard and Joel B. Cohen, "An Examination of the Fishbein–Ajzen Behavioral Intentions Model's Concepts and Measures," *Journal of Experimental Social Psychology* 17 (1981), pp. 309–39. Alternatively, the underlying salient beliefs for both A_{act} and SN could be considered as one set of activated beliefs that are combined to form a single, global A_{act}. One version of such a model was proposed by Paul W. Miniard and Joel B. Cohen, "Modeling Personal and Normative Influences on Behavior," *Journal of Consumer Research,* September 1983, pp. 169–80. For simplicity, however, we will follow the separate approach advocated by the theory of reasoned action.

48. Pat McIntyre, Mark A. Barnett, Richard Harris, James Shanteau, John Skowronski, and Michael Klassen, "Psychological Factors Influencing Decisions to Donate Organs," in *Advances in Consumer Research,* vol. 14, ed. Melanie Wallendorf and Paul Anderson (Provo, UT: Association for Consumer Research, 1987), pp. 331–34.

49. William O. Bearden and Randall L. Rose, "Attention to Social Comparison Information: An Individual Difference Factor Affecting Consumer Conformity," *Journal of Consumer Research,* March 1990, pp. 461–71.

50. Cited in Kenneth A. Longman, "Promises, Promises," in *Attitude Research on the Rocks,* ed. L. Adler and L. Crespi (Chicago: American Marketing Association, 1968), pp. 28–37.

51. Longman, "Promises, Promises," pp. 28–37.

52. For an interesting discussion of this issue, see Gordon R. Foxall, "Consumers' Intentions and Behavior: A Note on Research and a Challenge to Researchers," *Journal of Market Research Society* 26 (1985), pp. 231–41.

CHAPTER 7

1. Flemming Hansen, "Psychological Theories of Consumer Choice," *Journal of Consumer Research,* December 1976, pp. 117–42.

2. It is important to recognize that consumer decision making is actually a *seamless continuous flow of cognitive processes and behavioral actions.* Researchers "divide" this flow into separate stages and subprocesses for convenience in trying to research and understand the entire process and for helping to develop market strategies.

3. Joel B. Cohen, Paul W. Miniard, and Peter Dickson, "Information Integration: An Information Processing Perspective," in *Advances in Consumer Research,* vol. 7, ed. Jerry C. Olson (Ann Arbor, MI: Association for Consumer Research, 1980), pp. 161–70; Jerry C. Olson, "Theories of Information Encoding and Storage: Implications for Consumer Behavior," in *The Effect of Information on Consumer and Market Behavior,* ed. Andrew A. Mitchell (Chicago: American Marketing Association, 1978), pp. 49–60.

4. Richard W. Olshavsky and Donald H. Granbois, "Consumer Decision Making—Fact or Fiction?" *Journal of Consumer Research,* September 1979, pp. 93–100.

5. Peter H. Bloch, Daniel L. Sherrell, and Nancy M. Ridgway, "Consumer Search: An Extended Framework," *Journal of Consumer Research,* June 1986, pp. 119–26.

6. A similar notion is presented by Girish N. Punj and David W. Stewart, "An Interaction Framework of Consumer Decision Making," *Journal of Consumer Research,* September 1983, pp. 181–96.

7. Daniel Kahneman and Amos Tyersky, "Choices, Values, and Frames," *American Psychologist* 39 (1984), pp. 341–50; Christopher P. Puto, "The Framing of Buying Decisions," *Journal of Consumer Research,* December 1987, pp. 301–15; William J. Qualls and Christopher P. Puto, "Organizational Climate and Decision Framing: An Integrated Approach to Analyzing Industrial Buying Decisions," *Journal of Marketing Research,* May 1989, pp. 179–92.

8. James R. Bettman and Mita Sujan, "Effects of Framing on Evaluation of Comparable and Noncomparable Alternatives by Experts and Novice Consumers," *Journal of Consumer Research,* September 1987, pp. 141–54; Joshua L. Wiener, James W. Gentry, and Ronald K. Miller, "The Framing of the Insurance Purchase Decision," in *Advances in Consumer Research,* vol. 13, ed. Richard J. Lutz (Provo, UT: Association for Consumer Research, 1986), pp. 257–62; Peter Wright and Peter D. Rip, "Product Class Advertising Effects on First-Time Buyers' Decision Strategies," *Journal of Consumer Research,* September 1980, pp. 176–88.

9. Lawrence A. Crosby and James R. Taylor, "Effects of Consumer Information and Education in Cognition and Choice," *Journal of Consumer Research,* June 1981, pp. 43–56; John G. Lynch and Thomas K. Srull, "Memory and Attentional Factors in Consumer Choice: Concepts and Research Methods," *Journal of Consumer Research,* June 1982, pp. 18–37; Gabriel Biehal and Dipankar Chakravarti, "Consumers' Use of Memory and External Information in Choice: Macro and Micro Perspectives," *Journal of Consumer Research,* March 1986, pp. 382–405.

10. Gabriel Biehal and Dipankar Chakravarti, "Information Accessibility as a Moderator of Consumer Choice," *Journal of Consumer Research,* June 1983, pp. 1–14; Valerie S. Folkes, "The Availability Heuristic and Perceived Risk," *Journal of Consumer Research,* June 1988, pp. 13–23.

11. David B. Klenosky and Arno J. Rethans, "The Formation of Consumer Choice Sets: A Longitudinal Investigation at the Product Class Level," in *Advances in Consumer Research,* vol. 15, ed. Michael J. Houston (Provo, UT: Association for Consumer Research, 1988), pp. 13–18; John R. Hauser and Birger Wernerfelt, "An Evaluation Cost Model of Consideration Set," *Journal of Consumer Research,* March 1990, pp. 393–408; John H. Roberts and James M. Lattin, "Development and Testing of a Model of Consideration Set Composition," *Journal of Marketing Research,* November 1991, pp. 429–40.

12. John Howard and Jagdish N. Sheth, *The Theory of Buyer Behavior* (New York: Wiley, 1969); Prakash Nedungadi, "Recall and Consumer Consideraton Sets: Influencing Choice without Altering Brand Evaluations," *Journal of Consumer Research,* December 1990, pp. 263–76.

13. Sharon E. Beatty and Scott M. Smith, "External Search Effort: An Investigation across Several Product Categories," *Journal of Consumer Research,* June 1987, pp. 83–95.

14. Wayne D. Hoyer and Steven P. Brown, "Effects of Brand Awareness on Choice for a Common, Repeat-Purchase Product," *Journal of Consumer Research*, September 1990, pp. 141–48.

15. William Baker, J. Wesley Hutchinson, Danny Moore, and Prakash Nedungadi, "Brand Familiarity and Advertising: Effects on the Evoked Set and Brand Preference," in *Advances in Consumer Research,* vol. 13, ed. Richard J. Lutz (Provo, UT: Association for Consumer Research, 1986), pp. 637–42.

16. Kristian E. Moller and Pirjo Karppinen, "Role of Motives and Attributes in Consumer Motion Picture Choice," *Journal of Economic Psychology* 4 (1983), pp. 239–62.

17. Joel E. Urbany, Peter R. Dickson, and William L. Wilkie, "Buyer Uncertainty and Information Search," *Journal of Consumer Research,* September 1989, pp. 208–15.

18. Klaus G. Grunert, "Cognitive Determinants of Attribute Information Usage," *Journal of Economic Psychology* 7 (1986), pp. 95–124; C. Whan Park and Daniel C. Smith, "Product-Level Choice: A Top-Down or Bottom-Up Process?" *Journal of Consumer Research,* December 1989, pp. 289–99.

19. Mark I. Alpert, "Unresolved Issues in Identification of Determinant Attributes," in *Advances in Consumer Research,* vol. 7, ed. Jerry C. Olson (Ann Arbor, MI: Association for Consumer Research, 1980), pp. 83–88.

20. John U. Farley, Jerrold Katz, and Donald R. Lehmann, "Impact of Different Comparison Sets on Evaluation of a New Subcompact Car Brand," *Journal of Consumer Research,* September 1978, pp. 138–42; Srinivasan Ratneshwar, Allan D. Shocker, and David W. Steward, "Toward Understanding the Attraction Effect: The Implications of Product Stimulus Meaningfulness and Familiarity," *Journal of Consumer Research,* March 1987, pp. 520–33; Merrie Brucks and Paul H. Schurr, "The Effects of Bargainable Attributes and Attribute Range Knowledge on Consumer Choice Processes," *Journal of Consumer Research,* March 1990, pp. 409–19; Kim P. Corfman, "Comparability and Comparison Levels Used in Choices among Consumer Products," *Journal of Marketing Research,* August 1991, pp. 368–74; Noreen M. Klein and Manjit S. Yadav, "Context Effects on Effort and Accuracy in Choice: An Enquiry into Adaptive Decision Making," *Journal of Consumer Research,* March 1989, pp. 411–21; Rashi Glazer, Barbara E. Kahn, and William L.

Moore, "The Influence of External Constraints on Brand Choice: The Lone Alternative Effect," *Journal of Consumer Research,* June 1991, pp. 119–27.

21. Valerie S. Folkes, "The Availability Heuristic and Perceived Risk," *Journal of Consumer Research,* June 1988, pp. 13–23.

22. John W. Vann, "A Conditional Probability View of the Role of Product Warranties in Reducing Perceived Financial Risk," in *Advances in Consumer Research,* vol. 14, ed. Melanie Wallendorf and Paul Anderson (Provo, UT: Association for Consumer Research, 1987), pp. 421–25.

23. Scott Hume, "Seven-Up Stands Up to Cola's Challenge," *Advertising Age,* May 20, 1985, pp. 4, 92.

24. Narasimhan Srinivasan and Brian T. Ratchford, "An Empirical Test of a Model of External Search for Automobiles," *Journal of Consumer Research,* September 1991, pp. 233–42; Keith B. Murray, "A Test of Services Marketing Theory: Consumer Information Acquisition Activities," *Journal of Marketing,* January 1991, pp. 10–25.

25. Robert S. Billings and Lisa L. Scherer, "The Effects of Response Mode and Importance on Decision-Making Strategies: Judgment versus Choice," *Organizational Behavior and Human Decision Processes* 41 (1988), pp. 1–19; Peter Wright, "Consumer Choice Strategies: Simplifying versus Optimizing," *Journal of Marketing Research,* February 1975, pp. 60–67.

26. James R. Bettman and C. Whan Park, "Effects of Prior Knowledge and Experience and Phase of the Choice Process on Consumer Decision Processes: A Protocol Analysis," *Journal of Consumer Research,* December 1980, pp. 234–48; Cohen, Miniard, and Dickson, "Information Integration: An Information Processing Perspective," pp. 161–70; Wayne D. Hoyer, "An Examination of Consumer Decision Making for a Common Repeat Purchase Product," *Journal of Consumer Research,* December 1984, pp. 822–29; David J. Curry, Michael B. Menasco, and James W. Van Ark, "Multiattribute Dyadic Choice: Models and Tests," *Journal of Marketing Research,* August 1991, pp. 259–67.

27. James R. Bettman, *An Information Processing Theory of Consumer Choice* (Reading, MA: Addison-Wesley, 1979); Denis A. Lussier and Richard W. Olshavsky, "Task Complexity and Contingent Processing in Brand Choice," *Journal of Consumer Research,* September 1979, pp. 154–65; Merrie Brucks and Andrew A. Mitchell, "Knowledge Structures, Production Systems and Decision Strategies," in *Advances in Consumer Researech,* vol. 8, ed. Kent B. Monroe (Ann

Arbor, MI: Association for Consumer Research, 1981).

28. Bettman and Park, "Effects of Prior Knowledge," pp. 234–48; Hoyer, "An Examination of Consumer Decision Making for a Common Repeat Purchase Product," pp. 822–29.

29. James R. Bettman, "Presidential Address: Processes of Adaptivity in Decision Making," in *Advances in Consumer Research,* vol. 15, ed. Michael J. Houston (Provo, UT: Association for Consumer Research, 1988), pp. 1–4; Surjit Chabra and Richard W. Olshavsky, "Some Evidence for Additional Types of Choice Strategies," in *Advances in Consumer Research,* vol. 13, ed. Richard J. Lutz (Provo, UT: Association for Consumer Research, 1986), pp. 12–16; Wayne D. Hoyer, "Variations in Choice Strategies across Decision Contexts: An Examination of Contingent Factors," in *Advances in Consumer Research,* vol. 13, ed. Richard J. Lutz (Provo, UT: Association for Consumer Research, 1986), pp. 32–36; James R. Bettman and Michel A. Zins, "Constructive Processes in Consumer Choice," *Journal of Consumer Research,* September 1977, pp. 75–85; Bettman and Park, "Effects of Prior Knowledge," pp. 234–48.

30. Hoyer, "Examination of Consumer Decision Making," pp. 822–29; John Payne, "Task Complexity and Contingent Processing in Decision Making," *Organizational Behavior and Human Performance* 16 (1976), pp. 366–87; David Grether and Louis Wilde, "An Analysis of Conjunctive Choice: Theory and Experiments," *Journal of Consumer Research,* March 1984, pp. 373–85.

31. C. Whan Park and Richard J. Lutz, "Decision Plans and Consumer Choice Dynamics," *Journal of Marketing Research,* February 1982, pp. 108–15.

32. This terminology is borrowed from John Howard, *Consumer Behavior: Applications of Theory* (New York: McGraw-Hill, 1979).

33. Robert J. Meyer, "The Learning of Multiattribute Judgment Policies," *Journal of Consumer Research,* September 1987, pp. 155–73.

34. Wayne D. Hoyer, "An Examination of Consumer Decision Making for a Common Repeat Purchase Product," *Journal of Consumer Research,* December 1984, pp. 822–29.

35. James H. Myers, "Attribute Deficiency Segmentation: Measuring Unmet Wants," in *Advances in Consumer Research,* vol. 15, ed. Michael J. Houston (Provo, UT: Association for Consumer Research, 1988), pp. 108–13.

36. Lawrence W. Barsalou and J. Wesley Hutchinson, "Schema-Based Planning of Events in Consumer Contexts," in *Advances in Consumer Research,* vol. 14, ed. Melanie Wallendorf and Paul Anderson (Provo, UT: Association for Consumer Research, 1987), pp. 114–18.

37. This section was adapted from Bettman, *An Information Processing Theory of Consumer Choice.*

38. Anna Wilde Mathews and Nikhil Deogun, "Stung by UPS, Some Shippers Seek Alternatives," *The Wall Street Journal,* August 20, 1997, pp. B1, B2.

39. Ronald P. Hill and Meryl P. Gardner, "The Buying Process: Effects of and on Consumer Mood States," in *Advances in Consumer Research,* vol. 14, ed. Melanie Wallendorf and Paul Anderson (Provo, UT: Association for Consumer Research, 1987), pp. 408–10.

40. Hansen, "Psychological Theories of Consumer Choice," pp. 117–42 Bettman, *An Information Processing Theory of Consumer Choice.*

41. George A. Miller, Eugene Galanter, and Karl H. Pribram, *Plans and the Structure of Behavior* (New York: Henry Holt, 1960).

42. Robert M. Schlinder, Michael Berbaum, and Donna R. Weinzimer, "How an Attention Getting Device Can Affect Choice among Similar Alternatives," in *Advances in Consumer Research,* vol. 14, ed. Melanie Wallendorf and Paul Anderson (Provo, UT: Association for Consumer Research, 1987), pp. 505–9.

43. Dennis W. Rook, "The Buying Impulse," *Journal of Consumer Research,* September 1987, pp. 189–99.

44. See the Wirthlin Worldwide website at **www.decima.com/whatsnew/.**

45. Kevin Lane Keller and Richard Staelin, "Effects of Quality and Quantity of Information on Decision Effectiveness," *Journal of Consumer Research,* September 1987, pp. 200–13.

CHAPTER 8

1. For example, see Merrie Brucks, "The Effects of Product Class Knowledge on Information Search Behavior," *Journal of Consumer Research,* June 1985, pp. 1–16; Peter H. Bloch, Daniel L. Sherrell, and Nancy M. Ridgeway, "Consumer Search: An Extended Framework," *Journal of Consumer Research,* June 1986, pp. 119–26.

2. Sharon E. Beatty and Scott M. Smith, "External Search Effort: An Investigation across Several Product Categories," *Journal of Consumer Research,* June 1981, pp. 11–22.

3. For a complete discussion of these issues, see Howard Beales, Michael B. Mazis, Steven Salop, and Richard Staelin, "Consumer Search and Public Policy," *Journal of Consumer Research,* June 1981, pp. 11–22.

CHAPTER 9

1. Much of the material in this chapter is based on Walter R. Nord and J. Paul Peter, "A Behavior Modification Perspective on Marketing," *Journal of Marketing*, Spring 1980, pp. 36–47; J. Paul Peter and Walter R. Nord, "A Clarification and Extension of Operant Conditioning Principles in Marketing," *Journal of Marketing*, Summer 1982, pp. 102–17. For additional discussions of behaviorists' views on marketing and consumer behavior, see Gordon R. Foxall, *Consumer Psychology in Behavioural Perspective* (London: Routledge, 1990); Gordon R. Foxall, "The Explanation of Consumer Behaviour: From Social Cognition to Environmental Control," *International Review of Industrial and Organizational Psychology*, vol. 12, ed. C. L. Cooper and I. T. Robertson (New York: Wiley, 1997), pp. 229–87.

2. Behaviorists consider emotions or feelings not as cognitive events but as behaviors. For example, if someone is observed yelling and throwing books at a classmate, behaviorists would have no problem describing the person as angry. However, the idea that the person is angry is determined through observation of the behaviors. Alternatively, measures of the person's blood pressure or other physiological measures could be used. However, the behaviors of yelling and throwing are the problems to be analyzed and changed; the idea that there is an internal feeling called *anger* is believed to be impossible to prove or study scientifically by behaviorists. Today many behaviorists find self-report measures of cognitive events useful for providing supportive evidence in an analysis and for diagnostic purposes. However, self-reports alone of mental states and events are still considered less valuable than measures of observed behaviors.

3. Terence A. Shimp, Elnora W. Stuart, and Randall W. Engle, "A Program of Classical Conditioning Experiments Testing Variations in Conditioned Stimulus and Context." *Journal of Consumer Research*, June 1991, pp. 1–12.

4. Werner Kroeber-Riel, "Emotional Product Differentiation by Classical Conditioning," in *Advances in Consumer Research*, vol. 11, ed. Thomas C. Kinnear (Provo, UT: Association for Consumer Research, 1984), pp. 538–43.

5. For further discussion of this type of conditioning, see Terence A. Shimp, "Neo-Pavlovian Conditioning and Its Implications for Consumer Theory and Research," in *Handbook of Consumer Research and Theory*, ed. T. Robertson and H. Kassarjian (Englewood Cliffs, NJ: Prentice-Hall, 1991), pp. 162–87; Robert A. Rescorla, "Pavlovian Conditioning: It's Not What You Think," *American Psychologist*, March 1988, pp. 151–60; Gerald J. Gorn, "The Effects of Music in Advertising on Choice Behavior: A Classical Conditioning Approach," *Journal of Marketing*, Winter 1982, pp. 94–101; Richard A. Feinberg, "Classical Conditioning of Credit Cards: Credit Cards May Facilitate Spending," in *Proceedings of the American Psychological Association, Division of Consumer Psychology*, ed. Michael B. Mazis (Washington, DC: American Psychological Association, 1982), pp. 28–30. Also see Richard A. Feinberg, "Credit Cards as Spending Facilitating Stimuli: A Conditioning Interpretation," *Journal of Consumer Research*, December 1986, pp. 348–56; Francis K. McSweeney and Calvin Bierley, "Recent Developments in Classical Conditioning," *Journal of Consumer Research*, December 1985, pp. 310–15; Calvin Bierley, Francis McSweeney, and Renee Vannieuwkerk, "Classical Conditioning of Preferences for Stimuli," *Journal of Consumer Research*, December 1985, pp. 316–23; M. Carole Macklin, "Classical Conditioning Effects in Product/Character Pairings Presented to Children," in *Advances in Consumer Research*, vol. 13., ed. Richard J. Lutz (Provo, UT: Association for Consumer Research, 1985), pp. 198–203; Larry G. Gresham and Terence A. Shimp, "Attitude toward the Advertisement and Brand Attitudes: A Classical Conditioning Perspective," *Journal of Advertising*, 1985, pp. 10–17; Elnora W. Stuart, Terence A. Shimp, and Randall W. Engle, "Classical Conditioning of Consumer Attitudes: Four Experiments in an Advertising Context," *Journal of Consumer Research*, December 1987, pp. 334–49; Chris T. Allen and Chris A. Janiszewski, "Assessing the Role of Contingency Awareness in Attitudinal Conditioning with Implications for Advertising Research," *Journal of Marketing Research*, February 1989, pp. 30–43; Chris Janiszewski and Luk Warlop, "The Influence of Classical Conditioning Procedures on Subsequent Attention to the Conditioned Brand," *Journal of Consumer Research*, September 1993, pp. 171–89.

6. There are a number of other possibilities, such as punishment by the removal of a positive consequence. For complete descriptions of these processes, see Arthur W. Staats, *Social Behaviorism* (Chicago: Dorsey Press, 1975).

7. B. C. Deslauriers and P. B. Everett, "The Effects of Intermittent and Continuous Token Reinforcement on Bus Ridership," *Journal of Applied Psychology*, August 1977, pp. 369–75.

8. There are a number of other possible reinforcement schedules. However, we will limit our attention to continuous and ratio

schedules. Also, we will not deal with the consequences that the different schedules have on the pattern, rate, and maintenance of behavior. For a detailed treatment of these effects, see W. K. Honig, *Operant Behavior: Areas of Research and Application* (New York: Appleton-Century-Crofts, 1966).

9. Albert Bandura, *Principles of Behavior Modification* (New York: Holt, Rinehart & Winston, 1969), p. 120. This is a classic reference in the psychological literature.

10. This discussion of the three major types of modeling influences is based on Walter R. Nord and J. Paul Peter, "A Behavior Modification Perspective on Marketing," *Journal of Marketing*, Spring 1980, pp. 40–41.

11. Bandura, *Principles of Behavior Modification*, p. 167.

12. See Charles C. Manz and Henry P. Sims, "Vicarious Learning: The Influence of Modeling on Organizational Behavior," *Academy of Management Review*, January 1981, pp. 105–13. For discussions of model characteristics in advertising, see Michael J. Baker and Gilbert A. Churchill, Jr., "The Impact of Physically Attractive Models on Advertising Evaluations," *Journal of Marketing Research*, November 1977, pp. 538–55; "Models' Clothing Speaks to Ad Market: Study," *Marketing News*, November 22, 1985, p. 16; Lynn R. Kahle and Pamela M. Homer, "Physical Attractiveness of the Celebrity Endorser: A Social Adaptation Perspective," *Journal of Consumer Research*, March 1985, pp. 954–61.

13. Manz and Sims, "Vicarious Learning," p. 107.

14. Albert Bandura, *Social Learning Theory* (Englewood Cliffs, NJ: Prentice-Hall, 1977), p. 89. This book discusses a number of other variables affecting the modeling process.

15. Richard I. Evans, Richard M. Rozelle, Scott E. Maxwell, Betty E. Raines, Charles A. Dill, and Tanya J. Guthrie, "Social Modeling Films to Deter Smoking in Adolescents: Results of a Three-Year Field Investigation," *Journal of Applied Psychology*, August 1981, pp. 399–414.

16. Denise A. DeRicco and John E. Niemann, "*In Vivo* Effects of Peer Modeling on Drinking Rate," *Journal of Applied Behavioral Analysis*, Spring 1980, pp. 149–52; Barry D. Caudill and Thomas R. Lipscomb, "Modeling Influences on Alcoholics' Rates of Alcohol Consumption," *Journal of Applied Behavioral Analysis*, Summer 1980, pp. 355–65.

17. Trevor F. Stokes and Suzanne H. Kennedy, "Reducing Child Uncooperative Behavior during Dental Treatment through Modeling and Reinforcement," *Journal of Applied Behavioral Analysis*, Spring 1980, pp. 41–49.

18. Richard A. Winnett, Joseph W. Hatcher, T. Richard Fort, Ingrid N. Lechliter, Susan Q. Love, Anne W. Riley, and James F. Fishback, "The Effects of Videotape Modeling and Daily Feedback on Residential Electricity Conservation, Home Temperature and Humidity, Perceived Comfort and Clothing Worn: Winter and Summer," *Journal of Applied Behavioral Analysis*, Fall 1982, pp. 381–402.

CHAPTER 10

1. Robert C. Blattberg and Scott A. Neslin, *Sales Promotion: Concepts, Methods, and Strategies* (Englewood Cliffs, NJ: Prentice-Hall, 1990), p. 3.

2. J. Paul Peter and James H. Donnelly, Jr., *A Preface to Marketing Management*, 7th ed. (Burr Ridge, IL: Irwin, 1997), pp. 157–58.

3. "Study: Some Promotions Change Consumer Behavior," *Marketing News*, October 15, 1990, p. 12.

4. Alan Andreason, *Marketing Social Change* (San Francisco: Jossey-Bass, 1995), p. 7.

5. For further discussion, see Alan E. Kazdin, *Behavior Modification in Applied Settings*, 5th ed. (Pacific Grove, CA: Brooks/Cole, 1994).

6. Andreason, *Marketing Social Change*, p. 292.

7. Susan Caminiti, "What the Scanner Knows About You," *Fortune*, December 3, 1990, pp. 51–52. Also see Jeffrey Rothfeder et al., "How Software Is Making Food Sales a Piece of Cake," *Business Week*, July 2, 1990, pp. 54–55; Dom Del Prete, "Advances in Scanner Research Yield Better Data Quicker," *Marketing News*, January 7, 1991, p. 54; Howard Schlossberg, "IRI Expands Sales Tracking to Drugstores, Mass Merchandisers," *Marketing News*, May 27, 1991, pp. 1, 10.

CHAPTER 11

1. Adapted for this text from Jack Block and Jeanne H. Block, "Studying Situational Dimensions: A Grand Perspective and Some Limited Empiricism," in *Toward a Psychology of Situations: An Interactional Perspective*, ed. David Magnusson (Hillsdale, NJ: Lawrence Erlbaum, 1981), pp. 85–102.

2. C. Whan Park, Easwar S. Iyer, and Daniel C. Smith, "The Effects of Situational Factors on In-Store Grocery Shopping Behavior: The Role of Store Environment and Time Available for Shopping," *Journal of Consumer Research*, March 1989, pp. 422–33.

3. Adapted from William D. Crano and Lawrence A. Messe, *Social Psychology: Principles and Themes of Interpersonal Behavior* (Homewood, IL: Dorsey Press, 1982), p. 15.

4. For example, see Robert J. Graham, "The Role of Perception of Time in Consumer Research," *Journal of Consumer Research*, March 1981, pp. 335–42; Lawrence P.

Feldman and Jacob Hornik, "The Use of Time: An Integrated Conceptual Model," *Journal of Consumer Research*, March 1981, pp. 407–19; Jacob Hornik, "Situational Effects on the Consumption of Time," *Journal of Marketing*, Fall 1982, pp. 44–55; Jacob Hornik, "Subjective versus Objective Time Measures: A Note on the Perception of Time in Consumer Behavior," *Journal of Consumer Research*, June 1984, pp. 615–18.

5. See Fern Schumer Chapman, "Business's Push for More Daylight Time," *Fortune*, November 12, 1984, pp. 615–18.

6. See Debra A. Michal's "Pitching Products by the Barometer," *Business Week*, July 8, 1985, p. 45; Ronald Alsop, "Companies Look to Weather to Find Best Climate for Ads," *The Wall Street Journal*, January 19, 1985, p. 27; Fred Ward, "Weather, Behavior Correlated in New Market Test," *Marketing News*, June 7, 1985, p. 9.

7. See Jeff Meer, "The Light Touch," *Psychology Today*, September 1985, pp. 60–67.

8. See Mark Harris, "Evaluate Lighting Systems as a Marketing Device, Not Overhead," *Marketing News*, October 26, 1984, p. 1.

9. Carl P. Zeithaml and Valarie A. Zeithaml, "Environmental Management: Revising the Marketing Perspective," *Journal of Marketing*, Spring 1985, pp. 46–53.

10. See James H. Leigh and Claude R. Martin, "A Review of Situational Influence Paradigms and Research," in *Review of Marketing 1981*, eds. Ben M. Enis and Kenneth J. Reering (Chicago: American Marketing Association, 1981), pp. 57–74; Pradeep Kakkar and Richard J. Lutz, "Situational Influences on Consumer Behavior," in *Perspectives in Consumer Behavior*, 3d ed., ed. Harold H. Kassarjian and Thomas S. Robertson (Glenview, IL: Scott, Foresman, 1981), pp. 204–15; Joseph A. Cote, Jr., "Situational Variables in Consumer Research: A Review," Working Paper, Washington State University, 1985.

11. See Russell W. Belk, "The Objective Situation as a Determinant of Consumer Behavior," in *Advances in Consumer Research*, vol. 2, ed. Mary J. Schlinger (Chicago: Association for Consumer Research, 1975), pp. 427–38; Richard J. Lutz and Pradeep K. Kakkar, "The Psychological Situation as a Determinant of Consumer Behavior," in *Advances in Consumer Research*, vol. 2, ed. Mary J. Schlinger (Chicago: Association for Consumer Research, 1975), pp. 439–54.

12. Geraldine Fennell, "Consumers' Perceptions of the Product Use Situation," *Journal of Marketing*, April 1978, pp. 38–47.

13. Russell W. Belk, "Situational Variables and Consumer Behavior," *Journal of Consumer Research*, December 1976, pp. 157–64;

Kenneth E. Miller and James L. Ginter, "An Investigation of Situational Variation in Brand Choice Behavior and Attitude," *Journal of Marketing Research*, February 1979, pp. 111–23.

14. Miller and Ginter, "An Investigation of Situational Variation."

15. J. Edward Russo, Richard Staelin, Catherine A. Nolan, Gary J. Russell, and Barbara L. Metcalf, "Nutrition Information in the Supermarket," *Journal of Consumer Research*, June 1986, pp. 48–70.

16. Dennis L. McNeill and William L. Wilkie, "Public Policy and Consumer Information: Impact of the New Energy Labels," *Journal of Consumer Research*, June 1979, pp. 1–11.

17. These examples come from Skip Wollenberg, "P-O-P Campaigns Increase as Profiles of Shoppers Change," *Marketing News*, April 11, 1988, p. 25.

18. Joe Agnew, "P-O-P Displays Are Becoming a Matter of Convenience," *Marketing News*, October 9, 1987, pp. 14, 16.

19. J. Davis Illingworth, "The Personal Plus," *Marketing Insights*, Winter 1991, pp. 31–33, 45.

20. Ibid.

21. Antonio Fins, "Sunglass Huts: Thriving in Nooks and Crannies," *Business Week*, July 27, 1987.

22. Jeffrey A. Trachtenberg, "When a Mall's Biggest Retailers Fall, Surviving Shops Get an Unpleasant Jolt," *The Wall Street Journal*, October 25, 1990, pp. B1, B8.

23. "Hallmark Now Marketing by Color," *Marketing News*, June 6, 1988, p. 18.

24. Meryl P. Gardner and George J. Siomkos, "Toward Methodology for Assessing Effects of In-Store Atmospherics," in *Advances in Consumer Research*, vol. 13, ed. Richard J. Lutz (Provo, UT: Association for Consumer Research, 1986), pp. 27–31; Robert J. Donovan and John R. Rossiter, "Store Atmosphere: An Environmental Psychology Approach," *Journal of Retailing*, Spring 1982, pp. 34–57.

25. Michael Solomon, "The Missing Link: Surrogate Consumers in the Marketing Chain," *Journal of Marketing*, October 1986, pp. 208–18.

26. Ronald E. Milliman, "The Influence of Background Music on the Behavior of Restaurant Patrons," *Journal of Consumer Research*, September 1986, pp. 286–89.

27. Patricia Strand, "Bars Tap 'Cheers' Name," *Advertising Age*, March 11, 1991, p. 16.

28. Elizabeth Ames and Geraldine Fabrikant, "Rich Melman: The Hot Dog of the Restaurant Business," *Business Week*, February 11, 1985, pp. 73–77; Howard Riell, "Slumping Restaurant Industry Seeks New Marketing Ideas," *Marketing News*, February 18, 1991, pp. 2, 5.

29. Russell W. Belk, John Sherry, and Melanie Wallendorf, "A Naturalistic Inquiry into Buyer and Seller Behavior at a Swap Meet," *Journal of Consumer Research*, March 1988, pp. 449–70.

CHAPTER 12

1. Over 160 definitions of culture are reported in Frederick D. Sturdivant, "Subculture Theory: Poverty, Minorities, and Marketing," in *Consumer Behavior: Theoretical Sources*, ed. Scott Ward and Thomas S. Robertson (Englewood Cliffs, NJ: Prentice-Hall, 1973), pp. 469–520.

2. An important source is Grant McCracken, *Culture and Consumption: New Approaches to the Symbolic Character of Consumer Goods and Activities* (Bloomington, IN: Indiana University Press, 1988).

3. John F. Sherry, "The Cultural Perspective in Consumer Research," in *Advances in Consumer Research*, vol. 13, ed. Richard J. Lutz (Provo, UT: Association for Consumer Research, 1986), pp. 573–75.

4. Most consumer behavior textbooks focus on the content of culture, describing the values and lifestyles of consumers in different cultures. For example, see Leon G. Shiffman and Leslie Lazar Kanuk, *Consumer Behavior*, 4th ed. (Englewood Cliffs, NJ: Prentice-Hall, 1991); William L. Wilkie, *Consumer Behavior*, 2d ed. (New York: Wiley, 1990).

5. Ann Swidler, "Culture in Action: Symbols and Strategies," *American Sociological Review*, April 1986, pp. 273–86; McCracken, *Culture and Consumption*, pp. 73–74.

6. Craig J. Thompson, William B. Locander, and Howard R. Pollio, "Putting Consumer Experience Back into Consumer Research: The Philosophy and Method of Existential-Phenomenology," *Journal of Consumer Research*, September 1989, pp. 133–47; Craig J. Thompson, William B. Locander, and Howard R. Pollio, "The Lived Meaning of Free Choice: An Existential-Phenomenological Description of Everyday Consumer Experiences of Contemporary Married Women," *Journal of Consumer Research*, December 1990, pp. 346–61.

7. Margot Hornblower, "Advertising Spoken Here," *Time*, July 15, 1991, pp. 71–72.

8. David Kilburn, "Japan's Sun Rises," *Advertising Age*, August 3, 1987, p. 42.

9. Sidney J. Levy, "Interpreting Consumer Mythology: A Structural Approach to Consumer Behavior," *Journal of Marketing*, Summer 1981, pp. 49–61.

10. Morris B. Holbrook and John O'Shaughnessy, "On the Scientific Status of Consumer Research and the Need for an Interpretive Approach to Studying Consumption Behavior," *Journal of Consumer Research*, December 1988, pp. 398–402; Laurel Anderson Hudson and Julie L. Ozanne, "Alternative Ways of Seeking Knowledge in Consumer Research," *Journal of Consumer Research*, March 1988, pp. 508–21.

11. Susan Spiggle, "Measuring Social Values: A Content Analysis of Sunday Comics and Underground Comix," *Journal of Consumer Research*, June 1986, pp. 100–13; Russell W. Belk, "Material Values in the Comics: A Content Analysis of Comic Books Featuring Themes of Wealth," *Journal of Consumer Research*, June 1987, pp. 26–42.

12. Russell W. Belk and Richard W. Pollay, "Images of Ourselves: The Good Life in Twentieth-Century Advertising," *Journal of Consumer Research*, March 1985, p. 888.

13. Clifford Geertz, "Thick Description," in *The Interpretation of Cultures* (New York: Basic Books, 1973), pp. 3–30.

14. John F. Sherry, Jr., "A Sociocultural Analysis of a Midwestern American Flea Market," *Journal of Consumer Research*, June 1990, pp. 13–30; Russell W. Belk, John F. Sherry, Jr., and Melanie Wallendorf, "A Naturalistic Inquiry into Buyer and Seller Behavior at a Swap Meet," *Journal of Consumer Research*, March 1988, pp. 449–70.

15. Bruce Horowitz, "Retailers in Search of Customers for Life," *USA Today*, December 18, 1997, pp. 1A, 2A.

16. Wagner A. Kamakura and Jose Afonso Mazzon, "Value Segmentation: A Model for the Measurement of Values and Value Systems," *Journal of Consumer Research*, September 1991, pp. 208–18.

17. See the Levelor website at **www.levelor.com/new.html**.

18. This model is an adaptation and extension of the cultural process described by Grant McCracken (*Culture and Consumption*), who focused on how cultural meanings are first transferred to products and then passed on to individuals. The following discussion elaborates on McCracken's ideas and extends them into a systems model of cultural processes.

19. Grant McCracken, "Culture and Consumption: A Theoretical Account of the Structure and Movement of the Cultural Meaning of Consumer Goods," *Journal of Consumer Research*, June 1986, pp. 71–84.

20. McCracken, *Culture and Consumption*, p. 79.

21. Jeffrey F. Durgee and Robert W. Stuart, "Advertising Symbols and Brand Names That Best Represent Key Product Meanings," *Journal of Advertising*, Summer 1987, pp. 15–24.

22. Robert M. Schindler, "Symbolic Price Endings."

23. Elizabeth C. Hirschman, "The Creation of Product Symbolism," in *Advances in Consumer Research*, vol. 13, ed. R. J. Lutz (Provo, UT: Association for Consumer Research, 1986), pp. 327–31.

24. For a brief discussion of the meaning transfer aspects of the fashion system, see McCracken, "Culture and Consumption: A Theoretical Account."

25. Mihaly Csikszentmihalyi and Eugene Rochberg-Halton, *The Meaning of Things: Domestic Symbols and the Self* (Cambridge, UK: Cambridge University Press, 1981); Levy, "Interpreting Consumer Mythology"; Michael Solomon, "The Role of Products as Social Stimuli: A Symbolic Interactionism Perspective," *Journal of Consumer Research*, December 1983, pp. 319–29.

26. Seth Lubove, "Going, Going, Sold!" *Forbes*, October 14, 1991, pp. 180–81.

27. Russell W. Belk, "Possessions and the Extended Self," *Journal of Consumer Research*, September 1988, pp. 139–68.

28. Anne B. Fisher, "Coke's Brand-Loyalty Lesson," *Fortune*, August 5, 1985, pp. 44–46.

29. McCracken, *Culture and Consumption*.

30. For example, see Dennis W. Rook, "The Ritual Dimension of Consumer Behavior," *Journal of Consumer Research*, December 1985, pp. 251–64.

31. The last four rituals are described in McCracken, "Culture and Consumption: A Theoretical Account," pp. 71–84.

32. Sherry, "A Sociocultural Analysis."

33. Peter H. Bloch, "Product Enthusiasm: Many Questions, a Few Answers," in *Advances in Consumer Research*, vol. 13, ed. R. J. Lutz (Provo, UT: Association for Consumer Research, 1986), pp. 61–65.

34. Russelll W. Belk, "Gift-Giving Behavior," in *Research in Marketing*, vol. 2, ed. Jagdish Sheth (Greenwich, CT: JAI Press, 1979), pp. 95–126.

35. Michael R. Solomon, "Deep-Seated Materialism: The Case of Levi's 501 Jeans," in *Advances in Consumer Researech*, vol. 13, ed. R. J. Lutz (Provo, UT: Association for Consumer Research, 1986), pp. 619–22.

36. Lubove, "Going, Going, Sold!"

37. Some consumer researchers have written about such topics; see Belk, "Possessions and the Extended Self."

38. Terence A. Shimp and Thomas J. Madden, "Consumer–Object Relations: A Conceptual Framework Based Analogously on Sternberg's Triangular Theory of Love," in *Advances in Consumer Research*, vol. 15 (Provo, UT: Association for Consumer Research, 1988), pp. 163–68.

39. Edmund Sherman and Evelyn S. Newman, "The Meaning of Cherished Personal Possessions for the Elderly," *Journal of Aging and Human Development* 8, no. 2 (1977–78), pp. 181–92.

40. Thomas Reynolds and Jonathan Gutman, "Advertising Is Image Management," *Journal of Advertising Research* 24, 1984, pp. 27–37. For a similar viewpoint, see C. Whan Park, Bernard J. Jaworski, and Deborah J. MacInnis, "Strategic Brand Concept-Image Management," *Journal of Marketing*, October 1986, pp. 135–45.

41. Peter H. Farquhar, "Managing Brand Equity," *Marketing Research*, September 1989, pp. 24–33.

42. Russell W. Belk, "ACR Presidential Address: Happy Thought," in *Advances in Consumer Research*, vol. 14, ed. M. Wallendorf and P. Anderson (Provo, UT: Association for Consumer Research, 1986), pp. 1–4.

43. This section is adapted from Grant McCracken, "Who Is the Celebrity Endorser? Cultural Foundations of the Endorsement Process," *Journal of Consumer Research*, December 1989, pp. 310–21.

44. Joshua Levine, "The Sound of No Dealers Selling," *Forbes*, February 19, 1990, pp. 122–24.

45. Unfortunately, many foreign markets are not growing because of competition from television and home videos (box office receipts in Finland were down about 15 percent in 1990, for example). See Kathleen A. Hughes, "You Don't Need Subtitles to Know Foreign Film Folk Have the Blues," *The Wall Street Journal*, March 5, 1991, p. B1.

46. Hazel Rose Markus and Shinobu Kitayama, "Culture and Self: Implications for Cognition, Emotion, and Motivation," *Psychological Review* 98, no. 2 (1991), pp. 224–53.

47. Terrance H. Witkowski and Yoshito Yamamoto, "Omiyage Gift Purchasing by Japanese Travelers to the U.S.," in *Advances in Consumer Research*, vol. 18 (Provo, UT: Association for Consumer Research, 1991), pp. 123–28.

48. Thompson et al., "The Lived Meaning of Free Choice."

49. Carla Rapoport, "How the Japanese Are Changing," *Fortune*, September 24, 1990, pp. 15–22.

50. Laurel Anderson and Marsha Wadkins, "Japan—A Culture of Consumption?" in *Advances in Consumer Research*, vol. 18 (Provo, UT: Association for Consumer Research, 1991), pp. 129–34.

51. Yumiko Ono, "Japan Becomes Land of the Rising Mall," *The Wall Street Journal*, February 11, 1991, pp. B1, B6.

52. Russell W. Belk, "Materialism: Trait Aspects of Living in the Material World." *Journal of Consumer Research*, December 1985, pp. 265–79.

53. Ibid., pp. 265–80.

54. Marsha L. Richins and Scott Dawson, "Measuring Material Values: A Preliminary Report of Scale Development," in *Advances in Consumer Research,* vol. 17 (Provo, UT: Association for Consumer Research, 1990), pp. 169–75.

55. Scott Dawson and Gary Bamossy, "Isolating the Effect of Non-Economic Factors on the Development of a Consumer Culture: A Comparison of Materialism in the Netherlands and the United States," in *Advances in Consumer Research,* vol. 17 (Provo, UT: Association for Consumer Research, 1990), pp. 182–85.

56. For further discussion of these and many other examples, see David A. Ricks, *Big Business Blunders: Mistakes in Multinational Marketing* (Homewood, IL: Dow Jones-Irwin, 1983).

57. Lynne Reaves, "China's Domestic Ad Scene a Paradox," *Advertising Age,* September 16, 1985, p. 76.

58. "Global Advertisers Should Pay Heed to Contextual Variations," *Marketing News,* February 13, 1987, p. 18.

59. See Anne B. Fisher, "The Ad Biz Gloms onto 'Global,'" *Fortune,* November 12, 1984, pp. 77–80. The examples in this section are taken from this article. Also see Bill Saporito, "Black & Decker's Gamble on 'Globalization,'" *Fortune,* May 14, 1984, pp. 40–48.

60. For example, see "Levitt: Global Companies to Replace Dying Multinationals," *Marketing News,* March 15, 1985, p. 15; Theodore Levitt, *The Marketing Imagination* (New York: The Free Press, 1983), chap. 2; Theodore Levitt, "The Globalization of Markets," *Harvard Business Review,* May–June 1983, pp. 92–102.

61. Subrata N. Chakravarty, "The Croissant Comes to Harvard Square," *Forbes,* July 14, 1986, p. 69.

62. Christine Dugas and Marilyn A. Harris, "Playtex Kicks Off a One-Ad-Fits-All Campaign," *Business Week,* December 16, 1985, pp. 48–49.

63. Julie Skur Hill and Joseph M. Winski, "Goodbye Global Ads: Global Village Is Fantasy Land for Big Marketers," *Advertising Age,* November 16, 1987, pp. 22–36; Joanne Lipman, "Marketers Turn Sour on Global Sales Pitch Harvard Guru Makes," *The Wall Street Journal,* May 12, 1988, pp. 1, 10.

64. McCracken, "Culture and Consumption," pp. 71–84.

65. Steve Weiner, "How Do You Say L'eggs in French?" *Forbes,* November 27, 1989, pp. 73–79.

CHAPTER 13

1. Alecia Swasy, "Changing Times," *The Wall Street Journal,* March 22, 1991, p. B6.

2. Diane Crispell, "Guppies, Minks, and Ticks," *American Demographics,* June 1990, pp. 50–51.

3. Ibid.

4. Gretchen Morgenson, "Where Can I Buy Some," *Forbes,* June 24, 1991, pp. 82–86.

5. Thomas W. Osborne, "An American Mosaic," *Marketing Insights,* June 1989, pp. 76–83.

6. James W. Gentry, Patriya Tansuhaj, and Joby John, "Do Geographic Subcultures Vary Culturally," in *Advances in Consumer Research,* vol. 15, ed. Michael J. Houston (Provo, UT: Association for Consumer Research, 1988), pp. 411–17.

7. Thomas Moore, "Different Folks, Different Strokes," *Fortune,* September 16, 1985, pp. 65–72.

8. Joel Garreau, *The Nine Nations of North America* (Boston: Houghton Mifflin, 1981).

9. For a critical perspective on this approach, see Lynn R. Kahle, "The Nine Nations of North America and the Value Basis of Geographic Segmentation," *Journal of Marketing,* April 1986, pp. 37–41. For a more detailed discussion, see Del I. Hawkins, Don Roupe, and Kenneth A. Coney, "The Influence of Geographic Subcultures in the United States," in *Advances on Consumer Research,* vol. 8, ed. Kent B. Monroe (Ann Arbor, MI: Association for Consumer Research, 1981), pp. 713–17.

10. Blayne Cutler, "Welcome to the Borderlands," *American Demographics,* February 1991, pp. 44–49, 57.

11. Associated Press, "Survey: Age Is Not Good Indicator of Consumer Need," *Marketing News,* November 21, 1988, p. 6.

12. This discussion is based on Doris L. Walsh, "Targeting Teens," *American Demographics,* February 1985, pp. 20–25.

13. This discussion is based on Geoffrey Calvin, "What the Baby-Boomers Will Buy Next," *Fortune,* October 15, 1984, pp. 28–34.

14. William Dunn, "Wheels for the Baby Boom: Detroit Discovers Demographics," *American Demographics,* May 1984, pp. 27–29.

15. Russell W. Belk, "Yuppies as Arbiters of the Emerging Consumption Style," in *Advances in Consumer Research,* vol. 13, ed. Richard J. Lutz (Provo, UT: Association for Consumer Research, 1986), pp. 514–19.

16. This discussion is based on William Lazer, "Inside the Mature Market," *American Demographics,* March 1985, pp. 23–25.

17. Thomas Exter, "How Big Will the Older Market Be?" *American Demographics,* June 1990, pp. 30–32, 36.

18. Janet Neiman, "The Elusive Mature Market," *Ad Week,* April 6, 1987, p. 16.

19. For a complete work on this market, see Charles D. Schewe, *The Elderly Market: Selected Readings* (Chicago: American

Marketing Association, 1985). Also see Eleanor Johnson Tracy, "The Gold in the Gray," *Fortune*, October 14, 1985, pp. 137–38.

20. For example, see Janice Castro, "Is That You on TV, Grandpa?" *Time*, March 6, 1989, p. 53.

21. Joe Szezesny and Richard Woodbury, "A Nation on the Move," *Time*, April 29, 1991, pp. 30–31.

22. Jon Schwartz and Thomas Exter, "All Our Children," *American Demographics*, May 1989, pp. 34–37.

23. James P. Allen and Eugene Turner, "Where Diversity Reigns," *American Demographics*, August 1990, pp. 34–38.

24. Nancy Coulton Webster, "Multicultural," *Advertising Age*, November 17, 1997, pp. S1–S2, S6.

25. Cyndee Miller, "Toy Companies Release 'Ethnically Correct' Dolls," *Marketing News*, September 30, 1991, pp. 1–2.

26. Alix M. Freeman, "Heilemann, Under Pressure, Scuttles PowerMaster Malt," *The Wall Street Journal*, July 5, 1991, pp. B1, B4.

27. Sigredo A. Hernandez and Carol J. Kaufman, "Marketing Research in Hispanic Barrios: A Guide to Survey Research," *Marketing Research*, March 1990, pp. 11–27. Also see Webster, "Multicultural."

28. Cyndee Miller, "Hispanic Media Expand: TV Has Strongest Appeal," *Marketing News*, January 21, 1991, pp. 1, 10.

29. Rohit Deshpande, Wayne D. Hover, and Naveen Donthu, "The Intensity of Ethnic Affiliation: A Study of the Sociology of Hispanic Consumption," *Journal of Consumer Research*, September 1986, pp. 214–20.

30. Ricks, *Big Business Blunders: Mistakes in Multinational Marketing* (Homewood, IL: Dow Jones-Irwin, 1983), p. 70. Also see Edward C. Baig, "Buenos Dias, Consumers," *Fortune*, December 23, 1985, pp. 79–80.

31. The information in this section is from William O'Hare, "A New Look at Asian Americans," *American Demographics*, October 1990, pp. 26–31.

32. John Steere, "How Asian–Americans Make Purchase Decisions," *Marketing News*, March 13, 1995, p. 9.

33. Dan Frost, "California's Asian Market," *American Demographics*, October 1990, pp. 34–37.

34. Joan Myers-Levy and Durairaj Maheswaran, "Exploring Differences in Males' and Females' Processing Strategies," *Journal of Consumer Research*, June 1991, pp. 63–70; Floyd W. Rudmin, "German and Canadian Data on Motivations for Ownership: Was Pythagoras Right?" in *Advances in Consumer Research*, vol. 17 (Provo, UT: Association for Consumer Research, 1990), pp. 176–81.

35. Tom Peters, "Opportunity Knocks," *Forbes ASAP*, June 2, 1997, pp. 130, 132.

36. Alice Z. Cuneo, "Advertisers Target Women, but Market Remains Elusive," *Advertising Age*, November 10, 1997, pp. 1, 24.

37. Judith Waldrop, "Up and Down the Income Scale," *American Demographics*, July 1990, pp. 24–27, 30.

38. Ronald J. Faber, Thomas C. O'Guinn, and John A. McCarty, "Ethnicity, Acculturation, and the Importance of Product Attributes," *Psychology & Marketing*, Summer 1987, pp. 121–34; Lisa N. Penaloza, "Immigrant Consumer Acculturation," in *Advances in Consumer Research*, vol. 16 (Provo, UT: Association for Consumer Research, 1989), pp. 110–18, 121–34.

39. Larry Long, "Americans on the Move," *American Demographics*, June 1990, pp. 46–49.

40. Alan R. Andreasen, "Cultural Interpenetration: A Critical Consumer Research Issue for the 1990s," in *Advances in Consumer Research*, vol. 17 (Provo, UT: Association for Consumer Research, 1990), pp. 847–49.

41. Kalervo Oberg, "Cultural Shock: Adjustment to New Cultural Environments," *Practical Anthropologist* 7 (1960), pp. 177–82.

42. Raj Mehta and Russell W. Belk, "Artifacts, Identity, and Transition: Favorite Possessions of Indians and Indian Immigrants to the United States," *Journal of Consumer Research*, March 1991, pp. 398–411.

43. Richard P. Coleman, "The Continuing Significance of Social Class to Marketing," *Journal of Consumer Research*, December 1983, pp. 265–80. Much of the discussion in this part of the chapter is based on Coleman's view of social class as described in this excellent article.

44. Ibid.

45. James E. Fisher, "Social Class and Consumer Behavior: The Relevance of Class and Status," in *Advances in Consumer Research*, vol. 14, ed. Melanie Wallendorf and Paul Anderson (Provo, UT: Association for Consumer Research, 1987), pp. 492–96.

46. Adapted from Charles M. Schaninger, "Social Class versus Income Revisited: An Empirical Investigation," *Journal of Marketing Research*, May 1981, pp. 192–208.

CHAPTER 14

1. Lakshman Krishnamurthi, "The Salience of Relevant Others and Its Effects on Individual and Joint Preferences: An Experimental Investigation," *Journal of Consumer Research*, June 1983, pp. 62–72.

2. C. Whan Park and V. Parker Lessig, "Students and Housewives: Differences in Susceptibility to Reference Group Influences," *Journal of Consumer Research*, September 1977, pp. 102–10; William O. Bearden, Richard G.

Netemeyer, and Jesse E. Teel, "Measurement of Consumer Susceptibility to Interpersonal Influence," *Journal of Consumer Research,* March 1989, pp. 473–81.

3. John W. Schouten and James H. Alexander, "Hog Heaven: The Structure, Ethos, and Market Impact of a Consumption Culture," paper presented at the Annual Conference of the Association for Consumer Research, 1992.

4. William O. Bearden and Michael J. Etzel. "Reference Group Influences on Product and Brand Purchase Decision," *Journal of Consumer Research,* September 1982, pp. 183–94. The discussion in this section is based heavily on this excellent work.

5. David Brinberg and Linda Plimpton, "Self-Monitoring and Product Conspicuousness in Reference Group Influence," in *Advances in Consumer Research,* vol. 13, ed. Richard J. Lutz (Provo, UT: Association for Consumer Research, 1986), pp. 297–300.

6. For further discussion and an alternative approach to studying reference group influences, see Peter H. Reingen, Brian L. Foster, Jacqueline Johnson Brown, and Stephen B. Seidman, "Brand Congruence in Interpersonal Relations: A Social Network Analysis," *Journal of Consumer Research,* December 1984, pp. 771–83.

7. Julia M. Bristor, "Coalitions in Organizational Purchasing: An Application of Network Analysis," in *Advances in Consumer Research,* vol. 15, ed. Michael J. Houston (Provo, UT: Association for Consumer Research, 1988), pp. 563–68.

8. Jacqueline Johnson Brown and Peter H. Reingen, "Social Ties and Word-of-Mouth Referral Behavior," *Journal of Consumer Research,* December 1987, pp. 350–62; Peter H. Reingen. "A Word-of-Mouth Network," in *Advances in Consumer Research,* vol. 14, ed. Melanie Wallendorf and Paul Anderson (Provo, UT: Association for Consumer Research, 1987), pp. 213–17.

9. Dorothy Leonard-Barton, "Experts as Negative Opinion Leaders in the Diffusion of a Technological Innovation," *Journal of Consumer Research,* March 1985, pp. 914–26.

10. Bearden and Etzel, "Reference Group Influences," p. 184.

11. Joel Rudd, "The Household as a Consuming Unit," in *Advances in Consumer Research,* vol. 14, ed. Melanie Wallendorf and Paul Anderson (Provo, UT: Association for Consumer Research, 1987), pp. 451–52.

12. This section is adapted from Diane Crispell, "How to Avoid Big Mistakes," *American Demographics,* March 1991, pp. 48–50.

13. Sunil Gupta, Michael R. Hagerty, and John G. Myers, "New Directions in Family Decision Making Research," in *Advances in Consumer Research,* vol. 10, ed. Richard P. Bagozzi and Alice M. Tybout (Ann Arbor, MI: Association for Consumer Research, 1983), pp. 445–50; Jagdish N. Sheth, "A Theory of Family Buying Decision," in *Models of Buyer Behavior: Conceptual, Quantitative, and Empirical,* ed. J. N. Sheth (New York: Harper and Row, 1974), pp. 17–33.

14. Dennis L. Rosen and Donald H. Granbois, "Determinants of Role Structure in Family Financial Management," *Journal of Consumer Research,* September 1983, pp. 253–85; Irene Raj Foster and Richard W. Olshavsky, "An Exploratory Study of Family Decision Making Using a New Taxonomy of Family Role Structure," in *Advances in Consumer Research,* vol. 16, ed. T. K. Srull (Provo, UT: Association for Consumer Research, 1989), pp. 665–70.

15. William J. Qualls, "Household Decision Behavior: The Impact of Husbands' and Wives' Sex Role Orientation," *Journal of Consumer Research,* September 1987, pp. 264–79; Dennis L. Rosen and Donald H. Granbois, "Determinants of Role Structure in Family Financial Management," *Journal of Consumer Research,* September 1983, pp. 253–85; Charles M. Schaninger, W. Christian Buss, and Rajiv Grover, "The Effect of Sex Roles on Family Economic Handling and Decision Influence," in *Advances in Consumer Research,* vol. 9, ed. Andrew A. Mitchell (Ann Arbor, MI: Association for Consumer Research, 1982), pp. 43–47; Daniel Seymour and Greg Lessne, "Spousal Conflict Arousal: Scale Development," *Journal of Consumer Research,* December 1984, pp. 810–21.

16. Harry L. Davis, "Decision Making within the Household," *Journal of Consumer Research,* March 1976, pp. 241–60.

17. George P. Moschis and Linda G. Mitchell, "Television Advertising and Interpersonal Influences on Teenagers' Participation in Family Consumer Decisions," in *Advances in Consumer Research,* vol. 13, ed. Richard J. Lutz (Provo, UT: Association for Consumer Research, 1986), pp. 181–86.

18. George E. Belch, Michael A. Belch, and Gayle Ceresino, "Parental and Teenage Child Influences in Family Decision Making," *Journal of Business Research* 13 (1985), pp. 163–176; Ellen R. Foxman, Patriya S. Tansuhaj, and Karin M. Ekstrom, "Family Members' Perceptions of Adolescents' Influence in Family Decision Making," *Journal of Consumer Research,* March 1989, pp. 482–91.

19. Alvin Burns and Donald Granbois, "Factors Moderating the Resolution of Preference Conflict in Family Automobile Purchasing," *Journal of Marketing Research,* February 1977, pp. 68–77; Alvin C. Burns and Jo Anne

Hopper, "An Analysis of the Presence, Stability and Antecedents of Husband and Wife Purchase Decision Making Influence Assessment and Disagreement," in *Advances in Consumer Research*, vol. 13, ed. Richard J. Lutz (Provo, UT: Association for Consumer Research, 1986), pp. 175–80; Margaret C. Nelson, "The Resolution of Conflict in Joint Purchase Decisions by Husbands and Wives: A Review and Empirical Test," in *Advances in Consumer Research*, vol. 15, ed. Michael J. Houston (Provo, UT: Association for Consumer Research, 1988), pp. 442–48.

20. Kim P. Corfman and Donald R. Lehmann, "Models of Cooperative Group Decision-Making and Relative Influence: An Experimental Investigation of Family Purchase Decisions," *Journal of Consumer Research,* June 1987, pp. 1–13; Burns and Granbois, "Factors Moderating the Resolution of Preference Conflict," pp. 68–77; Pierre Filiatrault and J. R. Brent Ritchie, "Joint Purchasing Decisions: A Comparison of Influence Structure in Family and Couple Decision-Making Units," *Journal of Consumer Research,* September 1980, pp. 131–40.

21. Rosann L. Spiro, "Persuasion in Family Decision Making," *Journal of Consumer Research,* March 1983, pp. 393–402.

22. Ibid.; Dennis L. Rosen and Richard W. Olshavsky, "The Dual Role of Informational Social Influence: Implications for Marketing Management," *Journal of Business Research* 15 (1987), pp. 123–44.

23. Scott Ward, Donna M. Klees, and Daniel B. Wackman, "Consumer Socialization Research: Content Analysis of Post-1980 Studies, and Some Implications for Future Work," in *Advances in Consumer Research*, vol. 17 (Provo, UT: Association for Consumer Research, 1990), pp. 798–803.

24. George P. Moschis, "The Role of Family Communication in Consumer Socialization of Children and Adolescents," *Journal of Consumer Resaerch*, March 1985, pp. 898–913.

25. Gilbert A. Churchill, Jr., and George P. Moschis, "Television and Interpersonal Influences on Adolescent Consumer Learning," *Journal of Consumer Research,* June 1979, pp. 23–35.

26. Sanford Grossbart, Les Carlson, and Ann Walsh, "Consumer Socialization Motives for Shopping with Children." *AMA Summer Educators' Proceedings* (Chicago: American Marketing Association, 1988); Bonnie B. Reece, Sevgin Eroglu, and Nora J. Rifon, "Parents Teaching Children to Shop: How, What, and Who?" *AMA Summer Educators' Proceedings* (Chicago: American Marketing Association, 1988), pp. 274–78; Les Carlson and Sanford Grossbart, "Parental Style and Consumer Socialization of Children," *Journal of Consumer Research,* June 1988, pp. 77–94.

27. Ellen Graham, "Children's Hour: As Kids Gain Power of Purse, Marketing Takes Aim at Them," *The Wall Street Journal,* January 10, 1988, pp. 1, 24.

28. Karin M. Ekstrom, Patriya S. Tansuhaj, and Ellen Foxman, "Children's Influence in Family Decisions and Consumer Socialization: A Reciprocal View," in *Advances in Consumer Research,* vol. 14, ed. Melanie Wallendorf and Paul Anderson (Provo, UT: Association for Consumer Research, 1987), pp. 283–87; Elizabeth S. Moore-Shay and Richard J. Lutz, "Intergenerational Influences in the Formation of Consumer Attitudes and Beliefs about the Marketplace: Mothers and Daughters," in *Advances in Consumer Research,* vol. 15, ed. Michael J. Houston (Provo: UT: Association for Consumer Research, 1988), pp. 461–67; Scott Ward, Thomas S. Robertson, Donna M. Klees, and Hubert Gatignon, "Children's Purchase Requests and Parental Yielding: A Cross-National Study," in *Advances in Consumer Research,* vol. 13, ed. Richard J. Lutz (Provo, UT: Association for Consumer Research, 1986), pp. 629–32.

29. Susan E. Heckler, Terry L. Childers, and Ramesh Arunachalam, "Intergenerational Influence in Adult Buying Behaviors: An Examination of Moderating Factors," in *Advances in Consumer Research*, vol. 16 (Provo, UT: Association for Consumer Research, 1990), pp. 276–84; Patricia Sorce, Lynette Loomis, and Philip R. Tyler, "Intergenerational Influence on Consumer Decision Making," in *Advances in Consumer Research,* vol. 16 (Provo, UT: Association for Consumer Research, 1990), pp. 271–75; George P. Moschis, "Methodological Issues in Studying Intergenerational Influences on Consumer Behavior," in *Advances in Consumer Research*, vol. 15, ed. Michael J. Houston (Provo, UT: Association for Consumer Research, 1988), pp. 569–73.

30. For a review of these issues, see Michael D. Reilly, "Working Wives and Convenience Consumption," *Journal of Consumer Research,* March 1982, pp. 407–18. Also see Charles M. Schaninger and Chris T. Allen, "Wife's Occupational Status as a Consumer Behavior Construct," *Journal of Consumer Research*, September 1981, pp. 189–96; Charles B. Weinberg and Russell S. Winer, "Working Wives and Major Family Expenditures: Replication and Extension," *Journal of Consumer Research,* September 1983, pp. 259–63.

31. Gordon Green and Edward Welniak, "The Nine Household Markets," *American Demographics*, October 1991, pp. 36–40.

32. Martha Farnsworth Riche, "The Postmarital Society," *American Demographics,* November 1988, pp. 22–26, 60.

33. Ibid.

34. Martha Farnsworth Riche, "The Future of the Family," *American Demographics,* March 1991, pp. 44–46.

35. Diane Crispell, "Three's a Crowd," *American Demographics,* January 1989, pp. 34–38.

36. See Patrick E. Murphy and William A. Staples, "A Modernized Family Life Cycle," *Journal of Consumer Research,* June 1979, pp. 12–22.

37. For other approaches and discussion, see Frederick W. Derrick and Alane K. Lehfeld, "The Family Life Cycle: An Alternative Approach," *Journal of Consumer Research,* September 1980, pp. 214–17; Mary C. Gilly and Ben M. Enis, "Recycling the Family Life Cycle: A Proposal for Redefinition," in *Advances in Consumer Research,* vol. 8, ed. Andrew Mitchell (Ann Arbor, MI: Association for Consumer Research, 1982), pp. 271–76; Janet Wagner and Sherman Hanna, "The Effectiveness of Family Life Cycle Variables in Consumer Expenditure Research," *Journal of Consumer Research,* December 1983, pp. 281–91.

38. Martha Farnsworth Riche, "The Boomerang Age," *American Demographics,* May 1990, pp. 25–27, 30, 52.

39. Margaret Ambry, "The Age of Spending," *American Demographics,* November 1990, pp. 16–23, 52.

40. This section is adapted from Eugene H. Fram, "The Time Compressed Shopper," *Marketing Insights,* Summer 1991, pp. 34–39; Eugene H. Fram and Joel Axelrod, "The Distressed Shopper," *American Demographics,* October 1990, pp. 44–45.

CHAPTER 15

1. Marco R. della Cava, "Porsche Calls 911, Boxster, Japanese to the Rescue," *USA Today,* April 8, 1997, pp. 1B, 2B.

2. Russell I. Haley, "Benefit Segmentation: A Decision-Oriented Research Tool," *Journal of Marketing,* July 1968, pp. 30–35. Also see Russell I. Haley, "Beyond Benefit Segmentation," *Journal of Advertising Research,* August 1971, pp. 3–8; Russell I. Haley, "Benefit Segmentation—20 Years Later," *Journal of Consumer Marketing* 2 (1983), pp. 5–13.

3. Haley, "Benefit Segmentation: A Decision-Oriented Research Tool."

4. Joseph T. Plummer, "The Concept and Application of Life Style Segmentation," *Journal of Marketing,* January 1974, p. 33.

5. See W. D. Wells, "Psychographics: A Critical Review," *Journal of Marketing Research,* May 1975, pp. 196–213; John L. Lastovicka, "On the Validation of Lifestyle Traits: A Review

and Illustration," *Journal of Marketing Research,* February 1982, pp. 126–38.

6. www.sric=bi.com.

7. Russell W. Belk, "A Free Response Approach to Developing Product Specific Consumption Situation Taxonomies," in *Analytic Approaches to Product and Marketing Planning,* ed. Allan D. Shocker (Cambridge, MA: Marketing Science Institute, 1979).

8. Peter R. Dickson, "Person–Situation: Segmentation's Missing Link," *Journal of Marketing,* Fall 1982, p. 57.

9. Ibid., p. 61.

10. Text discussion based on Valarie Walsh and J. Paul Peter, "Claritas, Inc.: Using Compass and PRIZM," in J. Paul Peter and James H. Donnelly, Jr., *Marketing Management: Knowledge and Skills,* 5th ed. (Burr Ridge, IL: McGraw-Hill/Irwin, 1998), pp. 326–40. Reproduced with permission from The McGraw-Hill Companies.

11. It should be noted that the concept of "positioning" is somewhat ambiguous in the marketing literature and is used in a number of different ways. See John P. Maggard, "Positioning Revisited," *Journal of Marketing,* January 1976, pp. 63–73.

12. See Jack Trout and Al Ries, "The Positioning Era Cometh," in *Readings in Marketing Strategy,* ed. Jean-Claude Larreche and Edward L. Strong (Palo Alto, CA: The Scientific Press, 1982), pp. 141–51. Also see Al Ries and Jack Trout, *Positioning: The Battle for Your Mind* (New York: McGraw-Hill, 1981); Al Ries and Jack Trout, *Marketing Warfare* (New York: McGraw-Hill, 1986).

13. David A. Aaker and J. Gary Shansby, "Positioning Your Product." *Business Horizons,* May–June 1982, pp. 36–62. The discussion that follows is based on this work.

14. Shirley Young, Leland Ott, and Barbara Feigin, "Some Practical Considerations in Market Segmentation," *Journal of Marketing Research,* August 1978, p. 405.

CHAPTER 16

1. Richard L. Oliver, *Satisfaction: A Behavioral Perspective on the Consumer* (New York: McGraw-Hill, 1997). Also see Richard A. Spreng, Scott B. MacKenzie, and Richard W. Olshavsky, "A Reexamination of the Determinants of Consumer Satisfaction," *Journal of Marketing,* July 1996, pp. 15–32.

2. Ibid.

3. Marsha L. Richens, "Negative Word-of-Mouth by Dissatisfied Consumers: A Pilot Study," *Journal of Marketing,* Winter 1983, p. 69. Also see Jagdip Singh, "Consumer Complaint Intentions and Behavior: Definitional and Taxonomical Issues," *Journal of Marketing,* January

1988, pp. 93–107; Jagdip Singh, "A Typology of Consumer Dissatisfaction Response Styles," *Journal of Retailing,* Spring 1990, pp. 57–98.

4. Susan Fournier and David Glen Mick, "Rediscovering Satisfaction," *Journal of Marketing,* October 1999, pp. 5–23.

5. Steve Schriver, "Customer Loyalty: Going, Going . . . ," *American Demographics,* September 1997, pp. 20–23.

6. This discussion is based on Hans C. M. Van Trijp, Wayne D. Hoyer, and J. Jeffrey Inman, "Why Switch? Product Category—Level of Explanations for True Variety-Seeking Behavior," *Journal of Marketing Research,* August 1996, pp. 281–92.

7. This discussion is based on Brian Wansink, "Can Package Size Accelerate Usage Volume?" *Journal of Marketing Research,* August 1996, pp. 281–92.

8. Ibid.

9. These examples are taken from Ronald Alsop, "Color Grows More Important in Catching Consumers' Eyes," *The Wall Street Journal,* November 29, 1984, p. 37.

10. Hubert Gatignon and Thomas S. Robertson, "A Propositional Inventory for New Diffusion Research," *Journal of Consumer Research,* March 1985, pp. 849–67; Vijay Mahajan, Eitan Muller, and Frank M. Bass, "New Product Diffusion Models in Marketing: A Review and Directions for Research," *Journal of Marketing,* January 1990, pp. 1–26.

11. Mary Dee Dickerson and James W. Gentry, "Characteristics of Adopters and Non-Adopters of Home Computers," *Journal of Consumer Research,* September 1983, pp. 225–35. Also see William E. Warren, C. L. Abercrombie, and Robert L. Berl, "Characteristics of Adopters and Nonadopters of Alternative Residential Long-Distance Telephone Services," in *Advances in Consumer Research,* vol. 15, ed. Michael J. Houston (Provo, UT: Association for Consumer Research, 1987), pp. 292–98.

12. Elizabeth C. Hirschman, "Innovativeness, Novelty Seeking, and Consumer Creativity," *Journal of Consumer Research,* December 1980, pp. 283–95.

13. Gatignon and Robertson, "A Propositional Inventory," p. 861.

14. See Everett M. Rogers, *Diffusion of Innovations* (New York: Free Press, 1983).

15. Michael R. Solomon, "The Role of Products as Social Stimuli: A Symbolic Interactionism Perspective," *Journal of Consumer Research,* December 1983, pp. 319–29. Also see Morris B. Hollbrook and Elizabeth C. Hirschman, "The Experiential Aspects of Consumption: Consumer Fantasies, Feeling, and Fun," *Journal of Consumer Research,* September 1982,

pp. 132–40; Morris B. Hollbrook, Robert B. Chestnut, Terrence A. Oliva, and Eric A. Greenleaf, "Play as a Consumption Experience: The Roles of Emotions, Performance, and Personality in the Enjoyment of Games," *Journal of Consumer Research,* September 1984, pp. 728–39.

CHAPTER 17

1. Felix Kessler, "The Costly Coupon Craze," *Fortune,* June 9, 1986, pp. 83–84; Richard Gibson, "Recession Feeds the Coupon Habit," *The Wall Street Journal,* February 20, 1991, p. B1.

2. C. Whan Park, Bernard J. Jaworski, and Deborah J. MacInnis, "Strategic Brand Concept Image Management," *Journal of Marketing,* October 1986, pp. 135–45; Thomas J. Reynolds and Jonathan Gutman, "Advertising Is Image Management," *Journal of Advertising Research,* February–March 1984, pp. 27–37.

3. Kevin Higgins, "Billboards Put Nike Back in the Running," *Marketing News,* June 7, 1985, p. 7.

4. For example, see Katherine E. Jocz, ed., *Research on Sales Promotion: Collected Papers* (Cambridge, MA: Marketing Science Institute, 1984); James Cross, Steven W. Hartley, and Richard Rexeisen, "Sales Promotion: A Review of Theoretical and Managerial Issues," in *Marketing Communications—Theory and Research,* ed. Michael J. Houston and Richard J. Lutz (Chicago: American Marketing Association, 1985), pp. 60–64.

5. "McDonald's Olympic Promotion Gets the Gold," *Marketing News,* June 7, 1984, pp. 12–13.

6. Amie Smith, "CSPA Honors 1994 International Awards of Excellence Winners," *PROMO: The International Magazine for Promotion Marketing,* June 1994, p. 93.

7. "Guinness Taps Sales with Pub Giveaway," *PROMO: The International Magazine for Promotion Marketing,* June 1994, p. 14.

8. Mary Ann Falzone, "Survey Highlights Lower Costs, Higher Productivity of Telemarketing," *Telemarketing Insider's Report* (Special Report, 1985), pp. 1–2.

9. Stewart W. Cross, "Can You Turn a 1985 Salesperson into a TSR?" *Telemarketing Insider's Report,* April 1985, p. 2.

10. David Einhorn, "Dynamo of Direct Sales," *Marketing Communications,* February 1982, pp. 12–14.

11. Higgins, "Billboards Put Nike Back in the Running," p. 7.

12. Bart Ziegler, "Checkmate! Deep Blue Is IBM Publicity Coup," *The Wall Street Journal,* May 9, 1997, pp. B1, B4.

13. Donnelly Marketing, Inc., *The 16th Annual Survey of Promotional Practices,* 1994; Michael Wahl, "Eye POPping Persuasion," *Marketing Insights,* 1989, pp. 130–34.

14. W. E. Philips, "Continuous Sales (Price) Promotion Destroys Brands: Yes," *Marketing News,* January 16, 1989, pp. 4, 8.

15. Bill Robinson, "Continuous Sales (Price) Promotion Destroys Brands: No," *Marketing News,* January 16, 1989, pp. 4, 8; Chris Sutherland, "Promoting Sales Out of a Slump," *Marketing Insights,* Winter 1990, pp. 41–43.

16. Wahl, "Eye POPping Persuasion."

17. Junu Bryan Kim, "Marketing with Video: The Tape Is in the Mail," *Advertising Age,* May 22, 1995, p. S-1.

18. Joanne Lipman, "Ads on TV: Out of Sight, Out of Mind," *The Wall Street Journal,* 1991, pp. B1, B8.

19. Deborah J. MacInnis and Bernard J. Jaworski, "Information Processing from Advertisements: Toward an Integrative Framework," *Journal of Marketing,* October 1989, pp. 1–24.

20. Alan J. Bush and Gregory W. Boller, "Rethinking the Role of Television Advertising during Health Crises: A Rhetorical Analysis of the Federal AIDS Campaigns," *Journal of Advertising* 20, no. 1 (1991), pp. 28–37.

21. This section is adapted from John R. Rossiter and Larry Percy, *Advertising and Promotion Management* (New York: McGraw-Hill, 1987), pp. 129–64.

22. Rao Unnava and Robert E. Burnkrant, "Effects of Repeating Varied Ad Executions on Brand Name Memory," *Journal of Marketing Research,* November 1991, pp. 406–16.

23. Kevin Lane Keller, "Memory and Evaluation Effects in Competitive Advertising Environments," *Journal of Consumer Research,* March 1991, pp. 463–76.

24. James R. Bettman, *An Information Processing Model of Consumer Choice* (Reading, MA: Addison-Wesley, 1979).

25. Punam Anand and Brian Sternthal, "Ease of Message Processing as a Moderator of Repetition Effects in Advertising," *Journal of Marketing Research,* August 1990, pp. 345–53.

26. Banwari Mittal, "The Relative Roles of Brand Beliefs and Attitude toward the Ad as Mediators of Brand Attitude: A Second Look," *Journal of Marketing Research,* May 1990, pp. 209–19.

27. Cornelia Pechmann and David W. Stewart, "The Effects of Comparative Advertising on Attention. Memory, and Purchase Intentions," *Journal of Consumer Research,* September 1990, pp. 180–91.

28. Wahl, "Eye POPping Persuasion."

29. Aradhna Krishna, "Effect of Dealing Patterns on Consumer Perceptions of Deal Frequency and Willingness to Pay," *Journal of Marketing Research,* November 1991, pp. 441–51.

30. See Peter H. Webb and Michael L. Ray, "Effects of TV Clutter," *Journal of Advertising Research,* June 1979, pp. 7–12.

31. Laura Bird, "Loved the Ad, May (or May Not) Buy the Product," *The Wall Street Journal,* April 7, 1994, p. B1.

32. Alice Ann Love, "Companies Want to Cut Coupons, but Consumers Demand Bargains," *Marketing News,* May 12, 1997, p. 15; Raju Narisetti, "Down the Drain: Move to Drop Coupons Puts Procter & Gamble in Sticky PR Situation," *The Wall Street Journal,* April 17, 1997, pp. A1–A.

33. George E. Belch, "An Examination of Comparative and Noncomparative Television Commercials: The Effects of Claim Variation and Repetition on Cognitive Response and Message Acceptance." *Journal of Marketing Research,* August 1981, pp. 333–49; Cornelia Droge and Rene Y. Darmon, "Associative Positioning Strategies through Comparative Advertising: Attribute versus Overall Similarity Approaches," *Journal of Marketing Research,* November 1987, pp. 377–88; Cornelia Pechmann and S. Ratneshwar, "The Use of Comparative Advertising for Brand Positioning: Association versus Differentiation," *Journal of Consumer Research,* September 1991, pp. 145–60.

34. Richard L. Celsi and Jerry C. Olson, "The Role of Involvement in Attention and Comprehension Processes," *Journal of Consumer Research,* September 1988, pp. 210–24; Michael J. Houston, Terry L. Childers, and Susan E. Heckler, "Picture–Word Consistency and the Elaborative Processing of Advertisements," *Journal of Marketing Research,* November 1987, pp. 359–69; Deborah J. MacInnis, Christine Moorman, and Bernard J. Jaworski, "Enhancing and Measuring Consumers' Motivation, Opportunity, and Ability to Process Brand Information from Ads," *Journal of Marketing,* October 1991, pp. 32–53.

35. Alan G. Sawyer and Daniel J. Howard, "Effects of Omitting Conclusions in Advertisements to Involved and Uninvolved Audiences," *Journal of Marketing Research,* November 1991, pp. 467–74.

36. Mary Jane Schlinger, "A Profile of Responses to Commercials," *Journal of Advertising Research,* April 1979, pp. 37–46; David A. Aaker and Douglas M. Stayman, "Measuring Audience Perceptions of Commercials and Relating Them to Ad Impact," *Journal of Advertising Research,* August–September 1990, pp. 7–18.

37. See Andrew A. Mitchell and Jerry C. Olson, "Are Product Attribute Beliefs the Only Mediators of Advertising Effects on Brand

Attitude?" *Journal of Marketing Research,* August 1981, pp. 318–32; Meryl Paula Gardner, "Does Attitude toward the Ad Affect Brand Attitude under a Brand Evaluation Set?" *Journal of Marketing Research,* May 1985, pp. 192–98.

38. Thomas J. Olney, Morris B. Holbrook, Rajeev Batra, "Consumer Responses to Advertising: The Effects of Ad Content, Emotions, and Attitude toward the Ad on Viewing Time," *Journal of Consumer Research,* March 1991, pp. 440–53.

39. Scott B. MacKenzie, Richard J. Lutz, and George E. Belch, "The Role of Attitude toward the Ad as a Mediator of Advertising Effectiveness: A Test of Competing Explanations," *Journal of Marketing Research,* May 1986, pp. 130–43; Andrew A. Mitchell, "The Effect of Verbal and Visual Components of Advertisements on Brand Attitudes and Attitude toward the Advertisement," *Journal of Consumer Research,* June 1986, pp. 12–24; Pamela M. Homer, "The Mediating Role of Attitude toward the Ad: Some Additional Evidence," *Journal of Marketing Research,* February 1990, pp. 78–86; Douglas M. Stayman and Rajeev Batra, "Encoding and Retrieval of Ad Affect in Memory," *Journal of Consumer Research,* May 1991, pp. 232–39.

40. Laura Bird, "Loved the Ad. May (or May Not) Buy the Product," *The Wall Street Journal,* April 7, 1994, p. B1.

41. Richard E. Petty, John T. Cacioppo, and David Schumann, "Central and Peripheral Routes to Advertising Effectiveness: The Moderating Role of Involvement," *Journal of Consumer Research,* September 1983, pp. 135–46.

42. Celsi and Olson, "The Role of Involvement"; Deborah J. MacInnis and C. Whan Park, "The Differential Role of Characteristics of Music on High- and Low-Involvement Consumers' Processing of Ads," *Journal of Consumer Research,* September 1991, pp. 161–73.

43. Celsi and Olson, "The Role of Involvement," pp. 201–24; Deborah J. MacInnis and C. Whan Park, "The Differential Role of Characteristics of Music on High- and Low-Involvement Consumers' Processing of Ads," *Journal of Consumer Research,* September 1991, pp. 161–73; David W. Schumann, Richard E. Petty, and D. Scott Clemons, "Predicting the Effectiveness of Different Strategies of Advertising Variation: A Test of the Repetition-Variation Hypotheses," *Journal of Consumer Research,* September 1990, pp. 192–202; H. Rao Unnava and Robert E. Burnkrant, "An Imagery-Processing View of the Role of Pictures in Print Advertisements," *Journal of Marketing Research,* May 1991, pp. 226–31.

44. Manoj Hastak and Jerry C. Olson, "Assessing the Role of Brand-Related Cognitive Responses as Mediators of Communication Effects on Cognitive Structure," *Journal of Consumer Research,* March 1989, pp. 444–56; John L. Swasy and James M. Munch, "Examining the Target of Receiver Elaborations: Rhetorical Question Effects on Source Processing and Persuasion," *Journal of Consumer Research,* March 11, 1985, pp. 877–86.

45. Andrew A. Mitchell and Jerry C. Olson, "Are Product Attribute Beliefs the Only Mediators of Advertising Effects on Brand Attitude?" *Journal of Marketing Research,* August 1981, pp. 318–32; Meryl Paula Gardner, "Does Attitude toward the Ad Affect Brand Attitude under a Brand Evaluation Set?" *Journal of Marketing Research,* May 1985, pp. 192–98; Thomas J. Olney, Morris B. Holbrook, and Rajeev Batra, "Consumer Responses to Advertising: The Effects of Ad Content, Emotions, and Attitude toward the Ad on Viewing Time," *Journal of Consumer Research,* March 1991, pp. 440–53; Scott B. MacKenzie, Richard J. Lutz, and George E. Belch, "The Role of Attitude toward the Ad as a Mediator of Advertising Effectiveness: A Test of Competing Explanations," *Journal of Marketing Research,* May 1986, pp. 130–43; Andrew A. Mitchell, "The Effect of Verbal and Visual Components of Advertisements on Brand Attitudes and Attitude toward the Advertisement," *Journal of Consumer Research,* June 1986, pp. 12–24; Pamela M. Homer, "The Mediating Role of Attitude toward the Ad: Some Additional Evidence," *Journal of Marketing Research,* February 1990, pp. 78–86; Douglas M. Stayman and Rajeev Batra, "Encoding and Retrieval of Ad Affect in Memory," *Journal of Consumer Research,* May 1991, pp. 232–39.

46. Celsi and Olson, "The Role of Involvement," pp. 210–24; Hastak and Olson, "Assessing the Role of Brand-Related Cognitive Responses," pp. 444–56; Deborah J. MacInnis, Christine Moorman, and Bernard J. Jaworski, "Enhancing and Measuring Consumers' Motivation, Opportunity, and Ability to Process Brand Information from Ads," *Journal of Marketing,* October 1991, pp. 32–53.

47. Barry L. Bayus, "Word of Mouth: The Indirect Effects of Marketing Efforts," *Journal of Advertising Research,* June–July 1985, pp. 31–39.

48. Jon Gutman, "Analyzing Consumer Orientations toward Beverages through Means–End Chain Analysis," *Psychology and Marketing* 3/4 (1984), pp. 23–43.

49. See David Berger, "Theory into Practice: The FCB Grid," *European Research,* January 1986, pp. 35–46; Richard Vaughn, "How Advertising Works: A Planning Model," *Journal*

of Advertising Research, October 1980, pp. 27–33; Richard Vaughn, "How Advertising Works: A Planning Model Revisited," *Journal of Advertising Research,* February–March 1986, pp. 57–66.

50. Roberto Friedman and V. Parker Lessig, "A Framework of Psychological Meaning of Products," in *Advances in Consumer Research,* vol. 13, ed. Richard J. Lutz (Provo, UT: Association for Consumer Research, 1986), pp. 338–42.

51. Julie A. Edell, "Nonverbal Effects in Ads: A Review and Synthesis," in *Nonverbal Communication in Advertising,* ed. David Stewart and Sidney Hecker (Lexington, MA: Lexington Books, 1988); Werner Kroeber-Riel, "Emotional Product Differentiation by Classical Conditioning," in *Advances in Consumer Research,* vol. 11, ed. Thomas C. Kinnear (Ann Arbor, MI: Association for Consumer Research, 1984), pp. 538–43; Marian Chapman Burke and Julie A. Edell, "The Impact of Feelings on Ad-Based Affect and Cognition," *Journal of Marketing Research,* February 1989, pp. 69–83.

52. Meryl P. Gardner and Roger A. Strang, "Consumer Response to Promotions: Some New Perspectives," in *Advances in Consumer Research,* vol. 11, ed. Thomas C. Kinnear (Ann Arbor, MI: Association for Consumer Research, 1984), pp. 420–25.

53. Belch, "An Examination of Comparative and Noncomparative Television Commercials," pp. 333–49; William L. Wilkie and Paul W. Farris, "Comparison Advertising: Problems and Potential," *Journal of Marketing,* October 1975, pp. 7–15.

54. Coleman Lollar, "From Sales Gimmick to Global Reality," *Frequent Flyer,* November 1984, pp. 75–85.

55. Thomas J. Peters and Robert H. Waterman, Jr., *In Search of Excellence: Lessons from America's Best-Run Companies* (New York: Warner Books, 1982), p. 158.

56. Celsi and Olson, "The Role of Involvement," pp. 210–24; C. Whan Park and S. Mark Young, "Consumer Response to Television Commercials: The Impact of Involvement and Background Music on Brand Attitude Formation," *Journal of Marketing Research,* February 1986, pp. 11–24.

57. Marian C. Burke and Julie A. Edell, "Ad Reactions over Time: Capturing Changes in the Real World," *Journal of Consumer Research,* June 1986, pp. 114–18.

58. Thomas J. Reynolds and John P. Rochon, "Means–End Based Advertising Research: Copy Testing Is Not Strategy Assessment," *Journal of Business Research* 22 (1991), pp. 131–42.

59. Material for this section is derived from Jerry C. Olson and Thomas J. Reynolds, "Understanding Consumers' Cognitive Structures: Implications for Advertising Strategies," in *Advertising and Consumer Psychology,* ed. Larry Percy and Arch Woodside (Lexington, MA: Lexington Books, 1983), pp. 77–90.

60. For instance, see Thomas J. Reynolds and Alyce Byrd Craddock, "The Application of the MECCAS Model to the Development and Assessment of Advertising Strategy: A Case Study," *Journal of Advertising Research,* April–May 1988, pp. 43–54.

61. For example, see Thomas J. Reynolds and Charles Gengler, "A Strategic Framework for Assessing Advertising: The Animals vs. Finished Issue," *Journal of Advertising Research,* June–July 1991.

62. Barton W. Weitz, "Relationship between Salesperson Performance and Understanding of Customer Decision Making," *Journal of Marketing Research,* November 1978, p. 502. Also see Barton W. Weitz, "Effectiveness in Sales Interactions: A Contingency Framework," *Journal of Marketing,* Winter 1981, pp. 85–103. For other views on salesperson effectiveness, see David M. Szymanski, "Determinants of Selling Effectiveness: The Importance to the Personal Selling Concept," *Journal of Marketing,* January 1988, pp. 64–77; Gilbert A. Churchill, Neil M. Ford, Steven W. Hartley, Jr., and Orville C. Walker, Jr., "The Determinants of Salesperson Performance: A Meta-Analysis," *Journal of Marketing Research,* May 1985, pp. 103–18.

63. Barton A. Weitz, Harish Sujan, and Mita Sujan, "Knowledge, Motivation and Adaptive Behavior: A Framework for Improving Selling Effectiveness," *Journal of Marketing Research,* October 1986, pp. 174–91.

64. Harish Sujan, "Smarter versus Harder: An Exploratory Attributional Analysis of Salespeople's Motivations," *Journal of Marketing Research,* February 1986, pp. 41–49; Kaylene C. Williams and Rosann L. Spiro, "Communication Style in the Salesperson–Customer Dyad," *Journal of Marketing Research,* November 1985, pp. 434–42; Rosann L. Spiro and Barton A. Weitz, "Adaptive Selling: Conceptualization, Measurement, and Nomological Validity," *Journal of Marketing Research,* February 1990, pp. 61–69.

65. Albert C. Bemmaor and Dominique Mouchoux, "Measuring the Short-Term Effect of In-Store Promotion and Retail Advertising on Brand Sales: A Factorial Experiment," *Journal of Marketing Research,* May 1991, pp. 202–14.

66. Kapil Bawa and Robert W. Shoemaker, "The Effects of a Direct Mail Coupon on Brand Choice Behavior," *Journal of Marketing*

Research, November 1987, pp. 370–76; P. S. Raju and Manoj Hastak, "Consumer Response to Deals: A Discussion of Theoretical Perspective," in *Advances in Consumer Research,* vol. 7, ed. Jerry C. Olson (Ann Arbor, MI: Association for Consumer Research, 1980), pp. 296–301; Robert Blattberg, Thomas Biesing, Peter Peacock, and Subrata Sen, "Identifying the Deal Prone Segment," *Journal of Marketing Research,* August 1978, pp. 369–97.

67. For a review of various measures of advertising effectiveness, see David W. Stewart, Connie Pechmann, Srinivasan Ratneshwar, John Stroud, and Beverly Bryant, "Advertising Evaluation: A Review of Measures," in *Marketing Communications–Theory and Research,* ed. Michael J. Houston and Richard J. Lutz (Chicago: American Marketing Association, 1985), pp. 3–6. For a discussion of copy testing, see Benjamin Lipstein and James P. Neelankavil, "Television Advertising Copy Research: A Critical Review of the State of the Art," *Journal of Advertising Research,* April–May 1984, pp. 19–25; Joseph T. Plummer, "The Role of Copy Research in Multinational Advertising," *Journal of Advertising Research,* October–November 1986, pp. 11–15; Harold M. Spielman, "Copy Research: Facts and Fictions," *European Research,* November 1987, pp. 226–31.

68. Jeffrey A. Trachtenberg, "Viewer Fatigue?" *Forbes,* December 26, 1988, pp. 120, 122.

69. Lawrence D. Gibson, "Not Recall," *Journal of Advertising Research,* February–March 1983, pp. 39–46; Herbert E. Krugman, "Low Recall and High Recognition of Advertising," *Journal of Advertising Research,* February–March 1986, pp. 79–86; Jan Stapel, "Viva Recall: Viva Persuasion," *European Research,* November 1987, pp. 222–25.

70. Marvin E. Goldberg and Jon Hartwick, "The Effects of Advertiser Reputation and Extrem-ity of Advertising Claim on Advertising Effectiveness," *Journal of Consumer Research,* September 1990, pp. 172–79.

71. Jerry C. Olson, Daniel R. Toy, and Phillip A. Dover, "Do Cognitive Responses Mediate the Effects of Advertising Content on Cognitive Structure?" *Journal of Consumer Research,* December 1982, pp. 245–62; Arno J. Rethans, John L. Swasy, and Lawrence J. Marks, "Effects of Television Commercial Repetition, Receiver Knowledge, and Commercial Length: A Test of the Two-Factor Model," *Journal of Marketing Research,* February 1986, pp. 50–61; Daniel R. Toy, "Monitoring Communication Effects: A Cognitive Structure/Cognitive Response Approach," *Journal of Consumer Research,* June 1982, pp. 66–76.

72. Jon Gutman and Thomas J. Reynolds, "Coordinating Assessment to Strategy Development: An Advertising Assessment Paradigm Based on the MECCAS Approach," in *Advertising and Consumer Psychology,* vol. 3, ed. Jerry Olson and Keith Sentis (New York: Praeger, 1987).

CHAPTER 18

1. Vithala R. Rao, "Pricing Research in Marketing: The State of the Art," *Journal of Business,* January 1984, p. S39.

2. For an example of research on time as a resource, see France Leclerc, Bernd H. Schmitt, and Laurette Dube, "Waiting Time and Decision Making: Is Time Like Money?" *Journal of Consumer Research,* June 1995, pp. 110–119.

3. For a model and approach to measuring this cost, see Steven M. Shugan, "The Cost of Thinking," *Journal of Consumer Research,* September 1980, pp. 99–111. Also see Howard Marmorstein, Dhruv Grewal, and Raymond P. H. Fishe, "The Value of Time Spent in Price Comparison Shopping: Survey and Experimental Evidence," *Journal of Consumer Research,* June 1992, pp. 52–61.

4. See Ellen C. Garbarino and Julie A. Edell, "Cognitive Effort, Affect, and Choice," *Journal of Consumer Research,* September 1997, pp. 147–158. For research on the effects of mental budgeting, see Chip Heath and Jack B. Soll, "Mental Budgeting and Consumer Decision," *Journal of Consumer Research,* June 1996, pp. 40–52.

5. Rao, "Pricing Research," p. S39; Jerry C. Olson, "Price as an Informational Cue: Effects on Product Evaluations," in *Consumer and Industrial Buyer Behavior,* ed. Arch G. Woodside, Jagdish N. Sheth, and Peter D. Bennett (New York: Elsevier–North Holland, 1977), pp. 267–86; Valarie A. Zeithaml, "Issues in Conceptualizing and Measuring Consumer Response to Price," in *Advances in Consumer Research,* vol. 11, ed. Thomas C. Kinnear (Provo, UT: Association for Consumer Research, 1984), pp. 612–16; Kent B. Monroe and R. Krishman, "A Procedure for Integrating Outcomes across Studies," in *Advances in Consumer Research,* vol. 10, ed. Richard P. Bagozzi and Alice M. Tybout (Ann Arbor, MI: Association for Consumer Research, 1983), pp. 503–8.

6. Jacob Jacoby and Jerry C. Olson, "Consumer Response to Price: An Attitudinal, Information Processing Perspective," in *Moving Ahead with Attitude Research,* ed. Yoram Wind and Marshall Green (Chicago: American Marketing Association, 1977), pp. 73–86. Also see Jerry C. Olson, "Implications of an Information Processing Approach to Pricing

Research," in *Theoretical Developments in Marketing*, ed. Charles W. Lamb, Jr., and Patrick M. Dunne (Chicago: American Marketing Association, 1980), pp. 13–16.

7. Abhijit Biswas and Edward A. Blair, "Contextual Effects of Reference Prices in Retail Advertisements," *Journal of Marketing*, July 1991, pp. 1–12; Glenn E. Mayhew and Russell S. Winer, "An Empirical Analysis of Internal and External Reference Prices Using Scanner Data," *Journal of Consumer Research*, June 1992, pp. 62–70.

8. Peter R. Dickson and Alan G. Sawyer, "The Price Knowledge and Search of Supermarket Shoppers," *Journal of Marketing*, July 1990, p. 49.

9. Biswas and Blair, "Contextual Effects of Reference Prices."

10. Valarie A. Zeithaml, "Consumer Response to In-Store Price Information Environments," *Journal of Consumer Research*, March 1982, pp. 357–68.

11. For complete works on pricing strategy, see Kent B. Monroe, *Pricing: Making Profitable Decisions*, 2d ed. (New York: McGraw-Hill, 1990); Robert J. Dolan and Hermann Simon, *Power Pricing* (New York: Free Press), 1996.

CHAPTER 19

1. Robert J. Donovan and John R. Rossiter, "Store Atmosphere: An Environmental Psychology Approach," *Journal of Retailing*, Spring 1982, pp. 34–57.

2. For excellent discussions of these topics, see C. Samuel Craig, Avijit Ghosh, and Sara McLafferty, "Models of the Retail Location Process: A Review," *Journal of Retailing*, Spring 1984, pp. 5–36; Michael Levy and Barton Weitz, *Retailing Management*, 4th ed. (Burr Ridge, IL: McGraw-Hill/Irwin, 2001), chap. 8.

3. The information in this section is based heavily on Craig, Ghosh, and McLafferty, "Models of Retail Location," pp. 20–27.

4. Gary F. McKinnon, J. Patrick Kelly, and E. Doyle Robison, "Sales Effects of Point-of-Purchase In-Store Signing," *Journal of Retailing*, Summer 1981, pp. 49–63.

5. Joseph A. Bellizzi, Ayn E. Crowley, and Ronald W. Hasty, "The Effects of Color in Store Design," *Journal of Retailing*, Spring 1983, pp. 21–45. Also see Ayn E. Crowley, "The Two-Dimensional Impact of Color on Shopping," *Marketing Letters*, January 1993, pp. 59–69. Also see Gerald J. Gorn, Amitava Chattopadhyay, Tracey Yi, and Darren W. Dahl, "Effects of Color as an Executional Cue in Advertising: They're in the Shade," *Management Science* for further discussion of the use of color in marketing.

6. Ibid., Bellizzi, et. al., p. 43.

7. J. B. Wilkinson, J. Barry Mason, and Christie H. Paksoy, "Accessing the Impact of Short-Term Supermarket Strategy Variables," *Journal of Marketing Research*, February 1982, pp. 72–86. Also see Rockney G. Walters and Scott B. MacKenzie, "A Structural Equations Analysis of the Impact of Price Promotions on Store Performance," *Journal of Marketing Research*, February 1988, pp. 51–63; V. Kumar and Robert P. Leone, "Measuring the Effect of Retail Store Promotions on Brand and Store Substitution," *Journal of Marketing Research*, May 1988, pp. 178–85.

8. Ronald E. Milliman, "Using Background Music to Affect the Behavior of Supermarket Shoppers," *Journal of Marketing*, Summer 1982, pp. 86–91.

9. Ibid., p. 91. For additional support for these ideas, see Ronald E. Milliman, "The Influence of Background Music on the Behavior of Restaurant Patrons," *Journal of Consumer Research*, September 1986, pp. 286–89. Also see Richard Yalch and Eric Spangenberg, "Effects of Store Music on Shopping Behavior," *Journal of Consumer Marketing*, Spring 1990, pp. 55–63; Gordon C. Bruner II, "Music, Mood, and Marketing," *Journal of Marketing*, October 1990, pp. 94–104.

10. Information in this section is taken from Eric R. Spangenberg, Ayn E. Crowley, and Pamela W. Henderson, "Improving the Store Environment: Do Olfactory Cues Affect Evaluations and Behavior?" *Journal of Marketing*, April 1996, pp. 67–80.

11. This classification and all statistical information in this part of the chapter taken from Michael Levy and Barton Weitz, *Retailing Management*, 4th ed. (Burr Ridge IL: McGraw-Hill/Irwin, 2001) chap. 3.

12. Joseph Alba, John Lynch, Barton Weitz, Chris Janiszewski, Richard Lutz, Alan Sawyer, and Stacy Wood, "Interactive Home Shopping: Consumer, Retailer, and Manufacturer Incentives to Participate in Electronic Marketplaces," *Journal of Marketing*, July 1997, pp. 38–53.

13. "Will the Have-Nots Always Be with Us?" *Fortune*, December 20, 1999, pp. 288–89.

14. Mary Beth Grover, "Lost in Cyberspace," *Fortune*, March 1999, p. 127.

Glossary

accessibility The probability that a meaning concept will be (or can be) activated from memory. Highly related to top-of-mind awareness and salience.

accidental exposure Occurs when consumers come in contact with marketing information in the environment that they haven't deliberately sought out. Compare with **intentional exposure.**

accretion The most common type of cognitive learning. Adding new knowledge, meanings, and beliefs to an associative network.

acculturation The process by which people in one culture or subculture learn to understand and adapt to the meanings, values, lifestyles, and behaviors of another culture or subculture.

activation The essentially automatic process by which knowledge, meanings, and beliefs are retrieved from memory and made available for use in cognitive processing.

adopter categories A classification of consumers based on the time of initial purchase of a new product. Typically, five groups are considered: **innovators, early adopters, early majority, late majority,** and **laggards.**

adoption curve A visual representation of the cumulative percentage of individuals who adopt a new product across time.

adoption process An ambiguous term sometimes used to refer to a model of stages in the purchase process ranging from awareness to knowledge, evaluation, trial, and adoption. In other cases, it is used as a synonym for the diffusion process.

advertising Any paid, nonpersonal presentation of information about a product, brand, company, or store.

affect A basic mode of psychological response that involves a general positive/negative feeling and varying levels of activation or arousal of the physiological system that consumers experience in their bodies. Compare with **cognition.** See also **affective responses.**

affective responses Psychological responses consisting of four types: emotions, specific feelings, moods, and evaluations. These responses vary in level of intensity and arousal.

age subcultures Groups of people defined in terms of age categories (teens, elderly) with distinctive behaviors, values, beliefs, and lifestyles.

AIO An acronym for *activities, interest,* and *opinions.* AIO measures are the primary method for investigating consumer lifestyles and forming psychographic segments.

aspirational group A reference group an individual consumer wants to join or be similar to.

associative network An organized structure of knowledge, meanings, and beliefs about some concept such as a brand. Each meaning concept is linked to other concepts to form a network of associations.

attention The process by which consumers select information in the environment to interpret. Also, the point at which consumers become conscious or aware of certain stimuli.

attitude A person's overall evaluation of a concept. An affective response at a low level of intensity and arousal. General feelings of favorability or liking.

attitude-change strategies Processes for changing attitudes, including adding a new salient belief, making a salient belief stronger, and making a salient belief more positive. See **attitude** and **multiattribute attitude models.**

attitude models See **multiattribute attitude models.**

attitudes toward objects (A_O) Consumers' overall evaluation (like/dislike) of an object such as a product or store. May be formed in two quite different ways: a cognitive process that involves relatively controlled and conscious integration of information about the object or a largely automatic and unconscious response of the affective system.

545

attitude toward the ad (A_{ad}) Consumers' affective evaluations of advertisements themselves, not the product or brand being promoted.

attitude toward the behavior or action (A_{act}) The consumer's overall evaluation of a specific behavior.

attributes   Characteristics of the product. Can be tangible, subjective characteristics, such as the quality of a blanket or the stylishness of a car. Or can be tangible, physical characteristics of a product such as the type of fiber in a blanket or the front-seat legroom in a car.

automatic processing   Describes cognitive processes that tend to become more automatic—require less conscious control and less cognitive capacity—as they become more practiced and familiar.

baby boomers   The name for the very large cohort of people born in the United States during the years after World War II from about 1946 until about 1964. See **market segmentation.**

baseline   The level of consumers' responses prior to implementing a new strategy.

behavior   Overt actions that can be directly observed and measured by others.

behavioral intention *(BI)*   A plan to perform an action—"I intend to go shopping this afternoon." Intentions are produced when beliefs about the behavioral consequences of the action and social normative beliefs are considered and integrated to evaluate alternative behaviors and select among them.

behavior effort   The effort consumers expend when making a purchase.

behaviors   Specific overt actions directed at some target object.

belief   The perceived association between two concepts. May be represented cognitively as a proposition. Beliefs about products often concern their attributes or functional consequences. For example, after trying a new brand of toothpaste, a consumer may form a belief that it has a minty taste. Beliefs are synonymous with knowledge and meaning in that each term refers to consumers' cognitive representations of important concepts.

belief evaluation (e_i) Reflects how favorably the consumer perceives an attribute or consequence associated with a product.

belief strength (b_i) The perceived strength of association between an object and its relevant attributes or consequences.

benefits   Desirable consequences or outcomes that consumers seek when purchasing and using products and services.

benefit segmentation   The process of grouping consumers on the basis of the benefits they seek from the product. For example, the toothpaste market may include one segment seeking cosmetic benefits such as white teeth and another seeking health benefits such as decay prevention.

brand choice   The selection of one brand from a consideration set of alternative brands.

brand equity   The value of a brand. From the consumer's perspective, brand equity is reflected by the brand attitude based on beliefs about positive product attributes and favorable consequences of brand use.

brand indifference   A purchasing pattern characterized by a low degree of brand loyalty.

brand loyalty   An intrinsic commitment to repeatedly purchase a particular brand.

brand switching   A purchasing pattern characterized by a change from one brand to another.

categorization   A cognitive process by which objects, events, and people are grouped together and responded to in terms of their class membership rather than their unique characteristics.

category accessibility   The degree to which a consumer can activate a category of meaning from memory. A cognitive approach to describing modeling effects, where the process of viewing a model's behavior involves the activation of an interpretive schema.

central route to persuasion   One of two types of cognitive processes by which persuasion occurs. In the central route, consumers focus on the product messages in the ad, interpret them, form beliefs about product attributes and consequences, and integrate these meanings to form brand attitudes and intentions. See **peripheral route to persuasion.**

choice   The outcome of the integration processes involved in consumer decision making. See also **behavioral intention.**

choice alternatives   The different product classes, product forms, brands, or models available for purchase.

choice criteria   The specific product attributes or consequences used by consumers to evaluate and choose from a set of alternatives.

classical conditioning   A process by which a neutral stimulus (such as a new product) becomes capable of eliciting a response (such as positive affect) because it was repeatedly paired with a stimulus that naturally causes the response (such as sexy models).

cognition   The mental processes of interpretation and integration and the thoughts and meanings they produce.

cognitive activity The mental thought and effort involved in interpreting and integrating information, as in a purchase decision. Often considered as a cost.

cognitive dissonance A psychologically uncomfortable condition brought about by an imbalance in thoughts, beliefs, attitudes, or behavior. For example, behaving in a way that is inconsistent with one's beliefs creates cognitive dissonance and a motivation to reduce the inconsistency.

cognitive learning The processes by which knowledge structures are formed and changed as consumers interpret new information and acquire new meanings and beliefs.

cognitive processing The mental activities (both conscious and unconscious) by which external information in the environment is transformed into meanings and combined to form evaluations of objects and choices about behavior.

cognitive representations The subjective meanings that reflect each person's personal interpretation of stimuli in the environment and of behavior.

cognitive response The thoughts one has in response to a persuasive message such as support arguments or acceptance thoughts, counterarguments, and curiosity thoughts.

communication A type of behavior that marketers attempt to increase, involving two basic audiences: consumers who can provide the company with marketing information and consumers who can tell other potential consumers about the product and encourage them to buy it.

communication model A simple representation of human communication processes that focuses on characteristics of the source, message, medium, and receiver.

communication process The physical and social processes involved in transferring messages and meaning from a source to a receiver. See also **communication model.**

compatibility The degree to which a product is consistent with consumers' current cognitions and behaviors.

compensatory integration processes In decision making, the combination of all the salient beliefs about the consequences of the choice alternatives to form an overall evaluation or attitude (A_{act}) toward each behavioral alternative. See also **noncompensatory integration processes.**

compensatory rule A principle stating that in evaluating alternatives, a consumer will select the alternative with the highest overall evaluation on a set of criteria. Criteria evaluations are done separately and combined such that positive evaluations can offset (or compensate for) negative evaluations. This term is also called compensatory process,

compensatory integration procedure, and compensatory model. See also **noncompensatory integration processes.**

competitive advantage The degree to which an item has a sustainable, competitive, differential advantage over other product classes, product forms, and brands.

complete environment The total complex of physical and social stimuli in the external world that are potentially available to the consumer.

comprehension The cognitive processes involved in interpreting and understanding concepts, events, objects, and persons in the environment.

confirmation In consumer satisfaction theory, a situation in which a product performs exactly as it was expected to, that is, prepurchase expectations are confirmed.

conjunctive rule See **noncompensatory integration processes.**

consensual environment Those parts of the environment that are attended to and similarly interpreted by a group of people with relatively similar cultural and social backgrounds.

consideration set A set of alternatives that the consumer evaluates in making a decision. Compare with **evoked set.**

consumer acculturation The process by which people acquire the ability and cultural knowledge to be skilled consumers in different cultures or subcultures.

consumer behavior (1) The dynamic interaction of affect and cognition, behavior, and environmental events by which individuals conduct the exchange aspects of their lives; (2) a field of study concerned with (1); (3) a college course concerned with (1); and (4) the overt actions of consumers.

consumer decision making The cognitive processes by which consumers interpret product information and integrate that knowledge to make choices among alternatives.

consumer information processing The cognitive processes by which consumers interpret and integrate information from the environment.

consumer–product relationship The relationship between target consumers and the product or brand of interest. How consumers perceive the product as relating to their goals and values. Important to consider in developing all phases of a marketing strategy. See also **means–end chain.**

consumer promotion Marketing tactics, such as coupons and free samples, designed to have a direct impact on consumer purchase behavior.

consumer purchase mode The method a consumer uses to shop and purchase from store or nonstore alternatives.

consumer satisfaction   The degree to which a consumer's prepurchase expectations are fulfilled or surpassed by a product.

consumer socialization   How children acquire knowledge about products and services and various consumption-related skills.

consumption   Use of a product.

consumption situation   The social and physical factors present in the environments where consumers actually use and consume the products and services they buy.

content of culture   All the beliefs, attitudes, goals, and values shared by most people in a society, as well as the typical behaviors, rules, customs, and norms that most people follow, plus characteristic aspects of the physical and social environment.

continuous reinforcement schedule   A schedule of reinforcement that provides a reward after every occurrence of the desired behavior.

core values   The abstract, broad, general end goals that people are trying to achieve in their lives.

covert modeling   A type of modeling in which no actual behaviors or consequences are demonstrated; instead, subjects are told to imagine observing a model behaving in various situations and receiving particular consequences.

cross-cultural differences   How the content of culture (meanings, values, norms) differs among different cultures.

cross-cultural research   Studies in which marketers seek to identify the differences and similarities in the cultural meaning systems of consumers living in different societies.

cultural interpenetration   The amount and type of social interaction between newcomers to a culture (immigrants) and people in the host culture. Influences the degree of acculturation the newcomers can attain.

cultural meanings   The shared or similar knowledge, meanings, and beliefs by which people in a social system represent significant aspects of their environments.

cultural process   The process by which cultural meaning is moved or transferred among three locations in a society: the social and physical environment, products and services, and individual consumers.

culture   The complex of learned meanings, values, and behavioral patterns that members of a society share.

deal proneness   A consumer's general inclination to use promotional deals such as buying on sale or using coupons.

decision   A choice between two or more alternative actions or behaviors. See also **choice** and **behavioral intention.**

decision conflict   A situation in which family members disagree about various aspects of the purchase decision, such as goals and appropriate choice criteria.

decision making   See **consumer decision making.**

decision plan   The sequence of behavioral intentions produced when consumers engage in problem solving during the decision-making process. See also **behavioral intention.**

diffusion process   The process by which new ideas and products become accepted by a society. See also **adopter categories.**

disconfirmation   In consumer satisfaction theory, a situation in which a product performs differently than expected. See also **negative disconfirmation** and **positive disconfirmation.**

discriminant consequences   Consequences that differ across a set of alternatives that may be used as choice criteria.

discriminative stimulus   A stimulus that by its mere presence or absence changes the probability of a behavior. For example, a "50 percent off" sign in a store window could be a discriminative stimulus.

disjunctive rule   See **noncompensatory integration processes.**

disposition situation   The physical and social aspects of the environments in which consumers dispose of products, as well as consumers' goals, values, beliefs, feelings, and behaviors while in those environments.

dissatisfaction   Occurs when prepurchase expectations are negatively confirmed, that is, when the product performs worse than expected.

dissociative group   A reference group that an individual does not want to join or be similar to.

early adopters   The second group of adopters of a new product.

early majority   The third group of adopters of a new product.

elaboration   The extensiveness of comprehension processes. The degree of elaboration determines the amount of knowledge or the number of meanings produced during comprehension, as well as the richness of the interconnections among those meanings.

Elaboration Likelihood Model (ELM)   A formal model of how consumers comprehend and elaborate information. Two processes are possible, depending on the consumer's level of involvement: the central route and the peripheral route. See **elaboration, central route to persuasion,** and **peripheral route to persuasion.**

end goal The most abstract or most basic consequence, need, or value a consumer wants to achieve or satisfy in a given problem-solving situation.

enduring involvement The personal relevance of a product or an activity. See also **intrinsic self-relevance.** Compare with **situational involvement.**

environment The complex set of physical and social stimuli in consumers' external world.

environmental prominence The marketing strategy of making certain stimuli obvious or prominent in the environment.

episodic knowledge Cognitive representations of specific events in a person's life. Compare with **semantic knowledge.**

ethnic subcultures Large social groups based on consumers' ethnic backgrounds. In the United States, the important ethnic subcultures include African Americans or blacks, Hispanics, Asians, and Native Americans.

European Union (EU) An agreement among European countries designed to facilitate international commerce.

evaluation An overall judgment of favorable/unfavorable, pro/con, or like/dislike. An attitude toward an object such as a brand, an ad, or a behavioral act.

evoked set The set of choice alternatives activated directly from memory.

expectancy theory A possible explanation for modeling, a cognitive theory that suggests models influence an observer's behavior by influencing his or her expectations.

expertise High familiarity with a product category and specific brands and possessing substantial amounts of declarative and procedural knowledge organized in schemas and scripts.

exposure Occurs when consumers come into contact with information in the environment, sometimes through their own intentional behaviors and sometimes by accident.

extensive decision making A choice involving substantial cognitive and behavioral effort. Compare with **limited decision making** and **routinized choice behavior.**

external reference price Explicit comparison of the stated price with another price in advertising, catalogs, and so on.

extinction The process of arranging the environment so that a particular response results in neutral consequences, thus diminishing the frequency of the response over time.

family A group of at least two people formed on the basis of marriage, cohabitation, blood relationships, or adoption. Families often serve as a basis for various types of consumer analysis.

family decision making The processes, interactions, and roles of family members involved in making decisions as a group.

family life cycle A sociological concept that describes changes in families across time. Emphasis is placed on the effects of marriage, births, aging, and deaths on families and the changes in income and consumption through various family stages.

Fishbein Behavioral Intentions Model An earlier name for the **theory of reasoned action.**

fixed ratio schedule A type of reinforcement schedule where every second, third, tenth, and so on response is reinforced.

focal attention A controlled, conscious level of attention that focuses cognitive processes on relevant or prominent stimuli in the environment. Compare with **preconscious attention.**

Foote, Cone & Belding (FCB) grid A 2-by-2 grid developed by the Foote, Cone & Belding advertising agency for analyzing consumers and products. The FCB grid categorizes products based on consumers' level of involvement (high or low) and on whether consumers' dominant response to the product is cognitive or affective (think or feel).

form utility Utility that occurs when channels convert raw materials into finished goods and services in forms the consumer seeks to purchase.

four stages of acculturation Four levels of acculturation a newcomer to a culture could achieve, depending on the level of cultural interpenetration: honeymoon, rejection, tolerance, and integration stages.

free-form layout A store layout that permits consumers to move freely rather than being constrained to movement up and down specific aisles.

functional consequences The immediate outcomes of product use that can be directly experienced by consumers. For instance, a toothpaste may whiten your teeth.

functional (or perceived) environment Those parts of the complete environment that are attended to and interpreted by a particular consumer on a particular occasion.

funds access The ways consumers obtain money for purchases, such as cash, credit cards, checks, or loans. Primary marketing issues include the methods consumers use to pay for particular purchases and the marketing strategies used to increase the probability that consumers are able to access their funds for purchase.

general knowledge The meanings consumers construct to represent important informational stimuli they encounter in the environment. Compare with **procedural knowledge.**

geodemographic segmentation A segmentation approach that focuses on local neighborhood geography, demographics, and other market characteristics to classify actual, addressable, mappable neighborhoods where consumers live and shop.

geographic subcultures Large social groups defined in geographic terms. For instance, people living in different parts of a country may exhibit cultural differences.

global marketing An approach that argues for marketing a product in essentially the same way throughout the world.

goal hierarchy The end goal and the subgoals involved in achieving it.

grid layout A store layout where all counters and fixtures are at right angles to each other, with merchandise counters acting as barriers to traffic flow.

group Two or more people who interact with each other to accomplish some goal. Examples include families, co-workers, bowling teams, and church members.

heuristics Propositions connecting an event with an action. Heuristics simplify problem solving. For example, "buy the cheapest brand" could be a choice heuristic that would simplify purchase choice.

hierarchy of effects model An early model that depicted consumer response to advertising as a series of stages including awareness, knowledge, liking, preference, conviction, and purchase.

hierarchy of needs See **Maslow's need hierarchy.**

high involvement See **involvement.**

household The people living in a housing unit— a dwelling with its own entrance and basic facilities.

ideal self-concept The ideas, attitudes, and meanings people have about themselves concerning what they would be like if they were perfect or ideal. Compare with **self-concept.**

impulse purchase A purchase choice typically made quickly in-store with little decision-making effort.

inferences Meanings or beliefs that consumers construct to represent the relationships between concepts that are not based on explicit environmental information.

information acquisition situation Includes physical and social aspects of environments where consumers acquire information relevant to a problem-solving goal, such as a store choice or a decision to buy a particular brand.

informational reference group influence Information from a group that is accepted if the consumer believes it will help achieve a goal.

information contact A common early stage in the purchase sequence that occurs when consumers come into contact with information about the product or brand. This often occurs in promotions, where such contact can be intentional (consumers search newspapers for coupons) or accidental (a consumer happens to come into contact with a promotion while engaging in some other behavior). See also **exposure.**

information processing See **consumer information processing.**

information-processing models Used to divide complex cognitive processes into a series of simpler subprocesses that are more easily measured and understood.

information search Consumers' deliberate search for relevant information in the external environment.

innovativeness A personality trait regarding the degree to which a consumer accepts and purchases new products and services.

innovators The first group of consumers to adopt a new product.

instrumental conditioning See **operant coonditioning.**

integration processes The processes by which consumers combine knowledge to make two types of judgments. Attitude formation concerns how different types of knowledge are combined to form overall evaluations of products or brands. Decision making concerns how knowledge is combined to make choices about what behaviors to perform.

intentional exposure Occurs when consumers are exposed to marketing information because of their own intentional, goal-directed behavior. Compare with **accidental exposure.**

internal reference price The price consumers have in mind for a product.

interpretation processes The processes by which consumers make sense of or determine the meanings of important aspects of the physical and social environment, as well as their own behaviors and internal affective states.

interrupts Stimuli that interrupt or stop the problem-solving process, such as unexpected information encountered in the environment.

intrinsic self-relevance A consumer's personal level of self-relevance for a product. Cognitively represented by the general means–end chains of product–self relationships that consumers have learned and stored in memory. Compare with **situational self-relevance.**

involvement The degree of personal relevance a product, brand, object, or behavior has for a consumer. Experienced as feelings of arousal or activation and interest or importance. Determined by **intrinsic** and **situational self-relevance.** A *high-involvement* product is one a consumer believes has important personal consequences or will help achieve important personal goals. A *low-involvement* product is one that is not strongly linked to important consequences or goals.

ISTEA model A model for the process of developing a personal selling promotion strategy; stands for *i*mpression, *s*trategy, *t*ransmission, *e*valuation, and *a*djustment.

knowledge Cognitive representations of products, brands, and other aspects of the environment that are stored in memory. Also called *meanings* or *beliefs.*

laggards The last group to adopt a new product.

late majority The next-to-last group to adopt a new product.

level of competition A key aspect of the promotion environment for a product category. As competition heats up, marketers' use of promotions usually increases.

level of comprehension The different types of meanings consumers construct during interpretation processes.

levels of abstraction Levels of consumers' product knowledge ranging from concrete attributes to more abstract functional consequences to very abstract value outcomes.

levels of product knowledge Consumers' product knowledge in terms of abstraction–attributes, functional consequences, psychosocial consequences, and values. Also, consumers have knowledge about levels of products, including product categories, product forms, brands, and models. See **knowledge.**

lexicographic rule See **noncompensatory integration processes.**

lifestyle The manner in which people conduct their lives, including their activities, interests, and opinions.

limited capacity The notion that the amount of knowledge that can be activated and thought about at one time is quite small.

limited decision making A choice process involving a moderate degree of cognitive and behavioral effort. Compare with **extensive decision making.**

macro environment Large-scale environmental characteristics or features, such as the state of the economy, the political climate, or the season of the year. See **environment.**

macro social environment The broad, pervasive aspects of the social environment that affect the entire society or large portions of it, including culture, subculture, and social class.

marketing concept A business philosophy that argues organizations should satisfy consumer needs and wants to make profits.

marketing environment All of the social and physical stimuli in consumers' environments that are under the control of the marketing manager.

marketing strategy A plan designed to influence exchanges to achieve organizational objectives. From a consumer analysis point of view, marketing strategy is a set of stimuli placed in consumers' environments designed to influence their affect, cognition, and behavior.

market segmentation The process of dividing a market into groups of similar consumers and selecting the most appropriate group(s) for the firm to serve.

Maslow's need hierarchy A popular theory of human needs developed by Abraham Maslow. The theory suggests that humans satisfy their needs in a sequential order starting with physiological needs (food, water, sex) and ranging through safety needs (protection from harm), belongingness and love needs (companionship), esteem needs (prestige, respect of others), and self-actualization needs (self-fulfillment).

materialism A multidimensional value held by many consumers in developed countries; includes possessiveness, envy of other people's possessions, and nongenerosity.

meanings People's personal interpretations (cognitive representations, knowledge, or beliefs) of stimuli in the environment.

means–end chain A simple knowledge structure that links product attributes to more functional and social consequences and perhaps to high-level consumer values. Means–end chains organize consumers' product knowledge in terms of its self-relevance.

MECCAS model Attempts to simplify the difficult task of developing effective advertising strategies by identifying five key factors; stands for *means–end chain c*onceptualization of *a*dvertising *s*trategy.

metaphor An expression that helps one understand one thing in terms of another (money is like water that runs through my fingers). A metaphor can communicate both cognitive and affective meanings about a brand or company. Metaphors are important elements in marketing strategies.

micro environment Characteristics or features of the immediate, surrounding environment, such as the furnishings in the room where you are or the number of people close to you. See **environment.**

micro social environment Important aspects of consumers' immediate social environment, especially reference groups and family.

modeling See **vicarious learning.**

modern family life cycle The various life stages for modern American families, including the stages of the traditional family life cycle plus other stages found in modern culture such as divorce, single (never married), and single parents.

multiattribute attitude models Models designed to predict consumers' attitudes toward objects (such as brands) or behaviors (such as buying a brand) based on their beliefs about and evaluations of associated attributes or expected consequences.

multiple-baseline design Commonly used in applied behavior analysis, designs that demonstrate the effect of an intervention across several different behaviors, individuals, or situations at different times.

negative disconfirmation In consumer satisfaction theory, a situation in which a product performs worse than expected.

negative reinforcement Occurs when the frequency of a given behavior is increased by removing an aversive stimulus. See also **reinforcement.**

noncompensatory integration processes Choice strategies in which the positive and negative consequences of the choice alternatives do not balance or compensate for each other. See also **compensatory integration processes.** In evaluating alternatives using noncompensatory rules, positive and negative consequences of alternatives do not compensate for each other. Included among the types of noncompensatory integration processes are conjunctive, disjunctive, and lexicographic. The **conjunctive rule** suggests that consumers establish a minimum acceptable level for each choice criterion and accept an alternative only if it equals or exceeds the minimum cutoff level for every criterion. The **disjunctive rule** suggests that consumers establish acceptable standards for each criterion and accept an alternative if it exceeds the standard on at least one criterion. The **lexicographic rule** suggests that consumers rank choice criteria from most to least important and choose the best alternative on the most important criterion.

nonfamily households Unrelated people living together in the same household—about 30 percent of American households.

observability The degree to which products or their effects can be sensed by other consumers.

operant conditioning The process of altering the probability of a behavior being emitted by changing the consequences of the behavior.

opportunity to process The extent to which consumers have the chance to attend to and comprehend marketing information; can be affected by factors such as time pressure, consumers' affective states, and distractions.

overt consumer behavior The observable and measurable responses or actions of consumers.

overt modeling The most common form of vicarious learning; requires that consumers actually observe the model performing the behavior.

penetration pricing A pricing strategy that includes a plan to sequentially raise prices after introduction at a relatively low price.

perceived risks The expected negative consequences of performing an action such as purchasing a product.

peripheral route to persuasion One of two types of cognitive processes by which persuasion occurs. In the peripheral route, the consumer focuses not on the product message in an ad but on "peripheral" stimuli such as an attractive, well-known celebrity or popular music. Consumers' feelings about these other stimuli may influence beliefs and attitudes about the product. Compare with **central route to persuasion.**

personality The general, relatively consistent pattern of responses to the environment exhibited by an individual.

personal selling Direct personal interactions between a salesperson and a potential buyer.

person/situation segmentation Occurs when markets are divided on the basis of the usage situation in conjunction with individual differences of consumers.

persuasion The cognitive and affective processes by which consumers' beliefs and attitudes are changed by promotion communications.

physical environment The collection of nonhuman, physical, tangible elements that comprises the field in which consumer behavior occurs. Compare with **social environment.**

place utility Utility that occurs when goods and services are made available where the consumer wants to purchase them.

positioning See **product positioning.**

positioning by attribute Probably the most frequently used positioning strategy; associates a product with an attribute, a product feature, or a customer benefit.

positioning by competitors A positioning strategy where the explicit or implicit frame of reference is the competition.

positioning by product class A positioning strategy involving product class associations (for example, positioning a brand of margarine with respect to butter).

positioning by product user A positioning approach where a product is associated with a user or class of users.

positioning by use A positioning strategy where the product is associated with its use or application.

positioning map A visual depiction of consumers' perceptions of competitive products, brands, or models on selected dimensions.

positive disconfirmation In consumer satisfaction theory, a situation in which a product performs better than expected.

positive reinforcement Occurs when rewards are given to increase the frequency with which a given behavior is likely to occur. See also **reinforcement.**

possession utility Utility that occurs when channels facilitate the transfer of ownership of goods to the consumer.

postpurchase perceptions Consumers' thoughts about how well a product performed after purchase.

preconscious attention The highly automatic, largely unconscious selection of certain stimuli for simple cognitive processing. More likely for familiar concepts of low importance. Further processing tends to lead to **focal attention.**

prepurchase expectations Consumers' beliefs about anticipated performance of a product.

price elasticity A measure of the relative change in demand for a product for a given change in dollar price.

price perceptions How price information is comprehended by consumers and made meaningful to them.

problem representation Consumers' cognitive representation of the various aspects of the decision problem. Includes an end goal, a set of subgoals, relevant product knowledge, and a set of choice rules or simple heuristics by which consumers search for, evaluate, and integrate this knowledge to reach a choice.

problem solving A general approach to understanding consumer decision making. Focuses on consumers' cognitive representation of the decision as a problem. Important aspects of the problem representation include end goals, subgoals, and relevant knowledge. Consumers construct a decision plan by integrating knowledge within the constraints of the problem representation.

procedural knowledge Consumers' cognitive representations of how to perform behaviors. See also **script.**

product contact The actual behaviors consumers perform in coming into physical contact with products.

product knowledge and involvement Two very important concepts for understanding consumer cognition and affect; influence how consumers interpret and integrate information during decision making. See **knowledge, involvement, consumer decision making, interpretation processes,** and **integration process.**

product positioning Designing and executing a marketing strategy to form a particular mental representation of a product or brand in consumers' minds. Typically the goal is to position the product in some favorable way relative to competitive offerings.

product symbolism The various meanings of a product to a consumer and what the consumer experiences in purchasing and using it.

promotion clutter The growing number of competitive promotion strategies in the environment.

promotions Information that marketers develop to communicate meanings about their products and persuade consumers to buy them.

promotion strategies Strategies used by marketers to help them achieve their promotion objectives; include advertising, sales promotions, personal selling, and publicity.

psychographic segmentation Dividing markets into segments on the basis of consumer lifestyles.

psychosocial consequences Refers to two types of outcomes or consequences of product use: psychological consequences (I feel good about myself) and social consequences (Other people are making fun of me).

publicity Any unpaid form of communication about the marketer's company, products, or brand.

pull strategies Ways to encourage the consumer to purchase the manufacturer's brand, such as cents-off coupons.

punishment The process in which a response is followed by a noxious or aversive event, thus decreasing the frequency of the response.

purchase intention A decision plan or intention to buy a particular product or brand. See also **behavioral intention.**

purchasing situation Includes the physical and social stimuli that are present in the environment where the consumer actually makes the purchase.

push strategies Ways to enhance the selling efforts of retailers, such as trade discounts.

reciprocal system The idea that affect and cognition, behavior, and the environment cause and are caused by each other continuously over time.

reference group People who influence an individual's affect, cognitions, and behaviors.

reinforcement   A consequence that occurs after a behavior that increases the probability of future behavior of the same type.

reinforcement schedule   The rate at which rewards are offered in attempts to operantly condition behavior.

relevant knowledge   Appropriate or useful knowledge activated from memory in the context of a decision or interpretation situation.

respondent conditioning   See **classical conditioning.**

response hierarchy   The total list of behaviors a consumer could perform at any given time, arranged from most probable to least probable.

restructuring   A rare type of cognitive learning that occurs when an entire associative network of knowledge is revised., reorganizing old knowledge and creating entirely new meanings. Very complex and infrequent compared with **accretion** and **tuning.**

reversal design   An approach in which the problem behavior of a subject or group of subjects is first assessed to determine baseline performance. After a stable rate of behavior is determined, the intervention is introduced until behavior changes. The intervention is then withdrawn and reintroduced to determine if it is influencing the behavior.

rituals   Actions or behaviors performed by consumers to create, affirm, evoke, revise, or obtain desired symbolic cultural meanings.

routinized choice behavior   A purchase involving little cognitive and behavioral effort and perhaps no decision. Purchase could be merely carrying out an existing decision plan. Compare with **limited decision making** and **extensive decision making.**

sales promotion   A direct inducement to consumers to make a purchase, such as coupons or cents-off deals.

salient beliefs   The set of beliefs activated in a particular situation; may be represented as an associative network of linked meanings.

scanner cable method   A commercially available retail marketing research approach that documents household purchases by recording items scanned in supermarkets and other stores.

schema   An associative network of interrelated meanings that represents a person's declarative knowledge about some concept. Compare with **script.**

script   A sequence of productions or mental representations of the appropriate actions associated with particular events. Consumers often form scripts to organize their knowledge about behaviors to perform in familiar situations. Compare with **schema.**

segmentation   See **market segmentation.**

segmentation strategy   The general approach marketers use to approach markets, such as mass marketing or marketing to one or more segments.

selective exposure   A process by which people selectively come into contact with information in their environment. For instance, consumers may avoid marketing information by leaving the room while commercials are on TV.

self-concept   The ideas, meanings, attitudes, and knowledge people have about themselves. See also **self-schema.**

self-regulation   A form of ethical influence employed by marketers. Many professions have codes of ethics, and many firms have their own consumer affairs offices that seek to ensure the consumer is treated fairly.

self-schema   An associative network of interrelated knowledge, meanings, and beliefs about oneself. See also **self-concept.**

semantic knowledge   The general meanings and beliefs people have acquired about their world. Compare with **episodic knowledge.**

shaping   A process of reinforcing successive approximations of a desired behavior, or of other required behaviors, to increase the probability of the desired response.

shopping situation   The physical and spatial characteristics of the environments where consumers shop for products and services.

simplicity   The degree to which a product is easy for a consumer to understand and use.

situation   The ongoing stream of reciprocal interactions among goal-directed behaviors, affective and cognitive responses, and environmental factors that occur over a defined period of time. Situations have a purpose and a beginning, middle, and end.

situational involvement   Temporary interest or concern with a product or a behavior brought about by the situational context. For example, a consumer may become situationally involved with buying a hot water heater if the old one breaks. See also **situational self-relevance.** Compare with **enduring involvement.**

situational self-relevance   Temporary feelings of self-relevance due to specific external physical and social stimuli in the environment. Compare with **intrinsic self-relevance.**

skimming pricing   A pricing strategy that includes a plan to systematically lower prices after a high-price introduction.

social class   A status hierarchy by which groups and individuals are categorized on the basis of esteem and prestige.

social environment   Includes all human activities in social interactions.

socialization   The processes by which an individual learns the values and appropriate behavior patterns of a group, institution, or culture. Socialization is strongly influenced by family, reference groups, and social class.

social learning theory   One of a number of theories of human behavior.

social marketing   The application of commercial marketing technologies to the analysis, planning, execution, and evaluation of programs designed to influence the voluntary behavior of target audiences to improve their personal welfare and that of their society.

social stratification   See **social class.**

speed   Refers to how quickly the customer experiences the benefits of the product.

spreading activation   A usually unconscious process in which interrelated parts of a knowledge structure are activated during interpretation and integration processes (or even daydreaming).

store atmosphere   Emotional states that consumers experience in a store but may not be fully conscious of while shopping.

store contact   An important aspect of most consumer goods purchases; includes locating the outlet, traveling to the outlet, and entering the outlet.

store image   The set of meanings consumers associate with a particular store.

store layout   The basic floor plan and display of merchandise within a store. At a basic level, this influences such factors as how long the consumer stays in the store, how many products the consumer comes into visual contact with, and what routes the consumer travels within the store. Two basic types are *grid* and *free-form layouts*.

store location   Where a store is situated in a specific geographic area.

store loyalty   The degree to which a consumer consistently patronizes the same store when shopping for particular types of products.

store patronage   The degree to which a consumer shops at a particular store relative to competitive outlets.

subcultures   Segments within a culture that share a set of distinguishing meanings, values, and patterns of behavior that differ from those of the overall culture.

subjective or social norm *(SN)*   Consumers' perceptions of what other people want them to do.

subliminal perception   A psychological view that suggests attitudes and behaviors can be changed by stimuli that are not consciously perceived.

symbolic meaning   The set of psychological and social meanings products have for consumers. More abstract meanings than physical attributes and functional consequences.

theory of reasoned action   A theory developed by Martin Fishbein that assumes consumers consciously consider the consequences of alternative behaviors and choose the one that leads to the most desirable outcomes. The theory states that behavior is strongly influenced by behavioral intentions, which in turn are determined by attitudes toward performing the behavior and social normative beliefs about the behavior.

time utility   Utility that occurs when channels make goods and services available to the consumer when the consumer wants to purchase them.

trade promotion   Marketing tactics, such as advertising or display allowances, designed to get channel members to provide special support for products or services.

transactions   The exchanges of funds, time, cognitive activity, and behavior effort for products and services. In a micro sense, the primary objective of marketing, where consumers' funds are exchanged for products and services.

trialability   The degree to which a product can be tried on a limited basis or divided into small quantities for an inexpensive trial.

tuning   A type of cognitive learning that occurs when parts of a knowledge structure are combined and given a new, more abstract meaning. More complex and less frequent than **accretion.**

unconscious   An important characteristic of humans' cognitive systems where much "thinking" occurs below the level of conscious awareness.

unit pricing   Common for grocery products, a method using a shelf tag that indicates the price per unit for a specific good.

utilitarian reference group influence   Compliance of an individual with perceived expectations of others to obtain rewards or avoid punishments.

VALS™   An acronym standing for "values and lifestyles." VALS™ and GeoVALS™ are well-known psychographic segmentations marketed by SRI Consulting Business Intelligence.

value-expressive reference group influence   An individual's use of groups to enhance or support his or her self-concept.

values   The cognitive representations of important, abstract life goals that consumers are trying to achieve.

variable ratio schedule   Occurs when a reinforcer follows a desired consequence on an average at one-half, one-third, or one-fourth (and so on) of the time the behavior occurs, but not necessarily every second, third, or fourth time.

variety seeking A cognitive commitment to purchase different brands because of factors such as the stimulation involved in trying different things, curiosity, novelty, or overcoming boredom with the same old thing.

verbal modeling A type of modeling in which behaviors are not demonstrated and people are not asked to imagine a model performing a behavior; instead, people are told how others similar to themselves behaved in a particular situation.

vicarious learning Processes by which people change their behavior because they observed the actions of other people and the consequences that occurred.

word-of-mouth communication (WOM) Communication that occurs when consumers share information with friends about products and/or promotions such as good deals on particular products, a valuable coupon in the newspaper, or a sale at a retail store.

Name Index

Subject Index